T0307669

# THE RADICAL IN AMBEDKAR

ADVANCE PRAISE FOR THE BOOK

'Ambedkar, like Gandhi, provides a great subject for global and comparative studies. This volume aims to do just that, moving away from any spirit of uncritical adulation, and the result is a series of fresh perspectives on a man whose relevance to discussions of social justice and politics increases with every passing day. A timely collection of some truly powerful and incisive essays'—Dr Dipesh Chakrabarty, Lawrence A. Kimpton distinguished service professor, University of Chicago

'Taken together, these papers reposition Ambedkar as a global thinker addressing some of the most intricate problems that our world still wrestles with. Meticulous investigative essays, infectious concerns and combative advocacies admirably blend together in this volume suggesting several pathways of research and political action. The scholar-collective that the volume has brought together could not have been better in assessing Ambedkar's distinctive contribution in a comparative perspective particularly in relation to the struggles of the Dalits in India, the African Americans, and the Blacks in Africa'—Professor Valerian Rodrigues, Ambedkar chair, Ambedkar University Delhi

# THE RADICAL
# IN AMBEDKAR
## *Critical Reflections*

*Edited by*
## SURAJ YENGDE
## ANAND TELTUMBDE

PENGUIN
ALLEN
LANE

An imprint of Penguin Random House

ALLEN LANE

USA | Canada | UK | Ireland | Australia
New Zealand | India | South Africa | China | Singapore

Allen Lane is part of the Penguin Random House group of companies
whose addresses can be found at global.penguinrandomhouse.com

Published by Penguin Random House India Pvt. Ltd
4th Floor, Capital Tower 1, MG Road,
Gurugram 122 002, Haryana, India

First published in Allen Lane by Penguin Random House India 2018

Anthology copyright © Penguin Random House India 2018
Introduction copyright © Suraj Yengde and Anand Teltumbde 2018
The copyright for the individual pieces vests with the respective contributors

All rights reserved

10 9 8 7 6 5 4 3 2

The views and opinions expressed in this book are the authors' own and the
facts are as reported by them which have been verified to the extent possible,
and the publishers are not in any way liable for the same.

ISBN 9780670091157

Typeset in Bembo Std by Manipal Digital Systems, Manipal
Printed at Replika Press Pvt. Ltd, India

This book is sold subject to the condition that it shall not, by way of trade
or otherwise, be lent, resold, hired out, or otherwise circulated without the
publisher's prior consent in any form of binding or cover other than that in
which it is published and without a similar condition including this condition
being imposed on the subsequent purchaser.

www.penguin.co.in

This is a legitimate digitally printed version of the book and therefore might not
have certain extra finishing on the cover.

*To*
*the unknown and unsung millions who dared*
*Brahminical codes and helped build anti-caste rebellions,*
*some known and many unknown, in the history of caste*

# CONTENTS

# INTRODUCTION

## RECLAIMING THE RADICAL IN AMBEDKAR'S PRAXIS

Bhimrao Ramji Ambedkar, or Babasaheb Ambedkar as he is gratefully called by millions of his followers, may be unrivalled by any great in human history in terms of all conceivable markers of greatness. Whether it is the number of his busts and statues; pictures and posters, songs and ballads, books and pamphlets, conferences and seminars, roads, squares or localities named after him; or the numbers and sizes of congregations in his memory, there is no one who could even come close. Interestingly, even he is getting more and more distant from us with the passage of time, his legend is growing, diffusing the contours of a historical persona and thereby making him increasingly unavailable for us to draw lessons from.

Although he is known mainly for his struggle for the emancipation of Dalits and for writing India's Constitution, he had a number of other accomplishments that get largely marginalized. He is hardly remembered for his scholarship as one of the most educated persons of his times, for his works as an economist trained under the stalwarts of those days, as a talented journalist (he established four papers—*Muknayak, Bahishkrit Bharat, Janata* and *Prabuddha Bharat*—as organs for the various phases of his movement), for his founding of a trade union (the Municipal Kamgar Sangh in Mumbai), for his work as an educationist (he founded the People's Education Society and established colleges), for his advocacy of women's rights, his statesmanship, his internationalist vision, his authorship of books on varied subjects, his parliamentary debates and, lastly, his work as the reviver of Buddhism in the land of its birth. More than two decades ago, Upendra Baxi had written about his multifaceted contributions by describing as many as seven Ambedkars.[1] The multiple roles he played certainly inspire awe but make it as difficult to comprehend him because all of them do not necessarily cohere with each other. It certainly offers one multiple choices, a virtuous thing in our neoliberal times, to choose one's own Ambedkar. However, it becomes disadvantageous when he is seen as the beacon for the forward march of history.

Another problem with Ambedkar is that he became godhead for the Dalits. Not undeservedly, Ambedkar occupies the same place as Moses does for the Israelite tribes, whom he led away from Egyptian slavery across the Red Sea to their land. He is seen as a saviour, messiah and prophet by his people, the Ambedkarite Dalits, as he organized them into a formidable force and strove for their betterment against the entrenched interests of Hindu society on multiple fronts. In his lifetime itself he had won such epitaphs as 'Babasaheb' (lord father), Bhim Raja (King Bhim) and such others from his followers. They followed him without a whisper in converting to Buddhism, discarding the faith of their ancestors and happily giving him the epitaph of 'Bodhisattva' (one who has generated *Bodhicitta*, a spontaneous wish and compassionate mind to attain Buddhahood). When he died, a vacuum of leadership arose in the movement, there being none who could command the confidence of all the second-rung leaders. Soon the more ambitious of these leaders splintered the movement, and as they began facing attacks from the dominant communities, people developed nostalgic devotion for him.

There were other factors besides the intrinsic emotional feeling of Dalits that appear to have turned Ambedkar into an unsurpassable phenomenon in the world. When he died in 1956, the then Congress government under Jawaharlal Nehru as the prime minister would not even fly his dead body to Mumbai for cremation as desired by his family and followers. It demanded transportation charges for the aircraft and settled for half through hard negotiation, which then was paid by the Scheduled Caste Improvement Trust, founded by Ambedkar and then headed by Dadasaheb Gaikwad.[2] For the next eleven years, there was not even a small marker in his memory at the place where he was cremated. Only family members and some followers would pay homage there on 6 December every year, observing his death anniversary. The structure that stands as his memorial was constructed in 1967 with the money collected by his son during a special march he undertook from his birthplace in Mhow to Mumbai.

There were no roads, no statues or memorials erected for him, except perhaps in Mumbai, where the municipal corporation installed a statue at Cooperage and named the biggest road as Babasaheb Ambedkar Road. Dalits had to perform a nationwide satyagraha of unprecedented magnitude in 1964–65 demanding inter alia that his portrait be put up in the central hall of Parliament; still, the centre ignored this plea for more than a decade. The mass hysteria of devotion that one sees today cannot be entirely the making of the intrinsic emotion of the Dalit masses. Today, over two million people congregate annually at Chaitya Bhoomi, Mumbai, on 6 December, at Deeksha Bhoomi in Nagpur on Dussehra and in growing numbers at many other places associated with him that are being added each year. An entire almanac is developing around the life of Ambedkar that draws attention to the importance of each day for Dalits. The role of the state and the ruling classes in the making of this phenomenon is too stark to ignore.

## Communists, a Strange Yardstick

Ambedkar emerged as a cult figure even when he was alive, as the universal adaptation of the salutation 'Jai Bhim' (Victory to Ambedkar) indicates. Allegiance to Ambedkar became a prerequisite to gain acceptability among Dalits and with it the battle of one-upmanship was played out with competitive claims of being a real Ambedkarite. Ambedkar, Ambedkarite and Ambedkarism became the dominant markers of the Dalit universe, reinforcing the identitarian orientation among Dalits.

As a matter of fact, the first break-up of the Republican Party of India (RPI) happened because of this very issue. A section claiming that Ambedkar had advised to follow constitutional methods argued that the other section, by holding agitations demanding land for the landless, was going the communist way. This would be repeated after two decades in the form of the breaking away of the Dalit Panthers, which was an angry reaction by the Dalit youth to the bankruptcy of the RPI leadership. As the manifesto of the group had proposed a radical definition of 'Dalit' and spoke about revolution, it provoked a faction to condemn it as a communist document inimical to Ambedkarism, which, at that time, was projected as Buddhism. In both these significant splits, while the definition of Ambedkarism, interestingly, differed, the accusation of not being Ambedkarite centred on being a communist, which was considered the foremost enemy. This anti-communist theme would be skilfully played up by the new generation of university-educated Dalits to strengthen identity politics (caste versus class) under various guises.

The contention with communists developed along multiple strands in the Ambedkarite Dalit movement. Foremost was Ambedkar's persona and disposition: his religious upbringing (albeit in a radical stream of

Kabirpanth), the deep influence he gathered as a student in Columbia University, which contradicted the communist ideology,[3] and somewhat as a consequence of his inadequate exposure to communist theories.[4] Although he acknowledged the attraction of communism for the exploited masses of people as the science of liberation, it remained more or less as a threat rather than an opportunity in his scheme. This attitude was further reinforced by the alienating behaviour of the early communists in Mumbai: their upper-caste background and affiliation, Brahminical attitude and conduct in taking Marxist dictum as *ved-vakyas* (infallible universal doctrine) and near disdain of Ambedkar's struggles, which were seen as futile in the realm of the superstructure and divisive of the working class.

The colonial context also contributed immensely in keeping him away from communists: the opening up of political opportunities along communal lines laid a premium on the Dalit identity, the opportunity it held in extracting safeguards for Dalits as the third force in the contention of the two major communities of Hindus and Muslims, represented respectively by the Congress and the Muslim League.[5] Ambedkar as a pragmatist, moreover, would not be ready to give up the opportunity of short-term gains to Dalits in favour of the promise of long-term emancipation in communism. His ultimate refuge in the Buddha, which was expectedly followed by the mass conversion of his followers to Buddhism, appeared as the 'ultimate bulwark against communism', as observed by the prominent Ambedkar scholar Eleanor Zelliot.[6] All this may not be construed as his ideological anti-communism but his followers packaged it into a syllogism—concern for material issues is communist, Ambedkar was against communists and hence Ambedkarites should shun concern for material issues—to opportunistically free themselves to indulge in statist games for their narrow gains.

## The Postcolonial Political Economy

Postcolonial politics also duly reinforced these processes. The Congress under the facade of the Gandhian mass movement innately represented the interests of the incipient bourgeoisie without antagonizing feudal elements. After the transfer of power, it skilfully used the pro-people rhetoric of the freedom struggle to constitute the state that would serve this class. It continued with the same operative structure of the colonial regime in doing so. The new Constitution was created by the Constituent Assembly which barely represented 12 per cent of the population that possessed property and education.[7] It was essentially the last 1935 British Constitution (India

Act 1935).[8] With a masterstroke of the Gandhian strategy, Ambedkar was co-opted into the Constituent Assembly to be the chairman of its drafting committee.[9] They systematically projected him to be the maker of the Constitution so as to get the emotional buy-in from the lower strata of society, which was destined to be hit the hardest. Despite Ambedkar's disowning it within two years of its implementation,[10] the prowess of this strategy still operates with the Dalits.

The Congress surreptitiously drove its policies to promote the interest of the bourgeoisie, paradoxically packaging them as socialist. It began with the underhand incorporation of the Bombay Plan, prepared by the major capitalists in the country within the framework of the Five Year Plan,[11] which was identified with socialist planning. The land reforms followed by the capitalist strategy of the Green Revolution were implemented to carve out a class of rich farmers from the most populous Sudra caste as the link of the central party with rural areas. With increasing enrichment, the rising aspirations of this class could not be contained by the Congress, which resulted in the emergence of new political coalitions and in certain places the rise of regional parties of these neo-rich capitalist farmers. With electoral politics thus becoming increasingly competitive, threatening the electoral dominance of the Congress, there came the importance of the Dalit vote bank and the icon of Ambedkar as the lever to manipulate it. While on the one hand this process of development had intensified the class contradictions between Dalit farm labour and capitalist farmers that precipitated through the fault lines of caste into a new genre of atrocities, on the other, Ambedkar was becoming increasingly too important to be celebrated in a grand manner. This phenomenon is clearly discernible from the late 1960s but became strident post-1990s in neoliberal India.

The ruling classes, mainly represented by the Congress, had tended to ignore him after he resigned from the Nehru cabinet in 1951. But within a decade they realized Ambedkar's importance to their own sustenance. The land satyagraha of 1964–65 had awakened them to the imminent risk of Dalits realizing their material deprivation. Ambedkar had become a symbol of their collective aspirations. The ruling classes realized the strategic necessity of appropriating Ambedkar to achieve many of the emergent goals—containing the immediate risk of Dalits raising material demands, deradicalizing Ambedkar for the longer term, co-opting Dalit leaders, promoting identitarian politics among them and severally preventing the possibility of the Dalit movement drifting towards radicalism. The Congress prototyped the policy through Yashwantrao Chavan, the then defence minister, by offering Rajya Sabha membership to Gaikwad. Thereafter, the co-option of Dalit leaders in various forms and the iconization of Ambedkar became the order of the day. Today, the Hindutva dispensation under Narendra Modi, while brutally suppressing the voice of Dalits, has gone berserk in declaring that the places where Ambedkar set foot would be grandly memorialized.

After 1990, Ambedkar gained further importance as a means of placating Dalits, who would be most hit by the policies. Gandhi, who served as an icon for postcolonial India, was variously in conflict with the neoliberal ethos and therefore needed to be phased out and replaced by a new icon that represented modernity, free markets and success through sheer hard work. Ambedkar would outcompete anyone on these counts with little packaging. He was already painted as the greatest free market economist or monetarist by his own followers.[12] The government began promoting Ambedkar's image by encouraging universities to begin studies on Ambedkar through institutions like the Centre for Ambedkar Thought, Exclusion and Inclusion, Social Justice, etc., to house the growing numbers of Dalit PhDs in the social sciences and also to engage other scholars through seminars and conferences in their multiplier effect. This state promotion of and mass devotion to Ambedkar proved mutually reinforcing and set in an upward spiral.

This phenomenon was made possible by ensuring the availability of his writings and speeches. By the late 1970s, the Maharashtra government had begun to publish volumes of his works. His Marathi writings were mainly contained in his periodicals, which were collected by some people and published, but they were still scanty and fragmented. Ambedkar primarily wrote in English and, barring a few books, they were inaccessible to the common people. By 2000, most of his writings had been published in these volumes, igniting interest in academic circles, where until then hardly anything was known about him. This gave a fillip to Ambedkar research all over the world.[13] However, barring a few exceptions, this outpouring of literature has been largely hagiographic and of poor academic quality. In 1991, the government observed his birth centenary with year-long programmes.

In the UK, Ambedkarite organizations of the Dalit diaspora formed the Federation of the Ambedkarite and Buddhist Organizations (FABO), brought out four centenary souvenirs and started a quarterly journal called *New Era*. They undertook a campaign to donate busts of Ambedkar and volumes of his writings and speeches to noted universities and institutions in the UK and the US, including those associated with Ambedkar. It inspired Ambedkarite groups in the US, where organizations like Volunteers in Service to India's Oppressed and Neglected (VISION), the Ambedkar Center for Justice and Peace (ACJP), and the Ambedkar International Center had marked the existence of Ambedkarite activities. FABO has maintained its organized activities and been instrumental in getting the house at 10 King Henry Road in London where Ambedkar had stayed during 1920–23 as a student of the London School of Economics paid for by the Maharashtra government.

All these activities established the Ambedkar icon in a big way but lost the real Ambedkar to the Dalit masses. While the ruling classes used him as brand ambassador, Dalit scholars, instead of exposing this, rushed in with their hagiographies in support, which would completely obfuscate the radical contours of his persona. In the face of the pathetic state of Dalits—who continue to suffer the indignities and oppression they did a century ago, lingering significantly behind the non-Dalit population on every development parameter, paying exorbitant costs for the elevation of a few among them, increasing inequality among each other and facing the eventual loss of social investment and additionally bearing the burden of the capitalist–neoliberal developments—this paradoxical development should make any intellectual sit up and think through the process.

One factor that helped all these machinations of the ruling classes was the alienation of Ambedkarite Dalits from the communists. The Bolshevik revolution in Russia in 1917 inspired the urban educated middle class across the world, which began organizing the workers in organized industry. In India, this class naturally constituted Brahmins and other upper castes. Their cultural fidelity to the written word, tendency to closely map Indian society like European society and lack of understanding of the vast rural hinterland led them to ignore caste as the 'superstructure' that Marx had metaphorically described in his historical materialism.[14] In his early writing, Marx tended to depict a one-way causal relationship between the economic base and superstructure to stress his commitment to the principles of historical materialism. However, as his theory evolved and grew more complex over time, Marx reframed the relationship between base and superstructure as dialectical, implying that each influenced what happens in the other. That is, if something changes in the base, it causes changes in the superstructure, and vice versa. But Marxists in their materialistic enthusiasm failed to acquire this nuanced understanding and turned it into economic determinism. None other than Engels had to react to such a rampant misunderstanding of this metaphorical expression.[15] If it could cause such confusion in Europe sans any pervasive social divide such as caste, the havoc it caused in India can well be imagined.

This attitude of the Indian communists made them ignore Ambedkar's struggles as untenable and worse, divisive of the working class. Despite this, Ambedkar, whose ideological core disagreed with Marxist theory, still saw a possibility of common practice with the communists and joined hands with them at least in one of the historic strikes in Mumbai.[16] While the communists occasionally spoke against caste as a residue of feudalism, they never evinced the necessity of consciously combating it. This apathy of theirs towards caste could be easily attributed by the Ambedkarite movement to their Brahminical background. In the post-Ambedkar period, this historical divide and some of Ambedkar's exasperations with communism would be forged into an anti-communist syllogism by an opportunist Dalit leadership to widen the divide and land the Dalit movement in the enemy camp.[17]

## The Conception of the Book

The undertaking of this project in the midst of the euphoria over Ambedkar's 125th birth anniversary—much of it clearly state sponsored—was informed by the need to recover 'the real Ambedkar', at least in parts, from the hagiographic cobweb that has grown around him. We imagined whether we could take a dispassionate look at him, penetrating the mass of superlatives, hyperbole and folklore. The form of the book was essentially dictated by this objective: to call upon various people who could meaningfully take up different aspects of his contribution and subject it to objective scrutiny. It was too ambitious to attempt in a time where the slightest insinuation of lowering the scale of superlatives for him can be construed as blasphemy and lead to public outrage. We also realized the difficulty in communicating our objective to established scholars and expecting them to have a sharp turn of their thought process in the new direction contemplated by us. But even to make a start was a worthy task. This book may thus be taken as a modest beginning of the mega project of recovering the real Ambedkar, which may be useful in articulating the emancipatory project of Dalits and, in corollary, larger humanity.

This book is thus not a biographical addition to the plethora of texts on Ambedkar, nor is it a political rhetoric. It is meant to be a thoughtful exegesis of Ambedkar and Ambedkarite praxis. One of the ways, we thought, was to situate him within the expanded horizon of the emancipatory struggles of similarly placed people, unfortunately the most unexplored area in Ambedkar scholarship. It could facilitate the comparative assessment of his movement with others in situations akin to his. The people who immediately come to mind are African Americans, who right from their being uprooted from their African habitat and transported to the new world as slaves to their present-day problems have a glorious history of resistance. Every country had resistance movements by the socially oppressed sections in some or the other form, but the movement of African Americans is relatively better documented and longer lasting. It is, moreover, pertinent because Ambedkar spent his intellectually formative years in the buzzing Harlem neighbourhood of New York (1913–16) which coincided with one of the most crucial periods in Black American history. It was the time of the Harlem Renaissance, when Black American writers and thinkers were trying to separate those aspects of their existence that made them different from Whites by establishing themselves, drawing from the traditions of struggle and survival. In fact, they were struggling to free themselves from the White imagination which had defined their existence for them.[18] Columbia University was situated close to Harlem, where the leading black intellectual and civil rights activist W.E.B. Du Bois stayed. Du Bois had published his important book, *The Souls of Black Folk,* in 1903, which had become an instant success. It is unlikely that the bibliophile Ambedkar, said to have purchased more than 2000 books by then, did not know about him and the movement in general.

## Ambedkar and the Black Movement

Although Lama Choyin Rangdrol in his essay laments that the African-American movement sidelined Ambedkar, he himself gives evidence that in December 1942, the National Association for the Advancement of Colored People's (NAACP) magazine, the *Crisis*, had published a two-part series on India's Untouchables titled 'The "Negroes" of India'.[19] The article, written by Harry Paxton Howard, discussed untouchability in explicit detail and marvelled at Ambedkar's rise from the dregs of society to the position of India's labour minister. He went on to suggest Ambedkar's model should 'serve as a beacon-light not only to the Untouchables of India, but to pariahs and outcast peoples throughout the world—which might serve, indeed, as a new and militant program for Negroes in the United States'.[20] He further observed, 'Just as with American Negroes, they had to free themselves. The

"Great White Father" could not do it for them—especially when his more deep-rooted sympathies lay with their "Aryan" masters.'[21]

Surprisingly, there is no such reference to the African-American movement by Ambedkar. Eleanor Zelliot in her book observes: 'A direct comparison between the Negroes of America and Untouchables of India does not appear in Ambedkar's writings.'[22] One may see that the African Americans were not ideologically enslaved as the Dalits were and hence had a different trajectory of struggles. While they could express their raw anger against their forcible enslavement and the oppression of their masters, both individually as well as collectively, Dalits on their part were ideologically blinded not to see their oppression. They had internalized their placement in the caste hierarchy over millennia, believing it, like the others, to be their destiny. They were content with relying on gods to get them a better life in the next birth. When they were made aware of their unfair treatment, they did not rise with anger but looked up to the person who woke them up as their new messiah. Notwithstanding the differential psychological makeup and ontological experience of these two communities, the nature of their struggles had large existential similarities.

Ambedkar did make a comparison in his essay 'Slaves and Untouchables', pointing out the level of segregation and the degree of psychological damage suffered by them.

> Slavery was never obligatory. But untouchability is obligatory. The law of slavery permitted emancipation. Once a slave, always a slave was not the fate of the slave. In untouchability there is no escape. Once an untouchable, always an untouchable. The other difference is that untouchability is an indirect form of slavery. A deprivation of a man's freedom by an open and direct way is a preferable form of enslavement. It makes the slave conscious of his enslavement and to become conscious of slavery is the first and most important step in the battle for freedom. But if a man is deprived of his liberty indirectly he has no consciousness of his enslavement. Untouchability is an indirect form of slavery.'[23]

This comparison, however, is between slavery and untouchability, and Ambedkar may be right in presenting how the latter is more vicious than the former. But what is required is to compare African Americans with Dalits. In addition to the above-mentioned psycho-historical differences between the two, it may have to be acknowledged that the handicap of African Americans on account of their skin colour was more formidable than that of Dalits, who could anonymize themselves once out of their locale. As Ambedkar held, there was indeed no racial difference between Dalits and non-Dalits in India.

The similarities of their struggle are reflected in the similarities of their leaders' strategies. Like the Dalit movement, the movement of African Americans also threw up multiple leaders. The contemporary movement was dominated by two leaders, Booker T. Washington (1856–1915) and W.E.B. Du Bois (1868–1963), who sharply disagreed on strategies for Black social and economic progress. In his September 1895 speech, 'The Atlanta Compromise', which propelled him on to the national scene as a leader and spokesman for African Americans, Washington advocated Black Americans accept for a while the political and social status quo of segregation and preached a philosophy of self-help, racial solidarity and accommodation. He urged Blacks to accept discrimination for the time being and concentrate on elevating themselves through hard work and material prosperity within the Black community rather than through university education and voting rights. He believed in education in the crafts, industrial and farming skills and the cultivation of the virtues of patience, enterprise and thrift. Washington wanted Blacks not to aspire to be like Whites but be satisfied with things they could do. In other words, he was for the status quo. It was reflected in his famous slogan 'Cast down your bucket where you are'.[24] This, he said, would win the respect of Whites and lead to African Americans being fully accepted as citizens and integrated into all strata of society. It may be likened to the reformist approach reflected by the pre-Ambedkar Dalit leaders who thought that if Dalits gave up eating the meat of dead cattle or emulated upper-caste culture, it could impel the latter to rethink their practices. In terms of its status-quoist attitude, it is similar to the Gandhian approach as well. Many upwardly mobile Dalits reflect this instinctive notion that their acceptability among upper castes is due to their individual efforts to rise.

Du Bois, a towering Black intellectual, scholar and political thinker, vehemently disagreed with Washington's strategy, arguing that it would serve only to perpetuate white oppression. Du Bois advocated political action and a civil rights agenda (he helped found the NAACP). In addition, he argued that social change could be accomplished by developing the small group of college-educated Blacks he called the Talented Tenth:

> The Negro Race, like all races, is going to be saved by its exceptional men. The problem of education then, among Negroes, must first of all deal with the 'Talented Tenth.' It is the problem of developing the best of

this race that they may guide the Mass away from the contamination and
death of the worst.[25]

The Du Bois philosophy of agitation and protest for civil rights flowed directly
into the civil rights movement which began to develop in the 1950s and
exploded in the 1960s. In *The Souls of Black Folks*[26] Du Bois describes the
magnitude of American racism and demands its end. How close it appears
to Ambedkar who insisted that caste must be annihilated. On many counts,
Du Bois's approach comes close to Ambedkar's. His Talented Tenth is
what Ambedkar expected of select people reaching important positions in
the government with higher education and becoming a protective umbrella
for the interests of the Dalit masses. Right from the Mahad Conference, he
spoke of this expectation and focused most of his struggle on this issue. It
also informs his emphasis on higher education. Like Du Bois, he believed
in Dalits struggling for civil rights. Like Du Bois, Ambedkar identified the
problem of his people in his longish essay, 'Annihilation of Caste'.

Connecting the Dalit struggle with the African Americans' battle against
racism in America would have given the former a global context and also
expanded its support base. Such awareness is reflected among Black leaders.
James Baldwin, while emphasizing the uniqueness of the Black experience
in America, finds similarities between Blacks and oppressed groups in other
countries. As Stephen Spender writes: 'If the Negro problem is resolvable,
the only useful way of discussing it is to consider American Negroes in
a situation comparable to that of workers and Negroes elsewhere' (like
Dalits in India).[27] Even with hindsight, one can see that there was so much
for these movements to learn from each other. Ambedkar did have this
outlook when he drew upon the histories of other countries to buttress his
arguments. One of his expectations behind his conversion to Buddhism was
to connect Dalits with the larger Asian Buddhist fraternity. Contrary to his
hope, the orthodoxy in those countries did not welcome it, claiming that it
was not Buddhism but Ambedkar's own religion.[28]

The similarity between the caste system in India and racism in the US
had been noted by none other than Jotiba Phule, whom Ambedkar had
acknowledged as one of his three gurus. In 1873, Phule had dedicated his
book *Gulamgiri* (Slavery) to American abolitionists 'in an earnest desire that
my countrymen may take their example as their guide in the emancipation
of their Sudra Brethren from the trammels of Brahmin thralldom'.[29] It is
quite surprising not to find any reference in Ambedkar's writings to this
struggle. His correspondence with Du Bois in July 1946 was too late in the

day and consisted of mere enquiry about the National Negro Congress's petition to the UN, which attempted to secure minority rights through the UN Council. Ambedkar explained that he had been a 'student of the Negro problem' and that '[t]here is so much similarity between the position of the Untouchables in India and of the position of the Negroes in America that the study of the latter is not only natural but necessary'. In a letter dated 31 July 1946, Du Bois responded by telling Ambedkar he was familiar with his name and that he had 'every sympathy with the Untouchables of India'. Du Bois's interest in India turned up in editorials in the *Crisis* over the decades, as well as the novel *Dark Princess* published in 1928. His correspondence with Ambedkar, however, does not appear to extend beyond this letter.[30] It is surprising that there is no similar reference to the works of radical African-American leaders in Ambedkar's writings. As Kapoor observed, he 'was not influenced by the Black American struggle, though his stay in America coincided with an efflorescence of Black protest literature'.[31]

Despite a plethora of literature on and about Ambedkar, there is a serious dearth of a critical look at his multifaceted life. There is literature that either badly glorifies or nicely vilifies Ambedkar. These bipolar observations have harmed the Dalit movement the most. His scholarly acumen and scientific attitude have been seriously undermined. Thus, Ambedkar comes to us as a blurred figurine. While much of it may be rightly attributable to his liberal mould, the role of his devotees masquerading as followers casting him in hagiographic shallowness cannot be ignored. One finds Ambedkar eulogized for the wrong reasons: as a messiah for Untouchables, a Constitution maker, a Bodhisattva, a neoliberal free-market protagonist, a monetarist; he is also vilified unjustly as casteist, as a British stooge and a communist hater. Due to this, we witness a strange situation where Ambedkar becomes a reason for evocative conversations, heated debate and violent disapprovals and disagreements.

## Ambedkar and Gramsci

A parallel may be drawn from history. Writing on the occasion of the centenary celebration of Marx's birthday, Marx's sincere critic, a Marxist himself, Antonio Gramsci reminded the world of the 'stupidity' reining the fragments of Marx's thoughts. In the 4 May 1918 edition of *Il Grido del Popolo*, Gramsci begins by asking two hard-hitting questions—'Are we Marxists? Do Marxists exist?'—to the audience that was awed by the tentacles of the Marxist revolution without taking into account the paradigm shifts of socialist struggle. Taking a stab at the self-proclaimed directionless Marxists, Gramsci denounced the people in the celebratory quarters who relied on 'wild mumblings and stylistic affectation' to survive.[32] Gramsci was commenting in a similar vein as Ambedkar, who decried the idolizing of human personalities by their followers. In his 1943 speech commemorating the 101st birthday celebration of Ranade, Ambedkar decided to offer comments on three personalities of the times: Ranade, Gandhi and Jinnah.[33] His words have the profundity of universal application and paradoxically serve as a reminder to his own devotees who are increasingly rendering him inaccessible to others wanting to learn from him:

> No great man really does his work by crippling his disciple by forcing on them his maxims or his conclusions. What a great man does is not to impose his maxims on his disciples. What he does is to evoke them, to awaken them to a vigorous and various exertion of their faculties. Again the pupil only takes his guidance from his master. He is not bound to accept his master's conclusions. There is no ingratitude in the disciple not accepting the maxims or the conclusions of his master. For even when he rejects them he is bound to acknowledge to his master in deep reverence 'You awakened me to be myself: for that I thank you.' The master is not entitled to less. The disciple is not bound to give more.[34]

Gramsci invokes Thomas Carlyle much as Ambedkar does to define the fallibility of men. Both Ambedkar and Gramsci chose to place emphasis on history and how historical forces play a significant role in defining the virtues of great men. Other factors of greatness limited to individual attributes—valour, strength, natural ability, moral quality and intellect—were nominal in deciding the nature of greatness. The greatness of individuals emerges out of personal ego and insecurity. One wants to be great for two reasons: to silence critics who claim that individuals cannot be great, and to supervise the writing of historical records in one's favour.

Thus, we do not want to put a halo on another great actor of history and put him in the hollow box of greatness. Instead, we want to test his vision that changed the course of history. As Gramsci commented, referring to Marx as someone who 'signifies the entry of intelligence into the history of humanity, the reign of awareness', in a similar vein, Ambedkar epitomizes the summoning of intelligence to problematize history. Gramsci aligns the product of history being a continual interaction between economic forces. Like Marx, he firmly believes in the class divisions of society and it is these divisions that have the potential to completely subvert oppression by the formation of alliances. Although Gramsci believes in the socialist formulation of society that the present is an outcome of historical changes brought about through the struggle between classes, he considers Marx an important intervention in the history of ideas that radicalized change. Ambedkar, however, gives primacy only to the individual traits of 'great men', thereby conflicting with the prevailing theories of St Augustine, Carlyle, Marx and Henry Thomas Buckle who believed in the extra-human, that is, the power of factors beyond human capacity to make history.

Similarly, Dalit history is a rightful enquiry into the understanding of Dalit being, of the lost shipwreck of Dalit identity. History is not just a story of the past but a critical reflection to reify one's dislocation into a conflict with dominant groups. History is thus a confrontation, a warlike demeanour for the oppressed to deal with the appropriate criticism of their present condition. The morality that rests on a certain logic of defence is used to calibrate a targeted attack on the historiographical agency of the oppressed Dalit community. Here, the Dalit radical falls into the trap of reinventing history to confront Brahminism in the same zeitgeist and tools offered by Brahmins. The subaltern studies experiment is an exemplar of this impulse. The invention of myths and community stories replace the Hinduized form of dominance with that of Dalit assertion. One can observe an urgent mendacity where crude forms of narratives are brought out with a divisive gesture by taking popular myths to the gullible masses whose superstitious spiritualism is replaced with 'Ambedkar religion'. This profoundly articulate rebuttal promises a Dalit vision of the universal; however, without adequate critical engagement it falsifies the logic of relative rationalism—a pragmatic vision of shared radicalism—by falling into a cyclonic trap of self-dissonance. Or, as African-American thinker Cornel West suggests, 'generating romantic conceptions of the past to undergird self-esteem'.[35] The nostalgia and emotions that are presented through aggressive verbosity are evident in the behemoth of literature erupting every year, seen on bookstands and sold at every important Dalit gathering.

## Unlocking Ambedkarism

In contrast with Marx, Ambedkar does not have any single abiding thesis like historical materialism to offer. Rather, he is against any such proposition that human history is discernible through a certain set of laws. It is important to understand his ideological makeup in order to comprehend his responses to various events in time. Contrary to folklore, Ambedkar came from Mahar military aristocracy, for two previous generations both his paternal and maternal ancestors had served in the British military. His father had retired as subedar and was headmaster of the Normal School. He himself notes that the atmosphere at home was religious and his father got his children to sing Kabir's hymns (*dohas*). Although, after his father's retirement, when they shifted to Dapoli, he began experiencing the heat of untouchability, but all said and done, it was of a different degree from what an ordinary Dalit would face in rural India.

Shortly after, they left for Satara, where he had a bitter experience on account of his caste, although in the Satara school he met a kind Brahmin teacher who would not only share his food with him but also grant him his surname, 'Ambedkar'. From Satara, his father moved to Mumbai, settling in a chawl in a working-class locality in Parel. Ambedkar proved extraordinarily lucky in getting a scholarship from a maharaja for higher education in India, and thereafter for going to Columbia University for his postgraduate and doctoral degrees. Even after completing his education, he was lucky to get resources from another maharaja, the maharaja of Kolhapur. Columbia University marked a turning point in his career, not as much as it inspired him to get into public life (as he was not sure whether he would plunge into public life even on the eve of the Mahad struggle), but to open up the horizon of a world sans untouchability, to imbibe ideas of pragmatism and Fabian socialism from his teacher John Dewey, and to develop critical thinking. He used this opportunity to the hilt, putting in extraordinary hard work in completing his degree at Columbia, and shifted to London to quench his thirst of knowledge. He never revealed particular influences of the Fabian establishment in London but there was no doubt that his stay in London only reinforced what he had learnt from Dewey in Columbia.

One can thus see that Ambedkar was ideologically a pragmatist in his overall approach to social problems, a Fabian socialist in his political leanings and Buddhist in his personal spiritual makeup. One can further see that there were no conflict areas among the three aspects as they were containable within a broad liberal frame. This frame tended to reject Marxism, which inter alia attributed a scientific basis to human history. Ambedkar's greatness may be seen in not clinging to any doctrinal set or ism including Buddhism but stretching it to the limits to conform to the needs of the times. It may well be seen by critics as unprincipled pragmatism itself.

However, this trait opens up possibilities to extend him to any length towards the emancipatory goal. Unfortunately, Ambedkar is never understood in terms of this process and is taken as someone whose thoughts were cast in stone as gospel truth. It follows that whatever he did in the context of his time and space also should be taken as an incidental, transient subject to be evaluated and changed. If one agrees with this proposition, many of the confusions engendered by so-called Ambedkar scholars may be dispelled. Pragmatism does not respect consistency because it is always contextualized by circumstances and goal, both of which may be changeable. Ambedkar himself admitted it and dismissed consistency as the virtue of an ass. Therefore, extrapolating him beyond his times is not without its problems.

## The Issues of Ambedkarite Praxis

Ambedkar, in the course of his praxis, reflects his own understanding of state, religion, nation, imperialism, communism, revolution, violence, Buddhism, socialism, secularism, etc., each of which has a significant impact on the emancipatory politics of Dalits in varying degrees. The hagiographic waves unleashed by a mix of vote-bank politics and the nostalgia of Dalit masses that engulfed his memory prevented the undertaking of any serious review of his thoughts on these issues. The very emotional nostalgia, to the extent that it stems from the condition of their hopelessness, should impel us to think to what extent it is attributable to the failure of his followers in shouldering his legacy and to what extent to the legacy itself.

As a matter of fact, in his own life, Ambedkar had realized that his prescriptions for the problems of Dalits did not produce expected results. Whether it was political reservations, the logic of getting select Dalits to occupy bureaucratic positions or constitutional safeguards, many times he lamented that his methods were not working. In a speech at Agra on 18 March 1956, he expressed his frustration: 'Our community has progressed a little bit with education. Some persons have reached high posts after getting education. But these educated persons have betrayed me.'[36] Some of that may surely be due to his followers, but all of that cannot be dismissed in this way. If it has repeatedly happened over a long time, there is a case for the prescription itself. He did not live to see the aftermath of the conversion to Buddhism. However, his expectation to link Dalits with larger Buddhist communities in the world or making the entire country Buddhist has obviously not fructified. The biggest worrying factor is the ideological obfuscation of Ambedkar that has taken place during the last five decades.

It is not realized, but the straying of the Dalits in varied directions claiming his legacy must by far be the most damaging development. It is this loss of the ideological Ambedkar that has enabled right-wing Hindutva forces, the ideological opponents of what he stood for, to completely hijack him. It is time for people to sit up and examine what has gone wrong.

This project of critically reflecting on his praxis was conceived with this vision. While we expected that some beginning in this direction would be made by examining Ambedkar's views on some of the things listed above, the contributing scholars had their own way of choosing the issue to reflect upon. The cautionary preface that the volume stands for a critical examination of Ambedkar's praxis has obviously not worked fully, but as we imagined a modest beginning has certainly been made. We realized it was perhaps too ambitious to sublimate spontaneously from frigid hagiography to critical reflection. Nonetheless, readers would get a sense of déjà vu while reading most of the essays.

## Structure and Contents

The book contains a total of twenty-one essays which are divided into six sections: (1) Ambedkar's Struggle in the Global Perspective, (2) Ambedkar's Scholarship, (3) Ambedkar's Revolution, (4) Ambedkar and the Motifs of Freedom, (5) The Radical Humanism of Ambedkar and (6) Ambedkar, a Critical Radical Perspective.

In the first section, Ronald Hall and Nehra Mishra compare the Dalit and African-American movements through the water struggle movement—a novel way to understand the struggle of livelihood—by looking at Ambedkar's water satyagraha in Mahad and the current fiasco in Flint, Michigan. In their essay, 'Ambedkar and King: The Subjugation of Caste/Race vis-à-vis Colourism', they theorize the experiences of Dalits and African Americans viewed through a 'philosophical reconstruction' of the phenomenon of skin colour understood as 'colourism'. They have attempted to attribute the suffering of Dalits and African Americans to the mode of a colour-based institutionalized system. This system has the potential to posit a collective identification in the universal oppressive structures which otherwise localize the Dalit and African-American experiences. Hall and Mishra find this to be a drawback in raising the united Dalit–African American oppression 'to the level of necessary consciousness'. The authors' arguments would bring certain significant debates to the table.

Ashwin Desai and Goolam Vahed in their pioneering work on Ambedkar in the African context explore the contemporary issues of South African politics through Ambedkar's lens. They argue that all the nuances of decolonization in contemporary society remain critically unexplored, thus it is Ambedkar's critical antidote to caste structures that has the potential to speak to these issues in Africa. Although in the indentured framework caste was 'punctured and trespassed', Desai and Vahed argue that Ambedkar's idea of caste continues to inspire theories that address issues surrounding social and political inclusivity. Directing the critique against Gandhi's caste perspective in South Africa, they find experiences analogous to the contemporary South African political situation.

Gary Tartakov makes a case for the comparative framework between Dalits, African Americans and Jews as distinctively unique communities in their experiences of being criminalized, and how traditional hierarchy plays a role in the persecution and exploitation of Jews. Looking at the comparable experiences of criminalization and hierarchy attached to these three groups, Tartakov marshals a new comparative scholarship by forging the trio of oppression.

Kevin Brown's essay, 'African-American Perspective on Common Struggles', brings forth a much-needed statement on the comparative as well as interlocking connections that build up over the shared solidarities and historical connections of African Americans in the US and Dalits in India. Reviewing the historical as well as contemporary inspirations gained through each other's struggles, Brown charts the advantages of engaging with the solidarity struggles of these groups and expects that on the policy level as well as socioeconomic plane, Dalits and African Americans 'could draw inspiration and moral and legal legitimacy within their own country'.

Samuel Myers, Jr and Vanishree Radhakrishna compare the extent of hate crimes against African Americans in the US and atrocities committed against Dalits in India. The analysis aims to serve as a comparison between the economic, social and legal framework within which caste and race find their respective spaces in present-day India and USA.

Suraj Yengde delves into the understudied segment of Ambedkar's foreign policy. Locating the Dalit in the universal movement of civil rights, Yengde formulates a theory of Dalit universalism. The Dalit movement's lack of global appeal has to do with the failed policies of the Dalit social and political movements that did not export the Dalit cause across the world in their seventy years of history. By looking at Ambedkar's work in the international stream of human and sociopolitical rights' struggle, Yengde critically examines how Ambedkar and his movement neglected to build solidarities with the Black African nationalist movements and radical anti-imperialist movements across the globe.

In the second section, Partha Chatterjee writes about the less discussed questions of minorities through Ambedkar's analysis of the minority situation in caste-sensitive India. Chatterjee provides a tour de force within the politically nuanced thinking of Ambedkar. It is to the credit of Ambedkar's formal academic training, and his belief in it was incomparable to 'any other political leader in modern India'. Chatterjee surveys Ambedkar's evolving views from the 1920s to 1956 on the question of political rights of minorities. The changes in Ambedkar's views, Chatterjee argues, were set in certain republican constitutional values. Ambedkar's rationalist bearing brings a daunting critique to the foundations of modern society. Ambedkar's primary political concerns could be well drafted into his struggles for providing a legible and workable definition of 'minority'. It was not merely the calculus of demography that determined minority, according to Ambedkar, but also the experiences of subjugation and oppression. Thus, he formulated the 'special representation of minorities' as opposed to the widely accepted 'universal representation in the general body' which would provide representation in the government in addition to the legal measures. However, ignorance of Ambedkar's theory of minority rights has helped the Bharatiya Janata Party sideline the crucial Muslim vote bank by outwardly overlooking the Muslim minority. This could be possible, Chatterjee argues, due to the non-representation of Muslims in the reserved form of seats. Since Ambedkar's theory is widely accepted and incorporated in the makeup of Scheduled Castes (SCs), Chatterjee asks what can be done for the annihilation of caste.

Ambedkar was a busy man from his adolescence. As a student in Mumbai, New York or London, he had his hands full with gathering books and taking an overwhelming number of courses. After completing his studies and armed with the highest degrees in economics and law, Ambedkar found himself jostling between the legal profession, academics, social activism and at the same time advocacy with the British government to secure rights for Untouchables from the 1920s to the 1940s. Rohit De's essay, 'Lawyering as Politics: The Legal Practice of Dr Ambedkar, Bar at Law', digs into the legal registers of Ambedkar's career. By surveying newspaper reports and law cases, De offers some of the undiscussed aspects of Barrister Ambedkar. When the likes of Gandhi, Jinnah and Nehru were busy protecting the rights of the capitalists, Ambedkar consciously chose to fight the cases of workers and trade unions and became their chosen counsel. He took up cases of land rights, the working class and civil liberties in the colonial state. Ambedkar's law practice could be divided into four different primary fields: politics, community, the poor and constitutional practice. The position of Ambedkar as a counsel for Dalits, communists, maharajas and Chitpavan Brahmins, along with defending his clients on the questions of sex and social hygiene, is explored in this essay.

In the third section, Hira Singh underscores the importance and influences of studying Marx, Weber and Ambedkar. In his essay, he weds these thoughts to propose a radical rearrangement in anti-caste activism. He draws on the process of historical materialism as the primary motivator that initiated peasant revolts in the early 20th century, leading to the accession of princely states by firming up the class–caste equation in post-Independence India. Singh argues that Ambedkar's understanding of caste and its material relations reads closely with the Weberian distinction of 'status' as opposed to the economic centrism of class position in society. Weber's emphasis on the caste system as a primary Hindu institution that establishes Brahmin domination is placed alongside Ambedkar's thesis on the Brahmin supremacist position in the caste system.

The state promoted the myth that India is a constitutional democracy. This myth has been exploded by the accumulated democratic deficit of India over the last seven decades. Except for the ritual of periodic elections, which are managed by undemocratic parties with money and muscle power, on every conceivable count, the postcolonial regime would not qualify to be called a democracy. Was it really founded on Ambedkar's conception of democracy? Jean Drèze answers this question by presenting Ambedkar's radical conception of democracy in the essay 'Dr Ambedkar and the Future of Indian Democracy'. Ambedkar warned that the political democracy that India adopted would not last unless it was founded on social (the annihilation of caste) and economic democracy (socialism). Ambedkar may be rightly questioned about the practicability of his methods to achieve them, but the fact remains that what is claimed is light years away from Ambedkar's conception of democracy.

Chandraiah Gopani makes a claim for the 'invisible' Dalits who are left out in the process of democratic transformation. The lowest of the low remain out of the scope of development. Gopani finds the ignorance of these communities to be an unaddressed problem for the Dalit movement. The cross-caste solidarities among SCs do not take place owing to the dominance of numerically strong castes in various states. Due to this, the

Dalit castes that are left out are used by Hindutva groups and forced into their projects of violence. Such groups act vehemently against privileged Dalit castes because there is an absence of social endosmosis. The barriers created through prohibitions on intra-caste marriage and predetermined caste occupations push the oppressed community further into a lower order. Gopani directs his critique at the Dalit public and private intellectual discourse. A much-awaited interrogation of the frozen Dalit idiom is effectively handled in his essay, 'New Dalit Movements: An Ambedkarite Perspective'.

In 'Bisociative Revolution', Bronislaw Czarnocha proposes a utilitarian model drawing from Marxism and Ambedkarism that are 'connected as two independent concepts which are in close mutual interaction'. He defines this in the bisociative model of the 'Aha! Moment' also referred to as the Eureka Moment. Czarnocha adds that this concept brings a further informative argument to the telling of the Ambedkar and Marx question. The idea of the stand-alone positions of two categories as super categories without subduing each other and therefore merging with a 'compromise' theory is succinctly argued. Czarnocha emphasizes on moving beyond the intersectionality that places its focus on identity liberation movements and embracing a 'compromise' to dialectically synthesize class and caste struggles. Czarnocha argues that by eliminating certain aspects of Marxism and Ambedkarism, an 'effective integration' is possible so that they can be composed into one reading.

Anand Teltumbde in his essay, 'Strategy of Conversion to Buddhism: Intent and Aftermath', looks at Ambedkar's conversion to Buddhism as a strategy consistent with the goal of his life, which may be conceptualized in terms of a continuum ranging from the emancipation of Dalits (annihilation of caste) to the emancipation of mankind (liberty, equality, fraternity), and examines it on the touchstone of the outcome it produced. Ambedkar's interpretation of the Buddha was more an answer to the social and religious oppressions that his community was facing. Teltumbde distinguishes two forms of Buddhism in the Ambedkarite sense: existential and spiritual. The existential approach was a pragmatic approach which offered a new identity through neo-Buddhism—Navayana Buddhism. The spiritual was an individualistic and self-centred obsession with the ritualistic aspects of Buddhism. This attitude largely prevailed through the practices of vipassana and other meditation techniques.

In the fourth section, Anjani Kapoor and Manu Bhagavan explore Ambedkar's rigour with the idea of isolation in the tumult of differences in their essay, 'Beyond the Nation: Ambedkar and the Anti-isolation of Fellowship'. They look at the experiences of isolation in describing kinship-based national identity. Ambedkar's emphasis on a common humanity is argued in the extended analysis of his fight against the social, economic and grand political order.

Sukhadeo Thorat presents exhaustive data that questions the adaptability of caste and untouchability to the political and economic scene of post-Independence India. After surveying the data on caste factors and proffering a theoretical analysis, Thorat offers recommendations to deal with the problems of 'persistence of discrimination and atrocity'. It is in the economic empowerment of Dalits where Thorat seeks to find answers to the Dalit predicament. His approach is substantiated by empirical evidence from the field. He revisits Ambedkar's model of separate settlement to recover segregated Dalit communities in India who continue to occupy the lowest of each hierarchy—economic, social, welfare and rights-based mechanisms.

In the fifth section, Nicolas Jaoul marks the distinction between the ideal prototype of secular and religious citizenship in the political landscape of a modern nation state. He argues that Ambedkar's turn to religion towards the end of his life was to secure 'political autonomy from the state'. Jaoul juxtaposes the idea of religion as a moral sphere and the state as a liberal value institution. Ambedkar chose a more encompassing humanely spirited religion, Buddhism, over the limited axioms of state liberalism that the postcolonial Indian government proffered.

In 'A Derridean Reading of Ambedkar's *The Buddha and His Dhamma*' Rajesh Sampath puts Ambedkar's critical thought alongside that of Jacques Derrida. Sampath charts out the similarities of destructive mechanisms of supremacies that operated in both works. Referencing *The Buddha and His Dhamma*, Sampath aims to extend Ambedkar's analytical thought to the European philosophical traditions of which Ambedkar was a student. Looking at the Brahminical Hindu philosophy of supremacy, Sampath reads the caste system and patriarchal domination as a logocentric speech. Examining the twenty-two vows administered by Ambedkar on the day of his conversion to Buddhism, Sampath looks at the causes of justice, mercy and compassion that are part of Ambedkar's vista, which remains unexplored as a human rights tool. The modern human rights mechanisms that originate from the Judaeo-Christian understanding of human rights fail to measure the problem of caste.

The sixth section brings the book to a close. While one laments the lack of dialogue between the Dalit movement and the movement of African

Americans, particularly at Ambedkar's silence, one is surprised to note that it is Gandhi—who for the larger part of his social and political life opposed Ambedkar's project of annihilation of caste—has been adopted as the inspirational icon by African Americans. Lama Choyin Rangdrol in his essay, 'Strange Bedfellows Sideline Ambedkar', examines how religion is the undertone for the strange distance between Ambedkar and Black leadership. He explores the reasons for the Black community of America getting attracted to Gandhi's ideology and finds them in the elite Black Christians' culture of 'marginalization of a-hegemonic thought, represented by Gandhi's nemesis, Ambedkar'. He speculates that if the African Americans had followed Ambedkar's path and abandoned the 'slave religion of their New World' identity en masse, the act itself would have sent a shockwave throughout the world, it would have been 'a global shaming of Western imperialism's status quo'.

Hugo Gorringe looks at 'Ambedkar Icons' in his ethnographically rich documentation of Ambedkar's location as an icon in the public sphere. The author reports on the Tamil Nadu state and its political culture surrounding the deification of icons, looking closely at the Dalit political party Viduthalai Chiruthaigal Katchi (VCK—Liberation Panther Party, the largest Dalit party in the state) run by a charismatic leader, Thirumavalavan. This essay is an important statement in the growing Ambedkarite assertion that prioritized the deifying of an icon of the community over gaining material benefits that could play an important role in strengthening the condition of the Dalit community. Although Ambedkar as an icon has proffered a caste–intra-caste diversity to unify under a banner, this has also given opportunities of misappropriation to antagonistic Hindutva Brahminical groups. Iconization comes with benefits as well as challenges. Dead Ambedkar is undergoing these.

Anupama Rao in her essay, 'Ambedkar's Dalit and the Question of Caste Subalternity', considers the question of the global Dalit anchored in Ambedkar's philosophical quest to build a newer Dalit identity that was historically rooted and politically constructed. Ambedkar's Depressed Classes offered a move away from the colonial construction of minority based on religious identity to the material needs of the Dalit castes that lived a life of social deprivation, stratification and marginalization. Rao addresses the penultimate question in Ambedkar's political Dalit: 'How did historical comparison and global connection aid in staging Dalit life and the persistent agonisms that structured caste Hindu society?' This essay adds value to and simultaneously examines the critical Dalit thought that is available in mainstream discourse. Drawing on Ambedkar's hermeneutical reading of the caste situation, Rao argues that Ambedkar matured Marxism into heterodox Marxism by 'foregrounding the difference of untouchability and specifying outcaste politics'.

Ritu Sen Chaudhuri juxtaposes Ambedkar and Louis Dumont by offering a critical feminist reading interwoven through caste, gender and sexuality. Looking at Ambedkar's intervention and eventual 'subversion' of the Indological school of thought, Sen Chaudhuri questions the orientalist and non-orientalist framing of Dumont's and Ambedkar's respective analyses of the caste question. Sen Chaudhuri reviews Ambedkar's take on women's oppression charted in his extended terrain of scholarship on Hinduism, Brahminism and the sociological analysis of caste. She explores the relationship of caste and gender as forms of hierarchies to each other and suggests that Ambedkar's understanding of caste–gender–sexuality departs from the limited orientalist view to become a forceful act of political exercise.

We hope the readers will appreciate this modest attempt at examining Ambedkar's praxis from the standpoint of its impact on the course of Indian history.

Anand Teltumbde and Suraj Yengde
Sanquelim, Goa, and Cambridge, Massachusetts
October 2018

I

# AMBEDKAR'S STRUGGLE IN THE GLOBAL PERSPECTIVE

# AMBEDKAR AND KING

## THE SUBJUGATION OF CASTE OR RACE VIS-À-VIS COLOURISM

*Ronald E. Hall and Neha Mishra*

## Introduction

Some anthropologists contend that the original inhabitants of India, called the Dravidians, were dark-skinned.[1] The Dravidians were confronted by a light-skinned population called the Aryans, a nomadic group that arrived in the Indian subcontinent from west central Asia circa 1500 BCE.[2] The Aryans were a violent people who conquered the Dravidians upon their arrival in India. They invented a cultural structure to secure themselves and their descendants by inserting the concept of superior status for light skin into Indian society. The remaining Dravidian population eventually internalized the Aryan caste structure invented to standardize the latter's status quo, making it the dominant norm in Indian culture. Subsequently, the caste system constructed by the Aryans institutionalized the Aryan superiority ranking on the basis of purity suggested by light-coloured skin. This history of the Aryan caste system is gleaned from the Vedas, otherwise referred to as the books of knowledge.[3]

The term 'caste' is not of Indian origin. Formulated by the Portuguese in the 16th century, the word has roots in the Portuguese word *casta*, which literally refers to breed.[4] Varna, which finds mention in the Rig Veda, the oldest of the Vedas, referring to class, also means colour in Sanskrit and is essentially a colour system construct. Thus, those who insist that caste rather than skin colour is the reigning demographic in India are unaware of its origin. In the underlying modern-day existence of the Indian caste system there is little reference to and acknowledgement of skin colour by the educated elite as the tool by which all factions of

Indian society are organized. By said organized arrangement the Indian caste system then operates as a hierarchy of five distinct categories. The Indian population in its innate capacity associates these categories with different shades of skin. The highest or most superior caste is Brahmin, defined by and/or associated by the majority with light skin. Brahmins as a caste are represented by priests, teachers and judges of societal norms. Next in the order of rank is another light-skinned affiliated faction referred to as Kshatriya. Placed at an elevated level in the social hierarchy as power holders, royals and other warrior castes belonged to this faction. Light skin brings with it acceptability, desirability and power. Just below the Kshatriya in status is another light-skinned affiliated faction referred to as Vaisya, which consists of farmers and an assortment of merchants. In the caste system, the final and bottom-most in rank are the light-skinned Sudras, regarded as craftspersons and labourers.[5] These four aforementioned castes represented the formal caste structure. However, a fifth, lowest caste, exists, with a de facto inferior status—the people belonging to it are known as Untouchables. Unlike their upper-caste counterparts, Untouchables are affiliated with dark skin regardless of their skin colour.[6] While skin colours in each caste may vary, the higher castes are affiliated with light skin and the lower castes with dark skin.

The issue of colourism as a variant of racism manifested via skin colour remains controversial in conjunction with caste and race. Indian scholars contend that caste is a matter of birth. Internationally, others at the World Conference against Racism held in South Africa in 2001 contended that any discussions of racism should exclude caste. However, in both instances of race and caste, identity and/or inferiority cannot be established absent visual speculation. The most consistently applied trait in observations of race and caste is arguably that of skin colour.[7]

Aside from caste, race in America, as suggested by Michael Banton,[8] includes the assumed rights of a dominant Caucasian or light-skinned race group to exclude a dominant African-American or dark-skin-defined race group from sharing in the material and symbolic rewards of status and power.[9] This differs from ethnocentricity in that one's superiority is based upon a racial category.[10] The racial category of the dominant group in America is eventually rationalized as White supremacy and assumed as a natural order of the human biological universe.[11]

The most zealous proponents of race in America profess that light-skinned Caucasians are superior to dark-skinned non-Caucasian race groups, including African Americans and Indians.[12] They postulate that

Caucasian race groups have been endowed with the intellectual capacities necessary to bring about the advancement of civilization. This so-called 'advanced civilization' was initially a thinly veiled form of colonialism devoted to rationalizing the right of Caucasian race groups to embark upon a worldwide mission aimed at the exploitation of non-Caucasian peoples.[13] By way of race, Western dominance left no terrain or societal institution untouched, particularly in the modern era. After centuries of race-based privilege, race is sustained in the postmodern Western era to enable the confiscation of freedom, justice and equality from less aggressive groups. The ultimate outcome of skin colour as designate of race is global domination by a light-skinned power structure exacerbated by the Indian caste system.[14] This unprecedented historical arrangement prompted the urgency to banish the yoke of oppression, personified in the activism of Dr Bhimrao Ramji Ambedkar of India and the Reverend Martin Luther King Jr of the United States of America.

## Dr Bhimrao Ramji Ambedkar

Dr Ambedkar was born in Mhow in the Central Provinces, which is today known as Madhya Pradesh. The Ambedkar family was known to be of the Hindu Mahar caste. As members of this caste, they were regarded and treated as Untouchables. In an effort to provide for the family, the elder Ambedkar obtained employment with the British East India Company. Ambedkar's father had been a soldier in the Indian Army and eventually rose to the rank of subedar. He was an especially educated man, given his Untouchable status, displaying a value for scholarship by urging his children to learn as much as they could and put in their best efforts at school.[15]

Since he maintained some degree of status in the Indian Army, Ambedkar's father was in a position to advocate for his children's education at the local government school. While admission to school was an advantage for Untouchable-caste Indians, once enrolled, the treatment they were likely to encounter could be discouraging. They were often forced to sit outside the classroom. Such mundane basic tasks as getting a drink of water would require an Untouchable to ask a higher-caste member to pour it for them from a distance so as not to be personally polluted. The fact of an Untouchable student's thirst was irrelevant to members of higher castes, and thus they were subjugated by tradition and custom.[16]

In 1912, Ambedkar graduated from college, having earned degrees in economics and political science. Not much time later, his father died, on

2 February 1913. Shortly after, Ambedkar was granted a scholarship of $11.5 per month by Sayajirao Gaikwad III, the ruler of a princely state in Baroda, to study in the US. He enrolled at the American Ivy League's Columbia University in New York City, where he signed up for the graduate studies programme in political science.

Ambedkar eventually published his graduate studies dissertation, *The Evolution of Provincial Finance in British India*. He had previously published a work entitled *Castes in India: Their Mechanism, Genesis and Development*. Having completed his education in New York, he moved to London, England, where he got admission at the London School of Economics. There he studied law, which resulted in a doctoral thesis in economics. The beginning of the First World War and the expiration of his scholarship compelled Ambedkar to terminate his studies in England and return to India, where he was reintroduced to the ravages of caste discrimination. No longer willing to acquiesce to such treatment, he accepted work as a private tutor and an accountant. He also managed to start his own consulting business, but all these ventures failed due largely to the caste limitations he encountered as an Untouchable.[17]

With the help of influential friends, Ambedkar eventually acquired an appointment as a professor of political economy at the Sydenham College of Commerce and Economics in Mumbai. Later, he returned to England and again was able to continue his work with the support of friends. In 1923, he entered the University of London, authored a thesis titled *The Problem of the Rupee* and was awarded a DSc degree. This gave Ambedkar admission to the British Bar. On 28 June 1927, this lower-caste Indian, defined by his Untouchable status as dark skin affiliated, though relatively light-skinned himself, was officially conferred a PhD by Columbia University.[18]

## Martin Luther King, Jr

Martin Luther King was born Michael King on 15 January 1929.[19] Subsequently, in honour of the religious icon, Michael King's father changed his name from Michael to Martin Luther.[20] The King family was a key member of the Atlanta clergy; beginning with his grandfather, King was associated with a line of pastors who served the Ebenezer Baptist Church in Atlanta, Georgia. From 1960 until his assassination in 1968, King performed his duties as co-pastor of the church.

Before attending college, King was a student in the segregated Georgia public school system from which he graduated at the age of fifteen. Similar to Ambedkar, he displayed a keen intellect in his youth. As a young man, he was admitted to the premier HBCU (historically Black college and university) Morehouse College. HBCUs evolved on account of the fact that it was illegal for African Americans to attend a White college. In 1948, King graduated from Morehouse College having earned a BA degree. His matriculation conformed to the educational journey made earlier by his father and grandfather.

After Morehouse, King studied at the Crozer Theological Seminary in Pennsylvania. Although Crozer was a predominantly Euro-American institution, King was elected president of the senior class. In 1951, the institution awarded him a BD degree, giving him access to a fellowship at Crozer, which he used to pursue graduate studies at Boston University. Here, King studied theology and earned a doctorate in 1955. Education was not the sole turning point in his life, for, as a student at Boston University, he met his future wife in Coretta Scott. She was described as a 'woman of uncommon intellectual and artistic attainments'. Shortly thereafter, King and Scott were married. The union brought them four children: two sons and two daughters.[21]

In addition to his oratory as a clergyman, King authored numerous articles and books,[22] including *Stride toward Freedom: The Montgomery Story* (1958), *The Measure of a Man* (1959), *Strength to Love* (1963), *Why We Can't Wait* (1963) and *Where Do We Go from Here: Chaos or Community?* (1967). After being arrested, King wrote the well-known 'Letter from a Birmingham Jail',[23] dated 16 April 1963, which was to be a manifesto of the African-American struggle, culminating in the Alabama protest drives where he advocated for the registration of African Americans to vote. This act inspired the peaceful march on Washington, DC in 1963, where 2,50,000 people reportedly gathered to hear King's celebrated speech, 'I Have a Dream'.[24] Having gained considerable stature and recognition, King met with President John F. Kennedy and effectively campaigned for President Lyndon B. Johnson. For his work in civil rights, King was arrested, assaulted, awarded honorary degrees and eventually named 1963 Man of the Year by *Time* magazine.[25] By then, he stood as a leadership symbol of African-American freedom, justice and equality who was to be known by the entire world.

Both Ambedkar and King faced the most oppressive circumstances. While they each displayed keen intellects, neither entered educational institutions in their respective countries under normal conditions. Ambedkar was prevented from forming any close or normal associations with his scholastic peers as it was believed that Dalits were not worthy of receiving education. Similarly, King could not attend any college other than those started and maintained by the African-American community. While many such institutions, like Morehouse, were of high quality, they could not equal the financial prowess of the larger government-funded institutions. Thus, they were lacking in resources required by students.

Despite their subjection to formidable prejudice and rampant discrimination, Ambedkar and King made their way forward to become well educated. Ambedkar's journey was characterized by caste. King's journey was characterized by race. Both encountered considerable oppression not irrelevant to skin colour, that is, colourism. Rather than use their education to compensate for colourism or enrich themselves personally, both men devoted their lives to lifting untold numbers of their people from the oppression they had experienced as able young men. Among the most dramatic aspects of such oppression common to colourism was access to water.

## Oppression by Restricted Access to Water

In juxtaposing Ambedkar and King, it is critical to document the accessibility of water for both their peoples. Access to water is an effective metaphor for characterizing the struggle of the Indian Untouchable and African American to escape oppression for freedom, justice and equality in the new millennium. Access to public drinking locations has been limited by the various forms of race discrimination in America and caste discrimination in India that the oppressed populations in both countries have suffered for generations. In India, that suffering is illustrated in the confrontations associated with the Chavadar water tank,[26] a public facility situated in the vicinity of Mahad, a town in the Kolaba district of Bombay Presidency. The Chavadar tank contained a considerable volume of water replenished by rain and a number of natural local springs. The sides of the tank were reinforced by raised structures designed to contain the water. Around the tank there were lesser parcels of land owned by upper-caste Indians. Extending from their land was a municipal road circling the Chavadar tank. A short distance away were houses occupied by Untouchables. However, the tank was located in the hub of upper-caste Hindu influence as well as their residences. Complications arose because the 'touchable' lot did not allow Untouchable people from taking water from the tank. The reason for doing so wasn't just the fear that the water would get putrid or dirty with the touch of lower-caste

Untouchables but also the fear of equal status being established between them, hence challenging the old norm of the discriminatory Dharmashastras (scriptures), which maintained the inferiority of Untouchables.[27]

The history of the Chavadar tank is extensive and has conflicting accounts to the extent that its origin is unknown. When and by whom it was built is a matter of debate. However, in 1869, after a municipality was founded by the Mahad town authorities, the government assumed control of the tank's water, and since then it has been regarded as the property of the municipality, which defined it as a public tank. Yet, despite being regarded as a public tank, Untouchables were forbidden to drink from it or carry away water from it.[28] The designated water source for Untouchables was limited to the tank in their living space in Mahad, which was located a considerable distance from the centre of town and was difficult to access. This created a day-to-day struggle and hardship for the Untouchable population even for their basic right to drinking water.

Limiting Untouchables' access to water was a form of oppression that brought grave hardship and humiliation upon them. No Indian outside the Untouchable community objected with any consequence. Eventually, in 1923, the Legislative Council of Bombay adopted a policy which required that Untouchables got access to all public wells maintained by citizen tax revenues.[29] This resolution extended to bodies designated by the government including those brought by statutes as well as public schools, courts, offices and so forth. Therefore, according to Ambedkar:

> In pursuance of the foregoing Council Resolution the Government of Bombay are pleased to direct that all heads of offices should give effect to the resolution so far as it related to the public places, institutions belonging to and maintained by Government. The Collectors should be requested to advise the local bodies in their jurisdiction to consider the desirability of accepting the recommendations made in the Resolution.[30]

Bringing this governmental decision forward, the collector of Kolaba then provided a copy for the consideration of the Mahad municipality. In acting upon that, the municipality then adopted a relevant resolution, which it passed on 5 January 1924. In essence, the resolution established that the municipality had no objection to the Untouchables' use of the Chavadar tank.[31]

Following the adoption of the above resolution, Ambedkar led a contingent of Untouchables to a conference held in the district of Kolaba.

It took place on 18–20 March 1927 and was attended by more than 2500 Untouchable participants, whose excitement was apparent. Ambedkar gave a presidential address where he insisted that Untouchables should negate their 'dirty and vicious habits' and embrace their 'manhood' to the fullest extent. Various higher-caste Hindus attending the conference joined in advocating that Untouchables demand all that had been granted to them by law. This conference ended on a positive note.

However, during a subsequent gathering, it was noted that Untouchables encountered grave difficulties in accessing drinking water. Even at the conference, they had to buy water worth Rs 40 at the rate of 1 paisa per pitcher.[32] This was now unacceptable to Ambedkar. Thus, on 20 March, the conference attendees assembled at nine in the morning. They agreed upon the resolutions and the need to take action. Inspired by Ambedkar, they decided that they should visit the Chavadar tank and exercise their rightful access to it by law. They referenced the fact that their Hindu friends present had agreed to the resolution and to assist them. However, confronted with the prospect of dire consequences by the rigid upper castes, the Hindu attendees who had urged Untouchables to assert themselves hesitated, but the latter were undeterred by this. They were in fact inspired as in a call to arms. All 2500 Untouchable attendees, led by Ambedkar, marched through the streets to the amazement of onlookers. Determined never to submit, the Untouchable attendees proceeded to the well in Mahad, but, despite having been supported by the Hindus at the conference, were met in a ferocious attack by other Hindus, who appeared determined to defeat them. For the moment, the activists retreated.

Undeterred, they returned several months later. On 25 December, they renewed the struggle. However, the government had prohibited Untouchables from taking certain actions, a decree which Ambedkar honoured for the sake of legality. Seeking a legal alternative, he burned a copy of the *Manusmriti*, which introduced into the annals of Indian history the first battle of Untouchables for freedom, justice and equality. This struggle for water contains a metaphor: the oppression of Untouchables by caste is synonymous with the oppression of African Americans by race. Evident in the colourism relative to dark skin, the struggle for freedom, justice and equality for both is dramatically displayed in the African-American quest for water, in the historical as well as modern American era.[33]

Oppression due to denied access to water for African Americans was no less problematic when it came to attaining freedom, justice and equality than it was for the Indian Untouchable castes. During the post–Civil

War era, African Americans were officially free to drink water from fountains and various locations of their choosing by judicial decree. This was similar to the Indian Untouchables' gaining access to water by de jure documentation. However, despite the Civil Rights Acts of 1866 and 1875 and the Fourteenth and Fifteenth Amendments to the US Constitution, the decree was rendered meaningless. Denial of access to public and clean drinking water for African Americans became institutionalized by the quasi legislation historically referred to in America as the Jim Crow laws.[34] The Jim Crow laws were not laws per se but de facto customs contingent upon race that operated similar to the Indian caste system. It reduced African-American citizens in good standing to the status of second-class citizens. This lasted officially from 1877 to 1964, although in fact its strains are unofficially felt even today.[35]

Initially, African Americans were prohibited from using the same drinking facilities as Euro-Americans, similar to Indian Untouchables in areas designated for the upper castes. When travelling by public transportation under the Jim Crow laws, African Americans were assigned seats not where they chose to sit but always in the back of the bus, a humiliation that labelled them as 'less than'. Similar to the Untouchable community and caste in India, African Americans' access to water was subjugated by 'Coloureds Only' and 'Whites Only' signs posted at public water fountains. Rather than risk a breach of the Jim Crow laws, the Euro-American public preferred the thirst and humiliation of African Americans.

Local court decisions around the country resulted in the 1896 *Plessy vs Ferguson* decision, which officially segregated Americans by race per skin colour and, in effect, legally prohibited African-American citizens from drinking water from other than designated 'Coloureds Only' water fountains. No doubt, African Americans had legal access to public sources of water, but those sources were limited whereas their tax revenues, which provided for all public sources, were not. African Americans by race could only drink from designated sources as Untouchables in India by caste could only drink from designated sources. The unwritten objective in both instances was in fact the oppression of an entire group of people as inferior.[36]

The defining trait in India and America was differentiated as caste and race, but in commonality it was skin colour as skin colour was the affiliate of both caste and race. No less a body than the US Supreme Court supported the idea of dark-skinned African Americans being inferior, in the court's Dred Scott decision of 1857.[37] The court's official position was that African Americans are, as all dark-skinned peoples of the world, 'an inferior and subordinate class of beings'. The tenacity of this belief remains consistent in the modern era as observed in the predominantly African-American city of Flint, Michigan.[38]

Flint, Michigan, is located approximately 60 miles north of the predominantly African-American city of Detroit, Michigan. It was once known for its automobile industry which attracted numerous citizens from around the country to work in its plants. With competition from foreign auto manufacturers and deindustrialization, Flint was eventually subjected to a critical economic downturn, which culminated in Flint having primarily an African-American population. In an effort to 'save' money, the conservative Republican Party, under the leadership of the state's Republican governor, risked the health and well-being of African-American youth well into the foreseeable future by acting in a less-than-conducive manner.

A 72 inch water pipeline that was the source of Flint's clean water, provided by Detroit, was deliberately closed. Despite access to such water for decades without incident, the supply of clean water for an 'inferior' African-American population was deemed unnecessary by the political administration, and, indeed, this was secondary to other city concerns. In the aftermath, African-American residents of Flint were forced to drink unclean water laced with lead toxins, known to affect the intellectual development of children in particular. This created a toxic drinking water crisis for Flint, and complaints about the water to the city government and to the governor were ignored. Therefore, the official continuation of Jim Crow attitudes via denying access to clean water in Flint de facto sustains the subjugation of an oppressed African-American population who, because of the colour of their skin, share an affinity with the struggles of India's Untouchable population. In the aftermath is established a clear and potent strategy for delivering both populations from oppression, namely, juxtaposing the lives of Ambedkar and King who, by having non-White skin colour in common, encountered difficulty in accessing safe, clean water and were encouraged by considering the common foe of colourism as a metaphor for the struggle for freedom, justice and equality.

The commonality in their lives motivated Ambedkar and King along similar passages to free themselves and their people from the ravages of oppression. King was an admirer of India's Gandhi and his non-violent resistance to the British, which influenced his civil liberties movement,[39] though Gandhi was criticized by Ambedkar and Dalits for not acknowledging the real downtrodden status of the Dalit population in

India and rather choosing to call them Harijan ('God's favourite people'). Gandhi was arguing for the equality for all citizens while Ambedkar then was demanding special status and reservation for Untouchables, because he knew equity was what they needed after being oppressed for hundreds of years to come at par with others. It is likely that their disagreement was to some extent a function of the Western media in which Gandhi was memorialized. But the common focus on the termination of oppression by both men was no less apparent.

Following the American Civil War, President Abraham Lincoln declared African-American slaves to be free. Similar declarations to end oppression were made by Ambedkar in his drafting of the Indian Constitution. While laws were passed, Dalits as Untouchables in India and African Americans in the US continued to face oppression in their daily lives, as suggested by the modern-day events outlined above. This motivated some to seek a new direction in arming themselves in order to access their right to the dignity and respect denied to them by their oppressors. In America, African Americans organized the Black Panthers for a new direction. In India, there emerged the Dalit Panthers. Both fought for similar objectives, motivated by their goal to end blatant oppression. However, Gandhi and King, in the elimination of oppression, maintained their struggles in a religious context.

## Discussion

Juxtaposing Ambedkar and King is germane to freedom, justice and equality for their people and for the unification of their struggles in the context of skin colour, previously designated as colourism.[40] Colourism is not mere political abstraction reflected passively by culture, nationality, caste or race. Nor is colourism representative of some nefarious Western plot to hold hostage and oppress Dalits and African Americans by skin colour. It is, rather, a distribution of local political sensitivity to aesthetic, scholarly and cultural texts. It is an elaboration not only of a basic skin colour distinction but a perspective.[41] By such a perspective, scholarly discovery and/or philosophical reconstruction not only control but in some cases manipulate that which is manifestly different, as in caste and/or race. Dalit and African-American oppression is otherwise a phenomenon that is brought about overtly or covertly by the efforts of any individual political operative, but is generated by an uneven exchange with various sources of caste and race power, including political will power, intellectual will power, cultural will power and moral will power. Indeed, oppression by colourism does not represent India or America on the whole and as such has less to do with caste and race than with human coexistence.[42]

Because colourism by oppression is a cultural and political fact both at home and abroad, it exists not in some archival vacuum or demented fantasy. Quite to the contrary, it is apparent that what is thought or said about colourism follows certain intellectual prescriptions. It is evidenced by a considerable degree of nuance and elaboration seen as the mechanism of a broad, elusive colour-based superstructure. Thus, most Euro-Americans in the US and higher-caste Indians in India ignore the reality that African-American race rights and Indian caste rights are advocated in an oppressive context[43] since it does not address the core issue as to the reason of discrimination of a particular caste or race. The oppressive context then dilutes the universal nature of such discrimination based on colour. Euro-Americans and higher-caste Hindus overlook the explicit connection between that context and justifications for colourism, which keeps oppositional rhetoric for caste and race pure. Any effort at all to address the subject has been perceived as crudely iconoclastic.

But there is no negating the fact that those against colourism on a world platform have not made a serious effort to effectively bridge the quality-of-life gap between lower- and higher-caste citizens in India. Similarly, African Americans faced the same challenges led by King.[44] Yet, there will remain the perennial escape mechanism of saying that an activist less given to colourism is more concerned with freedom, justice and equality in the abstract as an ideological analysis. In other words, the argument can work quite effectively to block the larger and more intellectually threatening perspective of who benefits by apathy. In the aftermath is a form of colourism even more elusive and insidious than the oppression of Indian Dalits and African Americans taken together.

As it pertains to colourism in the new millennium, caste abusers and racists may say they are against colourism when what they really mean is individual colourism.[45] They refuse to recognize that upper-caste Indians and Euro-Americans benefit as a group from institutional and systemic colourism against all dark-skinned peoples of the world.[46] Thus, all upper-caste Indians in India and Euro-Americans in the US are nepotistic beneficiaries of an oppressive system that bestows upon them inherited 'rights' and privileges absent skill, talent and hard work. For these more 'fortunate' souls to admit their association with colourism would render it impossible for them to deny shared responsibility in the oppression of lower-caste Untouchables and inferior-race African Americans.

By way of the confines of daily life, upper-caste Indians and Euro-Americans as a group in the new millennium appear less than willing to address the existence of privilege while at the same time granting that by caste and race people are acutely disadvantaged.[47] They profess efforts for rights for the oppressed that focus on society's most prestigious and powerful institutions, stopping short of any effort that would limit the caste and race privilege that they benefit from. Such efforts are unspeakable in polite circles and buffer the privileges of power groups from mainstream discussion.

Because modern-day oppression via colourism is endemic in the institutions of India and America—including academia—the oppression of Dalits and African Americans prevails.[48] The polite façade and moral pretence of upper-caste Indians and Euro-Americans destines Dalit and African-American oppression to a longevity rivalled only by the native power group centrism from which it emerged. Thus, the privileged who dare acknowledge colourism prefer to do so in the context of some remote abstraction from self personally. They are instructed by cultural experience to ignore their privilege, much as males are taught to ignore the advantages of gender. Their inability to confront this crime predisposes them to a painful reality, that is, the tradition of colourism. Germane to that reality is an illusive cask of inherited assets that gives them daily advantage for quality of life by caste and race.[49] As a result, they necessarily perceive Dalit and African-American issues via different cultural and national interpretations and cannot acknowledge their own role in sustaining what is in fact an oppressive structure. Thus, oppression by colourism issues locally becomes secondary to caste and race issues because oppression in the end is beneficial to the universal status quo power configuration.[50]

The inability to acknowledge the advantages of colourism well into the new millennium suggests that Dalit and African-American oppression has still not risen to the level of required consciousness. At some level, both the persecuted groups have an astute awareness of the oppression attributable to the skin colour status quo. The result is an intellectual chasm between light-skinned beneficiaries and dark-skinned victims that has rendered colourism all but totally irrelevant to the interests and issues confronting dark-skinned people in the main. Extending from the denial of privilege by colourism is thus ignorance of oppression and the larger superculture from which it emanates.[51] Morality and contribution to oppression is measured by individual effort alone, which allows those so inclined to profess their morality despite their participating in oppression by caste and race.

As members of civil nations, higher-caste Indians and Euro-Americans must be held to a better standard of moral excellence. They have dignity and self-worth pertinent to individual merit. Colourism has not accommodated the oppressed in their efforts to sustain themselves.[52] That being so, 'self-determination' is rendered all but impossible for those so inclined. As an extension of 'individualization', self-determination gives the oppressed licence to have their issues incorporated into the mainstream of public discourse.[53] The fact that it has not been forthcoming lends credibility to the assertion of colourism. Among the more civil-minded there is then an urgent and ubiquitous need to purge colourism from the ethos of humanity for purposes of universal freedom, justice and equality. Such a purge in the new millennium is made apparent by the need for unification of the struggles of the Untouchable caste and so-called inferior African-American race. This can be regarded as a primary global initiative ultimately served by the juxtaposition of Bhimrao Ramji Ambedkar and Martin Luther King, Jr in reference to colour.

## References

King, Martin Luther King, Jr. 1958. *Stride toward Freedom: The Montgomery Story*. New York: Harper & Row.

King, Martin Luther, Jr. *The Papers of Martin Luther King* vol. 5, Threshold of a New Decade, January 1959–December 1960. https://kinginstitute.stanford.edu/king-papers/documents/my-trip-land-gandhi.

King, Martin Luther King, Jr. 1963. *Strength to Love*. New York: Harper & Row.

King, Martin Luther King, Jr. 1963. *Why We Can't Wait*. New York: Harper & Row.

King, Martin Luther King, Jr. 1967. *Where Do We Go from Here: Chaos or Community?* New York: Harper & Row.

Nobelprize.org. 2014.Martin Luther King Jr biography. http://www.nobelprize.org/nobel_prizes/peace/laureates/1964/king-bio.html. Retrieved 12 April 2016.

# CAN AMBEDKAR SPEAK TO AFRICA?

## COLOUR, CASTE AND CLASS STRUGGLES IN CONTEMPORARY SOUTH AFRICA

### *Goolam Vahed and Ashwin Desai*

Around the time that Francis Fukuyama heralded the 'end of history' in his 1989 essay in the American magazine *The National Interest*, Nelson Mandela was released from prison after almost three decades of incarceration. The South Africans' euphoria and expectations scoffed at Fukuyama's assertion. Our history had just begun. Apartheid had bounded us into tight racial boundaries to the extent that at its height some theorists wrote of a colour-caste system. From public toilets to the post office one had to constantly look upwards to the signs marked 'White' and 'Non-White'. By the time Mandela walked out of prison in 1990, much of petty apartheid, as it was dubbed, had eroded. But there was still history to be made, none more than the right for all South Africans to vote and redressing the inequalities imposed by apartheid.

Fast forward to 2018—the centenary of Mandela's birth and the African National Congress's (ANC) twenty-fourth year in power. Criticisms of the transition to democracy are everywhere, reaching back into the Mandela era. A high-ranking former member of Mandela's first cabinet, Ronnie Kasrils, called the period from 1990 a 'Faustian moment', that

> came when we took an IMF loan on the eve of our first democratic election. That loan, with strings attached that precluded a radical economic agenda, was considered a necessary evil, as were concessions to keep negotiations on track and take delivery of the promised land for our people. Doubt had come to reign supreme: we believed, wrongly, there was no other option; that we had to be cautious, since by 1991 our once powerful ally, the Soviet Union, bankrupted by the arms race,

had collapsed. Inexcusably, we had lost faith in the ability of our own revolutionary masses to overcome all obstacles.[1]

Some former ANC members, such as Julius Malema, leader of the Economic Freedom Fighters (EFF) political party, argued that the writing was on the wall from the very beginning. He stated at Oxford University in 2015:

> The deviation from the Freedom Charter was the beginning of selling out of the revolution. When Mandela returned from prison he got separated from Winnie Mandela and went to stay in a house of a rich white man, he was looked after by the Oppenheimers. Mandela used to attend those club meetings of those white men who owned the South African economy. The Nelson we celebrate now is a stage-managed Mandela who compromised the principles of the revolution, which are captured in the Freedom Charter.[2]

Writing in 2005, Patrick Bond argued:

> Notwithstanding official rhetoric to the contrary, South Africa suffered a durable replacement of racial apartheid with what can be considered 'class apartheid': systemic underdevelopment and segregation of the oppressed majority, through structured economic, political, environmental, legal, medical and cultural practices largely organised or codified by Pretoria politicians and bureaucrats. Patriarchy and racism remained largely intact in many areas of daily life, even if a small elite of women and black people were incorporated into state management and the accumulation of capital. Although slightly more expansive fiscal policies were adopted after 2000, Pretoria's neoliberal orientation has never been in doubt. There are many areas where evidence of class apartheid is irrefutable, not only locally but in South Africa's relations to its neighbours and the wider world. But where there is oppression, so does resistance inexorably emerge.[3]

It may be that we scoffed at Fukuyama too quickly. His point was that the collapse of the Berlin Wall did not just mark the end of the Cold War but signified the 'end point of mankind's ideological evolution and the universalisation of western liberal democracy as the final form of human government'. The English political philosopher John Gray labelled him the 'court philosopher of global capitalism'.[4] Adding to questions of genuflecting to global capitalism has been the whiff of corruption that has grown into a stench with the presidency of Jacob Zuma. At the heart of the scandal is a family that arrived from India in 1990, the Guptas. In a short space of time, they have accumulated fabulous wealth, mainly through tenders from state-owned enterprises. This led to allegations of state capture and the appointment of an official commission of enquiry. Meanwhile, the economic trajectory that the ANC has followed has created a small Black elite, while poverty and inequality have deepened. Unemployment is anything between 35 and 40 per cent, while some 13 million people (a quarter of the country's population) rely on meagre state grants to eke out a bare living.[5]

There is rebellion. Community protests demanding basic services are an everyday occurrence. A militant party, the EFF attracts increasing support among the young. And countrywide university protests in 2016 revealed an ideological resurgence. As the old liberation heroes are shown to have clay feet, students are reaching out to the radical literature of Martinican Marxist revolutionary Frantz Fanon, the charismatic Marxist Pan-Africanist Thomas Sankara and South African Black Consciousness leader Stephen Bantu Biko. The student movements' calls to decolonize the curriculum have led to renewed questions about the role of imperialist forces on the continent and local leaders who act as their henchmen rather than as representatives of those who voted them into power.

There is a deep sense that the postcolonial governments that arose in the wake of the national liberation struggles failed in their quest to break the shackles of Western imperialism. A growing body of work has pointed to the machinations of a comprador bourgeoise that acts in alliance with Western interests and against the interests of the poor and downtrodden in their home countries.

Are there voices from the Indian liberation struggle that can speak to these struggles that criticize the dominant national liberation movements, that strain against race and class oppression, that refuse to see the end of history as the global capitalist system? Why is this important for us writing in a South African context? The links between India and South Africa lie deep in the history of indenture and receive contemporary importance in BRICS (Brazil, Russia, India, China and South Africa). The thread that runs through these links is Mohandas Karamchand Gandhi who lived in South Africa from 1983 to 1914. His continuing influence was illustrated by the 2016 visit to South Africa of Indian Prime Minister Narendra Modi, who spent much time retracing Gandhi's steps and paying homage to him.[6]

But as Modi was sidling up to Gandhi, the halo was slipping. While in South Africa, Gandhi was obsessive about isolating Indian from African. For him a line needed to be drawn between the civilized (White and Indian) and the savage (African).[7]

Gandhi's time in prison provides a cameo of his approach to Afro-Indian relations. As Hofmeyr shows, his activism crystallizes in wanting Indians inside and outside prison 'not to be classed as native . . . "I have made up my mind to fight against the rule by which Indians are made to live with Kaffirs and others"'.[8] Gandhi petitioned the authorities to be given the same privileges as 'White' prisoners. He saw 'a boundary that could not be crossed and that is a line marked by the native'. Furthermore, those Indians who enjoyed the company of 'Natives' were 'addicted to bad habits'.

As a militant struggle against what some have labelled the transition from racial apartheid to class apartheid in South Africa gathered momentum—and in the process generated xenophobia against post-apartheid migrants from Africa and Asia, adding a new dimension to the already ambivalent relationship between African and Indian in Africa—it became clear that this was a politics that Gandhi could not speak to. Were there others in the Indian liberation movement that could relate to both the historical fight of the downtrodden and its present struggles? Could the struggles of the poor and oppressed in India help suture Afro-Indian relations on the continent we call home?

In researching our book on Gandhi, we began to read more widely about Indian political thought. Gandhi's contemporary and ideological rival Bhimrao R. Ambedkar is a name hardly known to the mass of South Africans, including the diasporic Indian population. Nor for that matter are some of Gandhi's other contemporaries, such as M.N. Roy, Bhagat Singh, J.P. Narayan or Ram Chandra. This despite the fact that, as many have pointed out, anti-colonial revolutionary thought in late colonial South Asia was not the monopoly of any one individual but 'the product of a global network of Indians' that included Sikhs, socialists, atheists, scholars, syndicalists, swamis, students, and even Soviet sympathizers.[9] While Gandhi has been portrayed as a 'revolutionary' in many senses, 'in the long history of Indian historiography, Maclean and Elam[10] further contend, he often represents the position *against* which "revolutionaries" were defined'.

We became immediately attracted to Ambedkar. Was there a politics *there* that could speak to Fanon's 'wretched of the earth' in Africa? Ambedkar's social location as a Dalit, his prescient critique of the Indian

National Congress (INC) and his refusal to countenance any compromise with caste, spoke both to the historical evolution of Indians in South Africa and to the contemporary politics of those who seek to smash the icons of colonialism, challenge the gods of liberation and conduct a radical anti-imperial struggle out of the 'dung-heap', to steal Ambedkar's phrase, of postcolonial dead ends.

We came to Ambedkar's work late but saw an immediate resonance in his writings in the African context. *Annihilation of Caste* (1944) is a case in point. In South Africa, the form and nature of Indian indenture meant that caste was punctured and trespassed both in marriage and in everyday social relations. The setting in Natal made it difficult to transplant the conventional caste system. Employers did not recognize caste, age or religiosity. It is not for nothing that the indentured were given numbers to denote their existence. All workers had to do the same work and were burdened with the same rules. While caste did not disappear, it was marked by many sites of transgression.

Yet, Ambedkar's ideas of caste continue to have relevance for as we move into the 21st century, new forms of social inclusion and exclusion, based around class, caste, religion and language are emerging amongst Indians.


## 'A Plea to the Foreigner'

It was not only in the past that we found Ambedkar nourishing our research and political sensibilities; he was also speaking to us in the present. Amongst his many works, we found Chapter IX of *What Congress and Gandhi Have Done to the Untouchables* (1946), entitled 'A Plea to the Foreigner', particularly relevant in the contemporary South African context. Protests over the past few years by a new generation of activists confronting South Africa's social, economic and political inequities, and global racism and neo-liberalism, provide, amongst other things, a critique of the Gandhian link. Whether this critique evolves into an insular African nationalism or a global anti-imperial politics remains to be seen.

Ambedkar argued in this work that most foreigners sided with the INC in the Indian struggle for independence and he attributed this to the 'propaganda' of the Indian press which 'does not give publicity to any news, which is inconsistent with the Congress prestige or the Congress ideology'. Newspapers survive on funding and those started by the Dalits did not receive support from business or government in the form of advertising revenue, making it difficult for them to survive. 'Will Congress' "Fight for Freedom" to make India free?' he asked.[11]

Here, parallels can be drawn with the South African transition where White capital and the Western countries threw in their lot with the ANC.

Ambedkar was concerned that the Congress 'far from planning for democracy is planning to resuscitate the ancient form of Hindu polity of a hereditary governing class ruling a hereditary servile class'. He made a distinction between the freedom of India and the freedom of the people of India. One did not guarantee the other. According to Ambedkar, 'the Fight for Freedom led by the governing class is, from the point of view of the servile classes, a selfish, if not a sham, struggle' since the governing class was 'struggling for freedom to rule the servile classes'.[12]

For Ambedkar, the governing class comprised 'principally of the Brahmins . . . whose allies had formerly included the Kshatriyas (warrior class) but now had support from the Banias (trading class)'. Ambedkar considered the change

> quite inevitable. In these days of commerce, money is more important than sword . . . That is one reason for this change in party alignment. The second reason is the need for money to run the political machine. Money can come only from and is in fact coming from the Bania. If the Bania is financing the Congress it is because he has realised—and Mr. Gandhi has taught him—that money invested in politics gives large dividends.[13]

Ambedkar saw society as characterized by a 'continuous struggle for power' between the ruling and 'servile' classes who suffered from an 'inferiority complex' and regarded the 'governing class as their natural leaders and themselves volunteer to elect members of the governing classes as their rulers'. He further argued that 'self-government and democracy become real not when a constitution based on adult suffrage comes into existence but when the governing class loses its power to capture the power to govern'. The transition was not making 'India safe for democracy' but freeing 'the tyrant to practise his tyrannies'.[14]

Ambedkar did not join the INC. He regarded 'deeply entrenched social inequities and caste loyalties' as 'serious obstacles to democratic participation and a shared sense of citizenship and nationhood'.[15] On caste, he wrote that it 'was not a physical object like a wall of bricks or a line of barbed wire which prevents the Hindus from co-mingling and which has, therefore, to be pulled down. Caste is a notion. It is a state of mind'.[16] Ambedkar was frustrated with the slow progress in addressing Dalit concerns. He wrote in his critique of Gandhi:

> Under Gandhism the common man must keep on toiling ceaselessly for a pittance and remain a brute. Gandhism, with its call of back to nature, means back to nakedness, back to squalor, back to poverty and back to ignorance for the vast majority of the people . . . Class structure in Gandhism is not an accident. It is its official doctrine.[17]

How analogous is this to recent developments in South Africa?

## The Negotiated Settlement in South Africa

The 1980s in South Africa was a period of persistent internal resistance to apartheid that refused to be crushed. In response, the apartheid government began a series of secret meetings with Nelson Mandela, then still a prisoner of the regime. Alongside this and sparked by White capital's meetings with the banned ANC, the ruling National Party (NP) engaged in talks with the ANC in exile. On the ANC's side there was a realization that as much as the regime was on the back foot it was nowhere close to defeat. The ANC's supplier of arms, the Soviet Union was crumbling and front-line African states that had supported it, such as Mozambique, Lesotho, Angola and Zimbabwe, were facing destabilization by the apartheid regime and were also keen to see a settlement.[18]

The ANC was not only open to negotiations; it was also keen to be seen as the predominant negotiating partner. Its strength in negotiations would be enhanced if it could produce a stable political environment. One of the challenges it faced was the internal resistance movement led by the United Democratic Front (UDF), formed in 1983, which, while swearing allegiance to the ANC, had its own leadership and was radicalized by the end of the 1980s. This was a mass-based movement whose constituents often acted on their own without reference to the top leadership.[19]

As John Daniel[20] put it, the UDF was 'a very different creature from its external progenitor', the ANC. In the process of 'orchestrating a national insurrection', rather than operating as 'a centralized entity', it 'practiced a robust and raucous form of participatory democracy in which a premium was placed on grassroots consensus and accountability. It was in most respects the antithesis of the essentially conformist ANC in exile'. The ANC was concerned that the UDF's radical potential would jeopardize a negotiated settlement. By now, Daniel argued, the ANC had become 'a tightly-knit, highly centralized vanguard party . . . with policy largely devised behind closed doors and then passed down to the lower ranks'.

With the release of Mandela, the environment was dominated by the ANC discourse of negotiation and compromise. As Dale McKinley shows:[21]

> The sheer pace with which the ANC leadership was traveling down the road of accommodation and negotiation instilled in its constituency the feeling there was no real alternative to a compromise settlement. This was further catalysed by the delegitimisation of socialist policies due to the collapsed economies of the USSR and Eastern Europe, and the accompanying confusion and demoralization experienced by movement socialists.

In the course of the transition, the ANC elbowed aside all other opposition, especially that from quarters seeking a more radical outcome to the transition from apartheid, absorbing the UDF, while the Congress of South African Trade Unions and even the South African Communist Party allied with the ANC as its junior partners.[22]

Two decades into post-apartheid South Africa, protests are mounting against the deepening contours of inequality and poverty. Militant community protests have become an everyday occurrence in the townships and shack settlements of the country. Alongside this, there have been insistent calls for the decolonization of the university curriculum and the removal of statues of people implicated in White racist rule. The statues of long-dead men like British imperialist Cecil John Rhodes and Gandhi are significant in moments of crisis. As Katherine Verdery tells us:[23]

> Desecrating a statue partakes of the larger history of iconoclasm. Tearing it down not only removes that specific body from the landscape, as if to excise it from history, but also proves that because it can be torn down, no god protects it . . . The person it symbolizes dissolves into an ordinary, time-bound person.

## Deconstructing Icons: Cecil John Rhodes

In March 2015, students at the University of Cape Town (UCT) demanded the removal of Cecil John Rhodes's statue. He was denounced as a racist and imperialist and the pioneer of a repressive system that saw Black workers dragooned into a migrant labour system. UCT Student Representative Council (SRC) member Ramabina Mahapa claimed that they wanted the statue removed because it 'represented what Rhodes stood for: racism and white supremacy'. The protesting students garnered massive support through a social media campaign called #RhodesMustFall.[24] The cause of this unrest was a man who butchered his way across the Limpopo and turned the area into his personal fiefdom, aptly named Rhodesia. Rhodes's desire for dominance was insatiable, dreaming of an imperial march from Cape to Cairo. During the anti-apartheid struggle in South Africa, Rhodes was a figure to be denounced and pilloried by Black South Africans as a representation of colonial pillage. Thus, any defence of Rhodes was likely to be muted.

But there was one sticky issue. None other than Nelson Mandela, the first President of non-racial South Africa, rescued Rhodes, dusted him off and gave him legitimacy by inaugurating the Mandela Rhodes Foundation. This followed the typical template of many post-1990 deals—Rhodes had the money, Mandela the prestige, and together they could help needy Black students get to Oxford University, so the argument went. Mandela gave Rhodes a new lease of life when he agreed to add his name to the Rhodes Foundation. At the inauguration of the Foundation in 2003, Mandela said: 'I am sure that Cecil John Rhodes would have given his approval to this effort to make the South African economy of the early 21st century appropriate and fit for its time.'[25] He used the same occasion to strongly condemn activists who suggested that White-run corporations should pay reparations to apartheid survivors.

However, protest against Rhodes runs much deeper than simply a demand for the removal of his statue. After the abolition of apartheid in 1994, a Truth and Reconciliation Commission (TRC) was established to highlight crimes against humanity in South Africa during the apartheid period. This time frame precluded the crimes of people such as Rhodes. Big business too was not required to properly bear witness to its long record of dispossession and exploitation.

Instead, the TRC gave multinational corporations like Anglo American and the Rupert empire a platform to dishonestly claim their long opposition to apartheid. While the TRC recommended a one-off 1 per cent corporate tax to raise money for victims of apartheid, the then Thabo Mbeki government rejected this on the grounds that the financial markets would interpret such a measure as anti-business.[26] In proposing the Mandela Rhodes Foundation, Mandela stated that 'the bringing together of these two names represents a symbolic moment in the closing of the historic circle; drawing together the legacies of reconciliation and leadership and those of entrepreneurship and education'.[27] According to Njabulo Ndebele, chair of the foundation, it represented

> a gesture of reconciliation between two historic moments: the moral ambiguities in the historical triumphs of colonialism and the transformative mandate of a modern democratic South Africa. The two names side by side engender unflagging energy, because the tension in their interaction is ultimately irresolvable as a constant spur to reflection on the possibilities, and the difficulties, of people living together in history.[28]

How quickly these words have come to be seen as quirky and quaint, of belonging to a time long past.

By raising the spectre of Rhodes, students at the UCT were in actual fact beginning to critique the contours and boundaries of the negotiated settlement itself which had kept intact the structures of White capitalist domination. Amit Chaudhuri makes the poignant observation:[29]

> From its start in South Africa, Rhodes Must Fall announced that it intended to address this unequal vision of the world as it manifests itself within universities—declaring itself 'a collective movement of students and staff members mobilising for direct action against the reality of institutional racism at the University of Cape Town. The chief focus of this movement is to create avenues for REAL transformation that students and staff alike have been calling for.'

The Rhodes statue was removed from the UCT but the movement spread to Oxford University where his statue stands at Oriel College. The university has thus far resisted removing it. These movements are not only about removing Rhodes's statue, but what he stood for, and this includes tackling institutional racism and decolonizing education.

Since 2015, students across South African campuses have been calling for a radical restructuring of the education system to incorporate 'free quality decolonized education'. The protests have at times been violent and bloody. By decolonized education, UCT student Athabile Nonxuba explained, they want education that embraces a curriculum that does not dehumanize Black students; stops undermining the thinking of Africans; allows them to be taught by decolonized African people; advances the interests of Africans rather than Eurocentric interests; stops valorizing the work of European thinkers like Karl Marx and instead introduces the ideas of Africans; and introduces African languages.[30]

With a new post-apartheid generation of young South Africans straining to have their voices heard, nostalgia for the struggle is not high on their list of priorities. In addition, twenty-four years have now passed and with a President (Jacob Zuma) in power from 2009 to 2017 who was persistently accused of corruption and talk of 'state capture' by a single family—the Guptas[31] who arrived from India in the 1990s—the ANC is fast losing its aura as a party of liberation. The Guptas reached deep into South African society, such that the term 'Zuptanomics' was coined to refer to the relationship between them and Zuma's family. Former public protector Thuli Madonsela's investigation into allegations of state capture led to her report of October 2016 which found that the family was involved in shady mining deals in coal, uranium, gold, platinum, diamonds and iron ore. They also allegedly benefited from official connections to secure lucrative state contracts and private loans.[32] Zuma used various legal channels to postpone Madonsela's recommendation that a commission of enquiry investigate this relationship, but the election of Cyril Ramaphosa as the new president of the ANC and of the country in February 2018 forced the issue.

## Mandela and White Capital

Following the protests around Rhodes, the critique of the Mandela moment has proceeded thick and fast in South Africa, both from the inside and the outside.

In Faust's parable, selling one's soul grants the attainment of short-term satisfaction: riches, fame and pleasure. But at some point down the line, the devil invariably comes to collect, and the price to pay is horrible. At first, the concessions Mandela made did not seem dramatic. It started with just one loan and the markets were satisfied that the ANC was not going to renege on paying the odious debt of the previous government.

The ANC duly swept to power in 1994, and with the world watching, Nelson Mandela was inaugurated as the first President of a democratic South Africa. It was expected that democracy would bring its own dividends, to be shared fairly among all South Africa's people. But, as time would show, this loan was but the beginning, not only of the acceptance but also an embrace of a severely damaging economic logic. And over the coming years, as the ANC government failed to deliver on an accelerated redistributive programme, there was a price to pay.

There is much resonance between young Africans' demands and Ambedkar's ideas. The South African transition has illustrated the poverty of relying on the market to level historical inequalities. In fact, it has led to a growing divide between rich and poor exacerbated by the commodification of basic services. These developments have renewed calls for a developmental state that is more interventionist and focuses on distribution rather than simply on growth. In this context Ambedkar has incredible resonance. In his monograph 'States and Minorities: What Are Their Rights and How to Secure Them in the Constitution of Free India', Ambedkar speaks of a model of economic development that he described as 'state socialism', calling for state ownership of land, free education, state planning of the economy and state provision of healthcare.

On the question of land ownership and violence, Ambedkar wrote in 'Buddha or Karl Marx':[33]

> As to violence there are many people who seem to shiver at the very thought of it. But this is only a sentiment. Violence cannot be altogether dispensed with. Even in non-communist countries a murderer is hanged. Does not hanging amount to violence? If a murderer can be killed, because he has killed a citizen, if a soldier can be killed in war because he belongs to a hostile nation why cannot a property owner be killed if his ownership leads to misery for the rest of humanity? There is no reason to make an exception in favour of the property owner, why one should regard private property as sacrosanct?

The agreements reached during the negotiated settlement in South Africa have meant that the promises made around creating a better life have been stymied.

Parallels can be drawn with Ambedkar's analysis of India, not just the need for the eradication of class-based disparities, but also his call for an end to caste and gender inequalities. As Arora points out, Ambedkar, 'more than any other leader of that movement, which would come to define all of independent India's heroes, understood that India's deeply entrenched social inequities and caste loyalties were serious obstacles to democratic participation and a shared sense of citizenship and nationhood'.[34] When he resigned from Nehru's cabinet in October 1951, Ambedkar stated that he had done so because the government's focus was excessively on economic rather than social development. According to Ambedkar, 'to leave inequality between class and class, sex and sex, which is the soul of Hindu society untouched and to go passing legislation relating to economic problems is to make a farce of our Constitution and to build a palace on a dung heap.'[35] Both in South Africa and India, there is a need to build societies that are socially inclusive and this means reducing racial, ethnic and class tensions, and addressing the concerns of women, migrants, refugees, people with disabilities and religious minorities.

Ambedkar's words of 1951 as well as his 'plea to foreigners' strike a chord in contemporary South Africa. The commanding heights of the economy are still mostly in White hands. Black capitalists emerge but have to hang on to the coat-tails of White capital. Meanwhile, lower down, the casual brutality of everyday life, replete with its own interior violence from rape to summary execution of suspected thieves and attacks on foreign nationals, relives the horrors of apartheid. Racism, among all segments of the South African population, is alive and well in the country, as is violent xenophobia and gender inequality and gender-based violence.

## The Present

South Africans are living in interesting times, witness to the attempted reclamation and ownership of history by younger Black Africans; and seeking to come to terms with the racist legacy of colonial warlords like Rhodes as well as participants in colonial structures, be they White, Black or brown, such as Gandhi, whose own statue in Johannesburg was desecrated in April 2015; the unfulfilled promises of political transformation in South Africa; and the economic consequences of the intrusion of neo-liberalism into post-democratic South African society. We are living not through the 'end of history' but history is on the march in South Africa and elsewhere, articulated so clearly by *Guardian* columnist Seumas Milne's *The Revenge of History* and French philosopher Alain Badiou's *The Rebirth of History* (2012), amongst others. Notwithstanding the surge of right-wing nationalism in the form of Donald Trump's victory in the US election in 2016 and Brexit, the referendum that resulted in victory for those that opted for the UK to leave the European Union, the movement against neo-liberalism is also gathering momentum.

We believe that Ambedkar speaks to these times. The rage that he displayed against caste and other inequalities has mostly been ignored. Ambedkar would likely have approved of young people's protests, for he believed in the 'insurrectionary duties of the citizen, one that he begins to articulate with unprecedented clarity in *Annihilation of Caste*. Indeed, the treatise forges a galvanizing relationship between the ethics of revolutionary annihilation and the creative energies of the people, between a people's immeasurable force and their spiritual capacity to constitute themselves anew'.[36]

While the ANC has become mired in allegations of corruption, what is inspiring is the form and nature of the opposition to the party's class apartheid. Most significant in recent times is the #FeesMustFall movement amongst university students who are demanding free and decolonized quality university education. At its heart is an ideology that seeks to attack class privilege while calling for a radical curriculum.

In response, the government of Jacob Zuma has sought to make increasing appeals to a crude racial nationalism, while it opens its doors to transnational capital. The ANC enhances the power of tribal chiefs while extolling the virtues of the modernizing effects of global capitalism. There is a parallel with India where, Achin Vanaik suggests, 'there has been a steady process of what the eminent historian Romila Thapar has called "syndicated Hinduism". This has entailed the more or less systematic consolidation of an ever-widening Hindu self-consciousness across castes'[37] that runs parallel to the drive to deepen capitalist social relations.

Rhodes has fallen in Cape Town, bringing into question Mandela's legacy. What kind of politics will emerge out of these fallen statues and embryonic student and community movements? Will it be an anti-imperialist, anti-racist global movement from below? One of the impulses of *Annihilation of Caste* is the

> need to posit a revolutionary subject through the general mobilisation
> of the multitude. The reclamation of authentic belief, the right to truth,
> and the ability to mobilise a shared and general will, Ambedkar insists,
> are inseparable from one another; together they constitute a people's
> movement towards free and revolutionary democracy'.[38]

Indian capital is busy buying up chunks of land in Africa and turning them into vast agricultural factories that export products back to India. Meanwhile, peasants in India are mired in debt to the extent that many see suicide as the only alternative. It is now more than ever that Ambedkar meets Fanon meets Sankara meets Biko. Their positing of a revolutionary subject not only speaks to the struggles from below spreading from Cape Town to the rural hinterlands of India, but can help facilitate links between them.

## References

Ambedkar, B.R. 1947. States and Minorities: What Are Their Rights and How to Secure them in the Constitution of Free India, Memorandum on the Safeguards for the Scheduled Castes submitted to the Constituent Assembly on behalf of the All India Scheduled Caste Federation. Available at http://www.ambedkar.org/ambcd/10A.%20Statesand%20Minorities%20Preface.htm.

Ambedkar, B.R. 2014. *Annihilation of Caste: The Annotated Critical Edition*. Edited by S. Anand. Introduction by Arundhati Roy. New Delhi: Navayana.

Badiou, Alain. 2012. *The Rebirth of History*. London: Verso.

Desai, Ashwin and Goolam Vahed. 2016. *The South African Gandhi: Stretcher-Bearer of Empire*. Stanford: Stanford University Press, and New Delhi: Navayana.

Fukuyama, Francis. 1989. 'The End of History?' *National Interest* (16): 3–18.

Milne, Seumas. 2012. *The Revenge of History: The Battle of the 21st Century*. London: Verso.

Rao, Rahul. 2015. On Statues, The Disorder of Things, 2 April 2016. Available at https://thedisorderofthings.com/2016/04/02/on-statues. Accessed 19 July 2017.

# CRIMINALIZED CASTES

## DALITS, AFRICAN AMERICANS
## AND THE JEWS OF CHRISTIAN EUROPE

### Gary Michael Tartakov

I

In an essay following the United Nations' Conference against Racism,
Racial Discrimination, Xenophobia and Related Intolerance held in Durban
in 2001, I made an extended comparison of Dalits and African Americans as
'stigmatized' or 'criminalized' communities, using those terms as descriptive
of their social situations. The title of the essay was 'Why Compare Dalits
and African Americans? They Are Neither Unique nor Alone'.[1]

My intention in that essay was to explain how each of these
communities underwent a 'hereditary stigmatization', by being marked for
discrimination on the basis of birth into supposedly separate and dangerous
populations within their respective nations. I wanted to demonstrate the
comparability of their identifications as what we call 'races' in the US
and 'castes' in India. The essay was composed for a pair of conferences[2]
arguing against the Government of India's official position in the Durban
conference, at the UN and internationally, that caste and race were not
comparable.

The point of the essay was to note that—as different as Dalits and
African Americans are as ethnic communities, and as different as the national
cultures within which they are located—what they have in common is not
their intrinsic characteristics, but their social and economic situations within
their host nations. They are each exploited as internal colonies within their
larger nations in distinctively similar ways.

One might say that I was following the lead of the Dalit Panthers in
their re-identification of the community that Ambedkar usually referred to

as 'Depressed Classes' or 'Scheduled Castes' as Dalit 'oppressed', in contrast
to the Brahminical pejoratives such as *achhut* (untouchable) or Gandhi's
paternalistic 'Harijan' (child of God). I wanted to emphasize that what
was most meaningful in explaining the social persecution and economic
degradation of both African Americans and Indian Dalits was not a matter
of their inherited characteristics but of their fellow citizens' ongoing efforts
to exploit them.

What the recognition of the comparability of 'race' and 'caste' would
have meant for Dalits at the Durban conference was acknowledgement from
the UN and the international community of their plight as a plundered
community. What I intended to note, besides this, was that it would be
beneficial for each of the two similarly oppressed communities to recognize
the commonality of their struggles. This would allow each to learn from the
resistance strategies of the other, and provide the potential for collaboration
in resisting their oppression in the globalizing worlds of commerce and
international politics.

Both African Americans and Dalits have been segregated and
terrorized, denied education, economic opportunity, healthcare and
political participation over centuries, and both continue to be exploited
economically and psychologically for the benefit of those the elites in their
respective societies have ranked above and against them.

# Dalits and African Americans[3]

## *In Practice: Comparable Experience*

As Dalits are consistently segregated in India's villages, African Americans
are largely segregated in their housing in the US. The elites' intention is
the same in each case: to separate this community from the others. The
segregation in housing is related to the insistence on a separation of the
communities as a whole into separate peoples. Its ultimate goal is the
restricting of marriage and childbearing and so effecting in practice the
ideal separation into what can be said to be separate lines of descent, called
separate races in the US and separate jatis or castes in India. If the caste
system opposed intermarriage among the castes going back to Manu, the
racial laws in the US forbidding 'interracial marriage' continued in effect
up to the Supreme Court case *Loving* vs *Virginia*, of 1967, invalidating
laws prohibiting interracial marriage, that then still existed in seventeen of
the nation's fifty states. The general populations in both places continue

this prescription in custom, very slowly being abandoned in the US and even more slowly in India, where murders within families to punish caste mixing—so-called 'honour killings'—are regularly noted in the news.

What the Government of India defines as an 'atrocity', as a 'shockingly cruel and inhumane' molestation of Dalits or Adivasis which does not always include murder, as what is called 'lynching' in the US does, but other than this most extreme degree of violence, they are similar examples of terrorizing discipline. Law enforcement and the gradual development of civil and human rights made public lynchings rare in the US by the second half of the 20th century, and yet we see a storm of controversy over the insistent repetition of police killings of unarmed Black men and women that have spawned the current Black Lives Matter movement, revealing that lynching of a sort continues in a modified form today. In India atrocities involving murder are common and rape, rationalized in terms of caste privilege, is rampant.

Education in the US, as in India, is mainly restricted by economic status—with public education theoretically free at the lowest levels—and is highly restricted by one's neighbourhood, and the income level of the neighbourhood. In both countries, a combination of residential and economic segregation results in severe limitation of education today, though this is much improved over the past, when both oppressed peoples were simply denied public education. As the laws of Manu called for the killing of any Sudra or lower-caste persons who heard the sacred Brahminical language, before the American Civil War it was punishable in the south of the US to teach Blacks to read.

The issue of higher education for both African Americans and Dalits is still controversial in both countries. Where the US has affirmative action programmes and India reservation to ameliorate what are de facto segregated and limited opportunities in higher education, neither has yet made more than token progress, despite the idealistic laws.

Economic opportunity is severely limited for both Dalits and African Americans in relation to other ethnic communities within their respective societies. Though American Blacks have a great deal more than India's Dalits due to the greater proportional wealth of the US, both are similarly confined to the lowest levels of their society's economy, the most demeaning, dangerous and unrewarding occupations and the highest levels of unemployment.

Though modern democracy has opened up the possibility of political participation and opportunity in the course of the previous century, both of these communities were—until the middle of that century—forbidden political participation. Though participation is now mandated in both places, it continues to be hedged around by discriminatory practices. Full participation is still so limited for both that success within the system as a whole is so remarkable as to require special recognition for being unusual. In India, where Dalits are guaranteed representation approaching their numbers in the society as a whole, control of those representatives remains corrupted by the terms of the Poona Pact—which made reserved seats for Dalits dependent on the caste Hindu majority rather than Dalit voters—while in some regions elected Dalits can be terrorized for taking the positions they are entitled to. In the US, Blacks are represented by only one of the two major parties and are a major target of disenfranchisement by the other.

The entire financial structure of both nations is constructed around the ability to pay the people of these two communities below what others are paid, while assigning a significant number to an unemployment that threatens the living standards of all who are employed.

In both cases, the social importance of everyone else is elevated to the degree that Blacks or Dalits are stationed beneath them, and they are treated as if significantly lesser in value. In each place, this works fully to the benefit of the elite, who gain in social status and economic benefit, while it works significantly less well for common folks, who gain in social status but also lose economically.

## In Theory: Contradictory Explanations

By contrast, the internal explanations of America's race system and India's caste system are quite different. Both traditions blame the malign status on the supposedly inherited traits of the individual, but in quite different terms. In India, one is said to be born into an 'Untouchable' caste (jati) due to karma's effect upon individual rebirth, resulting from caste mixing in a previous birth. It is an explanation peculiar to Brahminical theology with little meaning outside of India. American race theory is quite different, positing that Blacks have inherited an inferior genetic make-up that supposedly produces immoral and inadequate intellectual traits. On these bases the two systems are quite different. The Indian explanation is based upon a religious myth, while the American ideology is pseudo-scientific. And yet the practical reality is that both lead to the same sorts of social persecution and economic exploitation.

In both cases, it seems more appropriate to conclude that the economic and psychological exploitation of the stigmatized communities by their encompassing nation was a better explanation of the parallel social persecution and discrimination than traditional explanations of inherited personal characteristics.

In noting these parallels, I am following a series of scholars and political figures, going back in India to such well-known figures as Jyotirao Phule,[4] Lala Lajpat Rai,[5] B.R. Ambedkar[6] and, more recently, the Dalit Panthers. In America, noting the parallels goes back to anthropologists such as Gerald Berreman,[7] Joan Mencher[8] and Kathleen Gough[9] who, since the middle of the 20th century, have been pursuing the parallel in search of understanding both nations better.

## II

## The Jews of Christian Europe

What I want to do here is develop the comparison of the parallel social situations of Dalits and American Blacks by adding to it what I have learned since about a third 'stigmatized' and 'criminalized' hereditary community: the Jews of Christian Europe. I will then shift my focus from the commonality of similar persecution and exploitation to the importance of the 'criminalizing' or 'demonizing of identities' that is also characteristic of the actions of the host nations in all three cases. I have come to understand that this not only unites the three communities, but offers us a particularly sharp insight into the nature of social hierarchy and the means by which social elites may use such criminalization in the creation and maintenance of their broader social hierarchies.

Though it is seldom developed in general discussions of Western Europe's High Middle Ages, the period from about 1000 to 1400 CE, their elite employed a common description of the social world that divided it into separate compartments much like those of medieval India's varna system. The Europeans called their hierarchy the system of the Three Social Orders, and they will be recognized immediately by anyone familiar with Indian civilization when I use the most common manner of identifying them. The Three Orders—the Oratores, Bellatores and Laboratores—were those who prayed, those who fought, and those who laboured to support the other two. In their oldest textual formulations, in Bishop Adalbero of Laon's 11th-century poem to King Robert, we have:

Here below, some pray, others fight, still others work

and

> from the beginning, mankind has been divided into three parts, among
> men of prayer, farmers, and men of war.[10]

As offered with more detail elsewhere in that poem and by others in a
wide variety of contexts, we are informed that the 'farmers' or those who
'work' 'labour to support the other two'. And thus we can see how the
European formulation is almost a translation of the Purusha Sukta of the
Rig Veda, identifying three of the four varnas there—the Brahmin, the
Rajanya and the Sudra: those who pray, those who fight, and those who
labour to support the others—while omitting the Vaisha, the owners of
farms, who in the European version are included among those who fight
(the aristocracy who owned the great bulk of the land). The Three Orders
were hereditary and you will recognize them as Latin Christendom's priests,
aristocrats and commoners later installed in their political development as
the Three Estates of the earliest European parliaments that developed in the
13th century: the clergy, the lords, the commoners.

Both the European and Indian social systems are social hierarchies
rendered through economic systems, by the role of the lowest group,
whose occupation is to labour to support others who are not allowed to
labour.

## In Practice: Comparable Experience

What particularly caught my attention as I studied Europe's High Middle
Ages was that there was a fourth category, obsessively depicted in documents
of the time, that—like the panchamas of the chaturvarnya system—stood
not only below the others but outside the legitimate system of the Three
Orders as a supposedly antagonistic community, not included in the system
and yet attached to it. The position of the designated internal enemy,
which Manu attributed to the Chandala community and later Brahminical
authors attributed to the people we now call 'Dalits', was filled in the High
Middle Ages of Latin Christendom by the Jews, the only other religious
community allowed by Christians to exist in Western Europe after the year
1000, allowed only on the premise that they be treated as a dangerous and
malign opponent of the legitimate Christian society.

During the High Middle Ages and most of the time since, Western
Europe's Jews were treated in ways quite comparable to America's Blacks

under slavery and Jim Crow, and India's caste-persecuted Dalits. They too were segregated, terrorized, denied education, economic opportunity and political participation, and they too were exploited economically and psychologically. Though, as in the case of Dalits and African Americans, the details were quite unique to their particular beliefs and practices and their particular host civilization. And in striking contrast to the other two, a fraction of the medieval European Jewish community was able on occasion to accumulate significant wealth as agents of the royalty, who were legally their masters, despite the great majority languishing at the level of the Christian masses of the period.

As with the Chandalas and Untouchables, the segregation of the Jews into a separate birth community was fostered by laws forbidding the marriage or even sexual mixing of Jews with Christians, most famously established by the Church in the Fourth Lateran Council of 1215, but known in most places earlier.[11] Their segregation in public was further established in laws like those of the Fourth Lateran Council requiring Jews to wear distinguishing symbols on their clothing (Canon 68). Canon 68 even contains the complaint—which will sound familiar to anyone with experience of the caste system—that Jews 'do not blush to go forth better dressed' than Christians on some occasions.

European Christian violence against the Jews began when Christianity became the Roman empire's state religion in the 4th century and took on a hue of extreme terror with the Crusades to Palestine and the various expulsions from different Western European countries in the 13th to 14th centuries. And while the period from the Enlightenment to the mid-20th century saw Jews gradually integrated into Western European society, it was only to have them become the community around whom the terms 'genocide' and 'holocaust' were developed to explain the Nazi German slave labour and death camps of the Second World War in the late 1930s and early 1940s.

The great bulk of Europe's public schooling and all its higher education during the Middle Ages was Church based and so closed to Jews in the High Middle Ages, though it was Jews in Spain who made the translations of Greek, Hebrew and Arabic texts into Latin which became indispensable to the European universities of the era.

As both landholding and attesting to most legal documents required Christian oaths, Jews were largely excluded from most agricultural activities of the Western Christendom in the High Middle Ages. What made them infamous and anathema to the Christian Church and aristocracy (the Oratores and Bellatores) was their legal status as the king's slaves or serfs, and so those permitted to take interest on loans, which Christians were not allowed to take from other Christians. Some Jews thus acquired significant wealth by becoming the king's agents in bleeding his barons of significant amounts of their wealth, while others went into commerce or worked for those in banking and commerce. Jews were excluded from most urban occupations because the craft and merchant guilds were church related.

As nearly all the Western European nations of the Middle Ages were Christian kingdoms or empires, the Jews could not hold any court office or take part in even town governance, with the exception of those in the Arab-ruled kingdoms of southern Iberia and Sicily.[12]

Exploited psychologically for refusing to convert to Christianity, the Jews were obsessively persecuted by the Christian clergy, easing up only in the 19th century with the receding influence of the Church in European life, though public persecution was not ended until after the genocide of the Second World War.

## In Theory: Contradictory Explanations

The Jews of medieval Christian Europe were a relatively minor fraction of the population but received a disproportionately oversized theological interest. Constituting as little as 1 or 2 per cent of the population,[13] Jews had great symbolic significance as representatives of the Abrahamic faith from which Christianity evolved, who refused to follow the Christians into their 'new revelation', despite the fact that the Jews' sacred texts continued to compose the first three-quarters of the Christian Bible.

The medieval explanation for the persecution of the Jews in Western Europe was their refusal to recognize or worship the Christian deity, and indeed the claim by the Christian clergy, lasting down to the later part of the 20th century, that the Jews were collectively responsible for killing Christ, the Christian deity.[14]

Thus, we can see how the Jews were persecuted socially and exploited economically and psychologically in Christian Europe of the High Middle Ages, and even after that, in many of the same ways as Blacks in the Americas and Dalits in India. They only began to emerge from that social situation slowly in the 19th century with the growth of economic and political democracy. Democracy has made their economic and political persecution inefficient with the drive to create a more level field in which peoples of all creeds and nations can live and interact with a supposed equality of opportunity.

## III

## Criminalization and Hierarchy

The traditional explanation for the persecution and exploitation of the Jews of Christian Europe was different from that of either the African Americans or Dalits, and yet what resulted were quite similar forms of social persecution and related, if different, forms of economic exploitation. What all three have in common is the experience of being identified as illegitimate hereditary communities, separate communities within their nations, depicted by the elite as enemies of the nation, as criminal communities.

Why specify the elite when their vilification was taken up to a large extent by the nations as a whole? Because it is clear in each case that the definition came from the leading ideological sectors of society. In all three cases the vilification came most significantly through the priesthood. In India, this was the Brahmin caste, which developed the ideology of caste with themselves on top, declaring themselves most pure, and the 'lower' castes at the opposite end of their ritual purity. In the Americas, though, a growing number of clergy were among the abolitionists in the 19th century and later it was the clergy who blessed the slave system at the beginning and supported it with theological arguments across the centuries as slavery is accepted in the Christian Bible. In the case of the Jews of Christian Europe, it was the Church—Catholic and, later, Protestant as well—that preached antipathy toward the Jews.

Despite the historic shift of all three of these regions from their pre-modern monarchical, caste-, order- and race-driven hierarchical societies to modern democratic, capitalist societies—based on the ideals of social and economic equality of opportunity for all citizens—Jews, Dalits and African Americans have continued to endure degrees of their hereditary oppression into the present. Though it is significant how different the degrees of oppression are today: ranging from extreme in the case of the Dalits to strikingly reduced if still significant in the case of African Americans and relatively insignificant in the case of the Jews since the cataclysmic spike during the Second World War.

The main material explanation I offered for the persecution of Dalits and African Americans was the economic benefit gained by all those ranked above them through their exploitation. Whether or not their economic and psychological exploitation has been of the same benefit to all of those ranked above them, the perception of that benefit has been powerful.

But this explanation tells us little about the Jews of the High Middle Ages, whose numbers were quite limited and whose economic impact on the population as a whole was insignificant. Rather, it was the Jews' ideological importance—as the chosen enemy of the clerical caste—that made their presence important to the population (most of whom had never seen a Jew). Thus, it was the psycho-social value they offered as a criminalized (religious) community that was the Jews' primary impact.

As a criminalized community, Jews—like Blacks in the Americas and Dalits in India—appear to raise the social value of those in the legitimate communities ranked above them. Despite the ideal of social equality, our modern states are all still highly hierarchical in practice, both economically and socially. Besides their supposed material benefit to those ranked above them, Dalits and African Americans supply those at the lower end of their nations' social hierarchies with a social legitimacy they would not have without someone to look down upon as even less socially valuable than they are.

None of this is new to anyone familiar with any of these nations, where we can hear variations of the construction 'at least we are not [them]' coming from those among the devalued lower ranks. The point of raising it here is to focus upon the issue of social legitimacy. In the same way that elites seek to make use of foreign or 'external' enemies to establish unity within their nations—take Pakistan or China for India, or Russia for the United States—they seek to legitimize the hierarchical inequality within their nations by pointing to the existence of 'internal' enemies. And criminalized castes or races are—along with criminals, more generally, or those infected with communicable diseases or members of supposedly anti-national political parties or 'criminal' religions—the most important internal enemies.

The primary strategy by which economic elites divert attention from their economic (class) domination of their nations is to direct social attention towards non-economic divisions, the most important being caste, race, religion or region.

Where it appears rational to treat internal enemies, like criminals, as less than equal to legitimate citizens, it seems rational both to punish them and to limit their access to social benefits: their opportunities for employment, education, political participation or even healthcare.

The great problem this presents for a supposedly democratic society is that this rationale for limiting the benefits of those seen as enemies of the nation becomes the rationale for a hierarchy of benefits for all those within the nation. Those leading the nation are depicted as more worthy of benefits than those who are being led, who are valued less, and so depicted as deserving of less. The presence—the very supposition—of an internal enemy serves to legitimize the internal hierarchy by which differentiated social benefits, from wealth, education and political participation to healthcare and employment, are accepted as reasonable.

In the same way that the presence of an exploited caste seems to raise the material level of every caste above it, an illegitimate caste may seem to raise the value of every legitimate caste while actually buttressing, if not supplying, the rationale for the hierarchy that degrades the majority as it elevates the value of a minority, justifying a society with extreme ranges of both material and social inequality.

In Dr Ambedkar's terms, a chief strategy for a tyrannical elite to maintain its power is to identify an internal enemy community, to anchor and thus to rationalize and legitimize the 'graded inequality' over which it rules.

# AFRICAN-AMERICAN PERSPECTIVE ON COMMON STRUGGLES

## BENEFITS FOR AFRICAN AMERICANS COMPARING THEIR STRUGGLE WITH DALIT LIBERATION EFFORTS

### *Kevin D. Brown*

I have organized or joined in several academic journeys to India involving American scholars that are very familiar with the African-American experience. As part of those journeys, I have participated in over a dozen conferences or workshops in India over the past decade where the main topic was comparing and contrasting the African-American experience with racial discrimination in the US to the Dalit experience with caste-based oppression in India. In these various conferences and workshops, the question is almost always raised: what are the benefits of the cross-cultural comparison of the African-American struggle with that of the Dalits?

The answer to this question inevitably depends upon the purpose of making the comparisons. One might view the question in the context of traditional academic scholarship common in the US. Within this perspective there is a sort of assumption of an objective search for truth. Thus, the focus of the benefits of doing comparative work between the African-American and Dalit struggles is in an effort to add to human understanding of the nature of things. Under this guiding perspective, commentators doing comparative work might look at the similarities and differences between these two liberation struggles and raise questions about which group has progressed the furthest in their struggle for equality. One could do a comparison to try to judge which group has suffered more. One could also compare the struggle of the two groups and conclude that the cultural context of the historical struggle of these

43

two groups is so dissimilar that the comparison may not provide much
of a benefit at all. It is too much like comparing the proverbial apple to
the proverbial orange.

No one can deny that the history and culture of India are vastly
different from those of the US. Anyone who does a comparative inequality
scholarship quickly learns that oppression and subordination are local.
Each group that is struggling for liberation is responding to the unique
circumstances and situations impacting that group's struggle for justice.
Thus, the forms of oppression and subordination that African Americans
and Dalits encounter are radically different. This means that the experiences
of discrimination, oppression and subordination of African Americans are
qualitatively different from those of Dalits.[1] As a result, the question about
the benefits of such a comparison remains a legitimate one.

Without question, the central feature of the African-American
experience in the US has been their treatment as involuntary members of a
historically oppressed racial group. In other words, the core of this struggle
is one against White supremacy as it manifested itself in the US. Race was,
is and may always be the dominant feature of the historical experience of
African Americans. But any examination of how race functions for African
Americans must be understood from two different points of view, only
one of which is African American. Since the first Africans walked off the
first slave ship and into the Jamestown colony of Virginia in 1619, Blacks
have come face-to-face with laws, customs and social practices designed to
restrict or confine their social, political, economic and educational rights
and opportunities. The discriminatory practices and policies that African
Americans have faced in the US were 'justified' by rationales generated by
the dominant White community based upon their presumed superiority
and the presumed inferiority of Blacks. Against a background of nearly
400 years of racial domination, however, the descendants of the sons
and daughters of the soil of Africa in the United States and those non-
Blacks sympathetic to their cause formulated a counter discourse to that
based on the presumed substandard nature of African Americans. The
development of this counter-discourse was limited by and responsive to the
racial oppression experienced by the African-American community. This
alternative pattern of understanding always rejected the notion that there
was something wrong with Black people. Instead, the counter-discourse
was built upon the firm conviction that Black people were oppressed, not
inferior. Its central feature was, is and perhaps always will be dedicated to
the liberation of Black people from racial oppression. As James Forman

stated about the African–American experience, 'our basic history is one of resistance'.[2]

To answer the question about the benefits of a comparison of the African-American struggle with the Dalit struggle from the point of view of African Americans requires viewing the comparison from the perspective of the African-American system of belief that is centred on the historic struggle against racial oppression. This perspective does not purport to compare the struggles of African Americans with those of Dalits purely for the sake of the advancement of human knowledge. Rather, the question about the benefits of this comparison is a question about how it can aid the African-American community in its collective struggle against racial oppression. Despite the fact that Dalits and African Americans encounter different forms of oppression, there are a number of very significant benefits that those committed to African-American liberation can derive from engaging in this cross-cultural comparison and dialogue. For those interested in Dalit liberation, the same holds true. But that position is better articulated by scholars deeply embedded in the Dalit struggle. No doubt some of the benefits of this comparison may occur to both groups, but due to the differences in the socially constructed nature of each group's oppression, it is critical to note that the benefits will be unique to each of them. Indeed, it could very well mean that a strategy, policy or approach that will advance the interest of African Americans in the US may harm the interest of Dalits in India. The reverse could also be true.

In this essay, I will discuss some of the significant benefits for the African-American struggle that are obtained by comparing it to the Dalit struggle in India. Comparisons of the African-American struggle to liberation efforts on the Indian subcontinent, however, are not new. But the arguments to advance this cause in one era may not adequately take into account the conditions that exist in a later era. Thus, it may be that those who were viewed as allies of or groups sympathetic to African Americans in the past become reconceptualized in a later era, which places them in a negative light. This is the case when the African-American struggle is compared to liberation struggles on the Indian subcontinent.

The first comparison of the African-American struggle to conditions on the Indian subcontinent occurred during the antebellum era. Abolitionists in the US drew on comparisons between the treatment of Blacks in the US and the Indian caste system. This kind of comparison of the Black situation to caste in India was also advanced during the African-American struggle against segregation. From the perspective of the African-American struggle for its liberation, the benefit of these early comparisons to caste in India were tied to the efforts to demonstrate that the treatment of Blacks in the US violated the fundamental American belief in individual liberty, freedom, meritocracy and self-determination. Thus, if India's caste system is immoral because it limits a person's future at birth, then, by analogy, so is the treatment of Blacks due to slavery and segregation. The first part of this essay will briefly discuss these comparisons.

The original comparisons of the African-American struggles to the caste system in India were largely supplanted by a different type of comparison to liberation struggles on the Indian subcontinent during the unfolding of the 20th century. As the Indian nationalist movement against British domination led by Mahatma Gandhi progressed, the older caste-based comparisons yielded to a comparison of the African-American struggle against White supremacy in the form of segregation with the Indian nationalist struggle against White supremacy in the form of colonialism. With this kind of comparison, Blacks in the US would be allies of the Indian national struggle, which was primarily controlled by high-caste Hindus. Indeed, if one includes Japan and China, what developed during this period was described by Nico Slate as a 'coloured cosmopolitanism' with the coloured peoples of the world uniting against White supremacy. The second part of the essay will discuss this comparison.

India has been free of direct colonial rule for seventy years now. Yet the persistence of the comparison of the African-American struggle with the Indian nationalist struggle (and the larger 'colour cosmopolitanism' struggle against global White supremacy) has helped to obscure the comparison with the Dalit struggle. The third part of this essay will primarily highlight how leaders of the Dalit struggle have looked to the African-American struggle for inspiration and potential policies and programmes to pursue in the fight for Dalit liberation.

The fourth part will talk about some of the benefits that African Americans can gain by comparing their struggle with the Dalit struggle and engaging in cross-cultural dialogue with them. Such a comparison, however, abandons the typical perspective of the African-American community that views its struggle as one against oppression in the form of White supremacy and instead sees the obstacle of subordination, regardless of the source. Placing the African-American struggle in this different light may allow for a greater recognition and appreciation of the strengths and successes of the struggle that are normally obscured. In addition, it will point out that the gains from the African-American struggle against oppression can benefit other groups who are fighting against a form of oppression that is rooted in White supremacy.

## Early Historical Comparisons: African–American Subordination to India's Caste System

The initial comparisons in the United States of the African–American situation to issues of oppression in India were made during the antebellum period in the US by abolitionists, including Frederick Douglass, William Lloyd Garrison, Harriet Beecher Stowe and Charles Sumner.[3] In the south, the overwhelming majority of Blacks were chattel slaves. Even though Blacks were free people in the north that did not mean that northerners believed in racial equality. Although the extent of discrimination Blacks encountered varied from state to state, generally they were locked into the bottom of the racial system by custom, if not by explicit law.

The subordination of Blacks was also compared to the Indian caste system after abolition in the US. One of the most famous examples of this comparison is in the dissenting opinion of Justice Harlan to the 1896 US Supreme Court's infamous decision in *Plessy* vs *Ferguson*.[4] In *Plessy*, the Supreme Court upheld the doctrine of 'separate but equal'. Justice Harlan wrote separately to castigate his brethren for their decision. In perhaps the most famous passage from any opinion of a justice of the US Supreme Court in its entire history, Harlan stated, 'in the view of the constitution, in the eye of the law, there is in this country no superior, dominant, ruling class of citizens. *There is no caste here.* Our Constitution is color-blind and neither knows nor tolerates classes among citizens. In respect of civil rights all citizens are equal before the law (emphasis added)'.[5]

From the perspective of those concerned with the liberation struggle of Blacks in the US, invoking the Indian caste system was an effort to improve the chances of the success of that struggle. Since the caste system was principally understood as a hierarchical system of social division in which membership in an endogamous group was hereditary and permanent, it was in direct conflict with the commitment to individualism, equality, liberty and meritocracy that is at the core of American culture. Thus, the comparison of the situation of Blacks in the US with the Indian caste system allowed those who believed in racial equality to not only critique slavery in the south, but also racist attitudes in the north and the south towards Blacks by asserting that because of White supremacy the US was imposing a system that American core values had to reject as unjust.

## Comparison of African–American Condition with That of Indians in the US and Indian Nationalists Abroad

As the 20th century unfolded, the African–American experience with racism in the US was increasingly compared to the Indian nationalist movement for independence from British rule. As early as the 1850s, Black nationalist Martin Delany had described the situation of Blacks in the US as that of 'a nation within a nation'.[6] The legendary Black intellectual W.E.B. Du Bois put the same concept this way: 'The so-called Negro group . . . while it is in no sense absolutely set off physically from its fellow Americans, has nevertheless a strong, hereditary cultural unity born of slavery, common suffering, prolonged proscription, and curtailment of political and civil rights. [. . .] Prolonged policies of segregation and discrimination have involuntarily welded the mass almost into a nation within a nation.'[7]

The idea of the Black community in the US as a nation within a nation made the analogy of the situation of Blacks in the US to other people of colour suffering from colonialism, whether in Asia or Africa, more appropriate. In particular, it made the struggle by Indian nationalists against the British empire seem an apt comparison to the African-American struggle. As Slate has stated, it was 'at the height of empire and White supremacy, at a time when many African Americans and Indians found little in common, that forward-thinking individuals laid the groundwork for more inclusive conceptions of belonging and resistance'.[8] Indians and African-Americans were both categorized by the British and their American cousins as the 'darker races', which led the groups to 'engineer one of the most creative and politically significant redefinitions of racial borders . . . the invention of the colored world'.[9]

The Ghadar conspiracy brought the Indian cause for independence to the forefront for many Americans. It was perhaps the most prominent of the attempts to initiate a pan-Indian rebellion against British control of India during the First World War. The Ghadar group was centred in California and primarily made up of Punjabi Sikhs. A large number of Ghadar Party members had returned to India by 1915, mostly to the Punjab. During the First World War, the Ghadar Party attempted to spark an uprising against the British in India. The uprising failed and mass arrests of the party members followed in the Punjab and the Central Provinces of India. American intelligence officials also arrested several important Ghadar members in the US and put them on trial in San Francisco. These trials, which took place from November 1917 to April 1918, were the largest and most expensive in the US to date.

The Ghadar conspiracy became a subject of debate in the Black community of the US. For example, the *Crisis* magazine voiced its support for the Indian nationalists. The *Crisis* was the principal publication of the National Association for the Advancement of Colored People (NAACP) and was founded by Du Bois, who was its principal editor from 1910 until 1934. Commenting on the Ghadar conspiracy, the magazine indicated that the NAACP found the result was unjust because the Indians were struggling to free their country from a foreign power. A 1921 edition of the pro-communist African-American magazine the *Crusader*[10] commented on the Ghadar conspiracy, saying 'it is essential to the early success of our cause that the Negro seek cooperation with the Indian nationalists . . . and all other peoples participating in the common struggle for liberty and especially with those peoples whose struggle is against the great enslaver of the darker races—England'.[11]

Indians on the other side of the world also drew the analogy between the struggle by African Americans against White supremacy and their own struggle against the Anglo supremacy of colonialism. During Mahatma Gandhi's South African days, he distanced the struggle for equality of the Indians from that of the Black Africans. Gandhi had characterized Africans as uncivilized, troublesome, dirty and living like animals. He protested bitterly against a British effort to construct housing that would have integrated the Indian indentured servants with Blacks and spoke of the purity of the races and the need to ensure it was maintained.[12] However, Gandhi became an admirer of African-American educator Booker T. Washington. Gandhi's immense respect for Washington's ideas helped him overcome the racist views about Black people that he held when he was in South Africa. By the mid-1920s, Gandhi too was analogizing the South Asian situation under colonialism with that of the Blacks under segregation.[13] Several important Indian nationalists came to the US, in part to educate the Black community about their struggle for independence, including Lajpat Rai (known as the 'Lion of Punjab'), Kumar Gohsal and Haridas Muzumdar.[14]

In the words of Daniel Immerwahr, 'sending prominent blacks over to India became a sort of cottage industry in the 1930s and 1940s'.[15] Thus, in the mid-1930s, African-American intellectuals meeting with Gandhi in India included the following: Howard Thurman, a professor of religion at both the historically Black universities of Morehouse and Howard during his career;[16] Channing Tobias, chairman of the NAACP; and Benjamin Mays, the dean of the School of Religion at Howard University and President of Morehouse College from 1940 to 1967.[17] Mays would later teach and mentor many influential African-American activists, including Martin Luther King, Jr, Julian Bond and Maynard Jackson. When Thurman met with Gandhi, Gandhi told him that in Hinduism's ideal form, the caste system is a non-competitive and non-oppressive functional division of labour that does not imply hierarchy. Gandhi also said that the proper path was to reform Hinduism, not destroy the caste system. In describing his meeting with Gandhi, Thurman noted that Gandhi told him he used the term 'Harijans', meaning 'children of God', to refer to Dalits because he wanted to create in the minds of caste Hindus an acute contradiction that could only be resolved by transforming their attitude towards Dalits.[18] When Mays met with Gandhi they talked about non-violence, and about how the African Americans could learn from him about dismantling oppression.[19] In his autobiography, *Born to Rebel*, Mays pointed out the striking similarities between the oppression of Indians by the English and the oppression of African Americans, leading him to believe that 'the war against discrimination in the United States has been and must be waged by all Negroes—Black, White, tan—together'.[20] But Mays also raised the question of the treatment of Dalits with Gandhi. He came to believe that as bad as untouchability was in 1937, it would likely be abolished before segregation was legally abolished in the US.[21] Mays would also become a huge advocate of non-violence in the US. Other prominent Blacks, including Bayard Rustin and William Stuart Nelson, also went to India later on. And, of course, Reverend Martin Luther King, Jr visited India in 1959.

## Dalit Awareness of the African-American Community

The comparison of the African-American struggle with that of the Dalits is a different kind of comparison than comparing the African-American struggle with that of the Indian nationalists. From the perspective of African Americans, the rationale for the comparison is the same: advancing the African-American struggle against racial oppression. The type of comparison, however, is radically different. Rather than viewing the African-American struggle as one against White supremacy and using the analogy of a nation within a nation to draw comparisons with the colonial struggles, now the comparison is between minority groups that are oppressed within their own countries by a majority group. From the

African-American point of view, while the former comparison aligned the interest of African-Americans with the Indian national movement, which was principally dominated and controlled by upper-caste Hindus, the later comparison recast these upper-caste Hindus from the oppressed to the oppressors.

From the Indian side, one of the first major critics of the Indian caste system was Jotiba Phule. Phule is viewed as the foundational modern anti-casteist reformer.[22] He was an Indian activist, thinker and social reformer from Maharashtra. Phule belonged to a Sudra sub-caste, but sought to unite Sudras and Dalits. Phule knew, however, that Dalits had to bear the brunt of caste-based oppression.

Phule accepted the theory put forth by Friedrich Max Mueller, a German-born philologist, Orientalist and one of the first Western academics to study India. According to Mueller, the high-caste Hindus, especially the Brahmins, were White foreign invaders from Central Asia who conquered the northern part of India around 1500 BCE. These invaders, known as 'Aryans', imposed the caste system on the native people who were thought to have originally come from Africa. Phule asserted, 'since the advent of the rule of Brahmin for centuries (in India), the Sudras and the Ati-Sudras (Dalits) are suffering hardships and are leading miserable lives'.[23] He rejected the idea that Hinduism was a religion and instead argued that it was a set of superstitious beliefs based on a questionable mythology. He criticized the caste system and the religious, economic and social oppression that it visited upon the 'native' inhabitants.

Phule believed that in order to create a social system based on freedom, human dignity, economic justice and brotherhood, it was necessary to overthrow the old system. Phule laid out his criticisms of the caste system in his 1873 book entitled *Gulamgiri* (Slavery). This was one of the first published books by an Indian author to point out the oppressiveness of the caste system. Phule also made the connection of groups oppressed by the Hindu caste system with the Blacks in the US. Even though slavery was not an integral part of the Indian social system, Phule drew upon the American experience with equality and freedom in his critique of the caste system. The dedication to Phule's book read:

DEDICATED to THE GOOD PEOPLE OF THE UNITED STATES AS A TOKEN OF ADMIRATION FOR THEIR SUBLIME DISINTERESTED AND SELF SACRIFICING DEVOTION in the cause of Negro Slavery; and with an earnest desire, that my countrymen

may take their noble example as their guide in the emancipation of their
Sudra Brethren from the trammels of Brahman thralldom.[24]

According to Daniel Immerwahr, Phule hoped to strengthen the claim
against the injustice of the caste system by building upon the international
standing and success of the abolitionist movements.[25] With this book and
its dedication, the struggle against caste-based oppression in India and the
African-American struggle in the US were linked in the minds of progressive
Indians who would build on Phule's work.

One of Phule's sponsors was the maharaja of Baroda. The maharaja
shared Phule's interest in the US and visited Chicago during the World's
Fair in 1893. The maharaja returned to Baroda with American educators
and textbooks. He had them prepare an American curriculum for his use in
some of the schools in Baroda. So when a brilliant young Bhimrao Ramji
Ambedkar from the Mahar caste, a Dalit sub-caste, was presented to the
maharaja, he decided to send him to the US for higher education. Ambedkar
attended Columbia University from 1913 to 1916. He may very well have
been the first Mahar, if not Dalit, to study at an American university.[26]
Eventually, Ambedkar would not only receive a PhD in economics from
Columbia, but also a doctorate in science from the London School of
Economics, and he was called to the Bar at Gray's Inn in London. No one
has done more to liberate Dalits and the Dalit mind from the oppressive
mentality presented to it through Hindu religion than Dr Ambedkar. It may
be impossible to convey to the average American how significant a figure
Dr Ambedkar is for the Dalit struggle. As Anand Teltumbde put it, for the
Dalit masses, Dr Ambedkar is everything together, a first-rate scholar, a
Moses who led his people out of bondage, a Bodhisattva in the Buddhist
pantheon—he is like a god.[27]

There is no doubt that the time Dr Ambedkar spent in America
influenced him, and part of that experience was learning about the condition
of African Americans.[28] He did write a comparison of untouchability with
slavery, concluding that untouchability was an indirect form of the former
institution.[29] And the campus of Columbia University is very close to the
historically important Black neighbourhood of Harlem in New York.
During the time that Ambedkar was studying at Columbia, the population
of Blacks in Harlem increased significantly as Black migration from the
south to northern cities accelerated. This was also a period of substantial
immigration of Blacks from the West Indies to New York City.[30] While
Ambedkar was at Columbia just before the start of the Harlem Renaissance,

it would be hard to imagine that he didn't learn about the African-American struggles. In addition, Ambedkar would eventually become the first law minister of independent India, a cabinet-level position. In this capacity, he was the chair of the seven-member drafting committee for India's new Constitution. Many provisions in the Indian Constitution are drawn from the US Constitution.[31] When considering protections for minorities in India, Ambedkar also examined the Fourteenth Amendment as well as the US Civil Rights Acts of 1866 and 1875.[32]

In the 1940s, Ambedkar corresponded with Du Bois.[33] In October of 1947, Du Bois submitted a petition to the newly formed UN on behalf of the NAACP, accusing the US of human rights violations due to its discrimination against African Americans.[34] Ambedkar wrote to Du Bois to ask for a copy of this petition. In his letter, Ambedkar also noted, 'I have been a student of the Negro problem and have read your writings throughout. There is so much similarity between the position of the Untouchables in India and of the position of the Negroes in America that the study of the latter is not only natural but necessary.' Du Bois responded by stating he would send Ambedkar a copy of the petition once it was finalized and wrote, 'I have often heard of your name and work and of course have every sympathy with the Untouchables of India. I shall be glad to be of any service I can render if possible in the future.'

More recent evidence of the Dalit awareness of the African-American struggle was the creation of the Dalit Panthers in Maharashtra. Established on 29 May 1972 by a group of poets and writers, the Dalit Panthers movement was a response to violence and injustices faced by the Dalits at the hands of the Indian government and caste Hindus.[35] Although the Dalit Panthers were disbanded in March of 1977, the movement remains alive among the Indian Dalit community today. The organization and its history continues to influence progressive Dalit activists. During their five years of operation, the Panthers 'took to the streets as committed foot soldiers of the movement, took on the system, and provided relief to victims'.[36] The Dalit Panthers advocated for electoral boycotts and engaged in provocative displays of public dissent that sometimes resulted in violence between the Panthers and their opposing caste communities. In doing so, the Panthers disavowed the Gandhian principle of non-violence.

The creation of the Dalit Panthers was clearly inspired by the Black Panther Party in the United States.[37] The Dalit Panthers identified strongly with the 'militant literature, community service, and political struggle' of African Americans.[38] In fact, according to Vijay Prasad, the name Dalit

Panthers was chosen 'in honor of the Black Panther Party for Self-Defense and for the ethic of the Panther, who fights without retreat'.[39] The Dalit Panthers' 1973 manifesto acknowledges the work of the Black Panther Party:

> Due to the hideous plot of American imperialism, the Third World, that is, oppressed nations, and Dalit people are suffering. Even in the United States, a handful of reactionary whites are exploiting blacks. To meet the force of reaction and remove this exploitation, the Black Panther movement grew. From the Black Panthers, Black Power emerged. The fire of the struggles has thrown out sparks into the country. We claim a close relationship with this struggle.[40]

The manifesto also contained the Dalit Panthers' radical political agenda. The manifesto defined Dalits as 'members of scheduled castes and tribes, Neo-Buddhists, the working people, the landless and poor peasants, women and all those who are being exploited politically, economically, and in the name of religion'.[41] It specified that the enemies were those in possession of power and wealth including landlords, capitalists, moneylenders, those who indulge in religious or casteist politics, and the government. According to the Dalit Panthers, partial change was not enough. They sought a tidal wave of revolutions and felt that the only way to end Dalit oppression was through a complete, radical revolution of the Indian government, the caste system and the Hindu religion.

Another example of the awareness among Dalits of the struggle of African Americans is in the movement for 'Dalit capitalism'. Some social activists in India, including Gail Omvedt, argue that liberalization and globalization can empower Dalits as they undermine the Brahminical control over the economy.[42] Chandra Bhan Prasad, however, is widely credited with launching the idea of 'Dalit capitalism'. He is regarded by many in India as one of the most significant Dalit intellectual and political commentators.[43] Prasad was the first Dalit to have a regular column in a nationally circulating Indian newspaper. Though not central to the religious notion of pollution, economic exploitation has been built into the caste system. One must understand that the historical position of Dalits in the Indian caste system forbade them from engaging in entrepreneurial activities. Thus, Prasad challenges this traditional notion. He has asserted that in order for Dalits to successfully overcome the dominance of the caste Hindu they need to create a middle class based on education/white-collar jobs/professions. He also argues that the booming small-scale entrepreneurship sector provides an opportunity for the Dalit middle class to grow into an economic and social force. Prasad is quoted as saying:

> A few Dalits as billionaires, a few hundred as multi-millionaires and a few thousands as millionaires would democratise and de-Indianise capitalism. A few dozen Dalits as market speculators, a few Dalit-owned corporations traded on stock exchanges, a few Dalits with private jets, and a few of them with golf caps would make democratic capitalism loveable.[44]

Prasad believes that the caste system's focus on blood and occupational purity is dissolving under the impact of India's wealth creation endeavours.[45] Because free markets are based upon the logic of free individuals maximizing their gains/utilities, this has the potential to overcome caste-based bias. Prasad openly admits that Black capitalism in the US was his inspiration for Dalit capitalism.[46]

Prasad is also the mentor of Milind Kamble, founder of the Dalit Indian Chamber of Commerce and Industry.[47] As Kamble says to Dalits, 'to be a true follower of Ambedkar, become a "job-giver" not a "job-seeker". Do not fight capitalists but try to become one amongst them.'[48] According to research on Dalit entrepreneurs being conducted at the Center for the Advanced Study of India at the University of Pennsylvania, Dalit business is 'well represented in the manufacturing sector, producing cement pipes, copper tubes, automobile components, solar heaters and frozen food, as well as ethanol, and even high-rise buildings'.[49]

It is also important to note that many common Dalits have some familiarity with the African-American struggle. In my extensive travels in India, I have had many such interactions with Dalits where this was apparent. For example, I attended a rally of Dalit Christians in Mangalore in December 1996.[50] The Indian Constitution provides that governments can reserve jobs and seats in colleges and universities that receive government assistance for Dalits. However, the current provisions of the Constitution only allow Dalits who profess to be Hindus, Buddhists or Sikhs to qualify for reservations. Thus, Christian Dalits are excluded from these reservations. Over 80,000 Christian Dalits came together at a soccer stadium in Mangalore for a rally aimed at amending the Indian Constitution so that Dalit Christians would be eligible for reservations. There were only three main speakers at the rally; one of them professed to being a Dalit Panther. But the most striking aspect of the rally was that the only sign over the speaker's podium read 'We Shall Overcome'. This was taken directly from the civil rights struggle of the African Americans in the 1960s. Another example occurred when I led a group of thirteen American academics on a trip to India in October 2012. One of the places we visited was the rural village of Mohammadabad, a village for the lowest sub-caste of Dalits known as manual scavengers. Over 400 residents of the village attended activities to welcome our group. At one point, after singing one of their liberation songs, one of the residents asked the Americans to sing an American song. Indiana University Maurer School of Law professor Kenneth Dau Schmidt started our group off by singing 'We Shall Overcome'. As we began singing, the village residents demonstrated their familiarity with it joined us.

Recently, Dalit activists have also reached out to the Black Lives Matter movement for both support and for strategies and policies they should pursue.[51] This includes Dalit women activists who are organizing and protesting against sexual violence inflicted on them in India, which is often ignored by authorities.

## Benefits from an African–American Perspective of Comparing the African–American and Dalit Struggles

Many have criticized the citizens of the US for their lack of sufficient knowledge about international affairs or the history of other cultures and societies. Yet, a considerable amount of the past of the US led to the development of such a cultural orientation. For much of its time, the US has been isolated from most of the rest of the world by the barriers created by two huge oceans. But, more importantly, the US is unlike other countries because almost all Americans are from different parts of the globe or are descendants of people from other parts of the planet. In the US, people of different racial, ethnic and religious groups, some with traditions of long-standing grievances and animosities towards each other, live in relative peace and harmony. Margaret Thatcher, the former prime minister of the UK, noted this, 'No other nation has so successfully combined people of different races and nations into a single culture.'[52]

As a land of immigrants, one of the huge challenges the US faced from the beginning of the founding of the republic was to prevent ethnic or religious conflicts that had existed and did exist in Europe from being replicated on American soil. One of the principal ways to accomplish this objective was to stress that America was a new land where the old ways of the immigrants' prior homelands did not apply. Thus, America's culture deeply imbibed a belief that it was a new society, unique in human civilization. This anti-traditionalist strand helped to generate a view that strongly privileges what occurs in the US over what happens in the rest of the world and a concomitant lack of awareness and appreciation of the conditions that exist in other countries.

The African-American struggle has also been deeply influenced by this dominant American cultural notion of privileging national concerns. As noted earlier, the counter-discourse of the African-American perspective leads to a comparison of the socioeconomic conditions of the Black community in the US, primarily with those of the dominant non-Hispanic White community and other minority racial or ethnic groups. Thus, the normal analysis of the condition of the Black community in the US would make such comparisons as the median household income of Blacks in 2016 was $39,490, which was only 60.7 per cent of White family income and 48.5 per cent of Asian family income.[53] The 2016 unemployment rate for Blacks (8.4 per cent) was more than twice that of Asians (3.6 per cent), nearly twice that of Whites (4.3 per cent) and significantly higher than that of Hispanics (4.7 per cent).[54] And a much larger percentage of Blacks also live in poverty than any other racial or ethnic group. The poverty rate in the Black community stands at 27.2 per cent, in contrast to Hispanics at 25.6 per cent, Asians at 11.7 per cent and Whites at 9.9 per cent.[55]

Given that the African-American situation in the US has historically involved a tireless battle against racial oppression, this normal comparative framework makes sense. When these comparisons are done they are usually intended to illuminate the progress, or lack thereof, in the efforts of American society to eliminate the effects of current and past racial oppression due to White supremacy. But such comparisons carry with them an inherent difficulty and enduring problem for African Americans. No matter how much progress African Americans have made, in such a comparative framework they are almost always portrayed as being too poor, too unemployed, too undereducated, too short-lived, too under-represented or locked up behind prison walls too often. Even if progress on the road to racial equality is recognized, the almost always concomitant recognition is that African Americans still have a long way to travel before they reach their ultimate goal. Thus, the fire of victory celebrations for the accomplishments of African Americans is nearly always doused by the flood of despair that comes from the recognition that so much is left to be done.

Another downside of the normal comparative framework for understanding the African-American situation in the US is that it systematically fails to appreciate the strengths of the African-American community and the positive aspects of its struggle for racial liberation. Having discussed the awareness of the African-American struggle by those fighting for the liberation of Dalits, this section provides us with an opportunity to break out of the typical comparative framework for analysing and judging the African-American community. Discussing the benefits and advantages that African-Americans can obtain from a cross-cultural comparison of their struggle with that of Dalits places this discussion outside the mainstream of thought about the African-American struggle against White supremacy. But this comparison may also allow us to better appreciate more of the successes and strengths of the struggle of the Black community in the US that are obscured by the normal comparison of their condition to that of non-Hispanic Whites. It allows us to develop a fuller and more positive understanding of the African-American community than we get when our understanding is limited to the traditional framework.

## Positive Perspectives of the African-American Struggle

A reality that becomes clear for African Americans by comparing their struggle with that of Dalits is that other oppressed groups throughout the world take an interest in it. Indeed, as can be seen from commentators on the Dalit struggle in India, the African-American struggle sometimes functions as a source of hope, inspiration and insight for Dalit struggles against oppression. As noted above, Dalits have used the iconic phrase from the civil rights movement, 'We Shall Overcome', in some of their events. Inspired by African Americans, they created the Dalit Panthers and pursued Dalit capitalism. In other words, the African-American struggle against its racial oppression in the US is helping to inspire what may be the most oppressed group in human history in its liberation struggle. From the point of view of the African-American struggle, the recognition that other oppressed groups benefit from our struggle is significant. It means that the frustrations that African Americans may feel as a result of the lack of success in our struggle must be tempered with the positive realization that African Americans are helping to alleviate the sufferings of other oppressed people.

## Understanding the Value of the African-American Struggle

The reality that scholars and activists concerned about Dalit liberation draw upon strategies, policies and programmes used by African Americans suggests a second important pay-off to African-Americans from engaging in this comparative analysis. It is apparent that the benefits that stand to be derived from the African-American struggle are not exhausted by what happens in the US. This means that the struggle is more significant than is generally recognized from the normal comparative perspective. Thus, if African Americans succeed in obtaining equality, groups like the Dalits could draw inspiration and moral and legal legitimacy within their own country from that success.

## More Knowledge about the African-American Struggle

There are several ways in which understanding the African-American struggle is improved by comparing it with the Dalit struggle. As pointed out by Smita Narula, 'Meritocracy, equality, efficiency, and liberalism are the catchwords that resonate in both countries to either defeat or redefine constitutional pronouncements that were heretofore invoked to ensure substantive equality on the basis of race or caste.'[56] In attacking affirmative action, some Americans argue that race is irrelevant, as when Indians discuss attacks on reservations they argue that caste no longer matters. And the success of some members of subordinated communities because of affirmative action or reservations becomes a justification for the ending of such programmes in both countries. It may simply be that these are the counterarguments that are made against programmes that will benefit oppressed groups wherever they are in the world. Furthermore, in considering the successes and pitfalls of affirmative action policies of either country, African Americans and Dalits may be inclined to reconsider the structures and methodology of their respective approaches.[57]

## African-Americans Have Allies in the Global Struggle against Oppression

The comparison of the African-American struggle to the Indian struggle for independence showed that if the struggle against White supremacy is conceptualized as a global one, then African Americans and Indian nationalists are allies. But Indian independence (as is the case for any other country that gained its independence from colonial rule) makes it difficult to maintain such an alliance. The primary concerns of the leaders of any independent nation must be the interests of its own people. In short, given the current military, economic and international might of the US,

Indian support of the African-American struggle can only go so far before it damages its relationship with the US government. The comparison of the African-American struggle to that of the Dalits demonstrates that if the struggle African Americans are engaged in is against oppression within one's own country, as opposed to White supremacy, this will generate other allies for African Americans in their struggle. In other words, African Americans can bond with other groups struggling against oppression in their own countries whose support may prove vital to the success of the African-American struggle.

## Conclusion

There is little doubt that struggles against discrimination, oppression and subordination are local because they depend on the history of a specific group in a particular locale at a given time. As a result, it is clear that the struggle of African Americans against racism, prejudice and discrimination in the US is qualitatively different from the Dalits' struggle in India. Despite the differences in the situation of each group, a comparison of these two liberation struggles can provide significant benefits for both groups. Each group will have to decide what aspects of the other's fight for equality is helpful for it. But there is much insight, inspiration and support to be gained when they study the other's experiences.

# HATE CRIMES, CRIMES OF ATROCITY AND AFFIRMATIVE ACTION IN INDIA AND THE US

*Samuel L. Myers, Jr, and Vanishree Radhakrishna*

## Introduction

'Hate crimes' are crimes that result from a 'manifest prejudice based on race, religion, sexual orientation, or ethnicity . . . committed not out of animosity toward the victim as an individual, but out of hostility toward the group to which the victim belongs'.[1] Hate crimes in the US have not always been recorded officially. These crimes include infamous lynchings in southern states of Black men who dared to speak to White women.

'Crimes of atrocity' have come to be understood under international law as referencing genocide, crimes against humanity and war crimes. The legal meaning is found in the 1948 Convention on the Prevention and Punishment of the Crime of Genocide and subsequent treaties and encompasses the crime of ethnic cleansing. In particular, genocide is that component of atrocity crimes that targets individuals simply because of their group membership. The UN states:

> Genocide, according to international law, is a crime committed against members of a national, ethnical, racial or religious group. Even though the victims of the crimes are individuals, they are targeted because of their membership, real or perceived, in one of these groups.[2]

However, as used in the context of this essay, 'crimes of atrocity' means hate crimes committed by non-Scheduled Castes (SCs) or non-Scheduled Tribes (STs) against SCs or STs in India. The actions referenced are

61

considered to be shockingly cruel and inhumane and include rape, murder, and infliction of pain and suffering. The Scheduled Castes and Tribes (Prevention of Atrocities) Act of 1989 (PoA) and its rules in 1995 detail the specific acts perpetuated by non-SCs/STs against SCs or STs that would merit prosecution and include such indignities as forced drinking or eating of inedible or obnoxious substances, sexual exploitation, injury or common annoyances. Also essential in defining case discrimination is obstruction of access to public facilities like water wells and public education and access to the basic amenities of life.

The origins of caste-based atrocities are rooted in the notion of 'untouchability' in India. Relatively recent events that highlight the concept of caste-based atrocities include the Chundur massacre (1991), the Badanavalu killings (1993), the Kambalapalli carnage (2000) and the Khairlanji incident (2006). These events highlight historic hate crimes in India as outlined by Dr B.R. Ambedkar and are comparable to lynchings detailed by civil rights activist W.E.B. Du Bois. The result is that contemporary instances of hate crimes in both India and the US can be understood within the context of historic crimes against racial groups or castes.

The common defining feature about hate crimes in the US and crimes of atrocity in India is the role of racial or caste discrimination or prejudice as the motivation for the criminal act. Whether the hate crimes or crimes of atrocity take the form of rape, physical assaults, murders or violent attacks, the underlying motive is the prejudice against an individual because of the individual's group membership.

## Policy-induced Hate Crimes

Public policies designed to improve the social and economic well-being of marginalized groups may have the unintended consequence of provoking animosities among non-protected group members. These members may perceive that the policies that target specific racial, ethnic or tribal groups or members of lower castes inherently harm those who do not receive targeted protections. This perception might cause them to lash out at the protected group members and extract revenge.

A particular example of a policy that putatively may provoke unintended effects on the very groups it is intended to help is affirmative action. Majority-group opposition to affirmative action policies is arguably related to the real or perceived economic status of groups not covered by race-based or caste-based policies. Quite a bit has been written claiming that such policies provoke non-protected group members to engage in hate crimes. However, it is particularly difficult to test this hypothesis directly because conventional national crime data sets do not include measures of perceptions or beliefs of alleged perpetrators of violence against protected group members.

Field experiments and laboratory tests demonstrate that hostility towards race-conscious affirmative action programmes is rooted, in part, in racialized attitudes and beliefs among Whites.[3] The prevalence of more racialized beliefs among Whites is associated with higher opposition to race-conscious corrective programmes. The same research contends, however, that White beliefs about their relative disadvantage tend to be stronger in organizations with race-conscious affirmative action programmes than those without such programmes.

Not all groups, however, are likely to translate their opinions about affirmative action into hostility towards the beneficiaries of such action. Own-group discrimination is a common factor cited for why some groups excluded from affirmative action nevertheless support affirmative action programmes. For example, reports that Arab Americans, who face increasing discrimination in employment, tend to support race-conscious admissions policies.[4]

A good approximation, however, comes from own-group unemployment. Using non-protected group unemployment as a proxy for perceptions about the adverse impacts of affirmative action, one can empirically examine the putative relationship between: (a) White male unemployment and incidents of hate crimes against Blacks, and (b) unemployment among non-SCs/STs and crimes of atrocities against SCs and STs in India.

The essay begins with a historical rendering of legislation designed to punish hate crimes against African Americans in the US and Dalits in India. The legislation in both countries came about long after the hate crime problem had become widely publicized. In the US, at least, the hate crime legislation is very broad and includes gender identity, sexual orientation, disability, religion and race. But, the fact that the legislation mandates the collection of data motivates our empirical analysis.

We demonstrate that although the number and rates of reported crimes of atrocities against Dalits have been on the rise in India, in the US, hate crimes directed towards African Americans conspicuously declined after the election of Barack Obama; this was a period when unemployment rates were rising. We argue that the ambiguous relationship between reported hate crimes and economic indicators of potential opposition to affirmative action policies arises in part from the imprecise nature of hate crime data.

## Hate Crimes in the US

The Federal Bureau of Investigation (FBI) has collected information on hate crimes—a classic indicator of human rights abuse—since 1992. Some argue that federal officials do not view the police killings of unarmed civilians as hate crimes. Still, the official record seems to show no evidence of an escalation in the types of hate crimes that *are* reported to authorities.

Initially, the FBI recorded hate crimes that appeared to have been caused by prejudice based on race, religion, sexual orientation or ethnicity under the following offence categories: crimes against persons, murder and non-negligent manslaughter, rape (revised definition and legacy definition), aggravated assault, simple assault, intimidation, crimes against property, robbery, burglary, larceny-theft, motor vehicle theft, arson, destruction/damage/vandalism, crimes against society, and more. Absent from this list are police killings of unarmed offenders. Still, it is instructive to review what we know about these officially reported crimes.

With recent changes in legislation, hate crimes are now defined as any 'criminal offense against a person or property motivated in whole or in part by an offender's bias against a race, religion, disability, sexual orientation, ethnicity, gender, or gender identity'. Some hate crimes, like those based on sexual orientation, increased from 1016 to 1393 incidents from 1996 and 2001 and then declined to 1017 incidents in 2014. Race-based hate crimes declined steadily from 1996 until the present. Race-based hate crimes against Blacks declined from 3674 in 1996 to 2486 in 2002. There was a slight uptick in anti-Black hate crimes in 2008, the year of Barack Obama's election to his first term, rising to 2876. But, by 2014, the numbers had fallen again to 1621.

The incredible litany of publicly exposed incidents of police use of excessive force against African-American males in recent years is both a testament to the power of social media and an exposé of the deficits of state, local and federal government accountability. The brutalization of African-American males by law enforcement agents is not a new phenomenon. It was chronicled after the riots of the 1960s in the Kerner Commission report and remains a historical legacy of the power of law enforcement agencies over the lives and bodies of Black men. Whereas W.E.B. Du Bois used his brilliant essays published in the National Association for the Advancement of Colored People's (NAACP) the *Crisis* magazine to expose the horrors of lynching in early 20th-century America, contemporary movements such as

Black Lives Matter and their allies have used Twitter, Facebook, Snapchat, FaceTime and related social networking platforms—along with the ever-present video phone—to expose police excesses. The first issue of the *Crisis* in 1910–11 mentioned lynching several times; the second issue, of 1910–12, included a list of coloured men lynched without a trial from 1885 to 1910: 2425 in total.

Although the US belatedly ratified the International Convention on the Elimination of All Forms of Racial Discrimination (CERD) in 1994, it has failed to fully implement key elements of the treaty, according to the American Civil Liberties Union (ACLU). This failure is particularly evident in the area of criminal justice, where African Americans, Hispanics and American Indians are disproportionately stopped and frisked, arrested, incarcerated and sentenced to death. They are more likely to be denied bail, more likely to be tried as adults when they are juveniles and less likely to be employed once they are released from prison.

And, apparently—though not officially, as there is no uniform database for this—they are also more likely to be the victims of excessive police force. Just as there were no official lynching statistics in Du Bois's day, there are no reliable statistical indicators today on the police use of deadly force. Only recently has the US Department of Justice proposed a largely untested methodology for attempting to piece together what is known at the local level of police shootings.

Under J. Edgar Hoover's leadership, the FBI began to produce an annual report on major crimes and offences committed in nearly every city and state. This official report, dating back to 1932, highlights information on homicides, rapes, robberies, larcenies and auto thefts and is used by policymakers to gauge trends requiring corrective action.

Not surprisingly, official statistics are silent on the police's use of force against innocent African Americans. This has not prevented pundits and others from contesting whether there are in fact racial disparities in such action by the police. For example, in a widely criticized and unpublished report by a team of students led by Harvard economist Roland Fryer, evidence collected from several police departments did not show racially disparate uses of deadly force.[5] While others have pointed to various methodological flaws in the statistical analysis arising from one-sided police data, a more compelling objection is that there is no uniform federal database on police killings of unarmed citizens, despite the fact that for nearly a quarter of a century, there has been a federal mandate to collect such data. That we know so little about police killings of Black males is attributable to the lack of accountability on the part of local, state and federal law enforcement agencies.

Few observers, however, believe that anti-Black hatred in America has declined simply because *reported* hate crimes declined. It is well known that crimes of all types are seriously under-reported. Child maltreatment offences frequently go unreported by public officials legally mandated to report them.[6] What are known as index crimes—robbery, burglary, larceny, auto theft, murder, rape, assault and arson—also go unreported by victims or police.[7] Detecting, reporting and prosecuting hate crimes particularly require the involvement of law enforcement personnel. In a revealing analysis of the association between past lynchings (1882 to 1930) and contemporary law enforcement responses to hate crimes in the US, it has been reported that 'past lynching combined with a sizeable Black population largely suppresses (1) police compliance with federal hate crime law, (2) police reports of hate crimes that target Blacks, and in some analyses (3) the likelihood of prosecuting a hate crime case'.[8] In short, one cannot always believe officially reported hate crime statistics in part because the primary reporters are part of a long legacy of hateful activities.

This is just another illustration of why it is difficult to get a handle on the magnitude of racist acts in society. The extent of the looming crisis of continuing and unresolved racial divides in the US remains a matter of perceptions rather than careful empirical analysis.

## Case Study: Dylann S. Roof

One of the most horrific hate crimes in modern US history occurred on 17 June 2015. It took place at the Emanuel African Methodist Episcopal Church in Charleston, South Carolina, when Dylann S. Roof, a young, unemployed White male, systematically murdered nine African-American members of a Bible study class. Roof, a high-school dropout, confessed to the shootings and justified his acts as part of an effort to ignite a national race war. All indicators were that this White male was living on the margins of society, frequently using and abusing drugs and feeling angry at the advantages that African Americans and other non-Whites appeared to have gained at his expense and the expense of other Whites like him. The narrative of the angry White male would resonate, but for the fact that Roof was mentally ill.

The *New York Times* reported on 'how an awkward adolescent had progressed from reclusive consumer of internet hate to ruthless and remorseless jihadist' stating that unsealed psychiatric reports revealed a young man tormented by mental illness:

> The documents provide, for the first time, a multidimensional portrait of a withdrawn but strikingly intelligent misfit whose tastes ran to Dostoyevsky, classical music and NPR but who said his 'dream job' would be working at an airport convenience store. He exhibited disturbingly introverted behavior from an early age—playing alone, never starting conversations—but received little treatment for what defense experts later concluded was autism and severe social anxiety, with precursor symptoms of psychosis.[9]

Roof had repeatedly been arrested in prior months for other crimes and normally would have been prohibited from purchasing a lethal weapon. However, clerical errors apparently resulted in his prior arrests not being registered at the time of his application for a firearm. The Charleston massacre resulted in national outrage about gun availability, mental illness and auxiliary factors that seemed to explain away or diminish the explanation of White male unemployment as a contributing factor to violent acts of racism.

## Caste and Crimes of Atrocity in India

In India, according to Dr Ambedkar, 'Untouchables' are the descendants of 'Broken Men' (Dalit, in Marathi) who were the original inhabitant tribes that were conquered and forced to live as peripheral groups, relegated to guard the villages of the conquered. There was a clear non-acceptance of the original inhabitants by the conquered.[10] Article 17 of the Constitution abolished 'untouchability' in 1950. It is no longer defined under the Constitution.

SCs and STs are the only two groups covered under the PoA Act of 1989. Passed in furtherance of Article 17 of the Constitution, this Act seeks to:

(1)  Prevent the commission of offences of atrocities against SCs and STs
(2)  Provide for Special Courts for the trial of offences and
(3)  Provide for the relief and rehabilitation of victims.

An amendment to the Act in 2015 broadened its scope. Punishments under the act varied with the severity of the offence: from monetary fines to life imprisonment and even death.[11]

The prevalence of untouchability and caste-based atrocities in the present day strike a nerve at the very core of India's social identity and consciousness. Caste discrimination is a prevailing and entrenched bias that permeates Indian institutions even though it violates the constitutional mandate. It is based on the concepts of inferior and superior birth status. Atrocities in the form of violence against Dalits are manifestations of deep-rooted hatred and intolerance that are often directed towards the annihilation of entire Dalit families. Post the PoA Act, harrowing stories of suppression and extreme forms of human rights violations and stark insensitivity on the part of civil society to such happenings are among the striking paradoxes of modern India's social reality, for example, atrocities in the Chundur massacre (1991),[12] Badanavalu killings (1993),[13] Kambalapalli carnage (2000)[14] and Khairlanji incident (2006).[15] The Nagalapalli carnage, detailed below, is particularly relevant because it speaks not just about the plight of Dalits in Indian villages, but also about the dual discrimination based on gender and caste.[16]

The call for the annihilation of caste by Dr Ambedkar is countered by the resurgence of caste and discrimination in new communities. In 1932, Dr Ambedkar signed the Poona Pact to assuage his fears that the Hindu caste might massacre his people and to avert a genocide of sorts[17] if M.K. Gandhi's health was jeopardized. Forced to withdraw his demands for separate electorates for Untouchables, Dr Ambedkar fought for establishing equality and equal status, including the need for a strong federal structure, till the end of his life. His assertion that villages were 'cesspools'[18] of caste discrimination, based on bitter personal experiences, stands as a testimony against untouchability practices in Indian villages—a reality then as well as now.

Modern-day Indian villages are hubs of caste discrimination. A uniqueness of the Dalits' situation is their submergence in poverty. They are subject to large-scale atrocities[19] and sexual exploitation. Dr Ambedkar's fears of violence are being acted out on a daily basis. Dr Ambedkar resigned as the law minister in 1951, after his Hindu Code Bill was rejected by the Nehru government. The bill spoke of his rock-solid conviction that the recognition of women's right to equality was a priority in independent India. In this article, we have chosen to comment on atrocities on Dalits by closely examining the case of an assertive Dalit woman and her two sons, in Nagalapalli, a village in Kolar district of Karnataka.[20]

## Case Study: Crimes of Atrocity in Nagalapalli

The acknowledgement by Parliament in 1989 of the prevalence of atrocities and violence based on untouchability was a significant step towards addressing fundamental issues of abuse and violence against scores of citizens who are living in unequal circumstances socially, economically and politically. The PoA Act,[21] for the first time in Indian legislative history, formulated a new class of offences[22] by recognizing various forms of untouchability and created a presumption that every offence against an SC or ST person committed by someone who was a member neither of the SC nor ST group was inevitably and invariably based on caste prejudice.[23] It penalized wilful neglect of duties by public servants,[24] created a presumption as to group intentions to commit offences[25] and provided for the establishment of special courts to try cases under the PoA Act.[26]

### Demographics and Caste Composition

Nagalapalli is a village near Kyasamballi, 5 km from the Bethamangala police station limits of Bangarapet taluka in Kolar district of Karnataka. The total population of Kolar is 15,36,401.[27] SCs constitute 4,65,867 of the population, with 3,27,424 residing in rural areas.[28] Dalits represent 30 per cent of this population. The majority of the population of the village at the time of the incident consisted of the dominant Reddy caste, which owned twenty-five to thirty houses. SCs owned only five houses in the village. SCs and Reddys lived as neighbours as there are no separate settlements or SC colonies in Nagalapalli.

### History and 'Origin of Discord'[29]

Yashodamma belonged to the Adi Karnataka SC category and owned 3 acres and 17 guntas of land next to Vasanthareddy's property. Vasanthareddy belonged to the dominant Reddy community. There had been a dispute for over fifteen years between Yashodamma and Vasanthareddy regarding land. Yashodamma had the land surveyed and found that Vasanthareddy had encroached on her land. Yashodamma also owned about 3 acres of Inamti land granted by the government. Allegedly, the accused, Vasanthareddy, and his community members tried to coerce the victim to sell them all of her land. On the victim's persistent refusal to sell, her family alleges that she and her sons were threatened with death. The victim's family lodged several complaints of abuse and attacks at the police station in connection with this dispute.

Six months before the incident, Yashodamma's eldest son, D. Kumar, was allegedly abused and assaulted by Brahmanandareddy, Vasanthareddy and Gangireddy. Two days before the incident, on 24 April 2002, Brahmanandareddy and Puttappa allegedly abused and assaulted Dinesh. Due to the fear of an imminent attack from the dominant community, the victims moved from Nagalapalli. Yashodamma and Dinesh went to Bethamangala to live with D. Kumar. Chandrashekar moved to his wife's village in Lakkur. On the day of the incident, however, Vasanthareddy approached the victims and invited them to Nagalapalli to reconcile and compromise. Jayaramareddy went to Lakkur to invite Chandrashekar to join his mother and brother in this reconciliation. Yashodamma, Chandrashekar and Dinesh were taken into confidence, brought to Nagalapalli and allegedly led into a premeditated death trap.

### Trial Court Proceedings: Relevant Dates

| | |
|---|---|
| Date of offence | 26 April 2002 |
| Date of report of offence | 26 April 2002 |
| First Information Report (FIR) | 26 April 2002 |
| Date when FIR was handed to the court | 27 April 2002 |
| PoA sections added to FIR | 2 May 2002 |
| Date of inquest | 27 April 2002 |
| Post-mortem reports of the deceased | 27 April 2002 |
| Date of submission of charge sheet | 26 August 2002 |
| Charges framed by the court | 23 June 2003 |
| Commencement of recording evidence | 13 November 2006 |
| Date of closing of recording evidence | 1 September 2007 |
| Date of judgement | 19 October 2007 |

| Duration of the case | Years | Months | Days |
|---|---|---|---|
| | 05 | 01 | 23 |

## Failure of Judicial Process

(a) Although charges were framed under Section 3(2)(v) of the PoA Act by Judge Milind Dange in the first instance, Judge K. Shivaram completely ignored this important legal provision in his deliberations.

(b) The court declared eyewitness Muniyappa's evidence to be 'vague' without giving any reasons for the same. Similarly, eyewitness Bharatamma's evidence was turned down as 'not inspiring confidence' without giving any further clarification.

(c) The court did not comment on the evidentiary value of 'voluntary statements' made by some of the accused, on the basis of which weapons, clothes, vehicles and accessories were recovered.

(d) There was reliance on the statement that no bloodstains were found on the weapons, when the gap between the commission of the offence and the examination of the weapons by doctors was eleven months and nine days (26 April 2002 to 1 April 2003).

(e) When rejecting the evidence of D. Kumar, the judge drew the conclusion that the fifty-four persons against whom the complaint was made were inimical to D. Kumar. No reasons were given to substantiate this claim. Further, what was the court acknowledging in saying that 'even though there was an involvement of only about 6 to 8 accused, cases were registered against 54 persons'?

Frederick Douglass had this to say on the eve of America's Independence Day:

> This Fourth of July is yours, not mine. You may rejoice, I must mourn. To drag a man in fetters to the ground illuminated temple of liberty, and call upon him to join you in joyous anthems, were inhuman mockery and sacrilegious irony . . . I say it with a sad sense of disparity between us. I am not included within the pale of this glorious anniversary . . . the blessing in which you, this day rejoice, are not enjoyed in common. The rich inheritance of justice, liberty and prosperity and independence, bequeathed by your fathers, is shared by you, not by me. The sunlight that brought light and healing to you has brought stripes and death to me.

The caste carnage that took place in Nagalapalli, perpetrated by the dominant community that succeeded in taking the lives of all three members of a family, was sparked off predominantly because it was headed by an assertive Dalit woman who owned lands and sought to reclaim what was rightfully hers. The patriarchal hegemony and the inferior status of Untouchables in Nagalapalli sought to disentitle her and force her into compliance. The price she paid for standing up for her rights was her life and the life of her two sons.

These heinous anecdotes of recent history in Indian villages raise questions about the continued perpetration of violent crimes against Dalits despite the legislative attention and existence of provisions for strict legal enforcement. Specifically, it is worth examining the political and socioeconomic structures in rural settings that give rise to conflict and violence. Another lesson from Nagalapalli is the need to estimate the impact of gender on economic discrimination and violent crime.

## Descriptive Statistics on Hate Crimes in the US and Crimes of Atrocity in India

Figures 1 and 2 provide the initial core findings of the changes in hate crimes in the US from 1995 to 2015. Figure 1 reports the measures regarding victims. Figure 2 reports the measures regarding incidents. Whether the measure is victims or incidents, it is clear that over the period during which the FBI reported total, race-based, anti-Black or anti-White hate crimes, the numbers have faced a steady decline over the past twenty years. There is a sharp uptick in anti-race hate crimes between 2014 and 2015, but this is not attributable to the increase in anti-Black hate crimes. Thus, overall, the numbers of anti-Black hate crimes appeared to decline throughout 1995–2015.

### 1. Hate Crimes per Year

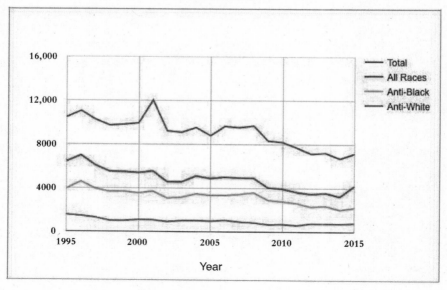

## 2. Hate Incidents Per Year

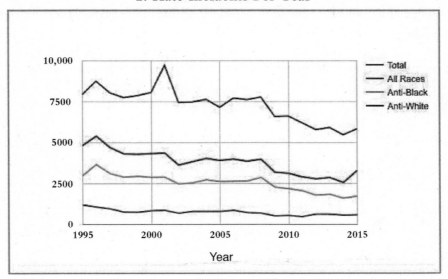

Figures 3 and 4, by way of contrast, report the numbers of crimes of atrocity in India over the same period of 1995–2015 against SCs and STs, respectively. Both figures show an initial spiking of reported crimes of atrocity from 2000 to 2002. For SCs, the number of reported crimes of atrocity increased steadily from 2005 with a sharp upturn after 2012. For STs, it levelled off after the peak of 2002 and then sharply increased after 2012.

Figures 3 and 4 show that there have been long-term increases in reported crimes of atrocity with several peaking periods. Moreover, both indicate that in India recent years have demonstrated upward spikes in crimes of atrocity, resulting in levels far higher than at any time during the entirety of 1995–2014. There is, however, a noticeable drop in the number of crimes of atrocity reported between 2014 and 2015, but the level in 2015 is still higher than any year before 2014.

In short, the US data shows long-term declines in reported hate crimes whereas the Indian data shows long-term increases.

The unemployment rates in the US for Black and White males between the ages of sixteen and twenty-four and White males of all ages are in Figure 5. The Black male unemployment rate is consistently higher than the White male rate. But the movements of these rates are the same: when one increases, the other also increases. When one falls, the other also falls. For example, from 2010 to 2015, Black male unemployment rates for persons sixteen to twenty-four years of age declined from nearly 35 per cent to 20 per cent. White male unemployment rates for the same age group dropped from almost 20 per cent to nearly 10 per cent. During the same period, the unemployment rate for all White males dropped from 10 per cent to about 5 per cent.

### 3. India's Incidence of Crime against Scheduled Castes[30]

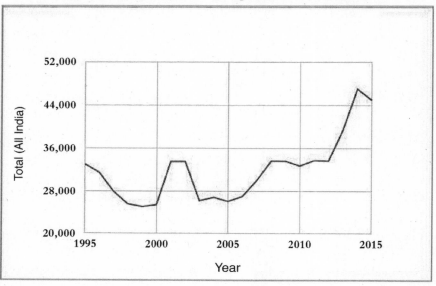

### 4. India's Incidence of Crime against Scheduled Tribes

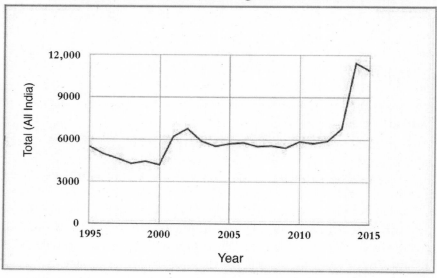

Unemployment rates in India are derived from various rounds of the National Sample Survey (NSS) and are not reported here for every year. However, it is clear from Table 1 in the Employment and Unemployment Situation among Social Groups in India report[31] that the urban unemployment rate is considerably higher than the rural rate.

## 5. Unemployment Rates in the US

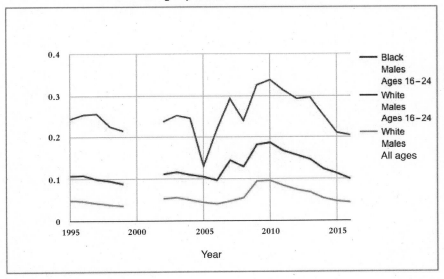

## The Relationship between Hate Crimes and Unemployment

We now turn our attention to the core question of this essay: how does the insecurity due to affirmative action faced by the non-preferred group—as measured by their unemployment rates—affect the level of hate crimes against the protected group? The rational model of economic behaviour posits that increases in the White male unemployment rate (or the relative White male unemployment rate) induce the perception that the protected group members—such as Blacks—are the culprits and thereby results in a higher number of anti-Black hate crimes. The model posits that when members of non-SCs/STs face higher unemployment rates, they too perceive that the culprit is affirmative action and preferences afforded to protected group members, resulting in an increase in crimes of atrocity directed towards members of SCs and STs.

## 6. Anti-Black Hate Crimes and Unemployment Rates in the US

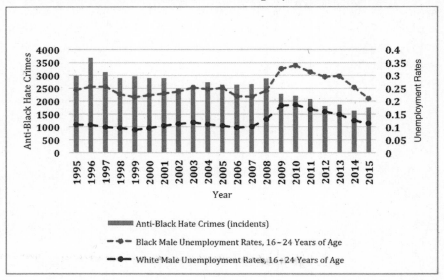

Figure 6 maps the time series of anti-Black hate crimes against the Black male unemployment rate and the White male unemployment rate for persons aged sixteen to twenty-four. Before 2005, it is difficult to discern any particular pattern in the data. After 2007–09 (the period of the great recession in the US), there is a sharp rise in White male unemployment as well as a sizeable increase in anti-Black hate crimes. From 2010 to 2015, there is a continuous drop in the young White male unemployment rate but not always a consistent drop in anti-Black hate crime. This figure provides the initial clue that the effects of White unemployment on anti-Black hate crimes are anything but obvious.

Another way to look at the relationship between economic insecurity and anti-Black hate crimes is to plot the overall unemployment rates against the level of anti-Black hate crimes. Figure 7 reveals that at low levels of unemployment, increases in the overall unemployment rates *reduce* anti-Black hate crimes. Only after unemployment is above 8 per cent or so does there appear to be a positive slope in the relationship between unemployment and anti-Black hate crimes.

## 7. Overall Unemployment Rates in the US

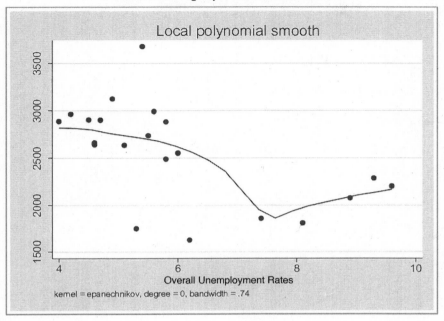

Figure 8 further underscores the non-linear relationship between the economic insecurity of Whites and the level of anti-Black hate crimes. Here, the plot is between the ratio of White to Black male unemployment rates for persons sixteen to twenty-four years of age and the level of anti-Black hate crimes. We have fitted the curve to a third degree polynomial function (R-square =0.6428) and demonstrate that only when White male unemployment rises to higher than half of Black male unemployment does there appear to be an upward relationship between relative unemployment and anti-Black hate crimes. Elsewhere along the curve, where young Black males' unemployment rates are more than twice the unemployment rates for young White males, the relationship between the economic insecurity of Whites and anti-Black hate crimes is inverse: higher relative insecurity reduces hate crimes.

## 8. Relative Unemployment Rates in the US

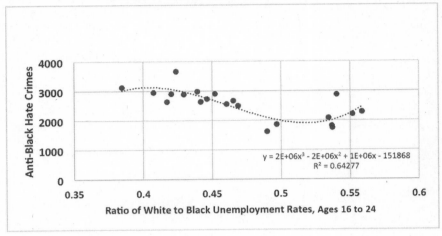

In summary, the relationship between (a) the economic insecurity faced by young White males triggered by increases in their unemployment rate or their unemployment rate relative to that of young Black males and (b) incidents of anti-Black hate crimes is not uniform. At best, the relationship is an inverse one when unemployment rates are low. When they are high or when the gap between Black and White unemployment rates narrows, then we do observe increases in anti-Black hate crimes with the increase in White insecurity.

Turning now to evidence on India, Figures 9 and 10 report the time series of crimes of atrocity and unemployment rates for persons other than those from households belonging to SCs, STs or Other Backward Castes. Between 1994 and 2000, unemployment rates for other males rose but the numbers of crimes against SCs and STs fell. Between 2000 and 2005, unemployment rates fell but the crimes of atrocity were slightly higher. Similar non-confirmatory results appear for other periods. These two figures provide little or no support for the claim that increases in economic insecurity among non-protected group members produce crimes of atrocity.

Figures 11 and 12 provide clearer evidence that increases in the unemployment rates for other males (rural or urban) do not produce higher levels of hate crimes against SCs or STs. Second-order polynomial equations are fitted producing R-squares of 0.587 and 0.688 with downward slopes.

## 9. Hate Crimes vs Unemployment of Other Rural Males in India

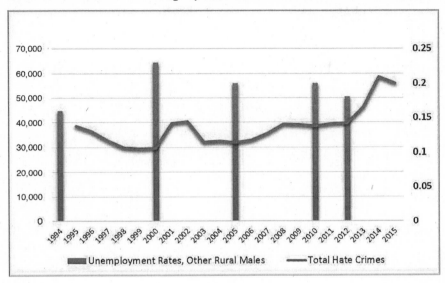

## 10. Hate Crimes vs Unemployment of Other Urban Males in India

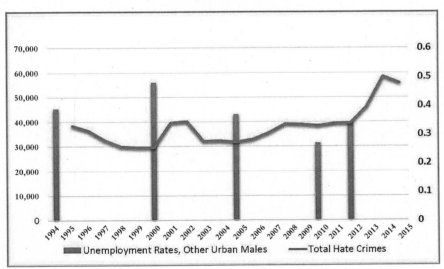

## 11. Urban Male Unemployment vs Hate Crimes in India

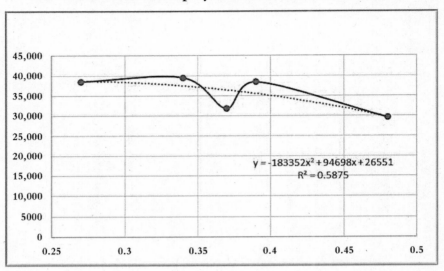

$y = -183352x^2 + 94698x + 26551$
$R^2 = 0.5875$

## 12. Rural Male Unemployment vs Hate Crimes in India

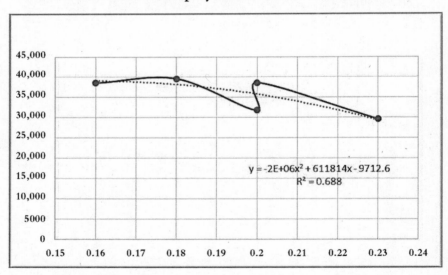

$y = -2E+06x^2 + 611814x - 9712.6$
$R^2 = 0.688$

By way of contrast, Figures 13 and 14 report the results of estimating the relationship between relative unemployment rates and hate crimes. For low rates of relative unemployment, there is an inverse relationship between the relative unemployment of other groups and crimes of atrocity against SCs and STs. For high rates of relative unemployment, increases in the relative unemployment of other groups produce higher levels of crimes against SCs and STs. This finding is consistent with the view that it is not the absolute level of unemployment or economic security that affects crimes against SCs or STs. It is the relative economic insecurity that matters. Anti-SC/ST sentiments may not translate into hate crimes until and unless the relative economic insecurity reaches a threshold. As seen in the US results, that threshold is quite high, suggesting that the standard rational economic model may not be particularly helpful in understanding the behaviour of those who perpetuate crimes against protected group members.

## 13. Ratio of Rural Others to SC Male Unemployment vs Hate Crimes

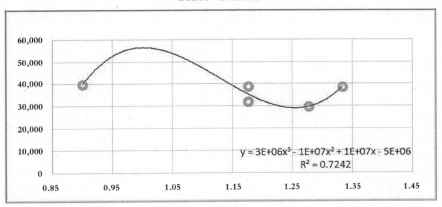

$$y = 3E{+}06x^3 - 1E{+}07x^2 + 1E{+}07x - 5E{+}06$$
$$R^2 = 0.7242$$

## Summary and Conclusions

Hate crimes against African Americans in the US are manifestations of deep prejudice based on racism. A comparison between atrocities against Dalits

## 14. Ratio of Urban Others to SC Male Unemployment vs Hate Crimes

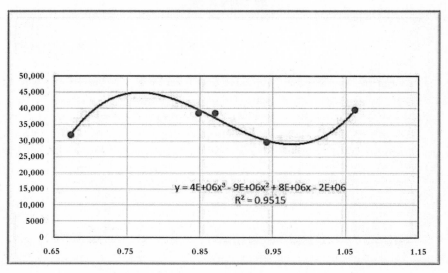

and racist hate crimes is especially germane since there has been increased media attention to violence based on hatred and intolerance against both communities, which face disabilities based on discrimination in all walks of life. Professor Derrick Bell deems racial discrimination a permanent institution, designed to keep the American economy in 'balance'.[32] A comparison of discrimination based on race in America and caste in India is useful—these are the two countries where legal protections are in place yet cases of violence and discrimination continue to escalate.

The essay has detailed a rationale for the empirical analysis that examines the relationship between hate crimes and unemployment. We demonstrate that the putative empirical relationship between hate crimes and affirmative action is tenuous at best. But we also point out some of the major flaws and measurement concerns related to the underlying data in the US and India.

The first major flaw and measurement issue is that one important form of hate crime is not included in the US data: the police use of deadly force against young African-American males. Strikingly, during the very years in which outward manifestations of racial hatred in America escalated, the FBI's official reports of anti-Black hate crimes declined. One can only speculate about why the official data does not coincide with popular beliefs and perceptions about the rise of anti-Black hatred in recent years.

A second methodological concern is that this theory pertains to hostility towards protected group members arising from the perception that affirmative action harms non-protected group members. However, we have not directly measured these perceptions in the US or India. Instead, we have used the empirical strategy of adopting a plausible proxy for economic insecurity: unemployment rates of non-protected group males. An interesting extension of this research might include the examination of other measures of economic insecurity—for instance, loss of property or decline in homeownership—or of gendered aspects of economic insecurity, for instance, female unemployment rates.

Nonetheless, our main finding, apparent in the data for both India and the US, is that racial hatred is not easily explained simply by economic insecurity—a pretext often used to justify opposition to race- or caste-conscious remedies to discrimination. While the conventional and widely held view is that affirmative action *causes* racial hatred, hostility and therefore hate crimes, the evidence in this essay does not support that view. At best, our results suggest that only in the most extreme cases of economic insecurity where non-protected group members unemployment relative to protected group members' unemployment is above some threshold does there appear to be an aggravating impact of economic insecurity on hate crimes. Over most of the range of unemployment rates, there does not appear to be an adverse impact of economic insecurity on hate crimes.

## References

Armstrong, David, Christian Davenport, Amanda M. Klasing, Martin Macwan, Manjula Pradeep, Sushma Vania, Allan Stam, and Monika Kalra Varma. *Understanding Untouchability: A Comprehensive Study of Practices and Conditions in 1589 Villages.* 2010. Washington DC: Navsarjan Trust and Robert F. Kennedy Center for Justice and Human Rights.

Arroyo, Luiz Antonio Salazar. 2010. 'Tailoring the Narrow Tailoring Requirement in the Supreme Court's Affirmative Action Cases'. *Cleveland State Law Review* 58: 649–84. Available at http://engagedscholarship.csuohio.edu/clevstlrev/vol58/iss3/6.

Ayres, Ian and Sydney Foster. 2007. 'Don't Tell, Don't Ask: Narrow Tailoring after Grutter and Gratz.' *Texas Law Review* 85 (3): 517–83.

Ayres, Ian and Sydney Foster. 1996. 'Narrow Tailoring.' *UCLA Law Review* 43 (6): 1781–1838.

Beltont, Robert. 1990. 'The Dismantling of the Griggs Disparate Impact Theory and the Future of Title VII: The Need for a Third Reconstruction.' *Yale Law and Policy Review* 8.2, Article 4: 223–256. Available at http://digitalcommons.law.yale.edu/ylpr/vol8/iss2/4.

Chakraborty, Debashis, D. Shyam Babu, and Manashi Chakravorty. 2006. 'Atrocities on Dalits: What the District Level Data Say on Society-State Complicity.' *Economic and Political Weekly* 41 (24): 2478–81.

Deshpande, Ashwini. 2005. Affirmative Action in India and the United States, Washington, DC: World Bank. https://openknowledge.worldbank.org/handle/10986/9038.

Deshpande, Ashwini. 2011. *The Grammar of Caste: Economic Discrimination in Contemporary India*. New Delhi: Oxford University Press.

Deshpande, Ashwini. 2000. 'Recasting Economic Inequality'. *Review of Social Economy* 58 (3): 381–99.

'Fullilove vs Klutznick: Do Affirmative Action Plans Require Congressional Authorization?' *Washington and Lee Law Review* 38 (4), Article 14: 1315–32. Available at http://scholarlycommons.law.wlu.edu/wlulr/vol38/iss4/14.

Galanter, Marc. 1984. *Competing Equalities: Law and the Backward Classes in India*. New Delhi: Oxford University Press.

Ghandnoosh, Nazgol. 2015. *Black Lives Matter: Eliminating Racial Inequity in the Criminal Justice System*. Washington, DC: The Sentencing Project. Available at http://sentencingproject.org/wp-content/uploads/2015/11/Black-Lives-Matter.pdf.

'How Race Impacts Post-Prior Job Prospects'. 26 February 2014. *Crime Report*. Available at http://thecrimereport.org/2014/02/26/2014-02-how-race-effects-post-prison-job-prospects.

Hoytt, Eleanor Hinton, Vincent Schiraldi, Brenda V. Smith and Jason Ziedenberg. 'Pathways to Juvenile Detention Reform: Reducing Racial Disparities in Juvenile Detention'. Annie Casey Foundation. Available at http://www.aecf.org/m/resourcedoc/aecf-Pathways8reducingracialdisparities-2001.pdf.

Jodhka, Surinder, S. 9 June 2017. 'Who Will Speak for the Villages?' *Tribune*. Available at http://www.tribuneindia.com/news/comment/who-will-speak-for-the-village/91267.html.

Joshi, Barbara, R. 1982. 'Whose Law, Whose Order: "Untouchables", Social Violence, and the State in India'. *Asian Survey* 22 (7): 676–87. Available at http://www.jstor.org/stable/2643703.

King, Ryan D. and Gretchen M. Sutton. 2013. 'High Times for Hate Crimes: Explaining the Temporary Clustering of Hate-Motivated Offending'. *Criminology* 51 (4): 871–94.

Leonard, Jonathan S. 1984. 'The Impact of Affirmative Action on Employment'. *Journal of Labor Economics* 2 (4): 439–63.

Military Leadership Diversity Commission. May 2010. 'Narrow Tailoring and Diversity Policy'. Issue paper 37. Legal Implications, version 2. Available at http://diversity.defense.gov/Portals/51/Documents/Resources/Commission/docs/Issue%20Papers/Paper%2037%20-%20Narrow%20Tailoring%20and%20Diversity%20Policy.pdf.

Omvedt, Gail. 20 August 2012. 'The Part that Parted'. *Outlook*. Available at http://www.outlookindia.com/magazine/story/a-part-that-parted/281929.

Osborne, Evan W. 2001. 'Culture, Development and Government: Reservations in India.' *Economic Development and Cultural Change* 49 (3): 659–85.

Pal, G.C., N. Sukumar and L. David Lal. 2011. *Atrocities against Dalits: Emerging Trends*. New Delhi: Indian Institute of Dalit Studies.

Radhakrishna, Vanishree. 2013. 'Affirmative Action and Social Justice: Reflections on the Judgments of the Supreme Court'. *Jindal Journal of Public Policy, Special Issue on Diversity, Discrimination and Social Exclusion in India and the USA* 1 (2): 117–23. Available at http://www.jgu.edu.in/public/journal/PDF/Chapter7_VanishreeRadhakrishna.pdf.

Reddy, O. Chinnappa. 2008. *The Court and the Constitution of India: Summits and Shallows*. New Delhi: Oxford University Press.

Roy, Arundhati. 2014. 'The Doctor and the Saint: An Introduction'. B.R. Ambedkar, *Annihilation of Caste*. New Delhi: Navayana.

Sheth, D.L. 1987. 'Reservations Policy Revisited'. *Economic and Political Weekly* 22(46): 1957–62.

Singh, Mahendra P. 1993. 'Are Articles 15(4) and 16(4) Fundamental Rights?' *SCC* (J) 3: 32–41.

Singh, Paramanand. 2010. 'The Ideal of Equality and Reservation Policy: A Critical Review'. *Law and (In) Equalities: Contemporary Perspectives*, eds. Mahendra Pal Singh and Swati Deva (1): 3–24. Lucknow: Eastern Book Company.

Ministry of Tribal Affairs. Annual Report 2005–06. Available at http://www.tribal.nic.in/writereaddata/AnnualReport/AR2005-06.pdf.

Weisskopf, Thomas. 2004. *Affirmative Action in the United States and India: A Comparative Perspective*. New York: Routledge.

## Cases

*Adarand Constructions Inc.* vs *Pena* 515 US 200, 227 (1995).

*Ajit Singh Januja* vs *State of Punjab* 2 SCC 715 (1996).

*Akhil Bharatiya Soshit Karamchari Sangh (Railway) Represented* vs *Union of India and Others* AIR SC 298 (1981).

*Albermarle Paper Company* vs *Moody* 422 US 405 (1975).

*Balaji* vs *State of Mysore* AIR SC 649 (1963).

*City of Richmond* vs *J.A. Croson & Co.* 488 US 469 (1989).

*Devadasan* vs *Union of India* AIR SC 179 (1964).

*Dothard* vs *Rawlinson* 433 US 321 (1977).

*Fullilove* vs *Klutznick* 448 US 448 (1980).

*Griggs* vs *Duke Power Company* 401 US 424 (1971).

*Grutter* vs *Bollinger* 539 US 506 (2003).

*Gratz* vs *Bollinger* 539 US 244 (2003).

*Indra Sawhney* vs *Union of India* Supp. (3) SCC 217 (1992).

*K.C. Vasantha Kumar* vs *State of Karnataka* AIR SC 1495 (1985).

*McDonnell Douglas Corp.* vs *Green* 411 US 792 (1973).

*Metro Broadcasting, Inc.* vs *FCC* 497 US 547 (1990).

*Regents of California* vs *Bakke* 438 US 265 (1978).

*Texas Department of Community Affairs* vs *Burdine* 450 US 248 (1981).

*Union of India* vs *Virpal Singh Chauhan* 6SCC 648 (1995).

*United States* vs *Paradise* 480, US 149 (1987).

*Vinod Kumar* vs *Union of India* 6 SCC 580 (1996).

*Wards Cove Packing Co.* vs *Antonio* 109 S. Ct. 2115 (1989).

*Watson* vs *Forth Worth Bank and Trust* 108 S. Ct. 2777 (1988).

*Wygant* vs *Jackson Board of Education* 476 US 267 (1986).

# AMBEDKAR'S FOREIGN POLICY AND THE ELLIPSIS OF THE 'DALIT' FROM INTERNATIONAL ACTIVISM[1]

*Suraj Yengde*

## Introduction

> 'Strange, isn't it, that the first common sense on the subject, strongly and publicly enunciated by a political leader of stature, comes from a spokesman of the Harijan Caste.'[2]

United States National Urban League leader, civil rights activist and labour organizer Lester B. Granger, while reflecting on global foreign policy programmes, invoked B.R. Ambedkar to describe the failing policies of peaceful coexistence and neutralism famous in the 1950s. This essay explores the historical intersectional struggle of Dalit rights in global politics. In order to understand it better, I suggest looking at the ideas of Ambedkar, one of the founding figures of modern Indian democracy, on national state formation. Various studies have commented on the international political imagination of Indian nationalist leaders, namely, Lala Lajpat Rai, Jawaharlal Nehru and M.K. Gandhi, alongside a stream of other privileged-caste leaders, M.N. Roy included. However, there is not a single study that analyses the international outlook of Ambedkar. The reasons have to do, perhaps, with ignorance about Ambedkar and the prejudice of the dominant privileged-caste academia.[3] The Brahminical historiography of India as well as the country's national narratives bears the responsibility for the egregious omission. This essay attempts to shed light on the global thinking of subalterns. With the story of Ambedkar, I wish to present the geopolitical thought process of marginalized groups to understand how under-represented groups envision(ed) their location in the international movements of human rights athwart civil and political representation.

In the post-Independence period, the Indian democracy bureaucratized the modus operandi of the social order. In the area of foreign policy especially, the Brahminical class was overwhelmingly appointed to the coveted posts of ambassadors, emissaries and experts, and in the state delegations to various committees of international government bodies. Foreign policy is the international mediation of a country's domestic policies with the rest of the world. It is an arena that guarantees global dialogue on mutual terms. Therefore, by promoting the Brahminical class, the postcolonial Indian state ensured strict control over the global scrutiny of its internal policies.

Extrapolating from this, we may ask what it means to look at the world through the lens of the marginalized. How do we reconcile the vision of the most oppressed under the hegemonic exclusionary theories of foreign policy? Or, simply put, do subalterns think of the global? By determining the position of the marginalized in the policy structures, close attention to Ambedkar's political philosophy illuminates the implications of such a global policy dialogue. This focus could help establish the citizenry of the marginalized community in terms of social, civil, cultural, economic and political human rights which are predominantly internationally influenced, globally inspired and in conversation with other countries. This will also help critically examine how the postcolonial Indian state, which was essentially inherited from the colonial regime, kept the foreign policy stance the same by excluding the marginalized community from its deliberations. It ensured that the internal strife between the majority and minority communities remained muted on international platforms.

## Internationalist Ambedkar

Ambedkar has been primarily confined to the emancipatory politics of the Scheduled Caste (SC) community of India, along with being bestowed with other laurels such as Constitution maker. However, little is spoken of his role in the colonial and postcolonial Indian foreign policy make-up and in international human rights movements. Ambedkar was a keen observer of India's foreign policy and it constituted one of the cornerstones of his political visions. The All India Scheduled Caste Federation (AISCF), in its election manifesto in 1951 authored by Ambedkar, had a column titled 'Problems of Foreign Policy', referring to the collapsing state of the Indian foreign programme. In it, Ambedkar made suggestions about the Kashmir issue that had been plaguing the South Asian region. He had also proposed India getting permanent membership of the United Nations Organization way back in 1951, making him perhaps the first person who considered India had a legitimate and rightful place in the international body.

Nationalist histories as well as the organized Left's counter-narratives overlooked these facets of the internationalist Ambedkar. Vernacular writings in India, which are rich in the narratives of the Ambedkar movement and the Dalit movement's 'counter publics',[4] also blatantly overlooked the Dalits' interface with international rights movements. Foreign policy was very dear to Ambedkar. He observed 'foreign affairs' to be the 'most important subject from [a] social, political and financial point of view'.[5] By taking a keen interest in foreign policy, Ambedkar was perhaps trying to extend his political constituency beyond India. This enthusiasm is seen in his efforts to communicate with other political movements, such as his famous letter to W.E.B. Du Bois, N. Sivaraj's[6] visit to the Pacific Relations Committee conference in Quebec as a representative of the AISCF in 1942 and the Buddhist country diplomacy with South East Asian countries, which he thought of in terms of potential solidarity to help the emancipatory struggle of the Dalits. Despite the eventual failures of all these measures, they serve as testimony to his international outlook. However, even though he led one of the world's most important civil rights movements, Ambedkar fell short of unifying it with other civil and political rights movements the world over. He confined his approach to state-sponsored organizations like the United Nations. This singular focus isolated the Dalit movement from other global social justice movements.

Ambedkar's international outlook matured during his stay in the US and the UK in pursuit of his education in the early decades of the 20th century. Eleanor Zelliot[7] argues that his vision towards the US had taken cues from non-Brahmin movement leaders like Jotiba Phule, who was inspired by America's initiative to abolish Black slavery. Maharaja Sayajirao Gaikwad had introduced the American education system after his visit to the US in 1893. The students who were being educated in Marathi, Hindi and English read about George Washington and Uncle Tom's Cabin instead of British-centred education. This benefited the anti-caste movement to draw inspiration from other parallel examples in the US and not the British empire.[8] Due to this American influence, Ambedkar was selected for a scholarship by the maharaja of Baroda to go to a university in the US and not the UK—then a general practice among Indians. Ambedkar's arrival in the US coincided with the era of the American Dream. It was a vibrant time for the US economy and appeals for social and political equality to ethnic groups like the Irish, Italians and Jews in New York were gaining momentum. The vibrancy of the Harlem Renaissance permeated the academic and social circles of New York, where Ambedkar was staying. Zelliot suggests that these observations helped Ambedkar build a theory of cultural unification as a prerequisite for the political and social unity of a nation.[9]

Upon Ambedkar's arrival in 1913 at Columbia University, which was in its 'Golden Age', the US was undertaking major reforms in the finance and banking system and management. Frederick Winslow Taylor had revolutionized management thinking with the publication of his book *The Principles of Scientific Management* (1911). The Federal Reserve System was established in 1913. The Ford automobile company was increasing its production. In 1914, President Woodrow Wilson officially declared his neutral position in the European conflict that led to the First World War. The communication gap was shrinking when Graham Bell telephoned San Francisco from New York in 1915, while 1916, Ambedkar's last year in the US, coincided with Wilson's second-term victory. Along with this, the Harlem neighbourhood in New York was expanding the artistic and cultural articulations of immigrant communities—Black and non-Black. The Black figures deliberated and presented their struggle through their experiences. This emphasized the emergence of a stronger identity movement that helped export the literary and musical creativity of African Americans to the world. The art-based movement offered an internationalist identity to the Black figures, who acted as ambassadors of Black culture, advocating for their rights. World famous figures such as Louis Armstrong, W.E.B. Du Bois, Alain Locke, Marcus Garvey, Duke Ellington, Paul Robeson and Claude McKay were the leading names that popularized their struggles in the literary canon, in newspapers and in performances on stage. It is unlikely that Ambedkar was ignorant about these developments. However, there is no direct evidence that he took interest in the social upheavals in his locale, and it is neither reflected in his early writings or speeches nor in the Dalit rights movement he launched in India.

Following his stint at Columbia, Ambedkar moved to London to pursue his DSc at the London School of Economics in 1916 and returned to India in 1917. His five years of education in Europe and America became one of the cornerstones of his grand public life, and was to shape the course of his struggle against the millennium-old oppression of Untouchables. Even after assuming his responsibility as a civil rights activist and as the leader of India's Untouchables, he had many occasions to travel overseas.

## Asserting the Indian Sovereign Right

In their attempts to construct an Indian image for the world, various works have been published that project the Brahminical classes (the Congress, socialists and communists) as anti-imperial. The 'Nehru doctrine', for example, receives enormous commentary, and almost every biographer of Nehru lauds his ingenuity towards strengthening Third Worldism.[10]

In contrast, Ambedkar is completely ignored as someone who had important insights to offer in international politics. However, he observed the dismal relationship among the former English colonies in the Commonwealth and demanded the 'status of equal partnership'—an equal share and role in its activities. If not, warned Ambedkar, it would herald the invocation of a new master–slave relationship; he rhetorically stated, 'No new masters, please!'[11] In the expanded thesis, 'India and the British Commonwealth', Ambedkar had pivotal observations on building a strong identitarian international character. The thesis also measured India's position in the Commonwealth, with Ambedkar denouncing its unfair representation, which had to do with India's negligible role in 'the making of events that bring on war and . . . in the making of terms which often instead of ending war only adjourn war'.[12] Ambedkar was trying to find ways to operate in the imperial government that was leading the First World War efforts by subordinating Indian interests.

From 1930 to the 1950s, the Independent Labour Party (ILP) formed by him made important interventions in asserting India's sovereign right. During the Second World War, the ILP critically commented on India's losing stand. It rejected outright Nazi Germany's proposition of the mono-race rule, that is, the idea of the Nordic race dominating over other races. It took serious offence to this position, considering it 'obnoxious' to the people of India.[13]

Foreign policy was among Ambedkar's principal grievances with independent India's general policies, leading to his frustrated resignation from the portfolio of law minister in Nehru's cabinet.[14] Ambedkar's relationship with the Congress and Gandhi was set on ambiguous lines. His criticism of Gandhi was followed by his acceptance of a position in the Constituent Assembly, and later, his standing by the Congress's policy of country first, and winding up with his resignation. There are various readings of this moment. Gail Omvedt argues that it was Ambedkar's commitment to a strong, centralized state that paved the way for his taking up the post in Nehru's cabinet, which came with no strings attached.[15] Sekhar Bandyopadhyay argues that owing to the AISCF's defeat in the 1946 elections, Ambedkar had few avenues in which to confront Congress. Thus, a hostile attitude would have alienated and further marginalized the Dalit constituency. This was an after-effect of the power struggle among the Dalit leadership that begun in 1917, leading to a fragmented version of Dalit political discourse. It was so shaken that Dalit politics was threatened with 'extinction' by the hegemonic Congress in the late 1940s.[16]

Anand Teltumbde sees it as Gandhi's strategic masterstroke to obligate Ambedkar by inducting him at his desperate moment into the Constituent Assembly and also the first all-party cabinet headed by Nehru. The former extended to making him chairman of the most important committee in the Constituent Assembly, giving him the epitaph of the maker of the Constitution. The strategy was to make the lowest strata of Indian society emotionally attach itself to the Constitution through its icon, Ambedkar. It was an ideal political choice.[17] Two years before Independence, in 1945, Ambedkar had 'wholly opposed' the proposal of the Constituent Assembly. He regarded it as the 'most dangerous project' which had the potential to incite 'civil war' in the country should it follow the upper-caste Hindu and Muslim dominance as decided by the Sapru Committee (Hindus and Muslims were offered fifty-one reserved seats each of the total of 160. This would have given them a larger footing in incorporating a majority in the Constituent Assembly).[18]

Ambedkar had indirectly created a space for himself in the elite circles of the Constituent Assembly by rejecting it outright in the first instance. In his rejection, he emphasized that the responsibility of the communal problem could not be entrusted to it. He believed it would not be a true representative body of the minorities who were to be chosen in joint electorates that were wholly dependent on caste Hindu votes and disproportionate sharing of seats between Hindus and Muslims.

Notwithstanding this, I argue that it was Ambedkar's best rhetorical tactic wherein he gestured to the Indian government that he was exploring the possibility of taking India to the United Nations. This move could have caused serious embarrassment to the Indian government as India was presenting itself as a nation that stood against racism and other forms of oppression, a tactic that worked for both Ambedkar and the Congress.

However, this relationship was short-lived. Nehru persisted in consciously ignoring Ambedkar, right from withdrawing his support to the Hindu Code Bill, to the important deliberations offered in various memorandums on the situation of minorities. On the other hand, Ambedkar couldn't build strategic alliances with other oppressed groups using his powerful political portfolio. And his radical strategy to take India to the United Nations remained a statement without any developments from the AISCF. Ambedkar chose instead to resign in protest from Nehru's cabinet.

The resignation made headlines the world over, with even the *New York Times* reporting the incident. Ambedkar stated in his resignation letter dated 10 October 1951:

> It may be said that my resignation is out of time and that if I was dissatisfied with the Foreign Policy of the Government and the treatment accorded to Backward Classes and the Scheduled Castes I should have gone earlier.

Additionally, India's 'colossal' expenditure on building defence capabilities, Ambedkar suspected, was owing to the grim foreign policy that was directed by the postcolonial elite Brahminical class, which participated in the framing of casteist policies in the deliberations in the United Nations. The recent unearthing of archival materials confirms this.[19]

The mid-20th century was divided by two ideologies that were racing to establish their dominance in the world—the imperialist division amongst capitalist countries on the one hand and the communism-inspired nationhood on the other, both of which had created a bipolar opposition. Ambedkar sympathized with India's 'dislike' for capitalism, but he feared that taken to its extreme it could lead to communism. His concern was that while avoiding capitalism, parliamentary democracy should not be weakened; if care were not taken, it would be 'like throwing the baby out of the bath but in emptying it of dirty water'.[20] This was also an outcome of his worries with communism which he found to be too dictatorial and violent and thus unsuitable to India's fragile democracy.[21]

He chose to not align with any 'isms' as stated in the AISCF election manifesto:

> the policy of the Party is not tied to any particular dogma or ideology such as *Communism, or Socialism, Gandhism, or any other ism*. The Party will be ready to adopt any plan of social and economic betterment of the people

irrespective of its origin and provided it is consistent with its principles. Its outlook on life will be *purely rational and modern, emperistic* and *not academic* [emphasis added].[22]

This approach makes a case for Ambedkar's strategic political pragmatism—aligning with socialist ideals[23] and at the same time not discarding capitalism. However, his socialist idealism was totally different from that of the socialists of privileged classes and castes—he kept them at arm's length in deciding strategies for reclaiming the rights of the Depressed Classes. This was a shift from his earlier position, when he had declared capitalism as one part of the Dalits' enemy duo, the other being Brahminism.[24]

## Ambedkar and the United Nations

Founded in 1920, the League of Nations preceded the formation of the United Nations. Ambedkar wanted it to be concerned with the issue of untouchability. In an interview to the *New York Times* in London on 30 November 1930, he centred untouchability as a global problem affecting the social and economic well-being of the world. He sought to bring it under the ambit of the League of Nations in the same vein as slavery and drug trafficking. He believed that the international standpoint on untouchability could bring about enough pressure for it to be eradicated. Ambedkar said, 'Nothing less than the aroused opinion of the world can do it.'[25]

The dealings between the United Nations and Ambedkar date back to the early years of its formation. He sought its intervention to address the problems faced by SCs by stating that the United Nations had jurisdiction over 'eight crore Scheduled Castes'. The working committee of the AISCF, under the chairmanship of N. Sivaraj, adopted a resolution on 17 January 1947 to submit a memorandum prepared by Ambedkar to the United Nations Assembly to highlight 'the sufferings of the Scheduled Castes in India against the Hindus for their acts of social, economic and political tyranny'.[26] The working committee instructed the president of the AISCF to ensure the delivery of the memorandum to the United Nations Secretary General and advised sending an AISCF delegation to the United Nations to present their grievances.[27] This was eventually halted as Ambedkar 'did not submit it'. He 'felt that it would be better to wait until the Constituent Assembly and the future Parliament was given a chance to deal with the matter'.[28]

Ambedkar perhaps chose to consciously oversee the potential of the 'upper-caste' state that was coming into being in postcolonial India. There were ample evidences of it during the parleys with the Cabinet Mission, the heat of which he had himself experienced. With all his compromises with the Congress to get into the Constitution and his ultimate prominent role in writing it, he could not go beyond the writ of the party. He realized his folly within two years when in 1953 he said the following words during a Rajya Sabha debate: 'Sir, my friends tell me that I made the Constitution. But I am quite prepared to say that I shall be the first person to burn it out. I do not want it. It does not suit anybody.'[29]

Facing the liberal as well as Hindu orthodoxy of the Congress at every turn, Ambedkar explicated that his alliance with the party was not amicable and not without conflict. Taking from this experience, he chose to induct an international lobby rather than overtly relying on the Indian government. Thus he started corresponding with other affected groups who were fighting for recognition in the United Nations (see p. 96 for the recorded communication with W.E.B. Du Bois). Ambedkar drew parallels with the Black population in the US, Indians in South Africa and SCs in India.

The efforts to draw inspiration from these groups and engage them in conversation reflected the working style of the Ambedkarite leadership. N. Sivaraj, in his presidential address at the AISCF conference in 1942, drew parallels with the world atrocities committed by colonizers and White men upon non-White peoples. Talking about the atrocities upon the 'Australian Bushman by the Colonizers, that of the Negroes by the Ku-Klax-Klan and of the Jews by the Nazis', Sivaraj submitted that these were comparatively 'less heinous than the suffering . . . subjected to Depressed Classes in the name of religion, caste and the like by the Hindus'. He remarked that it was 'slow poisoning'.[30] This remark came at a time when the League of Nations had acknowledged the issue of racism.

Post-Independence, the Indian government took on the White apartheid government in South Africa on the issue of racism that was affecting the rights and dignity of Indians in the country.[31] Almost twenty-four resolutions were passed by the United Nations in Nehru's presence.[32] In the fourth session of the United Nations General Assembly on 20 September 1949, India sought the intervention of the United Nations to offer justice to the South African Indian community.[33] In the midst of the diplomatic deadlock over India's stand on racism, Ambedkar drew attention in Parliament to the situation of the SCs, arguing that the 'tyranny and the constant and shameless resort to violence by Hindus . . . [was] far worse than the position of Indians in South Africa'.[34] He went on to add that the experiences of apartheid in South Africa were akin to the condition of Indian Untouchable groups. To impress upon the situation, he said that 'South Africa is replicated in every Indian village' as segregation was sanctioned in India.[35]

Even though he acknowledged the segregation, he did not make a conscious effort to establish links with the colonized groups of South Africa to make an international united front. In spite of the Dalit diaspora's vast presence in the British empire, Ambedkar did not reach out to these Indian groups striving for freedom from the colonial regime in their respective countries. Indian delegations would visit India to solicit support for their movement in the 1940s, meeting elite members of the Congress in New Delhi. As Ambedkar was part of the colonial government, it is difficult to imagine that he missed noticing these activities as they were part of the Indian state policy.

Experiencing repeated failures at the hands of the Indian government, Ambedkar sought to fight the battle on his own. Thus he started communicating with the leaders of the African-American struggle. He told the press in India that he was in conversation with African-American leaders in the US, mentioning W.E.B. Du Bois in particular, the foremost Black intellectual and civil rights activist 'who was fighting for political, economic and social rights of Negroes in that country'.[36] The two activists had famously exchanged letters, discussing an appeal to the United Nations to build a coalition to unify the struggle against dominating oppressive groups in their respective societies. Ambedkar wrote to Du Bois explaining his position:

> I have been a student of the Negro problem and have *read your writings throughout*. There is *so much similarity* between the position of the Untouchables in India and of the position of the Negroes in America that the study of the latter is not only natural but necessary.
>
> I was very much interested to read that the Negroes of America have filed a petition to the UNO. The Untouchables of India are also thinking of following suit. Will you be so good as to secure for me two or three copies of this representation by the Negroes and send them to my address. I need hardly say how very grateful I shall be for your troubles in this behalf [emphasis added].[37]

Du Bois promptly replied to Ambedkar and said that he too had read his works and was aware of him and 'of course have every sympathy with the Untouchables of India', expressing to offer 'any service . . . if possible in the future'.[38] After this exchange, there is no evidence of these two figures communicating with each other. There is also no record that the African-American community took the cause of the Untouchables' struggle to the United Nations alongside the topic of racism. However, Martin Luther King, Jr, after his India visit in 1959, 'sought to making a study of untouchability' and started collecting the relevant materials in this regard.[39] This effort too did not see the light of day.

The Indian Untouchable and the American Black connection can trace its provenance back to the 19th century when Phule sought to bring attention to the plights of the Sudras and Ati-Sudras to the world. Dedicating his book *Gulamgiri* (1873) to the abolitionists, referring to them as the 'Good People of the United States', Phule observed the condition of Negroes in America as a defining moment in the universal recognition of suppressed groups. Thus, the cause of Negro slavery was seen as similar to that of India's Untouchables.

Following this, several efforts were made to draw parallels between the two marginalized groups,[40] with Ambedkar himself stating that the struggle of Black Americans was similar to that of the SCs, that like 'Negros were "tyrannized by the white Americans", Scheduled Castes were tormented by the Caste Hindus'.[41] This departs from his earlier argument about the caste system being devoid of racial proliferation. In his two major works, *Castes in India: Their Mechanism, Genesis and Development* (1917)[42] and *Who Were the Shudras?* (1946)[43] Ambedkar rejected the racial logic of differentiation among caste groups. He argued in a 1917 paper that it was the 'imitation' of endogamy that was practised by the dominating Brahmin community which strengthened the purist tendency of the caste system and resulted in social inequality in society, caste being one of the leading factors.

The Black-centric magazine the *Crisis*, started by W.E.B. Du Bois and later edited by Roy Wilkins, carried stories of the 'Negroes of India' in its 1942 and 1943 editions, explaining the resonance between Indian Untouchables and the Negroes in the US. It credited Ambedkar for being 'one of the finest scholars of the country' and a 'single leader of sixty million untouchables'.[44] Ambedkar's stellar foreign policy acumen received accolades in African-American circles. Granger described Ambedkar as 'the best known leader of India's Harijan caste' in the established African-American newspaper the *New York*

*Amsterdam News*, and as the 'first Indian voice of authority to challenge Prime Minister Nehru's dream-eyed policy of "neutralism" for South Asia and "peaceful co-existence" with a rapaciously aggressive China'.[45] He also praised Ambedkar's statement and hoped that people like him, invoking a plural denomination as the 'Ambedkars', would be more successful with Nehru than 'Negro leaders have thus far been with President Eisenhower, Truman, or Roosevelt and their advisors'.[46]

## The Pragmatic Internationalist

The book *What Congress and Gandhi Have Done to the Untouchables* was primarily an international statement of an internationalist Ambedkar who was now turning to the world to seek justice for his community, a shift from his earlier stance of reliance on the Indian government. This was mainly the outcome of the political battles between the Congress and Ambedkar. Both were fighting to claim an 'exclusive space' for Dalit polity in India. The former, however, under facile intentions, chose to plot the subservient Dalits to 'represent' rather than lead the Dalit struggle. Thus, time and again, Ambedkar had to face obstacles that pushed him to initiate strategic steps which at times did not succeed.[47] He had to confront enormous barriers at the hands of 'Congress–High-class Hindu rule'[48]—a triumvirate of the Indian Congress, the Hindu Mahasabha and Gandhi.[49]

In the book, Ambedkar delineates the way orthodox Hindu groups dominated by Brahmins undermined every effort to genuinely eradicate the menace of untouchability.[50] He found no genuine concern in Gandhi or Congress-affiliated organizations like the Social Conference established in 1887 in Madras. The Social Conference focused on eradicating the social injustices imposed on Untouchable groups in India. According to Ambedkar, the 'Social Conference was a body which mainly concerned itself with the reform of the high-caste Hindu family'.[51] It did not believe in agitating for the abolition of caste and had no special interest in it as much as it did in child marriage and enforced widowhood. This was because the latter occurred in elite Brahmin families, thus making them personally invested in their eradication. Contrastingly, every attempt to include the issue of Untouchable emancipation was suppressed by the same band of caste elites. This suppression continued in important foreign policy interventions too, where the Depressed Classes were not involved in deliberating over the future of the country. This led to an irresponsible international outlook in the post-Independence phase and resulted in India's position with 'no friends, if not actual enemies'.[52] The AISCF observed three reasons for such incapacitation: one was due to the Kashmir issue, the second was the admission of communist China in the United Nations Organisation (UNO), and the third was its intervention in the Korean War in the 1950s.

On permanent membership to the UNO, the AISCF in its election manifesto of 1951 ridiculed India's position to 'fight the battle for' China's permanent membership in the UNO when China was self-sufficient. Instead it argued for India's permanent membership in the UNO.

> India is spending herself in fighting the battle of Mao as against Chiang Kai Shek. This quixotic policy of saving the world is going to bring about the ruination of India and the sooner this suicidal foreign policy is reversed the better for India.[53]

The manifesto also questioned the intentions of the Indian delegate fighting the battle for communist China, which had irrevocably caused antagonism between India and the US. During parliamentary proceedings in 1954, Ambedkar contended that Nehru was hostile towards the US due to the conflict of ideology which had fostered feelings of distaste in Nehru for anything that came from there.[54] The US, in those days, was an important ally to have on one's side because it had significant control over technology and global finance. Postcolonial India partially relied on US aid in terms of technical and financial assistance for reconstructing the economy via industrialization. Ambedkar was a proponent of industrialization as he foresaw it as an ideal way to improve the low productivity caused by archaic agricultural technologies.[55] He was leading infrastructure projects that relied on US technical expertise,[56] including the colossal Damodar Valley project. As a labour member in the viceroy's cabinet, Ambedkar established the Department for Irrigation and Navigation Commission (which was later renamed the River Control Board, Central Water Power Commission) to control the river and flood situation, advance irrigation and produce energy.[57] A team of four engineers from the US was invited to establish a 'technical team' to advise on the design and construction of the first two dams in India.[58]

Furthermore, there was a wise suggestion to seek every aid possible in order to strengthen the 'self' first before 'championing the cause of Asiatic countries'. This was a time of apotheosis for the Third Worldism that was gaining significant attention among the postcolonial elite who wanted to imagine their future void of Western interference. The Ambedkar-led party, however, had an alternative to offer to the enthusiastic objective of becoming an Asian power.[59] Ambedkar observed that the norm of 'Asia for Asiatics' was good insofar as colonialism was concerned but in the postcolonial condition this was a farcical principle where war and strife amongst Asians was turning the region towards totalitarian statehood; the Korean War, the China–Japan conflict and South East Asian instability were cited as examples. Ambedkar was also critical of India's policy on non-alignment. He held the view that non-alignment understated important American contacts that would strategically assist in development projects critical for an independent nation.[60] In the Rajya Sabha, he led a charge against Nehru's policy of peaceful coexistence, contending that it did not fare well, especially in the cases of Tibet, Indo-China and Korea. Ambedkar is reported to have rebuked this policy as purchasing peace 'at the price of portioning countries' to which he maintained strong objections.[61] Ambedkar warned Nehru that too much affection with communist Russia could be a harmful antidote to the politics of regionalism that was decided in the South East Asia Treaty Organization conference. Ambedkar had reservations about Russia's expansionist tendencies and said that Nehru's foreign policy ought to be examined in this context. The *Canberra Times* reported this news as a headline in its 28 August 1954 edition, as did another Australian paper, the *Armidale Express*.[62] Ambedkar again endorsed his commitment to pragmatism by overlooking the ideological imbalances his views had favoured. He preferred an alliance with the burgeoning imperial power America as long as it brought benefits to Indian development projects.

## Ambedkar's Spectre Haunts Brahmin Savoir Faire

Pondering over the current situation, one can see the Indian government's conscious suppression of caste dialogues at the United Nations. Post-Independence governments continued to maintain their hostility to engage with the issue on international forums. In 2001, at the World Conference against Racism in Durban, a delegation led by Omar Abdullah, then minister of state for external affairs in the Bharatiya Janata Party (BJP) government, strenuously rejected a resolution on caste.[63] Seventy-six paragraphs that mentioned caste were removed by the Indian government.[64] Their logic declared caste to be an internal matter which was adequately covered in the Indian Constitution. This is the excuse offered by the Indian government on every discussion of caste. The same applies to non-governmental discussions on Dalit human rights. Many international non-government organizations (NGOs) are barred by the Indian state from getting the affiliation of the Economic and Social Council, an executive body of the United Nations that endorses NGOs to deliberate in its proceedings. The Indian government's consistent blocking of Dalit solidarity groups focused on working towards caste-based issues gives it the notoriety of the 'longest pending NGO application' in United Nations history.[65]

Another glaring example is the Indian government's continuous disfavouring of UN-appointed independent experts' findings on caste. On 28 January 2016, Special Rapporteur on Minority Issues Rita Izsák-Ndiaye presented her report to the UN. The Indian representative dismissed the report, noting that it was unclear why 'minority status' had been applied to the caste system.[66] Izsák-Ndiaye had to clarify her position—she explained that the interpretative meaning of 'minorities' could easily cover the complex issues facing victims of caste discrimination throughout the world, saying it thus fell under her mandate.[67] This can be contrasted with Ambedkar's description of the situation of Scheduled Castes as much worse and vulnerable than the existing Indian minorities in 1947. He argued that SCs were more than a minority and that 'any protection given to the citizens and to the minorities will not be adequate for the Scheduled Castes . . . [they] would require special safeguards (against) the tyranny and discrimination of the majority'.[68]

## Dalit Movement's Blind Spots of Internationalist Vision

Given the ongoing theatrics between the Indian state on the one hand and the United Nations and civil society on the other, it arguably makes a stronger case to constitute a separate mandate on the issues of caste-based discrimination by having an independent body within the United Nations and other regional bodies like the European Union that exclusively concentrates on the rights and dignities of caste subjects. Currently, there is not a single organization that actively engages and consistently follows up with the international community on caste-related issues. It was, after all, Ambedkar's desire to work with the United Nations, which he was unsuccessful in achieving. Governments across various parties that express admiration for Ambedkar overlook the important Dalit intervention in the United Nations forum, including those who claim an affinity with his ideology.

The Bahujan Samaj Party formed the government in Uttar Pradesh four times and was also an active partner of the ruling powers at the centre. In spite of this, it did not consider launching an international policy-specific programme for developing alliances with other oppressed groups in the world. Barring Kanshiram's visit to the first International Dalit International Conference held in Kuala Lumpur on 10–11 October 1998, there have been no significant efforts to create an international outreach programme by the political Dalit leadership.[69] The visit of Kanshiram was not aimed at launching cross-border solidarity initiatives and efforts in that direction never took place.[70]

The post-Ambedkar leadership became severely disengaged with the issues of socialist policies like those concerning land, control over resources and production, which could have given them the desired platform to connect with other postcolonial countries' socialist movements fighting for a similar cause. A progressive Dalit socialist block would certainly have fit the Dalit struggle; it would not have remained an isolated bubble and instead become a global concern. By overlooking such political solidarities, the Dalit movements were unable to fix the fault lines of Ambedkar's misplaced pragmatic political solidarity projects that rejected untimely ideological anchors. While Ambedkar's approach helped India build its post-Independence development projects and increase its industrial capability in terms of technology and knowledge sharing, it also created a huge vacuum for the Dalit identity, which is now at the helm of NGOs, which, by virtue of their international presence, are privileged to describe Dalit identity to the rest of the world. International NGOs have been persistent in raising the issue of caste-affected citizens at the United Nations and on other international government and non-government platforms. Their understanding undermines the ideological categorization of the Dalit identity that emerges from the Dalit movement. The extraneous affirmation to identify caste within ambiguous frameworks of 'descent-based discrimination' has undermined an 'autonomous' categorization of caste violence and discrimination, and thereby its accountability in South Asia, Africa, Japan and other countries with Indian diaspora.

The impetuous refusal of the Indian state to acknowledge the issue of caste has led Dalit diaspora groups across the world to recognize the obnoxious state of affairs in the intransigent caste Hindu society. As caste-related incidents continue to occur in different countries, Dalit associations organize regular activities to raise awareness, making it a global concern. Groups inspired by Ambedkar across North America, Europe, the Middle East and the Far East are known as Ambedkar International Missions and Ambedkar International Associations.[71] These are run by professional expats who make a stronger case to theorize the shibboleth of caste among the diaspora.[72] There are also groups in the name of Ambedkar, Ravidas and Valmiki along with Dalit Christian churches that single-handedly inspire the diaspora movement of the marginalized.[73] Using advancements in technology and social media, these groups—whom I refer to as the 'Millennial Dalit diaspora'—place their activities in conversation with the Indian situation.

Annual lectures, gatherings on the important days of Dalit calendars and regular collections of funds to sponsor education-related projects in India explain the nature of these overseas Dalit groups. These are remarkable activities that remain unknown due to the organizational limitation of publication incentives and lack of interest within the scholarly world about such epochal activism. In addition, marginalized caste diaspora groups internalize the inter-group behaviour, thus ending up functioning as subordinate groups among the existing ethnic minority diaspora groups calling for a separate identity. This complex diversity hinges towards the reification of independent identities moving away from the common ethnic clubbing of divergent identities.[74] In spite of this and the efforts to establish a separate Dalit identity under the purview of ethnic diversity, there have been limited efforts by Dalit diaspora to make common cause with other oppressed groups.

## Conclusion

Ambedkar's engagement with African-American groups to solicit support for the Dalit cause at the international level and his simultaneous overlooking of African and other colonized spaces as potential partners hint at some of his shortfalls. His belief in pragmatism over ideological singularity—that is, relying entirely on one ideology—resulted in benefiting post-Independence Indian development programmes and policies. However, this came at the cost of his unfulfilled promise of creating international Dalit solidarity. As time passed, after two decades (1930 to 1950) of active political engagement on Indian foreign policy matters, he had to cede his interests in the area owing to the predominance of Nehru's overshadowing presence as the prime minister. Ambedkar confirmed that he had 'ceased to take the same degree of interest in the foreign affairs of the country which I used to take at one time'.[75]

Various policies and committees of the Indian foreign services have an inadequate representation of Dalit-nominated representatives. Ambedkar-inspired activism in foreign countries strives towards political intervention. The exclusion of historically marginalized communities from important interventions in India's foreign policy matters adds to the casteist make-up of the postcolonial bureaucratic order. Ambedkar's story as a staunch critic of postcolonial nationalism demands a critical appraisal of the postcolonial conditions in the global South countries. Dalit diaspora activism is yet to take a radical stand against the Indian state, which remains a passive agent in the face of persistent Dalit atrocities.

Ambedkar's famous statement to the Pacific Relations Committee detailed ten demands.[76] He was quick to add that athwart imperialism, racism, anti-Semitism and free traffic (refugees) there was an issue of untouchability which faced a larger risk of being ignored.[77] Ambedkar took a particularist view of the question of untouchability by withdrawing its notional international significance with other oppressed groups. This reaction was perhaps in response to the false propaganda of the ruling castes in India on the question of the problems of Dalits and untouchability. Nehruvian foreign policy ensured that race could be used as an important intervention to determine India's commitment to anti-imperialism. At the same time, it gave India an upper hand to not disclose its own fallacies of caste oppression and untouchability.

The global Dalit appeal as part of the world's oppressed communities was established by the Dalit Panthers, a radical Ambedkarite outfit in Maharashtra that not only marshalled an international solidarity initiative but aimed to connect across race, caste and national boundaries. They presented themselves as an inclusive category—the Dalits—with the worldly oppressed. As they declared in their manifesto:

> The Dalit Panthers aspire to join hands with the Dalits (oppressed) of the world which includes the oppressed and the exploited people in Cambodia, Vietnam, Africa, Latin America, Japan and even in US (specially with the Blacks).[78]

However, this effort has largely remained confined to literary rhetoric and is not an action-based programme. The Dalit Panthers, disabled by state oppression, could not seek out active collaboration with the aforementioned movements. While in politics, in later years, too, the leaders of the Dalit Panthers did not utilize their offices to build active partnerships with social movements around the world.

# II

# AMBEDKAR'S SCHOLARSHIP

# AMBEDKAR'S THEORY OF MINORITY RIGHTS[1]

## Partha Chatterjee

Everyone is claiming Ambedkar these days. Ranged from Left to Right on the ideological spectrum, parties, movements and leaders are trying to co-opt him for their own ends. Tailored by selective quotations and distorted interpretation, the Ambedkar on display in most public discussion is hardly recognizable to those who have taken the trouble to read his writings and speeches. Even though he was a prolific writer, Ambedkar was never careless or slipshod with his prose. Most of the important positions he took, no matter how controversial or unique, were based on serious research and close reasoning. One such was his much-debated stand on the question of minorities.

## Ambedkar on Minority Rights

Introducing one of his last political tracts, *Thoughts on Linguistic States*, Ambedkar admitted that his views had changed. His earlier statements on the subject had been made on the basis of fragmentary evidence, but the report of the States Reorganisation Commission had forced him to revise his views. Reminding his readers that consistency was the virtue of an ass, he argued that responsibility was more important than consistency. 'A responsible person,' he said, 'must have the courage to rethink and change his thoughts. Of course there must be good and sufficient reasons for unlearning what he has learned and for recasting his thoughts. There can be no finality in thinking.'[2] He might have added, however, that while all responsible thinkers are aware of the provisional nature of their knowledge and opinions, changes in their views always take place within a field defined by some basic concepts, the relations between those concepts, forms of acceptable argument or evidence, etc. that constitute a certain structure of thought. In Ambedkar's case too, we could argue, that while his views on particular topics did evolve, and while, unlike others, he was truthful enough to acknowledge that fact, he nevertheless retained a basic structure of political thought within which he revised his views in the light of new evidence or argument.

In this essay, I will attempt to survey Ambedkar's evolving views on the question of the political rights of minorities from the late 1920s to his death in 1956 and argue that he provides us with a theory of minority rights that, while being grounded within republican constitutional theory, radically challenges some of its liberal premises. In doing this, one must bear in mind that despite being more formally trained in academic social theory than any other political leader in modern India, Ambedkar's views were enunciated in the polemically charged field of political contestation: he did not always have the luxury of formulating philosophically rigorous theories. But then, that is a condition that holds for many canonical social and political philosophers. What is remarkable about Ambedkar in the context of modern Indian thinkers is his innate faithfulness to the academic method which values the reasoned unfolding of rational argument.

He makes the strategic context of his analysis quite clear in one of his early pronouncements on the methods of struggle. Writing in his journal *Bahishkrit Bharat* in 1927, he argued that untouchability could not be abolished by the mere spread of education or the expectation that orthodox Hindus would have a change of heart. The Depressed Classes (as Dalits were then called in the official terminology) would have to act in such a forceful way that Hindus would realize that it was dangerous to continue to practise untouchability. He reminded his Dalit readers that a struggle for cultural predominance was being waged between Hindus and Muslims in India in which the balance of power was in the hands of the Depressed Classes. They must use their strength judiciously to secure the most advantageous opportunities for gaining their social and political rights.[3] Commenting on the recent struggles in Mahad where Ambedkar had led a group of Untouchable activists to draw water from a public tank against the express prohibition imposed by orthodox Hindus, he brought up historical examples of Untouchable Mahar warriors fighting with immense bravery in the East India Company's army. This proved, he said, that they were born under the sign of the lion (*simha rashi*) and not of the sheep (*mesh*) or the goat. 'It is goats that are sacrificed, not lions.' What the Depressed Classes lacked was not bravery but the consciousness of their just rights. For that, they must organize politically to create a force that others would have to reckon with.[4]

This was the field of strategic politics in which Ambedkar's analysis of the intertwining of the rights of the majority with those of different minorities was carried out. There was always a reference to the real world of rival political claims against which his theoretical arguments were honed. Specifically, in the entire period leading up to India's independence, his arguments for the rights of the Untouchable castes as a minority were always presented in comparison with those made on behalf of the Muslim minority.

Analysing his efforts in this field of political contestation, Anupama Rao has pointed out with nuance and precision Ambedkar's extraordinary struggle to find an appropriate language to express the unique disability produced by untouchability and the incommensurable position of Dalits in relation to other minorities. Judging the matter from the standpoint of Ambedkar's lifelong project of the annihilation of caste and the emancipation of Dalits, one must agree with Rao that the Dalit as minority was an impossible category to realize.[5] But if we move away from the perspective of Ambedkar's intellectual biography and consider his contribution to political theory, we will find, as I will try to show, that his arguments added up to an original and robust theory of minority rights that made comparable, along a scale of rights, the positions of nationalities, minorities and minorities with special civic disabilities. Situated on a strong foundation of popular sovereignty, Ambedkar's theory went well beyond the terms of liberal constitutionalism. It also clarified the limits of what could be achieved by using the legal powers of the state.

## Simon Commission: The Franchise Question

The Indian Statutory Commission—a team of British parliamentarians led by John Simon—visited India in 1928 to seek the views of various parties, groups and individuals and recommend the forms of electoral representation to be included in the proposed constitutional reforms. The first full enunciation of Ambedkar's theory of minority representation is to be found in the statement he submitted on behalf of the Bahishkrit Hitakarini Sabha (or the Depressed Classes Institute of Mumbai) and in his oral evidence to the Commission.

His first theoretical move was to argue against the prevailing system of nomination by the executive of representatives from the minority communities. 'Election is not only correct in principle from the standpoint of responsible Government, but is also necessary in practice from the standpoint of political education. Every community must have an opportunity for political education which cannot well be secured otherwise than by the exercise of the vote.' He also added that if political reforms were introduced such that the government had to be responsible to the legislature, only elected members would be qualified to be ministers; if the Depressed Classes had only nominated members, they would not have the chance of getting a minister from their community. He dismissed the objection that electoral constituencies could not be formed for the Depressed Classes because their eligible voters were too thinly dispersed. How then, he asked, were Muslim and European representatives being elected? He agreed that under the present rules of suffrage, limited by property qualifications, very few people from the Depressed Classes would be eligible to vote. But the answer to this problem was not to deny them electoral representation but to lower the bar so that more voters from the underprivileged sections might become eligible.[6]

Ambedkar, on behalf of his organization, then extended this argument to make a theoretical claim. 'Franchise means the right to determine the terms of associated life,' he stated. In that case, 'those who by reason of their weak power of bargaining are exposed to the risk of having the terms of associated life fixed by superior forces in a manner unfavourable to them' must be given the franchise so that they could have a sufficient number of representatives to defend their interests. Ambedkar then goes on to make the point of principle: 'Indeed adult franchise is the only system of franchise which can be in keeping with the true meaning of that term.' He would be asked to elaborate on this claim during his oral evidence.[7]

In the interim, he argued, the Sabha would urge that the property qualification of voters from the Depressed Classes be set at the level that was currently in use for the Taluka Local Board elections in rural areas and Rs 3 rental per month in urban areas. Not surprisingly, he rubbished the argument that lowering the property qualification would give the vote to a mass of unintelligent people.

> Large property is not incompatible with ignorance. Nor is abject poverty incompatible with a high degree of intelligence . . . Consequently, the adherence of the Government to a high property qualification as an insurance against ignorance is nothing but a superstition, which is sedulously cultivated by the classes and fostered by the Government in order to deprive the masses of their right to the making of their Government.[8]

What is interesting here is that Ambedkar is not simply reiterating a general principle about the desirability of universal adult suffrage. Rather, he is making the case that adult suffrage is particularly crucial for the electoral representation of poor and property-less groups like the Depressed Classes because that is the only way they can secure the numbers to elect their representatives.

Asked to explain his position on the franchise, Ambedkar once again stated in clear terms the premise from which he was making his argument:

> *Dr Ambedkar:* The first thing I would like to submit is that we claim that we must be treated as a distinct minority, separate from the Hindu community. Our minority character has been hitherto concealed by our inclusion within the Hindu community . . . we must be regarded as a distinct and independent minority. Secondly, I should like to submit that the depressed classes minority needs far greater political protection than any other minority in British India, for the simple reason that it is educationally very backward, that it is economically poor, socially enslaved, and suffers from certain grave political disabilities, from which no other community suffers. Then I would submit that, as a matter of demand for our political protection, we claim representation on the same basis as the Mahomedan minority. We claim reserved seats if accompanied by adult franchise.
> 35. And if there is no adult franchise?
> *Dr Ambedkar:* Then we would ask for separate electorates.[9]

Three elements of the theoretical proposition have been introduced here: (1) the Depressed Classes are a minority community; (2) if they are allowed to vote under conditions of adult franchise, they must be given reserved seats in the legislature; and (3) if the voting qualifications fall short of adult franchise, they must have separate electorates from which they will elect their representatives. He also clarified that his acceptance of limited franchise was merely transitional; the correct principle always was adult franchise.

> *Dr Ambedkar:* Well, I would really insist upon adult suffrage. The lower the franchise the better; on that principle I would accept any lowering, but I certainly would not say I would be content with that.
> 110. Would you then extend adult suffrage to the aboriginal tribes and to the criminal and hill tribes?

*Dr Ambedkar:* Yes, I think so.

111. You would?

*Dr Ambedkar:* Yes.[10]

To quell any lingering doubts, Ambedkar was asked to clarify the general principle. Not surprisingly, he stated the general principle from the standpoint of the particular.

160. As regards adult suffrage, I suppose you are in favour of adult male and female suffrage?

*Dr Ambedkar:* Yes.

161. Do you think that is a practical proposition?

*Dr Ambedkar:* Very practical.

162. Do you think that the masses have attained any degree of political consciousness, so as to be able to use that political suffrage with any advantage to their community?

*Dr Ambedkar:* Speaking only on behalf of the depressed classes, I emphatically maintain that the depressed classes will exercise their vote in a most intelligent manner . . . Having regard to the fact that the canker of untouchability is before their minds every minute of their lives, and having regard to their being alive to the fact that political power is the only solvent of this difficulty, I emphatically maintain that the depressed class voter would be an intelligent voter . . .

165. Do you think you reflect the general opinion of your Institute in conveying this view to the Commission?

*Dr Ambedkar:* I think that would be the view of all poor communities.[11]

Ambedkar was also asked if separate electorates did not lead to communal tension. His answer was not evasive.

*Dr Ambedkar:* Even assuming it does lead to tension I do not see how you can get rid of it. Whether it does lead to tension is questionable, but I do not see in any case how you can get rid of it, having regard to the fact that society is divided into classes and communities.[12]

Connected to the franchise question was the issue of reserved seats in the legislature for minority communities. Here Ambedkar made another crucial claim of principle: the number of representatives from a minority community must not be determined merely by its population strength.

. . . the strength of the community cannot be taken as the sole factor in determining matters of this sort. The standing of a community is no less an important factor to be taken into account in determining its quota of representation. The standing of a community must mean its power to protect itself in the social struggle. That power would obviously depend upon the educational and economic status of the community. It follows from the recognition of the principle that the lower the standing of a community the greater is the electoral advantage it must get over the rest.[13]

His principle was clearly stated here: the weaker the social condition of a minority community, the greater the proportion of representation it should be allowed. He elaborated on this argument in his oral evidence before the Commission.

. . . I do not quite accept the principle of representation of minorities according to population in the legislature as though it was a museum of so many communities. A Legislative Council is more than a museum, it is a place where, for instance, social battles have to be fought, privileges have to be destroyed, and rights have to be won . . . I do not think at all in the fitness of things to confine the minority to proportional representation according to population. That means you are condemning a minority to be perpetually a minority without the power necessary to influence the actions of the majority.[14]

An important clause is added here to the principle: minority representation must be of sufficient size to effectively influence the actions of the majority. Ambedkar also added a further clarification to his concept of the minority.

I think we must be very careful about using the word 'minority'. I do not think simply because a community happens to be a community composed of small numbers it is therefore necessarily a minority for political purposes. A minority which is oppressed, or whose rights are denied by the majority, would be a minority that would be fit for consideration for political purposes.[15]

The implication, otherwise not obvious, was now clear. A community that was merely a numerical minority was not necessarily deserving of guaranteed political representation. In other words, a wealthy and powerful minority community did not need special political guarantees. Ambedkar sometimes mentioned the Parsis as a community that, although numerically small, was in no need of special protection. He might have added that the European population which had reserved seats in the provincial legislatures of India was not deserving of that privilege. The 'minority for political purposes' was necessarily a community that was in danger of being discriminated against by the majority. In his oral testimony, Ambedkar made several references to the protection of minority rights in the new democracies of Eastern Europe and the recognition of such rights by the League of Nations.

It is on the basis of these principles that Ambedkar made his specific claim to the number of seats to be reserved for the Depressed Classes in the Bombay Legislative Council. Even though by his calculation from the 1921 census figures the Depressed Classes were only 1.6 million, that is, 8.21 per cent, out of a total population of 19.5 million, while the Muslims were 1.2 million, that is, 6.15 per cent, he demanded that the Depressed Classes should have 22 reserved seats out of a total of 112 elected seats (19.64 per cent) in the Bombay legislature—the same number that the Muslims had been given. This was the number of seats that should be reserved for the Depressed Classes whether or not there was adult suffrage; the latter would only determine if there was to be a separate electorate for the minority community.

## Protection of Minorities

Apart from representation in the legislature, there was another set of protections that Ambedkar claimed on behalf of the minorities. Echoing John Stuart Mill, he argued that the mere fact that the legislature was periodically elected by the people was no guarantee that the people had the power to rule themselves, because electoral systems only ensured the rule of an active majority. Hence, minorities required the protection of the law against the tyranny of the majority. The need for such protections had been clearly recognized in the post-war constitutions of Eastern European countries. But the situation of the Depressed Classes in India was far more precarious than that of the minorities in European countries because they are 'a solitary case of a people who have remained fallen because their rise is opposed to the religious notions of the majority of their countrymen'. If minority protections are required in Europe where politics is far more secularized, they are even more essential in India 'where politics is nothing but theology in action'. Even though there were some among the leaders of

Hindu society who were critical of untouchability, that was no guarantee that the Depressed Classes would get justice. '. . . the fact is that laws and institutions require to be adapted not to good men but to bad. From this point of view, it is safer to grant the minority the necessary protection by the inclusion of guarantee clauses than to leave it unprotected on the fanciful ground that the tyrant majority has in it a few good men sympathetic to the minority.'[16]

Based on these justifications, Ambedkar, on behalf of his organization, demanded a set of clauses in the Constitution of the country to guarantee the civil rights of the Depressed Classes as a minority in the Bombay Presidency. These included a just grant from the state for their education, unrestricted recruitment into the armed forces and the police, and priority for a period of thirty years in recruitment to all posts in the civil services.[17] Explaining the demand, Ambedkar said in his oral testimony that the law was currently administered to the disadvantage of the Depressed Classes because the civil services and the lower courts were the preserve of orthodox Hindus.[18] He also emphasized that most ordinary members of the Depressed Classes were not particularly interested in constitutional questions regarding provincial autonomy, but were enormously concerned about getting the guarantees and protection of the law. As far as his personal views were concerned, Ambedkar was in favour of provincial autonomy and dyarchy at the central level.[19]

What is interesting is that nowhere in his arguments or demands did Ambedkar raise the question of preserving the distinct identity of the minority community. Clearly that is not what was relevant in any way for the Untouchable castes. If anything, it was the identity of inferiority and exclusion which had been thrust on them by the powerful Hindu majority that they were struggling to shake off. This is one of the most interesting aspects of Ambedkar's theory of minority rights because it runs along a very different course from the usual debates over minority rights which, for the most part, have been about cultural identity.

There were two crucial theoretical points that were raised by Ambedkar's initial presentation of his views on minority representation. First, he did not rely on a transcendental view of rights as flowing from divine providence or natural law or original social contract. Rather, he derived rights from a comparative and historical analysis of prevailing social conditions and demands made by rival groups. Second, his claim on behalf of the minority was not for religious toleration. On the contrary, he sought legal protection for the minority against the religious orthodoxy of the majority which sanctioned, indeed prescribed, discriminatory practices against the Untouchable minority. He claimed that only political power could remedy the situation for the minority. Hence, instead of state neutrality in matters of religion, he called for state intervention to abolish practices of discrimination sanctioned by religion.

## Round Table Conferences: Constitutional Protection of Minority Rights

I move next to the Round Table Conferences of British and Indian leaders convened in London in 1930–31 to discuss the proposed constitutional reforms. In his interventions at the conferences, Ambedkar reiterated his stated position on minority rights but, in the context of several contending proposals, sharpened his arguments.

Speaking in the plenary session of the first conference, boycotted by the Indian National Congress, Ambedkar emphatically stated that the British rulers of India could not be relied on to remove the evils in Indian society because they were mortally afraid of provoking resistance that might threaten their rule.

> We must have a Government in which men in power, knowing where obedience will end and resistance will begin, will not be afraid to amend the social and economic code of life which the dictates of justice and expediency so urgently call for. This role the British Government will never be able to play. It is only a Government which is of the people, for the people and by the people that will make this possible.
>
> [. . .] We feel that nobody can remove our grievances as well as we can, and we cannot remove them unless we get political power in our own hands [. . .] It is only in a Swaraj constitution that we stand any chance of getting the political power into our own hands, without which we cannot bring salvation to our people.[20]

This was as clear an enunciation as possible of Ambedkar's principled position that the Depressed Classes did not look upon the British as their protectors. They were looking forward to a truly representative government based on popular sovereignty and universal adult suffrage. The question, therefore, was: what was this swaraj constitution going to be?

Ambedkar dismissed the suggestion that untouchability was a social problem whose removal must await a prolonged process of social change.

He insisted that it was political power alone that could abolish such an oppressive system; in that sense, the question of untouchability was a political problem. Now that political power was about to shift from the British to the people of India, the Depressed Classes were prepared to join the process 'in the hope that we shall be installed, in adequate proportion, as the political sovereigns of the country along with our fellow countrymen. But we will consent to that on one condition and that is that the settlement of our problems is not left to time'.[21]

He then made a crucial theoretical intervention. Emancipation from untouchability must not be consigned to the ordinary business of law-making by a majority of elected representatives but made a fundamental right guaranteed by the Constitution itself.

> The Depressed Classes cannot consent to subject themselves to majority rule in their present state of hereditary bondsmen. Before majority rule is established their emancipation from the system of untouchability must be an accomplished fact. It must not be left to the will of the majority. The Depressed Classes must be made free citizens entitled to all the rights of citizenship in common with other citizens of the State.[22]

In other words, the participation of the Depressed Classes as a minority in an assembly of elected representatives had to be conditional upon the prior removal of the unique civic disability from which they suffered. The Depressed Classes were not merely victims of a set of discriminatory practices in religious life but were deprived of civic rights of free use of public places, employment and economic services that were open to other minorities. Unless those civic disabilities were removed, none of the provisions of minority representation would work for them.

> First of all, we want a fundamental right enacted in the constitution which will declare 'untouchability' to be illegal for all public purposes. We must be emancipated, so to say, from the social curse before we can at all consent to the constitution; and secondly, this fundamental right must also invalidate and nullify all such disabilities and all such discriminations as may have been made hitherto.[23]

Not only that, Ambedkar was insistent that a mere declaration of equal rights would be useless against the force of opposition that orthodox Hindu society could mobilize unless there were specific penalties imposed for the violation of the declared rights of the Depressed Classes. This claim led to a whole discussion in the subcommittee on minorities on whether a constitutional declaration of a fundamental right could be accompanied by an explicit list of penalties or whether that should be left to the making of appropriate laws. Ambedkar accepted the distinction but demanded that the subcommittee record his point that a mere paper declaration of the end of untouchability would be of no use unless followed by adequate legislation to impose penalties on those guilty of violating that right.[24]

When the first conference ended in January 1931 without an agreement on universal adult franchise, Ambedkar openly expressed his disappointment. The Motilal Nehru Report of 1928 on a new dominion Constitution had proposed legislatures elected by adult franchise, and all major Indian parties had agreed to that proposal. But now, Ambedkar pointed out, the liberals were reluctant to accept it. A future government of India elected by limited franchise would be 'a government of the masses by the classes'.[25]

Speaking at the second conference later that year, Ambedkar expressed the hope that 'with the help and support of Mahatma Gandhi' the supporters of adult franchise would prevail. He strongly opposed nominated members from the princely states in the federal legislatures, arguing that those states must, like the provinces, be represented by elected members. He argued against the special representation of trades, commerce, landholders, etc. If there was adult franchise, there should also be no need for the special representation of labour. Moreover, he rejected the current practice of nominated members from the bureaucracy constituting an official, predominantly European, bloc in the legislature.[26] All of these nominations and special constituencies were, for him, blatant examples of powerful minorities being doubly represented. In his view, special political representation was only justified for poor and socially powerless minorities that were threatened by an aggressive majority.

It is noteworthy that, given his position on minority rights, Ambedkar was very much in favour of an interventionist modernist state using its legal powers to bring about radical social change. Consequently, he was arguing not only for the use of political power to establish civic equality among all classes and communities but also for the explicit constitutional guarantee of penalties for infringement of those civil rights. It is not surprising that in his interventions at the conference, Ambedkar was more sympathetic to a relatively strong federal government within a structure of provincial autonomy and argued for federal intervention, including, as a last resort, the use of the army, in case a provincial government refused to carry out the orders of the federal executive or the federal court. In this context, he made repeated references to cases from the US where states had defied the orders of the federal government or the Supreme Court. He wanted constitutional provisions to avoid such events in a self-governing India.[27] Here too, his position was unlike that of, say, the Muslim League, which clearly favoured provincial autonomy with a weak centre. As we will see, he would take a somewhat different position later in the context of the Pakistan debate.

In the end, of course, as is well known, the Second Round Table Conference ended with a bitter confrontation between Ambedkar and Gandhi, not over adult franchise or the abolition of untouchability, but over whether or not the Depressed Classes were to be recognized as a minority. Gandhi agreed that there should be 'the most drastic legislation rendering criminal' the persecution of Untouchable people, but resolutely opposed the idea of separate electorates and reservation of seats in the legislature for the Depressed Classes. 'I can understand the claims advanced by other minorities, but the claims advanced on behalf of the Untouchables—that to me is the "unkindest cut of all".' He declared that Ambedkar's position was unrepresentative and claimed, with uncharacteristic bombast, 'that I would get, if ever there was a referendum of the Untouchables, their vote, and that I would top the poll'. Ambedkar, in his reply, reiterated the position of the Depressed Classes:

> Their position, to put it plainly, is that we are not anxious for the transfer of power; but if the British Government is unable to resist the forces that have been set up in the country which do clamour for transference of political power—and we know the Depressed Classes in their present circumstances are not in a position to resist that—then our submission is that if you make that transfer, that transfer will be accompanied by such conditions and by such provisions that the power shall not fall into the hands of a clique, into the hands of an oligarchy, or into the hands of a group of people, whether Muhammadans or Hindus; but that that solution shall be such that the power shall be shared by all communities in their respective proportions.[28]

## The Pakistan Question

It is not necessary to recount here the well-known story of the continued stand-off between Gandhi and Ambedkar over the British prime minister's 'communal award', Gandhi's fast in Yeravada prison in 1932 and Ambedkar's forced concession in the so-called Poona Pact by which he gave up his demand for separate electorates for the Depressed Classes (adult franchise, of course, not having been achieved). In the following years, Ambedkar did not abandon his principled position, already articulated at the Round Table Conferences, that any settlement between the Congress and the Muslim League over the communal question would only be an agreement between two powerful and organized parties. That settlement would not necessarily protect the rights of a poor and powerless minority such as the Untouchable castes, unless those rights were constitutionally guaranteed.

This position was elaborated in an ingenious way in Ambedkar's response to the Pakistan resolution of the Muslim League in March 1940. In the first edition of his book *Thoughts on Pakistan*, written only a few months after the Lahore resolution, Ambedkar proposed a crucial theoretical distinction. Thus far, he had consistently argued that there were many minority communities in India of which a few, such as the Muslims and the Depressed Classes, required safeguards such as special political representation to protect them from a tyrannical majority. Now he declared that whereas Untouchables, Christians and Parsis were minority communities, Muslims were a nation.[29] In the last pages of his book, Ambedkar remarked that this distinction did not immediately make a difference since a minor community and a minor nation would need the same safeguards against the oppression of the majority. However, in his introduction to *Thoughts on Pakistan* (presumably written after the book was finished) he argued that the Muslims, being a nation, deserved not merely special representation in an elected Parliament but 'self-determination'.[30] The point is worth our attention.

For Ambedkar, the distinction between a minority community and a nation hinged on the test of 'common destiny'.

> . . . a community, however different from and however opposed to other communities major or minor it may be, is one with the rest in the matter of the ultimate destiny of all. A nation on the other hand is not only different from other components of the State but it believes in and cherishes a different destiny totally antagonistic to the destiny entertained by other component elements in the State [. . .] It is this difference in the acceptance and non-acceptance of a common destiny which alone can explain why the Untouchables, the Christians and the Parsis are in relation to the Hindus only communities and why the Muslims are a nation.[31]

In other words, to align this proposition with the previous ones suggested by Ambedkar on the question of minority rights, minorities that were prepared to live under the same Constitution with the majority would require certain constitutional protections; those minorities that were poor and vulnerable might even need special political representation; but a minority possessed with a consciousness that made it thoroughly unwilling to live within the same constitutional state with the majority community would have to be granted the right to determine its own national destiny in another state. The principle of representation was still the same, reflecting Ambedkar's abiding faith in the sovereignty of the people. That is the principle on which his persistent arguments for adult franchise were based. It was also the principle that shaped his demand for separate electorates for minorities when the suffrage was restricted, since otherwise even elections to seats reserved for a minority community would be decided by voters from the majority group. The principle has to be pushed even further when one comes upon the case of a minority that has acquired the form of a nation: minority representation in such a case must become the determination by the community itself of the constitutional form under which it chooses to rule itself.

Ambedkar's response to the Pakistan demand considerably sharpened his arguments on minority representation as a matter to be determined by the community itself. Thus, reviewing the entire debate over joint and separate electorates in the context of Hindu and Muslim demands, he pointed out that guaranteed seats in the legislature for a minority community would necessarily create a statutory legislative majority of the majority community: there was no getting away from it.[32] But it was only where a minority community, or sometimes even a numerically larger but socially and economically weaker community, faced the prospect of being tyrannized by a hostile legislative majority—because the property qualification for voting would leave it in the minority within the general electorate—that the former would prefer the safeguard of separate electorates. Thus, not only did the Muslim minority in the different Indian provinces want separate electorates but so did the majority Muslims in Punjab, Sind, Bengal and the North-West Frontier Province, giving them statutory majorities in the legislatures of all those provinces. On the other hand, the minority Hindus in the Muslim-majority provinces preferred joint electorates.

A minority in one set of circumstances may think that separate electorates would be a better method of self-protection and may have no fear of creating against itself and by its own action a statutory majority based on separate electorates for the opposing community. Another minority or for that matter the same minority in a different set of circumstances . . . may prefer joint electorates to separate electorates as a better method of self-protection. Obviously the guiding principle, which would influence a minority, would be: is the majority likely to use its majority in a communal manner and purely for community purposes?[33]

The question then becomes one of tactical choice for a minority: which is the course that offers greater tactical flexibility in safeguarding its interests? In some cases, separate electorates may ensure a guaranteed representation of the community in the legislature. In others, joint electorates may offer the chance to the minority group to influence the election of candidates from the majority community. Ambedkar's position was clearly to insist that the choice should be left to the minority community. Indeed, he criticized the Communal Award of 1932 for thrusting separate electorates on Hindus in the Muslim-majority provinces when they did not want it.[34] Once again, his maxim was that the minority community must have the right to choose the constitutional form by which it preferred to participate in the rule of the people.

Ambedkar's specific analysis of the case for and against Pakistan, as presented in *Thoughts on Pakistan*, has been discussed by historians, most recently Faisal Devji and Venkat Dhulipala.[35] What is striking in Ambedkar's analysis is his concern with evaluating the feasibility of Muslim self-determination as a means to create a viable state of Pakistan, and as a consequence of that action, the strength of a truncated Hindu-majority state in India. He studied not only the demographic question but the financial resources, administrative capacity and the capability and morale of the armed forces to conclude that the creation of Pakistan, accompanied by the partition of Punjab and Bengal and a supervised exchange of population in certain areas, would in fact be the better solution for both Muslims and Hindus.[36] In the context of our discussion here, the important point to note is Ambedkar's distinction between the political significance of two kinds of minorities—those who must live within the same constitutional state with the majority community and those who want to separate. For the latter, there are, in fact, two tests that Ambedkar prescribes: one, that of 'common destiny', and the other, of state viability. By these two tests, Christians, Parsis and Untouchables in India could not claim self-determination as nations, whereas the Muslims could.

Ambedkar added three new chapters to his book when it was republished in 1945.[37] By then, the Pakistan demand had gained considerable strength. Ambedkar was particularly insistent on pointing out the emotions that were at play. In his book, he had tried to present as impartial an assessment as he could of the claims for and against Pakistan, including the shortcomings of the Muslim demand. But pointing out those weaknesses, he reminded his readers, and Hindu leaders in particular, would not shake the faith of those who had taken up the cause of Pakistan. 'Sentiment is a factor in politics,' he declared, and a realist observer would make a grave error by not accounting for it as a material fact.[38] Indeed, regardless of the historical or social foundations of nationalist politics in India, there was the irreducible element of political will that would determine the result. If two nations did come about, they would not be the result of predestination but deliberate design, he said.[39] Pointing out the Irish case where freedom had been won at the cost of partition, Ambedkar did not shy away from stating his own position: 'I prefer Freedom of India to Unity of India.'[40]

But even as Ambedkar upheld the Muslim case for separation, he did not abandon his fundamental principle of popular self-determination. How should the partition question be decided? Once again reminding his readers that a negotiated partition in Ireland had not put an end to the bitterness between Irish Catholics and Protestants, he argued that the fate of the various Muslim-majority provinces should be settled by a referendum of the whole people and not by back-room deals between British bureaucrats and Indian politicians.[41] Similarly, for Kashmir and Hyderabad—states where the majority of the population followed a different religion from their ruler—Ambedkar insisted that the question of their joining India or Pakistan could only be legitimately settled by self-determination of the people and not merely the ruler's signature on a piece of paper.[42] Again, recognizing that partition would still leave minorities in both new states, Ambedkar restated his familiar arguments on the need for constitutional safeguards of the remaining minorities.[43] Underlying the many specific arguments and recommendations he made in the course of a rapidly shifting political scene was a set of foundational principles, grounded in a conception of popular sovereignty, which shaped his theory of minority rights.

## The Final Move

As the leading figure in the drafting committee of the Indian Constitution and subsequently as the law minister in the Indian government, Ambedkar would, of course, play a historic role in giving shape to the new conception of citizenship and rights that would prevail in independent India. But in that role, he could no longer advocate or defend positions that were his own. Rather, he would have to speak in the collective voice of an emerging people or nation constituting its own power as a state. But immediately before that phase, Ambedkar did have one last chance to explain his fully elaborated position on minority rights in a memorandum submitted to the Constituent Assembly in March 1947.[44]

He called the new union of former British Indian provinces and Indian princely states 'the United States of India', perhaps reflecting the deep influence, more than was the case with any other major Indian leader of the time, which the history of the United States of America, marked by slavery, racial discrimination and the ongoing struggles for civil rights, had on him. True to the basic principles he had publicly upheld for over two decades, Ambedkar proposed that the Constituent Assembly proclaim a set of fundamental rights ensuring equal civic rights and the right to vote of all citizens, freedom of religion, and the legal prohibition of discrimination and forced labour or involuntary servitude. He also suggested that the new Supreme Court be given adequate powers to protect these fundamental rights of citizens.[45] In addition, he proposed that key industries and agriculture be taken over by the state.[46]

He also demanded several constitutional protections for minorities. One must remember that in March 1947 there was still a single Constituent Assembly, and although some form of partition was imminent, it was not yet decided that members belonging to the Pakistan provinces would set up a separate Constitution-making body. Thus, Ambedkar's proposals for minority political representation in the face of a communal majority must be read in that context.

A key feature of his proposal was to abandon the British system of making the cabinet responsible to a parliamentary majority and instead have the executive as well as the legislature at the Union and state levels elected for fixed terms.[47] He made this argument not on the ground that it was universally preferable to the British cabinet system but as a specific guarantee of minority rights in India. He explained his position as follows:

> The British System of Government by a cabinet of the majority party rests on the premise that the majority is a political majority. In India the majority is a communal majority. No matter what social and political programme it may have the majority will retain its character of being a

communal majority. Nothing can alter this fact. Given this fact it is clear
that if the British system was copied it would result in permanently vesting
Executive power in a communal majority.[48]

Consequently, he also made it a constitutional requirement that the cabinet
include representatives of the minorities elected by members of each
minority community in the legislature, while cabinet members from the
majority community were to be elected by the whole house. The reason,
once again, was that the British cabinet system did not impose any obligation
on the majority party to include members from the minority party in the
cabinet. If that system were to be followed in India, the majority Congress
party, perceived to be a Hindu party, would come to represent 'a governing
class' while the minority Muslim League would represent 'a subject race'.[49]
Hence, Ambedkar wanted to make it mandatory that the cabinet necessarily
include minority representatives elected by members of the minority
community in the legislature.

These provisions were, of course, on the assumption that Hindu and
Muslim political leaders were to choose a form of government within a
single constitutional framework. As Ambedkar had explained in his book
on the Pakistan proposal, were there to be a properly conducted partition of
the country, this particular problem of communal majorities and minorities
could be expected to go away. The proportion of Muslims left in India and
of Hindus in Pakistan would be too small and scattered for the continued
existence of exclusively communal minority parties. This would in turn take
away the lifeblood from the politics of majority communalism. Parties could
then be organized, Ambedkar argued, on a truly political ground, based on
contending social and economic platforms.[50] The problem of communal
politics, even if it did not disappear, would be much more amenable to a
resolution.

While Ambedkar's specific proposals on the constitutional protection
of the rights of religious minorities were contingent upon the manner of
the resolution of the Pakistan question, his proposals regarding the rights
of Scheduled Castes or SCs (as they were now called) were firmly in line
with the principles he had upheld for a long time. He explicitly set aside
the Poona formula and wanted election of SC members to the legislature
on the basis of a separate electorate and adult franchise. Explaining why he
was insisting on the separate electorate even when all adults would be able
to vote, Ambedkar pointed out that the Poona Pact method of having a
first round of primary elections for the reserved seats by Depressed Class

voters followed by a final election by the general electorate had shown that the candidate chosen by most Depressed Class voters did not necessarily win the final election. In other words, the very purpose of special political representation for the discriminated minority was defeated. Only separate electorates could ensure that the SCs would be able to elect representatives of their choice.[51] He repeated his claim that the SCs were a minority not to be assimilated into the category of Hindus and the method of their political representation should be left to their choice and not dictated to them by the majority.

> The system of electorates being a device for the protection of the minority, the issue whether the electoral system should be the joint electorate or separate electorate must be left to the wishes of the minority. If it is large enough to influence the majority it will choose joint electorates. If it is too small for the purpose, it will prefer separate electorates for fear of being submerged.
> [. . .] The majority, being in a position to rule, can have no voice in the determination of the system of electorates . . . In other words, the majority must look to the decision of the minority and abide by it.[52]

Ambedkar also inserted specific constitutional provisions for making the social boycott, used so widely against weak and vulnerable populations by the dominant majority in towns and villages, an offence punishable by law. Curiously, he also asked for the settlement of Untouchable peoples in areas completely separated from existing villages.

> It is the system of the Village plus the Ghetto which perpetuates Untouchability and the Untouchables therefore demand that the nexus should be broken and the Untouchables who are as a matter of fact socially separate should be made separate geographically and territorially also, and be settled into separate villages exclusively of Untouchables in which the distinction of the high and the low and of Touchable and Untouchable will find no place.
> [. . .] The proposal may be dubbed escapism. But the only alternative is perpetual slavery.[53]

It is likely that the proposal shows Ambedkar's extreme frustration with the slow pace of change brought about by the existing constitutional protections. This is not a move that is pursued later in Dalit politics. It is also important to note that Ambedkar used his intervention in these constitutional proposals for minority rights to make a strong plea for economic democracy. He actually argued for 'State ownership in agriculture with a collectivized method of cultivation and a modified form of State Socialism in the field of industry'.[54] He defended his argument on the ground that democracy could not stop with 'one man, one vote' but should be extended to 'one man, one value'. Leaving matters of the economy to the fickle will of a legislative majority would never achieve this since all democratic legislatures were subject to the influence of the economically powerful.

> Almost all Laws of Constitution which relate to countries which are called Democratic stop with Adult Suffrage and Fundamental Right [. . .] In other words, old time Constitutional Lawyers believed that the scope and function of Constitutional Law was to prescribe the shape and form of the political structure of society. They never realized that it was equally essential to prescribe the shape and form of the economic structure of society, if Democracy is to live up to the principle of one man, one value [. . .] All countries like India which are late-comers in the field of Constitution-making should not copy the faults of other countries.[55]

Ambedkar clearly realized that whereas the constitutional protection of the civic and political rights of SCs was essential, that alone would not lead to their emancipation unless they could be freed from their economic dependence on propertied Hindus, especially in rural society. The difficulty was that while legislating for economic democracy required a strong interventionist state, Ambedkar's concern for the protection of minority political rights pushed him to restrain and limit the powers of the legislative majority and the executive elected by that majority. His expanded view of minority rights, embracing a strong notion of economic equality, ran into this contradiction that Ambedkar was unable to resolve.

## The General Theory of Minority Rights

While Ambedkar's views on minorities were, broadly speaking, grounded in what might be called 'constitutional republicanism',[56] his theory of minority rights, rigorously spelt out over two decades of speaking and writing, goes well beyond, and is often in contradiction with, standard liberal theories of minority rights. As I have shown above, he had a general as well as a specific theory. His general theory of minority rights may be laid out as follows:

1. A minority community that has acquired the consciousness of being a nation, refuses to share a common destiny with the majority community, and has the territorial, administrative and financial viability of forming a state has the right to determine its own constitutional state form.

2. The Constitution must guarantee equal civic rights of all citizens, the right of all adults to vote and religious freedom, and must prohibit discrimination, involuntary servitude and the imposition of civic disabilities. The courts must have the power to impose penalties for the violation of civil rights. If necessary, the state must be given the power to intervene in institutions of property or religion to remove the civic disabilities that militate against the equal rights of all citizens.

3. A minority community that agrees to live in the same constitutional order with the majority must have guaranteed legal protections against discrimination by the majority.

4. A minority community that is poor and vulnerable must, in addition, have special political representation such that it is able to influence decisions made by a legislative majority. The specific form of that representation, such as the number of reserved seats in the legislature or a separate electorate, must be, in the main, determined by the minority community itself and not imposed on it by the majority.

These rights are, quite evidently, collective rights. Ambedkar does not make any significant attempt, like liberal political theorists, to reconcile a conception of minority rights with individual freedom and equality. Indeed, as is clear from his memorandum to the Constituent Assembly in March 1947, he believed that constitutional theory in countries like India must necessarily go beyond the liberal confines of Western democratic theory.

The foundational principle of Ambedkar's general theory is its abiding reliance on the collective autonomy and the will to self-representation of minority groups. Clearly, he believed this to be the irreducible element of political democracy. While fully acknowledging the inevitability of the presence of minorities in a state system based on territorial representation, he was insistent that in order to prevent the tyranny of a majority with absolute powers, it was necessary to have not only legally guaranteed protections for minorities but also appropriate procedures for their self-representation in the branches of government. In other words, democracy itself demanded that there be not only the universal representation of the general body of citizens but the special representation of minorities.

A key element in Ambedkar's general theory is his definition of a minority. As we have seen, he did not think that numbers were a sufficient determinant of minority status for political purposes. Only a group subject to discrimination and oppression by the majority could properly claim special rights of political representation. Such representation would enable the minority group to influence the government to make policies to remove those oppressive conditions, improve its social and economic status and claim its rightful position of equal citizenship. For most of his career, Ambedkar was busy with the struggle to establish the legal-constitutional rights of minorities, especially Untouchables. But as the independence of India became a reality and an assembly was formed to write a new Constitution, he began to explicitly recognize that the formal legal recognition of equal citizenship and special rights of representation in the branches of government were only the first steps towards achieving real equality. Most striking here is his call for economic democracy in the memorandum entitled 'States and Minorities' which I have presented earlier. In it, he spoke of the state taking in its possession all agricultural land and industry and creating a form of state socialism. This is the closest he comes to acknowledging that class exploitation is thoroughly intertwined with caste discrimination and that eliminating the latter will necessarily involve a struggle against the former. However, in light of the long and rich history of debate around the world since the nineteenth century on the question of state intervention in the economy, Ambedkar's defence of state socialism in 'States and Minorities' is extremely inadequate. Sadly, he did not get the opportunity to further develop his argument of economic democracy which could have added an entirely new dimension to his theory of minority rights.

As far as his general theory is concerned, it seems to me that his propositions for the legal-constitutional rights of minorities constitute a strong and original theory that is still relevant. It is worth remembering that in his own time Ambedkar strongly argued for deciding the partition issue through a referendum in the relevant provinces, an idea that was tossed about for a while among various Indian leaders but not implemented, except in the case of the North-West Frontier Province and Sylhet district in Assam. He also wanted the future of the princely states of Jammu and Kashmir and Hyderabad to be decided not by their rulers but a referendum among the peoples of those states, an idea that Nehru accepted in the case of Kashmir only to back away from it subsequently. On every question of the self-representation of minorities, Ambedkar took the consistently democratic position that the collective will of the minority group must take precedence. It is easy to see the force of this argument in the context of debates today over Kashmir or religious minorities or the demand for smaller states. Indeed, discussing the recommendations of the States Reorganisation Commission in 1955, he explicitly argued that if large states like Uttar Pradesh, Bihar, Madhya Pradesh and Maharashtra were divided up into smaller monolingual states, it would enable minority groups such as Muslims, SCs and Scheduled Tribes (STs) to have more effective political representation by virtue of their geographical concentration in certain parts of the existing states.[57] As far as linguistic minorities are concerned, Ambedkar's theory suggests that their demands be met by suitable territorial rearrangement of the federal units and, if necessary, a redistribution of powers between the Union and the states. In fact, his general theory of minority rights can supply strong democratic arguments today for smaller states, greater regional autonomy and even self-determination (as in the case of Kashmir).

An important issue that Ambedkar did not engage with sufficiently was that of inequalities and hierarchies within a minority group. One form of inequality is in property ownership, wealth and income. Ambedkar was aware of this problem as a barrier to the achievement of equality in general, as shown in his plea for economic democracy. This discussion, as I have pointed out, is neither adequate nor very persuasive. But there is another form of inequality that feminists in particular have pointed out, which is that perpetuated by patriarchy and which afflicts minority groups as much as the majority. Although Ambedkar himself did not make this point, it is nonetheless possible to use his theory to argue that if women acquire the organization and consciousness of a group oppressed by a social order of patriarchy, then irrespective of their numbers, they must be regarded as a minority entitled to special political representation. Of course, if this minority group is marked by caste and class divisions, then, as in the case of other minorities, Ambedkar's general theory must be modified by a more complex analysis which he himself did not provide.

On the subject of inequalities within an oppressed minority community, a question that has emerged recently is that of the disproportionately large share of reserved positions in government employment currently held by a few Dalit castes, leaving most of the others without the benefits of special protection. There is a further question here on whether the opportunity of reserved positions should be available to a second or third generation of Dalit families. Clearly, these were not problems that Ambedkar could have foreseen in the 1940s or 1950s. Nevertheless, his theory turns out to be powerful enough to supply an answer. If, as a result of the special protection, there does emerge a new hierarchy within a minority group, that question must be debated democratically within the group itself. If necessary, the existing rules and procedures of special protection may be revised, but only through a democratic decision of the minority group and not as a resolution imposed on it by the majority. The point is made clear by what may be called Ambedkar's specific theory of minority rights.

## The Specific Theory of Minority Rights

Ambedkar's specific theory of minority rights is an elaboration of Proposition 4 of his general theory. It can be stated in two propositions:

1. The specific legal–constitutional form of protection of minorities or their representation in the organs of government, involving questions such as the federal distribution of powers, the powers of a legislative majority, the procedures and quantum of special representation, etc., are matters contingent upon the particular circumstances of disability in which the minorities may be placed.
2. All such contingent choices of legal–constitutional form must be left primarily to the minority group itself and not imposed on it by the majority.

We have already seen how, in the context of the Pakistan question, Ambedkar explained why Muslims in Bengal chose to have separate electorates even when they were a numerical majority, while Hindus in Punjab wanted joint electorates even when they were a minority. Such choices, he argued, were tactical decisions that were best left to the minority groups themselves. Why was it not possible in India in the 1940s to adopt the general parliamentary principle that a government enjoying majority support in the legislature be allowed to rule without constraint? Ambedkar's answer was that the general principle assumed that a parliamentary majority was a political majority, an assumption that did not hold for India where a majority was always a communal majority. What was the difference?

A political majority is changeable in its class composition. A political majority grows. A communal majority is born. The admission to a political majority is open. The door to a communal majority is closed. The politics

of a political majority are free to all to make and unmake. The politics of
a communal majority are made by its own members born in it.[58]

And while in the context of the bitter Hindu–Muslim conflict in the 1940s
the communal majority was usually defined by religion, Ambedkar clearly
stated in 1955 that it could be made up of castes too.[59]

It is an interesting question, and one that is worth serious research,
how the idea of 'minorities' in post-Independence India has shrunk from
that more capacious definition to one that means only religious minorities,
and that too, in most cases, the Muslim minority. Perhaps the distinction
made in the Constitution, and subsequent legislation, between the rights
of religious minorities to their personal laws and over their religious and
educational institutions, on the one hand, and reserved positions for SCs
and STs in legislatures, government service and higher education, on the
other, was the watershed. However, that distinction has been blurred by
the extension of reservation benefits to Dalit Sikhs and neo-Buddhists,
and more recently, by decisions by several state governments to include
Muslims in their lists of 'Other Backward Classes' eligible for reservations.
Nonetheless, there is today a widespread use in ordinary political discourse
of the term 'minority' as a code word for Muslim.

Could it not be said that after the experience of more than six decades
of electoral democracy and competition among political parties based
on rival economic and social programmes, political majorities have now
replaced communal majorities in India? It is true that following the end
of the era of Congress dominance, a multiplicity of parties and coalitions,
with varying combinations of support from different classes and castes, have
formed majorities at the Centre as well as the States. Speaking of SCs,
various national and regional parties put up Dalit candidates in the reserved
constituencies and Dalit votes are frequently distributed over different
parties. Consequently, an arrangement such as separate electorates for SCs
is unlikely to make much difference today in Dalit representation in the
legislatures.

At the same time, it is also true that a major component of the electoral
strategies of political parties consists of calculations of caste and communal
arithmetic. There may no longer be permanent communal majorities as
in the 1940s, but successful political parties now strive to build political
majorities through the mobilization of caste and communal support. It is
even possible, as Ambedkar once imagined, for a combination of minority
groups to be brought together under parties or coalitions to form their own

government.[60] This produces a paradox for Ambedkar's theory, because it means that even with political majorities and special representation of SCs and STs, the co-option through political parties of the representatives of minority groups by the dominant majority has not come to an end. In other words, political representation in the organs of the state is not a sufficient condition for the emancipation of oppressed minorities.

There is another recent phenomenon in Indian politics on which, by applying Ambedkar's theory of minority rights, we gain a surprising insight. It was pointed out quite forcefully by the Rajinder Sachar Committee in 2006 that in the absence of reservations in government employment and educational institutions, the Muslim community had fallen behind SCs in improving their social, economic and educational status.[61] Even more alarming was the decision by the Bharatiya Janata Party (BJP) not to field a single Muslim candidate in the 2017 elections in Uttar Pradesh. Had there been, following Ambedkar's theory, some fifty or more reserved seats for Muslims in the Uttar Pradesh assembly, no party seeking to come to power in that state could have afforded to ignore them. In fact, special representation for the Muslim minority in the legislatures of India would have definitely set an obstacle before the BJP that is now attempting to create, after six decades, a permanent communal majority in the country.

I must conclude, therefore, that Ambedkar's theory, by insisting on a set of legal-constitutional provisions for the protection and special representation of minorities, makes it incumbent upon the state to create certain basic political conditions for greater equality of rights among its citizens. Curiously, the limits of Ambedkar's theory are reached in the case of SCs for whom, unlike religious minorities, the marks of being Dalit do not constitute a distinct cultural identity that they wish to preserve; on the contrary, it is precisely an identity they must find ways to renounce. Now that the formal conditions proposed by Ambedkar's theory have been met in the case of the SCs, the question arises: what are the next steps that must be taken not for the perpetuation but the annihilation of caste?

# LAWYERING AS POLITICS

## THE LEGAL PRACTICE OF DR AMBEDKAR, BAR AT LAW

### *Rohit De*[1]

'Legal practice and public service are thus the alternating currents in my life, I do not know on which current my life will end, whether AC or DC'—Dr B.R. Ambedkar, 1956[2]

Every eulogy to Dr B.R. Ambedkar mentions his training as a lawyer, but while his political engagements, his writings on history and economics, his role as legislator, law minister and constitutional drafter have all been extensively discussed, little is known about his career as a lawyer. This is surprising because Dr Ambedkar himself saw his legal practice as a dominant part of his life and had undergone considerable hardship to acquire the law degree.

Ambedkar initially gained admission to Gray's Inn to become a barrister in 1916. The ending of his Baroda scholarship required him to abandon his law studies and return to India to take up paid employment. Despite becoming a professor of economics at Sydenham College in Mumbai, Dr Ambedkar continued to lead a life of great frugality and took up private tuitions in order to save money to complete his education in London. He was able to complete his legal training and returned to Mumbai as a barrister in 1923, getting his *sanad* after borrowing money from a friend and setting up his practice in a small office of the Social Service League near BIT chawl, where he lived. Most biographies remain silent about his legal practice after this or refer to it in the most general terms.

S.R. Dongerkery, later the rector of Bombay University and a contemporary of Dr Ambedkar at the Bar, expresses some puzzlement about the fact that 'he did not remember briefing Ambedkar as an advocate in any suit'—his main recollection of Ambedkar's involvement at the Bar was as a member of the editorial committee of the *Bombay Law Journal* where he 'expressed strong views'.[3] Dongerkery's puzzlement comes from his encounters with Dr Ambedkar at the Bombay University Senate, where he impressed members with 'the soundness of his argument, the way he marshalled them, the clarity of mind and the forceful manner of speaking', but in spite of this and his sound legal knowledge, he did not command a larger practice at the Bar.[4] Dongerkery, without feeling the need to explain why he never briefed Ambedkar himself, opines that this was because his political and other activities as Dalit spokesman made heavy demands on his time and interfered in his legal practice. Whatever be the size and extent of his practice, it is clear this was not a testimony to Ambedkar's skills, which found appreciation in twice being invited to be a judge in the Bombay High Court.[5]

This essay seeks to reconstruct Dr Ambedkar's legal practice before the courts of the Bombay Presidency through newspaper articles, law reports and memoirs. This reconstruction is not merely to complete the record but to offer a way of understanding how Ambedkar's politics and ideas were shaped and reflected in his legal practice. It is a project of recovery; apart from a single remarkable but incomplete compilation, no such record exists.[6] It is also a project of reimagination—it seeks an underlying political philosophy that emerges from everyday acts of legal practice. The understanding of the lawyer and legal practice is that the lawyer takes all or any cases that come before her, and indeed, she can deploy any argument that would work for her client. However, through Ambedkar's practice, I wish to argue that lawyers, indeed committed lawyers, work within a political philosophy. This essay defines legal practice narrowly, as work done before courts and tribunals.

It opens with a discussion on what sets Ambedkar's practice apart from his contemporary lawyer-politicians. It then maps four different kinds of practice: cases involving political actors; cases involving intercommunity relations; work for poor and indigent clients; and finally, engaging with the spirit of the Constitution.

## Equality before the Law?

Political life in India from the late 19th century till Independence was dominated by men who had trained and practised as lawyers. This is a fact that is often noted but rarely commented upon. The domination of politics by legal professionals has been used as shorthand for class to attribute the bourgeoisie character of mass politics in India.[7] Others have suggested that the presence of lawyers led to the evolution of a certain moderate constitutional form of politics.[8] With Gandhi's critique of law and lawyers as enabling colonialism and the decision taken by the Congress to boycott British courts in the 1920s, politics was seen to move out of the courtrooms and on to the streets, leading to a meagre handful of studies on lawyering.[9]

This essay argues that the category of 'lawyer' does not account for the highly differential experiences of being a legal professional. In particular, Dr Ambedkar differed significantly from his most prominent lawyer-politician contemporaries, Gandhi, Jinnah and Motilal Nehru,[10] both in his decision to become a lawyer and in his experience in setting up practice. I use Gandhi, Jinnah and Motilal Nehru as perhaps the most visible lawyer-politicians, but the lawyer–public man–politician was a widespread phenomenon that included Dadabhai Naoroji, Badruddin Tyabji, Pherozeshah Mehta, N.G. Chandavarkar, Chittaranjan Das, H.S. Suhrawardy, Syed Hasan Imam and Mian Mohammad Shafi.[11]

Both Gandhi and Jinnah belonged to trading communities and families that saw an advantage in having a legally trained son, and both were supported by their families in their teens as they qualified as barristers in London. Motilal Nehru was born to a high-caste family which had been in government service for centuries, and studied law to join a brother who had already established a lucrative legal practice. In contrast, Dr Ambedkar took a self-conscious decision to train as a lawyer after he had completed several other qualifications and gained employment. He paid for his legal education through funds he raised himself. In several speeches, he would make his reasoning explicit, noting that the legal profession was the only one in colonial India that allowed one to remain independent of both the government and social forces. He turned down the position of a district judge with a promised promotion to the high court in three years even when he was living in straitened circumstances in a one-room chawl, on the grounds that judicial service would curb his independence.[12] He also turned down a lucrative offer by the nizam of Hyderabad to become the chief justice of Hyderabad state.[13]

Thus, Ambedkar faced great challenges in establishing a legal practice compared to his contemporaries. From the late 19th century, law had been seen as an overcrowded profession marked by 'the daily round of almost hopeless waiting at the Bar library in company of more than a hundred equally hopeless members of the learned brotherhood'.[14] Most young lawyers leveraged family and community networks for work. Jinnah's first case was representing his uncle, a Khoja merchant, in a commercial suit.[15] Gandhi, despite his poor oral advocacy skills, could draw upon family networks for work in Bombay and moved to South Africa to advise a Gujarati merchant firm.[16] Motilal Nehru joined the flourishing legal practice set up by his brother.

Ambedkar was aware of his disadvantage and lack of social capital and chose to join the Appellate Side of the Bombay Bar knowing that to be successful on the Original Side (which consisted of high-paying commercial work) one needed to be well networked with solicitors, already biased in favour of European solicitors who were believed to get a better hearing in court. They discriminated against Ambedkar on caste grounds, leaving him to search for work in the mofussil courts.[17] His cases were low in volume and value in the 1920s and he became a law professor in order to sustain a steady income. The contrast comes out starkly in a newspaper article that reported Jinnah representing an insolvency matter of Rs 2,57,000 on the same day that Ambedkar represented a retired Muslim schoolteacher in a breach of trust case valued at Rs 24.[18]

Lawyers from previously disempowered groups the world over found it hard to sustain private practice and had to turn to academia and government employment for a steady income.[19] Reflecting upon his choice of career, Dr Ambedkar said he 'knew there is no hope to gain from profession of legal practice as a lawyer because it depends on touchable people', but he chose legal practice because it provided 'liberty and free time to perform social work'.[20]

The legal profession was one of the few areas within colonial India where Indians were able to challenge the racial hierarchy. Indian advocates, both by sheer numbers and competence, had held their own against British lawyers. The judiciary was Indianized well before the higher echelons of the civil service or the army. While the profession allowed for some measure of equality between Europeans and Indians, Ambedkar's experiences are a reminder that it was not a level playing field for all Indians.[21]

Yet, Ambedkar's limited financial success in the legal profession and the securing of an independent source of income from teaching allowed him to become a different kind of lawyer. While his contemporaries took on 'political cases' or public interest cases only occasionally, the bulk of Ambedkar's practice consisted of such cases, making him one of the earliest precursors of India's civil rights lawyers.

## In Defence of Politics: Ambedkar and Political Parties

Dr Ambedkar's first major appearance in a criminal case was in the defence of Philip Spratt, a British communist who had been sent by the Comintern and one of the founders of the Communist Party of India. He was arrested for sedition within months of his arrival in Bombay for writing a pamphlet titled 'India and China', which was alleged to cause hatred and incite disaffection against the Government of India.[22] The pamphlet, printed in India and advertised in the Marathi and English press, was an approving study of the Kuomintang's use of violent means to secure independence in China and implicitly made the case for revolutionary change in India. It argued that Indians should follow the example of the Chinese to overthrow their foreign masters, who were described as 'murderers'.

In the trial itself, the defence was led by F.S. Taleyarkhan with Ambedkar assisting as a junior. The defence strategy was overtly political—drawing on precedents from both Tilak's and Annie Besant's sedition cases, the counsels argued that a man may criticize the government, even perversely and unreasonably, without coming under the operation of sedition.[23] The defence carefully said that Spratt's pamphlets challenged 'British imperialism' and not the 'government of India'. The term 'oppressor' was used not in a literal sense to mean the specific government in power, but in the popular sense of a people subjected to foreign rule—the freedom demanded was from British capital and 'imperialism' rather than the legal authorities under the Government of India Act.[24]

Spratt refused his privileges to be tried as a European with an all-White jury and his lawyers challenged the appointment of an all-European jury, leading to the final jury comprising Parsis, Hindus and Muslims. What played out in the courtroom was a skilled piece of legal theatre, allying Spratt with an Indian public and arguing that older definitions of sedition could not be reconciled with Indian desires for self-government. The association of prominent leaders' communities and ideologies demonstrated a united front. Jinnah had appeared in the bail application, Ambedkar (already a prominent figure as junior lawyer) worked in the trial and Sarojini Naidu would preside over a public meeting to celebrate Spratt's acquittal.[25] Spratt was acquitted amid thunderous applause in the courtroom.

What explained the defence of Spratt by men and women who disagreed with his methods and ideals? Indeed, Spratt's pamphlet described Indian nationalists as fools and 'servants of imperial masters', argued that non-violence was unwise and violence necessary for any fundamental social change. There is a clue in the celebrations which mention that the lawyers had secured the freedom to write, that is, to be critical of the colonial government.[26] What was at stake was not just Spratt's freedom but the question of civil liberties under the British.

Ambedkar's relationship with the Communist Party was complicated; he criticized them both for being upper caste dominated and for their advocacy of violence. Yet, there was a convergence of views over questions of economic policy and both competition and cooperation while organizing labour in Bombay.[27] Political disagreement apart, by the 1930s Ambedkar had emerged as one of the main lawyers for trade union leaders of all stripes. The most sustained involvement was in his defence of the leaders of the All India Textile Workers Conference, which had been charged with organizing an illegal general strike. The trade unionists charged were all communist or Left-aligned and included V.B. Karnik, Maniben Kara, B.T. Ranadive and Abdul Majid, among others.

The Trade Disputes Act of 1929 (which Ambedkar had been critical of) allowed strikes for very limited purposes, and an illegal strike was one which had objects greater than the furtherance of the trade dispute or was 'designed or calculated to cause severe, general and prolonged hardship on the community'. The attorney general alleged that at least four of the demands made by the trade unions—for the repeal of anti-labour legislation, freedom of speech, right to assembly, maternity benefits and employment insurance— could only be granted by the government and not employers. He referenced speeches made by the leaders to argue that they intended this mill strike to lead to a general strike, putting pressure on the government to meet their demands. Ambedkar's defence strategy was twofold. The first was to argue that the twenty-point list of demands made at the trade union conference contained general demands distinct from the object of the strike. The second was to challenge the claim that there would be a general strike and that the textile strike would cause 'prolonged hardship to the community'.[28]

This is one of the few cases where the transcript of Ambedkar's sharp cross-examination survives, showing how he established that the twenty demands were labour propaganda and not the intended requirement for settlement.[29] There was a distinction between the intention, which might have been to cause a general strike, and the actual strike which was limited to the textile industry. In the trial court, he deftly whittled down the argument that the textile strike would have caused significant economic hardship to the 'community'. He argued that the stoppage of work in the textile industry could cause external hardship, unlike, say, stoppage of work

in railways or transport, pointing to the fact that many countries existed
without a textile industry.[30]

The trial court acquitted all the trade unionists, agreeing with
Ambedkar's contention that a pecuniary loss to mill owners could not equal
'hardship to the community'. Taking a literal view of corporate ownership,
the magistrate held that the mills were limited companies whose stocks were
held by thousands of shareholders, so the eventual loss to an individual was
a small pecuniary amount, and acquitted the leaders.[31] Instrumental in this
acquittal was Ambedkar's pointed rebuttal of evidence. The prosecution
had witnesses representing tram and bus companies who claimed that they
suffered losses of close to Rs 28,000 because of the strike as the mill-hands
hands had left the city. However, Ambedkar, through cross-examination,
got them to admit that the receipts of the company were liable to great
fluctuations even in normal times. He was scathing in his interrogation of
T. Maloney, the head of the Bombay Mill Association, pointing out that
the reason the mill owners refused to negotiate was not the impossibility of
the workers' demands but the fact that the strike was led by people 'who
were of communist colour'.[32] Ambedkar succeeded in the acquittal and the
case built a strong relationship with Left trade unionists.

Ambedkar would independently defend B.T. Ranadive on sedition
charges before the Bombay High Court, arguing that the speech Ranadive
delivered in Marathi attacked capitalism and imperialism rather than the
government of Bombay.[33] He was a leading figure in the defence team
in the Chirner Forest case, where he worked with Congress stalwarts like
K.M. Munshi and B.G. Kher. The case rose from the suppression of the
forest satyagraha at Panvel which had led to a riot, indiscriminate police
firing and the death of four government servants. Forty-seven people were
charged with robbery, dacoity, unlawful assembly and murder. In his cross-
examination, Ambedkar attacked the reliability of prosecution witnesses,
adduced evidence of police torture and dissected the impossibility of the
prosecution case which had suggested that several thousand people were
in a conspiracy together. Brimming with irony, he pointed out that the
accused could not be charged with inciting the crowd to cut trees since that
was the goal of the satyagraha and the reason why the crowds had gathered
in the first place.[34]

Defending both communists and satyagrahis who had deliberately
chosen to work outside the frame of colonial law and within the limits of the
colonial legal system required a particular kind of deftness. Taken together,
the trade dispute and the Chirner Forest case showed that Ambedkar was

respected as a lawyer across the political fraternity, at equal ease and in demand for defending communist or Congress workers and bringing his considerable advocacy skills at parsing distinctions to find freedoms within a repressive legal system.

## A Community before Law: Ambedkar and Intercommunity Disputes

The rights of Indian subjects in colonial India rested on the ownership of property or their status on the basis of caste, community or religion. It is not surprising that a range of legal disputes were tied to questions of community identity.

Ambedkar's first prominent case involved the defence of the Dalit writer, publisher and printer of the 1926 book *Deshache Dushman* (Enemies of My Country). The Marathi book, authored by Keshav Jedhe, was a visceral critique of Brahminism and described Bal Gangadhar Tilak and Vishnushastri Chiplunkar as 'enemies of the nation' and 'children of asses' for their defence of Brahmin privileges. The book was banned and a local Brahmin lawyer filed defamation charges. Ambedkar's defence demonstrated his favourite legal strategy of parsing the fine distinctions in law. Realizing that the colonial legal system would not permit a defence of the merits of the claim, he pointed out that since two of the defamed were dead and the complainant was not a near relative, he had no basis to file the suit. Further, Ambedkar argued the attacks were really not aimed at the individuals but against the entire Brahmin community, who again could not be said to be represented by the complainant. The magistrate conceded that the attack was a 'mischievous one' but not illegal or one within his powers to supervise.

As Anupama Rao has noted, Dr Ambedkar continued to build up a civic notion of rights to challenge both religious democratization and a colonial order rooted in custom and identity.[35] This is clearly demonstrated in his leadership in the Chavadar Tank agitation in the late 1920s. In 1927, Dr Ambedkar led a satyagraha to gain access to water from the tank, exercising a right to the public resources maintained by the state, which was guaranteed by the Bombay legislature but not enforced due to social sanction. The satyagraha was met by violence, and upper-caste Hindus filed a court case arguing that the tank was private property. The filing of the court case and the restriction of the satyagraha on the grounds that the matter was sub judice led to Ambedkar's first public burning of the *Manusmriti*, obeying the grounds of the secular state while vowing to destroy Brahminical Hindu law.

As a defendant, he was actively involved in the strategy behind the case, which was to show that the tank was not private property. The first point, easily established, was that the tank legally belonged to the government and was vested with the Mahad municipality. The second was to prove that groups other than caste Hindus had been accessing it. While there was no Dalit house in the vicinity, the tank was near several Muslim homes. Dr Ambedkar wrote to the local advocate in Mahad that he needed an affidavit from a local Muslim butcher ('it must be a butcher') confirming he had used the tank.[36] The focus on the figure of the butcher is strategic; being a profession that involved working with dead animals, a butcher was often considered 'unclean' and evoked negative images in caste Hindu imaginations. To show that the tank had been used by a Muslim butcher would make upper-caste arguments about the 'purity' of the tank redundant. Ambedkar won at every instance as the case moved from the local trial court to the Bombay High Court. The trial courts gave the most powerful judgement, arguing that merely because the plaintiffs could show a long-standing custom of excluding Dalits, it conferred no legal right upon caste Hindus. The mere use of a 'public tank' by one class and non-use by another would not create legal rights of ownership.

The Chavadar case initially offered a new strategy to Ambedkar, and there was some talk of setting up an Institute for Civil Action that would pursue litigation to ensure public access for Dalits.[37] However, the experiences with the Bhuleshwar temple soon made the optimism fade. In 1929, Ambedkar became part of a movement to open up the Gaud Saraswat Brahmin–run Bhuleshwar temple and its attached tank to all communities. Around the same time, the priests of the temple approached the high court, arguing that they had been sacked by the temple owners and such an action could not be permitted because it was a public temple. Justice Mirza, drawing on evidence such as gifts from the public, maintenance of the priest from communal funds, and land records, held that the temple was not the private property of the founder's family and was to be placed in the receivership of the court until the state organized its administration.[38] At first glance, the judgement seemed to be a progressive one, declaring the temple to be a public space and therefore one that could be accessed by all. However, the trustees used the fact of the temple being in public receivership to declaim all responsibility for opening up the temple to Dalits, saying their hands were tied.

A furious Ambedkar wrote to the trustees, accusing them of parading the high court judgement and 'throwing them into the faces of those working for temple entry for untouchables' and decided to shift his strategy.[39] He made the stakes clear, stating that there would be a 'war' in the near future, as he had 'lost faith in the promises of Hindu leaders'. He said direct action was the only way of effectively solving the problem and promised that 1,00,000 Dalits would be ready to lay down their lives in a satyagraha to secure temple entry at Bhuleshwar.[40] He noted that the temple trustees were being duplicitous in expressing sympathy for the legitimate aspirations of Dalits but stating that their hands were tied by the high court judgement, a decision that Ambedkar described as being erroneous in law. A number of Dalit organizations took up Ambedkar's call, leading morchas and rallies to force entry into the Bhuleshwar temple, and were met by obstruction and violence.[41] Finally, in 1932, a combination of action on the streets and legislative compromises led to five major Bombay temples including Bhuleshwar being thrown open to all communities.[42]

The Chavadar Tank case took ten years in the court before a final decision was given and access was granted. In Bhuleshwar and other shrines, the turn to the streets had led to temple entry being granted in three years. It also became clear to Ambedkar that once a dispute became judicial, the parties lost control over the issue and they were prevented from using other strategies due to the question being sub judice. This meant the Chavadar litigation model was not repeated.

Any discussion of Ambedkar's legal engagement with communities would be incomplete without citing the Gore case, where, ironically, Ambedkar helped establish that the Chitpavan Brahmins, many of whom were implacably opposed to Ambedkar, were a distinct community. A wealthy Brahmin had died, leaving Rs 50,000 for the medical relief of persons belonging to 'his community'. The question arose whether 'his community' referred to Dakshini Brahmins (the wider description of Brahmins in south India) or Chitpavan Brahmins, the particular sect that the deceased belonged to. The executors argued that the definition of community could be governed by religious doctrine alone and cited Wilson on Indian castes to argue that there were officially two great classes of Brahmins with five orders each; 'community' could only mean one of these suborders.[43]

Dr Ambedkar and his colleagues argued that 'community' must be understood from social practice and quoted precedents from the Bombay High Court that had recognized that the Chitpavans were a community. Ironically, this was a case where the Chitpavans had brought a legal suit to challenge the right of other castes, in this case Palshe Brahmins, to access their temples. The court dryly noted, 'Dr Ambedkar simply cited the case to show that the Chitpavans regarded themselves as distinct from the Palshe community', both being Dakhini Brahmins. What does Ambedkar's defence of Chitpavan rights tell us? Was he merely obeying his duty as a lawyer to do his best for his client? It's clear that through his defence of Chitpavan rights, Ambedkar makes the case for the separateness of Untouchables from the Hindu fold as well as the existence of caste as a feature of Indian life.

The judge noted that subdivisions existed both within Muslims and Christians, and groups like Bohras or native Christians had to be regarded as distinct communities. Moreover, conceding that 'in a sense all Hindus are members of the same community', the court remarked that 'an orthodox Brahmin would be a little startled if he were told that he belonged to the caste community as an untouchable'.[44] Therefore, his defence of Chitpavan rights cut against the claims of the Congress and upper-caste Hindus that 'Dalits' were part of the Hindu fold and thus their needs could be addressed 'within' the community. These are the years when Ambedkar was active in the Round Table Conferences and the Franchise Committee, stating that the Depressed Classes would only consent to place themselves under majority rule in India if there were constitutional guarantees of equality and anti-discrimination and governmental measures to ensure free enjoyment of such rights as well as guaranteed representation in legislatures and public institutions. In particular, he argued for the infringement of rights of citizenship such as access to public transportation or schools to be made into a criminal offence.[45]

Even apart from the issue of temple entry, Dr Ambedkar stepped in to defend the secular civic conceptions of rights against the 'sentiments of a community'. He famously defended Professor R.D. Karve's journal *Samaj Swasthya* on charges of obscenity. Karve was the son of the famous social reformer Maharshi Karve, who had started India's first birth control clinic in 1921. The Gujarati journal edited by him and his wife addressed questions of sex and sexual hygiene quite frankly and came to the attention of the Crime Investigation Department. Ambedkar, in his defence, argued that Karve had certain views of sex and social hygiene and he was entitled to advocate them. Further, and quite radically for his time, he got the magistrate to concede that the taboo of silence on sexual matters should be ended. The magistrate, however, refused to admit that the liberty of writing on sexual matters could be a 'license'.[46] In his appeal, Ambedkar argued that under the Indian Penal Code the test for obscenity was that it should 'tend to deprave or corrupt a person who may in ordinary circumstances come to read it'. He pointed out that the magazine itself contained no general news and only published articles on social hygiene and would not find circulation among the general public. This echoed his defence in the Chirner Forest satyagraha, where he said a charge of incitement was irrelevant before a crowd which had gathered solely to perform the act.[47] Ambedkar lost the Karve case but continued to be engaged in the promotion of family planning. Shortly after, his party proposed a resolution in favour of birth control in the Bombay legislature.[48]

We also find Ambedkar engaged in individual rights against a majoritarian consensus in his defence of a Catholic man caught with a bottle of alcohol and charged with a violation of prohibition laws.[49] Prohibition of alcohol had been a major part of the Congress electoral plank and was imposed in Bombay in 1938 despite opposition from colonial officials and several minority communities.[50] The law was rooted in democratic legitimacy, and the loss to revenue and civil liberties was believed to be balanced by the general public welfare goals met by prohibition.[51] While the prohibition law would be struck down as unconstitutional for overstepping the legislature's powers in 1940, the cases of people arrested under the law for possession of alcohol continued to move through the courts. Ambedkar argued before the full bench of the Bombay High Court and established that the nullification of the prohibition law had in effect nullified all offences and charges against it. Not only did this set his client at liberty, the case had an impact on many others.[52]

Echoes of this strategy can be also found in his unsuccessful defence of a woman accused of being a brothel keeper. The Bombay Prostitution Act of 1923 did not abolish prostitution but sought to end its organized version and criminalize those who brought women into prostitution. In this case, the accused owned a house where the prostitute in question had met clients for a few hours. Ambedkar attempted to argue that the prostitute was an independent agent as evidenced by her short stay at the brothel and that the accused merely kept a brothel and was not a procuress. While Ambedkar's own views of sex work are complicated, in the court he did make an argument for the independent agency of sex workers.[53]

## A House of Justice: Lawyering for the Poor and Indigent

Dr Ambedkar argued a much smaller load of cases compared to his contemporaries. A recent attempt to collate all his published judgements could identify only thirty-two cases over twenty years, though there are several unreported ones that this chapter has tracked through newspaper sources.[54] Apart from the political cases discussed above and an occasional case about land transactions, the bulk of Ambedkar's practice consisted of representing indigent and working class clients. Given his connections with labour, it's unsurprising that several dealt with workmen's compensation, only a small fraction of which were reported.[55] The fact that in all cases Dr Ambedkar represented the worker is not a coincidence.

In the 1920s, politically minded labour lawyers around the world clearly made explicit decisions not to represent employers against workmen. Ambedkar defended railway workers charged with trespass while they were trying to prevent non-unionized workers from crossing the picket line.[56] He also frequently appeared in cases involving the death penalty where the accused was usually a poor man from a rural area with a surname suggestive of belonging to the Dalit or OBC (Other Backward Classes) communities.[57] Cases involving the death penalty usually had an automatic right of appeal in the high court; however, the absence of legal aid meant it was often difficult for the accused to secure the services of an appellate lawyer. It is clear that Dr Ambedkar was increasingly being approached in this regard.[58] It is perhaps his experience with the arbitrary nature of the death penalty, which disproportionately affects the poor and lower castes, that made him advocate for its abolition during the debates in the Constituent Assembly.[59]

As his biographer mentions, Ambedkar gained a reputation as a 'poor man's barrister' and gave legal advice for free or fought cases with nominal or no charges.[60] Clients who had come to Bombay for court cases were often fed and sheltered in his small apartment.

Ambedkar was also a supportive mentor to other Dalits entering the legal profession. D.G. Jadhav recounts that upon his election to the legislative assembly, he thought of quitting legal education and devoting himself to social work, but Dr Ambedkar urged him to complete his training and start an independent practice before he did so. Social work required 'honest men' who had an independent source of livelihood. Indeed, Ambedkar pointedly asked people to join politics rather than be paid for conducting social work.[61] This is the memory of Ambedkar that is remembered through folk songs like 'Tula Bheemana Vagh Banavalaye' and 'Vakil Doctor Jhali'.[62]

## Ambedkar and the Spirit of the Constitution

The 1940s saw a slowdown in Dr Ambedkar's legal practice as he grew increasingly drawn into national politics, serving as a member of the viceroy's executive council, drawing up plans for social security and labour reforms, negotiating with the Cabinet Mission and being elected to the Constituent Assembly. He ended the decade as chairman of the Drafting Committee of the Indian Constitution, steering India towards becoming a constitutional republic in 1950.

What did Ambedkar think of the Constitution he had drafted? In the 1950s he grew increasingly exasperated both at the timidity of the central government towards social reform and the tendency to ignore minority concerns. He exploded with rage at its failure to protect the rights of Scheduled Castes during the reorganization of linguistic states and famously said, 'I am quite prepared to be the first person to burn it out [the Constitution]. I do not want it. It does not suit anybody. But whatever that may be, if our people want to carry on, they must not forget that there are majorities and there are minorities, and they simply cannot ignore the minorities by saying, "Oh, no. To recognise you is to harm democracy." I should say that the greatest harm will come by injuring the minorities.'[63]

Ambedkar appeared in a single case involving constitutional law before the Supreme Court of India. He was hired by the maharaja of Kapurthala and other landed notables to challenge the constitutionality of the land reform and zamindari abolition acts in Madhya Pradesh, Bihar, Uttar Pradesh and Punjab.[64] Dr Ambedkar clearly accepted the case because it was a rare financially lucrative one at a time when he needed resources both for his political and social work. However, his arguments reveal a powerful case for constitutional interpretation that has continued to animate and save the Indian Constitution over the years.

The Constitution offered a narrow right to property, that is, property could be taken over by the state provided it met two requirements: that such acquisition was for public purposes and that compensation was provided for the same. Ambedkar argued that the enabling legislations failed to meet either condition. In order to protect these land reforms, Article 31A of the Constitution of India had been amended to immunize certain laws from the effects of fundamental rights and this had been upheld by the Supreme Court.[65] Assuming the court held the fundamental rights to be deleted for the Constitution as far as land reforms were concerned, how should it judge such cases?

Ambedkar argued that the court must recognize that structurally the Constitution aimed at 'securing the liberty and equality of people' and gave restricted powers to the state, therefore, the obligation to pay compensation for private property was implicit in the spirit of the Constitution. The courts dismissed the argument, holding that one could not take recourse to the 'spirit of the Constitution' when the provisions were explicit. Dr Ambedkar went on to argue that while the compensation provided by the laws was not illusory, it was grossly inadequate even compared to acquisition by the colonial state. The fact that the state had fixed the amount of compensation meant that it was the judge in its own cause and this again cut against the 'spirit of the Constitution'. Finally, he argued with 'some vehemence' that the laws as they stood did not operate on some public purpose. Under the land reform laws, the state merely constituted itself as a trustee for the distribution of certain interests between the haves and the have-nots. In fact, he contended that the land reforms failed the public purpose test for not being radical enough; they merely distributed land among smaller landowners and not the landless. In the absence of cooperatives or landless beneficiaries, these laws merely amounted to property being acquired to benefit certain private persons.

He asserted that the idea of 'public purpose' was not new and had a settled meaning when the Constitution was written, and it could not be construed in light of the generalities of the Directive Principles of State Policy. Ambedkar lost the case to a narrower, more textualist understanding of the Constitution, but his identification of the 'spirit of the Constitution' would continue to haunt the governments to come, leading to a final confrontation with Indira Gandhi in the 1970s when the Supreme Court would hold that 'the basic structure' of the Constitution could not be tampered with even through a procedurally perfect constitutional amendment. After the Emergency, the Supreme Court would turn to the 'spirit of the Constitution' to curb executive excesses and read the right to life to include the right to education, healthcare and livelihood (all concerns that motivated Ambedkar when he was in the Executive Council).[66]

Most fittingly, it evoked the spirit of the Constitution to read the 'due process of law' into it. 'Due process' prescribes a higher standard for the constitutionality of legislation, and due to fears of challenges, land reform laws had been explicitly excluded by the Constituent Assembly in favour of the narrower requirement of 'procedure established by law'.[67] Since his days in the US, Dr Ambedkar had been a fan of the Fourteenth Amendment to the US Constitution which helped guarantee freedom for African Americans. In his early law lectures, Ambedkar had reminded his students that such a clause was not found in the Constitution of other states, yet every civilized state sought to protect the life, liberty and property of its citizens from unwarranted attacks.[68] As chairman of the Drafting Committee, Ambedkar had to represent the consensus, but as a constitutional lawyer he was able to plant the intellectual seeds of a constitutional revolution of 'due process'.

## Conclusion: Practice as Politics

'We lawyers defend many things'—Dr B.R. Ambedkar, Rajya Sabha, 1953[69]

Under the common law tradition, lawyers are supposed to take on any client that comes before them, no matter the cause. Lawyering is an act of representation, that is, the lawyer is a mere agent for the client's interests. Dr Ambedkar, in his years in parliamentary opposition, faced with an obdurate government, would often disclaim his role in the making of the Constitution, noting with exasperation that he was a 'hack', merely following instructions. However, it is clear from the fragments of his legal career that he was not an ordinary lawyer, a mere representative of others' claims.

He was exceptional among his peers for having deliberately chosen to train as a lawyer because of the independence it would give him from governmental and societal control. He also faced obstacles that none of his peers did in gaining clients and making money from litigation. Kenneth Mack, in his study of the first generation of African-American lawyers, notes that minority lawyers have to perform a double act of representation, representing their clients as well as the community.[70] Ironically, the lack of Dr Ambedkar's commercial success in law allowed him greater time to develop his practice in political cases and representing the poor and indigent. Dr Ambedkar, perhaps more so than any of his peers, was the precursor of the committed human rights lawyer of today.

While Dr Ambedkar represented a range of clients, including political adversaries or those whose ideals he did not share, his legal strategies were not purely instrumental. There is a clear underlying legal philosophy that one can identify. During the colonial period, when working within the confines of the law, he argued that the offences they were charged with did not meet a strict interpretation of their legal definition. He preferred interpretations that were literal, almost minimalist, so that his clients may escape punishment. Yet, after Independence, recognizing that the Indian state was based on democratic legitimacy and the Constitution would emerge as a site of struggle, he urged against strict constructionist readings of the Constitution and advocated for 'the spirit of the Constitution'. For

Ambedkar, this was not merely the achievement of certain goals of justice but also a certain processual form of politics. In the Kameshwar Singh case, he made it clear that the 'spirit of the Constitution' could not be equated with the Directive Principles. Underlying his claim was his belief in constitutional morality, which sees the Constitution not just as a relationship between persons but between persons bound together by abstract rules.[71] Democracy could not be reduced to popular majoritarian rule, but required the consent of minorities, which could only be achieved if all groups agreed on certain processes to adjudicate that disagreement.[72] This is a lesson to be remembered as India is once again challenged by majoritarian forces contemptuous of institutional processes.

A question we must ask ourselves, particularly those of us who have been part of the legal academy, is why we have not looked at Dr Ambedkar as a legal scholar. His chairmanship of the Drafting Committee was not just an act of political patronage or strategic inclusion, but a recognition of his fine legal mind, his understanding of economics, necessary for a state committed to planned development, and his underlying legal philosophy. He delivered some of the earliest lectures on constitutional law in India and, as I outline, developed a clear line of both statutory interpretation and constitutional philosophy. However, Ambedkar's skills as a lawyer were put to use in several domains, which remain understudied, in particular his role as a law teacher and setting up and building legal education in Bombay. Ambedkar spent three years as a part-time teacher of mercantile law in Batliboi's Accountancy Training Institute. He then went on to become professor of law and later principal of the prestigious Government Law College of Bombay. Finally, he set up the Siddharth College of Law, which went on to train many from the early generations of Dalit lawyers.

The erasure of Ambedkar the lawyer prevents us from recognizing how legal practice, commitment to social justice and legal theory can have a productive relationship with one another and that lawyering can be rooted in the ethic of social and political justice.

# III

# AMBEDKAR'S REVOLUTION

# THREE MOMENTS IN THE ANNIHILATION OF CASTE[1]

## MARX, WEBER, AMBEDKAR

*Hira Singh*

## Introduction

On 15 August 2016, sixty-nine years after India's independence from colonial rule, Dalits in Gujarat organized a march from Ahmedabad to Una, chanting the slogan of equality and 'azadi' (freedom). Lack of freedom and equality, twin features of bondage to caste rule, is the persistent reality of the daily lives of Dalits in India to date. Against this context of lived reality, this essay proposes to critically examine three moments in the annihilation of caste conceptualized by Marx, Weber and Ambedkar to reflect on the basis of inequality and lack of freedom in the caste system and the possibility of its annihilation.

Karl Marx wrote in the *New-York Daily Tribune*:[2] 'Modern industry, resulting from the railway system will dissolve the hereditary divisions of labour, upon which rest the Indian castes, those decisive impediments to Indian progress and Indian power.'[3] What is relatively unknown is that some sixty years later, Max Weber wrote: 'Today, the Hindu caste order is profoundly shaken due to the railroads, taverns, changing occupational stratification, education, etc. It has been impossible to introduce caste coaches on the railroads in the fashion of the American railroads and waiting rooms [to] segregate "white" from "colored".' Desegregation of upper castes from lower castes, violating the ritual purity of the former, would eventually dissolve the caste system, was Weber's belief.[4]

Finally, reacting to the events leading to the signing of the Poona Pact in 1932, Ambedkar wrote that as long as Untouchables (now Dalits) remained in the 'Hindu fold' they would never be allowed to throw off the shackles of their subjugation. So he called upon his people to renounce Hinduism in favour of any religion which gives them equality of status and treatment.[5] His famous statement, 'I was born a Hindu because I had no control over this but I shall not die a Hindu', is indicative of his belief that an exit from Hinduism was an exit from the inequality and lack of freedom Dalits suffer from in the caste system. What happened?

## Marx on Dissolution of Caste

Marx's anticipation of dissolution of caste did not come true in its entirety, mainly because while the introduction of the railways and new technology weakened the traditional unity of agriculture and manufacture by decimating the latter (for instance, the ruin of Indian textiles), it was not able to destroy the existing social relations of production in agriculture, the dominant occupation in the economy. This was because colonial rule was not totalizing. The colonial state was not all-powerful. It was too weak to break the hold of the dominant class (and caste) in the countryside— the class of landlords with monopoly of economic power, political power, juridical authority and cultural power.

To elaborate in brief, if one looks at the map of India during colonial rule, there were two Indias shown in two different colours: British India in red and 'Indian India' in yellow. Indian India, covering two-fifths of the territory and a quarter of the population, was outside the direct jurisdiction of the colonial state. It was the domain of princely states. In what I have called the colonial mode of historiography,[6] Indian India was characterized as 'Indirect Rule'. Indirect Rule, it has been argued, is a conceptual tool of the colonial mode of historiography insofar as it attributes all agency to the colonial state and metropolitan capital, divesting colonized peoples of any agency, making them passive recipients of the former. In reality, rather than being passive recipients, colonized peoples resisted encroachment on their traditional rights by the colonized state, forcing it to compromise and make allowances. It was only between 1848 and 1856 that the colonial state, under pressure from English political economists, tried to dispense with traditional landlords, who were appropriating the surplus from two-fifths of the territory, depriving the metropolitan capital of immense gain. Following the advice of the political economists of the time (the most famous being James Mill, who occupied a position of eminence on the board of governors of the East India Company, the chief colonizing agent and ruling power on behalf of England until 1958), traditional landlords were declared social parasites and had to be dispensed with in the 'interest of Indian people'. Between 1848 and 1856 the Company gobbled up the territories of a number of princes and landlords, the last one being the Nawab of Oudh, along with over 250 landlords, in 1856, which was the main factor behind the Great Revolt of 1857.[7]

In the aftermath of the revolt, the colonial state restored the traditional powers and authority—economic, political and juridical—of all landlords, declaring them 'natural leaders' of the countryside (the very same landlords who were earlier denounced as social parasites!) and never ever did the Crown or the colonial state even think of messing with the traditionally dominant class and caste in the countryside. As a result, social divisions based on unequal social relations of production, foundation of caste and the caste system survived not only in Indian India, but in the whole of India. These social relations were the main target of the widespread peasant revolts in different parts of India between the 1910s and the 1940s, leading to the decline of feudal landlords and the end of colonial rule, culminating in the abolition of landlordism and the accession of princely states to the Union of India in the 1950s, and the changing caste–class equation in the countryside.[8]

It is argued that the relevance or irrelevance of Marx—Marxism, to be precise—to caste is not to be seen in terms of Marx's anticipation of the results of British colonial rule for the dissolution of caste. It should rather be judged in terms of the ability of Marxism to reveal the intrinsic connection between material conditions (economic and political) and the ideology (system of ideas, values—religious and secular) of the caste system within a historical perspective, which is conspicuously missing in mainstream sociology shackled by an ideological commitment to the Weberian legacy. It is further argued that Ambedkar's understanding of caste and the conditions of its annihilation is closer to that of Weber rather than Marx. I turn to that in what follows.

## Marx: Caste Division of Labour

> When the crude form of the division of labour which is to be found among the Indians, and Egyptians calls forth the caste-system in their state and religion, the historian believes that the caste-system is the power which has produced this crude social form.[9]

In December 1846, in his letter to Pavel V. Annenkov about Proudhon's book *The Philosophy of Poverty*, Marx writes that Proudhon did not understand division of labour correctly as he assumed it to be the same at all times: 'But was not the caste regime also a particular division of labour? Was not the regime of the corporations another division of labour? And is not the division of labour under the system of manufacture, which in England begins about the middle of the seventeenth century and comes to an end in the last part of the eighteenth, also totally different from the division of labour in large-scale modern industry?' ('Marx to Pavel V. Annenkov in Paris, 28 December 1846').[10]

In *The Poverty of Philosophy*, Marx writes:

> Under the patriarchal system, under the caste system, under the feudal and corporative system, there was division of labor in the whole of society according to fixed rules. Were these rules established by a legislator? No. Originally born of the conditions of material production, they were raised to the status of laws only much later.[11]

The relationship between the material conditions and caste division of labour is explained by Marx in *A Contribution to the Critique of Political Economy*: 'Legislation may perpetuate land ownership in certain families, or allocate labour as a hereditary privilege, thus consolidating it into a caste system.'[12]

For Marx, the division of labour in caste is not the product of a religious idea invented by the Brahmin. Rather, like the division of labour in non–caste societies, it is the result of the process of production, where human beings apply their labour to modify nature for producing goods to satisfy their needs. More importantly, rules governing a particular form of division of labour appear only after that division of labour has actualized on the ground. Marx writes:

> . . . the conversion of fractional work into the life-calls of one man, corresponds to the tendency, shown by earlier societies, to make trades hereditary; either to petrify them into castes, or . . . to ossify them into guilds. Castes and guilds arise from the action of the same natural law that regulates the differentiation of plants and animals into species and varieties, excepting that, when a certain degree of development has been reached, the heredity of castes and exclusiveness of guilds are ordained as a law of society.[13]

It is followed by a long footnote:

> The arts also have . . . in Egypt reached the requisite degree of perfection. For it is the only country where artificers may not in any way meddle with

the affairs of another class of citizens, but must follow that calling alone which by law is hereditary in their clan . . . In other countries it is found tradesmen divide their attention between too many objects. At one time they try agriculture, at another . . . commerce, at another . . . two or three other occupations at once.[14]

The restriction on occupational mobility is treated by Marx as a lack of freedom on the part of labourers, perhaps a characteristic of traditional societies. He continues:

In free countries, they mostly frequent the assemblies of the people . . . In Egypt, on the contrary, every artificer is severely punished if he meddles with affairs of state, or carries on several trades at once . . . since, they inherit from their forefathers numerous rules, they are eager to discover fresh advantages.[15]

The rule of following one's hereditary occupation, as found in caste in India, or its equivalent in Egypt, is not necessarily a negative feature compared to the division of labour in manufacturing in the capitalist mode of production. Marx writes:

It is only the special skill accumulated from generation to generation, and transmitted from father to son, that gives to the Hindu, as it does to the spider, this proficiency. And yet the work of such a Hindu weaver is very complicated, compared with that of a manufacturing laborer.[16]

What is very clear in Marx is that the division of labour or occupational specialization is not a mental abstraction but a product of the interaction between human beings and their natural surroundings. Division of labour, including priesthood, is not sacred but profane, not in the realm of the religious but grounded in materiality. He writes:

It is the necessity of bringing a natural force under the control of society . . . by the work of man's hand, that first plays the decisive part in the history of industry . . . Examples are, irrigation works in Egypt . . . The necessity of predicting the rise and fall of the Nile created Egyptian astronomy, and with it the domination of priests, as directors of agriculture.[17]

Ranganayakamma notes, 'Just as we do not know why castes emerged only in India, it is not known why these restrictions of occupations and severe punishments were present in only Egypt. We can grasp no more than that division of labour assumed such a form there.'[18] In order to understand the role of material conditions of production in division of labour in the caste system, it is important to be reminded of the basic fact that upper castes monopolized the ownership and control of all means of production and means of subsistence of lower castes; they excluded the latter not only from access to land, the most important means of production and subsistence, but also from cultural resources, the most vital being education. Excluding lower castes from education and vocations based on education was, and continues to be, a central theme of the caste system. Exclusion of lower castes from education in the caste system lasted for a much longer period than the excluding of slaves from education in the West in antiquity and modernity combined. Slavery criminalized any attempt by slaves to educate themselves as much as any attempt by a non-slave trying to educate the former. What was crime in slavery in the West was turned into sin in the caste system (an exercise in mystification), sanctioned by the sacred texts of Hinduism—the *Manusmriti* being the most infamous—turning what was in the realm of the profane into the sacred. Ironically, the very same sacred texts that held that it is by education one becomes human—hence the gratitude to the guru in the Hindu social order was considered the highest—excluded lower castes from education by birth (à la Ekalavya and Dronacharya in the Mahabharata). Is it mere coincidence that far fewer sociologists ever took a critical stand on these sanctions by sacred texts of Hinduism, compared to their outrage on the provision of limited affirmative action (like caste-based reservations) for the very same historically dispossessed and excluded people to partly make up for the systemic injuries perpetuated over millennia?

Very much like the division of labour in the caste system, the division of labour in slavery (and serfdom) was determined by the material conditions of production, that is, the monopoly of productive resources by masters in slavery and lords in serfdom, making slaves and serfs dependent on the former for their very subsistence. The secret of the division of labour in slavery, serfdom and the caste system lies in social relations of production. The class that owns and controls the means of production does not labour, but appropriates the labour or the produce of labour by those who are dispossessed of the right to own and control the means of production and the means of their subsistence. It was so in slavery, serfdom and the caste system. Indian exceptionalism that caste-based division of labour is religious—a product of the Brahmin's imagination—the argument central to mainstream sociology, is a myth.

Ambedkar famously argued that what distinguishes the division of labour aspect in the caste system is that it entails not only a division of labour but also a division of labourers (a variant of Indian exceptionalism!). The division of labourers in caste is not unique, if we remember that labourers even in advanced capitalism are divided according to race, ethnicity, religious affiliation and nationality. The division among labourers in pre-capitalist social economic formations (which is relevant to caste) is even more serious. It is because of social isolation due to the pre-capitalist mode of production—self-sufficiency of production and consumption unmediated by the market, accentuated by the lack of means of transportation and communication—discussed by Marx in *Eighteenth Brumaire of Louis Bonaparte* in the context of the small peasant producers in France in the mid 19th century. Being socially isolated, small peasant producers were unable to see the commonality of their interest with other peasants in opposition to the interests of the ruling class on a national level, and were therefore unable to beget a political organization in order to enforce their class interests. It was so in spite of the objective conditions that made them a class. Overcoming the division of labourers in class or caste is part of a political and ideological struggle rather than being taken for granted as a natural consequence of the objective conditions, a fallacy of the mainstream sociology wrongly attributed to Marx and Marxism.

It may be noted that while focusing on the material conditions, Marx does not ignore the role of religion in social formation in India. In 'The British Rule in India', he writes:

> This strange combination of Italy and of Ireland, of a world of voluptuousness and of a world of woes, is anticipated in the ancient tradition of the religion of Hindustan. That religion is at once a religion of sensualist exuberance, and a religion of self-torturing asceticism, a religion of the Lingam, and of the Juggernaut, the religion of the Monk and of the Bayadere.[19]

The question that is crucial is how to understand the relevance or otherwise of Marx and Marxism to explain the intrinsic connection between the economic, political and cultural, including religious, aspects in the caste system in its historical perspective. It must be stressed that Marxism and Marxism alone is equipped to accomplish this task. Mainstream sociology, given its characteristic approach to atomize the economic, political and cultural and ignore history is singularly flawed. Rather than explaining the caste system, it has significantly contributed to the mystification of caste by focusing on its ritual and symbolic boundaries, overlooking the material conditions—the foundation of these boundaries that produced caste in the first place and reproduced them over millennia.

With no risk of exaggeration, it must be admitted that neither Marxists (a minority in caste studies) nor non-Marxists (read anti-Marxists), including those specializing in Dalit studies (an overwhelming majority of whom are non-Marxists or explicitly anti-Marxist), have seriously engaged with the role of ideology in the caste system. Marxists have focused on the role of economic and political factors in caste and the caste division of labour without critically engaging with the role of ideology—the dialectical relationship between material conditions and ideology—in caste and the caste system.[20] Non-Marxists, on the other hand, have focused on ideology in isolation from economic-political conditions in caste ahistorically, eternalizing the role of ideas—religious ideas in particular—in caste and the caste division of labour.[21] Hence, they display a tendency to look for the legitimacy of caste in ancient Hindu scriptures going back to the Rig Veda period when neither caste nor the material conditions of its existence were yet developed. It should be stressed that Marx and Marxism did not and do not ignore the role of ideas in socioeconomic formations, including caste. They only relate the ideas of a particular epoch in a particular social economic formation to its material conditions. Ideas relating to caste (and varna), division of labour, inequality, exploitation and discrimination are not static. They change according to changing material conditions. That is what is missing in the mainstream and, by and large, in Dalit studies. Marxism fills in the gap.

A word about religion and caste. In brief, religion—religious ideas and rituals—plays an important role in shaping caste consciousness, the subjective dimension of caste. Is caste consciousness a mere reflection of the material reality of caste? Yes and no. Yes, insofar as the dominant castes use religious ideas and rituals and their agents—*pandas, pujaris, mahants* and yogis—to legitimize and mystify the existing social relations between upper and lower castes. These caste relations are rooted in the social relations of production and power which the dominant castes try to present as consensual, harmonious and interdependent. Do lower castes accept these ideas presenting caste as consensual and normal? Empirically rooted historical studies show that they don't. In many cases, they are not even aware of these ideas, which should come as no surprise, considering that lawgivers of caste prescribed the exclusion of lower castes from access to religious ideas and rituals enshrined in sacred Hindu scriptures that mainstream sociology and by default Dalit studies hold as the very essence of caste and the caste division of labour. The common refrain of mainstream sociology (including, regrettably, many in Dalit studies) is that Marxism with its emphasis on class is obsolete. It must be stressed to the contrary that if anything, Marxism and class analysis are indispensable in the current political ideological climate of the return of the mandir and masjid to the centre stage of political theatre in India (for return of the mandir to Indian politics, see Teltumbde[22]). For the demystification of caste, Marxism and Marxism alone provides an alternative to mainstream sociology which has singularly failed to understand and explain caste and the caste system.

To sum up, for Marx, the division of labour in the caste system is rooted in the social relations of production and property, legitimized by ideology—religious and secular. The social relations of production in caste were and continue to remain unequal and exploitative, necessitating extra-economic coercion exercised by the dominant caste, enabled by the monopoly of political–juridical power. The annihilation of caste and caste inequality is contingent on the annihilation of the unequal social relations of production restricting Dalits' access to the means of production and the means of their subsistence, political power and cultural resources, including education. As noted above, Marx's anticipation of dissolution of caste due to British rule in India did not come true in entirety for the reasons discussed above. Notwithstanding that, the Marxist perspective to see the intrinsic connection between the division of labour in caste, material conditions and ideology in the historical context is valid and relevant to understanding caste in the past as much as in contemporary times.

## Weber: Caste as Status

Distinguishing class from status is considered Max Weber's seminal contribution. According to Weber, status groups, unlike classes, are normally communities. As opposed to the 'purely economically determined class situation', status is determined by social honour. Property as such is not always recognized as a status qualification. Both the propertied and non-propertied may belong to the same status group. Caste as status is distinct from other status groups (master–slave or lord–serf). This is so since usurpation in the caste system is religious, in addition to being customary and legal. That sets caste apart from other status groups where usurpation is legal and customary.[23] What is often ignored is that in distinguishing status from class, Weber reduces class to purely economic terms—which is a distortion—and status, albeit caste, is seen as purely cultural in contrast to class. Ironically, Weberian sociologists turn it around to argue that it is in Marxism that class is purely economic! It must be noted that in Marxism, class—rooted in the social relations of production—is economic, political and cultural. It is economic insofar as it is based on one's relationship to the means of production and the means of subsistence, which may be disadvantageous. It is political insofar as unequal social relations of production are inevitably exploitative and coercive, and require monopoly of political power to maintain and reproduce them. Finally, they need control of cultural power to legitimize the existing social relations of production and the exploitation and coercion inherent in these relations. Separating economic power, political power and cultural power in class and status (caste) is myth-making.

Status stratification is opposed to stratification by market (the latter being the characteristic of class). Weber writes:

> The principle at work is that the market is restricted, *and the power of naked property per se, which gives its stamp to 'class formation'* is pushed into the background [emphasis added]. Where stratification by status permeates (antiquity and the Middle Ages), one can never speak of a genuinely free market competition, as we understand it today.[24]

Every rational economic pursuit, especially entrepreneurial activity, is looked upon as a disqualification of status. The market and its processes know no personal distinctions, only functional interests. If mere economic acquisition and naked economic power bearing the stigma of extra-status origin could bestow upon anyone the same honour as enjoyed by those who have earned it by virtue of style of life, the status order would be threatened to its very core. Precisely because of the rigorous reaction against the claim of property per se, the 'parvenu' is never accepted, without reservations, by the privileged status group. However, a succeeding generation of the 'parvenu' faces little resistance to acceptance by the status group. Having been educated in the conventions of their status group, they are easily assimilated provided that they have never besmirched status by their own economic labour.[25]

What Weber is saying is that in contrast to class, which develops in a market society (read capitalism), status belongs to pre-capitalist social formations. As such, success by one's own labour, which is the very essence of bourgeois (capitalist) ideology, is derided in status society. Weber's argument about education in the convention of the status group as a condition of admission and acceptance is well taken. The pre-eminent condition for that, however, is stabilization of the economic position, which makes training in the convention of status necessary and possible. Slave and serf could not be educated in the convention of the master and the lord. A landless labourer—invariably a lower caste—could not be educated in the convention of the Brahmin whose status qualification was to abstain from physical labour to earn his subsistence, while for the former engaging in physical labour was the very precondition of his survival.

It may be added that with the development of private property in the means of production came the distinction between physical labour and mental labour, the former associated with 'negative honour' and the latter with 'positive honour', to use Weber's terminology. The former, dispossessed of the means of their subsistence, had to engage in physical labour in order to survive—a disqualification to train in the convention of the latter. In Weber, positive honour and negative honour are culturally independent of economic and political power. In real history, positive honour and negative honour are precisely consequences of access to or denial of economic power and political power. Negative honour attached to lower castes was not a case of Indian exceptionalism rooted in Hinduism. Rather, it should be treated as a culturally specific case of the general rule of private property in the means of production.

## Weber: Division of Labour in Caste as Religious

Weber looks to the *Manuhhasya* to find the secret of caste and the caste system. Caste as a status group has a specific feature that makes it rather distinct from other types of status groups:

> Status distinctions in caste are guaranteed not only by conventions and laws, but also by rituals. This occurs in such a way that every physical contact between members of higher and lower castes results in ritualistic impurity (of the former)—a stigma that must be expiated by a religious act.[26]

Weber's view of caste is religious—a creation of Hinduism—and Brahmin-centric.

> Caste is a characteristic only of Hinduism . . . Caste, that is, the ritual rights and duties it imposes, and the position of the Brahmans, is the fundamental institution of Hinduism. Without caste there is no Hindu.[27]

He writes further:

> Caste is, and remains essentially social rank . . . by its very nature, caste
> is inseparably bound up with social ranks within a larger community . . .
> social rank in caste is determined with reference to Brahmans—the
> determination of the social rank of the castes by the social distance from
> other castes, and ultimately from the Brahman . . . in the last analysis,
> a rank position is determined by the nature of its positive or negative
> relation to the Brahman.[28]

Louis Dumont makes religion—Hinduism—the very essence of caste,
reducing caste hierarchy to an opposition of pure (Brahmin) and impure
(Untouchable). He argues that '. . . preoccupation with the pure and the
impure is constant in Hindu life'.[29] He admits that the opposition between
pure and impure is not the 'foundation' (within quotes in the original) of
society except in the intellectual sense of the term; it is by implicit reference
to this opposition that caste appears consistent and rational to those who live
in it. Opposition between pure and impure

> is manifested in some macroscopic form in the contrast between the two
> extreme categories: Brahmans and Untouchables. The Brahmans, being in
> principle priests, occupy the supreme rank with respect to the whole set of
> castes. The Untouchables, as very impure servants, are segregated outside
> the villages proper, in distinct hamlets (or at least distinct quarters). The
> Untouchables may not use the same wells as the others . . . access to Hindu
> temples was forbidden to them [and] numerous other disabilities . . . [I]n
> the setting of the opposition between pure and impure, the religious
> division of labour goes hand in hand with the permanent attribution to
> certain professions of a certain level of impurity.[30]

The religious nature of caste hierarchy stressed by Dumont finds strong
support among several scholars of caste. In the majority of societies it is
religion that provides the view of the whole. Hence, the ranking of castes in
India must be religious.[31] The unity of identity and difference—the unity of
purity and pollution—provides adequate grounds for defining the totality of
caste relations as a system.[32] On the contrary, as Dipankar Gupta has argued,
lower castes reject not only the opposition of purity–impurity as the basis
of occupational hierarchy in the caste system, but also the idea that upper
castes are pure.[33] Purity–impurity as the basis of occupational hierarchy in

the caste division of labour is strongly refuted by Berreman, among many others.[34]

The trouble with mainstream sociologists is that even when they write about political-economic dimensions, including the struggle for economic-political power that is central to the daily reality of caste in contemporary India as it was in the past, they continue to maintain that caste is status in the Weberian sense, that is, a cultural phenomenon exclusive of economic-political power. Weber's distinction between status and class rooted in cultural and economic power, respectively, was an ideological exercise, disconnecting the cultural from the economic and political, reducing class to purely economic terms and classifying caste as status, that is, cultural, albeit religious, in contrast to class. Uncritical acceptance of the Weberian position in mainstream sociology on caste mystifies caste. This is because the basis of caste hierarchy and its internal contradictions—rooted in the social relations of production—are a consequence of the intersection of the economic, political and cultural. It was so in the past. It is so in the present. To separate caste from the economic and political and see it purely or primarily as cultural, albeit religious, is a Weberian legacy. It is an obstacle to understanding caste and the conditions of its annihilation.

To sum up, as per the Weberian path to the annihilation of caste, the toilets in the Indian railways, notwithstanding the violence to the ritual purity of the upper caste they might have caused, did not dissolve caste. They could not. We may be reminded that upper castes were accustomed to violating their purity on their own by getting physically close to the very 'impure' bodies of Untouchables on a daily basis—that is, sexual contact between pure caste men and impure caste women—and purifying themselves by taking a terminal bath, the water for which was drawn from wells dug by the very same Untouchables.

In Weber, supremacy of the Brahmin owing to his ritual status is assumed a priori. In the real history of caste, supremacy of the Brahmin was not universal. As anthropological studies from the 1950s onwards demonstrate, Brahmins were not always, not everywhere, the dominant caste. Instead, it was the caste with the dominant position in ownership of land—the main form of property and the chief means of subsistence for the majority—that was dominant in a particular region at a particular time, for instance, the Rajputs in Rajasthan and many parts of Uttar Pradesh, Bihar and Madhya Pradesh until the end of the 1940s, the Jats in Haryana and Punjab, and the Marathas in Maharashtra. Brahmins held the dominant position in West

Bengal and parts of south India, mainly because of their dominant status in landownership, in addition to their ritual status. Ritual status alone was not sufficient and enough to make Brahmins the dominant caste at all places all the time.[35] More significantly, as Irfan Habib points out, the supremacy of the Brahmin was by no means essential for the continuance of the caste system.[36] Paraphrasing Marx, the Brahmin-centric view of caste is standing on its head. It is time to turn it upside down.

## Ambedkar: Caste as Essentially Religious

Between Marx and Weber, Ambedkar's understanding of caste and its annihilation is closer to the latter—that is, caste as essentially religious. Hence, the religious route to the annihilation of caste.

> One may join issue on every one of these premises on which rests the Socialists' case for economic reform having priority over every other kind of reform. One may contend that economic motive is not the only motive by which man is actuated. That economic power is the only kind of power no student of human society can accept. That the social status of an individual by itself often becomes a source of power and authority is made clear by the sway which the Mahatmas have held over the common man.[37]

See the similarity between Ambedkar above and Weber below:

> Economically conditioned power is not identical with 'power' as such . . . Man does not strive for power only to enrich himself, but frequently so also for social honour. Now, not all power entails social honour . . . In general, 'mere' economic power is by no means a recognized source of social honour. To the contrary, social honour may even be (and has been) the basis of economic and political power.[38]

It is interesting to note that Ambedkar never cites Weber. It is possible to imagine that two thinkers (here Weber and Ambedkar), sharing a common ideological premise, arrive at similar generalizations while remaining unaware of each other.

Like Weber, Ambedkar treats ritual purity and impurity as the very essence of the caste system. Accordingly, he is amused that common toilets in the Indian railways bringing the touchable-pure and Untouchable-impure castes in physical contact have not broken caste, ending caste discrimination, including untouchability. He wrote:

> It must be a source of silent amusement to many a non-Hindu to find hundreds and thousands of Hindus breaking caste on certain occasions, such as railway journeys and foreign travel, and yet endeavoring to maintain caste for the rest of their lives.[39]

As noted above, Hindus were 'breaking' caste routinely through more intimate physical contact between high-caste men and lower-caste women rather than breaking caste due to casual contact on certain occasions like railway travel. Violations of the rules of ritual purity and impurity were always rectified by rituals, so long as the material foundation of caste hierarchy was shielded by the existing production and property relations.

Alluding to the essentially religious character of caste, Ambedkar, like Weber, argued that caste is peculiar to Hinduism. He wrote:

> although there are castes among Non-Hindus, as there are among Hindus, caste has not the same social significance for Non-Hindus as it has for Hindus. Ask Mohammedan or a Sikh, who he is? He tells you that he is a Mohammedan or a Sikh as the case may be. He does not tell you his caste although he has one and you are satisfied with his answer. When he tells you that he is a Muslim, you do not proceed to ask him whether he is a Shiya or a Suni; Sheikh or Saiyad; Khatik or Pinjari. When he tells you he is a Sikh, you do not ask him whether he is Jat or Roda; Mazbi or Ramdasi. But you are not satisfied, if a person tells you that he is a Hindu. You feel bound to inquire into his caste. Why? Because so essential is caste in the case of a Hindu that without knowing it you do not feel sure what sort of a being he is. That caste has not the same social significance among Non-Hindus as it has among Hindus is clear if you take into consideration the consequences which follow breach of caste. There may be castes among Sikhs and Mohammedans but the Sikhs and the Mohammedans will not outcast a Sikh or a Mohammedan if he broke his caste. Indeed, the very idea of excommunication is foreign to the Sikhs and the Mohammedans. But with the Hindus the case is entirely different. He is sure to be outcasted if he broke caste. This shows the difference in the social significance of caste to Hindus and Non-Hindus. This is the second point of difference. But there is also a third and a more important one. Caste among the non-Hindus has no religious consecration; but

among the Hindus most decidedly it has. Among the Non-Hindus, caste
is only a practice, not a sacred institution.[40]

In an idealist approach, caste is a creation of religion. In reality, rooted
in production and property relations and enforced by coercion, caste is
profane. The twin myths that there is no caste without Hinduism, and there
is no Hinduism without caste, central to the idealist view, tend to mystify
caste by masking the real basis of caste, which lies in political economy.
Caste is not sacred, but profane.

Ambedkar wrote that caste will cease to be an operational force only
when inter-dining and intermarriage have become matters of common
course. A large majority of Hindus do not inter-dine or intermarry,
because intermarriage and inter-dining are contrary to their beliefs rooted
in religious, albeit sacred, scriptures. He argued, 'Caste is a notion, it is a
state of the mind. The destruction of Caste does not therefore mean the
destruction of a physical barrier. It means a notional change.'[41]

To the contrary, caste in the real world is more than an idea, more than
a state of mind, and the destruction of caste more than a notional change.
Caste is not mental, but material. Changing the notion without changing the
material conditions, which produced and reproduced caste over millennia, will
*not* annihilate caste. Changing the material conditions, most importantly, the
control of the means of production by the dominant caste(s) and dependence
of lower castes for their very subsistence on the former, is the only way to
realistically imagine the destruction of caste. The rest is fantasy.

## Epilogue: Ambedkar's Legacy

To conclude, I want to make two brief points in connection with Ambedkar's
lasting legacy. One, having been in existence over millennia, caste has been
normalized as the common sense of social life in India. Interrogating caste as
the norm, in theory and in practice, caste as common sense, as the vantage
point to look at society and the individual is a prerequisite, a necessary first
step to fight for annihilation of caste. Ambedkar took that necessary first
step: he interrogated caste as the norm, as the common sense of dominant
discourse and daily intercourse.

Two, at the Mahad Conference in 1928, Ambedkar said:

The responsibility of establishing equality by abolishing untouchability
that we have taken upon our heads must be discharged only by ourselves.

It will not be possible for others to do it . . . In order to remove obstacles from the path of our progress, we must take this responsibility on our head.[42]

Commitment to the continued struggle by Dalits for the abolition of untouchability and the establishment of equality between castes is as urgent today as it was in the 1920s, when Ambedkar made the above declaration. It may be added that the abolition of untouchability and the establishment of equality between castes cannot and should not be left to Dalits alone. Taking a leaf from the civil rights movement of the US in the 1960s, where Whites from the north and the south joined Blacks under the latter's leadership in their fight against racial inequality, non-Dalits must join Dalits under the latter's leadership for the abolition of untouchability and the establishment of caste equality.

## References

Marx, Karl. 1975. *Capital, Volume I.* Moscow: Progress Publishers.

Marx, Karl and Friedrich Engels. 1975. *Selected Correspondence.* Moscow: Progress Publishers.

Singh, Hira. 2014. *Recasting Caste: From the Sacred to the Profane.* New Delhi: Sage.

# DR AMBEDKAR AND THE FUTURE OF INDIAN DEMOCRACY[1]

## Jean Drèze

A few years ago, when a student from Delhi University asked Noam Chomsky what he thought about Indian democracy, Chomsky replied (echoing Gandhi's view of Western civilization) that 'it would be a good idea'. Had Dr Ambedkar been present, I am sure that he would have agreed. Indeed, Indian democracy today is a faint shadow of the hopes he had for it. He was well aware, of course, that his hopes might be dashed.

The future of Indian democracy depends a great deal on the revival of Ambedkar's visionary conception of democracy. This vision, I believe, also needs to be enlarged and updated in the light of recent experience.

## Liberty, Equality and Solidarity

The ultimate idea of democracy is often taken to be 'government of the people, by the people and for the people'. Ambedkar referred to this idea from time to time, but it does not seem to be his preferred definition of democracy, and it is worth reflecting on why this might be so. One possible reason is that for Ambedkar democracy was not just a form of government but also a way of life, or, as he put it, 'a mode of associated living'. Aside from this, defining democracy as 'government of the people, by the people and for the people' raises a troubling question—what kind of people are we talking about? Are they rational or irrational? Are they tolerant or intolerant? Are they equal or divided into castes? Are they compassionate or full of hatred? All this has an important bearing on what we might expect from government 'by the people'. For instance, what would that mean in a caste-ridden society? Ambedkar strongly felt that caste and democracy were incompatible, and that a plausible vision of democracy would have to include the annihilation of caste.[2]

Ambedkar's vision of democracy was closely related to his ideal of a 'good society'. He was clear about this ideal: on many occasions, he stated that he envisaged a good society as one based on 'liberty, equality and fraternity' (today we might prefer to call this 'liberty, equality and solidarity'). Democracy, as he saw it, was both the end and the means of this ideal. It was the end because he ultimately considered democracy as coterminous with the realization of liberty, equality and fraternity. At the same time, democracy was also the means through which this ideal was to be attained. Indeed, Ambedkar had great faith in the power of democratic practice. Among other inspiring definitions of the term, he once described democracy as 'a form and a method of government whereby revolutionary changes in the economic and social life of the people are brought about without bloodshed'.[3]

The expression 'liberty, equality, fraternity' goes back to the French Revolution. Ambedkar did not invent it, but nor did he adopt it lightly. The fundamental importance of liberty, equality and solidarity (and the relation between the three) was explained with characteristic clarity in three short sentences in one of his best-known speeches—his stirring address to the Constituent Assembly on 25 November 1949. He said:

> Without equality, liberty would produce the supremacy of the few over the many. Equality without liberty would kill individual initiative. Without fraternity, liberty and equality could not become a natural course of things.

These are prophetic words. At the risk of some simplification, they can be read as a forewarning of what would happen in capitalist countries, where equality was sacrificed for the sake of liberty, and in communist countries, where liberty was suppressed in the name of equality. They also indicate a way forward, whereby solidarity makes it possible to reconcile liberty and equality.

We can put this another way, building on the contrast between three basic modes of human association: coercion, competition and cooperation. Coercion is an infringement of liberty. Competition often undermines equality. Cooperation (more precisely, voluntary cooperation) is one way of reconciling liberty and equality, but it requires a certain amount of fraternity or solidarity. A good society, in this view, would be one based as much as possible on voluntary cooperation rather than coercion or competition. The scope for cooperation, however, depends on our ability to cultivate a spirit of solidarity not only within narrow circles such as the family but also in society at large. How far it is possible to foster values of solidarity is, I believe, one of the fundamental questions of our times.

Coming back to democracy, one implication of Ambedkar's broad view of it (as a state of liberty, equality and solidarity) is that the requirements of democracy are quite exacting. They go far beyond putting in place democratic institutions such as an electoral system and an independent judiciary. For instance, Ambedkar felt that democracy is not possible without ethics or what he called 'morality'—I shall return to that. Similarly, he often insisted that political democracy had to be linked with economic and social democracy. Here is one illustration:

> . . . political democracy cannot succeed where there is no social or economic democracy [. . .] Social and economic democracy are the tissues and the fibre of a political democracy. The tougher the tissue and the fibre, the greater the strength of the body . . . Parliamentary democracy developed a passion for liberty. It never made a nodding acquaintance with equality. It failed to realize the significance of equality and did not even endeavour to strike a balance between liberty and equality, with the result that liberty swallowed equality and has made democracy a name and a farce.[4]

This was a comment on the collapse of democracy in some European countries (such as Germany and Italy) at that time, but the critical importance of social and economic democracy was a recurring theme in Ambedkar's writings and speeches. In the speech quoted earlier, for instance, he argued that in order to 'maintain democracy not merely in form, but also in fact', we must 'make our political democracy a social democracy as well'. This idea, however, was quietly buried soon after his death and the democratic project in India was reduced to political democracy. This is one aspect of Ambedkar's political philosophy that needs to be revived today, even if we take a different view of the means that can be used to bring about economic and social democracy. Before elaborating on this, let me add a few words on other requirements of democracy as Ambedkar understood it.

## Rationality and Liberation

Ambedkar's passion for democracy was closely related to his commitment to rationality and the scientific outlook. At an obvious level, rationality is necessary for democratic government since public debate (an essential form of democratic practice) is impossible in the absence of a shared adherence to common sense, logical argument and critical enquiry. Rational thinking is even more relevant if we adopt Ambedkar's broad view of democracy as a state of liberty, equality and solidarity. Indeed, rationality is conducive if not indispensable to the realization of these ideals. A person who is deprived of liberty can afford to be irrational, since he or she is not in command in any case. But if we are to take control of our lives, rationality and a scientific outlook are essential.

There is also a close affinity between rationality and equality. For one thing, propaganda and manipulation are common tools of subjugation. The caste system, for instance, has been propped over the centuries by an elaborate edifice of irrational dogmas. The scientific outlook is essential to liberate and protect oneself from ideological manipulation. For another, the scientific spirit has a strong anti-authoritarian dimension. Authority rests on the notion that one person's view or wish counts more than another's. In scientific argument, this is not the case. What counts is the coherence of the argument and the strength of the evidence. In that sense, the scientific outlook is a protection against the arbitrary exercise of power.

Even fraternity (read solidarity), once defined by Ambedkar as 'a sentiment which leads an individual to identify himself with the good of others', has something to do with rationality.[5] Indeed, rational enquiry can be of great help in dispelling the prejudices that divide and oppose human beings. Science can also have a unifying influence in human affairs: the delights of scientific enquiry can be universally shared, irrespective of race, nationality, religion or other identities. As Bertrand Russell (1945) observed, 'in the welter of conflicting fanaticisms, one of the few unifying forces is scientific truthfulness'.

There is a view that reason and science are 'Western' notions, alien to the people of India, who have their own modes of knowledge. This view is bound to astonish anyone who has paid attention to the Buddha's teachings. Many centuries before Descartes, Buddha urged his followers to use their reason and think critically. In *Buddha or Karl Marx* Ambedkar includes the following in his summary of the essential teachings of the Buddha: 'Everyone has a right to learn. Learning is as necessary for man to live as food is . . .

Nothing is infallible. Nothing is binding forever. Everything is subject to inquiry and examination.'

This is not to deny that there are other modes of knowledge than rational argument and scientific discourse. That is the case not only in India but all over the world. For instance, no amount of rational argument can convey what a jasmine flower smells like. Direct experience is indispensable. Similarly, if you hold the hand of a child who has been wounded in a drone attack, you may learn something about the nature of war that no amount of scientific information on 'collateral damage' is likely to convey. In *The Buddha and His Dhamma*, his last book, Ambedkar gives a fine account of the distinction between *vidya* (knowledge) and *prajna* (insight). In the step from vidya to prajna, non-scientific modes of learning often play an important role. But this does not detract from the fundamental importance of rationality in individual enlightenment and social living.

One reason for bringing this up is that recent threats to Indian democracy include a concerted attack on rationality and the scientific spirit. This is one aspect of the Hindutva movement. This movement, I believe, can be interpreted as a sort of 'revolt of the higher castes': an attempt to reassert the traditional authority of the upper castes, threatened as it is by the expansion of political democracy in independent India. This reassertion of Brahminical authority in the garb of Hindu unity or even national unity involves a suppression of rational thinking and critical enquiry. That is the real significance of the seemingly irrational statements and actions of many political leaders of the saffron variety: the call for teaching astrology in universities, the substitution of myths for history, the search for Lord Ram's 'authentic' birthplace, the handover of research institutions to certified obscurantists, and so on. I doubt that Mr Murli Manohar Joshi really cared for the inclusion of astrology in the university curriculum when he was in charge of the Ministry of Human Resource Development, but what he possibly did care for was the nurturing of a spirit of submission to Brahminical obscurantism. Resisting this and other attacks on rationality is an important requirement of the defence of democracy in India today.

## Morality and Social Order

Aside from rationality, Ambedkar felt that democracy required ethics, or what he called morality. One aspect of this is the importance of 'constitutional morality', that is, of abiding by the spirit of the Constitution and not just its legal provisions. Going beyond this, Ambedkar felt that morality, in the sense of social ethics, was indispensable for the realization of liberty and equality. In the absence of morality, he thought, there were only two alternatives: anarchy or the police.

Among many other criticisms of the caste system, Ambedkar argued that it undermines social ethics and morality. In *Annihilation of Caste*, he wrote:

> The effects of caste on the ethics of the Hindus is simply deplorable. Caste has killed public spirit. Caste has destroyed the sense of public charity. Caste has made public opinion impossible. A Hindu's public is his caste [. . .] Virtue has become caste-ridden and morality has become caste-bound.

Ambedkar's emphasis on morality was well integrated with his commitment to rationality and the scientific spirit. In particular, he considered that morality was always subject to rational scrutiny. His attraction to Buddhism has to be seen in the light of his twin commitments to morality and reason. Not only did he regard the Buddha's Dhamma as compatible with (indeed committed to) reason, he also saw it as an expression of the ideal of 'liberty, equality and fraternity'. At one point, he stated that this ideal of his derived directly 'from the teachings of my master, the Buddha'. Towards the end of his life, he even seems to have nurtured the hope that Dhamma would become a universal code of social ethics.

In retrospect, Ambedkar's vision of Dhamma becoming a universal code of ethics was perhaps a little naive. I would even suggest that his devotion to the Buddha's teachings occasionally jarred with his commitment to critical enquiry and independence of mind. Having said this, his recognition of social ethics as an essential ingredient of democracy has not lost its relevance. If democracy is just political competition between self-interested individuals (as in, say, the median voter model), it will never succeed in bringing about liberty, equality and fraternity. In particular, it will never do justice to minority interests.

To illustrate, consider the problem of urban destitution in India—the plight of wandering beggars, street children, leprosy patients, the homeless and others. These people constitute a small minority and they have no political power whatsoever (most of them do not even vote). Nor are they likely to have any in the foreseeable future. This is the main reason why the problem remains almost entirely unaddressed. If this problem is to come within the ambit of democratic politics (and there are signs that this is beginning to happen), it can only be on the basis of ethical concern. This illustration pertains to a relatively confined aspect of India's social problems, but the potential reach of ethical concerns in democratic politics is very wide. If social ethics acquire a central role in democratic politics, a new world may come into view.

## Democracy and Socialism

Let me now return to Dr Ambedkar's fundamental concern with the link between political, social and economic democracy. As he saw it, political democracy alone would not go very far if glaring economic and social inequalities remained. A well-known expression of this concern was his historic speech to the Constituent Assembly, already quoted earlier:

> On the 26th January 1950, we are going to enter into a life of contradictions. In politics we will have equality and in social and economic life we will have inequality [. . .] How long shall we continue to live this life of contradictions? How long shall we continue to deny equality in our social and economic life? If we continue to deny it for long, we will do so only by putting our political democracy in peril.

Ambedkar's diagnosis raised the question of how this contradiction was to be removed. Since he had distanced himself in the same speech from extra-constitutional methods (including not only violence but also satyagraha), the answer presumably lay in democratic practice. However, Ambedkar himself warned that in an unequal society the democratic process might be captured by the privileged and powerful. Here is one expression of this fear:

> [It is a] hard fact of history that in every country there exist two classes—the governing class and the servile class between whom there is a continuous struggle for power [. . .] adult suffrage and frequent elections are no bar against [the] governing class reaching places of power and authority.[6]

At one stage, Ambedkar's answer to this contradiction was a socialist Constitution—a Constitution that would 'dislodge the governing class from its position' as he once described the 'principal aim' of a democratic Constitution. A socialist Constitution, he thought, would restrain economic disparities and enable the realization of economic and social democracy along with political democracy. His blueprint for a socialist Constitution was presented in 'States and Minorities', an early memorandum submitted to the

Constituent Assembly. This blueprint included constitutional protection for socialist principles such as state ownership of land and key industries.

In retrospect, this memorandum looks a little simplistic in some important respects. For instance, one would hesitate to advocate 'collective farming' with the same confidence today, in the light of recent evidence. However, this does not detract from the value of the larger idea of a socialist Constitution, helping to reconcile social and economic democracy with political democracy.[7] And some aspects of Ambedkar's blueprint are still relevant today.

Whatever its merits, Ambedkar's proposal of a socialist Constitution was a political non-starter. It had little chance of being accepted by the Constituent Assembly, where privileged interests were well represented. However, Ambedkar did not abandon the idea of constitutional safeguards for social and economic democracy. Ultimately, these were embodied in the Directive Principles of the Indian Constitution, which deal with a wide range of economic and social rights. The Directive Principles are indeed far-reaching, if one takes them seriously, as Ambedkar explained during the Constituent Assembly debates:

> In my judgment, the directive principles have a great value, for they lay down that our ideal is economic democracy [. . .] [Our] object in framing this Constitution is really two-fold: (i) to lay down the form of political democracy, and (ii) to lay down that our ideal is economic democracy and also to prescribe that every Government [. . .] shall strive to bring about economic democracy.[8]

As it turned out, however, the Directive Principles were not taken seriously in independent India. They were not enforceable in a court of law, and nor did electoral politics succeed in holding the state accountable to their realization, as Ambedkar had envisaged. We are left with a lopsided democracy, where reasonably sound institutions of political democracy coexist with fundamentally undemocratic social conditions. Contrary to Ambedkar's expectations, democracy in independent India has neither flourished nor perished. Instead, it has limped along, burdened by the 'contradiction' he had identified, which is still with us today.

## The Future of Indian Democracy

How would Dr Ambedkar feel about Indian democracy today, if he were able to take a look at it? Quite likely, he would be very disappointed.

He would certainly be appalled to find that the caste system, with all its horrors, is still alive. He would be dismayed, for instance, to hear that only 5 per cent of marriages today are inter-caste marriages, or that the majority of Brahmins admit to practising untouchability.[9] He would be equally dismayed by the continued subjugation of women in Indian society, and by other social inequalities that undermine democracy as he understood it. Political democracy did survive in some fashion, but social and economic democracy is still a distant goal. In fact, even political democracy is not in the pink of health. Old aberrations (the first-past-the-post system, a very odd notion of secularism, a series of anti-democratic laws, gross human rights violations, to cite a few) are yet to go away. Meanwhile, Indian democracy is facing new challenges, including extreme economic inequality, creeping authoritarianism, big-ticket corruption, the rapid growth of corporate power and the resurgence of Hindu majoritarianism—the biggest threat to democracy in India according to Ambedkar.

Having said this, there are also positive trends, in the form of the growth of democratic space and democratic spirit. A startling variety of social movements have flourished in India, and creative initiatives strive to expand the boundaries of political democracy year after year. The quality of Indian democracy is also gradually enhanced by a better representation of women in politics, wider opportunities for people's involvement in local governance and the spread of education among disadvantaged groups. The most encouraging trend is the growing participation of the underprivileged in democratic processes.

As discussed earlier, Ambedkar had a visionary conception of democracy, which needs to be rediscovered today. But going beyond that, we must also enlarge this vision in the light of recent developments. While Ambedkar was ahead of his time in stressing the link between political and economic democracy, perhaps he failed to anticipate the full scope of political democracy itself. Indeed, he thought of political democracy mainly in terms of electoral and parliamentary processes. Today, however, we are constantly discovering new forms of democratic practice, in which people are often able to participate, even if economic democracy is nowhere near being realized.

The basis of economic democracy also needs some rethinking with a little help from the libertarian socialist tradition. Ambedkar pinned his hopes for economic democracy mainly on state action: collectivization of agriculture, state ownership of key industries, central planning, and so on. This is understandable, considering that the developmental state seemed to have enormous potential at that time, not only in the Soviet Union but also in much of the developing world. However, the limits—indeed dangers—of state control of the means of production have now become clearer. At the same time, there is also greater clarity about the scope for expanding economic democracy through other means, such as worker management, producer cooperatives, non-profit associations, participatory planning and community control of environmental resources. The battle for economic democracy is far from lost but it requires a different approach from that envisaged by Ambedkar.

The state, of course, still has a role to play—for instance, by ensuring universal access to basic services and facilities. Among other 20th-century developments that were not fully anticipated by Ambedkar is the growth of the welfare state (for want of a better term) around the world. A significant proportion of the world population today lives in countries where healthcare, elementary education, social security and other basic services are guaranteed to everyone as a matter of right. These entitlements, aside from helping to eliminate poverty and insecurity, also create significant spheres of equality or at least relative equality in social life. This is one of the great achievements of the last century. It is also an example of how democratic struggles can bring about 'revolutionary changes in the economic and social life of the people', as Ambedkar put it. There is an important lesson here for India, where equality is still confined to the polling booth—in all other spheres of private and public life (even in jail), graded inequality is the norm.

To conclude, we have every reason to reassert the need to link political democracy with economic and social democracy, and the possibility of doing so. Indian democracy is still relatively young—seventy years is not a long time to make the transition from a society geared to the privileges of a small minority to one governed 'by the people for the people'. Ambedkar's thought is an invaluable guide on this unfinished journey. But it would be just as counterproductive to claim that he had the final word on democracy as to say that Marx had the final word on class. It would also be an insult to his appeal for critical thinking. The best way we can respond to this appeal is to enrich Ambedkar's profound ideas and insights with those of other schools of thought.

# References

Ambedkar, B.R. 1936. *Annihilation of Caste*, vol. 1 (self-published). Reprinted in Government of Maharashtra 1979–98.

Ambedkar, B.R. 1945. *What Congress and Gandhi Have Done to the Untouchables*, vol. 9. Mumbai: Thacker and Co. Reprinted in Government of Maharashtra 1979–98.

Ambedkar, B.R. 1948. 'States and Minorities: What Are Their Rights and How to Secure them in the Constitution of Free India, vol. 1.' Memorandum on the Safeguards for the Scheduled Castes submitted to the Constituent Assembly on behalf of the All India Scheduled Caste Federation. Reprinted in Government of Maharashtra, 1979–98.

Ambedkar, B.R. 25 November 1949. Speech to the Constituent Assembly. Reprinted in Government of Maharashtra, 1979–98.

Ambedkar, B.R. 1952. Conditions Precedent for the Successful Working of Democracy. Speech delivered at the Poona District Law Library. Reprinted in Bhagwan Das, 2010.

Ambedkar, B.R. 1957. *The Buddha and His Dhamma*, vol. 11. Bombay: People's Education Society. Reprinted in Government of Maharashtra, 1979–98.

Das, Bhagwan, ed. 2010. *Thus Spoke Ambedkar*. New Delhi: Navayana.

Government of Maharashtra. 1979–98. *Dr. Babasaheb Ambedkar: Writings and Speeches*, sixteen vols. Also available at http://www.mea.gov.in/books-writings-of-ambedkar.htm.

Kshirsagar, R.K. 1992. *Political Thought of Dr. Babasaheb Ambedkar*. New Delhi: Intellectual Publishing House.

Russell, Bertrand. 1945. *A History of Western Philosophy*. New York: Simon and Schuster.

# NEW DALIT MOVEMENTS

## AN AMBEDKARITE PERSPECTIVE

*Chandraiah Gopani*

## Introduction

The contemporary mobilization and struggles of Madigas in the Telugu-speaking region (Andhra Pradesh and Telangana), Mangs (Matangs) in Maharashtra, Arundhatiyars in Tamil Nadu, Madigas in Karnataka and Bhangis or Valmikis in north India, among others, bring to our attention an urgent need to address the exclusion and emerging inequalities among Dalits. These struggles critically interrogate 'understood' categories such as Scheduled Castes (SCs) and Dalits and invoke two different identities, that of 'visible' Dalits and 'invisible' Dalits (the invisibility referring to the marginalized among Dalits).

In both Dalit intellectual and political discourses, the issues and concerns of the most marginalized Dalits are either neglected or deliberately kept aside. Any attempt to raise the demands of these castes is further treated as anti-Ambedkar in spirit and detrimental to Dalit 'unity'. Given the urgent need for intellectual engagement and political attention, this essay is aimed at attempting to understand and outline the mobilizations and struggles for the subcategorization of reservation for SCs in various states. Further, it seeks to explain how B.R. Ambedkar understood and acted upon the untouchability and inequalities among Dalits and sought justice for numerically smaller castes among SCs. The essay draws upon sources for its analysis from three years of extensive fieldwork in Andhra Pradesh and Telangana and Ambedkar's writings and speeches and other published and unpublished materials.

A series of democratic struggles within Dalits by the most marginalized Dalits for greater recognition and redistribution have taken place from the mid-1990s in India. These struggles engage in understanding Dalit movements and politics from the bottom up. However, there are contested views and understandings of these 'new Dalit assertions'. The definition of SC assumes it to be a homogeneous identity. As such, it stays mute in addressing the diversities and differences of the constituent castes, particularly the numerically smaller ones. Therefore, the critical interrogation of this identity becomes an important intellectual discourse in contemporary Dalit movements and politics.

In 1975, the government of the state of Punjab took the decision to classify SCs into two categories in order to address the emerging economic, educational and employment disparities among them. Later, the Haryana government also initiated this process. However, the emergence of the Madiga Reservation Porata Samiti (MRPS), popularly known as the Dandora movement, in undivided Andhra Pradesh in 1994 for the sub-categorization of SC reservation soon created a nationwide debate. This movement inspired subsequent subcategorization struggles in Karnataka, Maharashtra, Tamil Nadu and other parts of India. All these struggles raised a number of questions in the public domain, which may be enumerated as follows:

1. Who are Dalits or SCs?
2. Can the SC category be divisible?
3. Is the SC category able to accommodate the differences and diversities among SCs?
4. Will the struggles for recognition of the 'smaller'[1] Dalit castes and their demands for redistribution of reservation benefits divide Dalit unity?
5. How does one understand the practice of untouchability among Dalits?
6. How do we address the demands of numerically smaller or minority SCs?

All these questions are either neglected or not deemed worthy of serious consideration by mainstream Dalit activists, leaders and intelligentsia. In fact, counter-mobilizations and arguments have come to the fore whenever the demands for subcategorization have arisen.

Among Dalits, manual scavengers (*safai karamcharis*) are considered the lowest of the low. Caste groups such as Mussahars in Bihar and Uttar Pradesh, Dakkalies, Gosangies and Gurram Malas in Telangana and Bhangis or Valmikis in various states are treated as untouchables within Untouchables. Untouchability forms part of the complex discriminatory

practices that impose social disabilities on persons by reasons of their birth
into certain castes. These practices include different forms of exclusion
and exploitation. The practice of untouchability in whatever degree and
whichever form has been adopted by Dalits, and segregation *among* them
is either normalized or excluded from discussion. These SCs are not in a
position to access government schemes, nor have they benefited much even
seventy years after independence from colonial rule. These caste concerns
are neither represented nor have they become part of the Dalit agenda.

Consequently, the Dalit discourse tends to focus around the castes that are
the most populous and educationally mobile, and their issues and aspirations
are well articulated. The intensity of the problem is such that there have been
'desperate' instances of political assertion (demands for subclassification of SC
reservations) in the form of self-immolations by individuals belonging to the
most marginalized Dalits in Tamil Nadu and undivided Andhra Pradesh. In
the wake of the categorization movement, the most marginalized castes have
also started to demand separate allocations of sub-plan funds to each caste
depending on their proportion in the population.

The contemporary Dalit movement is at a critical juncture. The all-
India phenomena of the struggle for subclassification of SC reservation and
the socioeconomic diversity of Dalits manifest themselves as an assertion
of multiple identities within Dalits and in the demand for equity within
the state-provided resources and opportunities. Overall, these new Dalit
assertions are engaged in critically understanding the meanings and broader
implications of social justice, representation, experience, untouchability and
leadership through the lens of the most marginalized Dalits and their life
experiences, thereby interrogating the hegemonic view of the dominant
Dalit castes. However, some scholars argue that this move leads to division
within Dalits while the protagonists argue that it deepens the Dalit
movement. It has also been argued in the recent past that the numerically
weaker castes within the SCs are mobilized by Hindu communal forces to
counter the Dalit movement and politics. Given the multiple articulations
in various states, it is necessary to critically engage with these emerging
issues and challenges and policy-level intricacies. The following section
deals with a critical understanding of the Dalit category.

## Interrogating the Category 'Dalit'

Today, the category 'Dalit' has become part of the local and global academic
and activist agenda across different sociocultural situations.[2] The word

'Dalit' often emerges in public discourse and most people refer to it in their writings, speeches, debates, discussions and analysis. Etymologically, Dalit (meaning depressed or broken people) originates from the root word *dal;* the adjectival form of dal is Dalit.[3] In Molesworth's Marathi-English dictionary (1975 reprint of the 1831 edition), the meaning of Dalit is generally given as 'ground', 'broken' or 'reduced to pieces'.[4] These English terms sum up the locations of a segment of Indian people who are discriminated against, excluded, exploited and humiliated in the name of caste and religion. People (SCs, Scheduled Tribes [STs] and Sudras [Other Backward Castes or OBCs] and all women) who were crushed and cramped and discriminated against by the Hindu religion and its caste hierarchy thereby positively asserted and declared themselves as Dalits. This identity was popularized with the emergence of the Dalit Panthers movement in Maharashtra during the middle of the 1970s. The movement advocated that Dalits be proud of their culture and history.[5]

The earlier Dalit nomenclatures, that is, Untouchable, outcaste, Panchama, Ati-Sudra, Avarna, Antyaja, Namasudra, Chandala, Parayar, etc. basically referred to an entire people as unseeable and unapproachable. The term 'Chandala' was used during different phases of Indian history and in different parts of the country. The British used the terms 'Depressed Classes' and 'Exterior Classes' for Dalits, thereby referring to the fact that they were kept away from Hindu society.[6] Gandhi preferred to call them 'Harijan', which literally means 'Children of God', a term he borrowed from the Gujarati Brahmin saint Narasi Mehta. Ambedkar had objections to the word because he found its implications derogatory and insulting (Harijan meant fatherless people).[7]

Dalit as a category in fact was used in the 1930s as the Hindi and Marathi translation of 'Depressed Classes'. It was used to refer to SCs during the British period. In the 1930s, a Depressed Classes newspaper titled *Dalit Bandhu* (Friend of the Dalit) was in circulation. The term was also used by Ambedkar in his Marathi speeches.[8] References to it are even found during the Nizam period between 1940 and 1955, for instance, in the name of an organization called the Dalit Jatiya Sangh and Dalit Sarsvat Parishat, a literary organization that was working for the upliftment of Untouchables. Ambedkar broadly described the term Dalit in his fortnightly, *Bahishkrit Bharat*, as an experience and condition of life that was characterized by the exploitation, suppression and marginalization of Untouchables by the social, economic, cultural and political domination of the caste Hindu Brahminical order. Ambedkar often deployed similar categories depending on the context; for instance, with the colonial state, he used the category of Depressed Classes, with caste Hindus he used the category 'Bahishkrit', meaning totally outcaste. In the domain of politics he used the term Scheduled Caste. Ambedkar, in an effort to politically radicalize and effectively mobilize Untouchables, used the term 'Pad Dalit', thereby referring to those who were crushed under the feet of the Hindu social order.[9]

Scholars have also referred to Dalits differently. Those using class analysis associated Dalits with categories such as peasants, agricultural labour, factory workers, etc. This kind of understanding can be seen in the writings of subaltern historiography and in movements such as the Dalit Panthers. Those who use the framework of religion have considered Dalits to be a part of the Hindu religious[10] order. In order to differentiate caste specificities, scholars also use the term 'sub-subaltern' to refer to Dalits while anti-caste thinkers are described as caste radicals.[11] The Dalit Panthers' manifesto defined the term in a broader sense. It included SCs, STs, neo-Buddhists, the working classes, landless and poor peasants, women and all those who were being exploited politically and economically and in the name of religion.[12] Similarly, the Dalit Mahasabha of Andhra Pradesh[13] has defined Dalits as the people who have been exploited and discriminated against across castes and are represented in the spheres of culture, economy and politics by their caste and religious locations within Indian society.[14] In Babu Rao Bagul's view, 'Dalit' is a revolutionary category for its hermeneutic ability to recover the emancipatory potential of the historical past of Dalit cultures and values. He argues that this category has a greater capacity to reach out to a larger section of people, being based on a materialist epistemology, and is not a mere linguistic construction. It is a category that is historically constructed through the revolutionary struggle of the Dalit.[15]

Gopal Guru argues that the category 'Dalit' is not a metaphysical construction. It derives its epistemic and political strength from the material and social experiences of the community. The category takes ideological assistance from the philosophies of Buddha, Marx, Phule and Ambedkar and in the process becomes man centred rather than God centred, unlike what is implicit in the Gandhian connotation of Harijan.[16] He further elaborated that it chose to radically distance itself from state-constituted categories such as SCs, STs and OBCs.[17] However, in practice, the identity 'Dalit-Bahujan' is also widely used in scholarly writings and public discourse, in which Dalit refers to SCs and Bahujan to Sudras or OBCs.[18] Although these categories appeal towards a unity and work towards a unified political goal, the existing historical and socioeconomic disparities and heterogeneity inevitably place limitations on the realization of the identity in everyday relationships between people. In order to recognize the lowest of the low within Dalits and take their deprivation into consideration, the Bihar government created a category called 'Maha Dalit'[19] for whom the government created special provisions. Scholars have also called the lowest of the low 'Ati Dalit'[20] by differentiating the smaller SC castes from the dominant SC castes.

However, the Dalit identity and the meaning it generates and the meanings people attach to it lie in the very objective condition in which the Dalit category operates. In the recent past, debates in academic writings and political discourse have equated it only with SC. As a result, the validity of Dalit becomes dependent on to what extent it can universally represent the realities of other identities that exist within it. There are many castes within SCs, such as Madiga, Mala, Adi-Andhra (Andhra Pradesh), Adi-Kannada, Holaya and Madiga (Karnataka), Pallar and Parayar (Tamil Nadu), Chamar (Uttar Pradesh, Bihar), Mahar and Matang (Maharashtra), Valmiki and Bhangi (Punjab) and so on. These identities too exist at the grassroots level and represent different degrees of socioeconomic inequality. The assertion of those identities can challenge the hierarchy and democratize social relations at various levels.[21] It is articulated at many levels among Dalits. This existence of multiple identities, both of the individual and the collective, certainly questions the validity and inadequacy of the top-down identities and categories.

The contemporary SC subcategorization movements by Madigas in Andhra Pradesh and Telangana, Arundhatiyars in Tamil Nadu, Mangs in Maharashtra, and Valmikis in Punjab raises historical challenges to the Dalit movement. These movements argue that different heterogeneous castes were legally clubbed into the SC category for administrative purposes that remained oblivious to subcategories. The category SC is used by the government for all welfare schemes and implementation of reservation benefits. In practice, this category is available only to a section of dominant and educationally mobile castes within Dalits. The demand therefore is that the SC categorization benefit the lowest among the low. Further, they ask how the SC category can be homogeneous when there are heterogeneous castes with specific socioeconomic conditions. They argue that the Dalit category may outwardly represent some historical and political commonality, but the problematic has to be addressed. The sociopolitical visibility of Mahars, Malas, Chamars, etc., tends to hegemonize the Dalit identity but the diverse sociocultural aspects of other Dalit groups below them are never focused upon. If untouchability is an important demarcation to distinguish savarnas[22] and avarnas (Dalits), the 'hierarchy of untouchability' among Untouchables (Dalits) makes the Dalit category more ambiguous. Therefore, one has to understand it in its multiple senses and in ever-changing conditions. The ability to stimulate the transformative politics of Dalits depends on the recognition of the lowest of the low among Dalits and the willingness to address the question of recognition and redistribution from its roots in order to consolidate Untouchables to fight against caste and class oppressions. The following section deals with hierarchies and inequalities among Dalits.

## Contesting Untouchability and Emerging Inequalities among Dalits

Untouchability is a by-product of the caste system and an inhuman practice imposed on Dalits in India. It prevails in various forms even seventy years after Independence. While its practise by upper castes is exposed and discussed, the existence of it among Dalits is either not noticed or is normalized. Many government, non-government and individual report writings are focused on documenting forms of untouchability with reference to upper castes. The purpose of the documentation and analysis of untouchability among Dalits is somehow felt as either unnecessary or unimportant.[23] But in the wake of assertions by smaller Dalit castes, the issue is being raised for public discussion. While it is true that untouchability has to be understood as a fallout of the caste system's rules and Brahminical ideology, the forms and degrees in which it operates within Dalits have to also be taken into consideration. One has to raise the question of why this hierarchy and untouchability exists among Untouchables. Will the struggle against upper-caste practices of untouchability automatically remove the caste hierarchy among Dalits? What is its root cause? Will discussing and fighting the inequalities and exclusions within Dalits lead to fragmentation among them? Do Dalits consider themselves a homogeneous group in rural India? Have contemporary Dalit writings been articulating this problematic? If not, why is there silence about it?

It is a fact that in every state the relatively most populous caste among Dalits is socially dominant and looks down upon others as inferior and certain others as Untouchables. Physical distance, lack of inter-caste marriages and inter-dining and separate burial grounds are visible practices among Dalits,[24] which is not any different from the practice of savarnas with Dalits as a whole.

However, when we talk about the hierarchy of untouchability, two things come to the fore.

1. Caste ideology, the root cause for such practices.
2. Agency (individual or group), which reproduces caste ideology and untouchability practices.

Therefore, while the hierarchy of untouchability is part of caste ideology, the role of agency has to be critically analysed. Here, the castes which carry or impose the practice of untouchability on fellow Dalits in any form and degree have to be exposed and challenged. There are sixty-two castes on the SC list in Andhra Pradesh, of which the numerically major ones are the Madigas and Malas. The socio-anthropological study conducted by T.R. Singh and P. Muthaiah clearly demonstrates the existing hierarchy among these two castes in the Telugu-speaking region. The following paragraphs explain the social hierarchy among them:

> It can be seen that the Mitha Ayyalwar caste is at the top of Dalit hierarchy while Dakkal at the bottom. The superiority in Dalit hierarchy flows from upward to downwards while inferiority from downwards to upwards. In the Mala hierarchy Mitha Ayyalwar is considered to be superior, standing at the top of the ladder. Mala Jangam and Mala Dasaries come from the priestly class and function as spiritual advisors to Mala satellite castes; they are also called Mala gurus. They consider Malas and Madigas inferior to them. In the Mala satellite castes Mala Jangam/Dasaries (in some cases) are at the top of Mala hierarchy. Next to them are Malas, Pambala, Masti and Gurram Malas in the descending order in the hierarchy. Syed Sirjul recorded that 'Gurram Malas are regarded as the lowest of all the Mala Sub-castes. It is considered to be a degraded branch of Mala satellite castes . . . Madigas rank next to Malas in the Dalit hierarchy. In the Madiga satellite castes the superiority flows from the Madiga guru, the Sangari to Dakkal and inferiority from Dakkal to Sangari. In the hierarchy of Madiga satellite castes, the Sangari's position is the highest. All satellite castes except Sangari are inferior to Madigas.[25]

And,

> T.R. Singh states that in some villages the Bindla and Verpula Madiga sub-castes not only claimed but also maintained superiority over other

Madigas. It is seen in villages, the Madiga, Bindla, Masti and Dakkal are inferior to Sangari in a discerning order. All the castes including the Madigas treat the Dakkal as untouchable. Here it is pertinent to mention that the Brahmanic invocation of superiority, inferiority and untouchability is located down to the Dakkal. The last man in the homo hierarchicus is then the untouchable of the untouchables.[26]

Jyotsna Macwan and Suguna Ramanathan bring to our attention the hierarchy and practice of untouchability among Gujarat Dalits. They observe that the

Dalit social world replicates the internal system of caste hierarchy of the savarna model. In this system, the Garodas play the role of priests, the Vankars and Rohits play the role of Kshatriyas (protecting the service castes dependent on them), and also of Vaishyas (Vankars engaged in the trade of woven cloth, the Rohits in the trade of hides, with both responsible for dead cattle). The Senvas, according to Randeria, perform menial tasks, like the Sudras in the Brahmanical system, and the Vankers and Rohits do not accept food and drink from the Senvas. The Turis, Tidgars and Senvas contest among themselves for superiority. The Bhangis, who are untouchables, are excluded from the services of the others, and are marginal in their sub-system. The dominant caste is the Vankers and Rohits, and the relationship between them is tense.[27]

Further, it is also argued that among the Rohits, conversion has played a less important role. The example is often citied of a Chamar group that converted to Catholicism and reconverted to its old Hindu identity when the Vankers refused to intermarry with them.[28] In 2006, the Action Aid groups published a report,[29] which is a product of an extensive survey of eleven states on existing forms of untouchability. It found more than a hundred forms of discriminatory practices. But they did not document the practices of untouchability or discrimination among Dalits. The documentary, released in 2007 and entitled 'India Untouched: Stories of a People Apart', directed by Stalin Kurup, also documents various forms of untouchability in different regions and religions. It, however, does not represent untouchability within Untouchables. Neither does *Broken People*, one of the important books that addresses the international audience on caste atrocities. In all these studies, Untouchables are more or less considered homogeneous, but in practical life it is not so. When we study and try to understand Dalits, one has to remember the hierarchy among them that leads to the practice of untouchability.[30]

In Tamil Nadu, there are four major caste groups among the state-enlisted SCs: Parayar, Pallar, Arundhatiyar and Chakkiliyar. They practise untouchability and discrimination amongst themselves. In a conversation I had with them, Arundhatiyar students narrated their experiences both with the upper castes (Thevars, Brahmins, Nadars, etc.) and with their fellow SCs, Pallars and Parayars. Tamil Nadu has villages where all Untouchables fought against upper castes for their right to enter temples, but the Pallars and Parayars did not allow the Arundhatiyars into the same temple, saying that they were impure. While academic and activist writings have so far largely focused on vertical untouchability, these examples prove the need to document and understand the horizontal untouchability within Dalits. A. Ramaiah observes:

> Taking into account the caste status ascribed to them and the life style they have been leading for the last several decades, the Chakkiliyars are below the Parayars in the caste hierarchy. It is believed that they originally held a high position but were later degraded. Their traditional occupations are sweeping, scavenging and removing dead animals, tanning and making footwear. They also play their drums and a wind instrument similar to the Shehnai. In some villages, the Pallars prefer the Chakkiliyars to Parayars to play drums on the occasion of their Kula Deivam (Clan God) festivals although they do not allow the latter inside their temple. However, the Parayars' interaction with the Pallars is very limited. The Chakkiliyars sweep the streets of the Pallars and, in turn, get food from them. They take away the dead cattle, remove their skin for making drums and consume their meat. All these activities are considered by the upper castes and the Pallars to be dirty, defiling and polluting. Hence, the Chakkiliyars are looked down upon. They have so far not challenged the caste supremacy of the Pallars. In general, inter-dining and inter-caste marriages between them and the Pallars are prohibited although the intensity with which these restrictions are observed varies from place to place.[31]

Meanwhile, in Punjab, there are disparities and hierarchy between Ad-dharmis, Balmikis and Chamars in terms of socioeconomic locations and access to reservations. The inequalities among SCs have to be understood in terms of their social locations and historical trajectory. To reduce the issue of recognition of the most marginalized to merely that of reservation is nothing but a side-lining of the hierarchy among Dalits. This is a real challenge to the contemporary Dalit movement. In 1976, the then chief minister, Sri Jalagam Vengal Rao of the Congress ruling government, organized the Andhra Pradesh State Harijan Conference on 10–12 April 1976. This conference was meant to understand and discuss the problems faced by SCs and the mechanisms for addressing them. Many academicians, politicians and bureaucrats attended and presented their opinions. One of the participants, anthropologist and professor L.P. Vidyarthi, argued:

> The term Scheduled Caste has been used as a blanket term to indicate a long list of backward castes though they suffer from distinct type of social disabilities, economic problems and face different socio-political problems. In order to eradicate the evils of untouchability and exploitation of the weaker section of India's population they need to be classified in terms of (1) core groups engaged in scavenging and allied occupations like the Bhangi, the Mehtar, the Hari, the Lalbegi ,etc. (2) Communities engaged in leather and allied works as for example, the Chamar (3) the artisan or skill specialized groups like the Pasi, the Turi (toddy tapper), the Mahali (Basket makers), the Bhogta, the Ghasi etc. and (4) the peripheral and landless agricultural labor communities like the Dusadh, the Musahar, the Rajwar etc.[32]

Vidyarthi therefore attempted to indicate the growing inequalities and existing disparities among SCs. In order to examine the implementation of reservations and disparities within SCs, the central government appointed the B.N. Lokur Committee to advise on the revision of the SC and ST list under the leadership of B.N. Lokur, the law secretary in 1965. The report concluded that there were some tribes and castes that were relatively advanced, hence de-scheduling those castes would help in distributing state provisions to the lower people. The committee recommended the de-scheduling of fourteen STs and twenty-eight SCs, depending on their development. The B.N. Lokur Committee received recommendations from various leaders and organizations to do the same with the Mala community from the SC list in Andhra Pradesh, which remains the best instance to prove that the Mala caste was relatively forward in 1965 itself. The committee stated:

> It has been in evidence for some time that a lion's share of the various benefits and concessions earmarked for the Scheduled Castes and Scheduled Tribes

is appropriated by the numerically larger and politically well organized communities. The smaller and more backward communities have tended to get lost in democratic processes, though most deserving of special aid. Though there is no escape from the larger and politically more conscious groups asserting themselves in the political field, it appears to us that, in matters of planning and development, distribution of benefits needs to be focused on the more backward and smaller groups on a selective basis. At one stage we thought of suggesting separation of political rights from developmental benefits but we are not making the suggestion since the political reservations are due to disappear shortly and since the idea cannot also be implemented within the present framework of the constitution. We would, instead, suggest that the various castes and tribes in the lists should be administratively classified or categorized so as to give higher priority in planning and development to the needier and lower priority for the comparatively advanced.[33]

Various committees and commissions observed the existing exclusion and growing disparities among SCs across India. Uttar Pradesh chief minister Rajnath Singh announced on 28 June 2001 a committee to re-examine arrangements for reservation of government jobs for SCs, STs and OBCs in the state. Named the Committee for Social Justice, it was headed by the minister for parliamentary affairs, Hukum Singh, and the minister for medical and health and family welfare, Ramapati Shastri, as its chairman and co-chairman respectively. Indian Administrative Services officer J.P. Vishwakarma functioned as the secretary. The committee observed that there were disparities within SCs and OBCs in accessing reservation opportunities and benefits of state policies. In view of this, the committee categorized Dalits into two schedules: Schedule A, comprising Chamars, Jatavs and Dhusias, and Schedule B, comprising sixty-five other castes in the SC category. Of the 21 per cent reservation available for Dalits, the committee recommended the reservation of 10 per cent for Schedule A castes and 11 per cent for those in Schedule B.[34] However, following many agitations by the Bahujan Samaj Party (BSP) and the Samajwadi Party (SP), it was withdrawn.[35]

In Karnataka, the Madiga Dandora Horata Samiti (MDHS) has been demanding the subcategorization of SC reservations. After many agitations and memorandums in 2005, N. Dharam Singh, the chief minister at the time, appointed the Justice A.J. Sadashiva Inquiry Commission to look into the methods of equitable distribution of reservation facilities among all SCs. The commission submitted its report in 2012 after an extensive study of the socioeconomic and political conditions and pattern of distribution of reservations among SCs. The commission recommended the sub-classification of SC reservation keeping the view that there were disparities in accessing reservation amongst the 101 listed SCs. The commission recommended reclassifying these castes into four groups: (1) Right community (2) Left community[36] (3) Touchable (4) Other Scheduled Castes, to avail 15 per cent reservation. Within the allotted 15 per cent, the commission allocated 6 per cent to the Left castes, 5 per cent to the Right castes, 3 per cent to the touchable castes and 1 per cent to other castes. There have been many agitations for the implementation of the recommendations of this commission.[37]

The Bihar state government also created special public policies for Maha Dalits in 2007. The Maharashtra government appointed the Lahuji Commission in 2003 to examine the unequal distribution of SC reservations among listed SCs and recommended appropriate remedies. The commission found disparities in and unequal access to reservation facilities and state policies and recommended a policy of equitable distribution among all SCs. Many Mang (Matanga) organizations have been mobilizing and demanding provisions for the subclassification of SC reservations and sub-plan funds. However, the government is yet to take proper steps for fulfilling their demands.[38]

The Tamil Nadu government in 2008 accepted recommendations from the M.S. Janardhanam Committee to provide separate reservations of 3 per cent for Arundhatiyars and Chakkiliyars and a few other sub-castes within the existing 18 per cent SC reservation. However, it has been challenged by some Parayars and Adi-Dravidas in the courts, where the case is now pending.[39]

Complaints also arose in other states that reservation had led to disproportionate benefits for certain sections of SCs at the cost of others within the same category. Accordingly, the central government appointed a commission headed by Justice Usha Mehra to look into the issue in undivided Andhra Pradesh. The Usha Mehra Commission, in its report submitted to the Union Ministry of Social Justice and Empowerment in May 2008, reportedly favoured the classification of SCs into subgroups with a view to uplifting the status of the deprived lot amongst them and recommended that the Constitution be amended suitably for the purpose. It observed that SCs were not a homogeneous group and said that in terms of traditional occupations, caste practices and the physical structure of villages, these castes differed from each other and as such there was apparently no homogeneity among them. The commission also said that its studies had shown that under the existing system there was no possibility of benefits reaching those at the bottom.

In the existing political situation, the ruling governments and parties have tended to focus on the development of the socioeconomically and numerically dominant castes within Dalits, such as the Malas in the Telugu region. Because of the numerical dominance of these castes and their ability to influence and negotiate with the government and political parties, castes such as the Dakkalis, Chindus, Mehatars, Mochis and Gosangies have neither become part of the negotiating agenda nor have they been politically taken into consideration. This affected their education, employment, development and political representation. Until the Dandora movement in 1994 demanded the status of various SCs and their representation in different fields, there was no discussion on these castes in the Telugu-speaking region.

However, it is shocking to hear that even seventy years after Independence, some of the caste groups do not have any legal proof of identification.[40] Historically, these castes are nomadic, moving from one village to another, performing various art forms and begging for their livelihood and survival. To acquire proof of identification of their caste and residential address, they are required to go through many hurdles to get the revenue divisional officer's approval, whereas the Malas and Madigas get it relatively easily from the mandal revenue officer. Because of the negligence of government personnel and the lack of understanding about these castes, they are pushed to take either Mala or Madiga caste certificates. There are many cases where people of the Chindu caste were given Madiga certificates and Netakanis were given Mala certificates.

Further, the population of these communities is misrecorded in government reports as being in thousands when they actually exist in lakhs. As a result, they are turned into a numerically minor SC caste. Consequently, their cultural and legal identity is pushed into invisibility; they are endangered and become a politically irrelevant force. When these smaller castes get certificates deeming them as either Mala or Madiga, it is difficult for them to compete in any public scheme given their historical backwardness, socioeconomic conditions and illiteracy. Therefore, while it appears that the submerging process helps in the broader project of the annihilation of caste, it has serious consequences for their historical specificities, justice and representation.

Recently, the Telangana government announced around 500 jobs for artists, along with a land distribution scheme.[41] While it is true that these are important both for the recognition of the contribution of artists towards the Telangana movement and to encourage their talent, the question remains, to what extent will these reach those at the bottom of the Untouchable hierarchy? The Andhra Pradesh government also announced financial assistance to Dalit students to study abroad. It is said that the already dominant Dalit castes have started to negotiate with the government for their own benefit.[42] It is therefore important and necessary to see whether or not the minority artistic communities will get their proportional representation in these employment and educational opportunities. As long as there is no separate allocation, there will not be any justice for them. In order to be more inclusive, the government should allocate the sub-plan funds according to the proportion of each caste group in the population. Given the existing scenario among Dalits, it is important to understand this through the framework given by the Ambedkarite philosophical praxis.

## Ambedkar on Justice for the Most Marginalized Dalits

B.R. Ambedkar was a synthesizer of anti-caste philosophy and struggles. His views on caste, untouchability, religion, democracy and the Dalit situation contain important insights to understand Indian society. His writings and struggles have become a source of inspiration for millions belonging to oppressed communities, particularly Untouchables. During his active political life, he also faced the problem of intra-caste conflicts within Dalits as we are experiencing today. In the Bombay Presidency, the differences and inequalities among Dalits came frequently in the way of Ambedkar's struggles. Ambedkar, being a visionary with a strong support base of Dalits across India, particularly the Mahars in Maharashtra, attempted to address the issue of intra-caste conflicts. He also tried to build a broader platform for all Dalits by attempting to include non-Mahar Dalit castes into his organizations, the All India Scheduled Caste Federation, the Independent Labour Party, etc. In response to his critics, Ambedkar said in one of his speeches:

> The critics also say that all the benefits of the Government schemes are being grabbed by the Mahars. Mr Nikalje of Mahar caste was nominated for the Mumbai Corporation. But when I found out that he is unable to perform to my satisfaction, I did not hesitate to nominate Mr P. Balu, a famous cricketer belonging to the Chamar community. In Satara city, the Mahars are larger in number, yet in the Municipality, the Government appointed members is from the Chamar Caste. It is through these instances

that one can see how the charges being made are totally baseless . . . If some individual Mahars turn out to be narrow-minded, please do not blame it on all the Mahars. I request the people from other castes to first carefully analyze the behaviors of Mahar leaders and then criticize. I am also ready to make blood relations with the people from Mang caste. In fact, I had a boy from the Mang caste in my own home. There is no difference between what I preach and practice. There is no inter-caste co-dining in the conferences organised by the National Congress. On the other hand, in the Depressed Classes Conference that I had organised, all castes dined together. What does this show? . . . It has also been alleged that the Mahars grab seats in the Council. Shouldn't we be sending the right people to the Council? It is their bad fortune that leaders like me have not emerged from non-Mahar untouchables. I have no interest in a council seat. If there are more able people in cases other than the Mahars, then they can take my seat and I will happily resign.[43]

Ambedkar, at the Round Table Conference of 1930–32, also spoke on behalf of all SCs where he asserted that SCs were a social minority who were historically deprived and discriminated against and who needed constitutionally mandated special policies. Hence, Ambedkar argued for all SCs as one group that commonly faced untouchability, exploitation and violation of human rights, for which he fought for special provisions, both in politics, education and the public services. During the Round Table Conferences and until his death, although there were differences among SCs, for Ambedkar, achieving constitutional guarantees for all SCs was the first and foremost concern, rather than sticking with addressing the internal problems.[44]

Contrary to this, the Congress and Gandhi were intent upon disqualifying Ambedkar's attempts to represent all SCs. Through his Harijan tours across India, Gandhi not only attempted to reach out to the outcastes, but also focused on the colonies of Bhangis to show that they were at the bottom of the pecking order. Gandhi wanted to prove that he stood by this category of people and not Ambedkar.

Even in these most challenging times, Ambedkar attended Round Table Conferences and fought for all Depressed Castes.[45] While he commented on minority representation, he maintained his vision to ensure justice would reach those who were most marginalized. He said, 'Any excess over this [over representation in public services and legislative bodies] cannot be tolerated, as it will be at the cost of the other communities.' Further, he said, '[W]eightage carved out from the share of majority shall not be assigned to one community only. But the same shall be divided among all minority communities equally or in inverse proportion to their (1) Economic Position, (2) Social status and (3) Educational advance'.[46]

In the contemporary Dalit movement, any attempt to discuss the discriminatory practices, inequalities and unequal access of SC reservations and state policies among SCs has been consistently resisted and treated as being against the Ambedkarite spirit and Dalit unity. This tendency can be seen in the arguments of the Mala Mahanadu[47] movement supporters and groups and individuals who are against the subcategorization of SC reservations across states. The Mala Mahanadu raised certain problematic arguments against the rationalization of the SC subclassification. Broadly, the arguments were:

1. SCs or Dalits are homogeneous. Hence, there should not be any division amongst them.
2. Rationalization of SC subclassification is unconstitutional; it divides SCs or Dalits.
3. Due to globalization and privatization, reservation in the public sector has become symbolic. Hence, instead of SC subcategorization, Madigas should fight for SC reservations in the private sector.
4. Those who have merit within SCs will get an opportunity (thereby implying that Madigas lack merit).
5. Madigas have a caste occupation, whereas Malas do not. The fact remains that Malas got early education and employment through Christian missionaries, which made them mobile and helped them gain access to modern opportunities.
6. If Madigas are backward, they may get some special packages but not the benefits of subcategorization of SC reservations.
7. Those demanding SC subcategorization are fighting against the Ambedkarite spirit and broader Dalit politics.

The Mala Mahanadu has organized many public meetings against the sub-categorization movement. Leaders such as Jupudi Prabhakar, Karem Shivaji and others organized the Malas under various Mala Mahanadu factions. It is also said that the Mala bureaucratic lobby worked at various levels in approaching courts and in stopping the government order in the Supreme Court.[48] Groups like the Rajyanga Parirakshana Committee, headed by Malas, and the Bahujana Vigyana Vedika organized public meetings and published small booklets. Hence, at most times, Mala Mahanadu activities were reactionary to the MRPS's activities. K. Balagopal observes:

> In any case, the Mahanadu plea is the kind of argument made first by the Brahmins and later by the other upper castes against reservations as such; give them help for economic upliftment and we too will learn to honour the dignity of labour, but do not branch our preserve of expanding knowledge and the status and opportunities it carries. The argument, as well as the answer to it, will become clearer if one goes below the Madigas to castes such as the Rellies, who have as their exclusive vocation scavenging in which they face no threat of competition. Nor do the Rellies have any scope for advancement, if they remain scavengers. It was also argued that, instead of fighting among themselves for sub-dividing their common quota, Dalits should jointly fight for increasing the SC quota, commensurate with the proportionate increase in Dalit population and for a proper implementation of reservations, including the backlog of unfilled vacancies. There is no reason, however, why the desire for justice inter se should wait upon the later task or tasks. The desire and the tasks can proceed together, provided both sides—particularly the more privileged side—makes sure that the struggle for subdivision and the response to it do not vitiate the atmosphere to the extent of making the united struggle for the common goals impossible . . . In any case, this is again no different in principle from the argument offered by the upper caste anti-reservationists; let us fight not over division of the existing job opportunities, but for the creation of more, the two struggles can well go together and the onus of making this possible lies on the more privileged and not the less privileged. To ask the disadvantaged to give up their just demand of equal opportunity in order to pave the way for the unity required for a common fight for greater opportunities is plainly unethical.[49]

Here, K. Balagopal raised the ethical dimension of the just demand of the Madigas and the unethical attitude of the Malas opposing the rationalization of SC subcategorization in the name of 'Dalit unity'. The prevailing Dalit leadership have also not initiated any method and negotiation to address the problem. So, it is argued that most of the so-called Dalit leaders belonged to the Mala community. This also made the Madiga youth and employees lose their trust in the Dalit leadership. According to Muthaiah, Malas and Madigas are historically not united culturally and there are practical and ritualistic differences among these communities. There are fifty-nine castes (in the Telugu-speaking region), among which the Malas and Madigas are the two majority castes. To understand the practices of untouchability amongst them, one has to see critically in order to understand the everyday relations among SCs. In the layer of social status, the Malas feel superior to other castes. Therefore, they also practise untouchability and discrimination against the Madigas. Inter-caste marriages have hardly taken place between them, and even if they do, have led to conflict. Therefore, the cultural differences and historical roots of inequality hint at the myth of Mala–Madiga unity. Unity between them did not exist even before the emergence of the Dandora movement. At the same time, it is a fact that both castes suffer untouchability at the hands of the upper castes and carry the common experience of suffering.

The historical inequalities made the Madigas mobilize on a large scale. After continuous struggles and agitations, the Justice Ramachandra Raju Commission recommended SC subcategorization in 1997. The Andhra Pradesh government passed a resolution on the rationalization of SC reservations in 2000 and the policy was implemented from 2000 to 2004. Manda Krishna claims that during this period, the Madiga community got more than 20,000 jobs.[50] However, in 2004, the Supreme Court set aside the subcategorization government order in the case of petitioner *E. V. Chinnaiah* vs *State of Andhra Pradesh Government and others*,[51] and recommended a constitutional amendment for reservations through SC subcategorization.

Following the Supreme Court judgement, on three occasions, all political parties unanimously passed a resolution for the amendment of SC subcategorization in the state assembly. Under Chief Minister Rajashekar Reddy, an all-party delegation also met the prime minister. Following the representation made by the delegation and subsequent agitations, the then United Progressive Alliance government appointed a single-person commission called the Justice Usha Mehra Commission. As mentioned earlier, this commission visited the three regions of the then united Andhra Pradesh, consulted many organizations and individuals and finally recommended SC subcategorization. However, the state and central governments are yet to initiate the constitutional amendment for the sub-categorization of SC reservations.

## Conclusion

New Dalit mobilization and assertion is being led by marginalized Dalits for dignified identity and equal share in state resources. These assertions carry the greater ability to democratize the Dalit movement and politics, provided these forces work for their social, economic and political emancipation and the annihilation of caste. Even many decades after Independence, the reservation policy is an important source of mobility for Dalits. However, due to the decline of the public sector in the face of rapid privatization and globalization, the future of the reservation policy is in danger. Though sub-categorization of SC reservation may not solve the structural discrimination of caste, it certainly creates opportunities for invisible Dalits and an enabling environment for broader solidarities amongst SCs for challenging common problems. Political parties are always playing an opportunistic role in the demands of most marginalized Dalits, depending on the numerical strength of these castes and their electoral strategies. The antagonism within Dalits against subcategorization is because of the deep-rooted hegemony of relatively advanced Dalit castes, which clearly indicates the multi-layered challenges to the Dalit movement and politics. Casteist practices are reproduced even among Dalits, the malaise being so deep-rooted that it threatens the unity of those who suffer its oppression the most. Hence, unless and until Dalit movements and politics recognize the hierarchy of untouchability, emerging inequalities and middle-class mobility among Dalits, the bid for unity and emancipation will remain in crisis. The existing imbalance in education, employment and representation among SCs clearly indicates the need for rationalization or subcategorization of reservation and sub-plan funds in order to reach the most marginalized groups.

Within the Dalit movement and among Dalit intellectuals and activists there is a feeling that supporting the subcategorization of SC reservation and building a broader Dalit politics are contradictory aims, but they are not contradictory; in fact, they are complementary. The sooner the remedy to the internal problems is achieved, the better the Dalit future will be. Dalit intelligentsia, activists and leaders should realize that understanding justice from the point of view of the most marginalized has a greater capacity to deepen the Ambedkarite philosophical praxis.

# BISOCIATIVE REVOLUTION

## THE EMERGENCE OF THE CONCEPT

*Bronislaw Czarnocha*

## Introduction

Right now, we have December 2016, and the US, rolling in the unexpected victory of Donald Trump, the President elect. The salient fact for our discussion is that one or two days after his election, it became clear that the so-called progressive Democrats lost the election due to the split within their party ranks along the axis of class economic struggle–identity struggle. As a result, most of the White working class voted for Trump, while the majority of women and minorities voted for Clinton (with an important exception of 53 per cent of White women voting for Trump). This, most probably, is the Left's last warning to find a true bridge between the identity struggles, in their manifold representations, and the socioeconomic class struggle. In doing so, they will be able to synthesize, or integrate, in theory and in praxis two independent yet closely connected battles to reach the necessary vision and strength to win. The second salient divide between these two separated axes of the struggle is the education level. Most workers who cast their vote for Trump lacked a college education, while the educated elite coalesced around Clinton.

I take this interesting convergence between the hypothesis of this presentation addressing the class struggle–identity politics divide in spring 2016, and the results of the American elections in autumn 2016 as an early confirmation of the correctness of the herein proposed route of reasoning.

I am proposing the new concept of bisociative revolution—revolution proceeding along two very different pathways, each with its own laws of development, drawing from two different motivational resources, and each reinforcing the other within the consciously constructed dialectical synthesis of both. The moment of synthesis, the 'Aha! Moment', is the rearrangement of structure, the act of revolution—the quantum jump.

The Polish Solidarity Movement of the 1980s provides the perfect example of bisociative revolution. Class struggle and a national liberation movement were the irreducible identity components (till the time of the military takeover).

The primary motivation for this chapter is the story of science scholar Rohith Vemula of Hyderabad Central University (HCU), which has played itself out over the winter and spring of 2016. As the standard media pattern unfolded, the essentially Dalit issue became eclipsed first by its generalization to human rights, then by fascism. At the beginning of the spring strike at Jawaharlal Nehru University (JNU) against the punishment of 'rustication' meted out to the majority of the Students Union, JNU's Kanhaiya Kumar acknowledged that the main reason for the recent rapid rise of Hindutva fascism is the divide between the Left and the Dalits.

The question, then, is how to create a coherent path of integration for the divide on both theoretical and practical levels. My aim here is utilitarian. I will be using only those essential principles, or components, of Marxism and Ambedkarism that are needed to participate in the path's construction. My aim is not a full comparison of both approaches, but of just those elements relevant to the task at hand.

## What *The Communist Manifesto* Is to the Capitalist World, *Annihilation of Caste* Is to Caste India

The starting point of this investigation is the statement of Anand Teltumbde (an 'organic Dalit intellectual', using Gramsci's formulation), the profound metaphor I was looking for: 'What *The Communist Manifesto* is to the capitalist world, *Annihilation of Caste* [B.R. Ambedkar] is to caste India. Why is this observation profound? *It goes to the very heart of the issue between the Dalits and the Left—the issue of the nature of the divide.* It suggests that the divide has two independent yet closely related conceptual frameworks: that of class struggle and that of the Dalit identity struggle in India. The metaphor, a statement of proportion, is suggestive of an as yet 'hidden analogy' between the two approaches and realities. The metaphor was formulated by Teltumbde in the introduction to Ambedkar's book, *Annihilation of Caste*, reprinted by a group of students in JNU. A communist group, Arvind Institute of Marxist Studies, critiqued it in its position paper for a seminar devoted to the caste question issue, in 2013.[1]

Teltumbde's text statement and the response to these comments by Abhinav Sinha of the Marxist-Leninist organization Bigur Mazdoor Dasta appeared in the background of the position paper for the conference,[2] not only showing us the extent of the divide but also offering suggestions on how to proceed with the construction of the pathway to connection.

As both a quantum physicist and mathematics teacher-researcher, the practitioner of two separate conceptual frameworks, I will be drawing from them as a guide for the formulation of the theory. One of them is the wave-particle duality of quantum mechanics, with special debt to the Schrödinger's Cat thought experiment exemplifying this duality. The other is Koestler's Bisociative Theory of the Act of Creation, which defines bisociation as 'spontaneous leap of insight . . . the bisociative act [which] connects previously [two or more] unconnected matrices of experience',[3] revealing at the same time the 'hidden analogy' between the two. Strong analogies between the two dual processes or objects are clearly visible. Let me add the third analogy to the collection, and that is the definition of the compromise as 'the composition of two rival principles in which part of each is sacrificed to make the composition possible'.[4] All three frameworks have the common quality of dialectically integrating different (opposing, or not) frames of reference, or discourses. To clarify the relation between Ambedkar's and Marx's intellectual pathways, we employ two theories of conceptual development, the Piaget and Garcia dialectical triad and Lev Vygotsky's Zone of Proximal Development (ZPD).

Of course, a careful reader will immediately ask what kind of a theoretical framework is one that is composed from three different disconnected pieces. And the answer is, of course, there is not yet a theoretical framework, as I am in the process of creating one. This situation of not having a theory because you are in process of creating one is a counter-example to the assertions of Sinha, who claims that we always do have a theory. Here we do not. We have three interesting observations that might bear an analogy and have a common pattern with each other that may lead to the theory.

## Posing of the Problem: Ambedkar and Marx

I will present here the central components of the problem from the Ambedkar and Marxist points of view.

In order to clarify the methodology of my approach and to outline the extent of the 'hidden analogy', it may be useful to provide a general description of the ZPD metaphor introduced by Vygotsky, the mental space environment within which learners develop new concepts, for instance, in mathematics or language. Its general borders, in the context of school learning, are denoted by spontaneous concepts anchored in daily experience and practice, and scientific concepts reflecting knowledge of the discipline.

The development of concepts proceeds in both directions, from spontaneous to scientific and from scientific to spontaneous. The best situation for such a development exists when spontaneous concepts are just 'below' the scientific, according to Vygotsky.[5] The corresponding metaphor from the Piaget point of view is that of the Piaget–Garcia (PG) Triad,[6] which describes the conceptual development, without the final scientific level necessarily being presented as in existence. The PG Triad then describes the conceptual development that leads to discovery, in fact, creative discovery.[7]

These two metaphors allow us to see the conceptual pathways of the two approaches. For Marx, the pathway led from the scientific concepts of the theory he first outlined in *The Communist Manifesto*, and completed in *Das Kapital*, to revolutionary practice. Ambedkar's pathway led from practice to the reality of Dalit liberation, which at some point became Buddhism, though incompletely. Each of them grasped the totality of the oppression they attacked. For Marx, it was in terms of the act of economic exploitation around which he built his theory. For Ambedkar, it was in terms of abolishing the full caste system together with its hierarchy. Yet, from the ZPD viewpoint, they were moving in opposite conceptual directions in the development of their particular struggles. Both identified the natural fighter for their causes—in one case, the proletariat, in the other case, the Untouchables. Both of them realized the need for international solidarity, but from significantly different points of view—Marx from the theory of capitalist development and Ambedkar from the necessity of the Dalit situation. Had their points of departure been within one conceptual framework, or within the ZPD, along one dimension, we could attempt to join them conceptually within that ZPD. However, we have here not one but two different conceptual frameworks: that of class struggle and that of the Dalit identity liberation struggle. What we have to find out is how the two are connected and connectable as two independent concepts in close mutual interaction. Moreover, we would like to do it in such a way that simultaneously provides both tactical and strategical clues for the struggle.

The difference between the two approaches has to do with where to focus one's primary attention—on the class struggle, which from the Marxist perspective is the primary focus of the struggle, or on Ambedkar's main focus, the altering of mental attitude out of which will come enlightened revolutionary liberation practice.

## Ambedkar: Annihilation of Caste

> Can you have economic reform without first bringing the reform of the social order?[8] [. . .] whereas the [. . .] conditions for socialist ideas centered on property have matured in Europe [circa 1936], they certainly had not matured in India, where religion, status and property are all sources of power and authority which one man has to control the liberty of the other. One is predominant at one stage; the other is predominant at another stage. If liberty is the ideal, and if liberty means destruction of the dominion which one man holds over another, then obviously it cannot be insisted upon that economic reforms *must be the one reform* to pursue.
>
> If the source of power and dominion is . . . social and religious, then social reform and religious reform must be accepted as the *necessary* sort of reform.

He states: 'The assurances of the socialist leading the revolution that he doesn't believe in caste, I am sure, will not suffice. The assurance must be coming from much deeper foundation, *namely the mental attitudes of the compatriots towards one another.*'

And then he continues: 'Can it be said that the proletariat of India, poor as it is, recognizes no distinction except rich and poor? Can it be said that the poor in India recognize no such distinctions of caste or creed, high or low? If they do, *what unity of front can be expected from such a proletariat in its action against the rich*? How can there be a revolution if the proletariat cannot present a united front?' [emphasis added]

These statements by Ambedkar must be supplemented by the general philosophy he coordinated through Buddhism (Ambedkar, Buddha or Marx). The Buddha's method was different. His method was to shift the mind of man, to alter his disposition, so that whatever man does, he does it voluntarily without the use of force or compulsion. We see that this approach, working through the mind, to shift the mind, plays the fundamental role in Ambedkar's praxis. This is distinct from Marx's approach which originates in the change in the 'matter' of socioeconomic conditions. This difference also manifests itself in Ambedkar's emphasis on the primacy of the individual ('Birth of an individual is not for service of the society, it is for his or her own emancipation'), as compared with Marx's view of the individual as a member of the class.

## The Caste Question and Its Resolution: A Marxist Perspective[9]

This position paper starts with a very strong assertion that 'No revolutionary project of making the Indian society exploitation-free can be made by excluding the caste question [. . .] The essence [of cast oppression] remains that of class-struggle and it gets expressed in a distorted manner as caste-struggle'.[10]

Below I offer some of the salient points of the paper. I have altered the language slightly, while retaining the substance.

- The Communist Party, while speaking about fighting untouchability, declared Ambedkar a separatist, opportunist and British supporter, though they totally lacked a concrete programme for elimination of caste and created caste-based prejudices. The fact that the Communist Party did not present a concrete programme for the elimination of caste is a separate issue.
- What was required to take along the Dalits was not to embrace Ambedkar by whitewashing reality, but rather to derive the concrete tasks of the prolonged struggle for the elimination of untouchability and the caste system within the task of the democratic revolution. The Communist Party failed to do this, and this was its lacuna.
- It is true that there was discrimination with the Dalit workers in the mill. They were not permitted to do certain kinds of work on the grounds of their untouchability. It is a separate issue that the Communist Party should have carried out a sustained work of education and propaganda on such issues and should also have presented the demands before the management.
- The caste system distorts and disfigures the class struggle in rural areas and breaks the unity of the broad toiling masses. Unlike rural areas, this is not the main obstacle for urban areas; though it is still an obstacle for the class unity of the urban toiling masses. Caste-based discrimination was never evidenced to be a problem for unity in any of the spontaneous or organized struggles waged by unorganized workers in recent times. Nevertheless, it has to be admitted that the walls of caste-based

discrimination and segregation exist even among the urban proletariat which is exploited by the trade union leaders of the bourgeois parties.

This repetitious pattern of the CPI(M)'s inaction in relation to the Dalits in critical moments precisely evidences the absence of the mental attitude called for by Ambedkar, and it ultimately underlies the thrust of their argument that class struggle is more fundamental than the caste liberation movement.

Prakash Louis[11] supports this charge; in relation to the question of Dalit mobilization, it has since been pointed out, however, that the CPI did not effectively take up the question of 'untouchability' and the caste-specific oppression of Dalits. Like those of the Socialist Party, the leadership and cadres of the CPI hailed from the upper and middle castes. Consequently, Dalit concerns remained peripheral in the CPI's campaigns.[12]

George J. Kunnath quotes a villager, a strong supporter of Maoists in Bihar:[13] 'When the Sangathan came here, it began among the *mazdur varg*. The cadres used to sleep and eat in the mud houses of the mazdur. It fought for the issues of the working classes—land and wages, as well as against social abuses, exploitation and the sexual abuse of women. But now that the Sangathan has got a foothold here, its ambition has grown into one of capturing state power. So they have started taking in people from the dominant castes, against whom we fought previously. As a result of the entry of the landowning castes into the Sangathan, it is hesitant to raise the issues of land and wages. For the last twenty years, wages have remained the same: 3 kilos of paddy for a day's work. The working class is no longer a priority for the Sangathan.'[14] This quote is important because it identifies a moment at which the Maoist guerillas in Bihar dropped Dalit issues from their central aims. It took place because the cadres of the movement started having the ambition of state power, which required the support of the higher castes.

We see here the battle between two very powerful principles grounded in very distinct philosophies of emancipation, operating on different general philosophical principles which propose not only different conceptual frameworks but also different methodological directions in their practical realization.

## Conceptual Reflection

A similar conceptual situation has been discussed by Etienne Balibar in the context of the duality between nationalism and class struggle which, as he seems to suggest, has reified into the nation-form as the compromise between the two:[15]

> The nationalization of the society to which we have referred [. . .] is the administrative (decentralization/centralization), economic and cultural [. . .] In these conditions, the nationalization of the society is a process of statization. But it also is a compromise—not just a more or less stable compromise between classes, but a compromise between two 'principles' themselves: between the principle of nationality and the principle of class struggle. This is the first factor of ambiguity in national identities and class identities, and a corollary of their reciprocal determination. It is the crises of the ultimate form assumed by that 'bourgeois state' which has been referred to as the 'Welfare State' [and/or the Socialist State of Eastern Europe]. It is the crisis of the relative integration of the class struggle, and classes themselves—into and by—the nation-form.[16]

Balibar thus formulates from two opposing principles, the principle of nationality and the principle of class struggle, their compromise in the nation-form. I would like to add that if the nation-form does not correspond to or does not change elastically with the 'justly formulated class needs of society', the revolution will continue with its revolutionary adjustments.[17]

Interestingly enough, Balibar picks up that dualism in the context of the discussion between race and class. He sees them as antinomic[18] poles that have not yet reified into their compromise as in the case of nationality and class. Balibar[19] states: 'We accept working hypothesis that "class" and "race" constitute the two antinomic poles of permanent dialectic, which is at the heart of modern representations of history.'[20]

This set of dual principles when augmented by the principle of race liberation and the principle of feminism by Black feminism produces a clue about how to deal with the tension between such opposing principles that we will apply to the class struggle–caste liberation duality.

According to Patricia Collins:[21]

> To me we must shift our discourse away from additive forms of oppression. Such approaches are typically based on two premises. First, they depend on either/or, dichotomous thinking [. . .] In spite of the fact that we all have 'both/and' identities, we persist in trying to classify each other in either/or categories. Either/or, dichotomous thinking is especially troublesome when applied to theories of oppression because every individual must be

classified as being oppressed or not oppressed. The both/and position of simultaneously being oppressed and oppressor becomes conceptually impossible.

In other words, the issue arises of how to satisfy or fulfil two opposing principles; how to construct their synthesis. Within the duality of simultaneously being the oppressed and oppressor, Audre Lorde suggests, 'The true focus of revolutionary change is never merely oppressive situations which we seek to escape, but that piece of the oppressor which is planted within each of us.'[22] This, of course, is closely related to Ambedkar's demand of the proper 'mental attitudes of the compatriots towards one another'. For Lorde, the liberation struggle must occur on both fronts simultaneously, inner and outer oppression. Similarly, I propose that the struggle within the system, the principle of class struggle and the principle of caste liberation, must be happening along both their axes in a well-coordinated manner. How to do it both in theory and in practice is the question we will address next.

First, though, I wish to say that we are moving beyond intersectionality. While accepting its emphasis on the relations between different frameworks, we are now focusing our attention more widely on the relationships between class struggle and race, nation, feminism and caste. In doing so, our focus is between the class struggle and the identity liberation movements, thereby pointing to the fundamental duality of the social and the individual in the contemporary world. The duality between feminism and race is part of the individual antinomic pole.

## Proposed Route to Solve the Problem

Is there a solution to the contradiction stated above? A solution in which neither of the two principles dominates the other? Teltumbde's 'What *The Communist Manifesto* Is to the Capitalist World, *Annihilation of Caste* Is to Caste India' suggests a fruitful approach by positing the two principles as independent pillars of the solution. The construction of that possible solution can be approached in two ways: the notion of the mutual principled 'compromise', which according to Webster's *Library of Universal Knowledge* (1969) is 'the composition of two rival principles in which part of each is sacrificed to make the composition possible'. This approach suggests the construction of the solution via dialectical synthesis. During the integration process, it is essential that certain aspects of each of the two principles be eliminated to achieve effective integration. It suggests that in the context of caste and class, Marxism and Ambedkarism must modify their respective structures to meet the contemporary requirements of the revolutionary strategy under which the two can be composed into one.

In no way is this a trivial task. The acceptance of the possibility that one of the central motivations for revolutionary struggle might be from the struggle against socio-religious oppression is very difficult to accept from the Marxist point of view as it is contradictory to the dialectics of historical materialism, which places itself squarely at the class struggle socioeconomic contradiction.

It is clear that Ambedkarism must no longer hold on to its claim of the mental or spiritual as priority in the path towards liberation, and, together with Marxism, must accept that both independent but interlocking struggles—the socioeconomic class struggle and the Dalit liberation struggle—are happening and should be happening simultaneously with generally the same strategical importance. The main question here is deriving the meaning of that language particle 'AND' that joins the two opposing principles.

## From Hamlet's 'To Be' OR 'Not to Be' Towards 'To Be' AND 'Not to Be' of Schrödinger's Cat

(From 'class struggle' OR 'caste struggle' towards 'class struggle' AND 'caste struggle', or how does one compose two different conceptual frameworks so that together they constitute a flexible yet powerful instrument of liberation.)

The research question is then: how does one formulate a theory of revolution utilizing two separate but closely related concepts: class struggle and caste struggle, or, more generally, class struggle and identity struggle. That is, how does one formulate a bisociative theory of revolution?

Bisociation is the term introduced by Arthur Koestler[23] in his book *The Act of Creation* as the theoretical definition for the 'Aha! Moment', or, as it is also known, the Eureka experience. 'The Aha! Moment is the spontaneous flash of insight, which [. . .] connects the previously unconnected frames of reference and makes us experience reality at several planes at once'.[24]

Unconnected frames of reference that become connected through the discovery of the 'hidden analogy' of the 'Aha! moment' can be called bisociative frameworks, that is, frameworks with the enhanced possibility of creativity. It is my contention that the theory of revolution based both on class struggle and caste struggle as two independent and interlocking principles is the bisociative framework, whose formulation as well as praxis promises large doses of creativity transpiring when working with them together to solve the problems encountered during revolutionary work.

Koestler's bisociation theory provides a framework from within which both the Marxist class struggle and the identity liberation movements can find mutually reinforcing resources that lead to a successful social revolution. This revolution is projected to 'wrench out class relationships' as well as 'abolish caste'. From the profound realization of the Black Liberation Movement,[25] 'We must see the connections between these categories of analysis and our personal lives.' The bisociative revolutionary framework bisociates between the unconnected matrices of social and individual experience, leading towards the creative self-realization rooted in both matrices, not limited by them but rather transcending them. The bisociativity of *The Act of Creation* is an optimistic concept or praxis that suggests new revolutionary strategical ideas as it throws new light on the traditional strategies derived from experience.

Equally important is the possibility of a new, more detailed understanding of previous events. The most significant here is the realization that Polish Solidarity was the integration of two independent yet interlocking movements: the workers' class struggle and the national liberation movement. Each movement had different aims, goals and different developmental timetables synthesizing across thirty-four years into the revolutionary 'Aha! Moment' of the Solidarity uprising of 1980–81.

The later collapse of the workers' movement component, leading to the 1989 agreements, revealed a fundamental divide between Poland's progressive intelligentsia and its workers at that point in time.

## What Is the Nature of the 'AND' That Joins the 'To Be AND Not to Be' of Schrödinger's Cat?[26]

We bring here the main conclusion from the Appendix, which tells us that a composition of two antinomies or the opposite states ↑ and ↓ has a collection of answerable questions. That collection is different, incompatible with collections of answerable questions for either state ↑ or ↓. And this is the meaning of the vilified Heisenberg assertion: 'What we observe is not nature in itself but [the aspect of] nature exposed to our method of questioning.' This discussion answers also the difficulty of Sinha, who, in his response to Teltumbde, asserts:

> Mr Teltumbde forgets the basic teaching of science: you can't escape theory; even those who claim to be purged of all theories are, in fact, putting forward a theory. In natural (hard) science too, one needs to take an a priori theoretical position, namely, the dialectical approach, otherwise they are obliged to fall in the pit of determinism or agnosticism, because at any given point, science cannot give answers for all questions.

That was the tragedy of the debate between the Copenhagen School formed by Heisenberg and Bohr and Einstein; a fetish for science always leads to this *disjunctive synthesis* of determinism and agnosticism (emphasis added).

We see from the discussion above that the disjunctive synthesis of determinism and agnosticism leads, as does the Schrödinger's Cat paradox, to a well-defined certainty for one variable and a related uncertainty to the non-commensurable observable. 'Determinism and agnosticism' lead to a new framework where both are tightly related to each other within the indeterminacy principle of complementarity, providing some knowledge and some absence of knowledge with a clear-cut relationship between the two as defined by the Heisenberg principle. And the pit between determinism and agnosticism is filled by human choice, which joins them. We see that the discussion between Bohr and Einstein was not a tragedy but a blessing in disguise. It opened pathways to new, purely quantum phenomena of entangled states and teleportation. Consequently, the correct philosophical assertion here is 'determinism AND agnosticism' and not 'determinism' or 'agnosticism' with the illusory pit in between.

Therefore, to answer the original question, the nature of 'AND', in this role, is very broadly a change of the conceptual framework governed by two opposite states, into a different framework where the opposites are irreducibly integrated within the new structure—pure yet precise dialectics.

This is the main clue we get for the composition of the principle of caste liberation with the principle of class struggle. How does this translate into class struggle and Dalit identity development? Each belongs to a separate domain just like the quantum particle and quantum wave. At present they are opposing each other. If class struggle is prior or central, identity development is secondary, and if identity development is primary then class struggle is secondary. One is the struggle for economic equality ($\uparrow$ state); the other is the struggle for equality of identity ($\downarrow$ state). To seek a connection between the two states may mean to take some composition of both, so that neither the class struggle nor the identity struggle are co-measurable (co-observable) separately. It must be some other concept that binds the components together.[27]

A 'real world' example of this concept was provided by Patricia Collins in her excellent exposition 'Towards the New Vision: Race, Class and Gender as Categories of Analysis and Connection'.[28] She describes the situation from her own experience as a teacher in the inner city, where parents of students presented a spectrum of social backgrounds with seemingly unsurmountable opposing differences. Collins recounts that: 'In spite of profound differences in our personal biographies, differences that in other settings would have hampered our ability to relate to one to another, we found that we were all deeply committed to the education of Black children.'[29] In other words, the concept of 'education of Black children' turned out to be much more binding than the concepts of separate identity that in different situational frameworks may have turned them apart. We see that the state of 'education of Black children' cannot be realized (formulated or measured) if each participant focuses on his or her) separate identity— both, 'the education of Black children' and the 'separate identity of parents', are not co-measurable simultaneously.

A framework formulated by Collins out of the experiences of Black feminism can be of help in the discussion of the effective synthesis of class and caste in the Indian context. Collins asserts that as a Black woman, she is in the intersection of race, gender and class oppressions, that she, in a different situation, can be impacted by all three axes of oppression, and that each, however, has a different social background and psychologically feels different. Thus, the different oppressions cannot be 'added', and the statement 'I am more (or less) oppressed than you', therefore, makes little sense. Instead, they can be qualitatively compared and the relationships between them can be and should be investigated. In this context, Collins proposes the axis of 'domination' or 'subordination' as the space for the symbolic dimension of oppression within which the useful comparisons can be constructed. In my opinion, another dimension—that of liberation— should be added to investigate the dynamic aspect of the relationship within domination and submission.

It is not surprising that in this context, Collins is one of the first academic intellectuals who recognized the inadequacy of dichotomous either-or Hamlet-like thinking. She proposes instead, like the Schrödinger's Cat thought experiment of quantum mechanics, the simultaneous presence of two or more different identities. For Collins, as well as for the structure of 'caste India', the simultaneity of being the oppressed AND being the oppressor is important.

For us, the relation between class oppression AND caste oppression is important, and in particular, those relationships that bind sufficiently strongly to eliminate the drive for separate actions within a particular context. For Collins, the context was 'the education of Black children'. What are those concepts or contexts for the economically exploited Indian proletariat of a village and the oppressed Dalits living in the same village?

With this question we start designing the answer to the question: how does one formulate a theory of revolution, based on two separate but closely related concepts, class struggle and caste struggle, or more generally, class struggle and identity struggle? That is, how does one formulate the bisociative theory of revolution?

## Initial Research Answers

We are looking for such theory/praxis (or praxis/theory) units of action, whose source lies in both the content of identity oppression for the Dalits and in more generalized class oppression, each as an independent source of motivation. In the course of the struggle for so defined a task, the mutual trust and necessary unity of concept/praxis may be forged. The revolutionary task, in the context of the bisociative theory of revolution, is the task which is composed out of the issue important from the Dalit liberation viewpoint and the issue that is important from the class struggle viewpoint. It could be the same task, or it could be a task made of two different components which were brought into close coordination. Consequently, we see here that the content of the proposed 'compromise' between the two principles is the creation of the socio/cultural/economic units of revolutionary action designed to address and to overcome both the socio/economic oppression of the worker simultaneously with the socio/cultural oppression of the Dalits, and not the distribution of seats in Parliament, nor the classical 'united front' approach.

The previous discussion suggests the choice of revolutionary tasks which validly engage both proletarians and Dalits. The tasks must have class struggle and caste struggle as independent but interlocking components, and this choice generalizes to any bisociative revolution—the tasks have to engage bisociative components having a valid relative connection.

Till now I have discussed the concept of the bisociative revolution which bisociates the class struggle with the identity movement struggle, such as with feminism or Ambedkarism. However, postulants of Collins who have come out from the Black feminist experience suggest going deeper with that connection to the very individual dimension of oppression that resides within each of us, for at least living our lives in a world full of oppressive structures. Consequently, the bisociative revolution bisociates the social class struggle with individual liberation in several different contexts. Social liberation and individual liberation exist together in a successful bisociative revolution.

## Strategies of the Bisociative Revolution

Our search for the solution of the contradiction between the Marxist class struggle and Ambedkar's version of the caste struggle, focused on Dalit identity development in India, might have a much wider application and usefulness as the question of and need for the proper reformulation of the Marxist theory of revolution has appeared in the context of several modern social revolutions.

BOLIVIA: Alvaro García Linera, the former vice president of Bolivia, one of the leaders of the revolutionary transformation in that country, offers the concept and reality of Indianismo, the identity revolutionary framework, in his book *Plebeian Power*, as the motivational source for the Bolivian revolution. Linera observes:

> In Bolivia [of 2005], the old Marxism is neither politically nor intellectually relevant, and critical Marxism, which comes from a new intellectual generation, has only limited and still narrow circles of production. In contrast, Indianism [a revolutionary identity movement] has little by little established itself as a narrative of resistance.

The question of the interaction between the two essentially different domains of struggle, the assertive struggle of Indianismo and the class struggle of Marxism, came to the forefront with the attempt of reconciliation [a compromise] that allows for 'the processes of local knowledge production' to be combined 'with the universal ones'.

The Bolivian example suggests that the identity movement, seeking identity liberation from the shackles of oppression, can successfully take the revolutionary path. At the same time, the example of the Bolivian revolution shows the conceptual and social limitations of the revolution based primarily on the identity framework. Thus, Linera, in 'Indianismo y Marxismo El Desencuentro De Dos Rasones Revolucionarias',[30] observes that 'Marxism came to form political culture [. . .] based on supremacy of the working class identity over and above other identities [. . .] and in the historical and class-based inferiority of the country's predominantly campesino [peasant] communities', and he quite correctly assesses the hierarchical, and therefore oppressive, nature of the Marxist cultural, intellectual and political milieu.

However, in the January–February 2006 issue of the *New Left Review* (p. 83), in Linera's action statement, just at the very beginning of his assumption of power in Bolivia, we find the assessment that 'In the case of the left pole, the mobilizing identity is predominantly ethnocultural, around which workers' identity is either dissolved [. . .] or complements indigenous leadership at the secondary level'. We see, from this viewpoint of hierarchical oppression, that the identity framework of Indianismo had preserved exactly the same hierarchical structure as its Marxist competitors. The Bolivian revolution lost the opportunity to learn. It had not learned the necessity of the new dialectical 'and'.

MEXICO: John Holloway,[31] coming from the background of the Zapatista Liberation Army's victory in Mexico, points out that the scientific socialism of Friedrich Engels, which developed into the theory of Vladimir Lenin's vanguard party, is the theory of the 'emancipation of the proletariat', but certainly 'not of its own self-emancipation'.[32] But for the Dalits to overcome their oppression, self-emancipation is necessary. Together with Linera, Holloway points to the separation of theory—such as developed by bourgeois intellectuals (Lenin)—and the experience of workers as one of the central characteristic obstacles along the way of revolution. The proposed approach eliminates this separation by synthesizing the identity development based on lived experience within with the structure of class struggle without.

POLAND: We start with the Polish Solidarity worker leader Lech Walesa, who provided evidence of the desperation of the Polish workers lacking a revolutionary theory that would help them fight the 20th-century Polish communist regime: '. . . and out of it should come out a book. It has to overturn the old theories. And, at the same time describe them, in order to overturn them.'[33]

The absence of theory accompanying revolutionary strategy in the Polish workers' struggle of the 1980s undermined the vision of the Polish Solidarity movement. It saw the self-governing workers' factory councils as the integral component of the self-governing Polish nation. The 'self-governing' component here belonged to the national liberation movement; rarely in history had the social justice agenda and the nationalist idea been in such a close, interlocking synthesis. This Polish socialist compromise was sharpened by the author to extend and focus the attention of the workers' control on the city–countryside divide, present in Poland's economic development at the time, by creating a socioeconomic domain that integrated the social dimension of workers' consciousness with the individual dimension of peasant consciousness, while creating an indivisible socio/economic unit.

Unfortunately, the martial law declared four months after that programmatic synthesis was reached at the 1st National Solidarity meeting undermined it, and the 'round table' compromise of 1989 was effectively emptied of workers' councils.

## Conclusion

The aim of the presented discussion has been to offer a constructive response to JNU's Kanhaiya Kumar, who realized that the reason for the increase of Hindutva fascism in India is the divide between the Left and the Dalits. In order to arrive at the bridge closing the divide between the two, we have sketched elements of the approach in terms of the discussion organized by the Arvind Institute of Marxist Studies in 2013 where Sinha and Teltumbde presented their arguments.

We have connected the discussion with the concept of the principled compromise proposed by Balibar and Wallerstein as well as with the intersectionality approach formulated by Black feminism and applied the two to the construction of the bridge for the divide between the two antinomies of caste and class. We asserted, on the basis of this discussion, that class oppression and Dalit caste oppression are distinctly different from each other yet two strongly interlocking forms which need to find similarly independent yet interlocking paths to liberation. We proposed, as the solution to this contradiction, the way of choosing, and organizing around, the revolutionary tasks that have two distinct components of class and caste.

To our surprise, after sketching the argument, we found that early Naxalite movement was already organizing itself around similar principles. Kunnath[34] discusses the 'Dalit capacity to object not only to the landlords but also to the Maoist organization itself. I present the Dalit critique of the Maoist struggle, their perceptions of how the Movement in its rise to power has neglected Dalit interests. A case study of a Maoist people's court illustrates the strategies employed by Dalit labourers in demonstrating their protest against their own organization. In the second part, I discuss how Dalit participation in the Maoist movement has enhanced their capacity to act collectively as a class on the one hand, and on the other, to express themselves through the idioms of their own caste identities.'[35] He further quotes from the conversation with Rajubhai, a villager and member of the Maoist movement in Bihar, who in no uncertain voice asserts the degree of negligence of Dalit's issues and presents us with the cause of this negligence:

> . . . but now that the Sangathan has got a foothold here, its ambition has grown into one of capturing state power. So they have started taking in people from the dominant castes, against whom we fought previously. As a result of the entry of the landowning castes into the Sangathan, it is hesitant to raise the issues of land and wages. For the last twenty years, wages have remained the same: 3 kilos of paddy for a day's work. The working class is no longer a priority for the Sangathan. (p. 128)

As soon as the Naxalite movement woke up to its ambition of power, the working class (and Dalits) was no longer its priority. That brings us again to the question of Holloway,[36] how to win revolution without taking power?

# References

Ambedkar, B.R. *Buddha or Karl Marx*. Published posthumously. Available at http://www.ambedkar.org/ambcd/20.Buddha%20or%20Karl%20Marx.htm. Accessed 18 July 2017.

Baker, William. 2016. 'Koestler Theory as a Foundation for Problem Solving', in B. Czarnocha, William Baker, Olen Dias and Vrunda Prabhu. 2016. *The Creative Enterprise of Mathematics Teaching-Research*. Sense Publishers.

Linera, Alvaro Garcia. 2014. *Plebeian Power*, Haymarket Books.

# STRATEGY OF CONVERSION TO BUDDHISM

## INTENT AND AFTERMATH

*Anand Teltumbde*

## Ambedkar's Vision behind Conversion

Babasaheb Ambedkar had made a historic declaration on 13 October 1935 at Yeola (in Nashik district) of his resolve to renounce Hinduism.[1] It provoked varied reactions. The orthodox Hindus were unmoved. In nearby Nashik, where they were being harassed for the past five years by the Kalaram temple entry satyagraha, they were exceedingly jubilant. The politically minded Hindus deplored it and felt threatened. Some had issued death threats to Ambedkar.[2] His own people were confused, some of them having openly opposed it.[3] The religious establishments of some minority communities were, however, enthused to make a bid to attract him towards them.

As a follow-up of this declaration and in order to have a blueprint for the tasks ahead, a conference titled Mumbai Ilakha Mahar Parishad (Mumbai Province Mahar Conference) was organized from 30 May to 1 June 1936 at Mumbai. It shared the venue with two more conferences, namely, the conference of Mahar ascetics and the conference of Matangs from the Bombay province. In the conference, Ambedkar made a detailed and passionate speech, which was published under the title 'Mukti Kon Pathe?' (Which Path to Salvation?).[4] Here he tried to systematically explain why Dalits needed to change their religion.[5] He had just developed this explanation in his celebrated text, *Annihilation of Caste*. His conclusion in *Annihilation of Caste* was that castes being mainly part of the rules of the Hindu religion, which were sourced from the *Dharmashastras* (Smritis and Puranas), could not be annihilated unless the *Dharmashastras* were destroyed. He divided the scriptures of the Hindu religion into two parts: the religion of rules and the religion of principles, the latter being provided in the Vedas and Upanishads, which he observed did not have much influence on the religion in practice. He assessed that the Hindus would never be prepared for destroying the *Dharmashastras* and hence he had decided for himself to renounce Hinduism. Ambedkar thus argued that there was no hope for Untouchables to live a respected life within Hinduism. The only way they could escape from their caste bondage was to renounce it.

In 'Mukti Kon Pathe?' Ambedkar outlined two considerations in changing religion— existential and spiritual.[6] In explaining the existential consideration, he mainly indicated the pitiful plight of Dalits. They suffered atrocities at the feeblest violation of the caste code as perceived by the caste Hindus. Ambedkar termed it a class conflict. He elaborated his point as follows:

> It is not a conflict between two individuals or two groups; it is a conflict between two classes. It is not a question of dominance or of injustice over one man; it is a question of dominance perpetrated by one class over the other. It is a question of injustice heaped by one class over the other [. . .] The examples of this conflict enumerated above openly prove one point, which is that this conflict arises when you insist upon equality with the upper classes while dealing with them [. . .] the cause of their anger is only one and that is your behavior demanding equality, which hurts their esteem.[7]

Ambedkar then concluded: 'The conflict between the touchables and the untouchables is of permanent nature and is going to last for ever. Because, according to them the religion that is responsible for assigning you the lowest rung, is *sanatan* (which does not have either origin or end). There cannot be any change in it.'[8] Coming to the existential aspect of this problem, he observed that the lack of strength of Dalits was the root cause of the perpetuation of this conflict. Dalits did not possess any of the three strengths human beings are expected to possess, namely, the strengths of numbers, wealth and mind.[9] They did not have the strength of numbers as they were a minority, divided into numerous castes and dispersed in villages. They did not have the strength of wealth because they did not possess land or businesses or pursue decent employment. They did not possess mental strength as they were inured to humiliation, insults and oppression by caste Hindus for centuries.[10] If Dalits relied upon their own strength, they could not hope to escape their prevailing miserable state.

He then compared them with Muslims, who were also a minority quite like Dalits. However, he said, Hindus would not dare to treat them like Dalits, because they very well knew that a Muslim had the backing of the entire Muslim community in India. If a Muslim is touched by a Hindu anywhere, the Muslim community from Kashmir to Kanyakumari would come out in support of him. The Hindus, however, would never hesitate in unleashing humiliation and perpetrating atrocities on Dalits on the slightest pretext because they know that Dalits do not have any such backing from anyone. Moreover, Dalits and their oppressors, both being seen as Hindus, leave no scope for others to intervene. Therefore, as he concluded, Dalits had to think in terms of supplementing their strength from the outside. This strength could come only through merging with some other religious community, by converting to its religion. He thus justifies his call for conversion as an existential necessity for Dalits. It followed that the religion they convert to should have a sizeable community in the country, with Islam, Christianity and Sikhism implicitly constituting his zone of consideration. And since he had been speaking about Islam all along since 1928, including in the speech under discussion, Islam appeared to be the religion of his choice.

The spiritual consideration in the change of religion was related with enhancing the worth of an individual. Since the Hindu religion did not have any place for an individual, it could not provide spiritual solace to anyone. According to Ambedkar, the real objective of a religion should be the spiritual development of individuals: '[B]irth of an individual is not for service of the society, it is for his or her own emancipation.'[11] He declared that a religion which did not grant an individual primacy was not acceptable to him.[12] He saw the necessity of three things for the development of an individual—compassion, equality and freedom—and observed that Hinduism did not have any of these.

Personally, Ambedkar rated the spiritual aspect of religion to be more important than the existential aspect. However, for the sake of Dalits, he would emphasize the existential utility of religion. It appeared that he was inclined to join one of the existing religious communities in India which would bring them the requisite strength to counter Hindu oppression. Although the Yeola declaration came in 1935, he had been variously advocating religious conversion to Dalits as a means of escaping caste bondage right from 1928 through his journal *Bahishkrit Bharat*.[13] *Bahishkrit Bharat* is replete with references which clearly indicate that he had almost reached the conclusion that without conversion to some other religion there was no escape for Untouchables from caste bondage.[14] Apart from the subject of conversion, he also dwelt upon which religion would be the best for Dalits to convert to. He had gone to the extent of rejecting Buddhism and Arya Samaj and indicating his preference for Christianity or Islam:

> By becoming Buddhist or Arya Samajist, there is not going to be any significant impact on the prejudices of the people who call themselves as belonging to upper varna (*uccha varniya*) and therefore we do not see much sense in accepting that path. If we want to successfully confront the prejudices of Hindus, we have to convert to either Christianity or Islam in order to secure the backing of some rebellious community. It is only then the blot of untouchability on Dalits will be washed away.[15]

Within less than two years, he eliminated Christianity and zeroed in on Islam. In the *Bahishkrit Bharat* edition of 15 March 1929, under the editorial 'Notice to Hinduism', Ambedkar exhorted Untouchables under the bold heading, 'If you have to convert, become Musalman'. After analysing the futility of becoming Buddhist and Arya Samajist, he also dismissed Christianity because 'even Christianity could not escape castes in India'. He might have known that the conversion of Dalits to Christianity would not make any difference to their social status. They would remain the same old Untouchables to not only Hindus but also to their upper-caste counterparts. He would explain that only the Muslim community could come to back them up with full support.[16] Even though he would keep saying that he had only decided to renounce Hinduism and not specified which religion to embrace, his rational choice of Islam was all too evident until 1936.

It might have been a stratagem to pressurize Hindus for reforms, which was his modest expectation in the Mahar conference. But the manner in which they reacted to the legitimate exercise of Dalits' civil rights left Ambedkar totally disillusioned. Even in the next Satyagraha Conference, organized in December, they cunningly aborted it.[17] Immediately after Mahar, he began speaking about conversion. Since the Morley–Minto Reforms (Indian Councils Act, 1909), the communal basis of sharing political power was formalized and even the separate status of Dalits and Adivasis from Hindus was insinuated by the Muslim League, Ambedkar saw a lever to bend Hindus by threatening to leave the Hindu fold. Interestingly, Hindus completely ignored them until the Yeola declaration.

## The Choice of Buddhism

However, the choice of religion that Ambedkar made in 1956 was quite contrary to this existential consideration.[18] It appears that his spiritual consideration eventually overwhelmed the existential one. Buddhism, which became his choice for conversion, was almost extinct in India save in the hilly areas of the north-east (West Bengal, Assam, Sikkim, Mizoram and Tripura) and the high Himalayan valleys (Ladakh district in Jammu and Kashmir, Himachal Pradesh and northern Uttar Pradesh), with a tiny population as its traditional followers. This did not qualify as satisfying the existential need of Dalits as he had outlined. While there is a reason to believe that Ambedkar made this choice after a serious study over more than two decades, the influence of Buddhism on him was public knowledge. It goes back to his early years, when he was introduced to the Buddha through his biography, which was presented to him to commemorate his having passed his matriculation examination. It was authored by Keluskar Guruji, a noted social worker of those times who had presided over the felicitation function. Since then, the influence of Buddhism on his mind would surface off and on. Even in 'Mukti kon pathe?', although he appeared to be extolling Islam and thereby gave an impression that Islam might be his choice for conversion, he ended his speech with the famous exhortation of the Buddha in the Mahaparinibbana Sutta—'Appo deepo bhava' (Be your own light).[19] It was not surprising that he ultimately chose Buddhism, ignoring his own rationale that the religious conversion of Dalits should serve their need of existential utility.

His choice of Buddhism was influenced as much by his own proclivities as by the external reactions from the potentially 'receiving' minorities, the upper-caste Hindus and Untouchable leaders. The Indian Christians immediately disapproved it as 'instrumental conversion' devoid of any spiritual content. Actually, what lay behind it was the upper-caste Christians' perceived threat from the mass influx of anti-caste Dalits to their hegemony. The Hindu Mahasabha (HMS) was palpably threatened and deployed a dual strategy to persuade Ambedkar against embracing any 'foreign' faith and threatened him against the conversion itself. Its ex-president B.S. Moonje had a compact with Ambedkar (called the Moonje–Ambedkar Pact) that before taking any decision he would confer with HMS leaders and other Hindu organizations. On 29 October 1935, the HMS had convened its extraordinary session in Bombay under the chairmanship of Madan Mohan Malviya, wherein many Dalit leaders—Jagjivan Ram, J.N. Mandal, Rasiklal

Biswas, Dharm Prakash, P.N. Rajbhoj, M.C. Rajah and Baloo Palwankar—were co-opted to oppose Ambedkar's declaration.[20] The Muslims, who were in contention with the Hindus for a greater share in political power, were elated by this heaven-sent opportunity. It is said that the nizam of Hyderabad offered a huge sum to Ambedkar if he converted to Islam.[21] The Buddhist leaders were more welcoming but it did not fit into the existential solution Ambedkar had in mind.[22] Buddhism would, however, appeal to him for its rationalism. Moreover, being a religion of Indian origin, it did not have the risk of denationalization associated with conversion to a 'foreign' religion.[23] With the latter consideration, he was rather inclined to accept Sikhism, which was also prompted by Moonje, who had agreed to support his demand to extend the safeguards available to Hindu Dalits if they converted to Sikhism. Ambedkar had also sent a thirteen-member team, a 'vanguard' of the conversion movement,[24] to Amritsar to study Sikhism and in the interim influenced the Sikhs to establish the Khalsa College in Mumbai. A section of the Akalis (Jat Sikhs), however, felt that the influx of a mass of Dalit converts would Dalitize Sikhism and opposed the proposal. After realizing that Sikh society also followed casteism, Ambedkar dropped the idea of joining the Sikh fold.

Ambedkar justified his choice of Buddhism in many ways. Buddhism, according to him, was the only religion most compatible with rationality and modern science.[25] He found that the emphasis on three principles—wisdom, as against superstition and supernaturalism; love and compassion in relation with others; and complete equality—unique to Buddhism.[26] Apart from its several superior attributes over other religions, as perceived by Ambedkar, there were other factors too that influenced his choice. One of the factors, as he later explained with nationalistic considerations, was the indigenous origin of Buddhism.[27] His rejection of Christianity and Islam, despite their egalitarian orientation, was as much due to their foreign origin as to the absence of their challenging something like the caste system. The only Indian religion, as seen by Ambedkar, that arose and grew out of the struggle against Brahminism and its offspring, the caste system, and never succumbed to it was Buddhism. He was the first to characterize it as a revolutionary and the most egalitarian of all religions. Christianity, Islam as well as Sikhism, which constituted his repertoire from existential considerations, had all compromised with caste in their communities in India.

In the political sphere, Ambedkar's efforts to project Dalit interests as the class interest of a vulnerable and stigmatized community based on the material consequences of exclusion—destitution, poverty and illiteracy— spelt the redefinition of the principle of minority, which was contrary to the colonial definition of religious communities as political actors. In order to fortify this argument, it was imperative to show Dalits as not belonging to the Hindu community. He accomplished it through his theory of untouchability, which showed Dalits not only as not belonging to Hinduism but also in an antagonistic relationship to Brahminical Hinduism throughout history. This theory was put forth in his essay, 'The Untouchables: Who Were They and Why They Became Untouchables', which was published in 1948. He propounded that Dalits (Untouchables) were a distinctive ethical and political community of Buddhists who became the Broken Men as they belonged to a group of wandering tribesmen defeated in battle as nomadic society gave way to settled agriculture. They were stigmatized as Untouchable as they had to eat the meat of dead cattle for survival and as they refused to accept Brahminism. Through this theory, he not only eased his political argument but also secured for Dalits a rich legacy and pride of being uncompromising warriors against the evil of Brahminism right from the very beginning. Buddhism was their original religion.[28] Ambedkar's choice of it was thus a mere return to a religion of the ancestors, a kind of homecoming.

It appears, in addition to the above, that certain circumstantial and temporal considerations also obviated his choice of 'foreign' religions. The communal situation in India had aggravated to inflammable levels after the 1940s. It was to soon culminate in the partition of India. Notwithstanding his assurance to Moonje, the choice of Islam, which most satisfied the existential consideration behind conversion, was out of the question as it would have created political upheaval with disastrous consequences for Dalits. At the same time, it may be argued that it could have been used to extract the most beneficial political-economic reforms for them. The consideration of Christianity too would have had similar consequences. There was no such danger with indigenous religions, which were considered by the hegemonic Hindus as just sects of Hinduism. In any case, they would never engender extraterritorial loyalties in the communities of their adherents. Ambedkar's choice of Buddhism therefore came as a great relief to the entire Hindutva movement.[29]

While these multifarious considerations certainly influenced his choice of Buddhism as a religion for Dalits,[30] the overriding reason, however, remained that it was seen as superior to all other religions. His repertoire interestingly was not limited by established religions and included even (anti-religion) Marxism, as he revealed later. Although Ambedkar was no Marxist, he never ignored its revolutionary promise to the contemporary world and particular attraction to the subaltern classes of which Dalits were a part. For him, Marxism was the 'given' best but for its 'negatives', which he had to transcend while making his choices. Therefore, he always used it as a benchmark, a measuring scale to validate his decisions. In the case of Buddhism, he made his evaluation public by demonstrating how Buddhism had all the positive content of Marxism and none of its pitfalls. He complained that while Marxism had shaken the religious system it had not provided a viable substitute. He accused it of using poverty as an excuse for sacrificing human freedom.[31] Buddhism, on the other hand, taught social freedom, intellectual freedom, economic freedom and political freedom and equality, not only between man and man but also between man and woman.[32] One may not agree with his understanding of Marxism or his projection of the Buddhist sangha as a model of communist society, which was brought about without resorting to bloodshed, unlike the Marxist revolution, but the fact remains that Marxism stayed the conceptual 'second best' to all his choices.

## Ambedkar's Navayana Buddhism

Ambedkar's thesis on the Buddhist origin of Untouchables as well as his attempt to convert Dalits to Buddhism interestingly had a precursor in the very similar attempts half a century before in Tamil Nadu. Pandit Iyothee Thassar (1845–1914), a native scholar, traditional medicine (siddha) practitioner and social reformer who struggled against the practice of untouchability and the concept of caste, had founded the Indian Buddhist Association in 1890,[33] which developed into a broad movement among Tamil Dalits in south India. Around the same time, a Ceylonese monk, Anagarika Dharmapala, had come to India and founded the Mahabodhi Society in 1891, which had a deep association with his attempts to reclaim Bodh Gaya for Buddhism. The Mahabodhi Society mainly attracted upper-caste people and did not have much to do with Untouchables.[34] Pandit Iyothee Thassar, however, was most concerned with the emancipation of Dalits. He established the Sakya Buddhist society at Madras in 1898 and conceived the idea of 'Tamil Buddhism'. This idea had burgeoned to construct an alternative discourse on Indian culture based on the Vedic tradition. In all the discourses on Tamil Buddhism, Iyothee Thassar emphasized the age-old contradiction between the so-called Untouchables and Brahmins. It was the animosity of the Brahmin community stemming from these contradictions that transposed the social stratum of ancient Buddhists to untouchability. He published a weekly magazine titled *Tamilian* from 1907 to 1914. Through this magazine and his other writings, Iyothee Thassar tried to arouse the consciousness of Untouchables and make them aware of their Buddhist antecedents.[35]

Although Ambedkar might not have been unaware of this movement,[36] it was not much help to him. When he decided upon Buddhism, his understanding of it was founded on a radical rejection of Hinduism and the caste system and a critical evaluation of existing versions of Buddhism.[37] He was painfully aware of the corruption of the Buddha's doctrines in practised versions of Buddhism. He therefore wanted to reconstruct his own version of Buddhism on the basis of the Buddha's rationalist thought to be a religion for modern society. Although he primarily chose it as a substitute of Hinduism for Untouchables, he wanted it to be a religion for all, which while meeting the spiritual needs of people would not conflict with the scientific ethos of modern times. He constructed such a Buddhism in *The Buddha and His Dhamma*[38] as a religion for modern civic society.[39] He wrote this book in the stylized form of gospel with the intent of creating a single text for neo-Buddhists (those who newly became Buddhist after following him) to read and grasp its essence. It so differed from the conventional understanding of Buddhism that it had to face flak from certain orthodox quarters.[40] After its publication, *The Mahabodhi*, a journal of the Mahabodhi Society of India, carried a review which termed it a dangerous book. 'Ambedkar's Buddhism,' said the reviewer 'is based on hatred as against the Buddha's based on compassion'. The title, pleaded the reviewer, should be changed from *The Buddha and His Dhamma* to *Ambedkar and his Dhamma*; for Ambedkar preached non-Dhamma as Dhamma for motives of political and social reform.[41] Another paper titled *The Light of Dhamma* (Rangoon) observed that although the author was a great and good man, the tragedy was that it was neither a great book nor a good book.[42] Buddhist monk Jivaka wrote: 'In India the movement started by Ambedkar was not Buddhism but a campaign for social reform under the name Buddhism . . . his book *The Buddha and His Dhamma* is misnamed for he preaches non-Dharma as Dharma . . . Ambedkar entered on his new religion with hate in his heart and his followers are still nourishing and fanning the flames of hate in the uneducated masses they lead.'[43] As against these, the noted Buddhist scholar and monk Bhadant Anand Kausalyayan defended the work as a creative interpretation that respects the spirit of the Theravada legend and precept.[44] In the introduction to *The Buddha and His Dhamma* Ambedkar himself indicated four deviations in his conception of Buddhism from the established understanding of it:

1.   The Buddha could not have had his first great realization simply because he encountered an old man, a sick man and a dying man. It is unreasonable and therefore false to assume that the Buddha did not have previous knowledge of something so common.
2.   The Four Noble Truths 'make the gospel of the Buddha a gospel of pessimism'. If life is composed entirely of suffering then there is no incentive for change.
3.   The doctrines of no soul, karma and rebirth are incongruous. It is illogical to believe that there can be karma and rebirth without a soul.
4.   The monk's purpose has not been presented clearly. Is he supposed to be a 'perfect man' or a 'social servant'?

These sweeping criticisms suggest that Ambedkar was not comfortable with conventional Buddhism and wanted to restructure it on a rational footing. To distance himself from all existing versions (*yana*) he called his Buddhism as Navayana Buddhism.[45] Several scholars have remarked upon and analysed this aspect of Navayana Buddhism. For example, Adele Fiske and Christoph Emmerich undertook a detailed analysis of Ambedkar's use of the traditional Buddhist texts in Pali in writing *The Buddha and His Dhamma*.[46] They examined his references in the original version of *The Buddha and His Dhamma* and observed patterns of alteration to the Buddhism in the Pali canon through omission, change in emphasis and changed meaning through interpolation or interpretation.[47] This critique may be simply answered by saying that Ambedkar himself never claimed any puritanical adherence to the old Buddhist canon. Rather, he purposefully subjected the latter to his rationalist scrutiny in order to transform Buddhism from a doctrine of individual salvation to a practice of collective emancipation in modern times. Moreover, Ambedkar did not intend Navayana for Dalits only; he meant it as a universal *vehicle* for the entire humanity.[48] Its goal is individual and collective emancipation from non-rational thought, economic exploitation and unjust social difference.[49]

Ambedkar was not happy with the contemporary state of Buddhism. He believed that Buddhism had great prowess to be the religion of the modern world and wanted it to perform that role. In his radical interpretation or interpolation of the Pali canon, he did believe that he was restoring what was originally preached by the Buddha.[50] For this radical departure from traditional Buddhism, his Buddhism was termed neo-Buddhism by others, which insinuated that Dalit converts were not Buddhists but Hindus with a different ideological stance.[51] Christopher Queen counters these insinuations by showing that activist Buddhism in many places in the world has used modern resources and methods to pursue 'this-worldly' change without being qualified as 'neo' Buddhism. Queen rather demonstrated that Ambedkar's transformations retained 'the central elements of the Buddhist vision'.[52] Many scholars observed that Ambedkar's Buddhism did not conform to any of the old Buddhist canons.[53] But the conformity to the revealed word has never been a characteristic of Buddhism. As Fiske and Emmrich rightly argued, 'orthodoxy is by far the lesser issue in the history of ruptures within the Buddhist tradition compared to the role of orthopraxy . . . If Ambedkar departed from any Buddhist tradition, it was on the grounds of a challenge to orthopraxy through his own ideas of political and social practice.'[54]

A keyword in Ambedkar's Buddhist discourse is 'justice', based on 'liberty, equality and fraternity', the slogan of the French Revolution that became the motto of bourgeois France. Therefore, his Navayana came to be seen as repackaged Western liberal thought. Ambedkar would invalidate this critique by saying that he had not picked up this slogan from the French Revolution but from 'my master', the Buddha. It is a different matter that there is no reasonable equivalent of such a saying in Buddhism that anticipated it to re-emerge in bourgeois France. Eugenia Yurolova's article, like Olivier Herrenschmidt's, echoes Ambedkar's statement that equality has no value without liberty and fraternity; that the three must coexist and do so only by following the Buddha's way. Ambedkar, Yurolova says, felt that democracy was the best form of government but not in its Western form, in which liberty had swallowed equality, producing class difference and a market ideologically supported by social Darwinism.[55]

Thus, Ambedkar's Navayana Buddhism represented a utopian vision of the world wherein mankind would experience 'liberty, equality and fraternity' all together. Drawing from what he wrote in relation to Marxism, it comes quite close to the Marxist utopia of communism, sans its methodological sophistication. Ambedkar's departure from existing versions of Buddhism reflected his desire to make it ideologically a perfect fit with modern rationality without forsaking the form of a popular religion with sets of symbols and rituals. It is noteworthy that he himself had written a booklet titled 'Buddha Puja Path' (Buddhist Way of Worship) for new converts to Navayana Buddhism. In both—the ideological as well as ritual aspects—however, Navayana Buddhism had to be antithetical to Hinduism. It was expected that it would be sans the unintelligible Brahminic mumbo-jumbo, elaborate rituals that entailed a waste of resources, obsessive individualistic orientation reflected in meditation, blindness towards injustice and exploitation, and so on. Seen this way, Navayana Buddhism in its ideological orientation may appear closer to Marxism[56] than any other ideological stream. However, the way it is practised by Dalits, it appears antagonistic to Marxism and friendly with Brahminic Hinduism.

## Impact on Dalit Converts

There are not many scientific studies to assess the impact of conversion on Dalits, although many people have made their impressionistic observations about this impact, which ranges from very negative to very positive.

Critiquing his conversion, one finds leftist intellectuals who think that it was a retrogressive step to adopt a religious identity in the mid-20th century, to a potentially revolutionary mass of Dalits. It has definitely weakened the movement for justice and equality and dimmed its prospects of achieving genuine social change. Its only impact has been the addition of one more identity, howsoever positively endowed or constructed, to people who already had a surfeit of them. It has thereby contributed to the aggravation of identity conflicts and enhanced the scope for identity politics by vested interests.[57] Besides these arguments against religious identity, there are many subsidiary arguments against Buddhism's ability to propel radical change. These arguments are primarily against historical Buddhism, which critics argue was essentially a path of individualistic salvation through a renunciation of the world. While Buddhism in itself did not subscribe to any of the social evils, at the same time it did not fight any of them, including the caste system and slavery.[58] Similarly, the eminent historian D.D. Kosambi pointed out that in the recruitment of monks, the candidate's social position was not entirely disregarded: '. . . runaway slaves, savage tribesmen, escaped criminals, the chronically ill and the indebted as well as aboriginal Nagas were denied admission into the order.'[59] Its radical orientation was limited to its own sphere of influence but because of its thrust towards renunciation, it did not have a proactive dimension to struggle against the social forces that sustain these social evils. Despite its domination for nearly a millennium, Buddhism could not dent the life-world of caste created by Brahminism, and when the latter resurged in the 8th century under the leadership of Adi Sankara, it disappeared without any trace in society. As such, they tend to dismiss any possibility of revolutionary change coming through the spread of Buddhism as imagined by Ambedkar.

Oblivious of these arguments of the detractors, the protagonists of conversion to Buddhism attribute the entire development of Dalits during the last five decades to Buddhism. Obviously this is an erroneous attribution insofar as while all Dalits have made progress, not all of them have become Buddhist even in name, leave aside in practice. One may have to prove that Dalit Buddhists have made significantly more progress than Dalits who have not become Buddhists. There is probably no evidence for this. In each geographical region, the most populous Dalit caste (Mahars in Maharashtra, Malas in Andhra Pradesh, Chamars in Uttar Pradesh, Parayars in Tamil Nadu, Holayas in Karnataka, etc.), irrespective of whether it has converted to Buddhism or not, has made significant progress in relation to other Dalit castes, which remains indistinguishable from the progress made by Dalit Buddhists in its vicinity or in Maharashtra, the prototype state for Dalit Buddhists. This may be true of tangible and measurable development, such as economic, educational, demographic and political development. However, the sociocultural, spiritual and psychological aspects are not measurable but they constitute the catalyst for other types of development. It is these developments which are aimed at through a change of religion. It is argued, for instance, that conversion to Buddhism provided almost an instantaneous increase in self-esteem and perception of self-worth among Dalits. While one may not dispute it, all these positives ought ultimately to result in some tangible development which is objectively measured.

Notwithstanding these broad-brush contentions between the protagonists and antagonists of conversion, one could assess the changes, if any, that have come as a result of Dalits converting to Buddhism. They may be best assessed in relation to what was expected by Ambedkar from this conversion. One of his objectives, as discussed before, was to merge the Dalit community with an existing community by becoming their co-religionists. This was obviously defeated by converting to Buddhism because Buddhism did not have any such community to absorb Dalits to resist atrocities by caste Hindus. The choice of Buddhism had basically overridden his initial existential consideration and highlighted the spiritual one, so as to become a precedent phase of the religio-cultural revolution for bringing about a 'socio-political' revolution as he contended.[60] Although he has not defined the contours of this religio-cultural revolution in clear terms, one can surmise them from the distinctive attributes of Buddhism because of which he chose it for conversion. They may be succinctly depicted by 'pradna, sheel, karuna': wisdom (scientific outlook), character (self-discipline), and compassion (encompassing equality and love for all). In order to create a new cultural paradigm as a prerequisite for imbibing these values, he gave twenty-two vows to his disciples.[61] One can probably assess to what extent this cultural paradigm has set in among the converts.

Outwardly there is a sea change observed among Dalits after 1956. There was a definite formation of an aggressive new cultural identity which expressed itself through massive celebrations of Ambedkar and Buddha Jayanti in place of Hindu festivals, new Dalit congregations in place of Hindu melas, new genre of songs and dramas, and so on. Growing congregations at an increasing number of places associated with events in Ambedkar's life have been astounding phenomena. The commemoration of the first initiation ceremony at Deeksha Bhoomi in Nagpur on Dussehra (paradoxically a Hindu festival), homage-paying to Ambedkar on his death anniversary at the Chaitya Bhoomi in Mumbai on 6 December, the observance of his birth anniversaries at his birthplace in Mhow in Madhya Pradesh and all over the country on 14 April, commemoration of the satyagraha at Mahad for asserting human rights on 25 December and the commemoration of the battle of Bhima-Koregaon on 1 January and other such ceremonies definitely stun anyone by the sheer magnitude. Then there is a huge market of exclusive cultural products in the form of songs eulogizing Ambedkar, along with bracelets, necklaces, clothes, flags and finally a great amount of literature—papers, magazines, pamphlets and books—reinforcing this identity. There is no doubt that the Ambedkarite movement has forged and fortified a new cultural identity for Dalits. But can one take it to mean the creation of a new cultural paradigm that Ambedkar expected through conversion to Buddhism?

We are facilitated by two studies devoted to this aspect. One is by Timothy Fitzgerald in 1994 and the other by Neera Burra in 1997. Both have studied the practices of Buddhists in Maharashtra and have come to a similar conclusion that the conversion has not significantly changed their way of life. For instance, Fitzgerald concludes his study saying that although rural Mahars have begun to refuse to perform traditional duties such as scavenging and have given up the practice of eating beef, their recognition and practice of sub-caste hierarchy and untouchability, absence of intercaste marriage, and worship of Hindu gods and goddesses is evidence that they practice 'the kind of Buddhism which has not really changed anybody or anything very radically'.[62] Burra's study of village life provides a still more devastating picture. Although 70 out of her 102 respondents classified themselves as Buddhist, none of them had taken Ambedkar's twenty-two vows. She found statues of Hindu gods and goddesses alongside pictures of Ambedkar and the Buddha in every household she visited. Over half the people she interviewed said that they prayed to all gods, including Hindu deities. She characterizes the religious practice of rural Mahars as fundamentally Hindu with a Buddhist exterior. While Mahars still observed most of the Hindu marriage rituals within the household, the marriage ceremony was performed in a Buddhist way. She observed that this dichotomy between private Hindu practice and public Buddhist practice marked other rituals as well.[63]

Burra is led to conclude this dichotomous behaviour as a 'symbol of identity transformation' rather than a true religious conversion. 'The Buddhist identity is important mainly for the outside world,' she writes. 'There is an attempt to emphasize one's distinctiveness and this is achieved by different methods. The inner core may remain Hindu but this in no way reflects a betrayal of the cause.'[64] This seeming dichotomy in the public and private behaviours of Dalits noted by Burra may rather be understood in terms of the old caste traditions. While their vulnerable lives impel Dalits to seek the security of their old gods and follow the old way of life in private, in public they essentially follow their collective caste practices. These practices reflect the political imperative of distancing from Hindus imbibed from the Dalit movement under Ambedkar. Since they were barred from going on pilgrimages and to jatras and temples, they developed their own substitutes through the central figures of Ambedkar and the Buddha, who just replaced their old gods in public. Viharas in place of temples, Buddhist places in place of old pilgrimage centres, Deeksha Bhoomi-Chaitya Bhoomi congregations in place of the old jatras, and so on. Even here the old Hindu modes appear to have been adopted unconsciously. For instance, not allowing people with footwear inside Buddha viharas or following gender segregation in all public places or avoiding non-vegetarian food in marriages, etc. can be easily traced to the Hindu practices.

The transformation of even cultural identity through conversion to Buddhism has been problematic. Since there was no existing Buddhist community to merge with, the Dalit identity of converts survived even after conversion. 'Dalit' itself is a construction for assimilating all ex-Untouchable castes, which was far from accomplished. Even conversion to Buddhism could not bind all Untouchable castes together. Ambedkar imagined that when he converted, all seven crore Dalits would at once follow suit.[65] This was not to be. What happened was that only Mahars in Maharashtra and to some extent similar castes of Dalits in other provinces followed him and became Buddhist. Buddhist thus became synonymous with Mahar. Even in terms of superfluous identity, the conversion failed to bring about any change. Buddhist still means Mahar in Maharashtra, Jatava in Uttar Pradesh, and so on. Even among these castes, the sub-caste consciousness has not been overcome. Most marriages used to take place within the same sub-castes and violations were resisted until at least the first educated generation. Although there was hope that second- and third-generation educated Dalits would override these differences, marriages across sub-castes among Dalits are still not widespread. Dalits still do not identify with scavenger castes (Bhangis) and treat them as Untouchables like others.

It may be imagined, as Ambedkar did, that if all the Dalit castes had converted to Buddhism it would have meant a big change in terms of binding all Dalits with a new identity. After all, de-casting Dalits is no mean achievement. If conversion could de-caste Dalits, casting off their primordial caste identity, they would have been able to forge a united struggle against the oppressive tendencies of civil society as well as the state. This contention could have set in motion the democratization of society. But this proved to be just wishful thinking. Conversion to Buddhism, like previous religious conversions, did not change anything for Dalits and as a result they carried on with their pre-conversion Hindu practices and beliefs. It could not even threaten Hindu chauvinist groups that are vehemently opposed to Dalits converting to Christianity or Islam but are happy with Dalits converting to Buddhism, as they treat the latter just as a sect of Hinduism. This is reflected in Hindutva forces' co-option of Ambedkar as the benefactor of the Hindus because he chose Buddhism instead of Semitic religions like Islam or Christianity.

The other impact of conversion to Buddhism was, interestingly, because of a legal technicality. As per the Moonje–Ambedkar Pact, if Ambedkar converted to Sikhism—an Indian religion considered to be a sect of Hinduism, Buddhism not being on the radar then—Hindus would support the extension of safeguards for Hindu Dalits to converts to Sikhism. But when the conversion took place after two decades to an Indian religion, the political situation had changed in favour of Hindus. The constitutional definition of Scheduled Castes (SCs), the official term for Dalits, was restricted to Hinduism. At its inception in 1950, the Constitution recognized only Hindu Dalits. Six years later, the relevant constitutional order (SC and ST Order [Amendment] Act 1956) was amended to include all Sikh Dalits on 25 September 1956, less than three months before Ambedkar led the conversion to Buddhism along with his followers. It would, however, make the Dalit converts lose their legal status as SCs and thereby most constitutional benefits tagged with it, including reservations. It also created a problem of identity. While Dalits enthusiastically followed the wishes of their Babasaheb and embraced Buddhism, they could not declare the same in official records. Those who declared it for ideological reasons were deprived of the constitutional benefits, such as concessions in school fees, scholarships and reservations in educational institutions and jobs as well as in politics. The conversion thus had a great negative impact on the economic and political development of Dalits. This problem told upon the conversion movement which appeared to almost stagnate during the intervening years. It took another thirty-four years for the constitutional order to be amended yet again in 1990 to include Dalit converts to Buddhism.[66] It has really picked up only after 1990, which removed the fear of losing constitutional concessions if one converted to Buddhism. Despite this upsurge, the Buddhist population still is just 8 million, 0.8 per cent of the Indian population. In Maharashtra, not all Mahars appear to have registered themselves as Buddhist as the Buddhist population stands at just 7 per cent of the state population.

Ambedkar left behind a legacy of his thoughts and institutions like the Peoples' Education Society (PES), Republican Party of India (RPI) (formed posthumously in deference to his wishes) and Bharatiya Bauddha Mahasabha (BMS).[67] Soon after his death, rivalry among Dalit leaders for one-upmanship began to surface. These leaders, however, could do so only by usurping Ambedkar's legacy. They had to project themselves as more devoted to Ambedkar than others to the Dalit masses to earn the acceptability of the latter. In this process, all that Ambedkar did or said was simplified and packaged, bereft of content or context, into wares to be traded in the political marts by charlatans. Buddhism, as the path of salvation shown by Ambedkar, with its spiritual and sentimental value, became the biggest victim of this symbolization. While everybody swore by it, the BMS, which was supposed to be the vehicle to propagate it among the masses, was left rudderless because it did not have direct political value. The presidentship of the BMS thus naturally came to his son Yashvantrao (Bhaiyasaheb) Ambedkar uncontested and remained with him until his death in 1977. The RPI, which began splitting from 1959,[68] had four major factions by 1970 in Maharashtra—under R.S. Gavai, B.C. Kamble, B.D. Khobragade and Y.B. Ambedkar—with many other leaders having already deserted it to join the Congress. By the 1970s, factionalism entered every

Dalit sphere and did not spare even the BMS. By then electoral politics had become competitive with the emergence of a class of rich farmers in rural areas and with it the regional parties that threatened the political monopoly of the Congress. Ambedkar, who was almost ignored until then, began to be iconized to woo Dalit voters. In 1967, Yashvantrao Ambedkar built a small stupa at the place where his father was cremated which helped institutionalizing congregations in Ambedkar's name. With their politics in a shambles, faced with assault by the caste Hindus, Dalits nostalgically began divinizing Ambedkar. When Bhaiyasaheb died, his widow, Meeratai Ambedkar, assumed the presidentship but had to face opposition from rival claimants. The BMS, following the RPI, split thereafter into numerous factions all over the country, barely any of them knowing Ambedkar's vision behind it or even Buddhism of *The Buddha and His Dhamma*.

No wonder, the masses were left to flaunt hollow symbols of Buddhism maintaining the Hindu core of their mode of living intact. Recently, a perceptive piece by a professor, who was educated and had later taught in Ambedkar's iconic college in Aurangabad, described the Buddhist practice in Maharashtra that captures the grim reality:

> The practice of Buddhism is limited to observing full-moon days and reciting three refuges at the time of weddings and other occasions. Panchsheel is just for chanting and not for practice. Giving names of the places with which Buddha's life was associated to their houses, is all that counts for the practice of Buddhism. Underneath the stupa-like structure atop a house of a modern Buddhist in Maharashtra, is the wealth of corruption. Buddhist temples are built on the material supplied by the contractors working in local self bodies; the expenditure is indirectly met by such local bodies. There is no sacrifice of any kind on the part of the followers with the result the structures so erected are found developing cracks, cracks in the base. The sermons on Buddhism do not inspire people, either they lack proper preparation or they lack inspirational quality. Buddha is supposed to be a God, and people ask for blessings from him in all events. This is the easiest way of following Buddhism.[69]

While the above may be taken as the practice of ordinary Buddhists, the class of upwardly mobile Dalits who wanted to distinguish themselves from the former have adopted the path of vipassana as truest Buddhism.[70] Through vipassana, a process of rapprochement between traditional Buddhists and Ambedkarite Buddhists has already set in and with that the radical vision of Ambedkar behind Buddhism is being systematically blunted. A few individuals have come out in the open in opposing this trend among Ambedkarite Buddhists.[71] They rightly argue that Ambedkar had not taken any vipassana course nor did he talk of meditation. All the radical Buddhist scholars like P.L. Narasu, Jagdish Kashyap, Bhadant Anand Kausalyayan and Rahul Sankritayan never preached vipassana. Notwithstanding these facts, vipassana has been steadily luring Ambedkarite Buddhists away from his Navayana vision of collective emancipation.

## Bulwark against Radicalism

Ambedkar was a liberal to the core, deeply influenced by the pragmatist ideas of his Professor John Dewey while in Columbia University and Fabian methods as alternatives to revolutionary Marxism, which he had reservations in accepting. Marxism ideologically violated his essentially religious persona. This ideological reservation was later amplified by his contention with practising communists in Mumbai.[72] While in his last days, Ambedkar elevated Marxism to the level of his ideal, Buddhism, in terms of the goal he problematized the former for its methodological reliance on violence and dictatorship. As a matter of fact, the other two anchors of Ambedkar's praxis, the state and religion, also have been anathema to Marxism. Thus, although it may be validly argued that Ambedkar did acknowledge Marxism as an emancipatory ideology with global mass appeal, his own ideological standing would not let him succumb to it. Rather, he would dissuade his followers from the lure of its promise. Eleanor Zelliot (1992), a devoted Ambedkar scholar, had termed Ambedkar's embracing of Buddhism an ultimate bulwark against communism.[73]

Kuber calls Ambedkar's conversion to Buddhism a 'self-deception', having channelled the whole movement of workers and peasants led by him into 'reactionary and metaphysical conceptions'.[74] Indeed, Ambedkarite Dalits have scrupulously observed the self-imposed taboo towards the struggles for livelihood issues—despite having neither land nor jobs to live with dignity—and have isolated themselves into cultural sectarianism. For instance, when after Ambedkar's death B.D. (Dadasaheb) Gaikwad wanted to take up the land struggle, he was accused of hobnobbing with the communists. The RPI then split and splintered, manufacturing a dichotomy between 'Ambedkarism' and Marxism. At that time, Ambedkarism was equated with constitutionalism. When the youth in the early 1970s, inspired by the worldwide wave of unrest, tried to articulate their response to the mounting incidence of atrocities and general deception by the ruling classes in the form of the Dalit Panthers, Buddhism was used to nip it in the bud. Smelling a communist influence in its manifesto, a section dissociated itself with the argument that the Ambedkarite path was Buddhism. From then on, whenever anyone tried to raise the material exploitation of Dalits, he/she was termed as an 'enemy'. On the contrary, self-proclaimed Ambedkarites blindly supported anything to do with Buddhism. The growing network of bhikkus and Buddha viharas in Maharashtra eloquently testify to these facts.

## Conclusion

History testifies that religious conversion has not helped Dalits escape their caste bondage. For over a millennium, Dalits converted to Islam, Christianity, Sikhism and numerous other sects, all of which were opposed to the caste system in theory. But in practice they could not ward off the caste virus and protect Dalits. Unlike the earlier conversions, conversion to Buddhism had a pronounced disadvantage inasmuch as there did not exist any Buddhist community to suppress the Untouchable identity of Dalits. Socioculturally, Dalits stayed as they were vis-à-vis others. On the contrary, they suffered deprivation on the economic and political fronts as they lost the constitutional benefits associated with their erstwhile identity for nearly thirty-four years. The only gain that could be seen is in the spiritual-psychological realm. The conversion to Buddhism suddenly made them a part of the rich legacy of rebellion, which in turn gave them a feeling of self-esteem and perception of self-worth. This change has manifested in the expression of a distinct cultural identity by Dalits but unfortunately, in the absence of any alternative framework, this expression remained subsumed within the familiar Hindu mould. While it did not threaten the caste system in structural terms, it still spelt the defiance of its order in processual terms. This defiance, with the emergence of middle castes (those defined as Backward Castes and Other Backward Castes) as new custodians of caste order in rural areas, has directly led to increasing violence against them.

Ambedkar's Navayana Buddhism was meant to be a radical ideological system, supposedly matching the radicalism of Marxism sans its assumed thrust on violence and dictatorial orientation. It was expected to imbue its adherents with a radical consciousness, marked by solidarity with the oppressed and disgust against the oppressors, the spirit of enquiry vis-à-vis tradition and customs, and so on. It is not clear whether convert Buddhists reflect this consciousness. Educated Dalits, who could be expected to lead the masses in cultural terms, rather reflect disorientation towards individualistic pursuits like vipassana, aspirations for Sanskritization, narcissistic attitudes, obsession with English education, disdain for Dalit masses and self-aggrandizement of various kinds. Ambedkar's dream of making Buddhist conversion a preparatory phase for political revolution gets more and more distant with every passing day.

# IV

## AMBEDKAR AND
## THE MOTIFS OF FREEDOM

# BEYOND THE NATION[1]

## AMBEDKAR AND THE ANTI-ISOLATION OF FELLOWSHIP

*Anjani Kapoor and Manu Bhagavan*

## Introduction

The practice of caste in Hindu traditions alienated Bhimrao Ambedkar right from his early childhood: from his faith, from his peers, and from society. Ambedkar's Dalit human, somewhat akin to Giorgio Agamben's homo sacer, was expunged from society and left in the alleys of isolation.[2] For Agamben, it is the repression of the stateless, the refugees and the marginalized that is the hallmark of the modern state and therefore its fundamental flaw. In this, the Italian philosopher in many ways echoes the primary concern of Ambedkar, who saw the threat to basic living brought on by imposed isolation as a matter of existential urgency. He had to confront the ways in which individual and society could be rethought to escape the interconnected enforced prisons of caste, religion and the modern state.

## The Isolated Self

Ambedkar's sense of isolation evolved from his searing personal experiences and the daily cruelties of the caste system. His handwritten autobiographical sketch 'Waiting for a Visa' is satirically titled to convey the realm of exclusion inhabited by Dalits. The ordeal faced by nine-year-old Ambedkar while travelling to Goregaon (Satara district) in the Bombay Presidency to visit his father left a permanent impression on his mind. His excitement to spend the summer vacation with his father was cut short when young Ambedkar was left stranded at the railway station with his older brother and his sister's son as no one came to receive them at their destination.

Seeing the children alone, the stationmaster came to enquire about their well-being but 'took five steps back'[3] upon learning that they belonged to the Mahar community.[4] No 'cartmen' (bullock carts) were ready to take the children to Goregaon for fear of getting polluted.

On the insistence of the stationmaster, one of the cartmen finally agreed to accompany the children by charging double the regular fare and walking all the way while Ambedkar and his siblings drove the cart. The children had to travel the complete distance without any water and in fear of the cartman. Ambedkar and his family finally reached his father's house the next morning, taking twelve hours to complete what was otherwise a three-hour journey. This childhood episode, in all its terror and odious degradation, helped Ambedkar realize the primacy of caste in South Asian society, and that even bodies—especially bodies—were 'Untouchable' before they were human.[5] While Ambedkar had faced indignities at school, such as when he had to wait for the school attendant ('peon') to open the tap for him to be able to drink water, 'this incident', he notes, 'gave me a shock such as I never received before, and it made me think about untouchability which, before this incident happened, was with me [as] a matter of course as it is with many touchables and Untouchables.'[6]

As is well known, through great rigour, Ambedkar worked his way to higher studies in New York and London. There he found himself an outsider in new contexts based more on race and culture, yet he found he could interact more freely with other students and teachers than he ever could have in India. He later wrote about his experience: 'The best friends I have had in my life were some of my classmates at Columbia and my great professors, John Dewey, James Shotwell, Edwin Seligman and James Harvey Robinson.'[7] So he perceived various patterns in the way discrimination was operationalized in society and wanted to understand the differences between them. Eventually Ambedkar prepared a major paper titled 'Castes in India: Their Mechanism, Genesis and Development', delivering it in 1916 at the anthropology seminar in Columbia University, New York. Coming from a highly segregated society, Ambedkar called endogamy (not race, occupation or culture) a fundamental characteristic of caste.[8] Eleanor Zelliot explains, 'These ideas are important in view of Ambedkar's later battle of separate rights for the Untouchables, a struggle based not upon a claim of different race or culture, but upon the removal, by special recognition, of disabilities incurred by isolation.'[9]

Shortly thereafter, Ambedkar had to interrupt his studies as his funding was over and he had to execute the bond on his scholarship.[10]

He returned to India and headed to the erstwhile princely state of Baroda to serve Sayajirao Gaekwad III, as the maharaja had paid for his studies at Columbia University. The maharaja of Baroda, well known for being progressive, wanted to appoint Ambedkar as the state's finance minister after he gained some administrative experience in various departments.[11] Yet, when Ambedkar reached Baroda, in spite of the maharaja's order, no one received him at the train station, a stinging reminder of the indignity he had suffered as a child. Ambedkar recalled, 'Five years of stay in Europe and America had completely wiped out of my mind any consciousness that I was an untouchable and that an untouchable wherever he went in India was a problem to himself and to others.'[12] Furthermore, he discovered no Hindu was ready to accept a Dalit as his tenant or as a guest in their hotel. As a result, Ambedkar masqueraded as a Parsi to take shelter at a local inn exclusively open to members of that community.[13] He writes:

> In this big hall on the first floor of the inn there were no fellow human beings to talk to [. . .] The whole hall was enveloped in complete darkness [. . .] I felt that I was in a dungeon and I longed for the company of some human being to talk to. But there was none. In the absence of the company of human beings I sought the company of books and read and read [. . .] But the chirping and flying about of the bats, which had made the hall their home, often distracted my mind and sent cold shivers through me reminding me of what I was endeavouring to forget, that I was in a strange place under strange conditions [. . .] I subdued my grief and my anger by the feeling that though it was a dungeon, it was a shelter and that some shelter was better than no shelter.[14]

But he soon found that there was no way to overcome his forced exclusion. Even in his state position, he was humiliated on a day-to-day basis— assistants would throw bundles of files at his desk, carpets were rolled up when he got up to go. Eleven days into his stay at the inn, he was confronted by angry Parsis armed with sticks. 'You arrant knave, you are the despicable untouchable we know,' they proclaimed.[15] He was charged with impersonating a Parsi, rebuked for polluting the hostel and ordered to vacate immediately. Ambedkar had nowhere to go. He sent a note to the maharaja, who referred him to the diwan (chief administrative officer), but to no avail. Tired, hungry and exhausted, he sat under a tree and burst into a flood of tears.[16] With a broken heart, Ambedkar left his job and the state the same day. There, then for the first time, he realized, 'a person who is an untouchable to a Hindu is also an untouchable to a Parsi.'[17]

## The Isolated Community

In 1919, Ambedkar was called to give evidence before the Southborough Committee dealing with the mechanics of franchise in light of the Montagu–Chelmsford Reforms.[18] For the first time in the political arena, Ambedkar talked about the hallmarks of caste in India. 'Each group,' he said, 'tends to create its own distinctive type of like-mindedness, but where there are more groups than one to be brought into political union, there would be conflict among differently like-minded. And so long as the groups remain isolated the conflict is bound to continue and prevent the harmony of action. It is the isolation of the groups that is the chief evil.'[19] How to overcome such isolation?

Ambedkar saw society as a collection of castes, each of which functioned as an interested group. He thought untouchability was not justified according to any legal code and rather drew its support from historical custom. He observed: 'Untouchability is an outward expression of the inner repulsion which a Hindu feels towards a certain person.'[20] The biggest problem of Dalits was the social isolation forced upon them by caste Hindus. Scriptural and social codes prescribing acts of commission and omission officially sanctioned the isolation of Dalits: 'The Untouchables must live in separate quarters away from the habitation of the Hindus. It is an offence for the Untouchables to break or evade the rule of segregation.'[21] Mincing no words, Ambedkar writes, 'The Hindus, therefore, are not merely an assortment of castes, but are so many warring groups, each living for itself and for its selfish ideal.'[22] The rules of secluding Dalits were just among the 'multitudes of commands and prohibitions'[23] to deter any common front against the caste system. 'All are slaves of the caste system. But all the slaves are not equal in status.'[24] He was clear about the consequences, 'Isolation means social segregation, social humiliation, social discrimination and social injustice. Isolation means denial of protection, denial of justice, denial of opportunity. Isolation means want of sympathy, want of fellowship and want of consideration.'[25]

## The Isolated Nation

Ambedkar asks: 'How can they [Dalits] end their social isolation? The one and the only way to end their social isolation is for the Untouchables to establish kinship . . . which is free from the spirit of caste.'[26] Citing Robertson Smith, Ambedkar clarifies that a 'kin was a group of persons whose lives were so bound up together, in what must be called a physical unity, that they could be treated as parts of one common life. The members of one kindred looked on themselves as one living whole, a single animated mass of blood, flesh and bones, of which no member could be touched without all the members suffering.'[27]

Kinship thus acts as an antidote to isolation. Where shared traits and similarities on the basis of language or culture could be found, barbed wire fencing off human from human could now be torn down. The act of touching in the Smith passage Ambedkar chooses to highlight still signifies violation, as it does within the caste system, but only by inverting the basic premise of untouchability. Whereas Dalits were prohibited from touching or being touched by the isolating edicts of caste supremacy and the fear of pollution, kinship insisted that to wrongly touch anybody within the community—none any longer marked by caste distinction—was to cause equal suffering amongst all. This shared suffering created empathy among all kindred, as well as unity of purpose.

Still, kinship could not be a *curative* for the poison of isolation. At best it could only slow it down. For Ambedkar, isolation would eventually overtake kinship precisely since kinship's ultimate manifestation, nationality, too relies upon the segregation of like-minded communities.

> Nationality is a social feeling. It is a feeling of a corporate sentiment of oneness which makes those who are charged with it feel that they are kith and kin. This national feeling is a double edged feeling. It is at once a feeling of fellowship for one's own kith and kin and an anti-fellowship feeling for those who are not one's own kith and kin. It is a feeling of 'consciousness of kind' which on the one hand binds together those who have it, so strongly that it over-rides all differences arising out of economic conflicts or social gradations and, on the other, severs them from those who are not of their kind. It is a longing not to belong to any other group. This is the essence of what is called a nationality and national feeling.[28]

In this conception, fellowship is the good that Ambedkar sees in kinship and it is anti-fellowship that is produced when kinship reaches its limits, the outer boundaries of the groups it seeks to create. Ambedkar discerns that kinship and its derivative nationality are therefore ultimately exclusionary.

Neither can fully end isolation since they both rely upon it. And this leads Ambedkar to conclude that the real solution he seeks to the problem of caste, and to all social ills, is to be found in a fellowship that goes beyond nationality.

## The Anti-isolation of Fellowship

*Ambedkar:* Gandhiji, I have no homeland.

*Gandhi:* You have got a homeland, and from the reports that have reached me of your work at the Round Table Conference, I know you are a patriot of sterling worth.

*Ambedkar:* You say I have got a homeland, but still I repeat that I am without it. How can I call this land my own homeland and this religion my own, wherein we are treated worse than cats and dogs, wherein we cannot get water to drink? . . . The injustice and sufferings inflicted upon us by this land are so enormous that if knowingly or unknowingly we fall a prey to disloyalty to this country, the responsibility for that act would be solely hers. I do not feel sorry for being branded as a traitor; for the responsibilities of our action lie with the land that dubs me a traitor. If at all I have rendered any national service as you say, helpful or beneficial, to the patriotic cause of this country, it is due to my unsullied conscience and not due to any patriotic feelings in me. If in my endeavour to secure human rights for my people, who have been trampled upon in this country for ages, I do any disservice to this country, it would not be a sin . . . I have been striving to win human rights for my people without meaning or doing any harm to this country.[29]

Here, in one of the first exchanges between Ambedkar and Gandhi, the former rejects territory and state as a means of achieving equality and justice. Instead, Ambedkar saw such worthy goals as attainable only through a universalistic framework such as that provided by 'human rights'.[30] While at first glance the concern in his conversation with Gandhi may be directed solely at the Dalit community, in fact, he specifically rejects such a narrow concern. Ambedkar is certainly after securing rights for his people, but he is attentive to the fact that such a limited objective would ultimately only be confounded by recalibrated forms of isolation. Justice for Dalits thus was by necessity to be found only through a type of social force that went beyond kinship, what Ambedkar called 'fraternity'.[31] 'An ideal society should be mobile, should be full of channels for conveying a change taking place in one part to other parts. In an ideal society there should be many interests consciously communicated and shared. There should be varied and free points of contact with other modes of association. In other words, there must be social endosmosis. This is fraternity, which is another name for democracy.'[32] In this complicated passage from Ambedkar's tour de force, *Annihilation of Caste*, Ambedkar lays out a triad of interrelated concepts that he sees as fundamentally antithetical to isolation: democracy, endosmosis and fraternity.

Ambedkar borrowed the concept of endosmosis from his mentor John Dewey to describe the fluidity of communication between social groups. Arun Mukherjee clarified that the term was used originally by Henri Bergson and later by William James to describe the interaction of the mind with nature. Dewey appropriated it as 'social endosmosis'—to break the barriers of stratification between the privileged and the subject class.[33] The notion of fluidity, for Ambedkar, becomes critical to end isolation. Such fluidity determined the extent to which life, both political and everyday, could be harmonious. The more connections that could be made, the greater the ability to create 'a new like-mindedness'.[34] Ambedkar expanded on Dewey's conviction of blurring the dichotomy between the privileged and the subject class to narrow the gap between the citizen and the human.

This is where democracy came in. For democracy, in Ambedkar's view, was not just a form of government, but a way of 'associated living, of conjoint communicated experience. It is essentially an attitude of respect and reverence towards fellow men.'[35] This concern for other people, fraternity, Ambedkar saw as the base value for a true ethics.[36] For Ambedkar, fraternity would also be a tool for reconstructing the idea of a nation based on inclusive democracy. The roots of such a democracy, according to Ambedkar, lay in the social relationships tied together in a society based on 'mutuality of sympathy and cooperation'.[37] The perils of choosing the political form of democracy without its social meaning became the highlight as well as warning in a major speech Ambedkar gave in the Constituent Assembly in 1949.

Political democracy cannot last unless there lies at the base of it social democracy. What does social democracy mean? It means a way of life which recognizes liberty, equality and fraternity as the principles of life. These principles of liberty, equality and fraternity are not to be treated as separate items in a trinity. They form a union of trinity in the sense that to divorce one from the other is to defeat the very purpose of democracy [. . .] Without equality, liberty would produce the supremacy of the few over the many. Equality without liberty would kill individual initiative. Without fraternity, liberty and equality could not become a natural course of things.[38]

Despite his use of terms associated with Western thought and despite his high personal regard for his mentor Dewey, Ambedkar rejected any claim that his vision derived from the Euro-American world.

Positively, my Social Philosophy may be said to be enshrined in three words: Liberty, Equality and Fraternity. Let no one, however, say that I have borrowed my philosophy from the French Revolution. I have not. My philosophy has roots in religion and not in political science. I have derived them from the teachings of my Master, the Buddha. In his philosophy, liberty and equality had a place; but he added that unlimited liberty destroyed equality, and absolute equality left no room for liberty [. . .] He gave the highest place to fraternity as the only real safeguard against the denial of liberty, equality; and fraternity was another name for brotherhood or humanity . . .[39]

Ambedkar's human, Arun Mukherjee writes, 'is not the atomistic isolated individual of Enlightenment thought, but the individual always already embedded in the social.'[40] The social, for Ambedkar, had to transcend any limitations of the local or the national, for it was only in the universal—the universal social—that democracy could find its full flowering.

Ambedkar gradually became more aware of the confusion that his use of the term 'fraternity' created. 'The word fraternity is not an adequate expression. The proper term is what the Buddha called "maitri".'[41] One of the ten virtues in Buddhism, *maitri* loosely translates into fellowship. A hand must be given not only to those who are friends, but to those who are foes as well. Moreover, the Buddha charged humanity with cultivating the spirit of maitri for all living beings.[42] 'Is not such maitri necessary? What else can give to all living beings the same happiness which one seeks for one's own self, to keep the mind impartial, open to all, with affection for every one and hatred for none?'[43]

In its universal and global extension, the flow of maitri surrounds and binds humanity together, opening associated living channels between not just communities, but nations as well. 'Conjoint communication' steadfastly moored to 'respect and reverence' could then, Ambedkar concludes, go beyond the limits of even kinship to forge a new harmonious human whole in balance with the natural world.

## Constituting Fellowship

Ambedkar was determined to make his vision of the whole human more than just airy talk. In the 1949 speech before the Constituent Assembly where he laid out his concept of social democracy, he also made clear the Constitution he helped shepherd to its moment of adoption was not an end in itself but rather a means to a larger end. It was the role and responsibility of everyone who believed in the document and the larger values for which it stood to actively participate in making the dream into reality.

He said, connecting the isolation of the self and that of the community with the liberation of fellowship: 'In India there are castes. These castes are anti-national: in the first place because they bring about separation in social life. They are anti-national also because they generate jealousy and antipathy between caste and caste [community and community]. But we must overcome all these difficulties if we wish to become a nation in reality. For fraternity [maitri] can be a fact only when there is a nation. Without fraternity, equality and liberty will be no deeper than coats of paint.'[44]

Significantly, Ambedkar did not believe that merely naming the isolationist effects of caste and theoretically celebrating the idea of fraternity would in themselves achieve anything, since India had also to move practically beyond kinship and community. He wrote: 'I am of [the] opinion that in believing that we are a nation, we are cherishing a great delusion. How can people divided into several thousands of castes be a nation? The sooner we realize that we are not as yet a nation in the social and psychological sense of the word, the better for us. For then only we shall realize the necessity of becoming a nation and seriously think of ways and means of realizing the goal.'[45] The Constitution, as a result, does not *establish* the nation, but rather provides the tools to help *achieve* it.

The constitutional lawyer Gautam Bhatia argues that there is in fact a 'golden triangle' in the Indian Constitution that represents the 'revolutionary potential' Ambedkar implanted as the heart of the document.[46]

1.  Article 15(2) prohibits any *citizen* from discriminating against *any other citizen*, on the basis of religion, caste, sex, race, or place of birth, with regard to access to shops, public restaurants, hotels, and place of public entertainment.
2.  Article 17 abolishes the practice of 'untouchability' in *any form*.
3.  And Article 23 prohibits human trafficking, *begaar*, and similar forms of *forced labour*.[47]

Bhatia points out that 'Each of these articles protects the individual not against the State, but against other individuals, and against *communities* . . . [T]he denial of human dignity, both material and symbolic, is caused not only by public power, but by *private* power as well—and the task of constitutionalism is not limited to satisfactorily regulating public power in service of liberty, but extends to positively guaranteeing human freedom even against the excesses of private power. The word 'fraternity' is as old as the French Revolution; but it is in the Indian Constitution that it first acquired sense and meaning.'[48]

The Indian Constitution, then, is a pathway to forming the nation, and thereby to transcending multiple forms of isolation, through which a broader fellowship can subsequently be imagined. But how then do we reconcile this with the India of today, which can seem quite removed from these objectives? Neither the strength and validity of Ambedkar's insights, nor the practical constitutional applications he provided to 'realize the goal' are diminished, in fact. This is because Ambedkar's golden triangle has until now not been properly understood and, in Bhatia's assessment, has actually been largely overlooked by the courts.[49] If it is properly set within the context of the larger strategic aim of maitri and effectively deployed, then the distant horizon perhaps may not be as far off as it may seem.

Should India manage to annihilate caste and get past the limitations of kinship and community to forge a true national spirit, then the Constitution also provides a mechanism to help cultivate broader human fellowship. Wedged into the Directive Principles, a relatively unique conceptualization that Ambedkar drew from Irish precedent, Article 40 stipulates that: 'The State shall endeavor to . . . maintain just and honorable relations between nations . . . [and] foster respect for international law and treaty obligations in the dealings of organized people with one another.'[50] The Directive Principles are not justiciable, meaning that they cannot be adjudicated, but Ambedkar did see them as enforceable. He said that 'whoever captures power will not be free to do what he likes with it. He cannot ignore them [. . .] [H]e will certainly have to answer for them before the electorate at election time.'[51] But he added significantly: 'What great value these directive principles possess will be realized better when the forces of right contrive to capture power.'[52] Ambedkar, in other words, envisioned the mechanisms of the Directive Principles to acquire their full meaning and potential only at such a *future* point when 'the forces of right' stand ready to exert their political will. These forces must of necessity be anti-isolationist, to give the nation coherence from within, and to build the bonds of fellowship from without.

## Conclusion

Ambedkar discerned that the defining feature of caste and the pillar upon which its system of oppression stood was isolation. Ambedkar saw that the bonds of community could overcome isolation and so saw benefit in the like-mindedness of kinship. Yet caste itself was built upon the like-mindedness of kinship, of a kind. While he believed that other types of kinship could be formulated free of caste, these he saw teleologically leading to the like-mindedness of nationality. This was not his destination of choice because he saw nationality ultimately reflecting many of the same kinds of tensions as those perpetuated by the like-mindedness of caste.

Ambedkar demanded that humanity therefore go beyond the nation, for only then could all the limits of kinship be transcended and the curse of isolation broken. To achieve this, a new like-mindedness was necessary, grounded in the triad of endosmosis, democracy and fraternity. The fluid communication between groups and the application of that communication on the basis of respect would ensure the destruction of exclusion and the creation of an integrated political space through which liberty and equality could take their fullest, most true, forms. Maitri, or fellowship, is the ultimate solution beyond the boundaries of caste, religion and state, the pathway of true liberation. Now as the world faces the dawn of a new global, authoritarian moment,[53] this prescriptive wisdom has never seemed more urgent.

## References

Ambedkar, B.R. 2013. *Ambedkar Speaks: Vol. 1: 301 Seminal Speeches*. Ed. Narendra Jadhav. New Delhi: Konark Publishers.

Ambedkar, B.R. 2016. *Annihilation of Caste: The Annotated Critical Edition*. Ed. S. Anand. New York: Verso.

Ambedkar, B.R. 1979. *Dr. Babasaheb Ambedkar: Writings and Speeches*. Ed. Vasant Moon. Vols. 1–17. Mumbai: Government of Maharashtra.

Ambedkar, B.R. 2004. *The Essential Writings of B.R. Ambedkar*. Ed. Valerian Rodrigues. New Delhi and Oxford: Oxford University Press.

Bhagavan, Manu. 2003. *Sovereign Spheres: Princes, Education, and Empire in Colonial India*. New Delhi: Oxford University Press.

Bhatia, Gautam. Why the Uniquely Revolutionary Potential of Ambedkar's Constitution Remains Untapped. Scroll.in. https://scroll.in/article/806606/why-the-uniquely-revolutionary-potential-of-ambedkars-constitution-remains-untapped. Accessed 25 February 2018.

Cabrera, Luis. '"Gandhiji, I Have No Homeland:" Cosmopolitan Insights from B.R. Ambedkar, India's Anti-Caste Campaigner and Constitutional Architect'. *Political Studies* 65.3 (1 October 2017): 576–93.

Constituent Assembly Debates, vol. 7. http://164.100.47.194/loksabha/writereaddata/cadebatefiles/C04111948.pdf. Accessed 19 March 2018.

# POLITICAL ECONOMY OF CASTE DISCRIMINATION AND ATROCITIES

## WHY DOES CASTE DISCRIMINATION PERSIST DESPITE LAW?

### Sukhadeo Thorat

## The Promise of Equality

The Indian Constitution overturned the legal and moral frameworks of caste and made justice, liberty, freedom, equality and fraternity the cardinal principles for the social, economic and political governance of the country. Article 15 of the Constitution promises equal rights to all citizens irrespective of caste, religion, race, sex or place of birth. Article 17 abolished untouchability and made its practise in any form illegal.

While the Constitution guarantees these fundamental rights, the Directive Principles of State Policy make it obligatory for the state to enact laws and frame policies based on the suggested principles to enable citizens to use these rights in practice.

In the case of Scheduled Castes (SCs) and Scheduled Tribes (STs), Article 46 directs the state in this way: 'The State is required to protect the Scheduled Caste and Scheduled Tribes from social injustices and all forms of exploitation.'

To give effect to the Constitution's provisions related to equality and freedom, the state enacted laws to secure fundamental rights for citizens. Accordingly, Parliament enacted the Untouchability (Offences) Act on 8 May 1955 (put in force on 1 June 1955) which prescribed punishments for restrictions on Untouchables in public spheres—economic, civil, cultural, religious and political. The Act was renamed in 1976 as the Protection of Civil Rights (PCR) Act, 1955.

Thirty-five years later, another Act called the Scheduled Castes and Scheduled Tribes (Prevention of Atrocities) Act was enacted in 1989 (amended on 4 August 2015) to provide legal safeguards to prevent any violent opposition by high castes in Untouchables' attempts to seek equal rights which they enjoy under the Constitution. It made thirty-five behaviours by people of high castes punishable.

## Persistence of Caste Discrimination Despite Law: Empirical Evidence

The Untouchability (Offences) Act (1955) has been in operation for sixty years and the Prevention of Atrocities Act (1989) for twenty years. The empirical evidence shows an improvement in access to civil, political and economic rights by former Untouchables in many spheres, but also points to the continuation of discrimination on a significant scale. While the positive changes bring former Untouchables closer to citizenship status, they remain citizens in the making as the legacy of the past continues.

In this essay, therefore, I intend to bring some insight into the persistence of caste discrimination and atrocities. I particularly examine four questions. First, where has discrimination been reduced or made absent and where does it still persist? We look at the nature of change in caste relations with respect to ex-Untouchables. Second, we look at the reasons for the persistence of discrimination with the help of both theories and facts. Third, we examine the reasons for the opposition of higher castes to the efforts of ex-Untouchables to secure equal rights, including the use of violent means. Finally, I suggest some measures for addressing the issue of caste discrimination and violence.

## Evidence of the Persistence of Caste Discrimination

The most widespread and blatant practice of untouchability in the public secular sphere relates to water and cremation or burial grounds—the bare necessities of life and death. Despite being common amenities that are managed and maintained by local governments, access to them continues to be governed by the notion of caste-based pollution and untouchability. In a survey conducted by Action Aid in 2006, in almost half the villages surveyed, Dalits do not have free access to common drinking water facilities.[1] In many of these villages, they are forbidden to touch the wheel or handle of a well or pump and must depend on the consent of *savarnas* to draw water and pour it into their pots. In several villages, Dalits are assigned a separate place on the riverbank (generally downstream of where upper castes bathe and wash) or on the edge of a pond meant only for 'Untouchables'. In nearly half the villages, Dalits have no access to the burial or cremation ground maintained with public funds. They have to use a designated separate place. In other words, segregation is maintained in life as well as in death.

The practice of untouchability continues to pervade the public sphere, including a host of state institutions and the social interactions that occur within them. In one out of four primary schools in rural India, Dalit children are forced by their teachers or by convention to sit apart from non-Dalits. As many as 40 per cent of schools practise untouchability while serving midday meals, with Dalit children being made to sit in a separate row while eating. Thus, instead of being a place where children imbibe the values of equality and fraternity, rural schools impress upon young minds and bodies the principles of segregation and discrimination, reproducing the hierarchies of caste and untouchability.

The same study found a similar hierarchy at the workplace: in nearly one-third of village panchayats, elected Dalit and non-Dalit members were made to sit apart. We found the same practices in police stations, with Dalits in more than one-fourth of the villages reporting that they were denied access to or were discriminated against in police precincts. It is appalling that the police, a state authority charged with the responsibility of upholding the laws against untouchability and investigating and prosecuting those who discriminate against Dalits, is itself a major practitioner of untouchability. How can the police forces protect the rights of Dalits when their own practices violate the law?

In other spheres of public life, the study found that the practice of untouchability, though still present, seems to be less common. These include access to polling booths, public transport, primary health centres and village panchayat offices. In more than 80 per cent of villages, Dalits do not experience untouchability when visiting these institutions or using their facilities. In about 10 per cent of villages, Dalits have to queue in separate lines at polling booths to cast their votes. We recorded some instances, though they appear to be fewer than in the past, where Dalits were not allowed to enter the booths to exercise their franchise. Since these are 'modern' secular activities directly managed by the state, one would expect that untouchability should have been completely eradicated from these spheres during the more than fifty years of free India.

As in the public sphere, the practice of untouchability continues to varying extents in different economic activities. Cinema halls seem to be marked by the lowest incidence of discrimination, where it is prevalent only in about 3 per cent of villages in the study. While 65 per cent had no cinema halls, the larger villages did. Perhaps the relative anonymity of Dalits in larger villages helps explain this low incidence. But in other spheres of economic life, Dalits continue to be discriminated against. In almost half the villages, barbers refuse to serve them. The practice of untouchability is somewhat less common with respect to the services of tailors, potters and carpenters. In one out of four villages, Dalits are discriminated against in these services.

Untouchability is more ubiquitous in the areas of food and its consumption—practices suffused with notions of purity and pollution. In every third village's restaurants and teashops, Dalits are served in separate glasses and plates kept for 'Untouchables'. In one village out of four, Dalits are not allowed inside hotels and teashops; they are served outside the premises in dishes kept aside for them. In one village out of three, Dalits are not allowed to enter shops. They have to make their purchases from outside without touching or examining the commodities for sale. The position of Dalits as commodity producers is no better. Nearly 28 per cent of milk cooperative societies practice untouchability. Almost the same situation is found in the case of wage employment.

All the evidence from this study shows that the notion of the market as a social equalizer is a myth; instead of ignoring caste and treating individuals as pure economic agents, market relations are based on the exploitation of caste inequalities. Dalits receive lower wages and are forced into ill-paid and arduous work because the market is not neutral.

*Economic Discrimination:* In the economic sphere, the former Untouchables faced discrimination in various markets, including the labour market in hiring, in the supply of inputs and services (required for farm and non-farm production) and in the sale of products by ex-Untouchable farmers and non-farm producers or businesspersons. In rural areas, ex-Untouchables are not hired in some professions such as cooking, in restaurants and the midday meal programme for children, and as waitstaff, and are hired for a lesser number of days and on lower wages than their higher-caste counterparts, while in the other spheres, they face forced labour.

In urban private employment, a low proportion of ex-Untouchables receive calls for interviews as compared to their higher-caste counterparts with the same or lower level of qualifications.[2] A National Sample Survey

(NSS)[3] found that in 2012 as compared to forward-caste employees, SCs earned 8 per cent less in the public sector and 20 per cent less in the private sector. The discrimination accounted for about 10 per cent and 24 per cent of the wage differential between SCs and the forward caste in the public sector and the private sector, respectively. Job discrimination accounts for a large part of the gross earning differences in urban areas as it is considerably more important than wage discrimination among regular salaried workers.

As regards farmers, a 2003 NSS survey indicated that almost 36 per cent of the observed differences in net income between SCs and higher-caste farmers and 64 per cent of the differences between SC and Other Backward Caste (OBC) farmers were accounted for by the discrimination perpetrated against SC farmers.[4] Using the same data set, another study found that inequality between castes accounted for 3–17 per cent of the overall inequality in net farm income.[5] Erstwhile Untouchables faced discrimination in buying agricultural land[6] and in the urban rental housing market.[7] Untouchables engaged in non-farm production and business faced a similar discrimination.

On the basis of the life histories of ninety Dalit entrepreneurs from thirteen districts in six states of India, Aseem Prakash[8] observed caste barriers faced by SC entrepreneurs and businesspersons in renting or buying strategically important physical space for their businesses, resulting in their having to shift their shops to their own caste locality and cater to consumers belonging to the same caste; difficulties in securing initial orders for business; compulsion to sell goods (particularly in the case of retailers of food and beverages) at lower prices than their higher-caste counterparts; the threat of their caste identity being invoked, resulting in negative publicity against them as impure sellers by higher-caste traders to prevent competition from them; discrimination from the state in the procurement of state resources like licences and other approvals; and lack of access to the social or caste network. Thus, while Dalits are able to enter the market as owners of capital, they experience numerous forms of discrimination, resulting in poor economic outcomes.[9]

This market-based discrimination affects the income of erstwhile Untouchables resulting from the barriers to their economic engagement. The 1994 and 2005 panel survey data of the National Council of Applied Economic Research found that at least one-third of the average income difference between high-caste Hindu and SC/ST households was due to the 'unequal treatment' of SC/ST attributes.[10] Non-market exchange is not free from discrimination. Studies provide evidence regarding discrimination faced by SCs in the receipt of goods and services supplied by the government or government-approved agencies in respect of food, nutrition, health services, education and public employment.[11] This empirical evidence shows that traditional restrictions faced by ex-Untouchables in the market and in non-market institutions have continued as remnants of the past in multiple spheres, thereby preventing SCs and STs from accessing various opportunities and facilities. Hence, a large part of the inequalities that we see in terms of ownership of assets, education, employment, civic amenities and income and poverty are due to economic discrimination.

## Why Caste Discrimination Persists and with What Motive

The empirical evidence presented above indicates that caste discrimination still persists to different degrees in numerous spheres of the social relationship between higher castes and ex-Untouchables. Caste discrimination cannot be without reason; it must serve some purpose. There must be economic, social and psychological motives for it. The fact that higher castes form groups and undertake collective action to deny equal rights to Untouchables indicates the fear of some kind of loss. Therefore, it is necessary to enquire about the motive behind the discrimination in order to understand its persistence.

Since discrimination is a ubiquitous practice in other societies based on group identities like race, colour, gender, ethnicity and social origin (caste), social scientists have developed theories about the reasons for it. The contributions mainly come from the US to explain discrimination related to race, colour and gender.

Way back in 1956, Nobel laureate economist Gary Becker provided the reason in response to a similar question, that White males discriminate against their Black counterparts because they have a taste for discrimination from which they derive utility, and this taste emanates from prejudices that an individual of one group holds against individuals of another group, in this case Blacks and women.[12] Another Nobel laureate, Kenneth Arrow, came up with an alternative reason in 1973, that people discriminate because they perceive that people from another group are, on an average, less productive and, therefore, they make their decisions about hiring and wages for the other group members on the basis of that belief, which may be wrong and may result in a discriminatory outcome.[13] Yet another Nobel laureate, George Akerlof, and his co-author, Rachel Kranton, bring in the fact of social categories or social identities and their norms into the realm of economic decisions.[14] The Identity Theory postulates that social categories and their norms determine how individuals in one social category would behave towards others, as individual decisions are socially framed. In its application to race and poverty, the Identity Theory implies that the behaviour of Whites towards Blacks is determined by group norms, which perpetuate a distinction of 'us' and 'them'. The Whites think of Blacks as 'them' rather than including them in the category of 'us all'. This division of norms on the basis of 'us' and 'them', or what authors call 'oppositional identity', results in discrimination.

In the Taste, Belief and Identity Theory, endorsed by Gordon Allport,[15] discrimination results from prejudice which is embedded in individual psychology—a psychology of prejudice, which produces stereotypical (false) beliefs by the dominant group about a subordinate group and which yields discriminatory behaviour towards the subordinate group, a view that is similar to the Taste Theory.

Social psychologists have provided more insights on the causes of prejudice and motives of discrimination. Herbert Blumer questions Allport's theoretical construct of prejudice as a set of individual feelings and argues that 'race prejudice exists in a sense of group position rather than in a set of individual feelings which members of one racial group have toward members of another racial group'.[16] Blumer shifts the locus of the origin of prejudice from individual beliefs to 'attitudes of group about the relative status and material benefits associated with membership in the group harbouring stereotypical beliefs toward the "other". The extent to which the dominant groups perpetuate advantage for their own and disadvantage for subordinate groups is a key factor for group outcomes'.[17] In Blumer's notion of prejudice, there are four basic types of feelings or attitudes that always seem to be present in (race) prejudice by the dominant group: 'a feeling of superiority, a feeling that the subordinate race is intrinsically different and alien, a feeling of proprietary claim to certain areas of privilege and advantage, and perhaps the most important, a feeling of fear that the subordinate race harbours designs on the prerogatives of dominant race.'[18] Thus, Blumer shifts the axis of prejudice away from individual sentiments towards collective interests in maintaining a relative group interest. The focus is on group position and group efforts (rather than on individual efforts) for material interest and high social status. Prejudice becomes an operative, mobilizing instrument for preserving the advantaged position of the dominant group. There are real (material) interests at stake in the efforts of the dominant group to preserve its privileged position, and also the more intangible and psychic benefit of a high status advantage.

Building on this, Darity, et al. brought in further insights into the role of economic or material interest in shaping (racial) identity norms.[19] These norms are shaped by the relative income gains from racist or non-racist or mixed strategies[20] in social interaction. Identity norms are determined by the relative income gains (or what the authors call the productivity of identity norms in social interaction) from each of the identity norms. The theory argued that the predominant purpose of most discriminatory identity norms is economic gain. It does not deny the motive of high social status for discrimination but argues that high social status also ultimately fetches economic gain, besides the utility or psychological satisfaction of being of high social status.

However, the main motive behind discrimination remains economic or material. The significant aspect of this theory is that by bringing relative income gains into the norm formation of racist, secular and mixed identity in social interactions, it captures the underlying condition that brings change, say, from racial norms to individual norms (non-racist norms) and mixed norms of discrimination, and makes the theory dynamic in nature. This helps to know how relative income gain would change the degree of discrimination.

There are obvious lessons in these theoretical insights for discrimination based on caste. In the Taste, Belief and Identity Theory, individual prejudice becomes the basis for discrimination. The group-based theory shifts the focus from individual psychological feelings to group feelings to explain prejudice. This prejudice is treated as an amalgam of attitudes of the dominant group towards a subordinate group. Racial identity norms would persist as long as they bring income gains and high social status for Whites in social interactions; this high social status also provides an avenue for material gains.

The discriminatory behaviour thus assumes a functional or instrumental role for the derivation of greater material benefit by the dominant groups at the cost of the subordinate groups. There is a twofold shift in focus in the group-based theory of discrimination: from an individual's prejudicial feelings to the group's prejudicial norms and also from the utility and psychological gains to more tangible material gains and high social status. These are the most valuable insights from the efforts made by social scientists to identify the motives for social discrimination, which are also relevant to caste. The group action by the dominant group is nothing but a politics of power to gain social and economic advantage.

*Caste and Discrimination:* Ambedkar is a leading commentator on the caste system and his analysis is more insightful than that of any other student of caste. His analysis of caste squarely falls in the group-based theoretical perspective. It not only presents the caste system as an empirical case for the group theory of prejudice and discrimination, but also brings new insights into the role of religious ideology in the formation of norms or beliefs that form group prejudice and discrimination. In Ambedkar's view, the caste system entails the division of Hindus into five social groups called 'castes' (with several sub-castes), with each of them being isolated through the rule of endogamy, the rule of marriage within one's caste, and restriction on social relations, making caste a separate, isolated and exclusive entity with some intercaste obligations of an exploitative nature. It fixes the economic (pertaining to occupations or property), civic and religious rights of each caste well in advance and makes them hereditary by birth. The rights are, however, assigned in an unequal and graded manner among castes, making 'graded inequality' the foundation of the caste system.

The castes consisting of members other than those belonging to the lower castes or Untouchables form the dominant groups, perpetuating a hierarchy of dominance by placing Brahmins at the top with all rights and privileges. The Untouchables located at the bottom, on the other hand, have no rights and bear the stigma of pollution, which makes them the subordinate group. The most unique feature of the caste system is the provision of a mechanism to enforce a system of excommunication and penalties for any deviation from the code. The fear of losing these privileges, which Blumer mentioned as the key feature of prejudice, is not left to chance by Manu but is fully protected through community policing.

However, the most unique feature of the caste system captured by Ambedkar is its religious roots. The system is considered to be of divine origin, receiving philosophical support from Hindu religious philosophy, ethics and morality. It is this double injection of moral and legal philosophy which imparts solidity to the institution of caste. The principle of graded inequality with privileges accruing to highest castes and disabilities to lower castes, particularly Untouchables, constitute the very foundation on which the structure of the caste system is erected, which is 'sanctified by the Hindu religious ethical, moral and legal philosophy, and made sacred, eternal, and inviolate'.[21]

By carefully scanning Brahminical literature like the Rig Veda, Bhagavad Gita, *Manusmriti* and other *smritis*, which form a storehouse of religious ideas and the source of the Hindu social order, Ambedkar generated ample evidence of its divine origin and philosophical base. It is indisputable that the Rig Veda laid down the theory of Chaturvarnya in what is known as the *Purushasukta*. It recognized the division of society into four groups as an ideal division. The lonely stanza (12) of the Rig Veda X 90, describes the sacrifice of the Purusa (a primeval giant), whose body was divided by the gods in order to create the world: 'His mouth was the Brahmin, His two arms were made the Warriors, His two thighs, that which was the Vaishya, from the His feet was born the Shudra.'

The Bhagavad Gita also upheld the varna system with considerable clarity. Its teachings can be summarized in the following four pronouncements made by Krishna.

(1) I myself have created the arrangement known as Chaturvarnya (that is, the fourfold division of society into Brahmins, Kshatriyas, Vaishyas and Shudras) assigning them different occupations in accordance with native capacities. It is I who am the maker of this Chaturvarnya. (Gita IV 13)

(2) Even if it may be easier to follow the occupation of another varna, yet to follow the occupation of one's own varna is more meritorious, although one may not be able to do so quite efficiently. There is bliss in following the occupations of one's varna, even if death were to result from performing it, but to follow the occupation of another varna is risky. (Gita III 35)

(3) The educated should not unsettle the faith of the uneducated who have become attached to their occupation. He himself should perform the occupation of his varna and make others perform theirs accordingly. An educated man may not become attached to his occupation. But the uneducated and dull-minded people who have become attached to their occupation should not be spoiled by the educated by putting them on a wrong path by abandoning their own occupation. (Gita III 26 and 29 )

(4) O Arjuna, whenever this religion of duties and occupations (this religion of Chaturvarnya) declines, then I myself will come to birth to punish those who are responsible for its downfall and to restore it. (Gita IV 7-8)

The *Manusmriti* advanced the original notion of the varna system, in fact converting the varna system into the caste system. It lent the force of law to the caste codes to be enforced by the state. It took away whatever little mobility or freedom people had with respect to occupation and property and social intermixing in the varna system. It fixed the occupation of the five castes and took away the freedom to change and made it hereditary. It brought endogamy—marriage within castes—and made caste separate and exclusive. But above all it founded the caste system on the principle of graded inequality.

Ambedkar says that to be intelligible is to be found out. Manu was neither afraid nor ashamed of being found out. He expressed his views in resonant and majestic notes. Manu states:

> But for the sake of the prosperity of the worlds, he caused the Brahmins, the Kshatriyas, the Vaisyas and Sudras to proceed from his mouth, his arms, his thighs and his feet.
>
> But in order to protect this universe, he assigned separate occupations (duties) to those who sprang from his mouth, arms, thighs and feet.
>
> To Brahmins teaching and studying (the Veda), to Kshatriyas protecting people, to Vaisyas tending cattle, trading, lending money and cultivating land and to Sudras one occupation only—to serve meekly the other three castes.

Manu added:

> Whatever exists in the World is the property of the Brahmins on account of the excellence of his origin. (I 99)
>
> But no collection of wealth must be made by the Sudra, even though he would be able (to do it), for a Sudra who has acquired wealth gives pain to Brahmins (X 129)

In Ambedkar's judgement, there is not much difference between the teachings of the Vedas, the Gita and the *Manusmriti*. The only difference one finds in that Vedas and the Bhagavad Gita deals with General Theory while the smritis are concerned with working out the particular details of that theory. But so far as the essence is concerned, all of them—the smritis, the Vedas and the Bhagavad Gita—are woven on the same pattern, the same thread runs through them and they are finally part of the same fabric.

The reason for this is obvious. The Brahmins, who were the authors of the whole body of Hindu religious literature, took good care to inject the doctrine of the social order formulated by them. Ambedkar argued that nothing was to be gained from picking and choosing between them. The philosophy of Hinduism would be the same whether one took the *Manusmriti*, the Vedas or the Bhagavad Gita,[22] summed up in Vedic Brahminism.

Thus, Manu's masterpiece was the society he constructed—an intellectual construction and a social creation. It was a hierarchical society, a society of privileges and of discrimination, a society of group ethics. It produced injustice, provoked immense suffering and human humiliations and frequently resorted to violence to impose its norms.

What was the motive behind this? Fernando Tola and Carmen Dragonetti captured it very well.[23]

> It was an ambition of acquiring power and authority, the covetousness to get for their undertakings workers to whom they had not to pay any salary, and the greed to become the owners of their riches and properties. In other words, the tendency to the exploitation of man by man so much inserted in human nature, and whereof history unfortunately gives so many instances, The ominous practice of slavery was defended not only in India but also in the West.

The Hindu social order was not developing with any spiritual thrust, but from a desire for power and economic and social greed and selfishness at the cost of the hunger, poverty and deprivation of Untouchables in particular. The motive was pure and simple, economic and high social status, there was nothing spiritual about it.

## How to Deal with the Persistence of Discrimination and Atrocity

Like other forms of discrimination, the motive behind caste discrimination is economic gain and high social status through the monopolization of resources and education. The group actions by the dominant group is for the preservation of privilege at the cost of denial of equal economic, social and political rights to ex-Untouchables and other low castes. The economic and social motives, with collective group action by high castes supported by religion, make it very difficult for Untouchables to secure economic and social rights and bring a positive transformation in the caste system. Therefore, despite sixty years of legal safeguards, caste discrimination and untouchability still persist. The issue is how to deal with this persisting discrimination. I review the present policies and try to reflect on solutions.

Broadly speaking, three sets of policies are used by the government to address the issues of untouchability and discrimination. These are:

(a) Laws against untouchability and atrocities
(b) Sensitization of people about the ills of caste and untouchability
(c) Legal safeguards against discrimination in employment, education and legislature through reservations and economic empowerment.

## Legal Safeguards and Their Limitations

The Untouchability (Offences) Act was enacted in 1955. It mainly provides protection against the denial of equal rights in public services and institutions. The Prevention of Atrocities Act (1989) provides safeguards against violent behaviour by high castes against Untouchables' efforts for accessing equal rights—thirty-five behaviours are listed as being against the law and punishable. In 2015, the Prevention of Atrocities Act was amended to cover more behaviours and strengthen its enforcement.

The studies quite clearly bring out the lapses in the implementation of the Act at various levels of its administration. The actual implementation of the Act deviates from the rule in a number of ways, including:

(a) Lack of on–the–spot visits to places where incidents have occurred
(b) Delays in filing FIRs
(c) Investigation by officers below the required rank
(d) Not registering cases under relevant sections of the Act
(e) Registering cases under sections which involve mild punishment
(f) Avoiding timely arrest of accused
(g) Delays in investigation
(h) Delays in filing charge sheets
(i) Acquittal by courts on procedural grounds rather than any substantial grounds.

It also emerged from the studies that among other reasons 'wilful negligence' on the part of officials to help people not of their social standing was one of the important reasons for the limited success of the laws. 'Wilful negligence', as described by the Ministry of Home Affairs circular and the Ministry of Social Justice and Empowerment, attributes the slow implementation of the law to bureaucratic resistance. The Standing Committee of the Ministry of Social Justice and Empowerment pointedly observed:

the officials attempted to dilute the spirit of the (PoA) Act at every stage—from non-registration of case, failure to investigate according to due process of law, not filing the charge sheet in court within the stipulated time, not giving relief and compensation to the victims, not providing protective and preventive measures etc.[24]

Thus, among other reasons, 'wilful negligence' on the part of officials was a significant factor in the deviation from the rules. Recognizing this, the 2015 Act made provisions for action against officials who purposefully avoided the implementation of the rules of the Act. There is a provision for conducting departmental enquiries against officers who violated rules in their investigation.[25]

What steps will make officials implement the Act as per the rules? How can officials and others in administration be sensitized to rise above caste affiliations and be secular and impartial? The monitoring of the Act as per its guidelines is the key issue that confronts us, for which measures are necessary on the part of the government.

## Transforming Codes and Norms Supportive of Caste

Ambedkar, more than anybody else, was immensely aware of the limitation of laws in eliminating caste discrimination and untouchability. He emphasized the need for legal safeguards against discrimination. Indeed, he worked hard to enact the Untouchability Act of 1955. But he was clear about the extent that the law could make a difference in a situation where the entire community was opposed to equal rights for Untouchables. In his famous lecture titled 'Ranade, Gandhi and Jinnah', which he delivered in 1943 at the Gokhale Institute in Pune, Ambedkar observed:

The idea of making the gift of fundamental rights to every individual, no doubt, is laudable. The question is how to make them effective. The prevalent view is that once rights are enacted in a law, then they are safeguarded. This again is an unwarranted assumption. An experience proves that rights are not protected by law but the social and moral conscience of society. If social conscience is such that it is to recognize the rights which the law chooses to enact, rights will be safe and secure. But the fundamental rights are opposed by the community. No Parliament, no judiciary can guarantee them in the real sense of the word. What is the use of fundamental rights to the Negros in America, to the Jews in Germany, and to the Untouchables in India? As Burke said, 'There is no method found for punishing the multitude. Law can punish a single solitary recalcitrant criminal. It can never operate against a whole body of people who are determined to defy it. Social conscience is the only safeguard of all rights fundamental or non-fundamental.'[26]

Ambedkar went on to add that:

there are no rights in the Hindu society which the moral sense of man could recognize. There are privileges and disabilities and the privileges for a few and disabilities for vast majority.[27]

Thus, the Hindu social order is characterized by the near absence of a social conscience supportive of equal rights and equal status to different castes, especially Untouchables, as it is based on the principle of inequality. The continued denial of equal rights and status to Untouchables is the outcome of this.

Ambedkar observed that if an individual violated a law, it could be dealt with legally, but if the whole community denied equal rights to lower castes, the law could not do much. In a village setting, the entire high-caste community can be against giving equal rights to Untouchables, and the laws have limitations in punishing the entire community. In fact, the Prevention of Atrocities Act has a provision of imposing fines on the entire high-caste village community but this has not worked and has politically and socially backfired.

The laws help prevent the disease, but do not cure it. What is the cure? Since there is a lack of social and moral conscience in Hindu society, there is a need to create one which is supportive of equal rights under the law through systematic programmes. This means purposeful efforts for change in the norms of behaviour that would support equal rights and status for untouchables. In Ambedkar's view, the development of a social conscience supportive of equal rights is the ultimate guarantee of equality. In *Annihilation of Caste*, Ambedkar argued:

People are not wrong in observing caste. In my view, what is wrong is their religion, which has inculcated this notion of caste. If this is correct, then obviously the enemy you must grapple with, is not the people who observed caste, but the Shastra which teach them this religion of caste. The real remedy is to destroy the belief in the sanctity of the Shastras. How do you expect to succeed, if you allow the Shastras to continue to mould the beliefs and opinions of the people? Reformers working for the removal of untouchability, including Mahatma Gandhi, do not seem to realize that the acts of the people are merely the results of their beliefs inculcated upon their minds by the Shastras and that people will not change their conduct until they cease to believe in the sanctity of the Shastras on which their conduct is founded.[28]

Unfortunately, this aspect has received less attention than it deserves when it comes to government action. Our main focus has been on laws and to some extent on economic empowerment, which is the right way, but very little focus is accorded to the transformation of norms and beliefs of people in favour of equality, which is equally important, as important as legal safeguards and economic independence. In the absence of this, traditional beliefs continue to influence the behaviour of higher castes towards Untouchables, which results in the denial of equal rights.

This also means that so far the focus has been on the victim, the sufferer, which is of course necessary. But equal focus is necessary on the accused, the people who practise discrimination, to bring about a change in their behaviour towards Untouchables, which is in fact the source of discrimination. There is no social engagement by the government with people who practise untouchability and oppose equal rights for Untouchables. Why do higher castes continue to practise discrimination? Why do they commit violence against Untouchables? How can their behaviour be transformed through proper programmes to make them supportive of equal rights? This is a challenge the government should meet through policies and schemes.

## Economic Empowerment of Dalits As a Solution

Inculcating social consciousness among higher castes in support of equality laws is necessary, but the process will be slow and long term. Besides, since discrimination against Dalits brings massive economic benefits to higher castes, an appeal to the social conscious is too weak a proposition to override the economic consideration. The economic progress of Dalits is therefore a prime alternative to make them independent. This has been attempted by the government through reservations and other policies to rescue them from the clutches of poverty and discrimination. The reservation policy in education and public jobs has helped reduce the dependence of Dalits on high castes and brought about some mobility among them.

However, this has happened on a limited scale. A large portion of Dalits who live in villages are poor, with most of them economically dependent on higher castes for employment as they lack agricultural land or business.

*Ownership of Assets:* At the all-India level, in 2012, among the total SC rural households, about 20 per cent were farmers. Another 14 per cent were small entrepreneurs or business households, whereas the corresponding ratio in urban areas was about 27 per cent. The Economic Survey of Private Enterprises for 2013 indicates that the share of SCs in the country's enterprise was 10 per cent, which is lower than their share in the population (16 per cent). A low incidence of ownership of income-earning assets by SCs results in high dependence on wage labour, at about 52 per cent, as compared to the corresponding figure of 32 per cent for OBCs and 21 per cent for Others. Similarly, in urban areas, about 21 per cent of SCs were casual wage labourers as compared to the corresponding figure of 15 per cent for OBCs and 6 per cent for Others. The erstwhile Untouchables also lack access to education and civic amenities. In 2014–15, the enrolment rate for higher education was 20 per cent for SCs as compared to 36 per cent for higher castes and 27 per cent of the all-India average. In 2011, the proportion of SC households without drinking water facilities was 68 per cent as compared to 57 per cent for Others. In addition, 77 per cent of SC households had no latrines in their homes as compared to a corresponding figure of 66 per cent for Others, and 41 per cent of SC households had no electricity as compared to the corresponding figure of 34 per cent for Others.

*Income and Poverty:* A low level of access to assets and a high dependence on wage labour result in low income and high poverty levels. In 2011–12, the monthly per capita consumption expenditure (MPCE) was about Rs 1297 for SCs, followed by Rs 1518 for OBCs and Rs 2239 for Others, with the corresponding all-India average being Rs 1645. The MPCE of SCs was only 58 per cent of higher castes, 85 per cent of OBCs and 79 per cent of the national average. Similar disparities are visible with regard to poverty.

In 2011, as compared to 12. 4 per cent of Others and 25 per cent of OBCs, 30 per cent of SCs were poor, with the corresponding all-India average figure being 23 per cent. The incidence of poverty among SCs was more than double as compared to Others. The proportion of underweight children among SCs was 51 per cent as compared to corresponding figures of 45 per cent for OBCs and 36 per cent for Others, while for those with anaemia was 74 per cent for SCs, 72 per cent for OBCs and 67 per cent for Others. The proportion of women with anaemia was 58 per cent among SCs, as compared to 51 per cent for Others. Thus, SCs suffered to a much greater degree than their higher-caste counterparts in all indicators of malnutrition.

This empirical evidence pertaining to caste-based discrimination and poverty indicates that despite an improvement to some degree, erstwhile Untouchables continue to face discrimination on a significant scale. The gap in human development between them and the rest of the population also persists. They are still far from attaining the status of full citizens, they are a 'part of Hindu society, but a part apart', as Ambedkar put it. There is a long way to cover the backlog of about 2200 years, which began with the codification of the *Manusmriti* in 186 BC.

Ambedkar had reflected on the implications of poverty and discrimination against Untouchables. In 1947 in *States and Minorities*, he suggested remedies to prevent the economic exploitation of Dalits, including the distribution of land to all of them by nationalizing land, along with the nationalization of key and basic industries and health, education and insurance. He suggested another set of safeguards that included reservations in government jobs, education and legislation as supplementary measures, for he believed that economic equalization would take away the power of higher castes to discriminate. But it would not eliminate their social power and hence discrimination altogether, and therefore he suggested the main package of safeguards against discrimination in jobs, education and legislature: reservation.

For rural areas, Ambedkar proposed separate villages for Dalits, first in 1943, then in 1946, and he finally retreated in 1947. He proposed separate settlements for ex-Untouchables away from high-caste settlements, with independent means of livelihood to delink Dalits from higher castes in villages geographically and economically. Ambedkar was of the view that the economic and demographic situation of Dalits and higher castes in villages was such that it did not allow Untouchables to secure equal rights, despite laws in their favour. Untouchables and higher castes live in close proximity on demographically and economically unequal terms. In this dependent relationship between two unequal groups, Ambedkar argued that equal access and justice for Dalits was nearly impossible. Therefore, he suggested a geographical and economic disconnect between high castes and Dalits, and argued for a separate settlement. His suggestion that Dalits move to cities was part of this strategy.

This is how Ambedkar made the case for separate living quarters and economic independence as a solution to the problem of untouchability and atrocities in villages.

> It is the close-knit association of the untouchables with the Hindus living in the same village which marks them out as untouchables and which enables the Hindus to identify them as being untouchables. [. . .] so long as the village system provides an easy method of marking out and identifying the untouchables, the untouchables have no escape from untouchability. [. . .] the untouchables therefore demand that the nexus should be broken and the untouchables who are as a matter of fact socially separate should be made separate geographically and territorially also, and be settled into separate villages exclusively of untouchables in which the distinction of the high and low and of touchable and untouchable will find no place.[29]

Ambedkar goes on to argue about the need for economic independence:

> The second reason for demanding separate settlements arises out of the economic position of the Untouchables in the village. That their condition is most pitiable—they are a body of landless labourers who are entirely dependent upon such employment. In the village . . . they cannot engage in any trade or occupation, for owing to untouchability no Hindu will deal with them. It is therefore obvious that there is no way of earning a living which is open to the untouchables so long as they live in a Ghetto as a dependent part of the Hindu village.[30]

He continues:

> A perpetual war is going on every day in every village between the Hindus and the Untouchables . . . The existence of a grim struggle between the Touchable and the Untouchables is however a fact. Under the village system, the Untouchable has found himself greatly handicapped in his struggle for a free and honourable life. It is a contest between the Hindus who are economically and socially strong and the Untouchables who are economically poor and numerically small. That the Hindus most often succeed in suppressing the Untouchables is due to many causes . . . the chief weapon in the armoury of the Hindus is economic power which they possess over the poor untouchables living in the village . . .

The proposal may be dubbed escapism. But the only alternative is perpetual slavery.[31]

All that Babsaheb Ambedkar had said in 1947 has come true. In the struggle to secure equal rights and dignity, Untouchables fight unequal battles and face atrocities and violence, and also social and economic boycott. Therefore, Ambedkar's demand for a separate village for Dalits with independent economic means of livelihood is more relevant today than before, as is his suggestion for migration to cities and towns. Urbanization takes away the oppressive feature of rural discrimination, atrocities and day-to-day humiliation due to urban settings, although discrimination in jobs, business, housing and other spheres will remain.

## Concluding Remarks

The problem faced by Dalits is too complicated. It is an economic problem, but not economic alone. It is intertwined with social discrimination and influenced by religious notions. It needs multiple interventions, legal and social transformations and economic empowerment; among these, however, economic empowerment is a must to relieve them from basic hunger and poverty, while dignity will come with its own speed.

The problems of untouchability and caste discrimination and atrocity, however, need to be top priorities in government policy and programmes, and in high-caste civil society. Presently, they are low in the pecking order. The removal of untouchability has not become a state-level issue of prime concern, importance and urgency. But it is as important as the problem of poverty. If poverty is the daily experience of hunger, discrimination is the daily experience of humiliation and contempt. It is a day-to-day experience which is absorbed by Untouchables under suppression and dominance. In fact, discrimination becomes a source of poverty and aggravates it. The denial of access to public amenities like water, economic rights like land, employment, trade and business, and discriminatory access to government schemes in some spheres, if not all, reduce access to sources of income for Dalits. Therefore, the eradication of untouchability and caste discrimination must become a central issue and an urgent matter.

It is essential for the purposes of nation rebuilding, which is heavily discussed today and considered to be of high importance. In this context it will be useful to recall Ambedkar, who says:

A nation is not a country in the physical sense, whatever degree of geographical unity it may possess. A nation is not a people synthesized by a common culture derived from common language, common religion or common race . . . Nationality is a subjective psychological feeling. It is feeling of corporate sentiment of oneness which makes those who are charged with it feel that they are kith and kin. [. . .] It is a feeling of 'consciousness of kind' which bind together those who are within the limits of kindred. It is longing (a strong feeling of wanting) to belonging to one's own group . . . This is the essence of what is called a nationality and national feeling.[32]

He goes on to say, 'Nation on the contrary is a spiritual reality binding people into a deep comradeship.' He emphasizes that 'nationality [is] a feeling of consciousness of kind, like-mindedness, possessing things in common in life of communication, participation and of sharing with all those who constitute one nation. In this sense nation is a society where there is an unlimited scope for "social endosmosis". Nation is a democracy, a mode of associated living, of conjoined communicated experience.'

Communication, participation and sharing with all those who constitute one nation is a key aspect of nationhood. It is made possible by fraternity and brotherhood. Fraternity encourages a mental attitude of fair play and equality towards one's fellow countrymen. In Ambedkar's view, equality is a precondition for nationhood and a feeling of oneness. He observed:

Fraternity and liberty are really derivative notions. The basic and fundamental conceptions are equality and respect for human personality. Fraternity and liberty take their roots in these two fundamental conceptions. Digging further down it may be said that equality is the original notion and the respect for human personality is a reflection of it. So that where equality is denied, everything else may be taken to be denied.

Today if ex-Untouchables face physical isolation (living in separate settlements), social isolation (from having social relations in many spheres of life—inter-dining and intercaste marriage), violence and contempt, we cannot say that we have fulfilled the necessary conditions to make a nation, namely, partaking of a common life of communication, sharing joys and sorrows with all those who constitute one nation, and equality and respect for all human beings.

We have to recognize that we are a nation in the making. We are a democracy in the making. A lot more effort will be necessary to achieve nationhood the way Ambedkar conceived the idea of the nation in the real sense of the term. A lot needs to be done to make Dalits full citizens with equal rights, at par with everyone else.

# References

Action Aid Study. 2000. See Sukhadeo Thorat and Prashant Negi. 2007. 'Exclusion and Discrimination: Civil Rights Violations and Atrocities in Maharashtra', working paper 2.2. Indian Institute of Dalit Studies, New Delhi.

Ambedkar, B.R. 1987. 'The Hindu Social Order: Its Essential Features'. In *Dr. Babasaheb Ambedkar: Writings and Speeches*, vol. 3. Mumbai: Government of Maharashtra.

Ambedkar, B.R. 1987. 'The Triumph of Brahmanism'. In *Dr. Babasaheb Ambedkar: Writings and Speeches*, vol. 3. Mumbai: Government of Maharashtra.

Ambedkar, B.R. 1946. 'Pakistan or the Partition of India'. In *Dr. Babasaheb Ambedkar: Writings and Speeches*, vol. 8. Mumbai: Government of Maharashtra.

Ambedkar, B.R. 1946. 'Scheduled Caste Settlement be Made at Par with Bantus (of South Africa)'. *Times of India*, 23 April 1946; *Dr. Babasaheb Ambedkar: Writings and Speeches*, vol. 17. Mumbai: Government of Maharashtra.

Buhler, G. 2006. *The Laws of Manu*. Delhi: Motilal Banarasidas Publishers.

Indian Institute of Dalit Studies. 2011. 'Mapping Caste-Based Atrocities in India with a Special Focus on Dalit Women'. Project Report 41.

Iyer, Lakshmi, Anandi Mani, Prachi Mishra and Petia Topalova. 2010. 'Political Reservation and Crime: Evidence from India'.

Modhok, Raahil. 2013. 'Reservation Policy and Criminal Behaviour in India: The Link between Political Reservation and Atrocities against Scheduled Caste and Tribes', *Issues in Political Economy* 22.

National Campaign on Dalit Human Rights. 2015. Fact-finding reports of fifty-two atrocity cases in Maharashtra prepared by civil society organizations, 2013-15.

National Commission for Scheduled Castes and Scheduled Tribes. 1990. 'Atrocities against Scheduled Castes and Scheduled Tribes: Causes and Remedies'. New Delhi: Government of India.

National Crime Records Bureau. 1995-2015. 'Crimes in India', Ministry of Home Affairs. New Delhi: Government of India.

National Human Rights Commission. 2002. 'Report on Prevention of Atrocities against Scheduled Castes and Scheduled Tribes'. New Delhi: Government of India.

National Commission for SC and ST. 1998. 'Third Report: 1994-95 and 1995-96'. New Delhi: Government of India.

Ramaiah, A. 2011. 'Growing Crime against Dalits in India Despite Special Laws: Relevance of Ambedkar's Demand for Separate Settlement'. *Journal of Law and Conflict Resolution*, 3.9.

Rao, Anupama. 2011. 'Violence and Humanity: Or Vulnerability as Political Subjectivity'. *Social Research* 78.2.

Scuto, Giuseppe. 2008. 'Caste Violence in Contemporary India'. Delhi, Haridwar, Munich.

Sharma, Smriti. 2015. 'Caste-based Crime and Economic Status: Evidence from India'. *Journal of Comparative Economics* 43.

Teltumbde, Anand. 2016. 'It Is Rare for Atrocities to Achieve the Event Status of a Khairlanji or Una'. Juggernaut blog. http://blog.juggernaut.in/khairlanji-teltumbde-interview.

Teltumbde, Anand. 2010. *The Persistence of Caste: The Khairlanji Murders and India's Hidden Apartheid*. New Delhi: Navayana.

Thorat, Sukhadeo, Nitin Tagade and Ajaya Naik. 2016. 'Prejudice against Reservations', *Economic and Political Weekly* 51.8.

Thorat, Sukhadeo and Prashant Negi. 'Caste Discrimination in Maharashtra: A Survey of Primary Village Level Studies, 1958 to 2000', working paper, Indian Institute of Dalit Studies, New Delhi.

Thorat, Sukhadeo. 2017. 'Untouchability, Caste Discrimination and Atrocities in Maharashtra: Analysis of Magnitude, Causes and Solutions'. Memorandum by Association for Social and Economic Equality. Pune: Sugava Prakashan.

# V

# THE RADICAL HUMANISM
# OF AMBEDKAR

# THE POLITICS OF NAVAYANA BUDDHISM

## REINTERPRETING AMBEDKAR'S TURN TO RELIGION

*Nicolas Jaoul*[1]

'Without religion our struggle will not survive'—Ambedkar's speech in Agra, 18 March 1956[2]

In October 1956, seven years after handing over the Constitution of India and five years after resigning from the Nehru cabinet to protest against its lack of commitment to social reforms, Ambedkar started the Navayana movement by 'converting' himself and several hundred thousand of his followers to Buddhism.[3] The 'new vehicle', Navayana Buddhism, was designed by him to free Dalits and eventually Indian society at large from the bondage of caste.[4] Since his studies at Columbia University in New York, Ambedkar was strongly influenced by the political philosophy of his teacher there, the philosopher John Dewey whose social liberalism was situated at the left of political liberalism. Although a liberal who saw in the liberal concept of political equality a milestone for Dalit emancipation, Ambedkar started expressing his concerns regarding the willingness of the Indian state to work for a truly democratic society as soon as independence was declared.

When he handed over the Constitution of the new-born Indian Republic in November 1949, Ambedkar's often-quoted speech spoke about the contradictions between political equality and economic and social disparities, which threatened the future of India's democratic institutions. But Ambedkar's decision to consecrate the rest of his life to Buddhism as soon as he left the Nehru cabinet in 1951 goes beyond this social democratic aspiration. The aim of this essay is to examine critically the different scholarly interpretations of Ambedkar's final turn to religious means of emancipation. As we will see, while some authors have simply understood the conversion as a religious pretext to achieve political purposes, others have started reflecting on its religious dimension as a political statement in itself. Therefore, how did the religious aspect of the conversion impact the political domain of Dalit emancipation?

While most scholars tend to take Ambedkar's political liberalism at face value, his embrace of Navayana directs us to reconsider his contribution. Indeed, Navayana represents an experimental political journey at the fringes of liberal politics. Anupama Rao has characterized it as the result of 'a forty year struggle to understand the co-constitution of politics and religion that produced caste'.[5] The choice of Buddhism enabled the appropriation of an ancient, prestigious Indian philosophy—a daring and powerful political claim for those who had been denied entry into Hindu temples and been considered unworthy of religion. Besides, this shift from the marginal religious sects of Dalits to a prestigious tradition also held a claim to universality that represented a powerful political statement on the part of the marginalized sections.

From a theoretical point of view, the political relevance of the conversion thus seems well established. But from an ethnographic point of view, what does the turn to religion imply for the Dalit movement? Seven weeks after *diksha* ('conversion' or more exactly, as I will discuss further, 'initiation'), Ambedkar passed away, leaving his followers the arduous task of putting Navayana into practice. Although carefully designed, it nevertheless remained an experimental religious prototype that sought to link together citizenship, revolutionary politics, spirituality and ritual functions.

In his perceptive account of Navayana, Martin Fuchs argues that 'even if simplistic, the naïve reactions of modernists who cannot accept religion as part of a modern agenda do point to some basic difficulty, even aporia, or rather, a bundle of dilemmas, which indicate an unresolved conundrum within the triangle of religion, politics, and social emancipation'.[6] I see Fuchs's remark as an invitation to take seriously Navayana's self-definition as a religion. According to a similar line of thought, the French sociologist of religion Michael Löwy[7] has, for instance, insisted on the often neglected spiritual dimensions of the theology of liberation in Latin America, thus taking issue with a purely secular interpretation that does not take into account their religious content. Although Ambedkar proposed with Navayana a highly secularized version of Buddhism, he nevertheless defined it as a 'Religion' with a capital R and insisted that it be recognized as such. Miguel Abensour's characterization of utopian discourse, not as the 'depreciation of the political' but rather as the 'complication of the political'[8] (my translation from the French), could help us think dialectically of Navayana's 'religious' experimentation with the 'political' and vice versa. In a more lengthy version of the present essay, my ethnography of the Navayana movement in Uttar Pradesh in the late 1990s highlights the practical issues that Ambedkarite activists face while seeking to conciliate their political aims with the more recognized and conventional aspects of 'Religion'.[9]

In this shorter theoretical discussion of Navayana, I show that Marx's positive understanding of Judaism in 19th-century Germany as an alternative to bourgeois citizenship brings relevant perspectives in order to understand Ambedkar's turn to religion as an attempt to stretch the political domain of emancipation beyond its bourgeois definition.

## Citizenship in Religious Clothing?

In his pioneering work on the Ambedkarite movement of Agra (Uttar Pradesh), the late Owen Lynch (1931–2013) wrote that Ambedkar wished to anchor citizenship and nationalism in moral values, thus pouring 'the new wine of political modernity into the old bottles of religious tradition'.[10] In a personal email correspondence some ten years ago, Owen confessed to me that this older formulation did not satisfy him any more. He said what was required now was for us to understand how the bottles transformed the content.[11] I shall take Owen's intuition as my point of departure and try to mobilize the way other authors' interpretations of Navayana can help us think about the manner in which the materiality of religion—that the image of the bottle puts before us—can help us understand how Dalit politics has been transformed by its experiment with religion.

As Anupama Rao's deep enquiry into Ambedkar's intellectual project testifies, a Marxian perspective provides an insightful and iconoclast understanding of his revolutionary aims, in comparison to a tendency of liberal scholarship to take his liberal politics at face value. Jaffrelot has, for instance, argued that Ambedkar's decision to devote the rest of his life to Buddhism was a manner of wrapping his liberal values in a religious discourse. On the one hand, Jaffrelot convincingly points out that in *The Buddha and His Dhamma*, written as a 'Buddhist bible' for the use of converts, Ambedkar gave central importance to the notion of Dhamma as civic morality. This was at the expense of the notions of karma that emphasized one's caste duties or dharma, and of the four noble truths in Buddhism, whose introspective and pessimistic content did not fit the purposes of the Dalit struggle. This attempt to secularize Buddhism, as highlighted by Jaffrelot, is indeed an important aspect of Navayana, but something is missed out. Jaffrelot argues that by redefining the Buddha's doctrine as 'liberty, equality, fraternity', 'Ambedkar selected the values within Buddhism that he had spotted in the Republican doctrine'.[12] To make this point, he quotes a speech originally reported by Ambedkar's biographer Dhananjay Keer that Ambedkar gave on the national radio in October 1954: 'Positively, my social philosophy,' he said, 'may be said to be enshrined in three words: liberty, equality and fraternity. Let no one, however, say that I have borrowed my philosophy from the French revolution. I have not. My philosophy has roots in religion and not in political science. I have derived them from the teachings of my master, the Buddha'.[13]

Jaffrelot, however, misses out a key point by ignoring the next sentence in which Keer concludes that Ambedkar's emphasis on religion was a manner of insisting on 'fraternity—which was another name for brotherhood or humanity, which was again another name for religion'.[14] What these two lines reveal is that although the continuities with liberal values are undeniable, Ambedkar was according to Keer somehow unsatisfied with them and thus searched in religion for the more encompassing human perspective that he could not find in citizenship. There is here a striking parallel with Marx's critique of the selfish bourgeois definition of citizenship, which Marx contrasts with the larger goal of 'human emancipation'.[15] What I mean to say is that unless we acknowledge that Ambedkar was dissatisfied with the liberal conception of citizenship, we cannot find a convincing explanation for his turn to religion. Jaffrelot's emphasis on the need to 'vernacularize'[16] Western ideas is unsatisfying in view of Ambedkar's assumed modernity. Simply wrapping Western ideas in a religious garb for the sake of cultural translation would mean that Ambedkar surrendered to the stereotyped imperialist divide between the religious East and Western secular modernity.[17] The risk presented by this cultural line of argumentation, if pushed to its logical ends, is to depict Navayana as a sort of orientalized version of citizenship. This fails to convey Ambedkar's reinscription of religion and thus does not capture its political significance.[18]

From the opposite direction, Navayana has also been interpreted as a form of 'Marxist Buddhism'.[19] There are, of course, explicit references to Marx in Ambedkar's Buddhist argumentation.[20] However, the assimilation of Navayana to 'Marxist Buddhism' also fails to convey 'the multidimensionality of Ambedkar's religious discourse'.[21] As argued by Yashwant Sumant, 'his understanding of religion was no doubt enriched by Marxist insights and yet his approach to religion was not essentially a Marxist one'.[22] Indeed, Gail Omvedt contrasts Ambedkar's real emphasis on religion with Marxism which 'was fundamentally uninterested in religion, in the critique of religion or in changes of religion'.[23] In another chapter, she also points out that in contrast to Marx and Weber, who believed that religion would die away, but similar to Durkheim's secular understanding of religion as 'society's self-consciousness',[24] Ambedkar considered that religion had a place in modernity, as *the main creator of the moral community* (emphasis in original).[25]

Durkheim's influence on Ambedkar, however, does not account for the emancipatory aspects of Navayana that both contain but also exceed the former's republican and secular perspective on religion's ethical function. Instead, the attempts to relocate the discourse of Dalit emancipation outside institutional politics lead us to take very seriously Navayana's convergence with Marx's early reflections on the political relevance of religion for the Jewish community in the context of 19th-century Germany. While Ambedkar often referred critically to the older Marx's economism as irrelevant to grasp the religious and cultural dimensions of caste exploitation, there is to my knowledge no explicit reference in his writings to Marx's earlier works. Nevertheless, these convergences provide major insights to reconsider Ambedkar's relationship with liberal political thought and to take into account his critical perspectives.[26]

In *On the Jewish Question*, Marx positively points to the religion of the Jewish minority as a politically significant and strategical point of friction with the German Christian state. Instead of urging Jews to give up their religion and opt for secular integration in German civil society, like Bauer—the German Jewish intellectual he criticizes—Marx looks at this religious difference as a political terrain from which to effectively push 'real, practical' political emancipation beyond the contradictions of bourgeois political equality.[27] Similarly, although the Indian state officially adopted secularism, which was an official statement of religious neutrality, Ambedkar rapidly found out while he served as law minister that the Nehruvian state's reformist agenda remained ineffective and uncommitted in creating a truly secular society.[28]

The political context of his decision to devote the rest of his life to the project of Buddhist conversion thus shows that Ambedkar's decision was, even though it had already been announced fifteen years before (in 1936), ultimately reconfirmed by his disillusionment with institutional politics. His resignation from the Nehru cabinet in 1951 was in protest against Nehru's lack of support for the Hindu Code Bill that he had prepared. The setback met by his attempt to strike legally against Hindu patriarchy which he considered the foundation of caste revealed that the Indian ruling class's Hindu conservatism had already outweighed the official doctrine of religious neutrality and secularism.[29] Therefore, Ambedkar became convinced that the new-born Indian state could not be trusted to protect society from the undemocratic Hindu social order. This disillusionment with institutional politics explains his decision to refocus his offensive on the religious reform of society.

Although there is no evidence that Ambedkar was influenced by Marx's reflection on the Jewish question or ever read the book, his turn to religion indicates a similar aspiration towards political autonomy from the state. However, the attempt to win Dalit political autonomy from the state was not without a cost. Leaving the Hindu fold meant giving up the official SC status, which entitled Dalit subgroups (jatis) to certain benefits. As a consequence, conversion meant giving up benefits in terms of education, public jobs, reserved seats in elected assemblies and protection against caste discrimination.[30] Ambedkar was ready to give up these measures of state welfare and economic improvement because he quickly understood the effects of upper-caste patronage that these policies enabled, which threatened to keep Dalits in a subordinate position. Ambedkar argued during a speech in Agra in March 1956 that it was advisable for Dalits to dissociate from any category reminiscent of untouchability, like SCs.[31] In this speech, he thus warned against state welfare in favour of a more autonomous definition of Dalits as Buddhists, unbound by state categories. He argued in his speech that Dalits should take this as an encouragement to renounce their state welfare benefits. He criticized these measures based on the criterion of untouchability as stigmatizing as well as debilitating, considering that the distribution of these resources had already started to encourage sycophancy among educated Dalits who sought the benefits of reserved jobs.[32]

In the press conference that he gave in Nagpur on the eve of his own conversion, he again clarified his stand. Answering the journalist who asked, 'What about the special concessions ensured by the Constitution to the

Untouchable class? They will be no more. What about that?',[33] Ambedkar reiterated that Dalits should become equal citizens rather than claim benefits that would perpetuate their traditional status as 'Untouchables'—'We will get all the concessions ensured for all citizens even after conversion. As of the question of special concessions, why do you worry about that? Whether you wish that we should remain Untouchables all the life to avail the special concessions given by the Constitution? We are striving to achieve *Humanism*.'[34] Interestingly, one can also note that his insistence on conversion as a means to reclaim autonomy from state categories thus conforms to the emancipatory process that Jacques Rancière[35] calls 'disidentification'.

## Examining Ambedkar's idea of 'Religion'

What now remains to be understood to do justice to Navayana's self-definition as a religion is the concessions that it makes to religiosity itself, which is where Ambedkar departs from Marx. Marx's purely strategical concessions to Jewish religion as a political attribute diverge from Ambedkar's positive apprehension of religion as an ethical resource for national life. In contrast to Ambedkar, who emphasized people's spiritual needs, Marx's view of people's religiosity remains doubly negative—it is both a result of suffering from economic exploitation and a symptom of the incompleteness of the project of political emancipation under the bourgeois state.

Zelliot underlines Ambedkar's spiritual concerns, reminding us of his earlier socialization with *bhakti* (devotional) Dalit religious sects and pointing to his erudite interest in Buddhist spirituality.[36] During his talk to the Buddhist Sasana Council of Burma in 1954, Ambedkar argued that 'like with the entry of Christianity in Rome, it was the poor and despised sections who needed religion'.[37] But he was also aware that popular religion in its existing form could harm prospects of emancipation. In his memoirs, his personal secretary reminds us that he equated Dalit religious practice with a culture of poverty and untouchability. Rattu tells us that he viewed bhakti cults as 'superstitions and blind faiths' and, borrowing Marx's famous formula, as the 'opium of helplessness'. 'He wanted to root out this disease from their minds, which he said was merely sentimental nonsense and made them impotent and which had stood in the way of their progress'.[38] Hence his intention was to replace subaltern religious life with a rational substitute that matched the Dalit movement's quest for modernity and self-respect.

Attempts have been made to draw parallels between Antonio Gramsci's and Ambedkar's emphasis on religion.[39] Although I consider that a Gramscian reading of the Dalit movement has many insights to offer, in my view there are also significant differences between Ambedkar's idea of Dalit emancipation and Gramsci's subaltern perspective. In *Prison Notebooks* Gramsci argues that popular religious praxis provides the cultural ground from which to instil a revolutionary consciousness into the peasant masses. Ambedkar's strategy was, on the contrary, to substitute a modernized version of Buddhism for popular religion. According to him, even the bhakti cults practised by Dalits had all become contaminated by caste, ideologically and practically.[40] In contrast with the Gramscian perspective, which seeks to differentiate and select from among existing religious notions and practices those that could be coherent with the Marxist philosophy, Ambedkar's strategy of religious substitution is somehow closer to the tabula rasa approach that Gramsci criticizes. By reconstructing a Dalit Buddhist past in his essay on the origins of untouchability, Ambedkar made a connection with a distant and forgotten past, but he also argued that Dalits had lost touch with this past, and he saw their present culture as the internalization of caste subordination.[41]

Besides the issue of rationality, which determined Ambedkar's preference for Buddhism among other established religions, the issue of respectability—offering Dalit converts a religion with a big 'R' that would enhance their social status—was an important factor in his willingness to depart from existing subaltern bhakti cults prevailing among Dalits. His emphasis on respectability explains a fundamental tension in Ambedkar's conception of Buddhism. While at times he defined Dhamma in opposition to religion as it existed, 'at some places he took Buddhism as a religion among others'.[42] This, according to Fuchs, was because he wanted Navayana to be recognized and respected as 'Religion'. As noted by Joel Lee, this shows that Ambedkar 'had acquiesced to the regnant taxonomy of religion—in which Hinduism, Islam, Buddhism, Sikhism and Christianity enjoyed status while the religious traditions of Lal Begis, Satnamis and so on did not—and committed himself to an emancipatory project *legible* in the terms of that taxonomy: conversion from one politically recognized religion to another'.[43] Therefore, Ambedkar's strategy was to gain respectability through the appropriation of a religion that was already recognized by Western discourses, to the detriment of existing Dalit cults that bore the stigma of caste subordination.

A few significant examples can help us see concretely the importance that Ambedkar gave to religious signifiers in order to build Navayana's respectability. Although wishing to downplay as much as possible the importance of the clergy in the *diksha* ceremony, he nevertheless acknowledged that Navayana could not do without the *bikshus* (Buddhist monks) if it were to obtain religious recognition. He also took pains to elaborate a diksha ritual, which was regarded as the first step of an initiation rather than an instant conversion, and an iconography, thus making formal concessions to established conceptions of 'Religion'. In his public speech in Sri Lanka in 1950, he reminded his audience that 'the first definite object of my visit is to see Buddhist ceremonial. Ceremonial is an important part of religion. Whatever rationalists might say, ceremonial is a very essential thing in religion'.[44] In February 1956, while preparing for the diksha, he wrote a booklet in Pali (the ancient language of Theravada Buddhist scriptures) and Marathi, titled 'Buddha Puja Path', which synthesized his findings on Theravada rituals in Sri Lanka. On the morning of his conversion, one of his followers who published a detailed chronology of his life reported that 'Babasaheb dresses up in white Kurta, Coat and special white Dhoti (loincloth) which he had specially arranged from Coimbatur, Tamil Nadu. He expresses his wish to Mr Godbole that homage (Shradhanjali) be paid to his father Ramji Ambedkar on this day as he was the man who cultured him in religion'.[45] Indeed, his father was a follower of the Kabir Panthi sect, which emphasized equality of all humans before god. These details show that Ambedkar did not simply make formal concessions to religion but also paid his homage to previous forms of Dalit spirituality.

He was nevertheless careful to select ritual symbols that were consistent with his political aims. Based on his research on the more ancient Theravada tradition of Sri Lanka and Burma, Gary Tartakov noticed that Ambedkar, selected images of the Buddha with open eyes, rejecting the more introspective-looking ones with closed eyes in order to propose a politically relevant image of the Buddha engaged with the world.[46] Politically, Navayana thus defines an ambivalent or grey zone between a 'respectable', liberal and bourgeois conception of religion tailored for Dalit citizens and political engagement. Navayana has thus lent itself to different interpretations and controversies, some emphasizing the needs for ritual consolidation,[47] while ethnographic observations have shown that the politicized Ambedkarite milieus that establish and fund the Boddh Vihars, recruit the bikshus and provide for their livelihood often themselves display a persistent anticlericalism.[48]

On a larger plane, the Navayana movement's inability to achieve its universal goal of transforming society as a whole has been characterized by Fuchs as a failure for having been 'pushed into its communalist corner, becoming a religion for Dalits only'[49] by the dominant discourse. In a similar vein, Partha Chatterjee emphasizes that Navayana has not helped Dalits escape their subaltern condition.[50] While it is a fact that Navayana has been ghettoized in subaltern communities and has become integrated into the ideological landscape of Dalits almost exclusively, these negative assessments fail to convey its meaning and political relevance for those concerned.

Studying a political movement of emancipation of the subaltern requires us to take into account the psychological impact of these claims to universality. The enunciation of the universal constitutes a subversive claim on the part of those who are constantly 'anthropologized', stigmatized as 'different' and 'communitarized' by the dominant discourse.[51] Marxist political philosophers like Balibar and Rancière advise us that the reclamation of universality constitutes a powerful statement of equality that challenges the elite's intellectual hegemony while requalifying politically the margins of society. Political ethnography can therefore help us understand how Navayana has fuelled these claims to universality and influenced Dalit political praxis. Ethnography requires us to pay attention in detail to the manners and effects of the enunciations of universal discourse by subaltern/minoritarian sections of society (for an ethnography of Navayana Buddhism in Maharashtra, see Johannes Beltz[52] and for Uttar Pradesh, see Jaoul[53]).

## Conclusion

In her editorial piece published in a national daily newspaper entitled 'Neo Buddhists Are Far Ahead of Hindu Dalits', the Ambedkarite sociologist Shura Darapuri highlights the benefits of conversion in terms of sex ratio, literacy rates, female literacy and employment. Based on the all-India figures of the 2001 census, she shows that in all these domains, Navayana practitioners have surpassed Hindu Dalits and Hindus in general. She thus concludes that 'it is definitely the result of change of religion which has liberated them from the bondage of caste and inferiority complex'[54] and enabled them to progress. Whether Buddhism produces adequate citizens or the better educated and economically better off among Dalits are attracted to Buddhism is like the question of the chicken and the egg. This undetermined relationship of causality in any case indicates a virtuous circle at work in the Ambedkarite movement's intimate link with education and upward mobility. Shura Darapuri's claim that Navayana favours the norms of citizenship, thus succeeding where the state itself is failing to educate and provide for its citizens' welfare, epitomizes the Ambedkarite movement's dual relationship to the state. By appropriating these statist goals, Navayana activists are not simply being good subjects of the state. They are challenging the state's official disqualification of Dalits as weaker groups entitled to state protection.[55] By redefining themselves as a religious minority, they are taking responsibility for their own progress and for establishing a truly democratic society. Navayana therefore implies the repoliticization of Dalit citizenship by 'inciting real people to reappropriate this universality that the state claims to carry'[56] (my translation from the French). It represents a political antidote to the state's attempts to equate citizenship with subordination to the state as passive 'citizen subjects'.[57]

If Navayana should not be mistaken for citizenship in oriental religious clothing, neither can it be reduced to a form of crypto-Marxism hidden beneath a cloak of religion. One major difference between Ambedkar's conception of Navayana and Marx's conception of religion for the Jewish minority is that while the latter explicitly opposed the religious domain of the oppressed minority to the statist domain of citizenship, Ambedkar also more conventionally considered religion a part of Dalit citizenship in independent India. Navayana thus defines a space at the fringes of the state's citizen subject and a more utopian project that encapsulates both the Marxian idea of a classless society and liberal ideas of a society composed of free, rational and ethical citizens.

However, based on Ambedkar's own insistence on the importance of religion for Dalits and their emancipation, as well as on Marx's insights regarding the political significance of the Jewish oppressed minority's religion, we ought to take seriously Navayana's self-definition as 'Religion'. Navayana lends itself to a plurality of social and political uses, in which revolutionary politics coexists with a more conventional idea of religion as an attribute of respectability, while also providing its practitioners with lifecycle rituals that are helpful for Dalits to distance themselves from the influence of Hindu priests. The effect has thus been the entrenchment of a political tradition of emancipation into the domestic sphere, which makes Navayana a source of political ferment in everyday life.

While swimming against the tide of popular religiosity in order to conform to Ambedkar's project, ethnographic accounts show that Navayana's attempt to replace popular religion with a rational substitute is nevertheless fraught by its own reticence in the face of religiosity. Although Ambedkar conceived his religious project as an ideological basis for the unification of Dalits as a religious minority (as well as for society at large in the longer run), in reality the issue of conversion has generated controversies and sustained divisions among Dalits. The political ethnography of Navayana thus brings to our attention the 'complication of the political'[58] that Ambedkarite Dalits encounter by seeking to implement in real life the religious prototype that Ambedkar crafted at the end of his life, without having the time to check how it was implemented. It teaches us that in its empirical and socialized version, emancipation requires struggles within the struggle and cannot be a homogeneous process, even less a sudden illumination, unlike the Paulinian myth of instant 'conversion'[59] which continues to run through the idealistic notion of 'emancipation'.

## References

Ambedkar, B.R. 1979. 'Ranade, Gandhi and Jinnah'. In *Dr. Babasaheb Ambedkar: Writings and Speeches*, vol. 1. Mumbai: Government of Maharashtra.

Ambedkar, B.R. 1990. *The Untouchables: Who Were They and How They Became Untouchables* in *Dr. Babasaheb Ambedkar: Writings and Speeches*, vol. 7. Mumbai: Government of Maharashtra.

Ambedkar, B.R. 1992. *The Buddha and His Dhamma* in *Dr. Babasaheb Ambedkar: Writings and Speeches*, vol. 11. Mumbai: Government of Maharashtra.

Ambedkar, B.R. Undated. 'What Path Salvation.' In Bhagwan Das, *Thus Spoke Ambedkar: On Renunciation of Hinduism and Conversion of Untouchables*, vol. 4, pp. 11–65.

# A DERRIDEAN READING OF AMBEDKAR'S *THE BUDDHA AND HIS DHAMMA*

*Rajesh Sampath*

## Introduction

In this essay, we will appropriate insights from Derrida's *Of Grammatology* (1967)[1] and transmute them in an application of a close textual reading of Ambedkar's *The Buddha and His Dhamma*.[2] That great work marks a quintessential moment contemporaneous with the great liberation movement in the South Asian context: one in which Ambedkar, in a mass conversion event, leaves Hinduism behind once and for all and embraces Buddhism as his new faith. Having studied Hinduism for decades[3] in an attempt to deconstruct its immorality, which founds the caste system as one of the most horrific forms of any social order in recorded human history, Ambedkar finally abandoned what he perceived as an opaque world religion born of a mixture of myth (the epics) and scripture (the Vedas and Upanishads) in antiquity and turns to Buddhism towards the end of his life.[4]

Our thesis is just as Derrida tries to show that in Eurocentric Western philosophy, history and science 'living speech' has been valued as presence as part of the 'epoch' of 'logocentrism'[5] and 'phallocentrism' while devaluing, debasing and misunderstanding writing as dead, empty, a false copy of living speech,[6] we will argue that Brahminical Hindu supremacy and its caste system is also a type of prioritized speech, logos (word/truth) and patriarchal domination that devalues, disintegrates, demeans and deplores the Dalit (formerly known as 'Untouchable') experience and intersectionally within it, women who are the most oppressed. Specifically, Derrida's 'grammatological' project tries to deconstruct how this speech-writing

293

distinction has reached its 'closure'[7] but not end in Western thought (particularly its philosophy) and while developing novel tools that are neither words nor concepts—namely, the 'trace, archive, supplement and différance (differing and delaying)'.[8] He tries to work within the Western system and epoch to carve out new possibilities of what is *other* to the metaphysics of speech, presence, logos (word/truth).

Analogously, we will examine the event of Ambedkar's conversion to Buddhism as a type of liberational exercise vis-à-vis the historical dominance, hegemony and ideology of Hindu caste that has pervaded Indian civilization and history. This will require a close analysis of Ambedkar's text while doing an unrelenting deconstruction of Hindu Brahmin supremacy and its unjust metaphysical conception of caste, which affects and corrodes social reality down to the core of the Hindu mind and spirit. We bracket our exercise as a phenomenological destruction of caste by way of an appropriation of Derridean grammatology and its critique of the history of Western metaphysics and its ontological underpinnings. What is other to the metaphysical traditions of the West—and its priority of 'being' as presence as logos, the truth of truth and phallocentric male heterosexual domination of women, and one can say exclusion and marginalization of LGBTQ too—is brought into dialogue as to what could be other to Hinduism and its malevolent 'truth' of the caste system. This way we can outline future contours to imagine how to revolutionize Indian society by way of Ambedkarite Buddhism, an event which has failed to occur since independence from British colonialism and the birth of the Indian nation. The crosswise application aforementioned as a marker of our method is this: we are trying to see Derridean deconstruction in the liberational event of Ambedkar's conversion to Buddhism, and inversely what is 'other' to Western metaphysics in Derrida's *Of Grammatology* finds its passage to alterity in the Buddhist transcendence of Hindu caste. Our objective is to make this method clearer in the course of our close reading of both texts separately and in relation to one another.

In the exergue of 'Part I: Writing Before the Letter' in *Of Grammatology*, Derrida already gives us some clues as to what his enterprise entails.[9] These initial reflections can be used as a pretext to frame—through a series of prefatory remarks in our own voice independent of Derrida's and Ambedkar's—how one can embark on a novel reading of Ambedkar's text. In many respects, Ambedkar's attempt at social revolution by way of Buddhist transcendence of the Hindu caste system remains an unfinished task.[10]

Derrida states:

This triple exergue is intended not only to focus attention on the *ethnocentrism* which, everywhere and always, had controlled the concept of writing. Nor merely to focus attention on what I shall call *logocentrism*: the metaphysics of phonetic writing (for example, of the alphabet) which was fundamentally—for enigmatic and yet essential reasons that are inaccessible to a simple historical relativism—nothing but the most original and powerful ethnocentrism, in the process of imposing itself upon the world, controlling in one and the same *order* . . .[11]

*The history of (the only) metaphysics,* which has, in spite of all differences, not only from Plato to Hegel (even including Leibniz) but also, beyond these apparent limits, from the pre-Socratics to Heidegger, always assigned the origin of truth in general to the logos: the history of truth of the truth, has always been—except for a metaphysical diversion that we shall have to explain—the debasement of writing, and its repression outside 'full' speech.[12]

Derrida will go to great lengths to say that his project is not to invert the hierarchy and make writing superior to speech just as speech has been superior to writing throughout the history of metaphysics as the long epoch of logocentrism. We offer two more long passages before returning to the previous two passages. Together, they will inform the analysis that outlines our pre-textual framework to foreground the conditions of possibility for reading the event of Ambedkar's conversion to Buddhism as an enigmatic 'text' in its own right. For us, the event of conversion is like a text that has yet to be deciphered beyond our normal, intuitive apperceptions of what conversion typically means—say a turning, repentance, awakening, revelation, realization, transmogrification, ecstatic mystical elevation or becoming a 'new Being'.[13] Our project does not speak from within the religious experience of conversion per se, whether Buddhist or any other major world religion. Rather, we are interested in a phenomenological deconstruction of various normative registers as to what might constitute any meaning whatsoever in the event of conversion for the larger task of what could possibly replace the Hindu metaphysical system of caste; this is why we have to focus squarely on Ambedkar's South Asian context of Hinduism and within it the event of conversion to Buddhism.

In returning to two more passages that we need for the start of our analysis, we quote Derrida again:

> Of course, it is not a question of 'rejecting' these notions; they are necessary and, at least present, nothing is conceivable for us without them. It is a question at first of demonstrating the systematic and historical solidarity of the concepts and gestures of thought that one often believes can be innocently separated. The sign and divinity have the same place and time of birth. The age of the sign is essentially theological. Perhaps it will never *end*. Its historical *closure is*, however, outlined.[14]
>
> Since these concepts are indispensable for unsettling the heritage to which they belong, we should be even less prone to renounce them. Within the closure, by an oblique and always perilous movement, constantly risking falling back within what is being deconstructed, it is necessary to surround the critical concepts with a careful and thorough discourse—to mark the conditions, the medium, and the limits of their effectiveness and to designate rigorously their intimate relationship to the machine whose deconstruction they permit; and, in the same process, designate the crevice through which the yet unnameable glimmer beyond closure can be glimpsed.[15]

The initial juxtaposition we have in mind for our hypothesis is that what Derrida says about 'closure' and the 'unnameable glimmer beyond closure that can be glimpsed' is linked to the mysterious event of Ambedkarite philosophical critique and the practical event of collective, publicly witnessed conversion—to imagine the passage from the dominant Hindu caste regime that has dictated over two millennia of history on the Indian subcontinent to a new epoch of freedom and transcendence via Buddhism. But also we must avoid the trap of merely replacing Hinduism with Buddhism, the actual religions and their theological contents, without eradicating the caste system. This would require a new type of thinking, perhaps heterodox to all extant religions and their incumbent theologies, to prepare the conditions for the final 'annihilation'[16] of caste—by working through the dilemmas Derrida confronts in challenging the dominant logocentrism of Western metaphysics and its priority of leaving speech, presence, the soul and the self in a realm beyond the West.

So let us pause here and discuss the Derridean themes to foreground the reading of Ambedkar's Buddhism and inversely how Ambedkar's Buddhism can expand into new domains beyond the history of Western metaphysics for which Derridean deconstruction marks the 'closure' but not end. We must expand and morph these concepts to understand the relation between the event of Ambedkarite Buddhist conversion and the destruction of the Hindu metaphysics of caste. We can set up a juxtaposition of Derridean deconstruction of Western metaphysics by way of his grammatological enterprise and our attempt at destruction and passage to the 'other' beyond Hindu metaphysics of caste.

To recapitulate some of the major ideas at the outset of *Of Grammatology*, Derrida speaks of a pervasive, omnipresent, and infinitely expanding 'Eurocentrism, Logocentrism, and Phoneticization'. Without these there would be no history of Western metaphysics and its a priori asymmetry of which full, living speech as presence has always debased, demeaned and denigrated writing when merely seeing it as false copy, death remnant that is inferior to full living presents and presence of breath, soul and life. Similarly, Hindu metaphysics prioritizes the idealized notion of the living soul and absolute Self but gradated in a cosmic movement of reincarnation and the transmigration of the soul from one living body that dies to another living body which does not remember the past body. But it does so ideologically in terms of this multifarious complex of diabolical forces—while perpetrating a metaphysical and idealized notion of supra-consciousness that transcends the senses, it actually only achieves empirical proof of such doctrines in the oppressive juridical-legal-political-social-cultural-economic system of caste which divides whole peoples into separate castes. In the Hindu mind, transcendence feeds off material oppression while not recognizing the hypocrisy of claiming a pure distinction between transcendence and immanence. In other words, announcing a distinction between transcendence and immanence is contradictory if one claims that immanence and the material realm are impure while transcendence and otherworldly asceticism are deemed pure, when in fact such transcendence depends on immanent commitments in the material world, such as the caste system. To begin with, without this primordial forgetfulness, no Hindu metaphysics would be possible.

This material domination structures everyday life down to the smallest details in a type of 'biopolitics' that works at the individual and general population levels.[17] But what Western thinkers like Foucault see as the general functioning of modern, Western and democratic capitalist systems changes form in the South Asian context. We need a more nuanced complexity to understand the modern, capitalist and 'democratic' South Asian context, particularly the Hindu supra-majority in India. To the 'disciplinary-anatomico techniques of power' that works at the infinitely complex and microscopic level of individual bodies in the process of 'normalization' and the macro-'biopolitical power' that exerts its administrative forces on entire populations, we have to add the cosmic-material caste power that exceeds the individual body and general population. Following Foucault, all three of these exceed the history of the social contract and all concepts of sovereignty that try to justify the nature of state and government. We are not talking about how states protect themselves from foreign threats while protecting their citizens from one another by upholding the rule of law.[18] Nor are we talking about the system of international law and associated rights and duties of nation states interacting at the global level that regulates their actions and behaviours based on certain universally recognized norms of human rights.[19] Furthermore, this goes beyond the issue of class measured by wealth, property, assets or purely economic definitions of class, particularly within the gross inequality that capitalist economies generate. For in the Hindu caste system that underpins Indian society, within each class could be multiple castes. It is in the level of both economic oppression (social-material poverty) and caste alienation and hegemony (vertical differentiation of higher castes that enjoy greater rights and privileges than lower castes) that the true problem arises.[20]

Now returning to the Derridean passages to unpack the mystery of caste we find some new patterns and resemblances in the cross-wise encounter of Derridean deconstruction of the Western tradition and our phenomenological destruction of the Hindu metaphysics of caste. And this will help us foreground any understanding of what the true meaning of the event of Ambedkarite Buddhist conversion turns out to be. For Derrida, the 'sign' and 'divinity' share the same 'birth' because on the one hand the arbitrary unity of a 'signifier' (word as speech or phoneticized writing) that corresponds to the 'signified' (mental image, concept, object) is the 'sign', but on the other hand what composes these signs and their relations and differences between one another is quite arbitrary. Presumably in recorded human history and consciousness with the birth of the first formal writing systems, there is nothing outside the sign to which internal consciousness can associate. But Derrida goes one step further than the breakthroughs of Saussurian linguistics.[21] Insofar as our normalized logocentric view of seeing writing as a secondary and inferior type of speech when compared to living speech, which is linked with being, presence, being as presence, being of presence and presence of being, as the only way to articulate the truth is quite revealing. It also shows that the concept of the divine—as exclusive ownership of truth and its revelation—requires its own type of power and exclusion. The 'ontological-theological'[22] constitution of Western metaphysics signifies the uncanny notion that Being is thought of in terms of Truth and Truth is equated with the Being of God, but in a way that has been obscured over and over again from pre-Christian Greek metaphysics to Christian medieval philosophical theology to various attempts to relate philosophy and theology in Western modern discourse.

Regardless, the non-divine or impure, mortal, fleeting and derivative can never speak on behalf of the divine on any interrelation of being, truth and the godhead. That sacrosanct prohibition becomes the condition of logical truth-telling, and this is instantiated by the history of metaphysics and therefore theology too as the philosophical and metaphysical justification of religion. Both the superiority of living speech and the concept of the divine require this exclusivity and this subtle but unthought notion that somehow non-phonetic (and hence non-Eurocentric) 'writing' as the lesser representation of speech, which itself is the pure representation of Truth, God, Being, whatever, is something that has to be contained. But this is exactly what Derridean deconstruction seeks to release from within and to upset the innate hierarchies and repressions that bind the sign with the divine. Nothing short of the eclipse and 'closure' but not end of the 'West' as we know it is at stake.

We can ask now the following question: how does all of this discussion about the Derridean deconstruction of Western philosophy and theology apply to our analysis of Hindu metaphysics before we turn to the event of Ambedkar's conversion to Buddhism and what that means for the 'annihilation' of caste? One can say that Hindu Brahminical superiority operates by its own Hindu-centric consciousness of caste akin to the Eurocentric bias of Western metaphysical prioritization of speech as logocentric presence. But the twist in the context of Hindu metaphysics is this: Brahminical supremacy writes 'caste' as a specious text or delusory language in which what is accorded to the highest caste, namely the Brahmins, is the innate ability to transcend bodily consciousness to arrive at the atman–brahman unity of supra-consciousness, the highest peak of wisdom.

Caste as a language separates the high caste as free and living speech of the soul and of breath, while the low caste incarnates in bodily signs the equivalent of what Western metaphysical history does with respect to living speech's domination and desecration of writing. The low caste, and furthermore the outside caste or Dalit (formerly known as Untouchable), is constantly debased in its bodily state from which the trapped soul cannot escape except at death. Death is the event of meaning that could escape the enclosed language of the body but such a meaning and hence liberation for the low caste/Dalit never arrives—it is delayed, in the transmigration of the soul that arrives at another body, and hence another system of signs. The low caste and Dalit become the text of the body that is encrypted, inscribed over and over again with the multitude of sins (past bad karma) for which the individual body of the low caste and Dalit must be punished. It is a constant reminder of what is 'Other' to the living soul of the divine life as presence in transcendence of the senses, namely the impurity of bodily existence itself. The social body of the caste system has to lacerate parts of the metaphysical body so that other parts can be deluded to think they can be free of any material reality. The self-mutilation of the social body in the form of caste conceals the ideological notion of a free, egalitarian social contract whose essence is that of 'liberty, fraternity and equality' for all. The secular, diverse, pluralistic, peaceful and free democratic society that India presents to the world as its sociopolitical reality is in fact false; that is what effective ideologies do, namely, presenting a reality that appears to be true while concealing a form of domination that the outside world cannot see.

The Dalit is equated with death, depravity, impurity and the demonic material forces of everyday life from handling defecation to corpses as antipodes to the purity of the divine. The divine is what the Brahminical caste incarnates in the so-called transcendental consciousness of the otherworldly ascetic being but not in obvious, everyday bodily, immanent terms. Or so it would seem. The Dalit is made to be associated with death as the one who carries the dead body and also handles human defecation as the excess, impure, remnant and trace that has to be expunged and washed away after incineration in order for the life of the whole to continue. Individuation is asymmetric in which the higher caste earns the privilege of total moral detachment to the point of concealing their immoral acceptance of the mass human suffering of the most oppressed, namely, Dalits, while the masses forfeit any type of individual freedom, mobility or liberation from station or caste. The book is written over and over again as the system of traces vanishes and reappears in the miracle of reincarnation.

What the sign and divine are in Western logocentric metaphysics that Derridean deconstruction dismantles, one can argue is the Brahminical non-bodily (hence specious and false) supra-consciousness as the preternatural, divine life, which requires the manufactured script of the caste in which what is lower is debased, made impure and repressed, just as death is from the living soul. Caste in the Hindu context is the logocentric metaphysicalization of the pure and impure whereby consciousness as a non-bodily sign of the high caste exists at the expense of bodily, scripted oppression of the lowest caste and outside—Dalit—caste as impure. Caste is this system of what one can refer to as 'sign-bodies', which are constantly being reproduced and destroyed in an endless cycle of misery and oppression in a textual regime of terror known as the Hindu caste system. The mythic function of these sign-bodies is to provide the matter for which the speech and writing of Hindu speculative wisdom is encrypted and inscripted, while erasing the trace of the origin of the brutality encrusted in the doctrinal movement known as the transmigration of the soul; whereas the Western system according to Derrida is merely the sign as the unity of an empty signifier (word-utterance) and signified (concept, mental image, thing, object).

Domination for Western thought is merely speech over writing when the former makes the latter an inferior, phoneticized version of itself. But something far more horrific is at work in the Hindu South Asian context. No other system is allowed to penetrate the inner cosmos of Hinduism which claims to be free, open, inclusive and accepting all forms of life (which should ideally include other religions as fascist Hindutva national consciousness tries to convince the world). But the claim is one thing, the lived reality another. For Hinduism claims a profound and mysterious, seemingly prehistoric antiquity and boasts of the 'longest living religious tradition,' even prior to the great monotheistic faiths whose texts emerged much later and, of course, Buddhism as an 'offshoot' of Hinduism.

With this foregrounding we can now turn to the event of the Ambedkarite conversion to Buddhism and link this to the final statement by Derrida within the passages we offered: namely, 'the crevice through which the yet unnameable glimmer beyond closure can be glimpsed'.[23] Here we can only offer some preliminary remarks as ways to differ, defer and delay a much larger reflection, one that will encompass the general ontological meaning of the event of Ambedkarite Buddhist conversion and what that signals as the destruction of Hindu metaphysics and a passage to another epoch that has yet to be experienced in the long history of Indian consciousness and its ancient roots in the Hindu oppression of caste. For this, we turn to the actual event of the mass conversion and Ambedkar's articulation of the vows read and recited by a large group of converts out of the Dalit identity on that momentous day of 14 October 1956.

## Ambedkar's Recitation of Vows at the Conversion

In particular we will quote vows 9, 10, 19 and 21 and analyse them in depth.

> 9. I shall believe in the equality of man.
> 10. I shall endeavour to establish equality.
> 19. I renounce Hinduism which is harmful for humanity and impedes the advancement and development of humanity because it is based on inequality, and adopt Buddhism as my religion.
> 21. I believe I am having a rebirth.[24]

One should look at all twenty-two vows individually and what they contain in their indivisible totality that constitutes the 'event' of conversion. But we will isolate these four to open the multidimensional complexity of the event by reading Derrida's *Of Grammatology*. The editors of the volume *The Buddha and His Dhamma: A Critical Edition* speak of a 'political theology'[25] that upsets the traditional, orthodox and monastic notion of Buddhism as 'other-worldly asceticism'.[26]

We are not going to try to understand this event from within Buddhist doctrines or as a new way to promote that particular world religion (and its miraculously and geographically diverse set of traditions, schools, cultures and languages). We do not claim any specialized knowledge of the 'other-worldly asceticism' of Buddhism or wish to engage in debates with early sociologists of religion like Weber; for some postcolonial critics could claim that the rampant Eurocentric racism of Western discourse that Derrida acknowledged for Western thought, philosophy and science in general runs amuck in these 20th-century Western sociologies and anthropologies of Eastern religions. With no aim to disrespect Buddhism, we simply bracket the fact that such a world religion currently speaks to hundreds of millions of people; it promises a peaceful and fulfilling way of life to detach from all the material desires that can lead to human suffering. However, for the Ambedkarite programme prior to the event of conversion, we cannot forget the project of social revolution and material transformation that can defeat the Hindu metaphysical calcification of the caste system and therefore dissolve the caste system once and for all. For that prioritization, we must turn to an analysis of the four specific vows we just quoted in light of our larger analysis of Derridean deconstruction of Western metaphysics and our non-dialectical critique of Hindu metaphysics of caste.

It is very hard to imagine from within Dalit consciousness and its subconsciousness,[27] which has been ingrained in the life-world and experiences of Dalits under an unspeakable and unjustifiable oppression and one that has lasted for millennia. If one is not Dalit (a false construct created by the master-order of Hindu Brahminical supremacy), then how can one understand the event of conversion from Hinduism to another religion like Buddhism? Similarly, it is extremely difficult to understand five centuries of African-American oppression from the slave trade to slavery to segregation to de-segregation and civil rights to the current age of mass incarceration, structural inequality and state-condoned homicide of innocent Black males and females. It is hard to imagine the enduring suffering of indigenous peoples everywhere and religious, linguistic, cultural minorities in every context and history, for example, the Tibetans in China and India and the Roma peoples and their long journey from South Asia to Europe. Anti-Semitism is a painful reminder of one of the longest-standing oppressions of people on earth, namely, the Jews.

But as an outsider to the Dalit peoples and now also an 'outsider' to the Hindu fold of caste in general, one must try respectfully, always in mindful, circumscribed ways not to fetishize Dalit suffering as purely an academic exercise. What was at stake for Ambedkar in his whole life and for which hundreds of millions of Dalits in India, South Asia and worldwide seek today is the final liberation from the oppressive regime of caste, which means its utter and total 'annihilation'. The task at hand is to think of the event of conversion in terms of a type of liberation theology sown through the vows that Ambedkar took on that fateful day with hundreds of thousands of other Dalits.

Vows 9 and 10 claim two things: (a) that one must announce and assert a fundamental belief in equality and (b) one must strive to create that equality. This is a paradox in itself. From one standpoint, one is being asked to believe something that does not exist within the Hindu social, political and metaphysical status quo—namely, the fundamental equality of human beings, which means the humanization of the notion of equality itself as not something abstract or constitutionally calcified. Rather, the issue is one of a genuine belief in the other as equal in essence to oneself which requires love, empathy, compassion and the elimination of all bias, prejudice and suspicion of essential difference. But this state does not yet exist and hence it requires something, some willpower, that must be strived for—a longing and yearning that is also met with a strident, radical movement to make this a reality.

The 'other-worldly asceticism' required for the belief in equality is connected to a this-worldly radical action to make equal individuals a reality. To have this built into the event of conversion means that the delay of a future equality (that has yet to be achieved) is overcome through an event of differentiation of the Hindu metaphysical presence of caste and another which is not that—a state of internal transcendental being where equality becomes, like theosis or becoming god, a type of unity between individual human beings. There is no place for caste hierarchy and 'graded inequality' and the immoral and amoral virtues of antipathy, hostility, amusement and sadism endemic in the high-caste mindset. Here the Derridean notion of 'différance' is itself altered, requiring a different grammatological set of concepts to understand its mysterious movement and temporalization in the event of the Ambedkarite Buddhist conversion.

Vow 19 brings in a stringent critique of the Hindu social order and the 'harm' it brings to the 'progress and development of humanity.' If the postcolonial critiques of academic elites borrowing from both the French post-structuralists and the German Frankfurt School include a suspicion of Western modernity and its ideas of enlightenment, progress and democracy, then we need to go deeper than those critiques. Coupled with this critique of Hindu metaphysics and its danger to humanity is a confession of Buddhism as the new religion; this is not a mere substitute for Hinduism. Something else is at stake, which culminates in the penultimate Vow 21 of confessing the experience of 'having a rebirth'.

We have to phenomenologically bracket what this all means: the event of 'confession' of an 'experience' of having a 'rebirth' so we do not get entangled in the dialectical relations one might think of when comparing and contrasting the following: namely the ideas of rebirth in Hindu metaphysics, which requires the material realm of caste domination as its basic infrastructure, and the Buddhist notion of rebirth which individualizes this down to a mysterious acontextual context of spiritual transcendence in monastic asceticism. If the punished body of the low caste is required in the false metaphysical transcendence of the former, then the complete evaporation of the body and its desires becomes the prerequisite for the latter in an indescribable mystical experience of inner unity of consciousness with a realm beyond decay and even death.

Rather, the critique of Hindu metaphysics of caste and the declaration of injury to 'humanity' seems to point to an Eastern conception of human rights that recognizes the vile and cruel system of oppression that caste represents and Hinduism embodies in a self-satisfying and narcissistic way, namely, as some superior form of human wisdom. Justice, mercy and compassion as Ambedkar says in many of his writings are missing from this ethereal, spiritual life-world known as Hinduism.[28] Instead, we need a new foundation to human rights whose indigenous voice relates to the event of Ambedkarite Buddhist conversion; that is, if we believe that the Judaeo-Christian roots of the UN Declaration of Human Rights in 1948, albeit with many signatories in the international context which included the East and Global South, are not sufficient to tackle the problem of caste in a manner that Indian society is compelled to eradicate its enduring presence. What can be Other to all previous conceptions of human rights that descend from the 20th century? That is a difficult question because one does not intend to dismiss the great declarations and conventions of so many rights instruments borne out by the UN over the course of the 20th and early 21st centuries. Those instruments are crucial and necessary to combat, for example, racism and xenophobia while fighting for indigenous and LGBTQ rights worldwide.

However, for overthrowing caste oppression and its intersectional experience of domination by gender, racial, ethnic, sexual, disabled and other minoritized groups, we must think philosophically about this question of the assertion of experiencing a 'rebirth'. If we read Ambedkar's vow by the letter, he states: 'I believe I am having a rebirth.'[29] Here we can only conclude with some speculations that are philosophical in nature but also pragmatic in hoping to articulate conditions to revitalize the Ambedkarite quest to 'annihilate' caste once and for all.

## Conclusion

Ambedkar's vow does not state one is having a rebirth but rather one 'believes they are having this rebirth'. Belief is the state of separation that does not dialectically consume the antithesis known as the Hindu metaphysics of caste but remains in a state as a suspended Other to the Hindu metaphysics of the socio-cultural-political-economic caste system. The meaning of the Other known as 'belief' is deferred and delayed so we do not speak of isolating an original presence from which to derive its truth or voice as presence. This of course comes straight out of Derridean deconstruction. But we do not stop there.

The experience of the rebirth therefore cannot be the movement-transition from the Hindu concept of rebirth to a new concept within the Buddhist fold. Rebirth therefore is not part of the line or the circle that one speaks of as the birth of one body with one soul and the death of that body as its occupant soul is born (reborn) in a new body. The movement of transition between epochs is something else. When one says they are having a rebirth, they are coming into being again, in the freshness and genesis of the new, not unlike a new baby being born (who was never embodied in a previous life), but this time as an adult, not the biological coming into being of a new life form—hence one speaks of a rebirth, not a first birth. The rebirth is the movement of the repetition of an a-original birth, not tied to any previous births (and deaths) that would otherwise occur in the movement of Hindu reincarnation. The origin evacuates itself from any sense and hence does not appear. But in this Buddhist event of conversion, one cannot speak of a rebirth of an original birth as presence, an origin that was originally present (and may have become past); but nor is it a future origin as present waiting to happen. The idea of the origin is crossed out altogether as to not permit the endless cycle of births and rebirths of bodies with souls as if one can point to an original moment that is repeated. It is not a point 'in' time as line or circle to pay homage to Derrida and therefore Heidegger before him. Without the line or the circle, Hindu metaphysics may still proclaim that it can go on in some non-Euclidean way, buried in the heart of its ancient wisdom texts of the Vedas and the Upanishads, but it would not be able to prove empirically that such wisdom points to real human experience without the catastrophically exploitative social reality known as the caste system. And that quite frankly is the whole point of the Ambedkarite critique.

Here we must expound even further, given the inspiration of Derrida and Heidegger, and prior to them, of Hegel, this passage of the movement-transition of epochs that will reorient the human being to another horizon of understanding Being by which we understand human relations between birth, death, time, movement, etc. And this will not be the logocentric encrustment of Hindu metaphysics and its interior engine that keeps it alive, namely, caste and reincarnation or the 'transmigration of the soul'. Rather, the 'belief in having a rebirth' in Vow 21 of the Ambedkarite Buddhist event of conversion opens up a new reality to be explored. There, being is stretched from beginning to end as a single event that is never present and hence not repeated like a video you play over and over again. Being-as-motion of the event of conversion in 'I believe I am having a rebirth' forces us to conceive the meaning of birth itself anew; one that is permanently divorced from an idea of an original birth in which a body is born with a previous soul (that inhabited a previous body that is dead) only to die itself in the future and thus repeating the cycle of being born–again and hence reborn. It is in this realm that perhaps we can 'glimpse through the crevice' the beyond of Hindu metaphysics of the caste system and its assemblage of time, origin, death and rebirth *while* re–occupying the event that announces the 'belief that one is having a re–birth'. A new sense of Being becomes necessary in order to achieve this passage to a realm beyond 'Western' and 'Eastern' metaphysics.

# VI

# AMBEDKAR, A CRITICAL RADICAL PERSPECTIVE

# STRANGE BEDFELLOWS SIDELINE AMBEDKAR

*Lama Choyin Rangdrol*

The fruitless intersection of Ambedkar and Du Bois has long been interpreted as a missed opportunity between individuals. It's reasonable to ponder that the underlying sociopolitical tectonics of marginalizing 'pro-Negro a-hegemonic thought' may also have contributed to the ensuing malaise. Was Ambedkar known to Negro America before the latter's adoption of his Indic nemesis as a non-violent icon? If so, what purpose and boon did the exclusion of Ambedkar bring to Negro identity at home and abroad? Is there a model evident in the slavocratic archive that parallels Ambedkar's verve and mendacity under caste-like fire? One might think not, given that slaves lacked the luxury of education which Ambedkar worked hard to achieve. And of Manu, tinder for Ambedkar's flame, what American slave doctrine could likewise outrage the heart of human dignity? These issues, and others, beg exposition in the Ambedkar–Negro discourse. The pulse of this essay seeks to bring forth this important perusal. It begins in the throes of a cultural renaissance not far from Columbia University, in Harlem, New York.

The early 20th-century Harlem Renaissance was an African-American attempt to define its own identity through the promotion of cultural, social and artistic works. Its efforts to mitigate the global circulation of Black minstrelsy caricatures lasted from about 1918 to the mid-1930s. This was an especially important endeavour due to the Whites' pervasive use of minstrel variety shows travelling abroad. The shows featured Whites wearing burnt cork on their faces to mimic the African-American complexion. Their content consisted of debasing slave mimicry, highlighted by song and dance, whose buffoonery affected the world's concept of postbellum slave life. The Renaissance, at its zenith, was embraced by Black writers internationally, especially francophones from African and Caribbean colonies living in Paris. The Renaissance was the first time Black America sustained an artistic movement powerful enough to gain the attention of international policymakers. Philanthropist A'Lelia Walker, daughter of Black haircare business millionairess Madame C.J. Walker, stood out as the Renaissance's significant patron.[1] She gave money to both local and national organizations, as well as facilitated the introduction of Black artists' works to White editors, publishers and patrons. Her Harlem townhome, named the Dark Tower, was often the scene of elaborate mixed-race socialite parties attended by the most prominent Black artists of the time. Recognized as the Renaissance's principal patron, 'A'Lelia's death in 1931 began a gradual decline of resources necessary to sustain the Renaissance movement.'[2]

African America's quest to influence international policy continued after the Harlem Renaissance's decline. Their longing for international relevance found new lodging in response to Italy's invasion of Ethiopia (1935). The Mussolini-led invasion was an unprovoked assault on an African nation. This added to the discussion of Europe's disregard for Africa that had led to slavery centuries earlier. Concerns about the mistreatment of segregated Black soldiers stationed internationally were also brought to the table.

The invasion prompted India's Gandhi, formerly an admirer of Mussolini, to decry the Italian incursion.[3] His amended claim was against imperial Europe's disregard for foreign sovereignty, which played into his stand against Britain's rule of India. The American government kept out of the matter. They feared Italy's dictator, Mussolini, would ally with Hitler if they intervened.

Given free rein, Italian machine guns mowed down poorly equipped Ethiopians. Mustard gas was also deployed on them. Every living thing was killed as the odourless, colourless gas descended on military and civilian targets. Why is this important to the discussion of African-American religion and Buddhism? Because the events that followed sealed African America's religious fate. America was committed to supporting Britain. They along with their allies left Ethiopia's emperor, Haile Selassie, to live in exile, looking for support on his own (1936–41). Selassie's lonely plight as an émigré served both African-American claims against White injustice and Gandhi's campaign against imperialism. Consequently, the disparate 'African-American Christian' and 'Gandhian Hindu Indian' causes joined in alliance. Gandhi's criticism of Aryan British rule merged perfectly with African-American baulk against Aryan American (Whites) segregation and lynching.

The combined opportunity for propaganda against Aryanism was a boon for both. This was in addition to the Aryan versus Aryan conflict raging between Hitler and the whole of Europe. It's fair to say that the fog of war made for peculiar distinctions and alliances in the Aryan world. The miasma separated Gandhi's Hindu Aryanism, British Aryanism, Hitler's Aryanism, Italian Aryanism and American Aryanism into a hierarchy of evils. By contrast, Gandhi's Hindu Aryanism was a lesser evil. When African America seized the opportunity to work with him, Hindu Aryanism invited itself in.

Gandhi's adverse opinion of Mussolini's imperialist romp in Africa was a globally strategic star for the Negro effort to cling to, a star that shone ever brightly having risen on both sides during the later Harlem Renaissance period.

In July 1930 the *Weekly* carries news of Marcus Garvey's praise for Gandhi's struggle in India and of Gandhi's encouragement of African Americans in their war against white racism.[4]

Hitler's sordid ambition provided an impetus for Mussolini to take action against African sovereignty, prompting Gandhi's subsequent disavowal. America's Black elites seized the opportunity. A bond of sorts was established between Gandhian and Negro interests. Hence, unbeknownst to many African Americans today, Hitler's actions set into motion a chain of events that led to Black America's relationship with Gandhi.

The incongruity of Gandhi's non-violence with 'untouchability's brutality' was an intra-Indic dilemma far removed from Jim Crow America. For the Negro, isolated and traumatized by Abrahamic occidental hegemony, untouchability was a pitiable horror incapable of relieving the American Jim Crow condition. The a-hegemonic virtue of an apostate Untouchable movement was inconceivable to most Negroes of the time. Unlike India's millennia of religious diversity, the Negro experience in America was one of forced monotheism (primarily Christianity) policed by lawless extra-judicial brutality. Aligning with Gandhi, the so-called God-believing 'saint', the 'Mahatma', the 'self-governance advocate/hero against European imperialism' was tactically relevant to the Negro dilemma; more so than the complexity of contending with Gandhi's claim to represent India's oppressed Untouchable masses. The mass movement in fact was being led by Bhimrao Ramji Ambedkar, himself an Untouchable.

The bond of new-found geopolitical necessity between the Negro–Gandhi bedfellows was strange. In essence, the lamenting oppressed Negro lauded a Brahminical casteist. Yet, the bond proved so powerful that

Ambedkar's mission was politically thrown under the bus. The African-American interest in Gandhi's globally relevant resistance to occidental imperialism won out. Consequently, Ambedkar's brilliant oration and visionary leadership were sidelined.

Undeterred by the 'world away' Negro–Gandhi communion, Ambedkar held his ground on Indian turf by delivering a blistering critique of Gandhi. Ambedkar's discourse was so charged that Gandhi eventually went on his now-famous hunger strike in 1932. His purpose was in part to sway public opinion against Ambedkar's determined mission—a point lost in Hollywood's 1982 $100 million-dollar grossing film on Gandhi.[5] Ambedkar's appeal for social justice was to no avail in the elite Negro mind. The Jim Crow Negro of the time was faced with tunnel vision, resulting from centuries of forced isolation in the American predicament. The sidelining of Ambedkar made Ambedkar virtually invisible to the globally remote Negro uplift movement.

## *Crisis* Magazine (1942): The Sticking Point

Global politics aside, evidence of suppressing Ambedkar in Black America is found in the annals of the National Association for the Advancement of Colored People (NAACP) publications. Without diminishing the Young Men's Christian Association's (YMCA) Colored Division and other Christian evangelical missions abroad, the NAACP let the cat out of the bag on Ambedkar's mission like no other in the Black community. In December 1942, the NAACP's *Crisis* magazine published a two-part series on India's Untouchables titled 'The "Negroes" of India'.[6] This is incontrovertible and gives rise to questioning the whereabouts of confluence with Ambedkarite thought during the forthcoming civil rights era. Other news outlets such as the *New York Times*, *Washington Post*, *Associated Press* and the *National* magazine reported on Ambedkar's activities. However, during the Jim Crow era they did not cater to primarily African-American audiences. In the *Crisis* article, author Harry Paxton Howard discussed untouchability in explicit detail. He marvelled at Ambedkar's rise from the dregs of society to the post of India's labour minister. He went on to suggest that Ambedkar's model should

> Serve as a beacon-light not only to the Untouchables of India, but to pariahs and outcast peoples throughout the world—which might serve, indeed, as a new and militant program for Negroes in the United States.

Similar Untouchable and African–American parallels continued throughout the piece. The author observes:

> Just as with American Negroes, they had to free themselves. The 'Great White Father' could not do it for them—especially when his more deep-rooted sympathies lay with their 'Aryan' masters.[7]

## *Crisis* Magazine (1942): 'Negroes of India', Part One

The fallibility of following Aryan dominance is documented in the above statement. It was a known pitfall. The responsibility of African Americans and Untouchables to uplift their respective communities was as clearly stated in 'The "Negroes" of India' as was recognition of Ambedkar's intellectual contribution to the discourse.

Before the Second World War, Aryanism was broadly defined as a 'supremacist doctrine' based on Indic discourse rather than a racial identity exclusive to Germans. Hitler's 1925 publication, *Mein Kampf* (My Struggle), expanded usage of the term to include his German volk whom he inspired to take 'upon themselves championship of the Aryan cause generally and on the global scale'.[8] Hitler's Aryanism also transcended German borders in 'the battle of Aryan Supremacy on this planet and for establishing Europe and the New World Order based on this supremacy'.[9] Lastly, Hitler's Aryanism transcended race, culture, religion and national identity by ascribing his inclusive label 'sub-Aryan' to all human beings in solidarity with eliminating the Jews.[10] Hence, through diabolical means and intentions, Hitler breached the Indic Aryan discourse by unleashing his expanded notion of Aryanism onto the world. *Mein Kampf* was extremely successful. It sold 2,40,000 copies before its author became German Chancellor in 1933, and sold evermore successfully thereafter until 1945 when its publication was banned. After a seventy-year ban it became an immediate bestseller in 2017 with 85,000 copies sold that year. As a result, the term Aryan has been used to popularly describe those who believed they are by birth or doctrine better than 'subordinate others'. By 1943, the definition of Aryanism had expanded to include (1) Hitlerism, (2) conservative and liberal White global supremacy in general, (3) European supremacy specifically (4) Judaeo-Christian manifest destiny, (5) Brahminical caste Hinduism, (6) anti-Semitic Islamic fundamentalism, (7) expressed as a critical view towards Tibetan Buddhism.[11] All were considered Aryan directly, indirectly through association or by influence. Today, the popularization of Hitler's expanded definition of Aryanism (White nationalism) has led to concerns about its presence in the American government.[12]

This deserves mention because it helps identify the Aryan substructure that belies today's concerns about American culture. The term 'Aryan' has been struck from the occidental vernacular that was once used to describe Euro-American culture's obsession with dominating people of colour. Today's overt expression of Aryanism is thought reprehensible. But the underlying presence of Aryanism in both Euro-American liberalism and conservatism is considered acceptable in its covert form of subliminal messaging. The image of the European Jesus is itself an Aryan representation inseparable from the founding and perpetuated ethos of America as a Christian nation.[13]

## Departure from Futility

Even though the Aryanization of indigenous lands in America is inarguable, there's more to 'religifying' Aryanism than meets the eye. African Americans would be wise to understand the inescapability of the Aryan hegemonic stratagem secretly celebrated by Whites in the triumvirate iconic mythos of Dr King, Gandhi and the Dalai Lama. To the Black mind, Dr King symbolizes domestic Judaeo-Christian moralism, Hindu Gandhi represents non-violence, and the Tibetan Buddhist Dalai Lama represents spiritual moralism. But all three religious figures and respective traditions are historically tied to Aryanism. King's Jesus and the Bible, Gandhi's Christian-tinged Hindu 'non-violence' ethic, and Tibetan Buddhism's 'white colored peace/purity and black colored wrath'[14] all subtly lent to an Aryan world view. Whether intentional or not, the use of such icons and metaphors advantage Aryan hegemony in the minds of the Western world's conquered masses. Where Blacks see redemption and salvation in the Jesus–Gandhi–Dalai Lama triumvirate, White powerbrokers see perpetuation of the Aryan pantheon and its hegemony. They're comfortable with it and demand the same of their victims of past conquest. Though the addition of a Hindu and Buddhist appears to contravene the Abrahamic aspect of occidental hegemony, the fact that the triumvirate itself is an occidental construct should not be lost.

The pertinent question is not Eurocentric Abrahamism. It is for whom and to what purpose the triumvirate has been created. If in the end White dominance remains intact, even if couched as occidental liberalism, it offers little to African America's liberation from occidental hegemony.

The purposeful or unwitting Black Abrahamic occidentalist identity—by any other name—negates a-hegemonic relief for Black minds immersed in perpetual dominance by descendants and beneficiaries of African enslavers. This is a critical insight necessary to accurately assess what was lost when Negro elites stifled Ambedkarite a-hegemonic intellectualism in the African-American continuum.

The occidental hegemonic model is nothing new in dominance theory. It is an expression of a long-standing humanistic phenomenon of conquest management. For example, it existed in Asiatic form vis-à-vis the Mongol conquest of continental Asia. And in Indic form used to justify the subordination[15] of subaltern fragments known to the Western world as untouchability. American occidentalism is merely an extension of Graeco-Roman conquest turned Catholic/Protestant Eurocentrism migrated to America during Europe's seafaring expansionism. The Persian variation that contested with occidentalism in the form of the Crusades is the foundation of Islamic domination theory. Occidental Judaeo-Christendom and Persian Islamification, despite contestation over dominance, are united through both Abrahamic doctrine and their participation in the enslavement of African people.

Ambedkar posits a reason for African America's amnesia concerning Arab enslavement:

> The Negro was imported as a slave by the Arabs into Asia long before he was introduced as a slave by the Europeans into America. Although this is so, Negro slavery in America and in the English Colonies has had a sorrowful history which has made people forget the importation of the Negro as a slave in Asia and quite naturally because Negro slavery in America as carried on by the Europeans was a most revolting thing.[16]

However, an in-depth comparative discussion on the theoretical framework of Euro-Persian Aryan hegemony's impact on the African continuum transcends the scope of this work. Suffice it to say that Eurocentric—Islamic inclusive—American Aryanism, even in its most liberal form, has not put forward an a-hegemonic plan to end its racialized dominion over African-American identity in the Western world. Likewise, the Islamicized world has not put forth a reparation plan to mitigate the conquest of African indigenousness that dates back to the dawn of humankind.

The role of White (Aryan) liberalism is to reward occidental-compliant people of colour with a modicum of comfort, security and resources for

acquiescing to its subtleties of dominance. The role of Hindu Aryanism is
to reward the same for complicity with untouchability. In response to the
aforementioned Aryan-American triumvirate, some may say, 'How dare
you insult the images of such great luminaries!' But a student of spiritual
literacy will investigate further by asking, 'Have there been other examples
of people of colour images used by Aryans as a double meaning?' Of course,
the Victorian era was an example. Not only were the images of pyramids,
pharaohs and African animism appropriated during the development of
Victorian-era Jim Crow, mummies were stolen from Africa and sold in mail
order catalogues. Pictures of African bishops adorned the Hitler–Mussolini–
complicit Vatican walls. Frederick Douglass's image was likewise prolifically
disseminated throughout American society, as Gates says, in a state 'of
being as a Black man in a White society in which one's blackness signifies
negation'.[17] And yet, at no time through the use of these and countless other
images has White dominance ever been capitulated on American soil. Nor
has the Black mind entitled itself to seek a-hegemonic apostasy from the
occidental-Abrahamic vestiges of slavery that reside therein.

The recalcitrance of White dominance begs even the most liberal
observer to wonder whether the injury of slavery can ever be healed
through reverence for Aryanism, subordination to the Euro-Aryan doctrine,
or by embracing the subtleties of the Euro-Aryan liberalized facade. The
African America a-hegemony will perhaps come from recognition of this
consideration and departure from its futility. To that end, 'The "Negroes"
of India' stands out as a significant recognition of Ambedkar's a-hegemonic
intellectualism visited upon pre–Civil Rights Negro American thought.

## Crisis Magazine Article (1942): Part Two

Part One of the Crisis magazine's 1942 issue, edited by Roy Wilkins,[18]
introduced the overarching presence of occidental hegemony and the
hegemonic constraint of caste Hindu Aryan domination that the 'Negroes
of India' live under. Part Two relieves the burden of wondering whether the
relevance of Ambedkar's work was clearly communicated. An affirmative
answer would validate further investigation into whether elite Black America
led popular attention away from Ambedkar's thought, as well as account in
part for the Crisis editor Du Bois's later divergence from Ambedkar:

Here the approaches of Du Bois and Ambedkar towards the liberation
of their people diverge. Whereas Du Bois emphasized cultural and racial

aspects, not completely ignoring the political aspect, Ambedkar believed that liberation could be achieved through political means. His demand for a separate electorate for his people which was conceded by the British and his disagreement with Gandhi over it shows the direction in which he wanted his struggle to move.[19]

The resulting deviation of purposes would eventually contribute to the occidental Abrahamic Negro elites' difficulty in identifying with the a–hegemonic virtue of Ambedkar's Buddhist movement.

In context, the NAACP's *Crisis* magazine was the Huffington Post of Black America from 1910 to 2003. Every Black college, business, political office and celebrity as well as every Black man and woman interested in straightened hair[20] subscribed to it. In its heyday it sold for 15 cents a month and boasted 100,000 subscriptions. Actual readership was greater due to the 'barbershop and beauty salon' phenomenon. One copy could pass through a hundred hands a week if placed in high-traffic Black businesses.

When Part Two appeared, the magazine's cover was graced with young and beautiful actress and civil rights activist Lena Horne. The article stated Ambedkar: (1) had become world famous 'despite slanders and attacks of "Aryan" Hindus and their spokesmen', and that (2) Gandhi was someone 'whom Ambedkar regards as a hypocrite'.[21]

The writer went on to say, 'The appointment of B.R. Ambedkar as Minister of Labor in the Viceroy's Cabinet is a harbinger of the future.'[22] And, he was right. Ambedkar has re-emerged in today's global scene; though to some he never left.

Finally, the author concedes the heart of India's Untouchable community is universal to humankind:

> For theirs is not only the hope of their own 60 millions—the former 'Untouchables.' It is the only hope of the masses of India as a whole. It is the only hope of the world.

Of note is his reference to the 'former "Untouchables"'. This acknowledges there were significant strides in the Untouchables' revisioning of identity within India and in the eyes of the world.

This small excerpt in Black America's most popular publication is irrefutable evidence that Ambedkar's relevance reached them. From it can be concluded that as early as 1942, African America was informed about Ambedkar and the great Untouchable uplift that was underway. It's clear his momentum was discussed in African America's most widely read magazine of the day. All the same, Ambedkar was sold down the river.

By 1942, the unholy alliance between Hindu caste Aryanism and implicit Aryanism in Black Christianity became a force to reckon with. The latter descended from slavemaster to slave during Euro-Aryan supremacist African enslavement institutionalism. Black elites could not play to Gandhi on the one hand and honour his most blistering a-hegemonic nemesis on the other. They made a choice. Their decision shaped African-American religion and its role in the forthcoming civil rights era.

. A closer reading of *Annihilation of Caste* suggests that Ambedkar had thought about leaving Hinduism as early as 1936.[23] However, it's fair to note that Ambedkar did not convert to Buddhism until 1956. At the time of the 1942 *Crisis* article, both Gandhi and Ambedkar were Hindus. The fracture in their relationship was squarely over the deplorable condition of untouchability. Therefore, rejection of Ambedkar's critique was rejection of Untouchable self-determination at the time. Gandhi, being from the elite bania caste, held sway over India—incomparable to the low-born yet highly educated Untouchable Ambedkar.

Black Christian leaders, who themselves enjoyed affiliation with America's dominant enslaving religion—Christianity—parlayed with Gandhi, who enjoyed high-caste privilege over millions of oppressed people. Their suppressive gatekeeping of the 'Ambedkar secret' reflected an adventitious politic rather than the championing of solidarity between mass oppressed people in America and Gandhi's world. The significance of Ambedkar's later (1956) and perhaps most effective a-hegemonic refuge in the morally persuasive teachings of Buddha and love was lost. In consequence, the most downtrodden human population on earth began confronting Hindu hegemony on their own in the context of liberating caste identity from their minds. Concurrently, the hegemonic-aligned African-American Gandhism identity—born of strange bedfellows—caused African America to continue treading water in the ocean of occidental self-negation. Thereby, they have yet to confront, let alone liberate themselves from, the vestiges of occidental/Persian Abrahamic hegemony in African-American identity and culture.

Dr King visited India in 1959. He witnessed its oppressed masses personally and was taken aback. In a 1961 speech he titled 'The American Dream', King implied occidental Abrahamism was not a prescription for human fraternity. He suggested the sum total of confluence among American and Indian people was greater than their divergence. Gandhism, gifted to him by a prior generation, was not enough to reach the lofty goal of his aspiration. His Promised Land was something that apparently included rather than avoided complexities of mitigating human suffering in India:

> The destiny of India and the destiny of every other nation is tied up with the destiny of the United States and the destiny of the United States is tied up with the destiny of India.[24]

## Truth Be Told: Mr Manu . . . Meet Mr Ham

The only question left to consider contemporarily is whether a throughline of suppressing a-hegemonic voices pre-existed Ambedkar and continues today. Dr Velu Annamalai, the president of the Ambedkar journal, comments in 2013:

> I called the King Center, several years back. I said, 'I want to talk to you guys.' They have a room called Gandhi Room, in the King Center. I said, 'I want to tell you the truth about this man.' Nobody would talk to me.[25]

Conversely, in 2017, a dramatic and perhaps stunning contrast to the civil rights sideline of Ambedkar occurred. Martin Luther King, Jr's son, Martin Luther King III, epically pivoted to the inclusion of Ambedkar. The occasion was a global conference in Bengaluru, India, organized by the Government of Karnataka in honour of the 126th birth anniversary of Ambedkar. An estimated 9000 delegates, speakers, academics and participants attended.[26] Having taken a commanding presence on stage amid distinguished luminaries, the invited guest speaker King III declared he believed his father, Martin Luther King, Jr, and Ambedkar were 'intellectually, philosophically, morally and spiritually cut from the same cloth'. He further declared, 'They were brother revolutionaries whose minds and hearts were driven by justice and compassion.'[27] King III's comments seemed in accord with his father's 1961 claim that the destinies of India and America are 'tied up'.[28] The son's declaration stood out as Ambedkar inclusive. His message harked back to the 1942 *Crisis* article's confluence between Untouchables and African-American interests. Seventy-five years of being strange bedfellows had come full circle. However, neither King the father nor his son's declaration arose to the prolific popularism of the father's 'Dream' speech associated with America's considerable self-interest in civil rights legacy.

King III's parity with Ambedkar did, however, marry African America's iconic Christian legacy with that of Ambedkar. With it came a new iteration of peculiarity: African America's continued affinity with Christianity's hegemonic reasoning used to justify slaveocracy. Whether enslaved Africans identified as Christian or not, '. . . they were still powerfully constrained by colonial governance because of the particular constitution of Christianity as a manifestation of imperial power'.[29] The peculiarity is not, therefore, Christian doctrine per se. It is the intractable role Christianity played in the foundation of imperial rule governing the land and peoples of the Americas.

In contrast, Ambedkar's a-hegemonic polity is organic to the subcontinent. He is neither invader nor conqueror. His affront is intra-religio-cultural. This is illustrated in his public burning of the casteist doctrine *Manusmriti* on 25 December 1927. Ambedkar's biographer Narendra Jhadav writes, 'Manu Smriti was a charter of rights for the so-called upper-caste Hindus but a bible of slavery for the untouchables.'[30] We do not see, nor can most fathom, the possibility of King, Jr or King III doing the same to the Bible, even though it was used to justify human denigration of their kith and kin Africans on the North American continent.

Ambedkar specifically locates justification of the origin of caste brutality in a story entailing the slaughter of Shambuka, a Sudra ascetic. Shambuka's illicit practice of upper-caste Brahminical ritual brings down mortal wrath. The ascetic is put to death by the raja to protect caste (chaturvarnya) boundaries. Ambedkar writes, 'Ram Raj was a raj based on chaturvarnya. As a king, Rama was bound to maintain chaturvarnya. It was his duty therefore to kill Shambuka, the Shudra who had transgressed his class and wanted to be a Brahmin.'[31] Ambedkar continues, 'That is why Manu-Smriti prescribes such heavy sentences as cutting off the tongue or pouring molten lead in the ears of the Sudra, who hears or recites the Vedas.' The gist of this explains Ambedkar's reasoning for a-hegemonic rejection of the *Manusmriti*. It also brings to light the parallel between Manu's justification of caste and Western Biblical justification for African enslavement. The latter is associated with Noah's curse of his son Ham.

The curse was that Ham's descendants would live in perpetual servitude because of Ham's insult to his father's dignity. European/American slavocratic colonials accused Africans of being Ham's biblical descendants. According to them, African enslavement was hence biblically justified. The supposed 'curse of Ham'[32] served as validation for slavery's brutal assault on African indigenousness and the dispossession of its people from their native land. On this Goldenberg writes, 'The Curse of Ham is the assumed

Biblical justification for a curse of eternal slavery imposed on Black people, and Black people alone.'[33]

African-American reverence for the Bible of American slavery, translated into English by King James of England (1611)[34] and carried onward by King George III (1738–1820),[35] stands in stark contrast to Ambedkar's rejection of the *Manusmriti*. African-American reverence for the imperial faith doctrine of enslavement began during slaveocracy and extends to as recently as 2017. On 25 August of that year, 3000 Christian ministers, including Martin King III, marched 'for justice' in rebuke of American president Donald J. Trump's presidency.[36] American, Christian, Jewish, Muslim and Sikh clergy marched in solidarity. However, the unifying principle among African-American ministers was the biblical doctrine and its civil rights legacy in the African-American mind.

Intra-hegemonic argumentation over the curse within the context of Christian imperialism intensified during slavery. A heated contest on the issue was penned a century prior to Michael King, Jr's adoption of Martin Luther's name[37] and his declaration on the issue of Ham's curse: 'They argue that the Negro is inferior by nature because of Noah's curse upon the children of Ham. Oh my friends, this is blasphemy.'[38]

Earlier evidence of antebellum disputation of the curse is found in the writings of escaped slave minister James (Pembroke) Pennington[39]— Pembroke being the birth name, 'Pennington' serving as nom de guerre[40] after Pembroke's successful escape from slavery, after which he travelled to Connecticut. He became the first African American to unofficially attend Yale Seminary School (1834–38). His negritic colour barred him from student rights to enroll in class or borrow books from the library.[41] Undaunted, he audited lectures while seated in the back of classrooms for four years.[42] Denied a degree, Pennington persevered on. He became a well-known minister, abolitionist and writer.[43] As an anti-slavery preacher he maintained his own stop on the Underground Railroad, officiated at Frederick Douglass's wedding, emphasized the role of education in breaking the bonds of slavery,[44] raised funds to pay for the Amistad Africans' return voyage,[45] travelled three times to England, Scotland and other parts of Europe, represented Connecticut at the World's Anti-Slavery Convention in London (1843), was awarded an honorary doctorate of divinity from Heidelberg University in Germany,[46] received exemplary praise as an African-American leader in the notes of feminist abolitionist Harriet Beecher Stowe's *Uncle Tom's Cabin* and authored one of the first African-American history books, titled *A Textbook of the Origin and History of the*

*Colored People* (1841). Heidelberg University continues to bestow the James W.C. Pennington Award even today.[47, 48]

*A Textbook of the Origin and History of the Colored People*[49] is nothing less than a sonorous ninety-six-page excoriation of both Ham's curse and its progenitors, written in a style similar to Ambedkar's rebuke of caste. His critique declares the Church and its theology so horrid, 'all the rebels in the world would catch the infection.'[50] Yet, despite Pennington's assault on Euro-Christian imperialism, he too remains in its orbit by suggesting that polytheism, not Christianity, is the African bane: 'Their Polytheism, was a grand error.'[51] Of Ethiopians he concludes, 'he is a heathen.'[52] In so saying, Pennington sides with biblical reasoning used to justify the abuse of his 'heathen' ancestors, thereby suggesting it is righteous for the enslaved African-American mind to be in accord with the 'infectious' hegemony of its captors. He is lost in duplicity—marooned in New World identity. He's robbed of ancient indigenous legacy, and Indic faith is beyond his reach. And yet, we also find within his range an interesting reduction of humanism in his tome. He acknowledges the 'like nature of minds'[53] that cannot be explained by antebellum biblical interpretation alone.[54]

Like Ambedkar's long-lived stomp of caste ego, Pennington's blistering assault on the 'noble Christian slave master' escapes the hangman's noose. Pennington defies his place redundantly, not only intellectually but circumstantially. At a time when penalties for slave insubordination were beating, mutilation and at times death, Pennington survives and thrives. He hides in plain sight, runs an Underground Railroad station, champions the Amistad group, raises funds on their behalf and bids them public farewell on the eve of their departure back to Africa. It is as though the demure Pennington were possessed by Blakeney's pimpernel double life of daring and wit.

Nonetheless, in contrast to King, Jr's conformist uplift, iconoclast Pennington falls into obscurity. The account of Pennington's work, and perhaps more significantly his unbridled mendacity, is allowed to sink into the quagmire of time. He's sidelined in a manner only redeemed by a slow re-emergence a century and a half later.[55]

## Truth's Aim

Dispensation of the Pennington model suggests that the sidelining of a-hegemonic thinkers is nothing new to the American experience. The sidelining of Ambedkar is simply 'par for the course'. Their truths are inconvenient. Both Ambedkar and Pennington are anathema and therefore branded reprobate to the perpetuation of dominance. Neither can be allowed to stand unchallenged. The stature and breadth of their intellectual discourse are a threat to the degradations that empires need to exist. The sidelining of Ambedkar is inherited therefrom. The breadth of his critique is unwanted.

Ambedkar's Buddhism, in particular, reeks of alienation in the American dominant cultural nexus. Were the Negroes to abandon the slave religion of their New World identity en masse, the act itself would have sent shock waves throughout the world. Not for the sake of Buddhism. Rather, the slave conversion's challenge would have been a global shaming of Western imperialism's status quo. The threat of Ambedkar's trajectory, then and now, is therefore onerously cataclysmic. His gargantuan contribution to human upliftment can barely breathe in the haughty air of the Western world view. The constellation of legacies ensnared by Western imperialism's suppression is the source that creates strange bedfellows indeed.

This is true not just in the case of Ambedkar, but from the period of American slaveocracy to the present. More study is needed to deconstruct the mechanism of Western imperialist racification and philosophication of the global human voice. Ambedkar's a-hegemonic belligerence is a minor yet relevant subplot. The development of stratagems to dispel the inertia imposed on the authentic migration of Ambedkar's voice is critical. Fulfilling Martin Luther King, Jr's declaration that the destinies of India and America are tied to one another is motivation enough. When King speaks of Indian and American mutuality, Ambedkar is invited in by default. What better advocate is there than one of Twain's 'Master of the Game' lead into the discourse on Ambedkar, whether intentional or not. Who speaks of King's dream 'for all God's Children' speaks for masses of the oppressed that inspirationally touched him during his 1959 tour of India.[56] Who else could he have been speaking of when he recounted his concern for India's 'millions going to bed hungry at night' and others having 'no beds to sleep in' or 'houses to go in'?[57]

The African-American mission to uplift global human dignity in confluence with Ambedkar would be wise to learn from past mistakes. To ignore or pander to luminaries that marginalize human dignity injures the global Dalit family as well as African America's dignified role in human redemption. However strangely the solidarity of the Ambedkar/King/ Pembroke message may appear, they are of one purpose. Pembroke targets the 'constitution of Christian imperialism'. King, Jr's Indo-American mutuality philosophically conjoins African America to Ambedkar's India. The reason and means of sidelining greatness end in this idea alone. As a consequence, Ambedkar is freed. Twentieth-century African-American political necessity takes its proper historical place as a bygone means to an end. The next generation on both continents is left an improved legacy rather than the shadow of neglect. Lest we never forget, these ideas are the Colossus, and we petty women and men walk under their legs. We are masters of our own fate. Though we inherit the shortcomings of past generations, the fault, dear friends, is not with them, but in ourselves if we do not embrace what's been given and transform it into what ought to be.[58]

For the sake of *causa future*[59] the prevailing notion of Ambedkar's miraculous landing in America is better understood by unfolding the pre-existing scenery of a backdrop as old as slavery. His fertile mind apprehends the elegance of constitutional promise. Concurrently, the inopportune timing of an Aryan war in Europe triggers the snapping shut of his voice in the American experience, particularly in the discourse of African-American upliftment.

Ambedkar's tremendous accomplishments were recognized in the heart of everyday African-American life via the *Crisis* newsletter, the bosom of which is slavery born. Erstwhile fate bound the Negro, desirous of global relevance, to his hegemon nemesis. Thereby Ambedkar's nobility and expressed affinity with Negro uplift was socially and politically guillotined. Through a reasonable analysis of empire what we find is not actions on the part of individuals. Rather, we find a century of event-oriented centrifugal record commingled with hegemonic and a-hegemonic writing, thoughts, actions and philosophies represented in Pennington, Twain, King, Mussolini, Gandhi, Ambedkar, Hitler, the Dalai Lama and all sorts of unlikely bedfellows.

Through the example of American slavocratic marginalization of a-hegemonic thought, namely, Pennington, we find Ambedkar's fall from American notoriety contiguous rather than coincidental. The fruitlessness of Du Bois's response is relieved of culpability that has perhaps been overbearing from the beginning. The tectonics of global empires was not, nor could it have ever been in his control. It is *political* tectonics of rigid empires clashing among themselves and crushing indigenous identities into oblivion that turned the wheels of history. Even the kings of Europe and India's rajas could not determine the fate of their reigns, let alone 19th-century a-hegemonic pro-Negro-dignity thought in American culture. Both Ambedkar and Du Bois were merely citizens entangled within the limitations of their respective empires. Marginalization beyond their control made the American sidelining of Ambedkar's a-hegemonic model not only possible but characteristic of an oppressed survival narrative deeply rooted in the tumult of continental imperialism. A sensible case can be made that the culprit of Ambedkar being ignored in the uplift of Negroes was 'slavocratic social engineering's vestige' rather than the fault of individuals. This view at least offers reasoning and perhaps forgiveness for such a tangled web of odd fellows strewn about multiple conquest idioms. To the extent this essay stimulates further interest in Ambedkar–Negro discourse as 'empire deconstruction', its perusal has served the enquiring reader. The rest is left to posterity and the enthusiasm of the academy.

# AMBEDKAR ICONS

## WHYS AND WHEREFORES

*Hugo Gorringe*

'Even the national leader Mahatma Gandhi doesn't have as many statues as revolutionary Ambedkar. Significantly, these statues are installed by people, not by the government. The birth and death anniversaries of Mahatma Gandhi are celebrated by the government, but the people have forgotten about that. Ambedkar is commemorated everyday—he is not a local leader, he has more than 10 lakh statues across India, he is the only Indian leader . . . There is a world famous university in London, their library is the largest in the world, they have portraits of two leaders in their reception—one is the portrait of Karl Marx, who is the great philosopher who provided communism to the world, and the other one is the portrait of the revolutionary Ambedkar'—Speech by Thirumavalavan, Dalit activist and member of Parliament, 10 August 2012[1]

## Introduction

When Fidel Castro, leader of the Cuban revolution, died in 2016, it emerged that he had left instructions that no statues, busts or memorials should be constructed in his honour. He is reported to have said that he was 'hostile to anything that resembles a cult of personality'.[2] Castro is not alone in such sentiments. Well before the Cuban had seized power in the island state, B.R. Ambedkar—the first law minister of India, eminent scholar and pre-eminent leader of India's lowest castes—voiced similar misgivings about hero worship. Both were inspirational activists as well as thinkers and saw their examples and ideologies as far more important than their image. If Ambedkar's experience is any guide, however, as the opening quote suggests, then Castro may find that his wishes are observed more in the breach than the practice. Not only has there been a proliferation of monuments to Ambedkar, but there is a whole politics that centres on them as seen in the quote above.

Standing on a makeshift stage at a busy intersection in Madurai—the temple city in south central Tamil Nadu—Thirumavalavan, the leader of the Viduthalai Chiruthaigal Katchi (VCK—Liberation Panther Party, the largest Dalit party in the state), was surrounded by a crowd of supporters some 3000-strong. They had gathered at short notice to condemn the desecration of statues of Ambedkar and local leader Immanuel Sekaran in the city a week earlier. Thirumavalavan's once fiery and electric speeches have been tempered by his entry into formal political institutions, but he delivered a rousing peroration on this occasion.

Ambedkar, he stressed, in the above quote, must be seen as a figure of national or international significance despite repeated attempts by non-Dalits to portray him as a caste or community leader. The central place he holds in the hearts of Dalit activists was emphasized by Adiveerapandian, a local VCK leader in attendance at the event. He was enthused by the speeches but saddened that the crowds were not larger. Some of his associates had been tempted to skip the demonstration, he told me, since it was scheduled for mid-afternoon on a working day. He had been irate at the mere suggestion: 'This is Ambedkar,' he claimed to have shouted at reluctant companions, 'you *have* to come' (field notes, August 2012).

Earlier that year, Thirumavalavan, then a member of Parliament, had brought Parliament to a standstill with an impassioned tirade against the inclusion of an old cartoon of Ambedkar in a school textbook. One supporter went so far as to state that this intervention alone was sufficient to justify his five-year term. If activists and supporters were delighted to have someone to stand up for Ambedkar, others were less impressed. Several critics thought that more could have been done to raise key issues in Parliament or organize Dalits at the grassroots. A non-political Dalit campaigner was damning in his indictment of the VCK:

The attention seeking impulse was driven by emotions but was not sustainable. The steps needed to secure social justice were not there. The uprising was born of centuries of exclusion, suffering, and pain so that when people felt that someone was addressing their issues they took heart. It was totally and utterly an emotional response. An emotional crowd and emotional group. (interview, March 2012)

Writing in the *Economic and Political Weekly* (EPW), Anand Teltumbde echoes this analysis and berates Dalit politicians for neglecting material concerns and injustices to focus on symbolic issues. 'The entire Dalit emotional charge,' he argues,[3] 'is concentrated in the Ambedkar icon.' As the comment about statues in the opening quote and the way in which parties rush to the defence of portrayals of Ambedkar illustrate, Dalit politics is overly focused on visual representations of the great man despite his exhortations against idolization. The preoccupation with form often undermines the substance of struggles against caste and has invited a powerful critique of symbolic politics. Even the most trenchant critics, however, accept that a degree of iconization is inevitable. To their minds, the key is to ensure that 'real' issues are not neglected in pursuit of symbolic goals. In this essay, I seek to navigate the varied debates and practices surrounding the iconization of Ambedkar. I begin with the compelling critique of Dalit symbolic politics, before seeking to place such practices in a wider context. The iconization of Ambedkar, I argue, has to be understood within the prevalent political culture. It is also important to stress that mobilization around statues need not entail empty symbolism and can serve to effect meaningful social change. In conclusion I bring the different strands of the debate together.

## Monumental Failures?

Against Thirumavalavan's celebration of the proliferation of Ambedkar statues, many Dalit activists who are disengaged from party politics are dismayed by the repeated compromises of elected Dalit representatives and their emphasis on symbolic rather than material concerns. Furthermore, the adoption of Ambedkar as the darling of the mainstream means that his image alone is no longer sufficient to distinguish between Dalit-focused and non-Dalit parties. Across the political spectrum, politicians line up to appropriate and honour Ambedkar but, in the process, the icon has been 'shorn of Ambedkar's vision of radical transformation'.[4] Where a statue or portrait once indicated engagement with Ambedkar's life and thought (if only at a basic level), it currently means little other than an attempt to woo Dalit votes. It is telling that most of the early statues of Ambedkar in the northern districts of Tamil Nadu were erected by the Pattali Makkal Katchi (PMK, Toiling People's Party) led by S. Ramadoss. The PMK sought to harness Dalit votes and did initially lend some support to struggles against untouchability. The superficial regard they have for Ambedkar's writing, however, is seen in their focus on securing benefits for the Most Backward Castes[5] and in subsequent campaigns against cross-caste marriages. That a virulently casteist party can embrace the icon of the foremost critic of the institution should give us pause for thought.

For political recognition to be meaningful, it must mean more than the reproduction of images and insincere statements of 'respect'. To campaign against caste marriages, ban beef, thrash Dalits engaged in tanning, and speak of the death of 'merit' whilst actively seeking to embrace Ambedkar as an icon renders the action hollow and serves to dishonour his legacy. In a powerful critique of Dalit politics in the northern state of Uttar Pradesh, an editorial in EPW went further in taking aim at Dalit parties that ostensibly maintain an Ambedkarite perspective. 'The primacy given to symbolism while utterly neglecting the *real* tasks of bringing about progressive social and economic change,' EPW insisted in an attack on the Bahujan Samaj Party policy, 'can only imply commitment to the status quo',[6] (emphasis added). Jakkaian, leader of the Arun-Tamizhar Viduthalai Peravai (Arunthathiyar Tamils Liberation Front), stressed the emotive power of memorials to Dalit heroes and suggested that Dalit leaders 'should do some work to find a place in history. But if you do too much then it will become an aversion for people. You can't do only this as your main agenda' (interview, March 2012). Indeed, Jakkaian here seems to be heeding the lesson handed out to the BSP by disillusioned voters. Gupta notes how once supportive followers began to see Mayawati's memorial construction 'as a waste of badly needed resources. Especially as the zeal she demonstrated in the pursuit was missing from her pursuit of her real task—building a more equitable society in UP'.[7] Pai similarly argued that Dalits in the late 2000s 'were disappointed that Mayawati preferred to spend crores of rupees on Ambedkar memorials and parks rather than on education, health and infrastructure'.[8]

The icon of Ambedkar is now ubiquitous. The blue-suited, constitution-bearing figure stands tall in cities, towns and villages and his portrait adorns innumerable walls, letterheads, posters and shirts. This undoubtedly serves as an inspiration to many, but it is as if the icon is expected to stand in for all the aspirations and demands of Dalit citizens and compensate for the lack of sustained action towards other ends. Teltumbde despairs of Dalit leaders who were exercised about an ancient cartoon whilst the culprits responsible for the massacre in Bathani Tola walked free.[9] In an echo of this controversy, VCK leaders in Madurai fell out with advocate P. Rathinam—who was instrumental in prosecuting those responsible for the Melavalavu murders in 1997—when he whitewashed a picture of their leader so as to condemn the acquittal of culprits from that case (interview, August 2012). Such episodes suggest that the focus on statues, memorials and posters substitute for, or displace, action for meaningful change. So has the Ambedkar icon lost its radical edge? Are Dalit politicians merely 'feigning deep devotion' to him?[10] How should we understand the dominant focus on iconography in the contemporary Dalit movement?

## Hero Worship As Political Culture

Addressing a meeting in 1943, Ambedkar remarked that: 'India is still par excellence the land of idolatry. There is idolatry in religion, there is idolatry in politics. Heroes and hero worship is a hard, if unfortunate, fact in India's political life. I agree that hero worship is demoralizing for the devotee and dangerous to the country.'[11] His scathing comments ring as true today as they did at the time. In his review of party politics across India, K.C. Suri notes how 'authority is centralised and personalised'.[12] Irrespective of ideology, most parties focus on image and style and foster a perception of leaders as heroes or semi-deities.[13] Price[14] argues that these 'person–centred aspects of Indian political behaviour' need to be explained by reference to culture, and points to the persistence of organizational aspects of monarchical culture, such as 'the conviction that daily well-being or relief from distress is dependent on discrete acts of mercy and generosity from superior beings, human or divine'.[15] Supporters and followers here are portrayed as responding 'to the person and not the message',[16] and engaged in acts of veneration or supplication rather than critical engagement with ideas.

Thus, we have such an abundance of icons celebrating leader figures that R. Gerritsen[17] concludes that 'images are as much part of political practice as they are a representation of it'. The proliferation of guru pujas (leader worship) and *jayanti* (birthday) processions suggests that this emphasis on visual culture extends beyond images to incorporate public performances. Given the propensity of established political parties to engage in forms of hero worship and iconization, Dalit movements seeking to compete end up replicating such modes of politics. As Ambedkar noted with regard to caste formation: 'It cannot be otherwise. Imitation is easy and invention is difficult.'[18] The absence of statues, posters and murals is read as inactivity and weakness by potential supporters, who put pressure on their own organizations to comply. This in itself, however, need not entail de-radicalization. Replication, as G. Karanth[19] notes, need not imply consent.

Indeed, in Dalit politics, N. Jaoul argues, 'the Ambedkar icon, symbolising Dalit pride, became a way to play out' the political assertion of the community.[20] S. Rege likewise describes participation in jayanti events as a form of cultural politics.[21] The problem arises when the Dalit counter-public is absorbed into the mainstream and becomes a mere echo or a wider politics of adulation. D. Karthikeyan cautions that such 'forms of self-expression of the Dalits could be seen as a combination of both defiance and complicity'.[22] Even as they lay claim to public space, he suggests, the replication of dominant modes of politics can result in the dilution of Dalit radicalism. S. Beth similarly finds that 'the transformation of Dalit *melas* such as Ambedkar Jayanti into a civic festival also serves to reinforce rather than disrupt or break existing social hierarchies'.[23] Identity politics of this kind, Teltumbde insists, 'can massage your ego, make you feel good, but cannot feed your hunger, or liberate you from bondage. It can give you statues and memorials, but not what those icons lived for'.[24] The celebration of Ambedkar as an icon, in this context, can go hand in hand with a neglect of his work and a reproduction of normal politics. Equally, however, symbolic assertion may be a powerful means of challenging marginalization. Drawing on Schwimmer, A. Cohen documents processes of '"symbolic competition" in which the apparently disadvantaged group rejects the symbolic code in which it is disadvantaged and replaces it by its own in which it is relatively powerful or to which it has exclusive access'.[25]

## Changing the Landscape

The celebration of Ambedkar, this reminds us, does more than simply mimic dominant modes of politics. At its most basic level it changes the look and feel of social space by introducing a Dalit figure into public space. This is important because the regimented and regulated nature of caste-based habitation and interaction serves to naturalize caste hierarchy. As H. Lefebvre argues: 'Political space is not established solely by actions. The genesis of space of this kind also presupposes a practice, images, symbols and the construction of buildings, of towns and of localized social relationships'.[26]

The symbolic exclusion of Dalits from the body politic thus takes a spatial form. Crucially, as D. Harvey argues, this symbolic order shapes patterns of thought and action that reproduce the dominant order.[27] R. Rawat accordingly, points to 'the constitutive role of space in the institution of untouchability and in Dalit political mobilization'.[28] Rege, likewise, argues that 'space and spatial strategies of appropriation, deployment and control have been of crucial significance in maintaining hierarchical relations of caste'.[29] Historically, and often still today, Dalits were relegated to settlements on the outskirts of main villages or confined to urban slums and settlements. The increased visibility of Dalit icons and concerns in both social and political spheres, as A. Rao notes, thus 'reflects the success of Dalit claims to human recognition'.[30] Contests over access to public spaces and symbolic disputes over the content of such spaces (billboards, posters, wall paintings and statues, for example), it follows, are central to Dalit struggles for representation and challenge both hegemonic social relations and the spatial patterns which sediment caste dominance.[31] Dalit symbolic assertion in this context, as an EPW editorial notes:

> memorialises an alternate pantheon of intellectual and political leaders . . . This Dalit Prerna Sthal, like the numerous other statues and memorials built by Mayawati, is thus both a site for archiving Dalit memory and history as well as establishing, in cold physical form, the actuality of Dalit presence in the national imagination.[32]

Dalit symbolic assertion, thus, is not simply an emotional spasm, but stakes a claim to recognition and serves to alter the social landscape. 'Wherever they are found, but especially in the slums and villages where they have proliferated since the 1990s,' Jaoul observes, 'the Ambedkar statues testify to a rising consciousness of constitutional rights among the unprivileged, and sometimes even to their ability to motivate local authorities to enforce them.'[33] Symbolic politics here involves a challenge to the status quo and is, as Rao insists, 'genuinely consequential'.[34]

Tartakov similarly refers to Ambedkarite statues and portraits as 'a materially powerful and socially significant instrument for change'.[35] For a start, Ambedkar offers a truly pan-Indian Dalit icon at a time when the trend is towards intra-Dalit differentiation. The social significance of Dalit iconography, though, is perhaps best seen in the reaction of castes above Dalits, who have responded to Dalit assertion with aggression. Reflecting on this, Rao interprets efforts by 'state and casteist forces' to destroy or desecrate Dalit symbols as 'symbolic annihilation that would be experienced by Dalits as forms of social death and invisibility'.[36]

Following caste violence in Tamil Nadu, for instance, the state government proposed to place Ambedkar statues in cages to prevent them being desecrated. The caging here was taken to represent the limits placed on Dalit assertion.[37] 'Defacement is forceful,' Gerritsen writes, 'as it symbolically destroys what your opponent cherishes most.'[38] Over the past year, statues of Ambedkar across the country have become a front-line of contentious politics. Whilst the Bharatiya Janata Party government seeks to lay claim to Ambedkar by building memorials and statues, dominant caste groups have sought to keep Dalits 'in their place' by targeting the symbols of Dalit assertion. The year 2018 has witnessed a series of desecrations.[39] The contests over meaning and the attempts to appropriate Ambedkar for a Hindutva agenda are most obviously visible in the installation of a 'saffron' statue in Badaun in Uttar Pradesh.[40] Dalit attempts to insert themselves into and democratize public space, thus, are met by obstacles that speak to the centrality of symbolic politics to political practice and boundary marking.

## The Symbolic Construction of Community?

Cohen emphasizes the importance of symbols to community formation and boundary marking.[41] The Ambedkar icon, thus, is at the heart not just of Dalit strategies, but of processes of mobilization more widely. As Teltumbde rightly notes, for assertive Dalits, 'Ambedkar's icon replaced their gods and symbolised their self-esteem, honour and prestige. It became their beacon, a rallying point to carry on with their emancipatory struggles.'[42] The icon was pivotal to efforts to overcome and invert the stigma marking the lowest castes. Ambedkar is, almost invariably, portrayed wearing a suit and tie and usually carrying a copy of the Indian Constitution in one hand. The effect, Tartakov[43] emphasizes, is to foreground Ambedkar's status as a modern, educated leader who rejects the hierarchies and superstitions of the past. The Western attire, moreover, clearly distinguishes him and 'symbolically places him in opposition to other Indian leaders'.[44] The evocative power of this distinction is seen in the 2016 blockbuster *Kabali*, when Tamil superstar Rajinikanth references the difference between Gandhi and Ambedkar in saying that his attire is intended to make a statement.

The icon of Ambedkar thus not only celebrates a historical figure, but serves as an aspirational role model for followers and as a unifying force for Dalit villagers. The symbol, Jaoul notes, 'links wider political struggles to local issues, emphasising that Dalit progress requires a relentless struggle at every level. Wherever the Ambedkar statue has been installed, Dalits have felt encouraged by this tangible symbol of success'.[45] The affinity Dalits feel towards Ambedkar is seen in the lengths to which they will go to erect and protect his statues. In Periyakulam in south-western Tamil Nadu, young Dalit activists installed a concrete statue of their leader in the late 1990s, but the government removed it as it did not have formal permission. A wave of violence and protests met this decision, compelling the state authorities to concede that a statue could be placed in the town centre if it was cast in bronze and, thus, less susceptible to desecration. Since such a statue would cost twenty times more than a concrete one, it was assumed that the issue would fade away. Instead, Muthulakshmi, an elderly Dalit woman from Periyakulam, captured the sense of common purpose and commitment in the community that led to a grand unveiling in 2000:

> The statue here was not erected by the government. There was a collection from the people. Whether people put in one rupee or whatever it was that tax-collection (*vari panam*) that enabled us to meet the government insistence that we have a bronze statue. That day, when it was unveiled, there was joy beyond measure. (interview, July 2012)

'The actual process of identifying and installing the statues,' as M. Loynd insists, 'is itself empowering'.[46] Nor can such events be described as empty symbolism, since they entail community building and consciousness-raising alongside the material construction. This point was brought home for me in an interview with Chidambaram Kalam—a VCK activist—in Madurai who was tasked with constructing a memorial to the victims of the Melavalavu massacre in which six Dalits, including the local panchayat president, were butchered in broad daylight in 1997. Chidambaram captured the twin processes of memorial and community building in this case:

> There was huge resistance to the memorial within the community. *Our* [Dalit] community tried to stop it. 'You will build this up now and then go away', they said; 'what are we to do? Do you not want us to have a livelihood or to have a life here?' They campaigned not to have a martyr's memorial there. The day we first went they said this. So for six months we not only built the memorial, but did movement work and converted those people into activists . . . I understood why they were scared but tried to build them into a movement. You can build a liberation monument, but that is nothing, you need to build a spirit amongst the people too. (interview, July 2012)

What Kalam indicates here is that such statues become living memorials that speak to current issues and debates and are tied into processes of identity formation and mobilization. Crucially, the Ambedkar icon is never allowed simply to fade into the background. At least twice a year, on his birth and death anniversaries, groups gather to pay their respects and celebrate; 14 April in particular is marked in grand style. Alongside the garlands, pots

of milk and processions to various statues there are the more intimate
festivals in Dalit localities across the country in which music is played,
books and pencils distributed to young scholars and a sense of belonging
created. Where Dalit organizations are most active, this is combined with
a concerted attempt to educate the masses about Ambedkar's life and
thought and inculcate a critique of caste hierarchies. This is not to say,
however, as we have seen above that such events may not be neutralized or
appropriated by groups seeking to attract Dalit votes rather than appreciate
Ambedkar. J. Beltz notes how the Rashtriya Swayamsevak Sangh, in their
efforts to reinvent themselves as disciples of Ambedkar and crusaders against
untouchability, present him as a Hindu leader fighting for reform of the
religion in flagrant disregard of his advocacy of conversion.[47] The 'saffron'
Ambedkar installed in Badaun marks the apotheosis of such trends. Less
fantastically, most politicians remember their 'commitment to social justice'
only for as long as it takes to be photographed draping an Ambedkar statue
or portrait with a garland of flowers.

## Not *Just* Symbolic Politics?

Symbols, Cohen posits, 'do more than merely stand for or represent
something else. Indeed, if that was all they did, they would be redundant.
They also allow those who employ them to supply part of their meaning'.[48]
What to Dalits may be a symbol of rebellion and mobilization is a superficial
means of attracting support for others. The icon of Ambedkar, this reminds
us, is open to various uses and interpretations. It is neither inherently
radical nor necessarily an empty symbol. Its import, in sum, rests on the
meanings that it is made to bear and how it is presented. The thoughtful
VCK leader Sindhanai Selvan captures the difference between posters used
for advertisement and those intended to encourage change:

> We should think what the posters are for and try and get a little message
> or slogan across in them. I first encountered this party through a slogan
> on a poster that said 'Adangu maru, athu meeru' (Refuse to submit, fight
> back). When I first read this my whole body tingled. 'Resist', 'Fight
> back'? Can anyone have posters saying this on them? At school we are
> told to be quiet and sit still, at work we are told to behave, in families we
> are disciplined and here was an invocation to ask questions and talk back!
> That is why I first joined the movement. A picture on a poster is fine to
> identify ourselves but it achieves little. (speech, April 2012)

Sindhanai, here, echoes Teltumbde in suggesting that there has been a shift from engagement to empty display in Dalit politics. From his perspective, the rationale for symbolic politics is to encourage thought, provoke debate and engage passers-by.[49] Contemporary posters and official statues, by contrast, have no wider message to impart, and they turn public space into an arena for self-promotion rather than dialogue. In his survey of Dalit attitudes towards Ambedkar, A. Thokder, likewise, argues that in politics 'the intentions behind his principled vision have been abandoned'.[50] Ambedkar himself cautioned against this dilution of principles in commenting on the early celebrations of his jayanti:

> Personally, I do not like the celebration of my birthday. I am too much of a democrat to relish man-worship which I regard as perversion of democracy. Admiration, love, regard and respect for a leader, if he deserves them, are permissible and should be enough for both, the leader and the followers. But worship of the leader is certainly not permissible. It is demoralising to both.[51]

The difference between respect and worship is critical here. As Ambedkar puts it: 'The former does not take away one's intelligence to think and independence to act. The latter makes one a perfect fool.'[52] A Dalit cultural event held on waste ground near a Dalit estate in Madurai offered a stark illustration of this. The evening involved plays, songs and speeches of variable quality:

> An actor had been made up and dressed to resemble the Ambedkar familiar to all from statues and murals, and he was drummed onto the stage amidst whistles and fireworks. For all the need to 'get on with the show', leaders clustered round to be photographed with the icon before the performance commenced. Baba Saheb took centre stage raised his right arm in a pose characteristic of countless statues and called out 'Jai Bhim', then the music went on and young men started cavorting around him in Tamil film style dance moves. It was all too much for one enthusiastic drunk who leaped up onto the stage and prostrated himself before 'Ambedkar' before running around the actor holding his ears with opposing hands as though worshipping a God, losing his lungi in the process, before being ushered off stage. (field notes, July 2012)

Ambedkar here is worshipped as an icon with scant regard for his teachings. Indeed, since Ambedkar was forced into the political mainstream by Dalit activists in the 1990s, politicians have sought to make 'perfect fools' of followers by divorcing the Ambedkar icon from his writings and the social reality of caste. As long-running editor of the journal *Dalit Drum* (*Dalit Murasu*), Punitha Pandian, puts it:

> Changing the society is different from electoral politics. You need a social revolution to change society. That will not occur in parliament or the Assembly. You can only pay lip service to it there. You can create some statues, you can create some Ambedkar parks, you can build some schools or something else, but you cannot change society. (interview, May 2012)

It remains to be seen whether Castro's wishes are honoured or not, but the experience of Ambedkar suggests that his supporters, opportunistic politicians and salespeople will soon defy his injunctions. All political parties in India today use Ambedkar's image and lay claim to his legacy as they seek to capture the Dalit vote. What the data above suggests, however, is that not all images are equal. There is, as Ambedkar noted, a difference between respect and worship. One suspects that Ambedkar would have nothing but scorn for the politicians who build grand monuments to him whilst neglecting the very real and pressing issues that Dalits confront on a daily basis. On the other hand, it is quite probable that he would be accepting—if not approving—of the community groups and movements that have harnessed his image to support their struggles for dignity and justice.

If the icon of Ambedkar is to retain its radical potential, then it must be wedded to sustained mobilization and critical engagement with social issues. Across India, Dalits revere Ambedkar as a deity and saviour. They treasure his image and venerate his statues. As Chidambaram Kalam noted, however, erecting a statue without also taking the time to build a political community renders the monument meaningless. If the innumerable statues are to honour Ambedkar instead of just depicting him, then it is time that as much attention was paid to his ideas as to his image. As Narendra Jadhav put it in a wide-ranging interview: 'It's perfectly fine to recognise Ambedkar but I am saying that it should be done in the right letter and spirit. It should not only be symbolic, it should be substantial.'[53]

# AMBEDKAR'S DALIT AND THE PROBLEM OF CASTE SUBALTERNITY[1]

*Anupama Rao*

Ambedkar's Dalit was a particular sort of historical subject, caught between a Buddhist past and a (Dalit) future, between historic discrimination and its redress. Ambedkar's investment in the exceptional subject, the Dalit, as also the universal subjects of rights, the political citizen, is a signal contribution to political thought. It derives from his immanent critique of caste (and untouchability), which plots the mutual entailments of politics and religion: (political) separation and Buddhist conversion, the two major events that define 'late Ambedkar', manifest that relation.[2]

Ambedkar did not merely address the relationship between the caste question and Indian democracy theoretically, but through a simultaneous commitment to programmes and policies instituted to produce caste equality. In essence, Ambedkar's efforts helped to resignify the violence of caste, whose effects lingered as so many forms of historic discrimination, into the object of affirmative action. Affirmative action policies assume a relationship between history, law and identity: rights are predicated on the assumption that historic injury requires correction in the present. Meanwhile, the perpetrators of past injury become the current beneficiaries of inherited privilege.[3]

However, constitutional commitments to redress have not resolved the caste question. Rather, they are at the heart of a governing tension in contemporary politics between the desire for radical equality on the one hand and its persistent failure on the other. Instead of excising contradiction from the field of politics, Ambedkar effected a signal transformation of the political, which consisted of investing law (and the Constitution) with the capacity to reveal the state's historic complicity with caste power.

Thus, Ambedkar's thought, which is evident in his activism as much as his writings, draws our attention to the gap between legislated redress and existential suffering and between the founding document and the equality it imagines. The recurrent staging of this aporia marks both the difficulties of annihilating caste and its urgent necessity.

## Introductory Remarks

My essay for this volume does two things. First, I address the omission of anti-caste thought (and an accounting of Ambedkar's Dalit) from the colonial–anti-colonial binary that has structured South Asian scholarship. Ignoring caste was crucial for enabling nationalism's universalist claims, and today the centrality of caste highlights the failure of that universalism and clarifies contemporary postcolonial politics. Critiques of caste and anti-caste thought were dismissed as parochial concerns during the interwar years, when nationalist mobilization dominated South Asian politics. Today it is the provincialism of interwar nationalism that is most striking. Anti-colonial critique was directed at imperialism, which was on the defensive during this time. In the interwar years, a variety of factors began to make imperialism less attractive to colonial rulers. In this context, nationalists could at times feel they had the wind of history in their sails, while anti-caste thinkers, by comparison, had to struggle much harder to make an impact. Reviled as spoilers of nationalist unity and as dupes of colonial power, they had no option but to look for global inspiration, whereas nationalists could concentrate on bolstering their demands for universal representation at home: if upper-caste nationalists focused on underlining their difference from colonial power, anti-caste thinkers harnessed their imagination of radical equality through acts of historical comparison.[4] Thus, the global context of the interwar period is relevant and necessary for understanding Ambedkar's efforts to make the phenomenon of untouchability historically specific but generalizable as inequality and discrimination.

This feeds into the related issue, which forms the bulk of this essay. If we want to shift our attention (and our explanation) away from political history in order to address issues of political subjectivity and historical identity, we need to turn to a different archive. We need to turn to the work of political philosophers and social theorists who are concerned with how history might intersect with theory to reanimate, or revivify conceptions of 'the political'. For them, the relationship between the experience of social marginality and trajectories of political enfranchisement and visibility cannot be explained through the normative language of political philosophy, which typically considers questions of freedom, liberty, sovereignty and morality without attending to material conditions, for example, relations of production (as also social relations) or agonism within the domain of the social. Thus, Judith Butler asks, 'What happens when the universal is wielded, precisely, by those who signify its contamination, by those socially excluded and marginalized?' Is it possible that 'conventional and exclusionary norms of universality can, through perverse reiterations, produce unconventional formulations of universality that expose the limited and exclusionary features of the former [. . .] at the same time that they mobilize a new set of demands'?[5]

One way to historicize Butler's question, which asks us to stretch the limits of our understanding of universality itself, is to turn to the interwar period. Broadly speaking, the interwar period had two connected yet contradictory developments. The internationalization of the minority question and the universalization of the working class organized around the poles of (historical) difference and equality, respectively, emerged as mutually entailed, if contradictory, processes with the breakdown of European empires and the emergence of Soviet Russia. The primacy of labour universalism for Marxist accounts of political subject formation meant that the proletariat was viewed as the paradigmatic figure associated with emancipatory politics, with workers' subjectivity assumed to be necessarily oppositional, if not radical.[6] Meanwhile, the period also witnessed the emergence of 'minority' identities, for example, Negro, Muslim and Jew, which assumed political pertinence in the context of imperial transition, and nation–state formation. These were figures whose concrete particularity troubled the constitution of the social whole, whose politicality, that is, the conditions by which their actions might be viewed as properly 'political', had to be established rather than assumed.[7] Another way to put this might be to echo Saba Mahmood, who argues that the idea of minority 'congeals within itself different forms of marginalization and precarity that are historically distinct, which in turn determines the kind of political struggles a minority can pursue in order to ensure its collective survival and well-being'.[8]

Ambedkar's Dalit is an underexplored or ignored actor in this story of convergent logics of class and minority; she has an affinity with similar figures whose emergence alters our imagination of a progressive politics predicated solely on the universalization of labour, yet does not remain untouched by it. As he tried to make a space for the distinctive history of caste (and the origin of untouchability), Ambedkar drew, at different times, on the figure of the Muslim, the Negro and the proletariat as close approximations of the Dalit.[9] While the proletariat provided him with a figure of universality associated with a distinct political practice— revolution—minority identity provided Ambedkar greater leeway to imagine a possible Dalit politics. What were the conditions of possibility (historical, conceptual) for such filiation? How did historical comparison and global connection aid in staging Dalit life and the persistent agonisms that structured caste Hindu society?

I address three interrelated issues by way of response: Ambedkar's concern with equivalence, that is, his interest in global historical comparison and his focus on equating untouchability with other forms of systemic exclusion (race, class) as these related to and refracted back on his understanding of competing inequalities in the Indian context (Dalits, Muslims); his commitment to thinking about agonism in/as history as a way to understand the genealogy of caste and untouchability at a time when he had turned away from the project of historical comparison towards nationalizing untouchability by rooting it in subcontinental history; and a brief meditation on the Dalit question as a problem for thought. My account is less exhaustive than instructive, and keeps in view key issues that preoccupied Ambedkar across his life: his concern with the phenomenological dimensions of deprivation, dispossession and dehumanization, that is, Ambedkar's enduring focus on experiences that signal the (sanctioned) withdrawal of social care. It is surely this aspect of Ambedkar's thought, the effort to organize his conceptual world to address the existential question of 'outcaste-ness', that must distinguish his thought from other Indian thinkers and from scholarly projects that seek to merely include him in the canon of global or Indian intellectual history.

## Equivalence

### Minority and the Colonial Franchise

Ambedkar's standoff with Gandhi over the 1932 Communal Award was the culmination of Ambedkar's extended engagement with colonial franchise and the politics of community.[10] His efforts to forefront the Depressed Classes as a political constituency, a minority with distinct needs, required him to refer to and distinguish his demands from the separate electorate for Muslims, which had been instituted in 1909 partly in response to the mobilization in this regard of the Aga Khan and his colleague Nawab

Mohsin-ul-Mulk since 1906. Demarcating the Depressed Classes as a distinct group with separate interests, that is, as non-Hindus, was essential to Ambedkar's effort.

In a series of representations before the Southborough 'and Simon Commissions, established to consider extension of franchise and the functioning of diarchy in the period between 1918 and 1928, respectively, Ambedkar argued that the Depressed Classes constituted a distinctive third constituency (along with Hindus and Muslims) with the need for political representation.[11] Two broad arguments characterized Ambedkar's position on Depressed Class representation during 1919–28. The first was that any demand for separate representation ought to be a fallback option in the absence of adult franchise combined with reserved representation. The second distinguished Depressed Class representation by emphasizing the civic and economic disabilities from which they suffered. Ambedkar thus argued from the position of a theory of representative government based on adult franchise to make demands on behalf of a heretofore unrecognized constituency, the Depressed Classes.

The significance of this move is both subtle and significant. Ambedkar was laying claim to what Etienne Balibar has called a 'right to politics' by challenging the exclusionary systems of colonial nomination and the property qualification in favour of universal franchise.[12] By emphasizing material deprivation and civic exclusion as the grounds for political marginalization of the Depressed Classes, Ambedkar was demanding a shift away from the focus on religious identity—the basis of colonial recognition for the separate Muslim electorate—to the contingencies of class. However, this definitional shift required a more expansive view of the franchise, one that transcended educational and property qualifications and subverted the colonial system of nominated representation. Universal enfranchisement was crucial for anti-colonial equality.

At the Southborough Commission, Ambedkar argued that Depressed Class representation was contingent on the extension of adult franchise. This was an important critique of colonial models of limited representation that articulated with, and reproduced, upper-caste hegemony. Instead, (universal) enfranchisement could be used proactively to reveal potential constituencies such as the Depressed Classes. Only then, Ambedkar suggested, could a subsequent reduction of the criterion of eligibility, that is, of the property (and taxation) qualification, enable substantive Depressed Class representation. In essence, a formal commitment to universal enfranchisement could open the door to policy measures to provide substantive equality for vulnerable minorities. So far as special representation was concerned, Ambedkar argued that reserved or communal seats could enhance Depressed Class representation in the Legislative Council but that communal electorates had a better chance of ensuring the selection of candidates who truly represented the community's interest.[13] For Untouchables, 'communal representation and self-determination are but two different phrases which express the same notion'.[14]

Ten years later, Ambedkar's representation to the Simon Commission marked a refinement of these arguments but now through a sustained critique of the Muslim separate electorate.[15] Distinguishing the Depressed Classes from the Muslims, Ambedkar described the former as 'educationally backward, that it is economically very poor, socially enslaved'.[16] As for Muslims, Ambedkar had argued before the Southborough Commission that Hindus could represent 'the *material* interests of the Mohammedans and vice versa'. Instead, material deprivation and social stratification united the Depressed Classes as an alternate constituency defined by a class interest: they required protection due to their low social and economic status, and weightage due to their small numbers.

The principle of weightage was first articulated in connection with the Muslim electorate to address demographic shifts in the Muslim constituency and to acknowledge their 'historical and political importance'. Instead, Ambedkar highlighted the socioeconomic status of the Depressed Classes to demand similar measures for them. Representing the Bahishkrit Hitakarini Sabha, Ambedkar argued that weighted representation was 'literally showered upon a community like the Mahomedans holding a stronger and better position in the county than can be predicated of the Depressed Classes. The Sabha protests against this grading of the citizens of a country on the basis of their political importance'.[17] Ambedkar argued that if the position of Muslims as a demographic majority in Sind, Bengal, Punjab and the Northwest Frontier Provinces was acknowledged, it would be clear that the Muslim-majority provinces were an 'ingenious contrivance' that 'involved the maintenance of justice and peace by retaliation'.[18] Hindu and Muslim minorities would be ruled by fear and anxiety since they could be held hostage for the behaviour of their co-religionists in other parts of the country: 'For if the Hindu majority tyrannized the Muslim minority in the Hindu provinces the scheme provides a remedy whereby the Mohammedan majorities get a field to tyrannize the Hindu minorities in the five Mohammedan provinces. It is a system of protection by counterblast against blast; terror against terror and eventually tyranny against tyranny.'[19] Ambedkar was arguing that the territorial principle allowed Muslims to challenge their minority status. This was prescient as it was politically potent.

In the latter half of the 1930s, Muslim politics challenged the politics of number and the demographic calculus that had been set in place by colonial technologies of objectification such as the census and limited franchise by claiming that Muslims were a nationality. While majority and minority were enumerated entities within the nation, the nation form was organized around affective bonds, the feeling of commonality. (Ambedkar addressed the difference between a politics of minority and of nationality in *Thoughts on Pakistan*, published in 1941.) So far as the Depressed Classes were concerned, Ambedkar's strategy was to present them as an as-yet-unrecognized interest group, a constituency. First, he argued that like Muslims, the Depressed Classes were minorities with a distinctive history, identity and set of interests that set them apart from the Hindu community at large. Next, he argued that deprivation and social marginalization, rather than religious identity, ought to form the basis of minority representation. Going yet further, Ambedkar characterized the relationship between caste Hindus and Untouchables as a 'fundamental and deadly antagonism'. He argued:

> The first thing I submit is that we [Untouchables, Depressed Classes] claim that we must be treated as a distinct minority, separate from the Hindu community: a distinct and independent minority. Secondly I should like to submit that the Depressed Classes minority needs far greater political protection than any other minority in British India for the simple reason that it is educationally backward, that it is economically very poor, socially enslaved and suffers from certain grave political disabilities from which no other community suffers. Then I would submit that, as a matter of demand for our political protection, we claim representation on the same basis as the Mahomeddan minority. We claim reserved seats if accompanied by adult franchise.[20]

Let us extrapolate the immense significance of these efforts. If the Depressed Classes, Hindus and Muslims could be said to constitute *three* distinct communities of interest, with the Depressed Classes forming 18 to 20 per cent of the population, then this third community disturbed the idea that only 'fixed permanent communities' existed in political space. The Depressed Classes were defined by the principle of socioeconomic status and material deprivation, rather than the primordial distinctions of religion. As a third community produced through practices of power and historic discrimination, the very existence of the Depressed Classes was a challenge to the colonial obsession with Hindu and Muslim communities as primordial communities and corporate political actors. At the same time, upper-caste Hindus' efforts to include the Depressed Classes within the general (Hindu) electorate could be shown to be purely instrumental. Ambedkar subverted the colonial discourse that equated religious community with constituency by suggesting a *fundamental* contradiction between Hindus and Untouchables. Instead, he was suggesting that the Depressed Classes were a community that Hinduism produced outside or apart from itself, in an act of 'agonistic intimacy'.[21]

Ambedkar's strategic engagement with the political theory of representative democracy preceded Ambedkar and Gandhi's historic confrontation in 1932, and the ensuing Poona Pact: this involved utilizing and enacting a shift from the discourse of universal franchise, to specifying the grounds on which political representation for the Depressed Classes could be justified, that is, through their separation from Hindus.

Recall that Ambedkar had advocated for the inevitability of Partition due to the power of the Pakistan idea predicated on the 'national feeling' prevalent among the Muslims in his texts, *Thoughts on Pakistan* (1941) and *Pakistan, or, The Partition of India* (1945). Ambedkar's understanding of the interrelation between Partition and the Dalit question underwent a shift as he began to realize what the fact of Pakistan would mean for the key stakeholders who sought to determine the future of India: the Congress, Muslim League and the colonial state. Ambedkar dated the Dalits' historic failure for recognition as a national minority to the period between 1944 and 1946.[22]

As late as 1944, Lord Wavell argued with Gandhi that the Scheduled Scheduled Castes (SCs) constituted a 'separate element in the national life of India'.[23] Yet resistance to separate SC representation was in place by 1942, when the Cripps Mission held that only religious minorities were entitled to separate representation.[24] Cripps's refusal to support SC demands for separate representation was described as a 'conspiracy of silence' between 'the Government, the Congress and even the Muslims'.[25] It was the immediate trigger for Ambedkar's establishment of the All India Scheduled Caste Federation (AISCF), formed at a Nagpur conference in July 1942.[26] The AISCF working committee argued that Dalits were a religious minority and described Congress hegemony as leading to 'the annihilation of our people as a political entity'.[27] Ambedkar strongly objected to the Cripps betrayal, arguing:

> Up to the declaration of 8th August 1940 His Majesty's Government's view was that the untouchables were a distinct and a separate element and that they constituted so important an element that their consent was necessary for any constitutional changes that may be desire.[28]

Ambedkar notes that although SCs had enjoyed political support from Muslims, the politics of Muslim nationalism now pitted Muslims against all other communities. He saw the Muslim League setting up 'a new equation of values . . . that the Muslims, whatever their numbers, are just equal as to the non-Muslims and therefore in any political arrangement the Muslims must get fifty percent'.[29] The Muslim League had trumped number with nationality.[30] Now it was imperative to find recognition for Untouchables as 'a separate element' in the national life of India. Physical separation was proposed through the establishment of SC villages on government wastelands and private lands overseen by a government-established Settlement Commission.[31] Village committees would form the basic AISCF organizational unit and provide funds through a tax on constituents.[32]

We know these efforts came to naught. In a telling reminder of Dalits' political negligibility, C. Rajagopalachari would argue that SCs had no claims on a separate democracy:

> The Scheduled Castes are evenly distributed all over India and are about ten per cent of the population . . . Thus distributed, they have to be part of the general population and cannot isolate themselves into a separate democracy. Nothing therefore follows from the argument even if conclusively proved that the Scheduled Castes do not stand behind the Congress and do not support its claim for political freedom.[33]

Ambedkar's argument that the Congress did not represent SCs was moot, since 'it may often be impossible to get minorities to agree to the claims for self-government which is majority rule even though the minorities be fully protected in their civil and political rights'.[34] Another text by K. Santhanam, *Ambedkar's Attack,* discounted SCs as a territorially dispersed minority: 'Whether there are 50 or 60 millions, it is of minor importance. I may point out that they are distributed almost evenly in all the villages of India. In each village they constitute a minority.'[35] Santhanam argued that SCs had to accept their position as lesser Hindus and an ineffective minority because they were defined neither by demographic concentration nor cultural distinction.[36]

## Minority between Race and Class

By the interwar period, anti-caste and anti-race thinkers had begun to think through 'class' to distinguish the complex histories (and the analytic purchase) of the categories of 'caste' and 'race'. Recall that the transformative character of class, arriving as it did with a latent model of revolutionary social change, had become very nearly standard because it had become transposed on to the idea of the Industrial Revolution, as something gradually emanating from Europe towards the rest of the world. Thus, the difference between race and class as models for historical comparison (with caste) can be captured by the idea of revolution that accompanied class analysis and working-class politics. Both anti-caste and anti-race thinkers would take advantage of the way in which class now offered a way to conceptualize social mobility, but as a form of social and political change rather than of purely individual luck or effort.

Ambedkar was no different. He was thinking about the similarities between caste, race and class throughout his struggle for Dalit rights. Ambedkar framed caste as a manifestation of the diverse forms of global inequality. This allowed him to transcend the parochial resolution of the caste question within a national frame. Like race, caste was a category that sharpened the perception of inequality, but it did not act as a progressive model for comparison, as class did for anti-caste thinkers. Instead, class was a category to argue for mitigating or overcoming inequality where caste was historically dominant in order to bypass the tendency of nationalists to render caste as an aspect of tradition and thereby safeguard it from reform. The fact that the model of revolution proved incapable of accommodating historical difference (caste, race) should not prevent us from appreciating its utopian impulse.

Below, I briefly discuss the role played by ideas of connection, comparison and commensuration in globalizing caste, as well as the limits of that exercise.

Nineteenth-century anti-racism drew on the concept–metaphor of caste as a complex structure of inherited privilege and sanctioned exclusion as a way of addressing the multiple effects of race thinking.[37] In a similar yet opposite set of moves, Jotiba Phule, the famous anti-caste thinker, drew on racial antagonism as a model for understanding caste and argued that a permanent and irreconcilable hostility between Brahmins and non-Brahmins characterized caste society from its inception. Phule's famous 1873 text, *Gulamgiri* was structured around an imagined affinity with the Emancipation Proclamation, and with figures such as George Washington and the Marquis de Lafayette, drew from race. For Phule, American republicanism appears to have been of one piece, with the Emancipation Proclamation completing the promise of the Constitution: Phule expressed his admiration of Abraham Lincoln for rescuing American Negroes from thralldom and exhorted upper castes to do the same for their Indian brethren. Phule also recognized race as the basis of Atlantic World slavery and argued that the Aryan–Dravidian distinction played a similar role in structuring the social antagonisms of caste.[38] This was followed by Phule's efforts to produce a combined and inclusive identity for the peasant and Untouchable castes and to make them visible as a demographically dense political collectivity as a community of 'shudra-atisudras'. (We see here the example of a political performative that sought to birth a new collectivity through the practise of naming.)

Fifty years later, W.E.B. Du Bois described the US during Reconstruction as a society defined by complex practices of unfreedom premised on worker discipline, acquisitive ideology and marketized social relations. His 1935 magnum opus, *Black Reconstruction*, locates the origins of modern racial capitalism in a legislated emancipation that was followed by Jim Crow, marking the failure of the all-too-brief experiment in American democracy.[39] Indeed, for Du Bois, the 'Negro problem' originates with the legal freedoms announced by the Thirteenth, Fourteenth and Fifteenth Amendments: formal equality was the enabling ground for the emergence of new forms of inequality. Du Bois argues that American democracy was haunted by its past; that it could only ever make an appearance as an 'abolition democracy'. This name marked the intimacy of a specific history (American slavery) with a universal idea (democracy).[40] By bringing these terms into proximity with each other, Du Bois offered a pithy reflection on the grounding contradictions of American democracy, its historical entanglement with enslavement, and unfreedom.

If *Black Reconstruction* signalled a turning point in Du Bois's thinking, so too did *Annihilation of Caste* mark a turning point in Ambedkar's oeuvre. The two texts were published a year apart, in 1935 and 1936, respectively. What unites these otherwise disparate texts is their authors' discovery of the logic governing a social order, race and Hinduism, respectively. Du

Bois had referred to the hardening of a 'caste system' when he associated the failure of emancipation with the rise of racial capitalism, and the emergence of a White and Black proletariat. *Annihilation of Caste* posited the intractability of caste when conceived within Gandhian rubrics of an ethicized Hinduism capable of doing justice to the Untouchable, figured by Gandhi as Harijan (lit. person of God). In the extended debate with Gandhi that was inaugurated by his text, Ambedkar argued that the abolition of untouchability was impossible without the annihilation of Hinduism, since caste and Hindu religion were mutually entailed. Ambedkar outlined the relationship between the religious and the political with great ferocity, underscoring the anaemic responses of social reformism when what was required was the annihilation of caste as a social formation predicated on violence and inequality. Ambedkar's focus on the annihilation of caste conjugates the violence of caste with a Hindu state, thus linking a specific history with a universal form. Ambedkar's reference goes further and draws on the revolutionary discourse of annihilating the state as a rubric for exterminating social differences of caste.

Ambedkar also wrote about the place of slavery in universal history starting with Rome, but ending with plantation slavery in North America, and a comparison of modern slavery with untouchability. He argued that slaves in ancient Rome were educated as they inherited their masters' status; they participated in Roman society as scribes, performers, musicians and skilled labour. Plantation slavery in the Americas was brutal, yet their status as value-producing property meant that there was some incentive to protecting slaves: 'Being property and therefore valuable, the master for sheer self-interest took great care of the health and well-being of the slave.'[41] Ambedkar argued that the slave's status as value-producing property entitled her to better protection than the outcaste whose labour, though necessary, was degraded and devalued and thus subject to extreme stigmatization. Ambedkar's comparison was powerful not simply because it was true but because it placed two exploitative orders against each other and argued that the inequities of caste were more severe than the legislated disenfranchisement of the American slave.

Let me stop for a moment to make three points about my narrative so far. The first is to underscore the inspiration of republicanism for Indian anti-caste thinkers. The second is the creative miscommunication of specific histories (of race and slavery, or caste and capital), the flattening of their complexity as these ideas travelled so that historical figures such as Lincoln, or Washington, who were compromised by their position on Atlantic

World slavery could become heroes in the anti-caste repertoire. The last has to do with the place of slavery as the organizing figure for unfreedom in republican thought, and the enormous significance of the image and ideology of enslavement on both sides of the Atlantic.

## Ambedkar and Marx

One reason slavery and untouchability functioned as sister concepts was that they organized systems of historic dispossession predicated on coerced, degraded or exploited labour. Their role as modes of production in global histories of capitalism (and associated discourses of labour, worth and value) was of keen interest to Ambedkar as it was for Du Bois. Phule, too, was a keen observer of the transformations effected by colonial capital. His numerous essays on agrarian distress reflect an acute awareness of the combined effects of native rent seeking and colonial surplus extraction on the peasantry; they depict the alienation of rural labour from its own labour power, and the commodification of social relations in a colonial economy.[42] One might go so far as to argue that in Phule's writings the politics of caste becomes legible in the context of colonial capitalism and the specific forms of abstraction to which capitalist society gave rise.[43]

While Ambedkar's relationship to Marx was complex and contradictory, it is also the case that Marx was an important agon, as important as M.K. Gandhi. Yet Ambedkar's relationship with Marx is often portrayed as that of rejection and refusal: Buddhist conversion (1956) preceded by evidence of the long-standing antagonism between Ambedkarites and communists is used to argue that theirs is an impossible relationship.

The divide between struggles organized around caste as opposed to class—between anti-caste activism and Left politics—has occasioned intense debate and discussion. Both organize around a critique of inequality, and each struggles for social justice. Yet they have 'emerge[d] as two very different radicalisms', a remark Marilyn Strathern has made about a different set of intellectual traditions, namely, feminism and anthropology.[44] Caste has been viewed as a 'traditional', ascriptive category, while class is viewed as a political identity produced by the onset of modern, capitalist transformation and the prevalence of culturally unmarked, free labour. Since developmentalism was an ideology shared by modernizers across the 19th and 20th centuries more generally, including by Eastern and Western communist parties alike, the relationship between caste and class was assumed to be one-way, with capitalist modernity enabling the remaking of caste into class. Thus, the effort to downplay a complex history of alliance and agonism between Ambedkarites and the Left has as much to do with party politics as it does with differences of ideology; it was shaped by the uneasy alliance between Congress and the communists regarding their perception of Ambedkar as anti-national, and it is immensely consequential for recovering lost possibilities of a heterodox, capaciously imagined Marxism that might have been produced in the encounter between Ambedkar and Marx, between caste and class.

For example, political scientist Raosaheb Kasbe argues in his text, *Ambedkar Ani Marx* (1985) that there was an effective ban on asking about the relationship between Ambedkar and Marx until the 1970s, when the Dalit Panthers reopened the issue when they challenged the status-quoism of Dalit politics, and its co-option by the Congress.[45] However, the Republican Party of India (RPI), which was formed soon after Ambedkar's death in 1956, had built an alliance with the Praja Socialists, the Shetkari Kamgar Paksha (Peasant and Workers Party), and the Samyukta Maharashtra Samiti. The RPI used the language of class and labour exploitation in its manifesto, positioning Dalits as the vanguard of the exploited classes in their struggle for total emancipation. The RPI was influenced by Dadasaheb Gaikwad, who was prominent in the Ambedkar movement since the Nasik satyagraha (1928–34) and worked closely with the communists to organize *bhumiheen* (landless) satyagrahas in 1956 and 1964. However, Gaikwad was sidelined by urban, upwardly mobile Dalits led by B.C. Kamble, who took control of the RPI after Ambedkar's death.

Of course, there is an even earlier phase of Ambedkar's writings and activism, where he appears receptive to Marxist analyses of the political economy of caste. This was evident in the model of caste–class unity championed by the Independent Labour Party (ILP) (1936–42), though it should be said that Ambedkar almost always aimed to triangulate between Fabian socialism and communism.[46] (The ILP was preceded by the formation of the Municipal Kamgar Sangh in 1935, which represented about 5 per cent of the 15,000 employees of the municipality. Efforts were also made to organize dockyard and railway workers in 1948.)

Ambedkar's Bombay was a critical node for intellectuals and activists interested in global communism and a crucial political arena for the Indian Communist Party.[47] Ambedkar's engagement with the communists was contentious. He struggled, during the 1930s and 1940s to define Dalit politics as he manoeuvred between the Maratha-led Congress and the Communist Party. After his death, the presence of the Shiv Sena would radically alter the state's political landscape and the Dalits' relationship with it. On the national level, Ambedkar's representation to the Simon Commission (1928), followed by the historic Poona Pact (1932) would see him branded as an imperialist stooge and castigated as anti-national at a time when the Congress was increasingly moving leftwards starting with M.K. Gandhi's and Jawaharlal Nehru's support for the accused in the Meerut Conspiracy Case, followed by the creation of the Congress Socialist Party (1934) as a caucus within the Indian National Congress. Anand Teltumbde argues, 'Even when they sympathized with the struggles of Dalits, the Communist Party of India never missed an opportunity to attack Ambedkar's leadership', often voicing the same criticism of him that emanated from the Congress (that he was a British stooge) and denigrating him for destroying the possibility of worker unity by introducing the caste question.[48] Thus, the silence about Ambedkar's relationship to Marx also had an unresolved national question on the status of caste and untouchability.

Ambedkar's commitment to social democracy and the state notwithstanding, it is clear that he had a rather complex relationship with labour politics. It is well known that he threatened to break the historic strike of 1928, which was organized by the Girni Kamgar Union (GKU) because the GKU refused to take heed of the caste differences between textile mill workers, or to support the entry of Dalit workers in the weaving department. It is also well known that Ambedkar played a critical role in the anti-khot agitation in the Konkan in 1928 together with communist leader S.V. Parulekar, and that he joined hands again with the communists to lead the massive strike against the Industrial Dispute Act in 1938.[49]

However, the precise nature of Ambedkar's engagement with Marx's thought remains understudied: instead, the connection between Ambedkar and Marx has been represented as a matter of party affinity rather than of political philosophy, as a struggle between Ambedkarites and communists. However, the more significant question is what Marxism meant and how it functioned as a 'structure of feeling' for making sense of everyday exploitation and the possibilities of social transformation.[50] One should insist on the difference between party politics, on the one hand, and Marxism as a form of thought keyed to human equality and emancipation on the other.

Could the Dalit replace the proletariat as the revolutionary subject of politics?[51] Well before Ambedkar's time, anti-caste thought existed as a set of critical practices organized around images of destitution and dispossession and the figures who perpetuated it, such as the cunning Brahmin priest, the moneylender or the upper-caste bureaucrat in colonial institutions. I am suggesting that such figures were repurposed for a heterodox Marxism that spoke on behalf of the exploited and the disenfranchised who demanded to be seen and recognized on their own terms as so many forms of life whose strange, deformed multiplicity indicted hegemonic social structures and whose concern with historic dispossession focused on the dignity of work and respect for labouring bodies.[52]

Ambedkar's great innovation was to draw on Marx to stage the conflict between Dalit subjectivity as caught between the ideas of caste-as-labour and caste-as-historical-identity. This audacious thinker of Dalit universality struggled with caste and class, stigma and labour as supplemental, yet incommensurable categories. Ultimately, the struggle for Ambedkar was to specify caste (and untouchability) as a peculiar kind of 'body history': as embodied experience and an existential condition. Thus, Ambedkar very often took a detour through 'class' and 'labour' but always in the interest of foregrounding the *difference* of untouchability and specifying outcaste politics. Rather than deriving a model of emancipation through labour, Ambedkar argued that outcaste labour was fated to be marginalized and hyper-exploited without a strong regime of rights. The response to Dalits' dilemma did not call for politicizing labour as such *via* the general strike. Rather, it required, as a first step, that Dalits enter the wage labour contract. Capitalist modernity was to be applauded because the ideas of abstraction and equivalence that were central to it also enabled Dalits to cast off stigma: by bringing Dalits within a field of abstract mediation, capital also emancipated them from the culturalism of caste.[53]

## Agonism

The detour through the global allowed Dalits' marginality to become visible as historical injustice but to what extent was the caste question distinctively Indian?[54] It was a formation that marked off 'Hindus from other peoples', an agonistic intimacy that structured history itself. While revolution provided the model of political agonism, Ambedkar's important text, *Revolution and Counter-Revolution*, staged the defeat of Buddhism by Brahminism as the deep history of untouchability. Unlike Islam, which was more recent, and which Ambedkar framed as a matter of competitive sovereignty (Hindus, Muslims), caste's relationship to Brahminism (and Brahminism's relationship to state power) was both more ancient and more pervasive. Ambedkar writes, 'The history of India is nothing but a history of mortal conflict between Buddhism and Brahmanism.' Brahmin power had emerged through the killing of a Buddhist king: the regicide of the Buddhist king Pushyamitra and the destruction of the Buddhist state was the originary moment which saw the birth of caste and Brahminism.[55]

Ambedkar understood the Brahmin's right to bear arms and to kill to be a defining feature of the sovereignty of caste. It recast the traditional understanding of the relationship between Brahmin and Kshatriya, and sacral and temporal power, respectively, and it was most a result of Ambedkar's familiarity with the history of Brahmin kingship in the Deccan under the Peshwai. Meanwhile, Ambedkar argued that the norms of vegetarianism, which was imposed on Brahmins, was influenced by the Buddhist commitment to non-violence. These norms were then deployed against Sudras and Untouchables in order to confirm their stigmatized status.[56]

The dehumanization of Dalits (as originary Buddhists) was located in this Indic past and challenged what might appear on first glance to be the shared history of Buddhism and Brahminism on the subcontinent. If the Dalit was the defeated, secret sharer of Hindu history, she was also its key protagonist who narrated the history of caste as a history of violence and being made a social outcast.[57] Meanwhile, Ambedkar distinguished his account of the Dalit Buddhist from the origin story of the birth of a fourth varna, the Sudras, from a class of degraded Kshatriyas excluded from the right to perform the *upanayanam* (thread) ceremony. Ambedkar argued that Sudra identity was unstable due to the desire for incorporation into the caste Hindu order, while the Dalit perspective was developed from their position of symbolic negation. Thus, Manu's caste laws and taboos were belated; their function was to justify the permanence of untouchability through the force of law in the aftermath of the violent defeat of the Sudras and the permanent outcasting of the Dalit Buddhist.

We should note here that Ambedkar's history of violence is both conjunctural and structural. Regicide inaugurated the cycle of violence that defined Brahmin counter-revolution. In short, this originary regicide altered the distribution of ritual and temporal power and challenged the king's sovereignty by making him dependent on the Brahmin.[58] As a consequence, the taboo on the Brahmin's right to bear arms and hold kingly power was also lifted.[59] With the destruction of Buddhism, the Brahmin's sovereignty was embedded in codes and taboos, such as the Laws of Manu, while the varna order became a prosthetic of Brahmin power. (Ambedkar was anticipating Louis Dumont's argument by nearly three decades when he argued that Brahmin power suborned the temporal power of kingship and subordinated the Kshatriya to the Brahmin.)

Ambedkar goes further, however, by showing how Brahmin power operated as social totality, so to speak, by controlling access to the instruments and means of violence. First, there was the fundamental divide between the 'touchables' and Untouchables, which operated on the principle of social repulsion. Second, a separation was enacted between Brahmin and non-Brahmin through the principle of 'graded inequality', with the *dvijas*, or twice-born (Brahmins, Kshatriyas), restricting majority access to power and social mobility. Thus, Brahminism was predicated on a history of violence, which was iterative and archaic: the antagonism between castes structured the agonistic politics of caste.

## Existence

When did it become possible to think of an end to, if not a beginning for, the profound inequities of caste?

When we discuss the social fact of Dalit existence as a problem for thought and not merely for social movement activism then we must also address the history of how and in what manner Dalit existence has been problematized. Ambedkar's effort to think through approximation, that is, through affinities between the Dalit condition and the global contexts of dehumanization, was one part of the story. Ambedkar's thinking also reprises the conversation between the abstract and the concrete by asking us to consider the place from where truly creative and expansive thinking can occur. Ambedkar reflects to us the torturous path of doing both. He is trying to think through the conditions of the everyday, and yet his commitment to a stance of liberal proceduralism and a uniformity of policy design means that his own thought carries signs of resistance, gestures that slow us down and ask us to think about the different scales across which he is thinking. (By comparison, his predecessor Jotiba Phule is interested in rich social description, but Ambedkar, while he also provides description, is not limited to it.) We can thereby convoke the social context that will allow situating Ambedkar's thought in its time and place. But thought is not reducible to the context in which it is conceived and expressed; ideas are both within and without history.

It is precisely the 'untimeliness' of Dalit thought that marks it off from history. Take for instance the concept or concept–metaphor of 'Dalit', which was conceived as a weapon for battles in which previous terminology was insufficient. Ambedkar uses *asprushya*, *bahishkrit* and *paddalit* (Marathi adjectives signifying untouchable, ostracized and broken underfoot, respectively), but the noun forms he uses in English are chiefly Depressed Classes and Untouchables. The entry of 'Dalit' into English language debates occurred much after Ambedkar's death, in the early 1970s, when the mainly juridical and political terminology of SCs was unlikely to resonate with the general public. It arrived not so much as nomenclature for marginal classes as an oppositional style that was simultaneously political and literary. The presence of the Marathi word in Anglophone contexts resisted swift classification, warning instead of an epistemic depth brought by relatively unknown interlocutors who were entering arenas they were previously excluded from. The public visibility of the term thus also made the social conditions that lay behind it legible but on the Dalit's terms and not the upper caste's.

This is a simple illustration of how political ideas, names and aspirations can appear to emerge from specific contexts that limit their forms of embodiment and modes of address, or, what might be called 'modes of enfleshment', but on closer examination force us to project a genealogy that is all too often fictive.[60] The delimitation of the scale and scope of an idea in its time appears rather different when its genealogy is scrambled. In this way, the problem of the Dalit as a problem of/for thought also asks us to rethink fundamental categories of social ontology and their relationship to historical time. We have turned to the interrelated issues of person, time and thought in an effort to ask what it means to say that Ambedkar inaugurates Dalit thought as critical thought. Should we say that 'Dalit' as a figuration of equality and equalization therefore has to enfold within itself different temporalities, its untimeliness promising resolution in the unforeseen future?

# AMBEDKAR BEYOND THE CRITIQUE OF INDOLOGY

## SEXUALITY AND FEMINISM IN THE FIELD OF CASTE

### Ritu Sen Chaudhuri

This is an attempt to read B.R. Ambedkar's writings in the context of a debate which begins just a year after his death, without any reference whatsoever to his oeuvre. The essay situates Ambedkar within the 'Indology versus Indian sociology' debate initiated by Louis Dumont in the inaugural volume of *Contributions to Indian Sociology*.[1] Dumont[2] begins his essay, co-authored by David Francis Pocock, saying that 'the first condition for a sound development of a Sociology of India is found in the establishment of a proper relation between it and classical Indology'.[3] They go on to explain the sociological significance of this 'methodological assertion': 'By putting ourselves in the school of Indology, we learn in the first place never to forget that India is *one*.' The credo of 'unity in diversity'—of languages, religions, castes and customs—thus gets grounded in the hegemony of the Hindu Sanskritic tradition (relegating tribal, Islamic and Christian traditions to the ideological periphery). Dumont's confidence in Sanskritic sources, accepting the views of the ancient Brahmin literati (only a minor faction of the elite), and his typically ahistorical approach have been subject to scathing criticism by postcolonial theorists as blatantly orientalist.

Bernard Cohn[4] argues that anthropological discourses in the decade after the Second World War have been shaped by colonial assumptions on the nature of Indian society.[5] In combination with the dominant functionalist framework of the discipline at the time, these assumptions had led to a focus on the centrality of caste and the perception of caste as a 'thing'. For decades together, Dumont's work provided the dominant theoretical framework for the post-war diaspora of fieldworkers. They could compare their observations from the scattered corners of India to ancient Sanskrit texts.

Unlike Dumont, Ambedkar's writings have been rather slow in finding their place in Indian academe. On the one hand, there has been a consistent tendency of overlooking the issue of caste, though for different reasons, both by nationalist and Marxist historiographers. On the other hand, the social sciences, in their ever-increasing research engagements with caste in the last fifty years, following the pathways of G.S. Ghurye and Dumont run through an insidious split between the 'theoretical Brahmins and empirical Sudras'.[6] There has been a regular marginalization of Dalits as a source of sociological knowledge. Silence about Dalit lives corroborates the systemic and institutional neglect of Ambedkar's theorization of caste and the oppressive nature of the Hindu (Brahminical) social order.

The current essay remains animated by three theoretical exercises. First, I try to juxtapose Ambedkar's writings to those of Dumont in terms of certain apparent points of convergence between them. Second, I conceive of how Ambedkar's work interrupts the Indological approach, turning it upside down. Third, following Ambedkar's critique of ancient Indological texts, I attempt to figure out a feminist approach to read the complicity of caste, gender and sexuality. The three theoretical exercises can be weaved together into a fragmentary chronicle of a critique foretold. Critique, unlike criticism, is not always tied to a particular text. Critique remains open to the realm of ideologies and discourses which produce and condition individual texts. Judith Butler's[7] take on the distinction between 'criticism' and 'critique', in a sense, releases the work of 'critique' from the secondariness (both logical and temporal) involved in 'criticism'. Butler holds that '. . . [c]riticism usually takes an object, and critique is concerned to identify the conditions of possibility under which a domain of objects appears'.[8] I talk about the logical foretelling of a critique, of the debate of Indian sociology and Indology, following Ambedkar. Let me begin with my first exercise of putting Dumont next to Ambedkar, following a discourse begun almost five decades earlier.

## Ambedkar, Dumont and Orientalism

In a late 'for a sociology of India' series of articles in *Contributions to Indian Sociology*, Timothy Fitzgerald haughtily asserts '. . . if you accuse Dumont of orientalism you come dangerously close to saying the same about Ambedkar'.[9] Fitzgerald tends to establish his claim in terms of what he calls '. . . a significant overlap between Ambedkar's critique of Hindu orthodoxy and Dumont's academic analysis of it'.[10] I concede that there are certain areas of seeming convergence between Ambedkar and Dumont. What I fail to understand, in Fitzgerald's enquiry, is the requirement for a binary distinction between a purely academic and a politically appealing position. Why should one consider Ambedkar's work, despite being 'worthy of respect as sociological theorising',[11] primarily as political activism?[12] Is it that activism necessarily dilutes sociological theorization? How would Fitzgerald in any way negotiate with the philosophy of praxis or the historical necessity of linking up thought with action? Assuming a narrow meaning of politics, he simply fails to understand the political import of academic writing.

Ambedkar's is a generation before Dumont. The social, political and intellectual contexts of the two thinkers are disparate. Yet, there are certain overlapping nodes between the two schemes of thought. Both Ambedkar and Dumont underscore the centrality of caste and Brahminic domination in the Indian social formation. They conceive of caste as a system and tend to chart out its structural insinuations. Caste, being a system, can only be understood in relation to other castes. Both hold Hindu ideology, untouchability and ritual status–power disjuncture as defining features of the caste system. Orientalism offers both thinkers the 'epistemological template' to articulate their specific positions. Yet, Ambedkar's schema is radically different from that of Dumont.

Ambedkar conceptualizes caste as a graded hierarchical structure, a despicable display of India's pre-colonial Hinduness grounded in the ancient shastras. In his critical analysis of caste, remaining responsive to the means of reproduction of caste both at the level of everyday living and societal structure, Ambedkar reveals the gendered nature of caste dominance. He holds that caste continues only in plural—always in relation to other castes—materializing into a system sustained by endogamy. Dumont's perspective on the caste system, on the other hand, was primarily concerned with the ideology of the caste system, which he considers a state of mind—a system of ideas and values, a formal, comprehensible, rational system. Caste is not a form of stratification but a special form of inequality, based on a single principle: the opposition of pure and impure, whose essence has to be deciphered by sociologists. He identifies hierarchy as the essential value underlying the caste system supported by Hinduism.

Fitzgerald condemns postcolonial theorists, especially Nicholas Dirks, Ronald Inden and Arjun Appadurai, for labelling Dumont as an orientalist. First, postcolonial theorists hold that Dumont reflects India, perpetually, as the colonized 'other' of the West. Second, repudiating the variegated negotiations between caste hierarchy and community involvements,

Dumont imposes a general anthropological significance to Brahminical dominance. Third, this resonates with the colonial conceptualization of caste based on the *Dharmashastras* (the *Manusmriti* being the canonical text), obfuscating the limitations of such textual analysis.

Fitzgerald attempts to salvage Dumont from the charge of orientalism in terms of two assertions. First, Dumont's theorization is not as such involved in the 'mystification of Indian institutions . . . Dumont's theory does not stand or fall only as a theory about India, but as a paradigm for comparative analysis'.[13] Let us recall, at this point, the basic argument of Dumont in *Homo Hierarchicus*.[14] He states that Indians (and, by extension, other non-modern people) are not 'individuals' in the Western sense of the term. Indians are irreversibly embedded in an essentially hierarchical web of obligatory social relations. 'As opposed to modern society, traditional societies, which know nothing of equality and liberty as values,' Dumont continues, 'which know nothing, in short, of the individual, have basically a collective idea of man and our (residual) apperception of man as a social being is the sole link which unites us to them, and is the only angle from which we come to understand them. This apperception is therefore the starting-point of any comparative sociology.'[15]

Dumont's 'paradigm for comparative analysis', thus, in the most unambiguous orientalist terms, pits the oriental 'holistic' other against the occidental 'individualistic' self. *Homo Hierarchicus* is followed by *The Genesis and Triumph of Economic Ideology* (the French title being *Homo Aequalis*), *Essays on Individualism* and *German Ideology: From France to Germany and Back*[16] outlining the growth of European individualist ideologies. In these volumes, amidst other things, Dumont reveals the limitations of the democratic ideology to comprehend the fact that social relationships place practical limits upon the rights of individuals. The two phases of his work reflect his exploration of the social consequences of the opposition between holism and individualism.

Second, Fitzgerald, as we have already seen, holds that there is a close continuity between Dumont's and Ambedkar's theorization. He says that it would be 'inherently problematic' to mark 'Ambedkar's analysis of his own society, though admittedly indebted in some ways to his western education' as orientalist.[17] Fitzgerald seems to be contending that if Ambedkar is not an orientalist then Dumont can never be so. This loose argument reflects Fitzgerald's failure to come up to the charge of orientalism.

Ambedkar is not an orientalist per se in a pejorative sense. This is not because he is analysing his own society. And the possibility of his being an orientalist does not simply flow from his Western education. Before going further into my arguments against Fitzgerald, I would quickly touch upon the extended notion of orientalism worked out by various postcolonial scholars following Edward Said. Fitzgerald seems to have missed it completely. The discourse of orientalism has mutated itself, adapting to the shifting needs of time and space. Edward Said's pioneering work posits orientalism[18] as a set of distorted fixities which the occident since ancient times has discursively levied on its exotic and inferior other, the orient, in order to dominate it. And 'the will to exercise dominant control . . . has . . . discovered a way to . . . rarefy, and wrap itself systematically in the language of truth, discipline, rationality, utilitarian value and knowledge'.[19]

Orientalist discourse being initiated as an instrument of colonial control disseminated far beyond that. As David Ludden observes, by the mid-19th century, orientalism 'became objectified by the ideology of science as a set of factualized statements about a reality that existed and could be known independent of any subjective colonizing will'.[20] Being detached from its colonial anchorage, orientalism could now address contending political commitments. By 1900, Indian nationalists (including Rammohan Roy, Bankim Chandra Chattopadhyay, Rabindranath Tagore, Mohandas Karamchand Gandhi, Jawaharlal Nehru and also Ambedkar, often in disparate terms) assumed orientalist formulations to refute the colonizers. The Indian intelligentsia and the discourse of nation building thus remain tied to the 'English epistemological authority'.[21] Quite in keeping with scientific developments and the shifting equations of world politics, the form and content of orientalism altered, so that it could continue regimenting the course of knowledge production on the East always in relation to the West. It could mark the disciplinary parameters of the social and natural sciences and humanities in India and South Asia. Pervading the fields of academia, orientalism functions as an 'epistemological template' even after the official decolonization of South Asian countries.[22]

Debjani Ganguly points out the real problem underlying Fitzgerald's argument—'there is an unresolved tension in his argument between the conception of orientalism as the ideological counterpart of British colonialism and orientalism as an epistemological template'.[23] Before going deeper into this argument, let me add a note to Ganguly's distinction between orientalism as the 'ideological counterpart' and as an 'epistemological template'. This distinction, far from being a binary opposition, provides us with an analytical tool to grasp the subtle ways in which the hegemonic discourse of orientalism works. The two ends of this distinction can operate in tandem with as well as in opposition to each other. Orientalism is dispersed rather than concerted, represented and performed rather than outwardly controlled, discursive rather than compulsive. It produces subjects rather than being applied by them. As Ganguly argues, 'orientalism constituted the theoretical horizon that enabled Ambedkar to articulate his specific critique of Hindu India.'[24] For example, Ambedkar's critique of the tyrannical Hindu social order resorted to democracy as the instrument of social transformation ensuring equality. The standard Western ideology considering democracy as an ideal form of modern government often presumes a typical tenet of orientalism that the societies of the East, remaining despotic at the very core, are resistant to democratization. If Ambedkar shares this discursive contour he does this to counter both orientalist and Brahminic hegemonies. 'The power of discourse is that it is at once the object of struggle and the tool by which the struggle is conducted.'[25]

Fitzgerald remains unable to appreciate the discursive mediations of orientalism in both Ambedkar's and Dumont's writings. Dumont's purpose is never explicitly colonial. Analysing Dumont's opus in terms of the discourse of orientalism does not undermine the import of his structural analysis of caste.[26] Yet, it permits us to place his contributions within certain key developments in the history of caste studies since colonialism. Dumont has 'resurrected colonial categories and arguments at a time when . . . India's postcolonial struggle to reinvent the nation and the state, and to find a basis for civil society . . . was hardly helped by the rebirth of colonial Orientalism in contemporary Western social science'.[27] Dumont's work provides the theoretical and ideological framework of understanding caste to the post-war regime of developmental and modernization theories.[28]

## Ambedkar and the Inversion of Indology

Dumont has bestowed the sociology of India with the task of staying in convergence with classical Indology, which in turn has given Indian society a unique feature: 'wholeness'. The effort to construct a unified 'sociology for India' is followed by the necessity of outlining the specificity of a discipline with regard to a geopolitical space (which happened to be a colony in the near past). The inherent assumption of this is that India, remaining so removed from the r(w)est of the world, is beyond the reckoning of general sociological theory. 'It was clear that the underlying hypothesis behind Dumont's social anthropology was to limit India to a cultural specificity that could not be reduced to a generic model of universal type, which is of course reserved for Dumont's perception of Europe/West.'[29] Yet it is not clear why Dumont needs to think of this wholeness at all. This totality is essentially a demand of the 'synthetic theory of caste' he has produced.

Partha Chatterjee, in his essay entitled 'Caste and Subaltern Consciousness', calls attention to the point that in *Homo Hierarchicus* Dumont invests much of his endeavour to defend his schema of the totality of caste relations as a system. What Dumont's theory needs is an external force to keep its parts coupled to the whole. And 'the force which holds together the different castes within the whole of the caste system is the ideological force of dharma'.[30] What better than the timeless and spaceless ancient Sanskritic/Brahminical texts and their Indological interpretation, reifying India in its Hinduness, could provide Dumont with this 'force of dharma'? Dumont's theory, Chatterjee continues, is one-sided. It obscures the multiple dimensions of the real which cannot be accommodated within a single, universal ideality called caste. Dipankar Gupta[31] also disproves (the existence of dharma as) the unified ideology of caste. Dumont himself had revised his argument along the same lines. In the preface to the revised English edition[32] of *Homo Hierarchicus*, he observed that '[a]t the most general level what our conclusion means is that hierarchical ideology, like egalitarian ideology, is not perfectly realised in actuality, or, in other terms does not allow direct consciousness of all that it implies'.[33]

Ambedkar develops his theory of caste much before Dumont, on the basis of his critical reading of ancient texts from the standpoint of the Dalit. He inverts the whole discourse of Indology grounded in Brahminical patriarchal hegemony. He marks a paradigmatic shift of perspective, of reading, from the bottom to the top and fractures the purported oneness of India. This has major implications for the epistemological dimensions of both Indology and history. The authoritative narrative of the Sanskritic great tradition which has fixated India into a whole is now burst asunder into multiple narratives unleashing oppressive relationships. 'There is no such thing as a caste: There are always castes . . . while making themselves into a caste, the Brahmins . . . created non-Brahmin caste . . . while closing themselves in they closed others out.'[34] Caste is fissiparous in nature, always operating in relation to other castes, as a system of graded hierarchy continuously foreclosing the options of equality for the other castes. It is curious that the debate on the interfaces of Indology and Indian sociology has never alluded to Ambedkar. Such ignorance and disregard is a symptom of the fact that the institutionalized scholarship on caste effaces the epistemic dimensions of the non-dominant caste and/or Dalit perspectives as inauthentic, non-knowledge.

Ambedkar tries to institute an identity for Dalits that would irrefutably be unlike that of Hindus. Steeped in the 'rational' theories of Western modernity, he seeks solutions to caste discrimination within the promises of democracy. A few points need to be clarified here. (A) The overall discourse of orientalism provides Ambedkar, much like other social reformers of his time, with the 'theoretical horizon' he needed to articulate his critique of the shastras. Recourse to orientalism does not automatically render Ambedkar subservient to the colonial mission. Orientalism as a hegemonic discourse marks the simultaneous operations of repression and production, hierarchy and equality. The ubiquity of orientalist discourse does not imply a dead end. In spite of providing a generic structure of thought orientalism remains open to a constitutive outside which might as well work against the overall structure of colonialism.[35] Ambedkar opens up such possibilities in his understanding of caste. (B) He theorizes a logical continuity between the study of society in India and the modern theories, saving the former from at least two predicaments of orientalist 'othering'—objectification and exoticization. Orientalist discourses objectify India as a homogeneous whole, purportedly unmediated by social and political forces. Orientalism exoticizes India, portraying it as so different from 'this-worldly' Western societies that the research of Indian social formation has to be rooted in ancient texts (prejudiced towards Brahminical supremacy grounded in the sheer purity of their caste)! (C) I read Ambedkar's oeuvre as a moment of questioning this radical separation of understanding Indian society from Western epistemological concerns. He demystifies the question of caste often 'idealized in essentialist nostalgia and domesticated in relation to a newly sheltered private sphere' by thinkers like Ghurye and Gandhi.[36] Ambedkar introduces the caste question into the public realm of democratic discourses. (D) Ambedkar's theorization of caste (origin, operation and systematization in complicity with patriarchy) remains entrenched in a series of negotiations with the dominant discourses of positivism and objectivity abided both by the European caste scholars and their upper-caste nationalist contenders.[37] It is astounding that positivistic epistemology has allowed both groups, while they seek historical 'truth' through the textual analysis of Indological Sanskrit scriptures (entangled in the orientalist concept of the glorious Hindu past), to endorse Brahminical hegemony. (E) Ambedkar's staunch critique of the authenticity of positivistic scholarship paves the way towards an alternative mode of production of historical knowledge.

I would mention two significant moments of this alternative history. First, Ambedkar was nuanced enough to concede the subjective-discursive-political mediations in the production of knowledge. The knowledge emerging from Brahminic subjectivities fails to go beyond their authoritative bias. Almost foretelling (three-quarters of a century earlier) the contentions of feminist standpoint theorists, Ambedkar posits the non-Brahmin subject positions as the authentic entry points to both comprehension and critical questioning about caste-based society.[38] Second, violating the 'canons of historical research', he gives himself the task of retrieving the history of untouchability without adequate evidential data, through 'trained imagination'.[39] Intricately following the Hindu shastras and smritis, Ambedkar often lands up in paradoxes and broken threads. He constructs the missing links of history of caste lying buried in a dead past through 'imagination', 'intuition' and the 'ability to make things up in one's own mind'.[40] He asserts that '[a] thesis would not be unsound merely because in some parts it is based on [a] guess'.[41] The veracity of his account is not actually a significant consideration for us. The political import of his theorization is that he unleashes caste from a reified existence, underlining its constructed nature, historicizing it and making it amenable to change. His opus marks the first academic effort to contrive the annihilation of the caste system through an understanding of its origin.

This brings me to the third section of my paper where I read the Ambedkarian inversion of Indology in terms of his subversive reading of ancient texts. His attempts, although inadvertently, place gender and sexuality at a pivotal point of outlining as well as annihilating the caste system.

## Subverting the Shastras: Structural Connivance of Caste, Gender and Sexuality

Ambedkar himself was not particularly concerned with questions of gender and sexuality. Perhaps he was not even aware of their intersecting points athwart caste. Ambedkar's work, opening up to multiple readings—including those of Dalit feminists—exceeds his authorial intentions. Feminists like Sharmila Rege, Anupama Rao, Gail Omvedt and Kalpana Kannabiran[42]—working on the arguments of Dalit feminist movements (since the 1990s)—have given Ambedkar's articulations a different spin. They have reclaimed Ambedkar to read caste–gender interfaces. Delineating the means of reproduction of caste both at the level of everyday living and societal structure, Ambedkar revealed the gendered nature of caste dominance. What I intend to underscore here is that the substructures of caste cannot be comprehended by the concept of gender alone. One has also to address the question of sexuality. I come to formulate a conceptual structure called the caste–gender–sexuality system[43] to address this issue.

Let me begin with a basic question. How are caste and gender, both as forms of hierarchy, related to each other? One way of relating the two modes of discrimination would be to think of how one mode might add on to the other. Following a simple logic of addition, one can see that the magnitude of oppression over a Dalit woman is more than that over a Dalit man. Another way of responding to the question would be to think of the relatedness of caste and gender in complex ways—sometimes adding up to each other while at times working against one another. One can also see the Dalit man practising sexism against upper-caste women.[44] To look at the structural links between caste and gender one has to think of how the recognition or celebrations of certain modes of sexuality (*anuloma* marriage) and inhibitions against other modes (*pratiloma* marriage) remain operative in the production of caste hierarchies, and also in turn how caste hierarchies reproduce these celebrations and inhibitions. To consider Ambedkar's contribution in these terms would necessitate the historical veracity of certain events. What I am proposing here is that Ambedkar's contribution in understanding the structure of the caste–gender–sexuality system highlights the political to such an extent that at times the question of historical veracity does not appear to be paramount. His description of the structure of caste has to operate for the annihilation of it. Thus, this also raises important questions regarding standpoints in historical and sociological understandings.

Sharmila Rege calls attention to Ambedkar's vindication of 'three operations central to the origin and development of caste . . . intra-group organization of reproduction, violent control of surplus woman's sexuality, and legitimating control practices through ideology'.[45] Let me elaborate upon Rege's points, corroborating them with a few others. First, endogamy establishes the authority of the Brahmin man in terms of the differential treatment of the surplus man and woman.[46] Ambedkar conceives the origin, range and apparatus of caste and its consequences for gender relations in Hindu society in his 1916 paper 'Caste in India: Their Mechanism, Genesis and Development'. '[E]ndogamy is the only characteristic that is peculiar to caste, and if we succeed in showing how endogamy is maintained, we shall practically have proved the genesis and also the mechanism of caste.'[47]

The structural challenge of endogamy, Ambedkar discerns, is to maintain a certain sex ratio within a caste. In this proposal, an elementary crisis arises out of surplus men and women. As Ambedkar observes, '[w]ith the traditional superiority of man . . . [w]oman . . . has been an easy prey to all kinds of iniquitous injunctions.'[48] He identifies three particular customs—sati, enforced widowhood and girl marriage—that resolve the problem of the 'surplus woman' through a cruel control of woman's sexuality. As sati and enforced widowhood were not imposed on the surplus man, he was allowed to remarry. To limit the competition for the consumption of a woman, man was permitted to get his wife from lower marriageable ranks. According to the anuloma marriage rules, Brahmin, Kshatriya and Vaishya men can marry women from their varnas and the remaining lower varnas while Sudra men can marry from only their varna. Sudras marrying upper-caste women is bitterly decried as pratiloma marriage. The impasse of the 'surplus woman' is thus resolved through the structure of endogamy—in terms of sati, enforced widowhood and girl marriage, the prohibition of pratiloma marriage and several other discriminatory practices. This demonstrates how repression of women's sexuality works as a vector of caste oppression.

Second, Ambedkar opens up other angles of the Hindu marriage law, pointing at its curious loopholes. Many forms of marriage substantiating the anuloma and pratiloma rules on the one hand 'are only euphemisms for seduction and rape' of women at large.[49] On the other hand, the sanction of seduction and rape, in terms of recognizing 'thirteen kinds of sons'[50] bred out of such intercourses, logically undermines the very system of varna. Following the *Manusmriti*, stumbling upon Riddle 19, Ambedkar identifies the logical slip. Leaning towards the sanction of seduction and rape, Manu did not disaffiliate the sons thus reproduced. He only changed the law of the child's varna. Sons borne from the permissible range of anuloma marriage achieve *pitra-savarnya* (father's varna). In the other cases the varna of the child is assigned to the *matra-savarnya* (mother's varna). This is a most revolutionary change in at least two ways. Ambedkar himself exposes how the change of the child's varna affects the system itself. '[N]otwithstanding the desire of the Brahmans to make it a closed system . . . [t]here are so many holes . . . in the varna system' to rent it open.[51] This generates possibilities of mobility and always turns caste mixed and composite. These possibilities remain grossly overlooked by caste scholars, including Dumont. I would like to draw attention towards yet another displacement involved in the story. What will be the impact of an increasing number of people identified in matra-savarnya on the varna system? Manu along with his commentators remains silent about this. Ambedkar did not deal with the issue either, which could have dealt an ultimate blow to the varna system.

Third, the entire apparatus—production and reproduction—of caste is based on violence against women. Grounded in his analysis of the *Manusmriti*, Ambedkar authors 'The Rise and Fall of the Hindu Woman: Who Was Responsible for It?'[52] He outlines the ideological, institutional and juridical foundations of caste, endorsing dominance over women, referring to the Brahminical scripture. The verses highlighted by Ambedkar symbolize the traits held by a *pativrata*, the venerated figure of a chaste, truthful and dedicated Hindu wife. In 'The Triumph of Brahmanism' Ambedkar maintained that Manu 'wanted to deprive woman of the freedom she had under the Buddhist regime. Manu was outraged by her license and in putting a stop to it he deprived her of her liberty'.[53] The woman was deprived of property, education and mobility. She was diminished to a piece of possession to be transacted upon. 'A wife was reduced to the level of a slave in the matter of property . . . In other matters woman was reduced by Manu to the same position as the Shudra'.[54]

Some scholars like Lata Mani[55] maintain that the notion that the *Manusmriti* has institutionalized the suppression of women is basically an orientalist edifice. It is directed towards the reformation of the 'barbaric tradition' of the colonized. They also thoroughly contest the authenticity of Ambedkar's idea of conversion of women and Sudras to Buddhism. My endeavour is not to remark on the veracity of Ambedkar's narrative. I do not consider the history of the origin of caste that Ambedkar proposes to be entirely accurate. 'One "fictions" history on the basis of a political reality that makes it true, one "fictions" a politics not yet in existence on the basis of a historical truth.'[56] Liberated from religious dictates, Ambedkar intends to explicate the structure of the caste system. The fulcrum of this structure is gender injustice. His theory has logically placed gender and sexuality at the focal points of both defining and defying the caste system. The caste–gender–sexuality prism helps in comprehending: (i) the causes and consequences of women's oppression and misogyny in Hindu India and (ii) the possibilities of annihilation of caste where 'woman' has been placed as a figure of disruption. Ambedkar signifies the 'paradigmatic moment' when the sacred–religious is transformed into mundane-political, a 'thought experiment' through which a Dalit intellectual theorizes the systemic injustice of the caste society.

Fourth, the caste system implicates both an ideological and institutional production of misogyny. Enquiring into the root of misogyny, Ambedkar condemns the decline of the social status and prestige of women under Brahminism. In 'The Triumph of Brahmanism: Regicide or the Birth of Counter-Revolution', he blatantly questions, 'What did Brahmanism want to achieve by having girls married before they had attained puberty, by denying the widow the right to marry again and by telling her to put herself to death by immolating herself in the funeral pyre of her deceased husband?'[57] Buddhism, for Ambedkar, was a Great Revolution. And Buddhism declined due to the Brahminical counter-revolution. He continues asking, 'Why was the widow, contrary to established practice, prohibited from marrying? Why was she required to lead a life of misery? Why was she disfigured?'[58] He explains '. . . girl marriage, enforced widowhood and Sati had no other purpose than that of supporting the Caste System which Brahmanism was seeking to establish by prohibiting intermarriage [. . .] Thus the superimposition of endogamy over exogamy.'[59]

Fifth, following from the previous four observations, the structural reproduction of caste occurs in a systematic alliance of unfair gender norms and sexual violence. In other words, the caste system is grounded in gender discrimination and sexual violence. The system operates through a complete control over the being-body of the woman, reducing her to a sub-huMan category. One can outline the caste–gender–sexuality system as a birth-related graded hierarchical structure of purity pollution and division of labour manifested in distinct ritual status and style of life. It is grounded in an 'inexorable' law of caste endogamy, working through a misogynistic ensemble of ideological and institutional arrangements, levying inequitable norms and practices on men and women—where women are violated simply 'by having to be women'.

## Trope of the Woman and the Annihilation of Caste

'Annihilation of Caste', the undelivered speech (1936), usually referred to as Ambedkar's utopia, allegedly opens up a field of impossibility. This is a point that Arundhati Roy[60] in her introduction to the piece refuses to agree upon. She rejects Ambedkar's utopianism, rightly reading in his arguments the influence of liberal Western discourses of progress and justice on the one hand and the Bhakti traditions of the anti-caste movement on the other. While accepting Roy's observation I make a plea for the retention of the utopia, which bears an emancipatory potential. Without the sense of utopia, how can one move towards something that is not there? Our language and culture remain mired in the system of caste. 'Caste . . . is a state of mind. The destruction of caste does not therefore mean the destruction of a physical barrier. It means a notional change.'[61] Perhaps a notional or ideological change logically requires a moment of utopia. Releasing utopia both from its derogatory and acclamatory connotations, one has to see it as a play of ideas, thinking something that has never been thought before: the annihilation of caste.

I attempt to read *Annihilation of Caste* from a feminist lens. This is to identify two specific instances where Ambedkar raises the woman question to subvert the logic of caste: first, his argument against the advocates of the chaturvarnya system, and second, his interpretation of intercaste marriage. Ambedkar conceives chaturvarnya as a ridiculous homogenization of the 'four thousand castes, based on birth, to the four Varnas, based on worth'. This is something logically untenable and has to crumble inevitably if not 'enforced by law'.[62] Ambedkar underscores that the advocates of chaturvarnya 'do not seem to have considered what is to happen to women in their system. Are they also to be divided into four classes? Or are they to be allowed to take the status of their husbands? If the status of the woman is to be the consequence of marriage, what becomes of the underlying principle of chaturvarnya, namely that the status of a person should be based upon the worth of that person?'[63] He problematizes the rudimentary logic of chaturvarnya by invoking the figure of the woman. On the one hand, Ambedkar critiques the event of abnegation of woman from the structure of chaturvarnya, while on the other hand he reinscribes woman with a political force. It is a force capable of questioning the very structure that repudiates her. He goes on to follow the logical consequence of applying chaturvarnya, the fourfold varna-based service option, to women. If chaturvarnya is implemented for women, Hindu society has to get accustomed to and accept women brewers and butchers (Sudras) and also women priests (Brahmins) and soldiers (Kshatriyas)! If women, abandoning their 'primordial' duties at home, come out to work in public, how will their sexuality be controlled? If their sexuality cannot be controlled how will the purity of caste be maintained? Ambedkar's critique of chaturvarnya can thus be logically extended to a critique of the gendered division of labour, gender roles and ultimately to the control over women's sexuality.

'[T]he real remedy for breaking caste,' Ambedkar asserts, 'is intermarriage. *Nothing else will serve as the solvent of caste*'[64] (emphasis in original). 'This emphasis on the sexual underpinnings of caste society is important,' as Anupama Rao observes, 'but what is more significant is Ambedkar's acknowledgment of desire between castes.'[65] Caste ideologies never allow intermarriage. Such unions are considered to be against 'nature'. The issue of inter-caste marriage raises the possibility that men and women of different castes might desire each other. Inter-caste marriages are to take place as acts of choice. This contains a liberatory possibility. We have already seen that to check the risk of increasing antagonism in consuming woman, the surplus man is allowed to marry girls from lower-caste ranks. Thus, inter-caste marriage is a prohibition for a few specific groups of people, namely, Sudras and Brahmin women. The question remains, when upper-caste men marry lower-caste women whose desire is being approved? Is it the desire of the man or the woman? Now, if inter-caste marriage is opened up, it would emancipate all women across castes. The annihilation essay (if one may call it so), as it establishes the issue of inter-caste marriage as the real remedy for breaking caste, foregrounds a possibility of emancipation for both upper-caste and Dalit women.

In this essay, I have put together Ambedkar's and Dumont's thoughts in an attempt to read an Ambedkarian critique of Dumont. Beyond the exercise of tracking down the similarity and difference between the two, I have a few specific points to make. Dumont's Indological approach circumscribes India within an orientalist empty time so much so that it remains beyond the grasp of Western sociological theories. Through his critique of Indological texts, remaining open to liberal democratic theories and turning the sacred-religious into the mundane/secular-profane Ambedkar has moved far beyond the narrowness of Dumont's approach. Far ahead of his time, Ambedkar advances a critical theory of caste as if extrapolating a nuanced critique of the conservative theories to be written after his death. While Dumont justifies the continuity of caste, valorizing it as the central organizing principle of Indian society, Ambedkar maps out its predicaments and produces a radical energy to annihilate it. Consistently critiquing the homogenizing principles of caste, Ambedkar reveals its fragmented nature riddled with inherent contradictions. In his attempt to analyse caste, inverting the canonical significance of Indological texts, Ambedkar reveals that the structure of caste is predicated upon gender discrimination and sexual violence. Following Ambedkar's subversive take on the discourse of Indology, I have attempted to formulate a feminist reading of the connivance of caste, gender and sexuality as it works in the social formation of India.

# References

Ambedkar, B. 2002. 'Caste in India: Their Mechanism, Genesis and Development'. In *The Essential Writings of B.R. Ambedkar*, ed. Valerian Rodrigues, pp. 241–62. New Delhi: Oxford University Press.

Ambedkar, B. 2002. 'Annihilation of Caste'. In *The Essential Writings of B.R. Ambedkar*, ed. Valerian Rodrigues, pp. 263–305. New Delhi: Oxford University Press.

Chatterjee, P. 1992. 'Caste and Subaltern Consciousness'. In *Subaltern Studies VI: Writing on Southeast Asian History and Society*, ed. Ranajit Guha, pp. 169–209. New Delhi: Oxford University Press.

Omvedt, G. 1991. *Violence against Women: New Movements and New Theories in India*. New Delhi: Kali for Women.

Tharu, S. and Niranjana, T. 1996. 'Problems for a Contemporary Theory of Gender'. In *Subaltern Studies IX*, eds. Shahid Amin and Dipesh Chakrabarty. New Delhi: Oxford University Press.

# ACKNOWLEDGEMENTS

Over the course of the three years involved in this project, we had immense support from all the contributors. We cannot thank them enough for their support and cooperation throughout the process of making of this book. We also thank the Department of African and African American Studies and the W.E.B. Du Bois Institute of African and African American Research, Hutchins Center, both at Harvard, for their support.

# APPENDIX

## THE STORY OF SCHRÖDINGER'S CAT (1935)

Schrodinger Cat (S–Cat) is a macroscopic metaphor for the microscopic kinematics of quantum states and related operators of for example, Spin ½. The Spin is taking place in two different spaces, 3dim Cartesian, or even better, real Euclidean space, where the actual measurements are occurring in 2 dim complex space, where wave functions of the Spin ½ and operators/observables live.

Spin ½ operators are chosen three $\downarrow$2x2 matrices ( ) that is linear operators on the two-dimensional complex numbers space. Each matrix corresponds to the measurement of the spin in one of three Cartesian directions/coordinates x, y or z in our three-dimensional space. The vectors of the 2 dim complex space are identified with experimentally verified states of the Spin ½ for electron. Whenever spin is measured by any of the Spin ½ operators, it has only 2 values, +1 (spin 'up'; aligning itself with the direction of the magnetic field that measures it) and −1 (spin 'down; anti-aligning itself with that field). This surprising feature is the quantum characteristic of the Spin ½, known as spin quantization. Any set of such two vectors is the base in that space. It is customary in physics to choose the states of the Spin ½ in z direction as the basis denoted by $|\uparrow>$ and $|\downarrow>$. These two vectors are the only eigenvectors of the operator. The only two possibilities that can be realized during the measurement of the Spin ½ in z direction. Any other vector in that space is the linear combination of those two, for instance, states like $|\uparrow> + |\downarrow>$. In fact, the state $|\uparrow> + |\downarrow>$ is the eigenvector of the operator σx, corresponding to the measurement of the spin in x direction. The measurement of spin components is governed by the consequences of the Heisenberg uncertainty relations, that this cannot be measured simultaneously, just as the position and momentum of the particle cannot be measured simultaneously.

Thus 'S-cat is dead and alive' is analogical to saying that the spin is in 'the linear combination of $|\uparrow>$ and $|->$ states', something like $|\uparrow+> + |\downarrow->$, that is, in the state analogous to the state of the operator σx. On the other hand, the state 'S-cat is alive' can be seen as analogous of $|\uparrow>$ and $|->$ - 'S-cat is dead'. To ask whether 'S-cat is alive' OR 'dead', $|\uparrow>$ or $|->$, of S-cat that is in the state 'S-cat is dead AND alive' is like asking for the measurement of the spin in z direction, by the state of the operator $\sigma x$. This cannot be done because of the Heisenberg principle. And it is why we get uncertain statistical results. If instead of this either/or question, we experimentally ask the question: What is the value of the spin in x direction, or metaphorically, is 'S-cat dead AND alive'? We will always get the same certain answer.

# NOTES

## INTRODUCTION

1. Upendra Baxi, 'Emancipation and Justice: Babasaheb Ambedkar's Legacy and Vision', in *Crisis and Change in Contemporary India*, eds. Upendra Baxi and Bhikhu Parekh (New Delhi: Sage, 1995), p. 124.

2. J.V. Pawar, *Ambedkarottar Ambedkari Chalwal, Khand I, 1956–1959* (Mumbai: Asmita Communication, 2002), p. 23.

3. Ambedkar was most impressed by Professor John Dewey, one of the progenitors of the philosophy of pragmatism, which fundamentally contradicted Marxism insofar as it did not think history is science. Any work on pragmatism can explain this contradiction. See, for instance, Darnell Rucker, 'Pragmatism versus Marxism: An Appraisal of John Dewey's Philosophy (review)', *Journal of the History of Philosophy* 16.1 (1978): 133–36.

4. Ambedkar's writings on Marxism never seriously engaged with the basics of Marxism: dialectical materialism, historical materialism and scientific socialism. They either refer to the practice of Marxists or a superficial notion of Marxist theory. His speech, 'Buddha or Karl Marx', wherein he compares them and concludes that the Buddha's path was superior to that of Marx, would also frustrate any serious Marxist. See for further discussion, Anand Teltumbde, *Bridging the Unholy Rift in B.R. Ambedkar, India and Communism* (New Delhi: LeftWord, 2017).

5. Ibid.

6. Eleanor Zelliot, *From Untouchable to Dalit* (New Delhi: Manohar, 1992), p. 137.

7. Jawaharlal Nehru, *The Discovery of India* (Allahabad: Penguin Books, 2004), p. 59.

8. 'Approximately 250 articles (out of 395 articles) were taken either verbatim or with minor changes in phraseology from the 1935 Government of India Act, and the basic principles remained unchanged.' S. Michael Brecher, *Nehru: A Political Biography* (London: Oxford University Press, 1959), p. 421.

9. Ambedkar was desperate to enter the Constituent Assembly but did not have members in the provincial assemblies to get elected. When he managed to get elected from the Khulna–Jessore constituency in East Bengal with the help of

Jogendranath Mandal, his partyman and an influential Dalit leader in undivided
Bengal, the 3 June 1947 Mountbatten Plan would annul his membership. In
such circumstances, the Congress decided to shelve its own plans and get him
elected to the Constituent Assembly before its next session convened. In view
of Ambedkar's tepid relationship with Nehru and Patel, it could only have
been Gandhi, the strategist extraordinaire, to influence this decision.

10. On 2 September 1953 during a debate on the power of the governor in
the Rajya Sabha, he retorted to the charge that he was the architect of the
Constitution, saying, 'My answer is I was a hack. What I was asked to do, I
did much against my will. . . . Sir, my friends tell me that I have made the
Constitution. But I am quite prepared to say that I shall be the first person to
burn it out. I do not want it. It does not suit anybody.' Vasant Moon, ed., *Dr.
Babasaheb Ambedkar: Writings and Speeches* vol. 15 (Mumbai: Government of
Maharashtra, 1989), pp. 860, 862.

11. 'The strategy of the government's Five Year Plans after Independence was
very similar to that of the Bombay Plan's. The first three Five Year Plans had
almost the same sectoral outlay pattern and together they can be described
as a scaled-down version of the Bombay Plan.' See Amal Sanyal, 'The
Curious Case of the Bombay Plan', http://citeseerx.ist.psu.edu/viewdoc/
download?doi=10.1.1.680.334&rep=rep1&type=pdf.

12. Balakrishnan Chandrasekaran, 'B.R. Ambedkar, the Greatest Free Market
Economist of India', https://swarajyamag.com/economics/b-r-ambedkar-the-
greatest-free-market-economist-of-india. See also, 'Ambedkar: The Forgotten
Free Market Economist', https://swarajyamag.com/economy/ambedkar-the-
forgotten-free-market-economist.

13. Credit needs to be given to Eleanor Zelliot (1926–2016) who through her
pioneering researches inspired American scholars to study India. One of
them is Gail Omvedt, who came to India and made it her home. Their
insightful researches have been great inspirations to scholars within and
outside India.

14. 'The changes in the economic foundation lead sooner or later to the
transformation of the whole immense superstructure.' Karl Marx, *A Contribution
to the Critique of Political Economy* (Moscow: Progress Publishers, 1977), https://
www.marxists.org/archive/marx/works/download/Marx_Contribution_to_
the_Critique_of_Political_Economy.pdf.

15. Engels's letter to J. Bloch, from London to Königsberg, written on 21
September 1890. *Historical Materialism (Marx, Engels, Lenin)* (Moscow: Progress
Publishers, 1972), pp. 294–96.

16. In 1938, Ambedkar's Independent Labour Party had played a leading part
along with communists in a massive one-day protest against the Industrial
Dispute Act in 1938. Rajni Kothari, *Caste in Indian Politics* (Hyderabad: Orient
Longman, 2004), p. 48.

17. See Anand Teltumbde, 'Introduction: Bridging the Unholy Rift', in, B.R. Ambedkar, *India and Communism* (New Delhi: LeftWord, 2017), pp. 9–80.

18. S.D. Kapoor, 'B.R. Ambedkar, W.E.B. Du Bois and the Process of Liberation', *Economic and Political Weekly* (27 December 2003): 5344–49.

19. The *Crisis* was founded in 1910 by Du Bois, Oswald Garrison Villard, J. Max Barber, Charles Edward Russell and Kelly Miller and edited by Du Bois.

20. Ibid.

21. Ibid, p. 378.

22. 'The American Experience of B.R. Ambedkar' in *From Untouchable to Dalit*, cited in S.D. Kapoor, 'B.R. Ambedkar, W.E.B. Du Bois and the Process of Liberation', *Economic and Political Weekly* (27 December 2003): 5344.

23. B.R. Ambedkar, 'Slaves and Untouchables', in *Dr. Babasaheb Ambedkar: Writings and Speeches*, vol. 5, ed. Vasant Moon (Mumbai: Government of Maharashtra, 1989), p. 15.

24. Booker T. Washington, *Up from Slavery: An Autobiography* (Cambridge: Riverside Press, 1928), p. 152.

25. W.E.B. Du Bois, 'The Talented Tenth', September 1903, http://teachingamericanhistory.org/library/document/the-talented-tenth.

26. W.E.B. Du Bois, *The Souls of Black Folks* (New York: Oxford University Press, 2007).

27. Cited in S.D. Kapoor, 'B.R. Ambedkar, W.E.B. Du Bois and the Process of Liberation', *Economic and Political Weekly* (27 December 2003): 5344–49.

28. Dhanajay Keer, *Ambedkar: Life and Mission* (Mumbai: Popular Prakashan, 1971), p. 521, with reference to the December 1959 edition of the journal *Mahabodhi*.

29. Vijay Prashad, *The Karma of Brown Folk* (Minneapolis: University of Minnesota Press, 2000), p. 26.

30. S.D. Kapoor, 'B.R. Ambedkar, W.E.B. Du Bois and the Process of Liberation', *Economic and Political Weekly* (27 December 2003): 5344–49.

31. Ibid.

32. Antonio Gramsci, 'Our Marx', in *The Gramsci Reader: Selected Writings 1916–1935*, ed. David Forgacs (New York: New York University Press, 2000), pp. 37–38.

33. Vasant Moon, ed., *Dr. Babasaheb Ambedkar: Writings and Speeches*, vol. 1 (Mumbai: Government of Maharashtra, 1979; reprint, 2014), pp. 205–42.

34. Ibid, p. 240.

35. Cornel West, *The Cornel West Reader* (New York: Basic Civitas Books, 1999), p. 523.

36. Dr Ambedkar's historical speech at Agra, translated by S.R. Darapuri, https://countercurrents.org/2016/08/26/dr-ambedkars-historical-speech-at-agra.

## PART I: AMBEDKAR'S STRUGGLE IN THE GLOBAL PERSPECTIVE

### Chapter 1. Ambedkar and King: The Subjugation of Caste or Race vis-à-vis Colourism

1.  N.H. Louwyck, 'The Dravidians'. *Mankind* 2.1 (1936): 226.
2.  P.T.S. Iyengar, 'Did the Dravidians of India Obtain Their Culture from Aryan Immigrants?' *Anthropos: Revue Internationale d'Ethnologie Et De Linguistique* 9 (1914): 1–15.
3.  Sucharita Sinha Mukherjee, 'Caste: Prehistory to 1200, South, Central and West Asia', in A. Stanton, *Cultural Sociology of the Middle East, Asia, and Africa: An Encyclopedia* (Thousand Oaks, CA: Sage, 2012).
4.  M.V. Chertoprud, E.S. Chertoprud, A. Saravanakumar, T. Thangaradjou and Yuri A. Mazei, 'Macrobenthic Communities of the Vellar Estuary in the Bay of Bengal in Tamil-Nadu in South India', *Oceanology* 53.2 (2013): 200–10.
5.  Ram Sharan Sharma, *Sudras in Ancient India: A Social History of the Lower Order Down to Circa A.D. 600* (New Delhi: Motilal Banarsidass, 1980).
6.  Gil S. Epstein, Dalit Gafni and Erez Siniver, 'Even Education Has Its Limits: Closing the Wage Gap', *Journal of Economic Studies* 42.5 (2015): 908–28.
7.  People's Union for Civil Liberties, 'A Debate on Caste and Race', 2001, http://www.pucl.org/reports/National/2001/debate.htm.
8.  M. Banton, 'The Arena of Racism', *New Community* 22.2 (1996): 350–51.
9.  H. Kitano, *Race Relations* (Englewood Cliffs, NJ: Prentice Hall, 1985).
10. M. Wilson, 'What Difference Could a Revolution Make? Group Work in the New Nicaragua', *Social Work with Groups* 15.2/3 (1992): 301–14.
11. N.K.M. Minor and L. McGauley, 'A Different Approach: Dialogue in Education', *Journal of Teaching in Social Work* 2.1 (1988): 127–40.
12. F. Welsing, *The Cress Theory of Color Confrontation and Racism* (Washington, DC: CR Publishers, 1970).
13. A. Daly, J. Jennings, J. Beckett and B. Leashore, 'Effective Coping Strategies of African Americans', *Social Work* 40.2 (1995): 4048.
14. C. Hyde, 'The Meanings of Whiteness', *Qualitative Sociology* 18.1 (1995): 87–95.
15. M.J. Ravindranath, 'Environmental Education in Teacher Education in India: Experiences and Challenges in the United Nations' Decade of Education for Sustainable Development', *Journal of Education for Teaching: International Research and Pedagogy* 33.2 (2007): 191–206.
16. Lian Kwen Fee, 'The Political and Economic Marginalisation of Tamils in Malaysia', *Asian Studies Review* 26.3 (2002): 309–29.
17. Mary M. Cameron, 'Transformations of Gender and Caste Divisions of Labor in Rural Nepal: Land, Hierarchy, and the Case of Untouchable Women', *Journal of Anthropological Research* 51.3 (1995): 215–46.
18. Ambedkar National Congress, 2016, http://anckarnataka.page.tl/Breif-History-Of-Dr-.-B-.-R-Ambedkar-.-.htm. Retrieved 12 April 2016.

19. Joshua F.J. Inwood, 'Contested Memory in the Birthplace of a King: A Case Study of Auburn Avenue and the Martin Luther King Jr. National Park', *Cultural Geographies* 16.1 (2009): 87–109.

20. Martin Luther King Jr., 'Biography of Martin Luther King Jr.', *Negro History Bulletin* 315. (1968): 3.

21. Teri S. Lesesne, 'The Long and the Short of It All: Nonfiction Books with Flair', review of *Martin's Big Words: The Life of Dr. Martin Luther King, Jr.* by Doreen Rappaport, *Voices From the Middle* 9.4 (2002): 53.

22. Johnny B. Hill, 'Resurrecting King: Re-considering Dr. King's Legacy on the 40th Anniversary of his Assassination', *Fellowship* 74.1–3 (2008): 30, 32–33. Retrieved 12 April 2016, from http://forusa.org/fellowship/2008/spring.

23. John H. Patton, 'A Transforming Response: Martin Luther King Jr.'s "Letter from Birmingham Jail"', *Rhetoric and Public Affairs* 7.1 (2004): 53–65.

24. Mark Vail, 'The "Integrative" Rhetoric of Martin Luther King Jr.'s "I Have a Dream" Speech', *Rhetoric and Public Affairs* 9.1 (2006): 51–78.

25. Martin Luther King, Jr, 'Man of 1963', *Negro History Bulletin* 27.6 (1964): 136–37.

26. M. Sridhar and Alladi Uma, 'Well, Isn't the Well Still the Issue?' *Intersections: Gender, History & Culture in the Asian Context* 34 (2014). http://intersections. anu.edu.au/issue34/sridhar_uma.htm. Retrieved 12 April 2016.

27. Anand Teltumbde, *Mahad: The Making of the First Dalit Revolt* (New Delhi: Aakar Books, 2016).

28. M. Sridhar and Alladi Uma, 'Well, Isn't the Well Still the Issue?' *Intersections: Gender, History & Culture in the Asian Context* 34 (2014), http://intersections. anu.edu.au/issue34/sridhar_uma.htm. Retrieved 12 April 2016.

29. Ibid.

30. B.R. Ambedkar, 'The Revolt of the Untouchables', Round Table India, 2012, http://roundtableindia.co.in/index.php?option=com_content&view= article&id=4834:the-revolt-of-the-untouchables&catid=116:dr-ambedkar& Itemid=128. Retrieved 12 April 2016.

31. Ibid.

32. Anand Teltumbde, *Mahad: The Making of the First Dalit Revolt* (New Delhi: Aakar Books, 2016).

33. B.R. Ambedkar, 'The Revolt of the Untouchables', Round Table India, 2012, http://roundtableindia.co.in/index.php?option=com_content&view= article&id=4834:the-revolt-of-the-untouchables&catid=116:dr-ambedkar& Itemid=128. Retrieved 12 April 2016.

34. Rachel D. Godsil, 'Race Nuisance: The Politics of Law in the Jim Crow Era', *Michigan Law Review* 105.3 (2006): 505–57, http://www.jstor.org/ stable/40041527. Retrieved 12 April 2016.

35. Annie Stopford and Llewellyn Smith, 'Mass Incarceration and the "New Jim Crow": An Interview with Michelle Alexander', *Psychoanalysis, Culture & Society* 19.4 (2014): 379–91.

36. James M. Reinhardt, 'The Negro: Is He a Biological Inferior?' *American Journal of Sociology* 33 (1927): 248–61.

37. W. Glasker, 'The Dred Scott Case', *Choice Reviews Online* (Supplement, August 2001), http://www.cro3.org/content/by/year. Retrieved 13 April 2016.

38. Virginia Historical Society, 'The World of Jim Crow', 2016, http://www.vahistorical.org/collections-and-resources/virginia-history-explorer/civil-rights-movement-virginia/world-jim-crow. Retrieved 12 April 2016.

39. Martin Luther King, Jr, *The Measure of a Man* (Philadelphia, PA: Christian Education Press, 1959).

40. Cynthia Sims and Malar Hirudayaraj, 'The Impact of Colorism on the Career Aspirations and Career Opportunities of Women in India', *Advances in Developing Human Resources* 18.1 (2016): 38.

41. L. Kass, 'The End of Courtship', *Public Interest* 126 (1997): 39–63.

42. A. Urrutia, 'The Development of Black Feminism', *Human Mosaic* 28.1 (1994): 26–35.

43. Tayler J. Mathews and Glenn S. Johnson, 'Skin Complexion in the Twenty-first Century: The Impact of Colorism on African American Women', *Race, Gender and Class* 22.1–2 (2015): 248–74.

44. Margaret Hunter, 'The Persistent Problem of Colorism: Skin Tone, Status, and Inequality', *Sociology Compass* 1.1 (2007): 237–54.

45. P. McIntosh, 'White Privilege: Unpacking the Invisible Knapsack', *Peace and Freedom* (July/August 1989): 10–12.

46. Nyla R. Branscombe, Michael T. Schmitt and Kristin Schiffhauer, 'Racial Attitudes in Response to Thoughts of White Privilege', *European Journal of Social Psychology* 37.2 (2007): 203–15.

47. Tracie L. Stewart, Ioana M. Latu, Nyla R. Branscombe, Nia L. Phillips and H. Ted Denney, 'White Privilege: Awareness and Efficacy to Reduce Racial Inequality Improve White Americans' Attitudes toward African Americans', *Journal of Social Issues* 68.1 (2012): 11–27.

48. K. Kilty and E. Swank, 'Institutional Racism and the Media: Depictions of Violent Criminals and Welfare Recipients', *Sociological Imagination* 34.2–3 (1997): 105–28.

49. J. Makkar and M. Strube, 'Black Women's Self Perception of Attractiveness Following Exposure to White Versus Black Beauty Standards: The Moderating Role of Racial Identity and Self-esteem', *Journal of Applied Social Psychology* 25.17 (1995): 1547–66.

50. J. Bendersky, 'The Disappearance of Blondes: Immigration, Race and the Reemergence of "Thinking White"', *Telos* 104 (1995): 135–57.

51. Rashawn Ray and Jason A. Rosow, 'The Two Different Worlds of Black and White Fraternity Men: Visibility and Accountability as Mechanisms of Privilege', *Journal of Contemporary Ethnography* 41.1 (2012): 66–94.

52. Jennifer Heller, 'Emerging Themes on Aspects of Social Class and the Discourse of White Privilege', *Journal of Intercultural Studies* 31.1 (2010): 111–20.
53. Monika Frejute-Rakauskiene, 'Contemporary Phenomenon of Racism and Its Manifestations in Public Discourse', *Filosofija Sociologija* 4 (2006): 13–19.

## Chapter 2. Can Ambedkar Speak to Africa? Colour, Caste and Class Struggles in Contemporary South Africa

1. Ronnie Kasrils, 'How the ANC's Faustian Pact Sold Out South Africa's Poorest', *Guardian*, 24 June 2013, https://www.theguardian.com/commentisfree/2013/jun/24/anc-faustian-pact-mandela-fatal-error. Retrieved 10 September 2017.
2. Ahmed Areff, 'Rich White Men Made Mandela Turn against the Revolution: Malema', News24, 26 November 2015, http://www.news24.com/SouthAfrica/News/rich-white-men-made-mandela-turn-against-the-revolution-malema-20151126. Accessed 28 September 2016.
3. Patrick Bond, *Elite Transition: From Apartheid to Neoliberalism in South Africa* (Scottsville: University of KwaZulu-Natal Press, 2005), p. 253.
4. Eliane Glaser, 'Bring Back Ideology: Fukuyama's "End of History" 25 Years On', *Guardian*, 21 March 2014, https://www.theguardian.com/books/2014/mar/21/bring-back-ideology-fukuyama-end-history-25-years-on. Retrieved 28 January 2018.
5. Ashwin Desai and Goolam Vahed, 'The Guptas, the Public Protector's Report and Capital Accumulation in South Africa,' *Alternation*, 24.1 (2017): 26–49.
6. Ibid.
7. Isabel Hofmeyr, 'The Idea of "Africa" in Indian Nationalism: Reporting the Diaspora in *The Modern Review* 1907–1929', *South African Historical Journal* 57.1 (2007): 76.
8. Ibid.
9. Kama Maclean and J. Daniel Elam, 'Reading Revolutionaries: Texts, Acts, and the Afterlives of Political Action in Late Colonial South Asia: Who Is a Revolutionary?', *Revolutionary Lives in South Asia: Acts and Afterlives of Anticolonial Political Action*, eds. Kama Maclean and J. Daniel Elam (London: Routledge, 2015), p. 6.
10. Ibid, p. 7.
11. B.R. Ambedkar, *What Congress and Gandhi Have Done to the Untouchables* (Bombay: Thacker, 1946), http://www.ambedkar.org/ambcd/41A.What%20Congress%20and%20Gandhi%20Preface.htm. Retrieved 3 December 2016.
12. Ibid.
13. Ibid.
14. B.R. Ambedkar, 'A Plea to the Foreigner: Let Not Tyranny Have Freedom to Enslave' in *What Congress and Gandhi Have Done to the Untouchables* (Mumbai: Thacker, 1946), http://www.ambedkar.org/ambcd/43.%20A%20Plea%20to%20the%20Foreigner.htm. Retrieved 3 December 2016.

15. Namit Arora, 'Caste Iron', *Caravan*, 1 November 2013, http://www.caravanmagazine.in/perspectives/caste-iron. Accessed 25 September 2013.

16. B.R. Ambedkar, *Annihilation of Caste with a Reply to Mahatma Gandhi*, third edition (1944).

17. Ania Loomba, *Colonialism/Postcolonialism*, second edition (London: Routledge, 2005), p. 196.

18. Ashwin Desai and Goolam Vahed, 'The Natal Indian Congress, the Mass Democratic Movement and the Struggle to Defeat Apartheid: 1980–1994', *Politikon* 42.1 (2015): 1–22.

19. Ibid.

20. John Daniel, 'The Mbeki Presidency: Lusaka Wins', *South African Yearbook of International Affairs, 2001–02* (Johannesburg: South African Institute of International Affairs, 2002), pp. 7–15.

21. Dale McKinley, *The ANC and the Liberation Struggle: A Critical Biography* (London: Pluto Press, 1997), p. 109.

22. Patrick Bond, *Elite Transition: From Apartheid to Neoliberalism in South Africa* (Scottsville: University of KwaZulu-Natal Press, 2005).

23. Katherine Verdery, *The Political Lives of Dead Bodies* (Columbia: Columbia University Press, 1999), p. 5.

24. Sipho Masondo, 'Rhodes Must Fall Campaign Gains Momentum at UCT', *City Press*, 23 March 2015, http://www.news24.com/SouthAfrica/News/Rhodes-Must-Fall-campaign-gains-momentum-at-UCT-20150323. Accessed 1 October 2016.

25. Reported in *Sowetan*, 26 August 2003. Quoted in Patrick Bond, 'US Empire and South African Subimperialism,' in *Socialist Register 2005: The Empire Reloaded*, eds. Leo Panitch and Colin Leys (New York: Monthly Review Press, 2004), p. 227.

26. Naomi Klein, 'Democracy Born in Chains', naomiklein.org, 13 February 2011, http://www.naomiklein.org/articles/2011/02/democracy-born-chains#endnote3. Accessed 9 October 2016.

27. Berkley Center, 'A Discussion with Professor Njabulo S. Ndebele, Chair of the Mandela-Rhodes Foundation', 29 October 2013, https://berkleycenter.georgetown.edu/interviews/a-discussion-with-professor-njabulo-s-ndebele-chair-of-the-mandela-rhodes-foundation. Accessed 7 October 2016.

28. Ibid.

29. Amit Chaudhuri, 'The Real Meaning of Rhodes Must Fall', *Guardian*, 16 March 2016, https://www.theguardian.com/uk-news/2016/mar/16/the-real-meaning-of-rhodes-must-fall. Accessed 7 October 2016.

30. Annit Evans, 'What Is Decolonized Education?' News24, 25 September 2016, http://www.news24.com/SouthAfrica/News/what-is-decolonised-education-20160925. Accessed 3 October 2016.

31. Goolam Vahed and Ashwin Desai, 'Stuck in the Middle? Indians in South Africa's Fading Rainbow', *South Asian Diaspora* 9.2 (2017): 147–62.

32. Ibid.

33. B.R. Ambedkar, 'Buddha or Karl Marx', published posthumously. Available at http://www.ambedkar.org/ambcd/20.Buddha%20or%20Karl%20Marx.htm. Accessed 18 July 2017.

34. Namit Arora, 'Caste Iron', *Caravan*, 1 November 2013, http://www. caravanmagazine.in/perspectives/caste-iron. Accessed 25 September 2013.

35. Anand Teltumbde, *Dalits: Past, Present and Future* (Routledge India, 2017), p. 83.

36. Aishwary Kumar, *Radical Equality: Ambedkar, Gandhi and the Risk of Democracy* (Stanford: Stanford University Press, 2015), p. 8.

37. Achin Vanaik, 'India's Landmark Election', in *Transforming Classes*, eds. Leo Panitch and Greg Albo (London: Merlin Press, 2014), p. 60.

38. Aishwary Kumar, *Radical Equality: Ambedkar, Gandhi and the Risk of Democracy* (Stanford: Stanford University Press, 2015), p. 9.

## Chapter 3. Criminalized Castes: Dalits, African Americans and the Jews of Christian Europe

1. Gary Michael Tartakov, 'Why Compare Dalits and African Americans? They Are Neither Unique Nor Alone', in *Against Stigma: Studies in Caste, Race, and Justice Since Durban,* eds. Balmurli Natrajan and Paul Greenough (Orient Blackswan: Hyderabad, 2009), pp. 95–137.

2. 'Beyond Durban: Caste and Race Dialogues', Symposium, Iowa City, 2002.

3. The 2009 essay, unlike the following section here, is richly documented.

4. Jyotirao Phule, *Gulamgiri*, 1873.

5. Lala Lajpat Rai, *The United States of America; A Hindu's Impressions and a Study* (Kolkata, 1916).

6. See B.R. Ambedkar, *What Congress and Gandhi Have Done to the Untouchables* (1945).

7. See Gerald D. Berreman, 'Caste and Race: Reservations and Affirmations', in *Against Stigma: Studies in Caste, Race, and Justice Since Durban*, eds. Balmurli Natrajan and Paul Greenough (Orient Blackswan: Hyderabad, 2009), pp. 47–77.

8. See Joan P. Mencher, 'The Caste System Upside Down, or, The Not-So-Mysterious East', *Current Anthropology* 15.4 (December 1974), pp. 469–93.

9. See Kathleen E. Gough, 'Caste in a Tanjore Village', in *Aspects of Caste in South India, Ceylon and Northwest Pakistan*, ed. E.R. Leach (Cambridge, 1960), pp. 11–60, 147–48.

10. Quoted in Georges Duby, *The Three Orders: Feudal Society Imagined*, trans. Arthur Goldhammer, foreword by Thomas N. Bisson (Chicago: University of Chicago Press, 1980), p. 13.

11. See https://sourcebooks.fordham.edu/basis/lateran4.asp.

12. This too was demanded in Canon 69 or the Fourth Lateran Council.

13. This is much smaller than either Blacks in the US population (14 per cent) or Dalits in India (17 per cent).

14. The most important acknowledgement of this persecution has been Pope John Paul II's apology in 2000 to the Jewish people and the Vatican Council's 'Nostra Aetate' declaration in 1965.

## Chapter 4. African–American Perspective on Common Struggles: Benefits for African Americans Comparing Their Struggle with Dalit Liberation Efforts

1. There are many writings drawing comparisons between African Americans and Dalits. See Gyanendra Pandey, *A History of Prejudice: Race, Caste and Differences in India and the United States* (2013); Mohan Dass Namishray, *Caste and Race: Comparative Study of B.R. Ambedkar and Martin Luther King* (2003); Arvind Sharma, *Reservation and Affirmative Action: Models of Social Integration in India and the United States* (2005); Laura Dudley Jenkins, 'Race, Caste and Justice: Social Science Categories and Anti-discrimination Policies in India and the United States', *Connecticut Law Review* 36.3 (2004); Clark D. Cunningham, 'After Grutter Things Get Interesting! The American Debate Over Affirmative Action Is Finally Ready for Some Fresh Ideas from Abroad', *Connecticut Law Review* 665 (2004); Smita Narula, 'Equal by Law, Unequal by Caste: The "Untouchable" Condition in Critical Race Perspective, 26 *Wisconsin International Law Journal* (2008): 255; Kevin Brown and Vinay Sitapati, 'Lessons Learned from Comparing the Application of Constitutional and Federal Discrimination Laws to Higher Education Opportunities of African-Americans in the U.S. with Dalits in India', *24 Harvard Blackletter Law Journal* 3 (2008).

2. See Stephen Tuck, *We Ain't What We Ought to Be: The Black Freedom Struggle from Emancipation to Obama* (Belknap Press, 2010), p. 2.

3. Daniel Immerwahr, 'Caste or Colony? Indianizing Race in the United States', *Modern Intellectual History* 4 (2007): 275, 277.

4. *Plessy* vs *Ferguson*, 163 US 537 (1896).

5. Ibid, 559 (Harlan, J. dissenting).

6. Martin Delany, *The Condition, Elevation, Emigration and Destiny of the Colored People of the United States* (1852).

7. W.E.B. Du Bois, 'Three Centuries of Discrimination', *Crisis* 54 (December 1947): 362–63.

8. Nico Slate, *Colored Cosmopolitanism* (Boston: Harvard University Press, 2012), p. 8.

9. Ibid, p. 65.

10. *Crusader*, September 1920. *Crusader* was founded as a Black communist magazine by Cyril Briggs, who had worked for the *Amsterdam News*. It published articles calling for African nationalism and was anti-colonial.

11. Gerald Horne, *The End of Empires: African Empires and India* (Philadelphia: Temple University Press, 2008), p. 45 (citing *The Crusader*, August 1921).

12. Sankaran Krishna, 'Gandhi, Ambedkar, and the Construction of the International', in *Race and Racism in International Relations: Confronting the Global Colour Line*, eds. Alexander Anievas, Nivi Manchanda and Robbie Shilliam (Routledge, 2014), pp. 139, 145.

13. Nico Slate, *Colored Cosmopolitanism* (Boston: Harvard University Press, 2012), p. 124.

14. Daniel Immerwahr, 'Caste or Colony? Indianizing Race in the United States', *Modern Intellectual History* 4 (2007): 282–83.

15. Ibid, pp. 292–93.

16. For Thurman's account of the trip, see Howard Thurman, *With Head and Heart: The Autobiography of Howard Thurman* (University of Michigan, 1979), pp. 103–36.

17. Gerald Horne, *The End of Empires: African Empires and India* (Philadelphia: Temple University Press, 2008), pp. 108–13.

18. Ibid, p. 133.

19. Ibid, p. 109.

20. Benjamin Mays, *Born to Rebel: An Autobiography* (1987), p. 153.

21. Gerald Horne, *The End of Empires: African Empires and India* (Philadelphia: Temple University Press, 2008), p. 109.

22. Daniel Immerwahr, 'Caste or Colony? Indianizing Race in the United States', *Modern Intellectual History* 4 (2007): 277.

23. Jotiba Phule, *Gulamgiri* (1873), p. 1.

24. Ibid.

25. Daniel Immerwahr, 'Caste or Colony? Indianizing Race in the United States', *Modern Intellectual History* 4 (2007): 278.

26. Mohan Dass Namishray, *Caste and Race: Comparative Study of B.R. Ambedkar and Martin Luther King* (2003), p. 71. The Mahars are a sub-caste living primarily in Maharashtra and adjoining states in India. In the early 1980s, they made up about 9 per cent of the population of the state of Maharashtra. They are the largest sub-caste of Dalits in the state.

27. Anand Teltumbde, *Ambedkar and Post-Ambedkar Dalit Movements* (1997).

28. M. Vain Chandola, 'Affirmative Action in India and the United States: The Untouchable and Black Experience', *Indiana International and Comparative Law Review* 3 (1992): 101, 118.

29. B.R. Ambedkar, 'Slaves and Untouchables', *Dr. Babasaheb Ambedkar: Speeches and Writings*, vol. 5, p. 15.

30. Nancy Foner, *In a New Land: A Comparative View of Immigration* (New York: NYU Press, 2005), p. 44.

31. Pratap Kumar Ghosh, *The Constitution of India: How It Has Been Framed* (Kolkata: World Press, 1966), p. 70.

32. D.C. Ahir, *Dr. Ambedkar and the Indian Constitution* (Lucknow: Buddha Vihara, 1973), chapter 3; and B.R. Ambedkar, *States and Minorities: What Are Their Rights and How to Secure Them in the Constitution of Free India* (Mumbai: Thacker and Co., 1947), pp. 14, 33. See also Daniel Immerwahr, 'Caste or Colony? Indianizing Race in the United States', *Modern Intellectual History* 4 (2007): 290.

33. See S.D. Kapoor, 'B.R. Ambedkar, W.E.B Du Bois and the Process of Liberation', *Economic and Political Weekly* 38 (27 December 2003–2 January 2004): 5344–46. These can both be found in *The Papers of W.E.B. Du Bois* (Sanford, N.C.: Microfilming Corporation of America, 1980), reel 58, frames 00467–00468.

34. Letter from W.E.B. Du Bois to Walter White (1 August 1946), in *The Correspondence of W.E.B. Du Bois: Selections, 1944–1963*, ed. Herbert Aptheker (1997), p. 163.

35. J.V. Pawar, *Dalit Panthers: An Authoritative History* (The Marginalised Publication, 2017).

36. Ibid.

37. Deepa S. Reddy, 'The Ethnicity of Caste', *Anthropological Quarterly* 78 (2005): 543, 551. See also Lata Murugkar, *Dalit Panther Movement in Maharashtra: A Sociological Appraisal* (Popular Prakashan, 1991), pp. 190–205; and Manan Desai, 'Caste in Black and White: Dalit Identity and the Translation of African American Literature', *Comparative Literature* 67 (2015): 94, footnote 1.

38. Janet A. Contursi, 'Political Theology: Text and Practice in a Dalit Panther Community', *Journal of Asian Studies* 52.2 (1993): 325–26.

39. Vijay Prashad, 'Afro–Dalits of the Earth, Unite', *African Studies Review* 43 (2000): 189, 197.

40. Dalit Panthers Manifesto, available at http://ir.inflibnet.ac.in:8080/jspui/bitstream/10603/14528/15/15_appendicies.pdf. Accessed 2 April 2018.

41. Ibid.

42. B.S. Chimni, 'Alternative Visions of Just World Order: Six Tales from India', *Harvard International Law Journal* 46 (2005): 389, 394.

43. Center for the Advanced Study of India at the University of Pennsylvania website, available at https://casi.sas.upenn.edu/visiting/prasad.

44. Subhash Gatade, 'Dalit Capitalism: The New Mantra to Move up the Social Ladder through Economical Enterprise', *The Weekend Leader*, 12 September 2012, http://www.theweekendleader.com/Culture/1341/money-beats-manu.html.

45. See Aseem Prakash, *Dalit Capital: State, Markets and Civil Society in Urban India* (Routledge, 2015), p. 3.

46. Centre for Civil Society website, http://ccs.in/people/chandrabhan-prasad; see also Nissim Mannathukkaren, *The Chimera of Dalit Capitalism*, *The Hindu*, 18 July 2013, http://www.thehindu.com/todays-paper/tp-opinion/the-

chimera-of-dalit-capitalism/article4926005.ece (though the author criticizes the embrace by Prasad of capitalism). See also, Milind Kamble stating his inspiration from Black capitalism in the US; Rama Lakshmi, 'New Millionaires Hope to Serve as Role Models for India's Lower Castes', *Washington Post*, 26 March 2011, https://www.washingtonpost.com/world/new-millionaires-emerge-as-role-models-for-indias-lower-castes/2011/04/03/AFesUMfD_story.html?utm_term=.55e91c16302d.

47. Nissim Mannathukkaren, 'The Chimera of Dalit Capitalism', *The Hindu*, 18 July 2013, http://www.thehindu.com/todays-paper/tp-opinion/the-chimera-of-dalit-capitalism/article4926005.ece.

48. Subhash Gatade, 'Dalit Capitalism: The New Mantra to Move Up the Social Ladder through Economical Enterprise', *The Weekend Leader*, 12 September 2012, http://www.theweekendleader.com/Culture/1341/money-beats-manu.html.

49. Rama Lakshmi, 'New Millionaires Hope to Serve as Role Models for India's Lower Castes', *Washington Post*, 26 March 2011, https://www.washingtonpost.com/world/new-millionaires-emerge-as-role-models-for-indias-lower-castes/2011/04/03/AFesUMfD_story.html?utm_term=.55e91c16302d.

50. For a discussion of Professor Brown's experience of this rally and other such experiences in India, see Vidya Bhushan Rawat, *Contesting Marginalisations: Conversations of Ambedkarism and Social Justice* (2017), pp. 263–64; see also Kevin Brown, 'African-Americans within the Context of International Oppression', *Temple International and Comparative Law Journal* 1.17 (2003): 14–15.

51. See BBC World Services, 'India's Dalits Find Allies in Black Lives Matter', 13 November 2015, https://www.bbc.co.uk/programmes/p037yt48.

52. Arthur Schlesinger Jr, *The Disuniting of America* (New York: W.W. Norton and Co., 1991), p. 78.

53. Black family income was also less than Hispanic household income ($47,675). In contrast, White non-Hispanic household income was $65,041 and Asian household income was $81,431. US Census Bureau, 'Income, Poverty, and Health Insurance Cover in the United States: 2016', 12 September 2017, https://www.census.gov/newsroom/press-releases/2017/income-povery.html.

54. US Bureau of Labor Statistics, 'Labor Force Characteristics by Race and Ethnicity, 2016', *BLS Reports*, October 2017, fig.4, https://www.bls.gov/opub/reports/race-and-ethnicity/2016/home.htm.

55. US Census Bureau, 'Poverty Status of People, by Age, Race, and Hispanic Origin: 1959 to 2016', table 3, https://www.census.gov/data/tables/time-series/demo/income-poverty/historical-poverty-people.html.

56. Smita Narula, 'Equal by Law, Unequal by Caste: The Untouchable Condition in Critical Race Perspective', *Wisconsin International Law Journal* 26 (2008): 255, 265.

57. Kyle Rene, '"This Seat's Taken": Affirmative Action Policy at Institutions of Higher Education in the United States and India', *Georgetown Journal of Law and Modern Critical Race Perspective* 3 (2011): 303, 320.

## Chapter 5. Hate Crimes, Crimes of Atrocity and Affirmative Action in India and the US

1. Federal Bureau of Investigation, https://fbi.gov/investigate/civil-rights/hate-crimes. On 23 April 1990, the US Congress passed the Hate Crime Statistics Act. This law required the attorney general to collect data 'about crimes that manifest evidence of prejudice based on race, religion, sexual orientation, or ethnicity'.

2. Framework for Analysis of Atrocity Crimes, United Nations, 2014. http://www.un.org/en/preventgenocide/adviser/pdf/framework%20of%20analysis%20for%20atrocity%20crimes_en.pdf.

3. Garriy Shteynberg, Lisa M. Leslie, Andrew P. Knight and David M. Mayer, 'But Affirmative Action Hurts Us! Race-Related Beliefs Shape Perceptions of White Disadvantage and Policy Unfairness', *Organizational Behavior and Human Decision Processes* 115.1 (2011): 1–12.

4. Christine Tamer, 'Arab Americans, Affirmative Action, and a Quest for Racial Identity', *Texas Journal on Civil Liberties and Civil Rights* 16.1 (2010): 101–28.

5. Roland G. Fryer, Jr, 'An Empirical Analysis of Racial Differences in Police Use of Force', National Bureau of Economic Research Working Paper Series 22,399, July 2016, http://www.nber.org/papers/w22399.pdf.

6. Sheila D. Ards, Samuel Myers and Chanjin Chung, 'The Effects of Sample Selection on Racial Differences in Child Abuse Reporting', *Child Abuse and Neglect: The International Journal* 22.2 (February 1998): 103–126.

7. Samuel L. Myers, Jr, 'Why Are Crime Rates Underreported? What is the Crime Rate? Does It Really Matter?' *Social Science Quarterly* 61.1 (June 1980): 23–43.

8. Ryan D. King, Steven F. Messner and Robert D. Baller, 'Contemporary Hate Crimes, Law Enforcement, and the Legacy of Racial Violence', *American Sociological Review* 74.2 (2009): 291–315.

9. Kevin Sack, 'Court Files Raise Question: Was Dylann Roof Competent to Defend Himself?' *New York Times*, 31 May 2017, https://www.nytimes.com/2017/05/31/us/church-shooting-roof-charleston-hate-crime-.html?_r=0.

10. Christophe Jaffrelot, 'Dr. Ambedkar's Strategies against Untouchability and the Caste System', Indian Institute of Dalit Studies working paper 8.4 (2009).

11. Smriti Sharma, 'Hate Crimes in India: An Economic Analysis of Violence and Atrocities against Scheduled Castes and Scheduled Tribes', February 2013, http://66.223.50.234/asrec/archive/papers/Sharma%20-%20Hate%20crimes%20in%20india.pdf.

12. Chundur is a village in Tenali district of Andhra Pradesh, where, following an altercation between a postgraduate Dalit youth and a Reddy boy in a cinema

theatre, the Reddys organized themselves in large numbers and killed eight Dalits. In order to get rid of evidence, they packed the bodies in gunny bags and dumped them in the Tungabhadra drain and irrigation canal. For a detailed discussion, see Kaplan Cannabin, 'Chundur: On the Road to Justice', *Economic and Political Weekly* 42.39 (29 September–5 October 2007): 3915–16.

13. Badanavalu is a village in Nanjangud taluka, 25 km from Mysore city, where, due to assertive temple entry by Dalits, the headmaster of a school, his son, an engineering graduate, and a clerk of the school were attacked and killed by a mob of twenty-five 'upper caste' Lingayats. For a detailed discussion, see Amrose Pinto, 'Badanvalu: Emerging Dalit Paradigm', *Economic and Political Weekly* 30.15 (15 April 1995): 797–99, and Janaki Nair, 'Badanavalu Killings: Signs for the Dalit Movement of Karnataka', *Economic and Political Weekly* 28.19 (8 May 1993): 912–13.

14. Kambalapalli is a village 40 km north of Chintamani, in Kolar district of Karnataka, where, based on a history of hatred and distrust, the Reddys doused inflammable materials on two houses belonging to the Holeyas (SCs), bolted the door from outside and set it on fire, charring to death seven persons between the ages of twenty-five and seventy. For a detailed discussion, see M. Azadi and S. Rajendran, 'Changing Nature of Caste Conflict', *Economic and Political Weekly* 35.19 (6–12 May 2000): 1610–12.

15. Khairlanji is a village in Bandara district of Maharashtra, where a Mahar (SC) family headed by an educated woman whose three children (two sons and a daughter) went to school and colleges bought a plot of land in Khairlanji next to 'upper-caste' lands. They were attacked by 70 'upper-caste' men and women, 'the boys were ordered to rape their mother and sister; when they refused, their genitals were mutilated and they were lynched. Surekha and Priyanka were gang-raped and beaten to death'. For a detailed discussion, see Arundhati Roy, 'The Doctor and the Saint: An Introduction', in B.R. Ambedkar, *Annihilation of Caste* (New Delhi: Navayana, 2014), pp. 18–20.

16. The plight of Dalit women has been recognized at the UN. The Convention on the Elimination of All Forms of Discrimination against Women (CEDAW), in its concluding comments, rebuked India and called for special attention at 'the ongoing atrocities committed against Dalit women and the culture of impunity for the perpetrators of such atrocities', CEDAW 37th session, 2 February 2007, http://daccessddsny.un.org/doc/UNDOC/GEN/N07/243/98/PDF/N0724398.pdf?OpenElement. Accessed 23 April 2014.

17. Gail Omvedt, 'A Part that Parted', *Outlook*, 20 August 2012, http://www.outlookindia.com/magazine/story/a-part-that-parted/281929. Accessed 11 October 2016.

18. Ibid.

19. Debashis Chakraborty, Shyam Babu, Manashi Chakravorthy. 'Atrocities on Dalits: What the District Level Data Can Say on Society–State Complicity', *Economic and Political Weekly*, 4 (24 November 2006): 2478–81.

20. Based on research conducted by Chandrashekar Aijoor, Vanishree Radhakrishna and Manoranjani for the Centre for the Study of Social Exclusion and Inclusive Policy, Bangalore, and acknowledging the guidance of Professor Japhet Shantappa, B.T. Venkatesh and Sri Venkatesh.

21. The objectives of the PoA Act as laid down in its preamble 'A11, 602n Act to prevent the commission of offenses of atrocities against the members of Scheduled Castes and the Scheduled Tribes, to provide for Special Courts for the trial of such offenses and for the relief and rehabilitation of the victims of such offenses and for matters connected therewith or incidental thereto.'

22. See Section 3 of the PoA Act.

23. Section 3 (1) of the PoA Act.

24. See Section 4 of the PoA Act.

25. See Section 8 of the PoA Act.

26. See Section 14 of the PoA Act.

27. Census 2011, http://censusindia.gov.in/2011-prov-results/indiaatglance.html. Accessed 19 April 2014.

28. Ibid.

29. Based on information provided by family members of victims in a study conducted by the National Law School of India University, Bangalore, and court records in *State* vs *Seethappa and Others*, SC No. 260/2002. The accused persons were acquitted at the trial court, and during appeal before the high court; the case was dismissed in 2015.

30. Data for India: National Crime Records Bureau, http://ncrb.nic.in/ StatPublications/CII/PrevPublications.htm; Smriti Sharma, 'Hate Crimes in India: An Economic Analysis of Violence and Atrocities against Scheduled Castes and Scheduled Tribes', February 2013, http://66.223.50.234/asrec/ archive/papers/Sharma%20-%20Hate%20crimes%20in%20india.pdf; 'Crime in India', National Crime Records Bureau. This data is based on complaints or FIRs filed with the police and not the cases convicted. An FIR is a written document prepared by the police when they receive information about the commission of a 'cognizable' offence from either the victim or by someone on his or her behalf. Debashis Chakraborty, D. Shyam Babu and Manashi Chakravorty, 'Atrocities on Dalits: What the District Level Data Can Say on Society–State Complicity,' *Economic and Political Weekly* 4 (24 November 2006): 2478–81.

31. Employment and Unemployment Situation among Social Groups in India, 2004–05, http://mospi.nic.in/sites/default/files/publication_reports/516_ final.pdf?download=1; Employment and Unemployment Situation among Social Groups in India, July 2009–June 2010, http://mospi.nic.in/sites/default/ files/publication_reports/nss_Report-543.pdf?download=1; Employment and Unemployment Situation among Social Groups in India, July 2011– June 2012, http://mospi.nic.in/sites/default/files/publication_reports/nss_ rep_563_13mar15.pdf?down load=1.

32. Derrick Bell, *Faces at the Bottom of the Well: The Permanence of Racism* (New York: Basic Books, 1992).

## Chapter 6. Ambedkar's Foreign Policy and the Ellipsis of the 'Dalit' from International Activism

1. This chapter is dedicated to the memory of Rajkumar Kamble (1954–2018), who pioneered the Ambedkar-inspired international Dalit movement.
2. L.B. Granger, 'Manhattan and Beyond', *New York Amsterdam News,* 11 September 1954, p. 16.
3. [Barring one exception] Vijay Gaikwad, *Dr Ambedkar's Foreign Policy and Its Relevance* (Mumbai: Vaibhav Prakashan, 1999). The author confesses in his preface that the book does not claim to be a complete research work.
4. Sharmila Rege argues that the emergence of 'counter-publics' in the popular Dalit discourse was to challenge Brahminical patriarchy. She finds 'booklet culture' consisting of humongous booklets produced in vernacular languages, and the music troupe ('gayan party') as authentic interpretations to understand the expression of the body politic. In these mediums too, there is no exemplified version of engaging with foreign policy dossiers and Ambedkar. Sharmila Rege, *Against the Madness of Manu: B.R. Ambedkar's Writings on Brahminical Patriarchy* (New Delhi: Navayana, 2013).
5. B.R. Ambedkar, 'Freedom Versus Freedom', *Dr. Babasaheb Ambedkar: Writings and Speeches*, vol. 1 (Mumbai: Government of Maharashtra, 1979, reprint 2014), p. 322.
6. N. Sivaraj was president of the AISCF. He had experienced the power of working with international allies. Ambedkar had deputed Sivaraj to represent the cause of the Untouchables as a Depressed Classes delegation at the Pacific Relations Committee hosted in Mont Tremblant, Quebec, in December 1942. Sivaraj made the demand for separate settlements in separate villages. The report of the 1942 conference also stated that the Depressed Classes representative desired prior assurance of special protection and opposed the idea of a Constituent Assembly that would undermine their representation. *War and Peace in the Pacific New York* (New York: International Secretariat, Institute of Pacific Relations, 1943), pp. 68–9. Also see N. Sivaraj 'Memoirs of Dr. Ambedkar', in N. Rattu, *Reminiscences and Remembrances of Dr B.R. Ambedkar* (New Delhi: Falcon Books, 1995), pp. 143–45; R. Kshirsagar, *Dalit Movement in India and Its Leaders, 1857–1956* (New Delhi: MD Publications, 1994), pp. 150–51.
7. Eleanor Zelliot, *From Untouchable to Dalit: Essays on the Ambedkar Movement* (New Delhi: Manohar, 1992).
8. Daniel Immerwahr, 'Caste or Colony? Indianizing Race in the United States', *Modern Intellectual History* 4.2 (2007): 278.
9. Ibid.

10. M.J. Akbar, *Nehru: The Making of India* (New York: Viking, 1988); A.B. Kennedy, 'Nehru's Foreign Policy', in *The Oxford Handbook of Indian Foreign Policy*, eds. D. Malone, C.R. Raja and Srinath Raghavan (Oxford: Oxford University Press, 2015), pp. 92–103.

11. 'Dr. B.R. Ambedkar and His Egalitarian Revolution: Social-Political, Religious Activities', in *Dr. Babasaheb Ambedkar: Writings and Speeches*, vol. 17, part 2, eds. H. Narke, N.G. Kamble, M.L. Kasare and A. Godghate (Mumbai: Government of Maharashtra, 2003b [reprint Dr. Ambedkar Foundation 2014]), pp. 310–11.

12. Ibid, p. 308.

13. Ibid, pp. 308–13.

14. 'Resignation Not Due to Illness', in *Dr. Babasaheb Ambedkar: Writings and Speeches*, vol. 17, part 2, eds. H. Narke, N.G. Kamble, M.L. Kasare and A. Godghate (Mumbai: Government of Maharashtra, 2003b), reprint Dr. Ambedkar Foundation 2014, p. 404.

15. Gail Omvedt, *Dalits and the Democratic Revolution: Dr. Ambedkar and the Dalit Movement in Colonial India* (New Delhi: Sage, 1994).

16. Sekhar Bandyopadhyay, 'Transfer of Power and the Crisis of Dalit Politics in India', *Modern Asian Studies* 34.4 (October 2000): 895.

17. Ambedkar was an incomparable intellect in the country and a perfect candidate for the position. He had demonstrated his calibre when he drafted a memorandum in 1947 on behalf of the AISCF that was viewed as a draft Constitution of India. The memorandum consisted of a Preamble, Fundamental Rights, Provisions for the Protection of Minorities, Special Responsibilities Regarding Higher Education and Separate Settlement, and Protection of Scheduled Castes. In spite of this he was excluded from the States Committee of the Constituent Assembly formed in 1947. See B.R. Ambedkar, 'States and Minorities, What are Their Rights and How to Secure Them in the Constitution of Free India', in *Dr. Babasaheb Ambedkar: Writings and Speeches*, vol. 1, ed. Vasant Moon (Mumbai: Government of Maharashtra, 1979 [reprint Dr. Ambedkar Foundation 2014]), Chapter 10.

18. B.R. Ambedkar, 'Communal Deadlock and a Way to Solve It', address delivered at the session of the All India Scheduled Caste Federation held in Bombay on 6 May 1945' in *Dr. Babasaheb Ambedkar: Writings and Speeches*, vol. 1, ed. Vasant Moon (Mumbai: Government of Maharashtra, 1979 [reprint Dr. Ambedkar Foundation 2014]), p. 360.

19. V. Thakur, 'When India Proposed a Casteist Solution to South Africa's Racist Problem', Wire, 4 April 2016, https://thewire.in/27045/exploring-casteism-in-indias-foreign-policy. Accessed 4 April 2016; On the theme of postcolonial Brahminical elitism in international relations, see Krishna Sankaran, 'A Postcolonial Racial/Spatial Order: Gandhi, Ambedkar and the Construction of the International', in *Race and Racism in International Relations: Confronting*

*the Global Colour Line,* eds. Alexander Anievas, Nivi Manchanda and Robbie Shilliam (New York: Routledge, 2015), pp. 139–156.

20. 'Dr. B.R. Ambedkar and His Egalitarian Revolution: Struggle for Human Rights', in *Dr. Babasaheb Ambedkar: Writings and Speeches,* vol. 17, eds. H. Narke, N.G. Kamble, M.L. Kasare and A. Godghate (Mumbai: Government of Maharashtra, 2003 [reprint Dr. Ambedkar Foundation 2014]), p. 396.

21. B.R. Ambedkar, 'Buddha and Karl Marx', in *Dr. Babasaheb Ambedkar: Writings and Speeches* vol. 3, ed. Vasant Moon (Mumbai: Government of Maharashtra, 1992 [reprint: Dr Ambedkar Foundation 2014]), pp. 441–64.

22. 'Dr. B.R. Ambedkar and His Egalitarian Revolution: Struggle for Human Rights', in *Dr. Babasaheb Ambedkar: Writings and Speeches,* vol. 17, eds. H. Narke, N.G. Kamble, M.L. Kasare and A. Godghate (Mumbai: Government of Maharashtra, 2003 [reprint Dr. Ambedkar Foundation 2014]), p. 388.

23. Ambedkar's work on economics, for example, is understood in the context of individual development in relation to national development as a collective.

24. Anand Teltumbde, 'Bridging the Unholy Rift', in B.R. Ambedkar, *India and Communism* (New Delhi: LeftWord Books, 2017).

25. C.A. Selden, 'Prince and Outcast at Dinner in London End Age-Old Barrier', Special Cable to *New York Times,* 30 November 1930, p. 1.

26. 'Dr. B.R. Ambedkar and His Egalitarian Revolution: Struggle for Human Rights', in *Dr. Babasaheb Ambedkar: Writings and Speeches,* vol. 17, part 2, *Dr. Babasaheb Ambedkar: Writings and Speeches,* vol. 17, eds. H. Narke, N.G. Kamble, M.L. Kasare and A. Godghate (Mumbai: Government of Maharashtra, 2003 [reprint: Dr Ambedkar Foundation 2014]), p. 358.

27. N. Sivaraj, while presiding over the iconic All India Conference of the Depressed Classes in 1942, which was a precursor to the AISCF, had assured the gathering that the problem of the Untouchables would be taken to the 'Grand Tribunal of the United Nations'. He was so confident in this endeavour that he affirmed to the conference 'we will receive consideration which has not hitherto been bestowed on [us] by the British Government', referring to the rights granted to the Untouchables. N. Sivaraj, 'Address by the President Rao Bahadur N. Sivaraj', *Report of the Proceedings of the Third Session of the All Indian Depressed Classes Conference, Nagpur, 18 and 19 July 1942* (New Delhi: Gautam Book Centre, 2009), p. 25.

28. B.R. Ambedkar, 'Statement by Dr. B.R. Ambedkar in Parliament in Explanation of his Resignation from the Cabinet, 10 October, 1951', *Dr. Babasaheb Ambedkar: Writings and Speeches,* vol. 14, part 2 (Mumbai: Government of Maharashtra, 1995 [reprint: Dr Ambedkar Foundation 2014]), p. 1320.

29. Ambedkar's Rajya Sabha speech delivered on 2 September 1953.

30. N. Sivaraj, 'Address by the President Rao Bahadur N. Sivaraj', *Report of the Proceedings of the Third Session of the All Indian Depressed Classes Conference, Nagpur, 18 and 19 July 1942* (New Delhi: Gautam Book Centre, 2009), p. 22.

31. B. Pachai, *The International Aspects of the South African Indian Question 1860–1971* (Cape Town: Struik, 1971).

32. Goolam Vahed, 'India and South Africa at the United Nations, 1946–1955', *AlterNation*, Special Edition 15 (2015): 54 –84.

33. 'India, South Africa and the U.N.O.', *Indian News Chronicle*, 25 September 1949, http://www.sacp.org.za/docs/history/dadoo-38.html. Accessed 25 March 2016.

34. 'Statement by Dr. B.R. Ambedkar in Parliament', p. 1320.

35. B.R. Ambedkar, 'An Appeal to Join the Republican Party of India', in *Dr. Babasaheb Ambedkaranchi Samagra Bhashane*, vol. 10, ed. P. Gaikwad (Nagpur: Kshitij Publications, 2016, eighth edition), p. 197.

36. 'Dr. B.R. Ambedkar and His Egalitarian Revolution', in *Dr. Babasaheb Ambedkar: Writings and Speeches*, vol. 17, part 2, eds. H. Narke, N.G. Kamble, M.L. Kasare and A. Godghate (Mumbai: Government of Maharashtra, 2003a [reprint: Dr Ambedkar Foundation 2014]), p. 359.

37. Daniel Immerwahr, 'Caste or Colony? Indianizing Race in the United States', *Modern Intellectual History* 4.2 (2007): 275–301; B.R. Ambedkar, 'Letter from B.R. Ambedkar to W.E.B. Du Bois, ca. July 1946', W.E.B. Du Bois Papers (MS 312), Special Collections and University Archives (University of Massachusetts Amherst Libraries, 2017).

38. W.E.B. Du Bois, 'Letter from W.E.B. Du Bois to B.R. Ambedkar, July 31, 1946', *W.E.B. Du Bois Papers (MS 312)*, Special Collections and University Archives (University of Massachusetts Amherst Libraries), http://credo.library.umass.edu/view/full/mums312-b109-i133. Accessed 21 March 2018.

39. Letter to William Stuart Nelson, 7 April, 1959, Martin Luther King, Jr. Papers Project, Stanford University.

40. Vijay Prashad, 'Afro-Dalits of the Earth, Unite!', *African Studies Review* 43.1 (2000): 189–201.

41. 'Dr. B.R. Ambedkar and His Egalitarian Revolution: Struggle for Human Rights', in *Dr. Babasaheb Ambedkar: Writings and Speeches*, vol. 17, part 2, eds. H. Narke, N.G. Kamble, M.L. Kasare and A. Godghate (Mumbai: Government of Maharashtra, 2003 [reprint: Dr Ambedkar Foundation 2014]), p. 260.

42. Ambedkar, 'Castes in India: Their Mechanism, Genesis and Development'.

43. B.R. Ambedkar, 'Who Were the Shudras? How They Came to be the Fourth Varna in the Indo-Aryan Society', in *Dr. Babasaheb Ambedkar: Writings and Speeches*, vol. 3 (Mumbai: Government of Maharashtra, 1987 [original publication: 1946; reprint, Dr Ambedkar Foundation, 2014]).

44. H.P. Howard, 'The "Negroes" of India', *Crisis,* December 1942, p. 378.

45. L.B. Granger, 'Manhattan and Beyond', *New York Amsterdam News*, 11 September 1954.

46. Ibid.

47. Sekhar Bandyopadhyay, 'Transfer of Power and the Crisis of Dalit Politics in India', p. 900.

48. Ibid, p. 915.

49. Ibid, p. 909.

50. B.R. Ambedkar, 'What Congress and Gandhi Have Done to the Untouchables', in *Dr. Babasaheb Ambedkar: Writings and Speeches*, vol. 9, ed. Vasant Moon (Mumbai: Government of Maharashtra, 1990 [reprint, Dr Ambedkar Foundation, 2014]).

51. B.R. Ambedkar, 'Annihilation of Caste', in *Dr. Babasaheb Ambedkar: Writings and Speeches*, vol. 1, ed. Vasant Moon (Mumbai: Government of Maharashtra, 1979), pp. 41–42.

52. 'Dr. B.R. Ambedkar and His Egalitarian Revolution', in *Dr. Babasaheb Ambedkar: Writings and Speeches*, vol. 17, part 2, eds. H. Narke, N.G. Kamble, M.L. Kasare, A. Godghate (Mumbai: Government of Maharashtra, 2003), p. 395; Ambedkar, 'Statement by Dr. B.R. Ambedkar in Parliament', p. 1321.

53. 'Dr. B.R. Ambedkar and His Egalitarian Revolution', in *Dr. Babasaheb Ambedkar: Writings and Speeches*, vol. 17, part 2, eds. H. Narke, N.G. Kamble, M.L. Kasare, A. Godghate (Mumbai: Government of Maharashtra, 2003), p. 397.

54. B.R. Ambedkar, 'International Situation', in *Dr. Babasaheb Ambedkar: Writings and Speeches*, vol. 15 (Mumbai: Government of Maharashtra, 1997 [reprint: Dr Ambedkar Foundation, 2014]), pp. 874–86, 875–81. In addition, Ambedkar had refused to offer insights on the ailing foreign policy in the later part of his life to the public. In response to a request from Marathi newspapers like *Kesari* and *Maratha*, Ambedkar stated in his letter dated 15 July 1954 that due to the overhauling influence of Nehru on the nation's mind, any opinion contrary to Nehru's was unwelcome as it was 'one man's traffic in public affairs it was very difficult to maintain one's interest in the foreign affairs', 'Dr. B.R. Ambedkar and His Egalitarian Revolution', in *Dr. Babasaheb Ambedkar: Writings and Speeches*, vol. 17, part 2, eds. H. Narke, N.G. Kamble, M.L. Kasare, A. Godghate (Mumbai: Government of Maharashtra, 2003), p. 386.

55. B.R. Ambedkar, *States and Minorities What Are Their Rights and How to Secure Them in the Constitution of Free India*, in *Dr. Babasaheb Ambedkar: Writings and Speeches*, vol. 1, ed. Vasant Moon (Mumbai: Government of Maharashtra, 1979), pp. 381–452.

56. Martin Luther King, Jr had also expressed a similar view about the extension of US technical assistance to India in 1959 to tackle unemployment and India's development growth. King, 'My Trip to India', *Ebony*, July 1959, pp. 84–92.

57. 'Flood Control Use of Atomic Power' in *Dr. Babasaheb Ambedkar: Writings and Speeches*, vol. 17, part 2, eds. H. Narke, N.G. Kamble, M.L. Kasare, A. Godghate (Mumbai: Government of Maharashtra, 2003 [reprint: Dr Ambedkar Foundation, 2014]), pp. 387–88.

58. 'Multi-purpose Development of Damodar Valley, Labor Member's Speech at Calcutta Conference', in *Dr. Babasaheb Ambedkar: Writings and Speeches*,

vol. 10, ed. Vasant Moon (Mumbai: Government of Maharashtra, 1991 [reprint, Dr Ambedkar Foundation, 2014]) p. 289.

59. *Indian News Chronicle.*

60. Eleanor Zelliot, *From Untouchable to Dalit: Essays on the Ambedkar Movement* (New Delhi: Manohar, 1992), p. 84.

61. L.B. Granger, 'Manhattan and Beyond', *New York Amsterdam News*, 11 September 1954. Also see 'Election Manifesto of the Scheduled Castes Federation', in *Dr. Babasaheb Ambedkar: Writings and Speeches*, vol. 17, part 2, eds. H. Narke, N.G. Kamble, M.L. Kasare and A. Godghate (Mumbai: Government of Maharashtra, 2003 [reprint: Dr Ambedkar Foundation, 2014]).

62. 'Dr. Ambedkar Warns Pandit Nehru on "Communist Giant"', *Canberra Times*, 28 August 1954; 'Warning to Nehru', *Armidale Express*, 28 August 1954.

63. Vijay Prashad, 'Afro-Dalits of the Earth, Unite!', *African Studies Review* 43.1 (2000): 189–201; Vijay Prashad, 'Cataracts of Silence: Race on the Edge of Indian Thoughts', in *Claiming Power from Below Dalits and the Subaltern Question in India*, eds. M. Bhagavan and A. Feldhaus (New Delhi: Oxford University Press, 2008), pp. 133–50.

64. 'Dalit Women Fight: Dr Ruth Manorama Speaks on the History of Dalit Women's International Advocacy', YouTube https://www.youtube.com/watch?v=U-_nKGQ9K5Q.

65. 'IDSN application for ECOSOC Status—the longest pending NGO application', http://idsn.org/wp-content/uploads/pdfs/Briefs/IDSN_ECOSOC_Application_Fact_Sheet_October_2014.pdf. Accessed 10 February 2016.

66. D. Mitra, 'Stung by UN Report on Caste Discrimination, India Cries Foul', Wire, 25 March 2016, http://thewire.in/2016/03/25/stung-by-un-report-on-caste-discrimination-india-hits-back-25909. Accessed 30 March 2016.

67. Rita Izsák-Ndiaye, *Report of the Special Rapporteur on Minority Issues*, Human Rights Council, thirty-first session agenda item 3 A/HRC/31/56, 2016.

68. Ambedkar, *States and Minorities*, pp. 382–84.

69. 'We need to become ruling class if we want to form a casteless society', *Bahujan Sanghatak,* New Delhi, 16 November 1998,http://www.ambedkar.org/News/rulingclass.html. Accessed 19 March 2018.

70. Kanshiram mentions the Dalit diaspora in his classic *Chamcha Age: An Era of Stooges* (1982) as another category of stooges who try to use their influence to subjugate to the hegemonic power structures of the Brahminical political parties. Perhaps because of this we can assume that Kanshiram did not initiate any significant steps towards establishing an international anti-caste movement.

71. The list of US-based Ambedkarite organizations is: Ambedkar International Mission, Ambedkar International Center, Ambedkar Association of North America, Ambedkarite Buddhist Association of Texas, Boston Study Group, Ambedkarites International Mission Society, Canada, Ambedkarites

International Co-ordinating Society, British Columbia, Canada, many Ambedkarite Guru Ravidass Organizations in the US and Canada.

72. The first intervention to the United Nations was made by E.V. Chinniah on behalf of the Untouchables to the UN Secretary General U. Thant on 6 December 1968. Chinniah was the editor of *Prajabandhu*, a fortnightly journal started in 1971 and published from Hyderabad. Chinniah authored a Telugu biography of Ambedkar titled *Dr Ambedkar Jeevitha Charitra* and also represented the cause of Dalit rights at the International Conference on Human Rights at Washington. Following his intervention, the second testimony was delivered by Laxmi Berwa to the UN Sub-commission on Human Rights (1982), Bhagwan Das to United Nations Commission on Prevention of Discrimination of Minorities held at Geneva (1983). Laxmi Berwa, 'Globalizing the Dalit Issue', *Dalit International Newsletter* (June 1996): 9.

73. Although increasingly large in number, there is no accurate statistical caste census of Indians living abroad. It is commonly argued that in the post-Mandal era there has been a swift rise in the population of Dalits and OBCs who benefited from the reservation movement and enrolled in higher educational institutions. From the pipeline of Indian IT personnel, many Dalits joined the trade and came into diaspora spaces. However, owing to the lack of organizational reach or discomfort of identifying the self as a Dalit, many have remained in the diaspora closet.

74. Vivek Kumar, 'Dalit Diaspora: Invisible Existence', *Diaspora Studies* 2.1 (2009): 53–74.

75. 'Dr. B.R. Ambedkar and His Egalitarian Revolution: Struggle for Human Rights', in *Dr. Babasaheb Ambedkar: Writings and Speeches*, vol. 17, part 2, eds. H. Narke, N.G. Kamble, M.L. Kasare, A. Godghate (Mumbai: Government of Maharashtra, 2003a [reprint: Dr Ambedkar Foundation 2014]), p. 386.

76. These demands were later published in booklet format entitled 'Mr. Gandhi and the Emancipation of the Untouchables', in *Dr. Babasaheb Ambedkar: Writings and Speeches*, vol. 9, ed. Vasant Moon (Mumbai: Government of Maharashtra, 1990 [reprint: Dr Ambedkar Foundation, 2014, original publication date: 1943]).

77. Ibid, p. 397.

78. N. Slate, 'The Dalit Panthers: Race, Caste, and Black Power in India', in *Black Power, Beyond Borders*, ed. N. Slate (New York: Palgrave Macmillan, 2012), pp. 127–43.

## PART II: AMBEDKAR'S SCHOLARSHIP

## Chapter 7. Ambedkar's Theory of Minority Rights

1. I am grateful to Akeel Bilgrami, Gopal Guru, Mahmood Mamdani, Aditya Nigam, Anand Teltumbde and Suraj Yengde for their comments on an earlier

draft. This paper was presented at a seminar at the Centre for Studies in Social Sciences, Calcutta. I am grateful to those who participated in that very useful discussion.

2.  B.R. Ambedkar, preface of 'Thoughts on Linguistic States', *Dr. Babasaheb Ambedkar: Writings and Speeches*, vol. 1, ed. Vasant Moon (Mumbai: Government of Maharashtra, 1989), pp. 139–40.

3.  Dhananjay Keer, *Dr. Ambedkar: Life and Mission* (Mumbai: Popular Prakashan, 1971), p. 82.

4.  'Mahad yethil dharmasangar wa asprishya vargachi jababdari', *Bahishkrit Bharat*, 20 May 1927, in *Dr. Babasaheb Ambedkar: Writings and Speeches*, vol. 19, pp. 129–40. I am very grateful to Rahul Sarwate for guiding me through these articles in Ambedkar's Marathi journal. As is now widely known from recent events in Maharashtra, Ambedkar visited Bhima-Koregaon in January 1927 to commemorate the heroic achievement of Mahar soldiers belonging to the Company's army in defeating the Peshwa's forces there in 1818.

5.  Anupama Rao, *The Caste Question: Dalits and the Politics of Modern India* (Berkeley: University of California Press, 2009), pp. 118–60.

6.  Statement submitted by Ambedkar on behalf of the Bahishkrit Hitakarini Sabha to the Indian Statutory Commission, 29 May 1928 (hereafter 'Statement'), *Dr. Babasaheb Ambedkar: Writings and Speeches*, vol. 2, eds. Vasant Moon and Hari Narke, (Mumbai: Government of Maharashtra, 2005), pp. 439–40.

7.  Statement, *Dr. Babasaheb Ambedkar: Writings and Speeches*, vol. 2 (Mumbai: Government of Maharashtra, 2005), p. 441.

8.  Ibid.

9.  Evidence of Ambedkar before the Indian Statutory Commission on 23 October 1928 (hereafter 'Evidence'), *Dr. Babasaheb Ambedkar: Writings and Speeches*, vol. 2 (Mumbai: Government of Maharashtra, 2005), p. 465.

10. Ibid, p. 471. When asked about the criminal tribes, Ambedkar admitted that there might be some reservations about granting voting rights to all members of that community, but he had no doubts that the aboriginal tribes should have adult franchise.

11. Ibid, pp. 476–7.

12. Ibid, p. 472.

13. Statement, *Dr. Babasaheb Ambedkar: Writings and Speeches*, vol. 2 (Mumbai: Government of Maharashtra, 2005), p. 437.

14. Evidence, *Dr. Babasaheb Ambedkar: Writings and Speeches*, vol. 2 (Mumbai: Government of Maharashtra, 2005), p. 471.

15. Ibid, pp. 478–9.

16. Statement, *Dr. Babasaheb Ambedkar: Writings and Speeches*, vol. 2 (Mumbai: Government of Maharashtra, 2005), pp. 442–46.

17. Ibid, p. 442.

18. Evidence, *Dr. Babasaheb Ambedkar: Writings and Speeches*, vol. 2 (Mumbai: Government of Maharashtra, 2005), pp. 468-69.
19. Ibid, p. 476.
20. 'Dr. Ambedkar at the Round Table Conferences' (hereafter RTC), Plenary Session, 20 November 1930, *Dr. Babasaheb Ambedkar: Writings and Speeches*, vol. 2 (Mumbai: Government of Maharashtra, 2005), p. 505.
21. RTC, 20 November 1930, *Dr. Babasaheb Ambedkar: Writings and Speeches*, vol. 2 (Mumbai: Government of Maharashtra, 2005), p. 506.
22. RTC, 'A Scheme of Political Safeguards for the Protection of the Depressed Classes in the Future Constitution of a Self-governing India', Appendix to Report of Subcommittee No. III (Minorities) submitted by Ambedkar and Rao Bahadur R. Srinivasan, *Dr. Babasaheb Ambedkar: Writings and Speeches*, vol. 2 (Mumbai: Government of Maharashtra, 2005), p. 546.
23. RTC, Subcommittee No. III (Minorities), 31 December 1930, *Dr. Babasaheb Ambedkar: Writings and Speeches*, vol. 2 (Mumbai: Government of Maharashtra, 2005), p. 532.
24. RTC, Subcommittee No. III (Minorities), 16 January 1931, *Dr. Babasaheb Ambedkar: Writings and Speeches*, vol. 2 (Mumbai: Government of Maharashtra, 2005), pp. 538–40.
25. RTC, Plenary Session (General Review), 19 January 1931, *Dr. Babasaheb Ambedkar: Writings and Speeches*, vol. 2 (Mumbai: Government of Maharashtra, 2005), p. 597.
26. RTC, Federal Structure Committee, 16 September 1931, *Dr. Babasaheb Ambedkar: Writings and Speeches*, vol. 2 (Mumbai: Government of Maharashtra, 2005), pp. 602–11.
27. RTC, Federal Structure Committee, 22 October 1931, *Dr. Babasaheb Ambedkar: Writings and Speeches*, vol. 2 (Mumbai: Government of Maharashtra, 2005), pp. 635–48.
28. For the full exchange, see RTC, Minorities Committee, 8 October 1931, *Dr. Babasaheb Ambedkar: Writings and Speeches*, vol. 2 (Mumbai: Government of Maharashtra, 2005), pp. 659–63.
29. B.R. Ambedkar, *Thoughts on Pakistan* (Mumbai: Thacker, 1941), pp. 337–9.
30. Ibid, pp. 4–5.
31. Ibid, p. 338.
32. Ibid, p. 99.
33. Ibid, p. 100.
34. Ibid, pp. 101–02.
35. Faisal Devji, *Muslim Zion: Pakistan as a Political Idea* (Cambridge, Massachusetts: Harvard University Press, 2013), pp. 166–200; Venkat Dhulipala, *Creating a New Medina: State Power, Islam, and the Quest for Pakistan in Late Colonial North India* (New Delhi: Cambridge University Press, 2015), pp. 120–93.

36. I have discussed Ambedkar's analysis of the Pakistan demand in Partha Chatterjee, *The Politics of the Governed: Reflections on Popular Politics in Most of the World* (New York: Columbia University Press, 2004), pp. 4–20.

37. B.R. Ambedkar, *Pakistan or the Partition of India* (Mumbai: Thacker, 1945).

38. *Pakistan or the Partition of India,* reprinted in *Dr. Babasaheb Ambedkar: Writings and Speeches*, vol. 8, ed. Vasant Moon (Mumbai: Government of Maharashtra, 1990), p. 365.

39. Ibid, p. 354.

40. Ibid, p. 367.

41. Ibid, pp. 396–403.

42. Ibid, pp. 371–72.

43. Ibid, pp. 379–80.

44. B.R. Ambedkar, 'States and Minorities: What Are Their Rights and How to Secure Them in the Constitution of Free India' in *Dr. Babasaheb Ambedkar: Writings and Speeches*, vol. 1, pp. 381–449.

45. Ibid, pp. 392–94.

46. Ibid, pp. 396–97.

47. Ibid, p. 398.

48. Ibid, p. 413.

49. Ibid.

50. 'Pakistan or the Partition of India', reprinted in *Dr. Babasaheb Ambedkar: Writings and Speeches*, vol. 8, ed. Vasant Moon (Mumbai: Government of Maharashtra, 1990), pp. 352–8.

51. B.R. Ambedkar, 'States and Minorities: What Are Their Rights and How to Secure Them in the Constitution of Free India', *Dr. Babasaheb Ambedkar: Writings and Speeches*, vol. 1, pp. 421–22.

52. Ibid, p. 424.

53. Ibid, pp. 425–26.

54. Ibid, pp. 396–27.

55. Ibid, pp. 412.

56. Aishwary Kumar, *Radical Equality: Ambedkar, Gandhi, and the Risk of Democracy* (Stanford: Stanford University Press, 2015).

57. B.R. Ambedkar, 'Preface', *Thoughts on Linguistic States* in Vasant Moon, ed., *Dr. Babasaheb Ambedkar: Writings and Speeches*, vol. 1 (Mumbai: Government of Maharashtra, 1989), p. 169.

58. Ibid, p. 169.

59. Ibid, pp. 167–68.

60. B.R. Ambedkar, 'Communal Deadlock and a Way to Solve It', *Dr. Babasaheb Ambedkar: Writings and Speeches*, vol. 1 (Mumbai: Government of Maharashtra, 1989), p. 374. Ambedkar identified this as one of the desirable outcomes that could be expected from a proper distribution of reserved seats for minorities in the legislature.

61. Prime Minister's High Level Committee (Chair: Rajinder Sachar), *Social, Economic and Educational Status of the Muslim Community of India: A Report* (New Delhi: Ministry of Minority Affairs, Government of India, 2006).

## Chapter 8. Lawyering as Politics: The Legal Practice of Dr Ambedkar, Bar at Law

1. Early versions of this paper were presented at Columbia University and the Nehru Memorial Museum and Library. I am grateful to the Ambedkar International Conference for giving me an opportunity to expand this paper and to Jun Yan Chua for helping me locate some of these materials. I am grateful to the editors and Sandipto Dasgupta, Sudhir Krishnaswamy, Sukhadeo Thorat and Anupama Rao for their comments.

2. Dr Ambedkar, Addressing a Session of Political Scientists Parliament at Jalandhar, 15 October 1956, as cited in Nanak Chand Rattu, ed., *Reminiscences and Remembrances of Dr Ambedkar* (New Delhi: Samyak Prakash, 2017), p. 79.

3. 'Dr Ambedkar as I Knew Him', Nanak Chand Rattu, ed., *Reminiscences and Remembrances of Dr Ambedkar* (Falcon, 1995), p. 146.

4. Ibid.

5. He was offered the position of a district judge in 1923 with a promise of promotion to high court in three years. He was again invited to be a high court judge in 1942. 'Speech by Dr Ambedkar at the AISCF Rally at Jullunder, 1951', Nanak Chand Rattu, ed., *Reminiscences and Remembrances of Dr Ambedkar* (New Delhi: Samyak Prakash, 2017), p. 77.

6. Vijay B. Gaikwad, ed., *Court Cases Argued by Dr. Babasaheb Ambedkar* (Thane: Vaibhav Prakashan, 2012).

7. Mithi Mukherjee, *India in the Shadows of Empire: A Legal and Political History, 1774–1950* (New Delhi: Oxford University Press, 2010).

8. Samuel Schmittenher, 'A Sketch of the Development of the Legal Profession in India', *Law and Society Review* 3.2/3, Special Issue Devoted to Lawyers in Developing Societies with Particular Reference to India (November 1968– February 1969): 337–82.

9. A.G. Noorani, *Indian Political Trials, 1757–1947* (Oxford: Oxford University Press, 2005); Julia Stephens, 'The Politics of Muslim Rage: Secular Law and Religious Sentiment in Late Colonial India', *History Workshop Journal* 77.1 (2013): 45–64; A.G. Noorani, *The Trial of Bhagat Singh: Politics of Justice* (Konark Publishers, 1996).

10. While Jawaharlal Nehru did qualify at the bar, he appeared in only a handful of cases in the early part of his career and once in the INA trial of 1945.

11. The majority of presidents of the Congress party and the Muslim League had their roots in the legal profession.

12. 'Speech by Dr Ambedkar at the AISCF Rally at Jullunder, 1951', Nanak Chand Rattu, ed., *Reminiscences and Remembrances of Dr Ambedkar* (New Delhi: Samyak Prakash, 2017), p. 77.

13. 'Ambedkar's Connection with Hyderabad Recalled', *The Hindu*, 20 January 2015, http://www.thehindu.com/news/cities/Hyderabad/ambedkars-connection-with-hyderabad-recalled/article6783123.ece.

14. P.C. Ray, *The Life and Times of C.R. Das* (Calcutta: Oxford University Press, 1927), p. 16.

15. Rohit De, 'The Legal Career of Mr Jinnah', 1 November 2010, http://blog.mylaw.net/a-brilliant-advocate-man-of-unimpeachable-integrity. Accessed 5 June 2017.

16. Charles di Salvio, *The Man before the Mahatma: M.K. Gandhi, Attorney at Law* (New Delhi: Random House India, 2012); Arvind Narrain, 'My Experiments with Law: Gandhi's Exploration of Law's Potential', *NUJS Law Review* 6 (2013): 273.

17. Dhananjay Keer, *Dr. Ambedkar: His Life and Mission*, fourth edition (Mumbai: Popular Prakashan, 2009), p. 51.

18. *Times of India*, 'Rash Speculation: Insolvent's Discharge Refused', 9 January 1929, p.17.

19. The increasing body of work on African–American and women lawyers in the US confirms this. See, for instance, Karen M. Tani, 'Portia's Deal', *Chicago-Kent Law Review* 87 (2012) on women lawyers, and Kenneth Mack, *Representing the Race: The Creation of the Civil Rights Lawyer* (Harvard University Press, 2012). Cornelia Sorabji, India's first female barrister, finally found employment with the government-run Court of Wards.

20. Dr Ambedkar, *Bahishkrit Bharat*, 3 February 1928.

21. Mitra Sharafi makes the case for linking professional and ethnic identities. Mitra Sharafi, 'A New History of Colonial Lawyering: Likhovski and Legal Identities in the British Empire', *Law & Social Inquiry* 32.4 (2007): 1059–94.

22. *Times of India*, 'Inciting Hatred against the Government', 22 November 1927.

23. *Emperor* vs *Philip Spratt*, 30, *Bombay Law Reporter* 315, 1928.

24. *Times of India*, 'No Intention of Attacking British Rule', 23 November 1927.

25. *Times of India*, 'Bail Application: Spratt's Trial Next Session', 27 September 1927, p. 9; *Times of India*, 'Mr Spratt's Acquittal', 25 November 1927.

26. *Times of India*, 'Philip Spratt Acquitted', 25 November 1927.

27. There is considerable writing on the subject, but see Gail Omvedt, 'Non-Brahmans and Communists in Bombay', *Economic and Political Weekly* 8.16 (21 April 1973), and Anupama Rao, 'Stigma and Labour: Remembering Dalit Marxism', *India Seminar,* May 2012, http://www.india-seminar.com/2012/633/633_anupama_rao.htm.

28. *Times of India*, 'Did the Accused Intend to Bring About a Countrywide Strike', 5 October 1934, p. 11.

29. *Times of India*, 'Strike Secretary as Witness', 23 August 1934.

30. *Times of India*, 'Alleged Instigation of an Intended Strike', 28 August 1935.

31. *Times of India*, 'Trade Disputes Act Case', 27 August 1935.

32. *Emperor* vs *A.A. Alwe*, Criminal Appeal No. 592 of 1934, Bombay High Court, (1935) 37 BOMLR 892.

33. *Times of India*, 'Labour Agitator's Appeal Lost', 7 August 1934.

34. *Times of India*, 'Alleged Torture of Witness', 25 June 1931.

35. Anupama Rao, *The Caste Question: Dalits and the Politics of Modern India* (Berkeley: UC Berkeley Press, 2009).

36. Letter from Dr Ambedkar to Martand Vaidya, 24 January 1928. Surinder Ajnat, ed., *Letters of Ambedkar* (Jalandhar: Bheem Patrika Publications, 1993).

37. Civil liberty organizations such as the American Civil Liberties Union and the Haldane Society in the UK had been set up recently.

38. *Times of India*, '*Barashankar Prabhashankar* vs *Naraindas Janakidas and Another*', 9 April 1929.

39. *Times of India*, Letter to the editor by S.N. Dabholkar, 20 November 1929.

40. *Times of India*, 'Temple Entry in Bombay: Leaders Call for Direction Act', 15 November 1929.

41. *Times of India*, 'Untouchables at Free Fight at Bombay Temple Gates: Fight at Temple, Untouchables Beaten', 24 March 1930.

42. *Times of India*, 'Leading Bombay Temple Open to Untouchables', 26 September 1932.

43. *Janardhan Govind Gore* vs *Attorney General of Bombay*, Suit No. 510 of 1938, decided on 6 December 1938, in Vijay B. Gaikwad, ed., *Court Cases Argued by Dr. Babasaheb Ambedkar* (Thane: Vaibhav Prakashan, 2012), pp. 96–102.

44. Ibid.

45. 'A Scheme of Political Safeguards for the Protection of the Depressed Classes in the Future Constitution of a Self-governing India', Dr B.R Ambedkar and Rao Bahadur R. Srinivasan, IOR/Q/RTC/24, India Office Records, British Library, London.

46. *Times of India*, 'Circulation of Alleged Obscene Literature: Charge against Professor', 21 March 1934.

47. *Times of India*, 'Prof Karve's Fine Upheld', 14 August 1934.

48. Harish Narke, ed., *Speeches and Writings of Dr. Ambedkar*, vol. 2, second edition (New Delhi: Dr Ambedkar Foundation, 2014), p. 263.

49. *Emperor* vs *Saveur Manuel Dantes*, Vijay B. Gaikwad, ed., *Court Cases Argued by Dr. Babasaheb Ambedkar* (Thane: Vaibhav Prakashan, 2012), pp. 130–36.

50. Ambedkar himself had opposed the government's prohibition policy since the 1920s, as he correctly identified that the heavy taxation and restrictions were fuelling an illicit market in liquor. Salim Yusufji, ed., *Ambedkar: The Attendant Details* (New Delhi: Navayana, 2017), p. 54.

51. See Rohit De, *A People's Constitution: Law and Everyday Life in the Indian Republic* (Princeton University Press, 2018).

52. Ibid.

53. *Emperor* vs *Vithalba Sukha*, Criminal Case No. 16 of 1928 (First Criminal Sessions 1928), Vijay B. Gaikwad, ed., *Court Cases Argued by Dr. Babasaheb Ambedkar* (Thane: Vaibhav Prakashan, 2012), pp. 23–25.

54. Vijay B. Gaikwad, ed., *Court Cases Argued by Dr. Babasaheb Ambedkar* (Thane: Vaibhav Prakashan, 2012). Gaikwad's collection is the first of its kind and a remarkable resource, yet has some errors such as the inclusion of cases fought by S.K. Ambedkar.

55. Most cases of workmen's compensation were decided by the commissioner of workmen whose decisions were not reported. Only appeals from this body to the high court are extant. For instance, *Ahmedabad Cotton CoI* vs *Bai Budhian Rajaram*, First Appeal No. 162 of 1926, Decided on 17 December 1926, Vijay B. Gaikwad, ed., *Court Cases Argued by Dr. Babasaheb Ambedkar* (Thane: Vaibhav Prakashan, 2012), pp. 6–7.

56. *Times of India*, 'Charge of Criminal Trespass: Strikers Fined', 5 September 1935.

57. See, for instance, *Times of India*, 'Death Sentence Confirmed: Murder of Villager in Bijapur District', 24 April 1937; *Times of India*, 'Death Sentence Confirmed: Murder of Brothers', 29 June 1938; *Times of India*, 'Murder of Inamdar: Death Sentence Confirmed', 19 August 1938; *Narayan Ramchand Jarag* vs *Emperor*, Criminal Appeal 196 of 1947, Vijay B. Gaikwad, ed., *Court Cases Argued by Dr. Babasaheb Ambedkar* (Thane: Vaibhav Prakashan, 2012).

58. *Times of India*, 18 September 1926; *Times of India*, 24 April 1937; *Times of India*, 29 June 1938.

59. *Times of India*, 'Abolish Death Penalty', 4 June 1949.

60. Dhananjay Keer, *Dr. Ambedkar: His Life and Mission*, fourth edition (Mumbai: Popular Prakashan, 2009), p. 67.

61. Salim Yusufji, ed., *Ambedkar: The Attendant Details* (New Delhi: Navayana, 2017), p. 94.

62. I am grateful to Suraj Yengde for bringing this to my attention.

63. Dhananjay Keer, *Dr. Ambedkar: His Life and Mission*, fourth edition (Mumbai: Popular Prakashan, 2009), p. 450.

64. *State of Bihar* vs *Shri Kameshwar Singh*, AIR 1952 SC 252.

65. *Shankari Prasad Singh Deo* vs *Union of India*, 1952 SCR 89.

66. For a survey, see Granville Austin, *Working a Democratic Constitution: The History of the Indian Experience* (New Delhi: Oxford University Press, 2003); Sudhir Krishnaswamy, *Democracy and Constitutionalism in India: A Study of the Basic Structure Doctrine* (New Delhi: Oxford University Press, 2011).

67. *Maneka Gandhi* vs *Union of India*, 1978 SCR (2) 621; *Manoj Mate*, 'The Origins of Due Process in India: The Role of Borrowing in Personal Liberty and Preventive Detention Cases', *Berkeley Journal of International Law* 28.216 (2010).

68. Ambedkar, 'Notes on Acts and Laws', https://archive.org/stream/Ambedkar_CompleteWorks/52C1.%20Notes%20on%20Acts%20and%20Laws%20PART%20III_djvu.txt. Accessed 10 July 2017.

69. Dhananjay Keer, *Dr. Ambedkar: His Life and Mission*, fourth edition (Mumbai: Popular Prakashan, 2009), p. 449.
70. Kenneth Mack, *Representing the Race: The Creation of the Civil Rights Lawyer* (Cambridge, MA: Harvard University Press, 2012).
71. Pratap Bhanu Mehta, 'What is Constitutional Morality?', *Seminar* 615 (2010): 17–22; Andre Béteille, 'Constitutional Morality, Economic and Political Weekly 43.40 (4 October 2008): 35–42. The idea was operationalized by the Delhi High Court in its judgement decriminalizing sodomy in the Naz Foundation Case.
72. Ibid.

## PART III: AMBEDKAR'S REVOLUTION

## Chapter 9. Three Moments in the Annihilation of Caste: Marx, Weber, Ambedkar

1. This is a revised version of the paper presented at the Preconference Session on 'Caste in Modern India', Annual Meetings of South Asian Studies, University of Wisconsin, Madison, 2016. My thanks to Uday Chandra, organizer of the Preconference, for inviting me to present the paper and to other presenters and participants for their comments. Special thanks to Frehiwot Tesfaye for patiently listening to and providing critical feedback. The responsibility for the views is entirely mine.
2. Karl Marx, 'The Future Results of the British Rule in India', in *The First Indian War of Independence 1857–1859*, Karl Marx and Friedrich Engels (Moscow: Progress Publishers, 1978).
3. Ibid, p. 32.
4. Max Weber, *The Religion of India: The Sociology of Hinduism and Buddhism*, trans. Hans H. Gerth and Don Martindale (New York: The Free Press, 1958), p. 30.
5. B.R. Ambedkar, *Annihilation of Caste*, Introduction by Arundhati Roy (London, New York: Verso, 2014).
6. Hira Singh, *Colonial Hegemony and Popular Resistance: Princes, Peasants, and Paramount Power* (New Delhi: Sage, 1998).
7. P.C. Joshi, ed., *Rebellion 1857: A Symposium* (New Delhi: Peoples Publishing House, 1957).
8. Hira Singh, *Colonial Hegemony and Popular Resistance: Princes, Peasants, and Paramount Power* (New Delhi: Sage, 1998).
9. Karl Marx and Friedrich Engels, *The German Ideology* (Moscow: Progress Publishers, 1976), p. 63.
10. Karl Marx, *The Eighteenth Brumaire of Louis Bonaparte* (Moscow: Progress Publishers, 1975), p. 32; M. Ranganayakamma, 'Marx on Caste', *Frontier*,

18–24 January 2004, http://www.ranganayakamma.org/Marx%20on%20Caste.htm. Retrieved 15 October 2016.

11. Karl Marx, *The Poverty of Philosophy* (Moscow: Progress Publishers, 1955), p. 118; M. Ranganayakamma, 'Marx on Caste', *Frontier*, 18–24 January 2004, http://www.ranganayakamma.org/Marx%20on%20Caste.htm.    Retrieved 15 October 2016.

12. Karl Marx, *A Contribution to the Critique of Political Economy* (Moscow: Progress Publishers, 1970), p. 201.

13. Karl Marx, *Capital: A Critical Analysis of Capitalist Production*, ed. Friedrich Engels (London: Lawrence and Wishart, 1967), p. 321.

14. Ibid, pp. 321–22, footnote 3.

15. Ibid.

16. Ibid, p. 322.

17. Karl Marx, *Capital: A Critical Analysis of Capitalist Production*, vol. 1, ed. Friedrich Engels (London: Lawrence and Wishart, 1967), p. 481.

18. M. Ranganayakamma, 'Marx on Caste', *Frontier*, 18–24 January 2004, http://www.ranganayakamma.org/Marx%20on%20Caste.htm. Retrieved 15 October 2016.

19. Karl Marx, 'The British Rule in India', in Karl Marx and Frederick Engels, *The First Indian War of Independence 1857–1859* (Moscow: Progress Publishers, 1978), p. 13.

20. T.O. Beidelman, *A Comparative Analysis of the Jajmani System* (Locust Valley, NY: Monographs of the Association for Asian Studies, 1959); Berreman, 'Stratification, Pluralism, and Interaction: A Comparative Analysis of Caste', in *Caste and Race: Comparative Approaches,* eds. Anthony de Reuck and Julie Knight, pp. 45–91 (London: J&A Churchill, 1967); and Claude Meillassoux, 'Are There Castes in India?', *Economy and Society* 2 (1973): 1.

21. Partha Chatterjee, 'Peasants, Politics and Historiography', *Social Scientist* 120 (1983); 'Caste and Subaltern Consciousness', in *Subaltern Studies, Writings on South Asian History and Society,* ed. Ranjit Guha (New Delhi: Oxford University Press, 1982–89); 'The Manifold Uses of *Jati*', in *Region, Religion, Caste, Gender and Culture in Contemporary India,* ed. T.V. Sathyamurthy (New Delhi: Oxford University Press, 1996); Nicholas Dirks, *Castes of Mind: Colonialism and the Making of Modern India* (Princeton: Princeton University Press, 2001); Edmond Leach, 'Caste, Class and Slavery: The Taxonomic Problem', in *Caste and Race: Comparative Approaches,* eds. Anthony de Reuck and Julie Knight (London: J&A Churchill), pp. 5–16.

22. Anand Teltumbde, 'Return of the Mandir', *Economic and Political Weekly* 53.10 (10 March 2018).

23. Max Weber, 'Class, Status, Party', in *From Max Weber: Essays in Sociology*, eds. Hans Gerth and C. Wright Mills (New York: Oxford University Press, 1958), pp. 186–87.

24. Ibid, pp. 192–93.

25. Ibid, p. 192.

26. Ibid, p. 189; Max Weber, *The Religion of India: The Sociology of Hinduism and Buddhism*, trans. Hans H. Gerth and Don Martindale (New York: Free Press, 1958), pp. 39–40.

27. Max Weber, *The Religion of India: The Sociology of Hinduism and Buddhism*, trans. Hans H. Gerth and Don Martindale (New York: Free Press, 1958), p. 29.

28. Ibid, pp. 30–31.

29. Louis Dumont, *Homo Hierarchicus: The Caste System and Its Implications*, transl. into English by Mark Sansbury (Chicago: University of Chicago Press, 1980), pp. 24, 37.

30. Ibid, pp. 24, 37, 44, 46–47, 49.

31. T.N. Madan, 'Louis Dumont and the Study of Society in India', in *Caste, Hierarchy, and Individualism: Indian Critiques of Louis Dumont's Contributions*, ed. R.S. Khare (New Delhi: Oxford University Press, 2006), p. 80.

32. Partha Chatterjee, 'The Manifold Uses of Jati', in *Region, Religion, Caste, Gender and Culture in Contemporary India*, ed. T.V. Sathyamurthy (New Delhi: Oxford University Press, 1996), pp. 170–71.

33. Ibid.

34. Gerald Berreman, 'Stratification, Pluralism, and Interaction: A Comparative Analysis of Caste', in *Caste and Race: Comparative Approaches*, eds. Anthony de Reuck and Julie Knight (London: J&A Churchill, 1967).

35. M.N. Srinivas, *Caste in Modern India and Other Essays* (Bombay: Asia Publishing House, 1962); T.O. Beidelman, *A Comparative Analysis of the Jajmani System* (Locust Valley, NY: Monographs of the Association for Asian Studies, 1959); Rajendra Singh, *Land, Power, People: Rural Elite in Transition, 1801–1970* (New Delhi: Sage). See also, Louis Dumont, *Homo Hierarchicus: The Caste System and Its Implications*, transl. into English by Mark Sansbury (Chicago: University of Chicago Press, 1980).

36. Irfan Habib, *Essays in Indian History: Towards a Marxist Historiography* (London: Anthem Press, 2003), p. 173.

37. B.R. Ambedkar, 'Annihilation of Caste', in *Dr. Babasaheb Ambedkar: Writings and Speeches*, ed. Vasant Moon (Bombay: Government of Maharashtra, 1979), p. 44.

38. Max Weber, 'Class, Status, Party', in *From Max Weber: Essays in Sociology*, eds. Hans Gerth and C. Wright Mills (New York: Oxford University Press, 1958), p. 180.

39. B.R. Ambedkar, *Annihilation of Caste*, Introduction by Arundhati Roy (London, New York: Verso, 2014), pp. 299–300.

40. Ibid, p. 65.

41. Ibid, p. 68.

42. Anand Teltumbde, *Mahad: The Making of the First Dalit Revolt* (New Delhi: Aakar, 2016), pp. 213–14.

## Chapter 10. Dr Ambedkar and the Future of Indian Democracy

1. An earlier version of this paper was published in *Indian Journal of Human Rights*, 9 January–December 2005.
2. Similar questions would apply to the idea of democracy as 'government by discussion'.
3. B.R. Ambedkar, 'Conditions Precedent for the Successful Working of Democracy', 1952, unpublished paper cited in G.R. Madan, *India's Social Transformation*, vol. 2 (New Delhi: Allied Publishers, 1996), p. 178.
4. From 'Labour and Parliamentary Democracy', a lecture delivered on 17 September 1943 to the All India Trade Union Workers' Study Camp in Delhi, partly reprinted in Chapter 3 of Valerian Rodrigues, ed., *The Essential Writings of B.R. Ambedkar* (New Delhi: Oxford University Press, 2002).
5. The nature of this sentiment is discussed in Ambedkar's 'Philosophy of Hinduism', *Dr. Babasaheb Ambedkar: Writings and Speeches*, vol. 3 (Government of Maharashtra, 1979–98). Ambedkar also used the term 'solidarity' from time to time, for instance in his speech of 25 November 1949 to the Constituent Assembly, quoted earlier.
6. The quote is from 'Plea to the Foreigner', Chapter 9 of the second edition of *What Congress and Gandhi Have Done to the Untouchables*, reprinted in *Dr. Babasaheb Ambedkar: Writings and Speeches*, vol. 9 (Mumbai: Government of Maharashtra, 1979–98); this is also the source quoted in the next sentence.
7. If not collective farming, the Constitution of India could have provided for radical land reform. In the initial scheme of things, however, property was a fundamental right, making land reform very difficult. In contrast, extensive land reforms took place in the early 1950s in Jammu and Kashmir (J&K), where it was possible to expropriate the landlords without compensation. Radical land reforms in J&K were immensely popular and laid a lasting basis for a relatively prosperous and egalitarian rural economy, with very low poverty rates by Indian standards. Beyond land reform, government policy in J&K before 1956 (when the Constitution of J&K was ratified) was strongly influenced by *Naya Kashmir*, the socialist manifesto adopted by the National Conference party in 1944. Even as India missed the boat of land reform, it seems J&K narrowly missed that of a socialist constitution. On these matters, see Sehar Iqbal, 'Social Impact of State Development Policy in Jammu and Kashmir: 1948 to 1988', PhD thesis, UNESCO Madanjeet Singh Institute of Kashmir Studies, University of Kashmir, Srinagar (2018).
8. Intervention in the Constituent Assembly debates, 19 November 1948, http://164.100.47.194/loksabha/writereaddata/cadebatefiles/C19111948.html.

9. Rukmini S., 'Just 5 per cent of Indian Marriages Are Inter-caste: Survey', *The Hindu*, 13 November 2014, based on the India Human Development Survey 2011–12.

## Chapter 11. New Dalit Movements: An Ambedkarite Perspective

1. Castes which are socially treated as low or minor or have no representation in education, employment or politics and are relatively underdeveloped compared to other castes within Scheduled Castes.
2. Gopal Guru, ed., *Atrophy in Dalit Politics* (Mumbai: Vikas Adhyayan Kendra, 2005), p. 66.
3. See Sir Monier Williams, *Oxford Sanskrit English Dictionary* (Oxford, 1964), p. 471.
4. Eleanor Zelliot, *From Untouchable to Dalit* (New Delhi: Manohar, 2005), p. 267.
5. Prakash Louis, *Political Sociology of Dalit Assertion* (New Delhi: Gyan Publishing House, 2003), p. 145.
6. Ibid, p. 135.
7. Ibid, p. 140.
8. John C.B. Webster, 'Who Is a Dalit', in *Dalits in Modern India*, ed. S.M. Michal (New Delhi: Sage, 2007), p.76.
9. Gopal Guru, 'The Politics of Naming', *Seminar* 471 (November 1998): 16.
10. Generally, if Dalits convert to Christianity, they are legally considered to be in the OBC (C) category in the Telugu-speaking region. This means that to claim the status of Scheduled Castes, they are forced to remain identified as Hindus. So, this legal category culturally bound the Dalits in the Hindu fold.
11. Kancha Illaiah, 'Caste or Class or Caste-Class: A Study in Dalit Bahujan Consciousness and Struggles in Andhra Pradesh in 1980s', working paper submitted to the Centre for Contemporary Studies, Nehru Memorial Museum Library, New Delhi, 1995. See also Anupama Rao, *The Caste Question* (New Delhi: Permanent Black, 2010), pp. 39–80.
12. Gail Omvedt, *Dalit Visions* (New Delhi: Orient Longman, 2008), p. 72.
13. Nagaraju Papani, ed., *Dalita Pratighatana Poratala Ninadam* (Hyderabad: Jabali Publications, 2013), pp. 74–79.
14. U. Sambashiva Rao, *Dalita Rnanninadam* (Hyderabad: Idireeta Publications, 2005), p. 11.
15. Ibid, p. 15.
16. Gopal Guru, ed., *Atrophy in Dalit Politics* (Mumbai: Vikas Adhyayan Kendra, 2005), pp. 69–71.
17. Ibid, p. 72.
18. See Kancha Illaiah, *Why I Am Not a Hindu* (Kolkata: Samya Publications, 2007), pp. vii–ix.

19. See George Kunnath, 'Compliance or Defiance? The Case of Dalits and Mahadalits', *Journal of the Anthropological Society of Oxford* 5.1 (2013): 36–59.

20. See Badri Narayan, 'Democracy and Identity Politics in India: Is it a Snake or a Rope', *Economic and Political Weekly* 50.16 (18 April 2015): 61–65.

21. See K.Y. Ratnam, 'The Dalit Movement and Democratisation in Andhra Pradesh', working paper 13 (Washington DC: East-West Center 2008).

22. Savarnas are broadly defined as those people who are not outcastes or untouchables, that is, who are within the fold of the varna system. Sudra caste people who live in mainstream villages along with upper-caste Hindus are also included in this group.

23. The practice of untouchability against Arundhatiyars and Chakkiliyars in Tamil Nadu by Parayars and Pallars is largely neglected in public and social media discussions. This was visible in the case of the untouchability wall at Sandiyar raised by Parayars against Arundhatiyars.
https://roundtableindia.co.in/index.php?option=com_content&view=article&id=9296:uproot-untouchability-wall-erected-by-parayars-in-sandaiyur&catid=119:feature&Itemid=132.

24. See 'Understanding Untouchability: A Comparative Study of Practices and Conditions in 1589 Villages' (Washington, DC: Navasarjan Trust, Gujarat, and the Robert F. Kennedy Center for Justice and Human Rights, 2010). In this study, they have documented non-Dalit on Dalit (vertical) discrimination and Dalit on Dalit (horizontal) discrimination.

25. P. Muthaiah, *Sub-Caste Conflict and Dalit Movement in Andhra Pradesh* (Hyderabad: Anveshi, 2006), p. 4.

26. See T.R. Singh, *The Madiga: A Study in Social Structure and Change* (Lucknow: Ethnographic and Folk Culture Society, 1969), pp. 31–39.

27. See Jyotsna Macwan and Suguna Ramanathan, 'Resolving Dalit Identity: Vankars, Chamars, Valmikis', in *Dalit Assertion in Society, Literature and History*, eds. Imtiaz Ahmad and Shashi Bhushan Upadhyay (New Delhi: Orient BlackSwan, 2010), p. 22.

28. Ibid, p. 24.

29. Ghanshyam Shah, Harsh Mander, Sukhadeo Thorat, Satish Deshpande and Amita Baviskar, eds., *Untouchability in Rural India* (New Delhi: Sage, 2006).

30. Ibid, pp. 13–14.

31. A. Ramaiah, 'Social Democracy in Indian Villages: The Experience of Dalits in Southern Tamil Nadu', in *Dalit Assertion in Society, Literature and History*, eds. Imtiaz Ahmad and Shashi Bhushan Upadhyay (New Delhi: Orient BlackSwan, 2010), p. 60.

32. See 'Andhra Pradesh State Harijan Conference', 1976, pp. 124–25.

33. B.N. Lokur Advisory Committee, *Revision of the Lists of Scheduled Castes and Scheduled Tribes* (New Delhi: Department of Social Security, 1965), p. 8.

34. A.K. Verma, 'UP: BJP's Caste Card', *Economic and Political Weekly* 36.48 (1 December 2001): 4452–55.

35. Bharat Bhushan, 'Modi's "Jumla" Nailed: How the BJP Tampered with Reservations in the Past', Catch News, 28 October 2015, http://www.catchnews.com/politics-news/modi-s-jumla-nailed-how-the-bjp-tampered-with-reservations-in-the-past-1445878883.html.

36. There are two major Scheduled Castes in Karnataka: Holeya and Madiga. The higher ritual status of the Holeyas as compared to the Madigas is reinforced by the fact that the former belongs to the right-hand section of castes, while the latter to the left-hand. The division into right- and left-hand is found in Karnataka. The left-hand castes appear to be the various specialist artisan castes known as Panchala in old Mysore, of which the Madiga is the last, and the right-hand castes appear to be those with a more generalized occupation, such as cultivation, of which the Holeya is the last.

37. *The Hindu*, 'Sadashiva Commission recommends internal reservation among SCs', 15 June 2012, http://www.thehindu.com/news/cities/bangalore/sadashiva-commission-recommends-internal-reservation-among-scs/article3528992.ece.

38. See B.S. Waghmare, 'Reservation Policy and the Plight of Matangs in Maharashtra', *Indian Journal of Political Science* 71.3 (July–September 2010): 923–46.

39. S. Viswanatham, 'Separate Slice', *Frontline*, 16 January 2009, http://www.frontline.in/static/html/fl2601/stories/20090116260110500.htm.

40. Interview with Banala Mangesh on 12 February 2015 at Nomula village, Ranga Reddy district, Telangana. He is a leader of the Dakkali Hakkula Porata Samiti. I also interviewed Gajaveli Ganapathi on 7 August 2014 at Hyderabad. Ganapathi is a leader of the 'Forum for Numerically Smaller Scheduled Castes welfare'.

41. Sushil Rao, 'Telangana to Have Official Folk Artistes', *Times of India*, 15 March 2015, https://timesofindia.indiatimes.com/city/hyderabad/Telangana-to-have-official-folk-artistes/articleshow/46570213.cms.

42. Interview with Gajaveli Ganapathi, 7 August 2014, Hyderabad. Ganapathi is a leader of the 'Forum for Numerically Smaller Scheduled Castes welfare' in the Telugu-speaking region.

43. Marathi speech at a public meet at Mangwada, Pune (20 July 1927), published in *Bahishkrit Bharat*, 29 July 1927. See *Dr. Babasaheb Ambedkar: Writings and Speeches*, vol.18, pp. 56–9, and Narendra Jadhav, ed., *Ambedkar Speaks*, vol. 3 (New Delhi: Konark), pp. 61–62.

44. Most of Ambedkar's writings and speeches addressed all Untouchable castes as one group. In 'Who Are Untouchables . . .' we don't get an adequate exposition as to why hierarchy and untouchability practices exist among SC subgroups.

45. Alistair McMillan, *Standing at the Margins* (New Delhi: Oxford University Press, 2005), pp. 81–88, B.R. Ambedkar, *Speeches at Round Table Conference* (New Delhi: Critical Quest, 2011), pp. 3–40.

46. Vasant Moon, ed., *Dr. Babasaheb Ambedkar: Writings and Speeches*, vol. 1 (Mumbai: Government of Maharashtra, 1989), pp. 401–02.

47. Mala Mahanadu is an organization established by P.V. Rao against the rationalization or subcategorization of SC reservations in the Telugu-speaking region. There are many Mala Mahanadu groups in both Andhra Pradesh and Telangana.

48. Panthukala Srinivas made a documentary called 'Dandora' (2006) in which he documented the for and against agitations on the subclassification for SC reservations in Andhra Pradesh. Parts of the documentary are available on YouTube.

49. K. Balagopal, 'A Tangled Web; Subdivision of SC Reservations in AP', *Economic and Political Weekly* 35.13 (25 March 2000): 1078.

50. Manda Krishna Madiga interview, 25 February 2015, Hyderabad.

51. *E.V. Chinnaiah* vs *State of Andhra Pradesh and others*, Case No. Appeal (civil) 6758. The Supreme Court judgement of 5 November 2004, the bench comprised N. Santosh Hegde, S.N. Variava, B.P. Singh, H.R. Sema and S.B. Sinha.

## Chapter 12. Bisociative Revolution: The Emergence of the Concept

1.  Anand Teltumbde, 'To the Self-obsessed Marxists and the Pseudo Ambedkarites', 2013, https://www.countercurrents.org/teltumbde030413.htm.

2.  Abhinav Sinha, 'Response to Anand Teltumbde: To the Self-proclaimed Teachers and Preachers', *Red Polemique*, 5 April 2013.

3.  Arthur Koestler, *The Act of Creation* (Hutchinson & Co: London, 1964).

4.  The New Webster Library of Universal Knowledge, 1969.

5.  Lev Vygotsky, *Thought and Language* (MIT Press, 1987), p. 194.

6.  Jean Piaget and Roland Garcia, *Psychogenesis and the History of Science* (Columbia Press, 1987).

7.  In general, scientific concepts are those concepts that constitute the structure of a fully developed theory or domain. For example, algebra deals with expressions of the type $2x+1$; such expressions are scientific concepts of the subject which acquire their meaning of 'educate, agitate, organize' from algebraic structure. On the other hand, the expressions $2\times5+1$, $2\times6+1$, etc. are spontaneous concepts of arithmetic, of which $2x+1$ is a generalization. Thus, in the case of Ambedkar's approach, spontaneous concepts are those of the Dalit's everyday caste experience, while scientific concepts, as I see it, are in Ambedkar's rendition of Buddhism. The engine of the transition between the two is Ambedkar's 'educate, agitate, organize' slogan.

On the other hand, the scientific concepts of Marxism are organized around the class struggle, which is the manifestation of a basic contradiction of capitalism, the exploitation of the worker by the capitalist. The spontaneous concepts are generated by the daily life of the worker and it is the development of class consciousness that leads from the second to the first.

8. B.R. Ambedkar, *Annihilation of Caste* (London: Verso, 2014), p. 231.
9. 'The Caste Question and Its Resolution: A Marxist Perspective', http://english.arvindtrust.org/archives/199.
10. CPI(M)M/L Position Paper on Caste, 2013, http://english.arvindtrust.org.
11. Prakash Louis, *People Power: The Naxalite Movement in Central Bihar* (Delhi: Wordsmiths, 2002).
12. Ibid.
13. George J. Kunnath, *Rebels from the Mud Houses: Dalits and the Making of the Maoist Revolution in Bihar* (Taylor and Francis, 2012), p. 45 (Kindle edition).
14. Ibid, p. 128.
15. Etienne Balibar, *Politics and the Other Scene* (London: Verso, 2002).
16. Ibid, p. 65.
17. The perfect example of such adjustment was the post-revolutionary period of the 1920s in Soviet Russia, when the social and economic policy of the Soviet state oscillated between the swing to the right of Lenin and Bukharin's New Economic Policy and the radically left Stalinist collectivization.
18. An antinomy is a contradiction between two beliefs or conclusions that are in themselves reasonable—this creates a paradox. Here, the reference is to race and class. The structure of race is essentially different from the structure of class, although they criss-cross.
19. Etienne Balibar, 'Class Racism', in *Race, Nation, Class: Ambiguous Identities*, eds. Balibar and Wallerstein (London: Verso, 1991).
20. Ibid, p. 91. Modern representations of history involve the dialectical interaction between racism and class struggle. On the one hand, class conflicts are often displaced by racism due to its predisposition, according to Balibar. Similarly, one needs to investigate how class relationships determine the effects of racism on society.
21. Patricia Hill Collins, 'Towards a New Vision: Race, Class and Gender as Categories of Analysis and Connection', Center for Research on Women, Department of Sociology and Social Work, Memphis State University, 1989.
22. Audrey Lorde, *Sister Outsider* (Ten Speed Press, 2007), p. 123.
23. Arthur Koestler, *The Act of Creation* (London: Hutchinson & Co, 1964).
24. Ibid, p. 45.
25. Patricia Hill Collins, 'Towards a New Vision: Race, Class and Gender as Categories of Analysis and Connection', Center for Research on Women, Department of Sociology and Social Work, Memphis State University, 1989.
26. See Appendix (p. 377) for the theoretical background.

27. Just as the operator of energy of quantum oscillator is the sum p2 + q2, yet neither p nor q can be measured in the state of 'p2 + q2'.
28. Patricia Hill Collins, 'Towards a New Vision: Race, Class and Gender as Categories of Analysis and Connection', Center for Research on Women, Department of Sociology and Social Work, Memphis State University, 1989.
29. Ibid, p. 43.
30. Indianism and Marxism: Mismatch of two revolutionary points of view (rationales).
31. John Holloway, *Change the World without Taking Power* (Pluto Press, 2002).
32. From Paulo Freire's *Pedagogy* point of view, the Leninist approach relies on the concept of 'banking' education as opposed to 'problem-posing' and problem-solving education. 'Banking education' is defined as the education where students are passive and receive information from a teacher in a similar way as a bank receives money deposits. Problem-posing education is, on the other hand, focused on students actively formulating the problems in their lives and learning and solving them in action.
33. Lech Walesa, Interview in *Playboy*, February 1982.
34. George J. Kunnath, *Rebels from the Mud Houses: Dalits and the Making of the Maoist Revolution in Bihar* (Taylor and Francis, 2012).
35. Ibid, p. 14.
36. John Holloway, *Change the World without Taking Power* (Pluto Press, 2002).

## Chapter 13. Strategy of Conversion to Buddhism: Intent and Aftermath

1. 'I am born with a blot of untouchability as I did not have control over it. Nevertheless, I will not die as Hindu,' he thundered in a speech delivered in the Mumbai Area Depressed Classes Conference. See *Dr. Babasaheb Ambedkar: Writings and Speeches*, vol. 18, part 1 (Mumbai: Government of Maharashtra, 2002), p. 430.
2. Dhananjay Keer, *Dr Ambedkar: Life and Mission* (Mumbai: Popular Prakashan, 2005), pp. 257–58.
3. Many Dalit leaders in Vidarbha, like Ganesh Akkaji Gavai, Raosaheb G.M. Thaware and Hemchandra Khandekar, opposed Ambedkar's call for conversion. While Gavai and his associate, Thaware, were under the spell of Hindu leaders like B.S. Moonje and K.B. Hedgewar and had joined the Hindu Mahasabha in 1933 and 1941 respectively (Khandekar becoming a member of its executive), Khandekar was a follower of the Mahanubhav sect who joined the Congress. See Gail Omvedt, *Dalits and the Democratic Revolution: Dr Ambedkar and the Dalit Movement* (New Delhi: Sage, 2014), and Anand Teltumbde, *Mahad: The Making of the First Dalit Revolt* (New Delhi: Aakar, 2016), pp. 66–72. Even Kisan Fagoi Bansode, who had followed Ambedkar

after his emergence on the scene, parted ways with him after his conversion call (Omvedt op. cit.). Even his closest associate, B.D. (Dadasaheb) Gaikwad was not pleased with the conversion. See B.R. Ambedkar, *Correspondence* (letter no. 215, dated 29 July 1954, to B.D. Gaikwad in Hari Narke, ed., *Dr. Babasaheb Ambedkar: Writings and Speeches*, vol. 21 (Mumbai: Government of Maharashtra, 2006), p. 408.

4. In English, 'Which Way the Liberation?'

5. The need for conversion to a different religion has reverberated throughout the anti-caste movement. This historic need was expressed by predecessors of Ambedkar like Jotiba Phule and contemporaries like Swami Achhutanand and Mangu Ram. Their respective efforts came into being as Sarvajanic Satya Dharma (1889), Adi Hindu Dharma (1922) and Adi Dharma (1926). Apart from the difference in their names, there is nothing contrasting among them and, in fact, all of them are governed by common similarities. Their philosophy was parallel to Vedic philosophy. They denounced the theory of rebirth and varnashram. See Dinesh Ram, 'The Tao of Liberation', http://www.combatlaw.org/information.php?article_id=1004&issue_id=36.

6. In fact he says: 'As it [conversion] should be considered from social viewpoint and religious viewpoint, it also should be considered from existential and philosophical viewpoints.' However, elaborating these viewpoints later in the speech, he focuses on only the existential and spiritual. See *Dr. Babasaheb Ambedkar: Writings and Speeches*, vol. 18, part 1 (Mumbai: Government of Maharashtra, 2002), p. 495.

7. Ibid, p. 495–96.

8. Ibid, p. 496.

9. Ibid, p.497.

10. Ibid, p. 497.

11. Ibid, p. 500.

12. Ibid, p. 501.

13. After the Mahad conference, Ambedkar had started *Bahishkrit Bharat* in 1927 under his own editorship. The earlier paper, *Muknayak* (leader of the mute), which he had started in January 1920 was basically edited and run by his comrades as he had to go back to England to complete his education.

14. Vasant Moon, ed., *Dr. Babasaheb Ambedkaranche Bahishkrit Bharat (1920–1929) ani Muknayak (1920)* (Mumbai: Government of Maharashtra, 1990). 1 July 1927p 51 (5), 4 November 1927 p 112 (2).

15. Ibid, 29 July 1927, p 76 (6)

16. Ibid, 15 March 1929, p. 244 (2).

17. In the first Mahad Conference, 19–20 March 1927, when the Dalits marched to the Chavadar Tank to exercise their legal right to access public water sources, goons of the caste Hindus attacked some of the delegates as they were returning home. In the second Satyagraha Conference, 25–27 December 1927,

some orthodox Hindus fraudulently obtained a court injunction against the Dalit accessing the Chavadar Tank, contending that it was a private property. See Anand Teltumbde, *Mahad: The Making of the First Dalit Revolt* (New Delhi: Aakar, 2016).

18. Much before the formal declaration to embrace Buddhism, Ambedkar's attraction to it was quite public. In 1948, Ambedkar republished P. Lakshmi Narasu's *Essence of Buddhism*. In 1950, Ambedkar wrote his famous essay entitled 'Buddha and the Future of His Religion' in the journal *Mahabodhi* and indicated the need of a gospel to guide the new converts. The essay was a turning point for Dalits insofar as they now knew Ambedkar's choice.

19. See *Dr. Babasaheb Ambedkar: Writings and Speeches*, vol. 18, part 1 (Mumbai: Government of Maharashtra, 2002), p. 525.

20. Christophe Jaffrelot, *Dr Ambedkar and Untouchability: Analysing and Fighting Caste* (Delhi: Permanent Black, 2005), p. 125.

21. Ibid.

22. An Italian monk, Lokanatha, had paid a visit to Ambedkar's residence at Dadar on 10 June 1936 and tried to persuade him to embrace Buddhism. In 1937, he published a pamphlet addressed to the Depressed Classes, 'Buddhism Will Make You Free', from his press in Ceylon. Mangesh Dahiwale, ed., *Ambedkar on Buddhism* (Pune: Jambudwip Trust, 2016), p. 8.

23. Ibid, p. iv.

24. Ibid.

25. The rationality of Buddhism is acknowledged by many scholars. As regards its compatibility with modern science, Einstein, as originally cited by Paul Carus in his popular book *The Gospel of Buddha* (Kessinger Publishing, 2003), is said to have remarked, 'Buddhism will be the only religion that can survive amidst the questioning of religions by modern science.' This quote, proudly repeated by the protagonists of Buddhism, however, appears to be spurious. But another quote of Einstein in *Albert Einstein: The Human Side*, eds. Helen Dukas and Banesh Hoffman (Princeton: Princeton University Press, 1954) indicates that Einstein did think of Buddhism as the most suitable religion of the future.

26. In May 1956, in a BBC talk titled 'Why I Like Buddhism and How It Is Useful to the World in Its Present Circumstances', he said: 'I prefer Buddhism because it gives three principles in combination, which no other religion does. Buddhism teaches prajna (understanding as against superstition and supernaturalism), karuna (love between people against a slave and master relationship) and samata (equality).'

27. In relation to his choice of religion for conversion, Ambedkar had explained: 'I will choose only the least harmful way for the country. And that is the greatest benefit I am conferring on the country by embracing Buddhism; for Buddhism is a part and parcel of Bharatiya culture. I have taken care that my conversion will not harm the tradition of the culture and history of this land.' Quoted

in Dhananjay Keer, *Ambedkar: Life and Mission* (Mumbai: Popular Prakashan, 1971), p. 498.

28. Dr. Ambedkar argued this hypothesis in his book, *The Untouchables: Who Were They and Why They Became Untouchables?* Reproduced in *Dr. Babasaheb Ambedkar: Writings and Speeches*, vol. 7 (Mumbai: Government of Maharashtra, 1990).

29. Dhananjay Keer, *Ambedkar: Life and Mission* (Mumbai: Popular Prakashan, 1971), p. 503.

30. He rather believed that Buddhism was the best religion for mankind, which would attract many non-Dalits after its revival. He had even declared his ambition to make the entire country a Buddhist country. (See D.C. Ahir, *The Legacy of Ambedkar* [New Delhi: BR Publishing Corporation, 1990], p. 155.) The thesis in 'Annihilation of Caste' is based on such an expectation.

31. B.R. Ambedkar, 'Buddha or Karl Marx' in *Dr. Babasaheb Ambedkar: Writings and Speeches*, vol. 3, ed. Vasant Moon (Mumbai: Government of Maharashtra, 1987) pp. 456–58.

32. Ken and Visakha Kawasaki, 'Buddhism in India: Lifting the Curse of Untouchability', http://home.earthlink.net/~brelief2/bud_ind.html.

33. Paul Carus, referred to above as the author of *The Gospel of Buddha*, who had a connection with the International Buddhism and Theosophical Society, was the first president of the Indian Buddhist Association.

34. Bhagwan Das, *Revival of Buddhism in India and Role of Dr Baba Sahib B.R. Ambedkar* (Lucknow: Dalit Today Prakashan, 1998), p. 13.

35. G. Aloysius, *Religion as Emancipatory Identity: The Buddhist Movement among the Tamils under Colonialism* (New Delhi: New Age Publishers, 1998).

36. Rattamalai Srinivasan, Ambedkar's lieutenant in Madras province, and Iyothee Thassar were related through marriage—Srinivasan's sister was the wife of Iyothee Thassar and Iyothee Thassar's son later married Srinivasan's daughter.

37. Valerian Rodrigues, 'Buddhism, Marxism and the Conception of Emancipation in Ambedkar', in *Dalit Movements and the Meanings of Labour in India*, ed. Peter Robb (New Delhi: Oxford University Press, 1993), pp. 299–338.

38. First published in 1956 and reproduced in *Dr. Babasaheb Ambedkar: Writings and Speeches*, vol. 11 (Mumbai: Government of Maharashtra, 1992).

39. Martin Fuchs, 'A Religion for Civil Society? Ambedkar's Buddhism, the Dalit Issue and the Imagination of Emergent Possibilities', in *Charisma and Canon: Essays on the Religious History of the Indian Subcontinent*, eds. Vasudha Dalmia, Angelika Malinar and Martin Christof (New Delhi: Oxford University Press, 2001), pp. 250–73.

40. Even to a mere suggestion of Ambedkar that 'a Buddhist "Bible" should be compiled so that converts to the faith could develop a proper understanding of the Buddha's teaching' (made in his essay entitled 'Buddha and the Future of His Religion' published in the journal *Mahabodhi* in 1950), Sangharakshita,

an English monk working in India, published his rejoinder in the same journal in 1952 saying that it would be 'fraught with danger to the entire Buddhist movement' . . . [such compilation] 'only be gained at the cost of Buddhism ceasing to be Buddhism . . . Something might indeed be spread by such means, but it would not in truth be Buddhism, however prominently it might display that sacred name . . . this would be to pollute the pure and living waters of the Dharma with the dead carcass of dogmatism'.

41. Dhananjay Keer, *Ambedkar: Life and Mission* (Mumbai: Popular Prakashan, 1971), p. 521, with reference to *Mahabodhi*, December 1959.

42. Ibid, with reference to *The Light of Dhamma*, January 1959.

43. 'Bhikkhus Who Lead Lay Lives', *The Buddhist* 1959–60, p.157, quoted in Heinz Bechert, *Buddhismus, Staat und Gesellschaft*, vol. 1, pp. 57–58.

44. See Ven. Bhadant Anand Kausalyayan, *The Buddha and His Dhamma*, Hindi edition (Mumbai: People's Education Society, Siddharth College, 1971). In this book Ven. Bhadant Anand Kausalyayan has traced sources in the Pali canon for Ambedkar's original unreferenced text of *The Buddha and His Dhamma*. They are: Bauddhacharita (90), Anguttar Nikaya (28), Digha Nikaya (27), Majjhima Nikaya (4), Samyutta Nikaya (22), Khuddaka Nikaya (232), Dhammapada (210) and others (22), Dhammapada commentary (5) and Vinaya Pitaka (19).

45. For a useful analysis of Ambedkar as a modern or postmodern man, see Christopher Queen, 'Dr. Ambedkar and the Hermeneutics of Buddhist Liberation,' in *Engaged Buddhism: Buddhist Liberation Movements in Asia*, eds. Christopher S. Queen and Sallie B. (State University of New York Press, 1996), p. 45.

46. See Adele Fiske and Christoph Emmrich, 'The Use of Buddhist Scriptures in B.R. Ambedkar's *The Buddha and His Dhamma*', in *Reconstructing the World: B.R. Ambedkar and Buddhism in India*, eds. Surendra Jondhale and Johannes Beltz (Oxford: Oxford University Press, 2004). Also a paper by Virginia Hancock, 'New Buddhism for New Aspirations: Navayana Buddhism of Ambedkar and His Followers', available at http://www.manushi-india.org/pdfs_issues/PDF%20145/Buddhism%2017-25.pdf.

47. Ibid, Fiske and Emmrich.

48. Ambedkar certainly wanted all Dalits to embrace Buddhism at the first stage and thereby de-caste themselves from their primordial caste identity. Through this they would be able to counter the orthodox religiosity of Hinduism and annihilate caste. The transformation of the Dalit community from a fragmented and hopeless lot to a cohesive and confident people in this process would certainly catalyse the conversion of others to Buddhism and make India a Buddhist country.

49. Surendra Jondhale and Johannes Beltz, eds., *Reconstructing the World: B.R. Ambedkar and Buddhism in India* (New Delhi: Oxford University Press, 2004), p. viii.

50. Pradeep Gokhale for one argues that while Ambedkar's Buddhism is a reconstruction of traditional Buddhism, 'it may or may not be so for original Buddhism', *Reconstructing the World: B.R. Ambedkar and Buddhism in India*, eds. Surendra Jondhale and Johannes Beltz (New Delhi: Oxford University Press, 2004), pp. viii, 124; Beltz, *Reconstructing the World: B.R. Ambedkar and Buddhism in India*, eds. p. 261; Christopher Queen, *Reconstructing the World: B.R. Ambedkar and Buddhism in India*, p. 146.

51. For instance, see Gail Omvedt, *Buddhism in India: Challenging Brahmanism and Caste*, third edition (London, New Delhi: Thousand Oaks, Sage, 2003), pp. 2, 3–7, 8, 14–15, 19, 240, 266, 271; Adele Fiske and Christoph Emmrich, 'The Use of Buddhist Scriptures in Dr. B.R. Ambedkar's "The Buddha and his Dhamma"'; *Reconstructing the World: Dr. Ambedkar and Buddhism in India*, eds. Surendra Jondhale and Johannes Beltz (New Delhi: Oxford University Press, 2003), pp. 97–119.

52. Adele Fiske and Christoph Emmrich, 'The Use of Buddhist Scriptures in Dr. B.R. Ambedkar's *The Buddha and His Dhamma*', in *Reconstructing the World: Dr. Ambedkar and Buddhism in India,* eds. Surendra Jondhale and Johannes Beltz (New Delhi: Oxford University Press, 2003), pp. 97–119.

53. Surendra Jondhale and Johannes Beltz, eds., *Reconstructing the World: B.R. Ambedkar and Buddhism in India* (New Delhi: Oxford University Press, 2004), pp. 86–92.

54. Among all the religions, Buddhism with its atheistic, rationalistic and dialectic approach is compared favourably with Marxism. Even the Dalai Lama, like the head of Mahayana Buddhism, would call himself half-Buddhist, half-Marxist, indicating the affinity between the two. But beyond these superficial similarities in approach, it must be recognized that they are different. The difference may largely be attributable to their periods of birth.

55. Gauri Viswanathan, *Outside the Fold: Conversion, Modernity, and Belief* (New Jersey: Princeton University Press, 1998), p. 224.

56. The scholars' opinion is contrary to the popular understanding that Buddhism fought against casteism. For instance, the Dutch Buddhologist Professor Zürcher writes, 'In modern popularizing writings, one often reads that "egalitarian" Buddhism was essentially a "protest movement" against the Brahminical caste system. It is true that the Buddhist view of caste is different from and more rational than the religious justification which one finds in Brahminism. But neither the Buddha himself, nor any premodern Buddhist teacher after him has combated the caste system' (E. Zürcher, *Boeddhisme* [Leiden: Sinologisch Instituut, 1974], p.49).

57. D.D. Kosambi, *The Culture and Civilisation of Ancient India* (Vikas Publishing House, 1997), p. 179. In his study on slavery in ancient India, the Marxist historian Dev Raj Chanana noticed the stark contrast between the actual history of Buddhist social practice and the more 'progressive' picture given

by modern writers who fail to register the existence of serfdom in connection with the Buddhist monasteries: 'On reading the modern works concerning the Buddhist order in India one gains the impression that no slave labour was employed in the monasteries. One would be inclined to believe that all the work, even in the big monasteries like [those] of Kosambi or Rajagriha, was carried out by the monks themselves. However, a study of Pali literature shows clearly that the situation was otherwise' (Dev Raj Chanana, *Slavery in Ancient India* [New Delhi: People's Publishing House], p. 81).

58. Ambedkar believed that all major social and political revolutions have been preceded by cultural and religious revolutions, and so in order to bring about revolutionary change in the societal structure, a kind of religio-social revolution in the form of mass conversion to Buddhism was necessary.

59. Twelve of these twenty-two vows are positive expressions of commitment to the Buddhist way and ten are negative expressions that proscribe observance of the Hindu way of life.

60. Timothy Fitzgerald, 'Buddhism in Maharashtra: A Tri-Partite Analysis—A Research Report', in *Dr. Ambedkar, Buddhism and Social Change*, eds. A.K. Narain and D.C. Ahir (B.R. Publishing Corporation, 1994), p. 20.

61. Neera Burra, 'Buddhism, Conversion and Identity: A Case Study of Village Mahars', in *Caste: Its 20th Century Avatar*, ed. M.N. Srinivas (New Delhi: Penguin Books India, 1997), pp. 160–68.

62. Ibid, p. 168.

63. Discussion with Purushottam Khaparde, Shankarrao Sonavanem and Gomaji Tembhare at Wardha on 1 May 1936. See *Dr. Babasaheb Ambedkar: Writings and Speeches*, vol. 18, part 1 (Mumbai: Government of Maharashtra, 2002), p. 469.

64. Satish Deshpande, 'Heavens Can Wait', *Tehelka* 5.20, 24 May 2008.

65. In 1955, Ambedkar founded the Bharatiya Bauddha Mahasabha (BMS, the Indian Buddhist Association) with the objective of propagating Buddhism. It was supposed to manage the religio-social affairs of Buddhists after conversion. It had to manage a strong interface between the Sangha and Buddhist lay community. Because of his sudden demise within two months after conversion, he could not, however, even put forth the functional model of the BMS for the post-conversion era.

66. When B.C. Kamble went out and formed his faction as *durusta* RPI against B.D. Gaikwad.

67. Dr Manohar Jilthe, 'Dr. Ambedkar's Dhamma: Revolution', 24 May 2008, http://www.ambedkarmission.org/cat/news/articles_item.asp?NewsID=35.

68. Vipassana, a meditation technique propagated by the Burmese master Sayagyi U Ba Khin and represented by S.N. Goenka, has struck firm roots in Maharashtra, mainly through its Vipassana International Academy in Dhammagiri near Igatpuri, where courses are offered round the year.

69. See Vinod Vanjari, *Buddhapranit Kranti ani Vipassana* (Pune: Sugawa Prakashan, 2002). It says S.N. Goenka's vipassana is trying to confuse elite Dalits and gradually 'Hinduize' them by subjecting them to all sorts of mesmerism.

70. See Anand Teltumbde, Introduction, 'Bridging the Rift', in *B.R. Ambedkar, India and Communism* (New Delhi: Left Word, 2017).

71. Eleanor Zelliot, *From Untouchable to Dalit* (New Delhi: Manohar, 1992) cited in W.N. Kuber, B.R. Ambedkar. op. cit., p. 88.

72. W.N. Kuber, *Dr. Ambedkar: A Critical Study* (New Delhi: People's Publishing House, 1973), p. 307.

73. The Dalit Panthers Manifesto was considered to be based on the Communist Manifesto; see Dipa Mahanuwar, 'Dalit Panther Ek Shodh', *Navshakti*, 21 November 1976.

74. See Anand Teltumbde, *Dalits: Past, Present and Future* (London: Routledge, 2016), p. 91.

## PART IV: AMBEDKAR AND THE MOTIFS OF FREEDOM

## Chapter 14. Beyond the Nation: Ambedkar and the Anti–isolation of Fellowship

1. Versions of this chapter were presented at the Quest for Equity: Revisiting Ambedkar, Reclaiming Social Justice conference held in Bengaluru, India, in 2017; and at the seminar of the Committee for the Study of Religion at the CUNY Graduate Center in Fall 2017. The authors are grateful to the participants and organizers for their critical feedback. This chapter is dedicated to the memory of Eleanor Zelliot.

2. Giorgio Agamben, *Homo Sacer: Sovereign Power and Bare Life*, trans. Daniel Heller-Roazen (Stanford, California: Stanford University Press, 1998).

3. Christophe Jaffrelot, *Dr. Ambedkar and Untouchability: Fighting the Indian Caste System* (New York: Columbia University Press, 2005), p. 3.

4. Mahar was one of the communities treated as Dalits in the Bombay Presidency.

5. For more on the role of the body in colonial India, see *Confronting the Body: The Politics of Physicality in Colonial and Post-Colonial India*, eds. James H. Mills and Satadru Sen (London: Anthem Press, 2004).

6. B.R. Ambedkar, 'Waiting for a Visa', in *Dr. Babasaheb Ambedkar: Writings and Speeches*, ed. Vasant Moon, vol. 12 (Mumbai: Government of Maharashtra, 1993), p. 671.

7. Eleanor Zelliot, *Ambedkar's World: The Making of Babasaheb and the Dalit Movement* (New Delhi: Navayana, 2013), p. 69.

8. B.R. Ambedkar, 'Castes in India: Their Mechanism, Genesis and Development' in *Dr. Babasaheb Ambedkar: Writings and Speeches*, vol. 1,

ed. Vasant Moon, (Mumbai: Government of Maharashtra, 1979), p. 8. Eleanor Zelliot suggests that Ambedkar observed distinctions between White and Black America. He argued that Dalits suffered from social discrimination, rather than racial bias, and as a result could more effectively make their claims to equality through political and educational means (pp. 81–82). For more on Ambedkar's American experience, see Eleanor Zelliot, *From Untouchable to Dalit: Essays on the Ambedkar Movement* (New Delhi: Manohar, 2001).

9.   Eleanor Zelliot, *Ambedkar's World: The Making of Babasaheb and the Dalit Movement* (New Delhi: Navayana, 2013), p. 69.

10.  Ambedkar completed an MA degree and his Ph.D. from Columbia University, New York. In 1916, he joined the London School of Economics and also enrolled at Gray's Inn for the Bar-at-Law.

11.  Cf. Manu Bhagavan, *Sovereign Spheres: Princes, Education, and Empire in Colonial India* (New Delhi: Oxford University Press, 2003).

12.  B.R. Ambedkar, 'Waiting for a Visa', in *Dr. Babasaheb Ambedkar: Writings and Speeches*, vol. 12, ed. Vasant Moon (Mumbai: Government of Maharashtra), p. 673.

13.  Ambedkar's closest friend and occasional benefactor, Naval Bhathena also belonged to the Parsi community.

14.  B.R. Ambedkar, 'Waiting for a Visa', in *Dr. Babasaheb Ambedkar: Writings and Speeches*, vol. 12, ed. Vasant Moon (Mumbai: Government of Maharashtra, 1993), p. 675.

15.  Dhananjay Keer, *Dr. Ambedkar: Life and Mission* (Mumbai: Popular Prakashan, 1962), p. 34.

16.  Ibid.

17.  B.R. Ambedkar, 'Waiting for a Visa', in *Dr. Babasaheb Ambedkar: Writings and Speeches*, vol. 12, ed. Vasant Moon (Mumbai: Government of Maharashtra, 1993), p. 678.

18.  Government of India Act, 1919 allowed for limited self-government in India.

19.  B.R. Ambedkar, 'Evidence before the Southborough Committee', in *Dr. Babasaheb Ambedkar: Writings and Speeches*, vol. 1, ed. Vasant Moon (Mumbai: Government of Maharashtra, 1979), p. 249.

20.  B.R. Ambedkar, *The Essential Writings of B.R. Ambedkar*, ed. Valerian Rodrigues (New Delhi, Oxford: Oxford University Press, 2004), p. 347.

21.  Ambedkar generalized the codes to be followed by Dalits in an Indian village. B.R. Ambedkar, 'Untouchables or the Children of India's Ghetto', in *Dr. Babasaheb Ambedkar Writings and Speeches*, vol. 5, ed. Vasant Moon (Mumbai: Government of Maharashtra, 1989), p. 21.

22.  Ambedkar, *Annihilation of Caste*, 246.

23.  Ibid, 305.

24. Ibid, 295.

25. B.R. Ambedkar, 'Untouchables or the Children of India's Ghetto,' in *Dr. Babasaheb Ambedkar: Writings and Speeches*, vol. 5, ed. Vasant Moon (Mumbai: Government of Maharashtra), pp. 415–16.

26. Ibid, p. 413.

27. Ibid.

28. B.R. Ambedkar, 'Pakistan or Partition of India', in *Dr. Babasaheb Ambedkar: Writings and Speeches*, vol. 8, ed. Vasant Moon (Mumbai: Government of Maharashtra, 1990), p. 31.

29. Dhananjay Keer, *Dr. Ambedkar: Life and Mission* (Mumbai: Popular Prakashan, 1962), pp. 166–67.

30. Early on, Ambedkar was exasperated with what he called 'paper rights' at the Round Table Conference convened by British Prime Minister Ramsay McDonald in 1930 to discuss the future of India. 'What I am saying is this, that the constitution may give me certain rights, but I know that 99 per cent of the people in India are not going to allow me to exercise those rights. What is the use of those paper rights to me unless the constitution provides that if anyone infringes my rights he is liable to certain penalties?' Quoted in Arun P. Mukherjee, 'B.R. Ambedkar, John Dewey, and the Meaning of Democracy', *New Literary History* 40.2 (22 November 2009): 361. By the late 1940s, Ambedkar came to see the universalisms at the heart of the human rights project as helpful to the removal of the deep-rooted localized customs of discrimination. Global consensus about behavioural norms, he thought, would be effective in ending dehumanizing practices informed by regional historical practices.

31. Cf. Aishwary Kumar, *Radical Equality: Ambedkar, Gandhi, and the Risk of Democracy* (Stanford, California: Stanford University Press, 2015), especially Chapter 7.

32. B.R. Ambedkar, *Annihilation of Caste*, p. 260. Zelliot notes: 'It is in the basis of Ambedkar's politics that American influence seems strongest. Behind all of Ambedkar's separatism—separate political parties for backward classes, special reservation of seats in political assemblies and in government jobs—there was a strong, unwavering belief in the power of democratic institutions to bring social equality.' Eleanor Zelliot, *From Untouchable to Dalit: Essays on the Ambedkar Movement* (New Delhi: Manohar, 2001), p. 83.

33. Arun P. Mukherjee, 'B.R. Ambedkar, John Dewey, and the Meaning of Democracy', *New Literary History* 40.2 (2009): 352. For further discussion of endosmosis, Ambedkar, Dewey, Bergson, and James, see J. Daniel Elam's manuscript, 'World Literature for the Wretched of the Earth: Anticolonial Aesthetics, Postcolonial Democracy', cited with permission. Also see Luis Cabrera's engagement with Ambedkar's concept of social fluidity in the treatment of linguistic states. Luis Cabrera, '"Gandhiji, I Have No

Homeland": Cosmopolitan Insights from B.R. Ambedkar, India's Anti-Caste Campaigner and Constitutional Architect', *Political Studies* 65.3 (2017): 576–93.

34. B.R. Ambedkar, 'Evidence before the Southborough Committee', in *Dr. Babasaheb Ambedkar: Writings and Speeches*, vol. 1, ed. Vasant Moon (Mumbai: Government of Maharashtra), p. 249. Cf. Cabrera, '"Gandhiji, I Have No Homeland."'

35. Ambedkar, *Annihilation of Caste*, 260.

36. Aishwary Kumar makes the case that fraternity was the core concept of Ambedkar's world view. See *Radical Equality*.

37. Ambedkar talked about the prospect of democracy in India on Voice of America in 1956. B.R. Ambedkar, *Ambedkar Speaks: Vol.1: 301 Seminal Speeches*, ed. Narendra Jadhav (New Delhi: Konark Publishers, 2013), p. 297.

38. B. Shiva Rao, V.K.N. Menon and Subhash C. Kashyap, *The Framing of India's Constitution*, vol. 4 (New Delhi: Universal Law, 2006), p. 944.

39. B.R. Ambedkar, *Ambedkar Speaks: Vol.1: 301 Seminal Speeches*, ed. Narendra Jadhav (New Delhi: Konark Publishers, 2013), p. 57.

40. Arun P. Mukherjee, 'B.R. Ambedkar, John Dewey, and the Meaning of Democracy', *New Literary History* 40.2 (2009): 348.

41. Ambedkar uses the spellings 'maitree' and 'maitri' interchangeably in his different writings. B.R. Ambedkar, 'Riddles in Hinduism: An Exposition to Enlighten the Masses', in *Dr. Babasaheb Ambedkar: Writings and Speeches*, vol. 4, ed. Vasant Moon (Mumbai: Government of Maharashtra, 1987), p. 283.

42. B.R. Ambedkar, 'The Buddha and His Dhamma', in *Dr. Babasaheb Ambedkar: Writings and Speeches*, vol. 11, ed. Vasant Moon (Mumbai: Government of Maharashtra, 1992), p. 297.

43. Ibid, p. 129.

44. Shiva Rao, *The Framing of India's Constitution*, p. 945.

45. Ibid.

46. The Supreme Court of India has recognized a 'golden triangle' in the fundamental rights chapter of the Indian Constitution, made up of Articles 14, 19(1) and 21. Gautam Bhatia's view is that there is another 'golden triangle' in the fundamental rights chapter that has largely gone unnoticed. For more, see Gautam Bhatia, 'Why the Uniquely Revolutionary Potential of Ambedkar's Constitution Remains Untapped', Scroll.in, https://scroll.in/article/806606/why-the-uniquely-revolutionary-potential-of-ambedkars-constitution-remains-untapped. Accessed 25 February 2018.

47. Ibid.

48. Ibid. Of course, Ambedkar does not locate fraternity in the French Revolution, but rather in concepts of the Buddha, and the more appropriate term is 'maitri'.

49. Ibid.

50. Manu Bhagavan, *The Peacemakers: India and the Quest for One World* (Noida: HarperCollins, 2012), p. 129.

51. *Constituent Assembly Debates, Volume VII*, http://164.100.47.194/loksabha/writereaddata/cadebatefiles/C04111948.pdf.

52. Ibid.

53. Manu Bhagavan, 'We Are Witnessing the Rise of Global Authoritarianism on a Chilling Scale', Quartz.com (blog), http://qz.com/643497/we-are-witnessing-the-rise-of-global-authoritarianism-on-a-chilling-scale. Accessed 9 December 2016.

## Chapter 15. Political Economy of Caste Discrimination and Atrocities: Why Does Caste Discrimination Persist Despite Law?

1. Ghanshyam Shah, Harsha Mander, Sukhadeo Thorat, Satish Deshpande and Amita Baviskar, *Untouchability in Rural India* (New Delhi: Sage, 2006).

2. Sukhadeo Thorat and Paul Attewell, 'The Legacy of Social Exclusion: A Correspondence Study of Job Discrimination in India's Urban Private Sector', in Sukhadeo Thorat and Katherine S. Newman, *Blocked by Caste: Economic Discrimination in Modern India* (New Delhi: Oxford University Press, 2010).

3. Sukhadeo Thorat and S. Madheswaran, 'Graded Caste Inequality and Poverty Evidence on the Role of Economic Discrimination', *Journal of Social Inclusion Studies* 4.1 (2018): 3–29.

4. Sukhadeo Thorat and Nidhi Sadana, 'Income and Productivity of Scheduled Castes, Scheduled Tribes and High-Caste Farmers', working paper, Indian Institute of Dalit Studies, New Delhi, 2013.

5. Ashish Singh, 'Do Returns to Farming Depend on Caste? New Evidence from India', MPRA paper no. 26526, Indira Gandhi Institute of Development Studies, Mumbai, 15 November 2010.

6. Sukhadeo Thorat and Katherine Newmen, 'Caste Discrimination in Rural Markets', in *Blocked by Caste: Economic Discrimination in Modern India* (New Delhi: Oxford University Press, 2010).

7. Sukhadeo Thorat, Anuradha Banerjee, Vinod Mishra and Firdaus Rizvi, 'Urban Rental Housing Market: Caste and Religion Matters in Access', *Economic and Political Weekly* 1 26–27 (2015): 47–53.

8. Aseem Prakash, *Dalit Capital: State, Markets and Civil Society in Urban India* (New Delhi: Oxford University Press, 2015).

9. Ibid.

10. Vani Kant Borooah, Nidhi Sadana Sabharwal, et al., *Caste, Discrimination, and Exclusion in Modern India* (New Delhi: Sage, 2015).

11. 'Role of Discrimination and General Factors in Access to Government schemes for Employment, Food, Health, Land and Forest in the Poorest Areas in India', research report, Indian Institute of Dalit Studies, New Delhi, 2013.

12. Gary Becker, *The Economics of Discrimination* (Chicago: University of Chicago Press, 1956).

13. Kenneth Arrow, 'The Theory of Discrimination', in *Discrimination in the Labour Market*, Orley Albert Rees, ed. (Princeton: Princeton University Press, 1973).

14. Rachel Kranton, *Identity Economics: How Our Identities Shaped Our Work, Wages and Well-being* (New Jersey: Princeton University Press, 2010).

15. Gordon Allport, *The Nature of Prejudice* (New York: Wesley Publishing Company, 1954).

16. Herbert Blumer, 'Race Prejudice as a Sense of Group Position', *Pacific Sociological Review*, Spring 1.1 (1958): 3.

17. Ibid, pp. 3–4.

18. Ibid.

19. William Darity, Mason Patrick and James Stewart, 'The Economics of Identity: The Origin and Persistence of Racial Identity Norms', *Journal of Economic Behaviour and Organization* 60.3 (2006): 283–305.

20. 'Mixed strategy' is understood as a situation where discriminatory and non-discriminatory actions coexist.

21. B.R. Ambedkar, 'Philosophy of Hinduism', in *Dr. Babasaheb Ambedkar: Writings and Speeches,* vol. 3 (Mumbai: Government of Maharashtra, 1987), p.129.

22. Ibid.

23. Fernando Tola and Carmen Dragonetti, *Brahmanism and Buddhism: Two Antithetic Conceptions of Society in Ancient India* (Buenos Aires: Institute of Buddhist Studies Foundation, 2009).

24. 'The Sixth Report of the Standing Committee on Social Justice and Empowerment on the Scheduled Castes and Scheduled Tribes (Prevention of Atrocities) to consider Amendment to the Act, Lok Sabha Secretariat, 2014–15.

25. Preventions of Scheduled Caste and Scheduled Tribes Act, 2015, Amended, Ministry of Social Justice and Empowerment.

26. B.R. Ambedkar, 'Ranade, Gandhi and Jinnah', in *Dr. Babasaheb Ambedkar: Writings and Speeches*, vol. 1 (Mumbai: Government of Maharashtra, 2014).

27. B.R. Ambedkar, 'Mr Gandhi and the Emancipation of the Untouchables', in *Dr. Babasaheb Ambedkar: Writings and Speeches*, vol. 9 (Mumbai: Government of Maharashtra, 1943, reprint 1991).

28. B.R. Ambedkar, *Annihilation of Caste* (Mumbai: Bharat Bhusan Printing Press, 1936).

29. B.R. Ambedkar, 'States and Minorities: What Are Their Rights and How to Secure Them in the Constitution of Free India', in *Dr. Babasaheb Ambedkar; Writings and Speeches*, vol. 1 (Mumbai: Government of Maharashtra, 1947).

30. Ibid.

31. Ibid.

32. B.R. Ambedkar, 'Mr Gandhi and the Emancipation of the Untouchables', in *Dr. Babasaheb Ambedkar: Writings and Speeches*, vol. 9 (Mumbai: Government of Maharashtra, 1943 reprint 1991).

## PART V: THE RADICAL HUMANISM OF AMBEDKAR

Chapter 16. The Politics of Navayana Buddhism: Reinterpreting Ambedkar's Turn to Religion

1.   I dedicate this article to Owen Lynch (1931–2013). I thank Mariam Mufti and Alpa Shah for their precious help in transforming my written Frenglish into proper English and therefore for helping me to formulate the arguments more clearly.
2.   Nanak Chand Rattu, *Last Few Years of Dr. Ambedkar* (New Delhi: Amrit, 1997), p. 73.
3.   Ambedkar himself converted a huge crowd of several thousand Mahar caste fellows (3,00,000 is the minimum estimation). Conversions continued thereafter, mostly among the Mahars of Maharashtra as well as in other pockets of northern India. According to the 2001 census, Mahars formed 75 per cent of the actual Buddhist population of India, which numbered 0.8 per cent of the total Indian population, according to the census. In 2011, the figure of 0.8 per cent remained stable, totalling 9.7 million.
4.   The name 'Navayana' (new vehicle) was not chosen by Ambedkar himself; his intention was to create not a new Buddhist sect but a modern adaptation of Buddhism that he considered closest to the Buddha's original doctrine. He himself chose to name it simply 'Buddhism' or 'Buddha's Dhamma' to highlight its ethical aspects. Nevertheless, he invented the word 'Navayana', which he pronounced during a press interview on the eve of his conversion in Nagpur. He said: 'The New Buddhists will follow the teachings of religion which have been given himself by Bhagwan Buddha. They will not entangle themselves in the schism of Buddhism. It is because it has created sects like Mahayan and Vajrayan. This is in a way "Navayana" (New Path)' (Vijay Mankar, *Life and the Greatest Humanitarian Revolutionary Movement of Dr B.R. Ambedkar: A Chronology* [Nagpur: Blue World Series, 2009], pp. 491–92). Considering the innovative aspects of what is also often referred to as 'Ambedkar Buddhism', many authors including myself have adopted the word 'Navayana', but it remains contested in the Navayana movement itself, where many practitioners still prefer to talk of 'Buddhism' in conformity with Ambedkar's wishes.
5.   John Kinsey, *The Empty Circle: B.R. Ambedkar, Karl Marx, and the Return of Buddhism to India* (Saarbrücken: VDM Publishing, 2009), p. 121.
6.   Martin Fuchs, 'Buddhism and Dalitness: Dilemmas of Religious Emancipation', in *Reconstructing the World: B. R. Ambedkar and Buddhism in India*, eds. Surendra Jondhale and Johannes Beltz (New Delhi: Oxford University Press, 2004), p. 287.
7.   Michael Löwy, *La Guerre Des Sieux: Religion Et Politique En Amérique Latine* (Paris: Editions du Félin, 1998).
8.   Miguel Abensour, *L'utopie De Thomas More à Walter Benjamin* (Paris: Sens and Tonka, 2000), p. 43.

9.  Nicolas Jaoul, 'Citizenship in Religious Clothing? The Politics of Navayana Buddhism in Uttar Pradesh', *Focaal: Journal of Global and Historical Anthropology* 76 (2016): 46–68.

10. Owen M. Lynch, *The Politics of Untouchability: Social Movements and Social Change in a City of India* (New York: University of Columbia Press, 1969), p. 143.

11. Email communication in 2005, exact date not available.

12. Christophe Jaffrelot, *Dr Ambedkar, Leader Intouchable Et Père De La Constitution Indienne* (Paris: Presses de Sciences Po, 2000), p. 202 (English version: Christophe Jaffrelot, *Dr Ambedkar and Untouchability: Analysing and Fighting Caste* [New Delhi: Permanent Black, 2006]).

13. Dhananjay Keer, *Dr Babasaheb Ambedkar: Life and Mission* (Mumbai: Popular Prakashan, 1971), p. 459.

14. Ibid.

15. Karl Marx, *On the Jewish Question,* www.marxists.org/archive/marx/works/1844/jewish-question, 1843.

16. Christophe Jaffrelot, *Dr Ambedkar, Leader Intouchable Et Père De La Constitution Indienne* (Paris: Presses de Sciences Po, 2000), p. 202.

17. Peter van der Veer, *Imperial Encounters: Religion and Modernity in India and Britain* (Princeton, NJ: Princeton University Press, 2001).

18. The paradoxes of a full-fledged culturalist interpretation of Navayana can be illustrated by two examples. In a challenging and puzzling postmodern reading of Ambedkar, the Ambedkarite literary critic D.R. Nagaraj has argued that the conversion casts into question Ambedkar's convictions as a modernist. Nagaraj thus assumes that Ambedkar's turn to Navayana epitomizes his renunciation at the end of his life to 'the social science mode of reasoning'. The author seeks to reconcile posthumously Ambedkar with Gandhi, even qualifying the religious tone of his book *The Buddha and His Dhamma* as Ambedkar's late 'epistemic rebirth' (D.R. Nagaraj, *The Flaming Feet: A Study of the Dalit Movement in India* [New Delhi: Permanent Black: 2010], p. 163). It has to be noted that the expression refers somewhat ironically to a reconciliation of Ambedkar with Brahminical notions like rebirth, although he explicitly rejected these beliefs in this book. More recently, a culturalist critique of Ambedkar has turned Nagaraj's argument on its head to contend that Navayana's intervention in the Brahminical domain of India's 'great tradition' allegedly failed due to his cultural inability to grasp its philosophical essence, both as a modernist and as an 'Untouchable' (Ananya Vajpeyi, *Righteous Republic: The Political Foundations of Modern India* [Cambridge, MA: Harvard University Press, 2012]). For a critique of Vajpeyi's chapter on Ambedkar, see Nicolas Jaoul and S. Anand, 'Outcasting Ambedkar', *The Hindu*, 4 June 2013, www.thehindu.com/books/outcasting-ambedkar/article4778738.ece.

19. John Kinsey, *The Empty Circle: B.R. Ambedkar, Karl Marx, and the Return of Buddhism to India* (Saarbrücken: VDM Publishing, 2009).

20. The more explicit Marxist influence of Navayana lies in Ambedkar's comparison of Buddhism and communism, where he highlighted the utopian and emancipatory dimension of Buddhism. In an unpublished and annotated text, which was posthumously published, 'Buddha or Karl Marx', as well as in a public speech that he delivered at the world conference on Buddhism in Kathmandu in November 1956, Ambedkar acknowledged that Buddhism shared the fundamental goals of Marxism, that is, the abolition of private property and economic exploitation of men by men. He recognized Marx's philosophy as the most sophisticated theory of human emancipation. However, he claimed that Buddhism proved 'superior' in offering the possibility to establish communism without having to impose it by means of violence and state coercion, which to him represented a shortcut to communism and even an impasse. B.R. Ambedkar, 'Buddha or Karl Marx', in *Dr Babasaheb Ambedkar: Writings and Speeches*, vol. 3 (Mumbai: Government of Maharashtra, 1987), pp. 441–65.

21. Yashwant Sumant, 'Situating Religion in Ambedkar's Political Discourse', in *Reconstructing the World: B.R. Ambedkar and Buddhism in India*, eds. Surendra Jondhale and Johannes Beltz (New Delhi: Oxford University Press, 2004), p. 63.

22. Ibid, p. 69.

23. Gail Omvedt, *Buddhism in India: Challenging Brahmanism and Caste* (New Delhi: Sage, 2003), p. 254.

24. Gail Omvedt, 'Confronting Brahmanic Hinduism: Dr Ambedkar's Sociology of Religion and Indian Society', in *Reconstructing the World: B.R. Ambedkar and Buddhism in India*, eds. Johannes Beltz and Surendra Jondhale (New Delhi: Oxford University Press, 2004), p. 51.

25. Ibid, p. 50.

26. Omvedt notes that Durkheim 'believed that the religion of the future would be rationalistic, ethical, and universalistic religion that would provide a moral base for the importance of the individual—a kind of 'civic religion,' of which he saw the symptoms in the worship of 'reason' at the time the French Revolution'. Ibid, p. 51.

27. Karl Marx, *On the Jewish Question*, www.marxists.org/archive/marx/works/1844/jewish-question, 1843.

28. Although a more systematic study of Ambedkar's relationship to Marxism is required, the heuristic value of these parallels has already been demonstrated by Anupama Rao's fine intuition by comparing Ambedkar's attempt to obtain a minority status for Dalits with Marx's idea of the general strike as a manner of giving visibility to labour. 'In a sense, Ambedkar saw the separate electorate as akin to the general strike. Ambedkar sought to mobilize the negative power of the Depressed Classes in the same way that the general strike revealed the secret

of Capital: that Capital necessarily includes labor even though it is invisible' (2009:137) Thus, similar to the general strike that highlighted the value of labour which the capitalist economy underrated, as soon as Dalits threatened to leave Hinduism, Hindus would start realizing the essential place occupied by them within this religion that in spite of excluding them, it could not do without them—to perform certain tasks without which Brahminical so-called purity could not be assured. Interestingly, this argument converges with Louis Dumont's thesis on purity and impurity in Hinduism (Louis Dumont, *Homo Hierarchicus: The Caste System and its Implications* [Chicago: Chicago University Press, 1970]).

29. For a recent critique of the Nehruvian state, see Perry Anderson, *The Indian Ideology* (New Delhi: Three Essays Collective, 2012).

30. Officially, Buddhist converts were meant to lose the benefits of positive discrimination, since only Hindu and Sikh Untouchables were eligible in the Scheduled Caste category. However, in practice, Buddhist converts continued to benefit from these measures by registering themselves as Scheduled Castes. Eventually, in 1993, the Buddhists became eligible for Scheduled Caste status.

31. I could access the content of this speech that Ambedkar made at the Ram Lila Maidan in Agra on 18 March 1956, thanks to Owen Lynch who generously gave me access to his fieldwork notes, in which he noted down the Hindi newspaper *Dainik Sainik's* report published on 19 March, which summed up Ambedkar's speech (Owen Lynch's fieldwork notebooks, dated 1964, pp. 1943–46).

32. Interestingly, this manner of disqualifying a category of citizens on the pretext of their special entitlement to measures of state welfare which Ambedkar criticized in this speech brings to our attention certain parallels with what Marshall noted in his study of early welfare legislation in England, where 'The Poor Law treated the claims of the poor, not as an integral part of the rights of the citizen, but as an alternative to them—as a claim that could be met only if the claimants ceased to be citizens in any true sense of the word [ . . . ] The stigma which clung to poor relief expressed the deep feelings of a people who understood that those who accepted relief must cross the road that separated the community of citizens from the outcast company of the destitute' (T.H. Marshall, *Citizenship and Social Class: And Other Essays* [Cambridge: Cambridge University Press, 1950], p. 88). Even though the case of Dalits in independent India is one of symbolic disqualification on the grounds of their identification to state welfare rather than disenfranchisement in the true legal sense, the parallel with Marshall's argument raises the question whether this is purely coincidental or if it could be explained by Ambedkar having come across his book, which was published six years before this speech. The same question arises regarding Ambedkar's relationship to Marx's works, as discussed above.

33. Vijay Mankar, *Life and the Greatest Humanitarian Revolutionary Movement of Dr B.R. Ambedkar: A Chronology* (Nagpur: Blue World Series, 2009), p. 491.

34. Ibid.

35. Jacques Rancière, *Aux Bords Du Politique* (Paris: La Fabrique Editions, 1998). (English translation: Jacques Rancière, *On the Shores of Politics* (London: Verso, 2005).

36. Eleanor Zelliot, 'B.R. Ambedkar and the Search for a Meaningful Buddhism', in *Reconstructing the World: B.R. Ambedkar and Buddhism in India*, eds. Surendra Jondhale and Johannes Beltz (New Delhi: Oxford University Press, 2004).

37. Ibid, p. 26.

38. Nanak Chand Rattu, *Little Known Facets of Dr. Ambedkar* (New Delhi: Focus Impressions, 2001), p. 163.

39. Cosimo Zene, 'Subalterns and Dalits in Gramsci and Ambedkar: A Prologue to "Posthumous" Dialogue', in *The Political Philosophies of Antonio Gramsci and B.R. Ambedkar: Itineraries of Dalits and Subalterns* (New York: Routledge, 2013).

40. Yashwant Sumant, 'Situating Religion in Ambedkar's Political Discourse', in *Reconstructing the World: B.R. Ambedkar and Buddhism in India*, eds. Surendra Jondhale and Johannes Beltz (New Delhi: Oxford University Press, 2004).

41. B.R. Ambedkar, 'The Untouchables: Who Were They and How They Became Untouchables', in *Dr. Babasaheb Ambedkar: Writings and Speeches*, vol. 7, ed. Vasant Moon (Mumbai: Government of Maharashtra, 1990).

42. Martin Fuchs, 'Buddhism and Dalitness: Dilemmas of Religious Emancipation', in *Reconstructing the World: B.R. Ambedkar and Buddhism in India*, eds. Surendra Jondhale and Johannes Beltz (New Delhi: Oxford University Press, 2004), p. 289.

43. Joel Lee, 'Jagdish, Son of Ahmad: Dalit Religion and Nominative Politics in Lucknow', *South Asia Multidisciplinary Academic Journal* 11 (2015): 7, special issue 'Contemporary Lucknow: Life with "Too Much History"', samaj.revues. org/3919?lang=fr.

44. D.C. Ahir, *The Status of the Laity in Buddhism* (New Delhi: Sri Sat Guru Publications, 1996), p.145.

45. Vijay Mankar, *Life and the Greatest Humanitarian Revolutionary Movement of Dr B.R. Ambedkar: A Chronology* (Nagpur: Blue World Series, 2009), p. 492.

46. Gary Tartakov, 'The Navayana Creation of the Buddhist Image', in *Reconstructing the World: B.R. Ambedkar and Buddhism in India*, eds. Surendra Jondhale and Johannes Beltz (New Delhi: Oxford University Press, 2004), pp. 151–85.

47. D.C. Ahir, *The Status of the Laity in Buddhism* (New Delhi: Sri Sat Guru Publications, 1996); D.C. Ahir, 'The Bhikkhu Sangha and the Revival Movement', in *Buddhism in India after Dr. Ambedkar (1956–2002)* (New Delhi: Blumoon Books, 2003).

48. Johannes Beltz, *Mahar, Buddhist and Dalit* (New Delhi: Manohar, 2005); Nicolas Jaoul, 'Citizenship in Religious Clothing? The Politics of Navayana Buddhism in Uttar Pradesh', *Focaal: Journal of Global and Historical Anthropology* 76 (2016).

49. Martin Fuchs, 'Buddhism and Dalitness: Dilemmas of Religious Emancipation', in *Reconstructing the World: B.R. Ambedkar and Buddhism in India*, eds. Surendra Jondhale and Johannes Beltz (New Delhi: Oxford University Press, 2004), p. 292.

50. Partha Chatterjee, *The Politics of the Governed: Reflections on Politics in Most of the World* (New Delhi: Permanent Black, 2004).

51. Etienne Balibar, *Le Citoyen Sujet Et Autres Essais d'Anthropologie Philosophique* (Paris: Presses Universitaires de France, 2011); Jacques Rancière, *Aux Bords Du Politique* (Paris: La Fabrique Editions, 1998).

52. Johannes Beltz, *Mahar, Buddhist and Dalit* (New Delhi: Manohar, 2005).

53. Nicolas Jaoul, 'Citizenship in Religious Clothing? The Politics of Navayana Buddhism in Uttar Pradesh', Focaal, *Journal of Global and Historical Anthropology* 76 (2016).

54. Shura Darapuri, 'Neo Buddhists Are Far Ahead of Hindu Dalits', *Dalit Liberation*, 7 May 2008, dalitliberation.blogspot.fr/2008/05/neo-buddhists-are-far-ahead-of-hindu.html.

55. Anupama Rao, *The Caste Question: Dalits and the Politics of Modern India* (Berkeley: University of California Press, 2009).

56. Miguel Abensour, *La Démocratie Contre l'Etat: Marx Et Le Moment Machiavélien* (Paris: Presses Universitaire de France, 1997), p. 16.

57. Etienne Balibar, *Le Citoyen Sujet Et Autres Essais d'Anthropologie Philosophique* (Paris: Presses Universitaires de France, 2011).

58. Miguel Abensour, *L'utopie De Thomas More à Walter Benjamin* (Paris: Sens & Tonka, 2000).

59. Alain Badiou, *Saint Paul: The Foundation of Universalism* (Stanford: Stanford University Press, 2003).

Chapter 17. A Derridean Reading of Ambedkar's *The Buddha and His Dhamma*

1. Jacques Derrida, *Of Grammatology*, trans. Gayatri Spivak (Baltimore: Johns Hopkins Press, 1974).

2. Ambedkar's preface of 1956 was written before the posthumous publication of the work. See Aakash Singh Rathore and Ajay Verma, eds., *B.R. Ambedkar: The Buddha and His Dhamma: A Critical Edition* (Oxford: Oxford University Press, 2011).

3. See, for example, his dissertation on caste, *Philosophy of Hinduism* (three volumes) and *Annihilation of Caste*. See 'Introduction: Historical Overview, 1919–55', in *B.R. Ambedkar: Perspectives on Social Exclusion and Inclusive Policies*,

eds. Sukhadeo Thorat and Narender Kumar (Oxford: Oxford University Press, 2008), p. 1.

4. The author has to admit the awkwardness of enjoying, appropriating, relishing, embellishing and expanding on the critiques of Western philosophers when they attempt to surpass a major world religion like Christianity, say, Nietzsche. Yet the critique based on distended time is not quite what it appears to be because it is not possible to understand Nietzsche's critique in his time for the following reasons: (a) one is not of his time and one does not descend from his 19th century Western-centric gentile-dominated religion of Christianity; and (b) feeling a postcolonial sting of critiquing a non-Western religion like Hinduism knowing full well that people who descend from the Indian subcontinent and claim to be Hindus were the product of colonial Christian oppression. We need to work through this asymmetry as to why one might feel bad (perhaps 'guilty') about critiquing Hinduism today precisely when many Indians and people everywhere of Indian descent, who comprise the majority of that world religion, still feel the legacy of Western–Christian colonial oppression. Could one be 'racist', for example, for attempting to destroy the religion of a non-Western people, who founded Hinduism, which managed to survive Western colonial oppression? And what if that critic was of Hindu origin and from Indian ancestry? If Nietzsche, the son of a Lutheran minister who died when he was young, spoke of the 'bad conscience' in his magisterial critique of Christianity in On the Genealogy of Morals (1886), then one needs to speak of the alterior 'bad conscience' of that Nietzschean bad conscience in critiquing a postcolonial survivor of oppression, namely, the world religion known as Hinduism which is alive and well today. On 'bad conscience', see Friedrich Nietzsche, On the Genealogy of Morals, trans. Walter Kaufmann (New York: Vintage Books, 1989), p. 57. We will work through this issue in our investigation and at least be mindful of it when performing an unrelenting critique of Hindu metaphysics in the spirit of Ambedkar's original and powerful critique of the caste system. And to confess the author was born a Hindu and raised as such but is no longer, having converted out of it just like Ambedkar did.

5. Jacques Derrida, Of Grammatology, trans. Gayatri Spivak (Baltimore: Johns Hopkins Press, 1974), p. 4.

6. See all of Of Grammatology.

7. Jacques Derrida, Of Grammatology, trans. Gayatri Spivak (Baltimore: Johns Hopkins Press, 1974), p. 5.

8. Ibid, pp. 19, 24.

9. Although our focus in this paper is on Of Grammatology and hence the 'early' Derrida that launched deconstruction as a major enterprise in the Western intellectual world, one could turn to the very late lectures on bestiality, animality and sovereignty to unpack them and apply them to a deconstruction of Hindu Brahminical supremacy and how it operates outside the 'law'. Even

though the Indian Constitution 'bans untouchability and discrimination on
the basis of caste', it did not exactly eliminate the caste system as the basic
anatomy of Indian society and culture, not only for the Hindu majority but
other religious minorities too, while the state politicizes the issue of caste to
achieve its various goals. The conditions and sources that perpetuate caste,
exceed the law, and to understand Brahminical supremacy we need to see it
as an admixture of animality and sovereignty that reigns supreme in Indian
society and the South Asian diaspora worldwide. Ambedkar himself knew the
hypocrisy of a Constitution, which he chaired in its drafting, that promotes
'liberty, equality, and fraternity', and the lived material and social reality that
creates just the opposite: namely, the caste system in a cruel and unusual form
of daily oppression that is tantamount to a gross human rights violation on a
mass scale. We need to examine the non-dialectical tensions in the heart of
this hypocrisy to see what makes it work. We reserve those reflections for a
future work. For now, we offer this long quote where Derrida states: 'For the
current representation, to which we are referring from the start, sovereign and
beast seem to have in common their being-outside-the-law. It is as though
both of them were situated by definition at a distance from or above the laws,
in non-respect for the absolute law, that they make or that they are but that
they do not have to respect. Being-outside-the-law can, no doubt, on the one
hand (and this is the figure of sovereignty), take the form of being-above-the-
laws, and therefore take the form of the Law, with a capital L, the condition
of the law, were before, above, and therefore outside the law, external or even
heterogeneous to the law; but being-outside-the-law can also, on the other
hand (and this is the figure of what is most often understood by animality or
bestiality), [being-outside-the-law can also] situate the place where the laws do
not appear, or is not respected, or gets violated.' See Jacques Derrida, *The Beast
and the Sovereign*, vol. 1, trans. Geoffrey Bennington (Chicago: University of
Chicago Press, 2009), p. 17. These reflections are absolutely fascinating. If they
are interpreted in deeper and even more creative ways, breaking open the non-
dialectical aporias and their asymmetrical patterns, beyond what Derrida could
offer, we can examine the seemingly infinitesimal complexity of what the
phenomenon of caste actually is and the processes, mechanisms and dynamics
by which it produces and reproduces itself over time in myriad ways. Caste is
truly a multi-headed monster which may not be 'animal, bestial, or sovereign'.
It is 'other' to Derridean discourse itself.

10. Not only does Hindu nationalism dominate the current ruling party and many
    Hindus around the world, the caste system remains in place within the South
    Asian context and the worldwide diaspora of Hindus. Going back to a much
    earlier European context, as early as the first decades of the 19th century,
    Hegel seems to have captured the dialectically twisted nature of the caste
    system in his *The Philosophy of History:* 'Instead of stimulating the activity of a

soul as their centre of union, and spontaneously realizing that soul—as in the
case in organic life—they petrify and become rigid, and by their stereotyped
character condemn the Indian people to the most degrading spiritual serfdom.
The distinctions in question are the *Castes*. In every rational State there
are distinctions which must manifest themselves. Individuals must arrive at
subjective freedom, and in doing so, give an objective form to these diversities.
But Indian culture has not attained to the recognition of freedom and inward
morality; the distinctions which prevail are only those of occupations, and civil
conditions.' See G.W.F. Hegel, *The Philosophy of History*, trans. J. Sibree (New
York: Colonia Press, 1899), p. 144.

11. Jacques Derrida, *Of Grammatology*, trans. Gayatri Spivak (Baltimore: Johns
    Hopkins Press, 1974), p. 3.

12. Ibid.

13. These registers are from Christian theological sources, which themselves are
    divided between so many traditions: Orthodox, Catholic, Protestant, etc. See
    Paul Tillich's *Systematic Theology*, vol. 1 (Chicago: University of Chicago Press,
    1973). Here, Tillich discusses Christian revelation in terms of man becoming a
    new Being. In orthodox theology, the idea of 'theosis' emerges, which means
    'becoming God'. See Vladimir Lossky, *The Mystical Theology of the Eastern
    Church* (New York: St Vladimir's Seminary Press, 1976), p. 9.

14. Jacques Derrida, *Of Grammatology*, trans. Gayatri Spivak (Baltimore: Johns
    Hopkins Press, 1974), p. 13.

15. Ibid, p. 14.

16. This is in reference to Ambedkar's great work, *Annihilation of Caste* (1936).

17. Foucault defines biopolitics as: 'If the development of the great instruments of
    state, as *institutions* of power, ensured the maintenance of production relations,
    the rudiments of anatomo- and bio-politics, created in the eighteenth century
    as *techniques* of power present at every level of the social body and utilized
    by very diverse institutions (the family and the army, schools and the police,
    individual medicine and the administration of collective bodies), operated
    in the sphere of economic processes, their development, and the forces
    working to sustain them. They also acted as factors of segregation and social
    hierarchization, exerting their influence on the respective forces of both these
    movements, guaranteeing relations of domination and effects of hegemony.'
    See Michel Foucault, *The History of Sexuality*, vol. 1, trans. Robert Hurley
    (New York: Vintage, 1990), p. 141.

18. If one were to analyse Ambedkar's works and contrast them with the self-
    justifying political philosophies of the social contract found in Hobbes, Locke,
    Rousseau, Kant, Hegel and Rawls, we could then show how the theory of
    the social contract and the constitutional law of India is at complete odds with
    the immoral reality of caste; the latter of which exposes the baser instincts
    of humanity that the Western social contract philosophers scarcely began

to uncover within the Western historical experience, even after colonialism began.

19. One can think of the UN Declaration of Human Rights of 1948 as a classic platform.

20. Ambedkar diagnoses this brilliantly in *Annihilation of Caste* where he talks about 'graded inequality'. See S. Anand, ed., *B.R. Ambedkar, Annihilation of Caste: The Annotated Critical Edition* (London: Verso, 2014), p. 234. Perhaps an in-depth comparison and contrast on what major Western Marxist thinkers from Lukács to Sartre have said about the complexity of the phenomenon of class, class consciousness, false consciousness, and ideology in relation to economy and the state and what Ambedkar means by the caste 'division of laborers' within each division of labour is sorely needed.

21. Jacques Derrida, *Of Grammatology*, trans. Gayatri Spivak (Baltimore: Johns Hopkins Press, 1974), pp. 7, 31.

22. This is a phrase that Heidegger coined and Derrida picked up on as well throughout his corpus. For more on this concept, see Iain Thomson, *Heidegger on Ontotheology: Technology and the Politics of Education* (Cambridge: Cambridge University Press, 2005).

23. Jacques Derrida, *Of Grammatology*, trans. Gayatri Spivak (Baltimore: Johns Hopkins Press, 1974), p. 15.

24. Aakash Singh Rathore and Ajay Verma, eds., *B.R. Ambedkar, The Buddha and His Dhamma: A Critical Edition* (Oxford: Oxford University Press, 2011), p. xxii. We will take up this issue of a 'political theology' later in the essay. In their caustic introduction, the editors go on to make a provocative critique of elitist, academic, left-leaning postcolonial theorists who wholly ignore Dalit perspectives when writing their critique of Western modern concepts like the 'enlightenment' as part of the legacy of colonialism. The editors argue that those same 'subaltern' critics in academia (from predominantly high castes) are suspicious of radical attempts to canonize Ambedkar's thought in modern academic disciplines such as 'philosophy, political science, and sociology'. And from traditional theological circles in Buddhism, Ambedkar's 'unorthodoxy' is troubling because of his liberation projects that look at actual historical and material suffering for the purpose of real social transformation. See Rathore and Verma, p. xxiii. In other words, Ambedkarite studies—that link Buddhism to a new material revolution—faces a double exclusion in the contemporary academic context. Thus in our minds *The Buddha and His Dhamma: A Critical Edition* is ripe for a Derridean investigation about the margins, the displaced centre and dilapidated presence, the trace and the supplement, and 'différance', or differing/delay, when pondering the mystery of the event of Buddhist conversion. This is about the critique of origins, original presence and their relationship to linear time as sequences of past, present and future. Furthermore,

beyond the 'political theology' embodied in the event, we must enquire ontologically what that means for the deconstruction of Hindu metaphysical endorsement of the inequality necessary for the caste system to persist. For that purpose, we will rely on Derrida's *Of Grammatology*. Derrida's critique of Western logocentric foundations of metaphysics is akin to Ambedkar's critique of this triple exclusion in the South Asian context: the event of Ambedkarite Buddhist conversion and the future of Indian society requires a simultaneous radical-critical response to Buddhist other-worldly monastic asceticism, Hindu metaphysical concepts of caste, and postcolonial, leftist critics of Western modern notions of enlightenment, science and rational progress, which those critics claim are artefacts of colonialism.

25. Ibid.

26. By alluding to this phrase we recapitulate the inspiration of Max Weber's pioneering works on the sociology of religion. In particular, his short insertion titled 'The Other-Worldliness of Buddhism and its Economic Consequences' in *Economy and Society: An Outline of Interpretative Sociology* is illustrative. See Max Weber, *Economy and Society*, eds., Guenther Roth and Claus Wittich (Berkeley: University of California Press, 1978), p. 627. Weber states: 'At the opposite extreme from religious ethics preoccupied with the control of economic affairs within the world stands the ultimate ethic of world-rejection, the mystical illuminative concentration of authentic ancient Buddhism (naturally not the completely altered manifestations of Buddhism in Tibetan, Chinese, and Japanese popular religions). Even this most world-rejecting ethic is "rational," in the sense that it produces a constantly alert control of all natural instinctive drives, though for the purposes entirely different from those of inner-worldly asceticism.' Presumably, Weber is contrasting this 'other-worldly asceticism' with the 'inner-worldly asceticism' of the early Puritans and other Protestant sects descending from Calvinism, which he famously argued bears an eerie resemblance to what will eventually inform the 'spirit of capitalism' from the late 18th century to modern industrial capitalism. See Max Weber, *Protestant Ethic and the Spirit of Capitalism*, trans. Peter Baehr and Gordon C. Wells (New York: Penguin Books, 2002).

27. In another project we can consider a return to Freudian psychoanalysis and its Lacanian structural variation, which had an enormous influence on Derrida's and Foucault's generation in the 1950s and 1960s, but apply it to a study of the complex phenomenon of caste. To understand the relation between the conscious and unconscious that undergirds the birth of Hindu metaphysics and justification of caste would be an enormously speculatively rich project that we will have to defer to a later date.

28. See *Annihilation of Caste*.

29. Aakash Singh Rathore and Ajay Verma, eds., *B.R. Ambedkar, The Buddha and His Dhamma: A Critical Edition* (Oxford: Oxford University Press, 2011), p. xxii.

## PART VI: AMBEDKAR, A CRITICAL RADICAL PERSPECTIVE

## Chapter 18. Strange Bedfellows Sideline Ambedkar

1. 'A'Lelia Walker, the daughter of millionaire, Madame C. J. Walker, inherited her mother's estate [. . .] the fact remains that she was one of the largest patrons of the time.' Adam R. Schaefer, *The Harlem Renaissance* (Heinemann Library, 2003), p. 37.
2. 'Harlem Renaissance Timeline: 1931, A'Lelia Walker dies at age 46. Less money available for artists and writers. End of the Harlem Renaissance', Adam R. Schaefer, *The Harlem Renaissance* (Heinemann Library, 2003), p. 44.
3. 'By the time Mussolini invaded Abyssinia (Ethiopia) in the mid-1930s, Gandhi (as well as Churchill, Shaw and other former admirers), completely disavowed Il Duce.' *International Business Times*, 'Mussolini and Gandhi: Strange Bedfellows', 3 March 2012.
4. Ruben Gowricharn, *Caribbean Transnationalism: Migration, Pluralization, and Social Cohesion* (Lexington Books, 2006), p. 149.
5. *Gandhi* (1982), box office data, DVD and Blu-ray sales, movie news, cast and crew information, The Numbers, https://www.the-numbers.com/movie/Gandhi#tab=summary. Retrieved 27 February 2018.
6. H.P. Howard, 'The "Negroes" of India', *Crisis*, December 1942, p. 377.
7. Ibid, p. 378.
8. Alexander Shtromas, *Totalitarianism and the Prospects for World Order: Closing the Door on the Twentieth Century* (Lexington Books, 2003), p. 153.
9. Ibid.
10. Ibid. 'The first and most important task of the twentieth century's struggle is . . . the elimination from life . . . to whatever race—Aryan or sub-Aryan . . . the Jews.'
11. 'The Nazi Connection with Shambhala and Tibet', Alexander Berzin, May 2003. '. . . Haushofer used the widespread presence of the swastika in India and Tibet as evidence to convince Hitler of this region as the location of the forefathers of the Aryan race.' http://www.berzinarchives.com/web/en/archives/advanced/kalachakra/shambhala/nazi_connection_shambhala_tibet.html.
12. 'The "Unite the Right" march in Charlottesville has brought the issue of white nationalism to the top of the nation's agenda—specifically, whether white nationalists are part of the White House staff.' Politifact, 15 August 2017, http://www.politifact.com/truth-o-meter/article/2017/aug/15/are-there-white-nationalists-white-house. Retrieved 7 October 2018.

13. It has spread throughout our country and the image is reinforced every Sunday. Psychologically, it has a subliminal effect. See Dr H.C. Felder, *The African American Guide to the Bible* (Author House, 2015), Part 2, Chapter 10.

14. 'White represents the enlightened activity of pacifying . . . Black represents the enlightened activity of wrath . . . forceful methods', https://bit.ly/2FVvjW5. Retrieved 7 August 2018. Also, the 'most common meaning of the colors are as follows . . . White = water, peace . . . Black = wrath'. Ellen Pearlman, *Tibetan Sacred Dance: A Journey into the Religious and Folk Traditions* (Inner Traditions, 2002), p. 69.

15. Vis-à-vis the *Manusmriti* Shambuka in the Ramayana.

16. B.R. Ambedkar, 'Roots of the Problem', in *Untouchables or The Children of India's Ghettos* (1956), http://bit.ly/1dMnXnW. Retrieved 26 February 2018.

17. John Stauffer, Zoe Trodd, Celeste-Marie Bernier and Henry Louis Gates, Jr, *Picturing Frederick Douglass: An Illustrated Biography* (Liveright, 2015), p. 211.

18. Roy Wilkins participated in the March on Washington (August 1963) and the Selma to Montgomery Marches (1965), and was awarded the Presidential Medal of Freedom (1967). He became executive director of the NAACP in 1964.

19. S.D. Kapoor, 'B.R. Ambedkar, W.E.B. Du Bois and the Process of Liberation: Perspectives', *Economic and Political Weekly*, 27 December 2003, p. 5348, http://www.columbia.edu/itc/mealac/pritchett/00ambedkar/timeline/txt_kapoor_2003.pdf. Retrieved 5 August 2018.

20. Most African Americans have tightly curled hair. 'During times when African Americans accepted white cultural ideas about how hair should look, they straightened their hair with pomades, creams, and hot combs as well as chemical straighteners.' Victoria Sherrow, *For Appearance's Sake* (Greenwood Publishing Group, 2001), p. 146.

21. H.P. Howard, 'The "Negroes" of India', *Crisis*, December 1942, p. 20.

22. Ibid, p. 378.

23. 'Still, at the 1935 Yeola conference, Ambedkar renounced Hinduism. In 1936, he published *Annihilation of Caste* that set out the reasons for why he had done so.' B.R. Ambedkar, *Annihilation of Caste: The Annotated Critical Edition*, ed. S. Anand (New Delhi: Navayana, 2014), p. 73, https://bit.ly/2NXOpz4. Retrieved 7 October 2108.

24. Martin Luther King, 'The American Dream', Lincoln University, 6 June 1961.

25. Video: Dr Velu Annamalai—Dalit: The Black Untouchables of India, http://bit.ly/1dDZyQg. Retrieved 9 March 2013.

26. 'The Police Intelligence report came true with around 9000, 8000 and 8000 people attending the conference on 1st, 2nd and 3rd day respectively.' What went into organizing the Ambedkar Conference, Citizen Matters, P. Manivannan, 7 August 2017, http://bengaluru.citizenmatters.in/ambedkar-

international-conference-2017-organising-bangalore-20649. Retrieved 29 March 2018.

27. *Indian Express*, 'Martin Luther King, Jr, Ambedkar were brother revolutionaries: Martin Luther King III', 22 July 2017, http://indianexpress.com/article/india/martin-luther-king-jr-ambedkar-were-brother-revolutionaries-4761958. Retrieved 27 February 2018.

28. Martin Luther King, 'The American Dream', Lincoln University, 6 June 1961.

29. Sylvester A. Johnson, *African American Religions, 1500–2000: Colonialism, Democracy, and Freedom* (Cambridge University Press, 2015), p. 137.

30. Narendra Jadhav, *Untouchables: My Family's Triumphant Escape from India's Caste System* (University of California Press, 2007), p. 40.

31. B.R. Ambedkar, *Annihilation of Caste: Annotated Critical Edition*, Introduction by Arundhati Roy, ed. S Anand (New Delhi: Navayana, 2014), p. 153.

32. 'Ham, the father of Canaan, saw his father [Noah] naked and told his two brothers outside.' Genesis 9:22, New International Version.

33. David Goldenberg, *The Curse of Ham: Race and Slavery in Early Judaism, Christianity, and Islam* (Princeton University Press, 2009), p. 168.

34. 'We have great hope that the Church of England shall reape [sic] good fruit thereby . . .' King James Version, Dedicatorie, 1611.

35. Thomas Jefferson on George III: 'Christian king of Great Britain determined to keep open a market where MEN should be bought & sold he has prostituted his negative . . .' 'Declaring Independence: Drafting the Documents, Jefferson's "original Rough draught" of the Declaration of Independence', https://www.loc.gov/exhibits/declara/ruffdrft.html. Retrieved 15 March 2018.

36. Atlante Millow, 'Thousands of Ministers March for Justice and Peace, Against "Political Laryngitis"', Trice Edney Wire News, 29 August 2017, https://bit.ly/2KculX8. Retrieved 9 March 2018.

37. Was Martin Luther King, Jr. born with a different name? Yes, he was born Michael King on 15 January 1929 and a few years later his father, also Michael King, changed his name to Martin Luther King, Sr, in honour of the great Protestant reformer, and his son's name was also changed to Martin Luther King, Jr. King Center, http://www.thekingcenter.org/faqs. Retrieved 9 March 2018.

38. Paul's Letter to American Christians', Martin Luther King, Jr, Delivered at Dexter Avenue Baptist Church, Montgomery, Alabama, on 4 November 1956.

39. James W.C. Pennington, *Autobiography, The Fugitive Blacksmith, or, Events in the History of James W.C. Pennington: Pastor of a Presbyterian Church, New York, Formerly a Slave in the State of Maryland, United States* (London: Gilpin, 1850). See also James W.C. Pennington, *A Text Book of the Origin and History of the Colored People* (Hartford: L. Skinner, 1841).

40. French for assumed name; name of war.

41. Kurt Schmoke, 'The Dixwell Avenue Congregational Church, 1829–1896', *New Haven Colony Historical Society Journal* 20.1 (May 1971): 6. Schmoke published this essay while a senior in Yale College. He was Senior Fellow at the Yale Corporation until June 2002. See also, 'Dr Rev. Pennington', *Frederick Douglass' Paper*, 14 August 1851.

42. 'He could sit in the back of the classroom and listen. A degree was out of the question. Hungering for an education, Pennington took what was offered and made the most of it.' Mike Cummings, 'In the Shadows No More: Divinity School Honors Minister James W.C. Pennington', *Yale News*, 30 September 2016.

43. 'Project Chronicles History of Black Students at Yale Divinity School', *Notes from the Quad*, Yale University, 4 November 2012. Retrieved 12 January 2013.

44. 'Sterling [Divinity School Dean] said Pennington's story is an important episode in Yale's history', Mike Cummings, 'In the Shadows No More: Divinity School Honors Minister James W.C. Pennington', *Yale News*, 30 September 2016.

45. Christopher Webber, *American to the Backbone: The Life of James W.C. Pennington, the Fugitive Slave Who Became One of the First Black Abolitionists* (New York: Pegasus Books, 2011).

46. Heidelberg University, founded in 1386, as an academic centre for theologians and law experts throughout the Holy Roman Empire—the site of Martin Luther's April 1518 debate that launched Europe's Reformation, associated today with fifty-five Nobel laureates.

47. 'James W.C. Pennington, who in 1849 received an honorary doctorate from Heidelberg University . . . It was the first time that an African American received this highest academic honor from a European university.' The James W.C. Pennington Award of the Heidelberg Center for American Studies and the Faculty of Theology of Heidelberg University, http://www.hca.uni-heidelberg.de/forschung/pennington_en.html. Retrieved 16 March 2018.

48. Ibid.

49. James W.C. Pennington, *A Text Book of the Origin and History of the Colored People* (Hartford: L. Skinner, 1841).

50. Ibid, pp. 17–18.

51. Ibid, p. 32.

52. Ibid, p. 34.

53. A phrase extrapolated from Buddhist esotericism in the Lamaist tradition. Technically: 'the nature of mind is nowhere to be seen in any direction, nor is it limited to any place or any particular conceptual imposition. Essentially: the fact human beings can understand one another is evidence their minds share a "likeness" irrespective of thoughts they have about themselves and others.'

54. There is a possibility that Pennington encountered the philosophical school of Schopenhauer during his European travel.

55. 'Sterling [Divinity School Dean] said Pennington's story is an important episode in Yale's history', Mike Cummings, 'In the Shadows No More: Divinity School Honors Minister James W.C. Pennington', *Yale News*, 30 September 2016.

56. 'On 3 February 1959, King, his wife, Coretta Scott King, and Lawrence Reddick, began a five-week tour of India.' India Trip (1959), Martin Luther King Jr. and the Global Freedom Struggle, http://kingencyclopedia.stanford.edu/encyclopedia/encyclopedia/enc_kings_trip_to_india. Retrieved 13 March 2018.

57. Martin Luther King, Jr speech, 'Remaining Awake Through a Great Revolution', Martin Luther King, Jr Research and Education Institute, Stanford, https://kinginstitute.stanford.edu/king-papers/publications/knock-midnight-inspiration-great-sermons-reverend-martin-luther-king-jr-10. Retrieved 15 March 2018.

58. Modernization of Julius Caesar, Act 1, Scene 2, Shakespeare, (1599), 'Like a Colossus . . .'

59. Latin: the future cause.

## Chapter 19. Ambedkar Icons: Whys and Wherefores

1. Data was collected over ten months in 2012 during fieldwork funded by the Economic and Social Research Council (ESRC) (Grant RES-062-23-3348), in and around Madurai district, central Tamil Nadu. All speeches and interviews were conducted in Tamil and translated by the author. I am grateful to the ESRC for their support and to Karthikeyan and the volume editors for their advice and encouragement.

2. *Daily Nation*, 'Cuba Will Ban Naming of Statues after Fidel: President Raul Castro', 4 December 2016, http://www.nation.co.ke/news/world/Fidel-Castro-s-dying-wish--No-statues-in-his-name/1068-3474190-eyu77mz. Retrieved 16 December 2016.

3. Anand Teltumbde, 'Bathani Tola and the Cartoon Controversy', *Economic and Political Weekly* 47.22 (2012): 10.

4. Ibid.

5. The 'Most Backward Classes' represent the most disadvantaged members of the Backward Caste communities. In socioeconomic terms they resemble Scheduled Caste communities, but for the fact that they have not experienced untouchability. Following the recommendations of the second Backward Classes Commission in Tamil Nadu, the DMK Government set aside 20 per cent of the Backward Class allocation for the 'Most Backward Classes' in 1989. The Vanniyar agitation is seen to have played a key role in this policy. P. Radhakrishnan, 'Ambasankar Commission and Backward Classes', *Economic and Political Weekly* 24.23 (1989): 1265–68.

6. *Economic and Political Weekly*, 'Misplaced Symbolism', 44.34 (2009): 7.

7. S. Gupta, 'BSP at the Crossroads', *Economic and Political Weekly* 44.26 and 44.27 (2009): 22.

8. S. Pai, 'New Social Engineering Agenda of the Bahujan Samaj Party: Implications for State and National Politics', *South Asia* 32.3 (2009): 352.

9. Anand Teltumbde, 'Bathani Tola and the Cartoon Controversy', *Economic and Political Weekly* 47.22 (2012).

10. Ibid, p. 11.

11. B.R. Ambedkar, *Dr. Babasaheb Ambedkar: Writings and* Speeches, vol. 1, ed. Vasant Moon (Mumbai: Government of Maharashtra, 1979), 230.

12. K.C. Suri, 'Party System and Party Politics in India', in *Political Science: Volume 2: Indian Democracy,* eds. K.C. Suri and A. Vanaik (New Delhi: Oxford Scholarship Online, 2013), pp. 209–52.

13. B. Bate, *Tamil Oratory and the Dravidian Aesthetic* (New York: Columbia University Press, 2009; A. Wyatt, *Party System Change in South India: Political Entrepreneurs, Patterns and Processes* (London: Routledge, 2010).

14. P. Price, 'Kingly Models in Indian Political Behaviour', *Asian Survey* 29.6 (1989): 559.

15. Ibid, p. 571.

16. P. Arora, 'Patterns of Political Response in Indian Peasant Society', *Western Political Quarterly* 20.3 (1967): 652.

17. R. Gerritsen, 'Canvases of Political Competition', *Ethnos* (2013): 2.

18. B.R. Ambedkar, *Dr. Babasaheb Ambedkar: Writings and Speeches,* vol. 1, ed. Vasant Moon (Mumbai: Government of Maharashtra, 1979), p. 19.

19. G. Karanth, 'Replication or Dissent? Culture and Institutions among "Untouchable" Scheduled Castes in Karnataka', *Contributions to Indian Sociology* 38.1–2 (2004): 192.

20. N. Jaoul, 'Learning the Use of Symbolic Means', *Contributions to Indian Sociology* 40.2 (2006): 192.

21. S. Rege, 'Interrogating the Thesis of "Irrational Deification"', *Economic and Political Weekly* 43.7 (2008).

22. D. Karthikeyan, 'Contentious Spaces: Guru Pujas as Public Performances and the Production of Political Community', in *From the Margins to the Mainstream: Institutionalising Minorities in South Asia*, eds. H. Gorringe, R. Jeffery and S. Waghmore (New Delhi: Sage, 2016), p. 197.

23. S. Beth, 'Taking to the Streets: Dalit Mela and the Public Performance of Dalit Cultural Identity', *Contemporary South Asia* 14.4 (2005): 408.

24. Anand Teltumbde, 'Maestro of Identity Politics', *Economic and Political Weekly* 49.40 (2014): 30.

25. A. Cohen, *The Symbolic Construction of Community* (London: Tavistock, 1985), p. 60.

26. H. Lefebvre, *The Production of Space* (Oxford: Blackwell, 1991), p. 245.

27. D. Harvey, *The Urban Experience* (Oxford: Blackwell, 1989).

28. R. Rawat, 'Occupation, Dignity, and Space: The Rise of Dalit Studies', *History Compass* 11 (2013): 1060.

29. S. Rege, 'Interrogating the Thesis of "Irrational Deification"', *Economic and Political Weekly* 43.7 (2008): 17.

30. A. Rao, *The Caste Question* (Ranikhet: Permanent Black, 2009), p. 272.

31. H. Gorringe, 'Out of the *Cheris*: Dalits Contesting and Creating Public Space in Tamil Nadu', *Space and Culture* 19.2 (2016): 164–76.

32. *Economic and Political Weekly* 46.44–45, 'Marginalisation, Memory and Monuments', 2011: 7–8.

33. N. Jaoul, 'Learning the Use of Symbolic Means', *Contributions to Indian Sociology* 40.2 (2006): 204.

34. A. Rao, *The Caste Question* (Ranikhet: Permanent Black, 2009), p. 195.

35. G. Tartakov, 'Art and Identity: The Rise of a New Buddhist Imagery', *Art Journal* 49.4 (1990): 416.

36. A. Rao, *The Caste Question* (Ranikhet: Permanent Black, 2009), p. 205.

37. D. Karthikeyan and H. Gorringe, 'Rescuing Ambedkar', *Frontline,* May 2012. Accessed 1 March 2013.

38. R. Gerritsen, 'Canvases of Political Competition', *Ethnos*, 2013, p.12.

39. C. Teja, 'Ambedkar Statue Demolished by Miscreants in Andhra Village, Residents Protest', *News Minute*, 19 April 2018, https://www.thenewsminute.com/article/ambedkar-statue-demolished-miscreants-andhra-village-residents-protest-79884; Q. Ahmad, '"Saffron" Ambedkar Statue Installed in Uttar Pradesh's Badaun, Opposition Cries Foul', News18, 10 April 2018, https://www.news18.com/news/india/saffron-ambedkar-statue-installed-in-uttar-pradeshs-badaun-opposition-cries-foul-1712987.html; *Times of India,* 'Now, B.R. Ambedkar's Statue Vandalised in UP's Meerut', 7 March 2018, https://timesofindia.indiatimes.com/india/now-b-r-ambedkars-statue-vandalised-in-ups-meerut/articleshow/63200890.cms; 'A Day Before Birth Anniversary, Another Ambedkar Statue Vandalised', NDTV, 14 April 2018, https://www.ndtv.com/india-news/a-day-before-birth-anniversary-another-ambedkar-statue-vandalised-1837423.

40. Q. Ahmad, '"Saffron" Ambedkar Statue Installed in Uttar Pradesh's Badaun, Opposition Cries Foul', News18, 10 April 2018, https://www.news18.com/news/india/saffron-ambedkar-statue-installed-in-uttar-pradeshs-badaun-opposition-cries-foul-1712987.html. Retrieved 16 May 2018.

41. A. Cohen, *The Symbolic Construction of Community* (London: Tavistock, 1985).

42. A. Teltumbde, 'Bathani Tola and the Cartoon Controversy', *Economic and Political Weekly* 47.22 (2012): 10.

43. G. Tartakov, 'Art and Identity: The Rise of a New Buddhist Imagery', *Art Journal* 49.4 (1990).

44. Johannes Beltz, 'The Making of a New Icon: B.R. Ambedkar's Visual Hagiography', *South Asian Studies* 31.2 (2015): 255.

45. N. Jaoul, 'Learning the Use of Symbolic Means', *Contributions to Indian Sociology* 40.2 (2006): 200.

46. M. Loynd, 'Understanding the Bahujan Samaj Prerna Kendra: Space, Place and Political Mobilisation', *Asian Studies Review* 33.4 (2009): 478.

47. Johannes Beltz, 'The Making of a New Icon: B.R. Ambedkar's Visual Hagiography', *South Asian Studies* 31.2 (2015).

48. A. Cohen, *The Symbolic Construction of Community* (London, Tavistock, 1985), p. 14.

49. A. Teltumbde, 'Bathani Tola and the Cartoon Controversy', *Economic and Political Weekly* 47.22 (2012).

50. A. Thokder, 'Photos: In India's Dalit Colonies, Ambedkar Continues to be an Inspiration 125 Years after His Birth', Scroll.in, 9 July, 2016, http://scroll.in/article/808095/photos-the-hero-worship-of-br-ambedkar-in-indias-dalit-colonies. Accessed 29 August 2016.

51. B.R. Ambedkar, *Dr. Babasaheb Ambedkar: Writings and Speeches,* vol. 17 (part II), eds. H. Narake, N. Kamble, M. Kasare and A. Godghate (Mumbai: Government of Maharashtra, 2003), p. 83. Available at http://www.mea.gov.in/Images/attach/amb/Volume_17_02.pdf.

52. B.R. Ambedkar, *Dr. Babasaheb Ambedkar: Writings and Speeches,* vol. 1, ed. Vasant Moon (Mumbai: Government of Maharashtra, 1979), p. 231. Available at http://www.mea.gov.in/Images/attach/amb/Volume_01.pdf.

53. M. Jain, 'The Narendra Jadhav interview: "Caste System Is the Most Brilliantly Administered Scam in History"', Scroll.in, 25 August 2016, http://scroll.in/article/814721/the-narendra-jadhav-interview-caste-system-is-the-most-brilliantly-administered-scam-in-history. Accessed 29 August 2016.

## Chapter 20. Ambedkar's Dalit and the Problem of Caste Subalternity

1. This essay draws on and reformulates the earlier arguments in 'Ambedkar and Indian Democracy', in *Decolonisation and the Politics of Transition in South Asia*, ed. Sekhar Bandhopadhyay (Hyderabad: Orient BlackSwan, 2016); and 'Anticaste Thought and Conceptual De-Provincialization: A Genealogy of Ambedkar's *Dalit*', in *Postcolonial Horizons*, eds. Gary Wilder and Jini Kim Watson (New York: Fordham University Press, 2018).

2. The question why Ambedkar converted to Buddhism requires a separate essay. Recall that Buddhist conversion comes after Ambedkar has drawn on secular, political mechanisms (franchise, reservations) to hold upper castes responsible for historical violence against Dalits. Elsewhere I have argued that we ought to see Buddhist conversion as Ambedkar's most political act, and a critique of

both religion and secularism given Ambedkar's unique understanding of the supplementarity of religion and politics on the subcontinent. I draw there on Marx's important text, 'On the Jewish Question', which stages the relationship between minority and universality as a problem that can be illustrated by counterposing the public recognition of the Jew as religious minority who is granted social exceptions, against the project of human emancipation through the ownership and control over the material means of existence. What happens, I ask, when public religion becomes a mechanism for exacerbating political antagonism, rather than deflating it.

3.  Iris Marion Young has argued that debates about group preferences tend to convert questions of historic injustice, which are essentially political questions, into demands for distributive justice predicated on perfecting policy design. Iris Marion Young, *Justice and the Politics of Difference* (Princeton, NJ: Princeton University Press, 2011). Young is right to alert us to affirmative action as an act of depoliticization. Rather than agree with Young that affirmative action politics is no politics at all, we could instead argue that the politics of identity has a different set of consequences for law and for politics: historic inequality is an issue that is typically decided in the courts so far as affirmative action is concerned, while demands for rights and recognition typically occur (and recur) in the agonistic space of 'politics'. Thus law and politics are mutually entailed, but they also operate as sites of friction and conflict.

4.  The fact that South Asian scholarship has reproduced this narrative, even and especially in its more critical variants, should give pause. If Western theory has tended to treat caste as a form of non-political difference, a manifestation of hierarchy that contrasts with Euro-American conceptions of equality, scholarship on caste's historicity has also had the unfortunate effect of parochializing caste. Together and separately, the two positions reprise caste as a form of subcontinental 'difference'.

5.  Judith Butler, 'Restaging the Universal: Hegemony and the Limits of Formalism', *in Contingency Hegemony Universality: Contemporary Dialogues on the Left*, eds. Judith Butler, Ernesto Laclau and Slavoj Zizek (London and New York: Verso, 2000), pp. 40–41.

6.  Marx's thought was conditioned by classical liberalism, which equates liberty with the right to private property, on the one hand, and by French republicanism, which viewed the idea of equality as a response to enslavement and un-freedom on the other. These two histories, the exclusionary right to property, and the commitment to radical human equality activates an internal tension in European intellectual history, which is also reflected in Marxist thinking. Marx argued that we must assume that political equality has reached the status of common sense, that is, that formal equality is a social fact before we can address the antagonism of labour versus capital. I bring this up here to suggest that the equation of the proletariat as a revolutionary political subject

is specific to a North Atlantic story. Or, one might argue that the primacy of labour—and the proletariat as the figure of a collective universality—is historically specific, even as it is interpretively overdetermined.

7.  The understanding of the relationship between majority and minority exceeded demographics and was seen to be constituted by antagonistic relations between groups or communities.

8.  Saba Mahmood, *Religious Difference in a Secular Age: A Minority Report* (Princeton, NJ: Princeton University Press, 2016), p. 65.

9.  At times, Ambedkar compares Untouchables with the abject figure of the Jew, and describes Untouchables as 'miserable', 'spent' and 'sacrificed'. This comes up when he contests earlier ideas, including Phule's, which posited caste as a form of racial distinction, for example, Aryans versus Dravidians. Ambedkar, who was writing against the backdrop of Nazism and race thinking, was adamant that castes were neither racially distinct nor separated by nationality. He disputed colonial ethnographers on this point though he was not above resorting, at other times, to questionable techniques such as phrenology or nasal classification to make a point. See 'Brahmins versus Kshatriyas', in *Dr. Babasaheb Ambedkar: Writings and Speeches*, vol. 3, and B.R. Ambedkar, 'Who Are the Untouchables' in *Dr Babasaheb Ambedkar: Writings and Speeches*, vol. 7.

10. See Anupama Rao, *The Caste Question: Dalits and the Politics of Modern India* (Berkeley, CA: University of California Press, 2009), Chapter 3.

11. For the first time, in 1911, the census contained three subcategories under the denomination 'Hindu': Hindus; Animists and Tribals, and the Depressed Classes or Untouchables. At the First Round Table Conference in 1931, Ambedkar and Rao Bahadur Srinivasan argued that the term 'non-caste' or 'non-conformist Hindus' was more appropriate than the insulting term 'Depressed Classes'. However, the term was used until the current terminology of Scheduled Castes came into effect in 1935.

12. Etienne Balibar argues that 'the signification of the equation man = citizen is not so much a definition of a political right as the affirmation of a *universal right to politics.*' Etienne Balibar, '"Rights of Man" and "Rights of the Citizen": The Modern Dialectic of Equality and Freedom', in *Masses, Classes, Ideas: Studies on Politics and Philosophy Before and After Marx* (London: Routledge, 1994), p. 49.

13. Supplementary Written Statement of B.R. Ambedkar, *Dr. Babasaheb Ambedkar: Writings and Speeches*, vol. 1.

14. Evidence before Southborough Committee, *Dr. Babasaheb Ambedkar: Writings and Speeches*, vol. 1, p. 270.

15. Ambedkar was labelled a 'British stooge' for agreeing to be a member of the Bombay Committee of the Simon Commission, which was boycotted by the Congress and the Muslim League. He eventually submitted a book-length rejoinder criticizing the Simon Commission's recommendations. See *Indian Statutory Commission*, vol. III, Appendix D, pp. 87–156.

16. Evidence of Dr Ambedkar before the Indian Statutory Commission on 23 October 1928, *Dr. Babasaheb Ambedkar: Writings and Speeches*, vol. 2, p. 465.

17. Statement concerning safeguards for the protection of interests of the Depressed Classes as a minority in the Bombay Presidency and the changes in the composition of and the guarantees from the Bombay Legislative Council necessary to ensure the same under Provincial Autonomy, submitted by B.R. Ambedkar on behalf of the Bahishkrit Hitakarini Sabha (Depressed Classes Institute) to the Indian Statutory Commission, 29 May 1928, *Dr. Babasaheb Ambedkar: Writings and Speeches*, vol. 2, pp. 438–39.

18. Report on the Constitution of the Government of Bombay Presidency, presented to the Indian Statutory Commission, *Dr. Babasaheb Ambedkar: Writings and Speeches, vol.* 2, p. 320.

19. 'A Report on the Constitution of the Government of Bombay Presidency', presented to the Indian Statutory Commission, *Dr. Babasaheb Ambedkar: Writings and Speeches*, vol. 2, p. 319.

20. Evidence of Dr. Ambedkar before the Indian Statutory Commission on 23 October 1928, *Dr. Babasaheb Ambedkar: Writings and Speeches*, vol. 2, p. 465. Ambedkar also submitted his own report to the (Simon) Indian Statutory Commission (vol. III Appendix D, pp. 87–156).

21. Some years later, Ambedkar would describe conversion from Hinduism as an aspect of 'class struggle', and underscore its necessity as a form of social inclusion if Dalit Mahars were to resist their marginality in his May 1936 speech to the Bombay Presidency Mahar Conference. Yet Buddhist conversion could not be reduced to the instrumentality of number or political interest. Neither was the Navayana Buddhism to which Ambedkar and Dalit masses converted available as an existing religion. As it took shape in the posthumously published *The Buddha and His Dhamma* (1957), Navayana was Ambedkar's creation.

22. Sekhar Bandyopadhyay, 'Transfer of Power and the Crisis of Dalit Politics in India, 1945–47', *Modern Asian Studies* 34 (2000): 893–942; Anupama Rao, *The Caste Question*, Chapter 3; Ramnarayan Rawat, 'Making Claims for Power: A New Agenda for Dalit Politics in Uttar Pradesh, 1946–48', *Modern Asian Studies* 37 (2003): 585–612; and Dwaipayan Sen, 'No Matter How, Jogendranath Had to be Defeated: The Scheduled Castes Federation and the Making of Partition in Bengal, 1945–1947', *Indian Economic and Social History Review* 49 (2012): 321–64.

23. 'The Cabinet Mission and the Untouchables', *Dr. Babasaheb Ambedkar: Writings and Speeches,* vol. 10, p. 538.

24. Sir Stafford Cripps was a left-wing politician in Winston Churchill's War Cabinet who came to India in March 1942 and offered Indian leaders dominion status after the war and eventual political independence if India supported the British war effort. Congress stopped talks with the Mission and began the

massive Quit India movement after the demand for immediate self-rule was not met.

25. 'Report of the Proceedings of the Third Session of the All-India Depressed Classes Conference', Nagpur, 18 and 19 July 1942, address by AISCF president Rao Bahadur N. Sivaraj, p. 24.

26. Ibid. A conference of the Samata Sainik Dal was held on 20 July as well as the second session of the All-India Depressed Classes Women's Conference.

27. Ibid, p. 23.

28. Ibid, pp. 31–32.

29. Ibid, pp. 32–33.

30. 'Pakistan, or the Partition of India', *Dr. Babasaheb Ambedkar: Writings and Speeches*, vol. 8.

31. 'Report of the Proceedings of the AIDC Conference', p. 5. The demand arose again on 23 September 1944 at a meeting of the working committee of the AISCF in Bombay.

32. Office bearers of the executive committee had to pay an annual fee of Rs 10, while members of the village, taluka and district committee paid Rs 5 per annum. AISCF Constitution, January 1955.

33. Chakravarti Rajagopalachari, *Ambedkar Refuted* (Bombay: Hind Kitabs, 1946), pp. 5–6.

34. Ibid, pp. 8–9.

35. K. Santhanam, *Ambedkar's Attack: A Critical Examination of Dr. Ambedkar's Book* What Congress and Gandhi Have Done to the Untouchables (New Delhi: Hindustan Times Press, 1946). Santhanam, a Congress activist between 1920 and 1942, was a member of the All-India Congress Committee as well as the Tamil Nadu Congress Committee. He was a Congress member of the Central Assembly when he resigned from his post in 1942.

36. The interwar status of Hindus and Muslims as 'majority' and 'minority' was structured along axes of agonism that have continued relevance for postcolonial politics. The claim that Muslims are the Dalits of neoliberal Hinduism, which is sometimes made, is a first approximation in analysing this process. However, the dialectic of de- and re-politicization affects Dalit and Muslim communities differentially, with *externality* and *negative sociality* structuring divergent paths to minoritization.

37. Demetrius Eudell, 'Not Only Natural but Necessary: On Ambedkar and the Caste/Race Dialectic'. Unpublished paper presented at Ambedkar@125 conference, 21–23 July 2017, Bengaluru.

38. For an extensive engagement with Phule's rewriting of history, Anupama Rao, *The Caste Question: Dalits and the Politics of Modern India* (Berkeley, CA: University of California Press, 2009), esp. Chapter 1.

39. The American Civil War (1861–65) ended in an uneasy peace brokered between the slave South and the industrializing North. The United States

Army remained in the American South to demobilize civilian militias, maintain civic order and ensure the emancipation of four million slaves. Broadly speaking, the period of Reconstruction (1865–77) was a period of social and political reorganization predicated on readmitting the southern states into the Union while producing the institutional conditions and the ideological grounds for a non-slave society. This brief period of full civil and political rights for African Americans was followed by the institution of Jim Crow. Jim Crow *legislated* African-American disenfranchisement through restrictions on social mobility (labour, housing and education) and the franchise. The Jim Crow period witnessed numerous atrocities on Black life, some spectacular, such as public lynchings. The period came to an end with the beginning of the civil rights movement in the 1950s, but is typically seen to have ended with the passage of the Civil Rights Act (1964) and the Voting Rights Act (1965). It is in this period, between 1890 and 1940, that events such as the Great Migration (of African Americans to the North) began to reshape the country's perception of race and racism. Scholarship in the period, especially that of the (in)famous 'Dunning School' led by Columbia University Professor William A. Dunning played an important role in painting Reconstruction as a failure due to the collective action of vengeful Republicans bent on humiliating the South, northern carpetbaggers and ignorant African Americans. Among other things, *Black Reconstruction* is a profound refutation of the arguments of the Dunning School.

40. 'Abolition democracy' was a way to conceive the civic and political personhood of Black workers through their education, control over capital and political rights. W.E.B. Du Bois, *Black Reconstruction 1860–1880* (New York: Free Press, 1998), pp. 184–87.

41. B.R. Ambedkar, 'Slaves and Untouchables', *Dr. Babasaheb Ambedkar: Writings and Speeches*, vol. 5, ed. Vasant Moon (Mumbai: Government of Maharashtra, 1988), p. 117.

42. For an argument about Phule as both a critic and a beneficiary of the transformations effected by colonial capital (and the cotton economy of western India), see Anupama Rao, 'Word and the World: Dalit Aesthetics as a Critique of Everyday Life', *Journal of Postcolonial Literature* 53.1–2 (2017): 147–61. (There, I note the remarkable similarity between Phule's descriptions of agrarian indebtedness, and theoretical arguments about real and formal subsumption by Jairus Banaji, that takes the Deccan's agrarian situation as a paradigmatic example.)

43. When I speak of social abstraction, I have in mind Marx's explanation of how the commodity form comes to stand in for social relations of exchange and exploitation, so that a critique of the social must also necessarily proceed through the critique of political economy.

44. Marilyn Strathern, 'An Awkward Relationship: The Case of Feminism and Anthropology', *Signs* 12.2 (Winter, 1987): 289.

45. For an analysis of Dalit political culture and the Dalit Panthers, see Anupama Rao, Chapter 3, *The Caste Question: Dalits and the Politics of Modern India* (Berkeley, CA: University of California Press): 182–216.

46. Jayashree Gokhale, *Concessions to Confrontation: The Politics of an Indian Untouchable Community* (Bombay: Popular Prakashan, 1993); Gail Omvedt, *Dalits and the Democratic Revolution: Dr. Ambedkar and the Dalit Movement in Colonial India* (New Delhi: Sage, 1994).

47. M.N. Roy was sent to Tashkent by Lenin in 1921 to head the Asiatic Bureau of the Comintern to train an army of Indian revolutionaries. By May 1922, Roy had started publication of the *Vanguard of Indian Independence*, and begun to communicate with the Maharashtrian Marxist Shripad Amrit Dange after reading Dange's text, *Gandhi versus Lenin*. The two maintained a steady communication aided by the arrival of Charles Ashleigh of the British Communist Party to Bombay on 19 September 1922. Charles Ashleigh was joined in Bombay by Philip Spratt, who was asked in 1926 to journey to India (together with Ben Bradley and Lester Hutchinson) as a Comintern agent at the behest of Clemens Dutt, elder brother of R.P. Dutt, the well-known theorist of the British Communist Party and author of *India Today* (1949). Spratt had been encouraged to launch the regional Workers and Peasants Parties as a cover for building the nascent Communist Party of India. In Bombay, key members of the Workers and Peasants Parties managed to infiltrate the Girni Kamgar Union (Textile Workers' Union) in 1928, just before the city's historic general strike of that year. By 1929, key Maharashtrian Marxists—G. Adhikari, S.A. Dange, S.V. Ghate and S.S. Mirajkar—had been arrested in the Meerut Conspiracy Case on the charge of treason, together with Muzaffar Ahmed, P.C. Joshi, Philip Spratt, Shaukat Usmani and others.

48. Anand Teltumbde, 'Introduction', B.R. Ambedkar, *India and Communism* (New Delhi: Leftword Books, 2017). Teltumbde's point is supported by Sanjay Seth, who argues that as Marxists became anti-colonialists, they came to embrace Marxism as a more robust variant of nationalism due to Marxism's commitment to social equality, self-determination and territorial sovereignty. This enabled a dual commitment to internationalism *and* national liberation, or what B.T. Ranadive later called 'left nationalism'. Seth argues, 'In accepting anticolonialism, the difference between national form and class substance was also blurred, so that in form *and* substance, nationalism was declared nationalist. Thus anticolonialism in this perspective was more than merely bourgeois-democratic struggle, and socialism could be achieved through that political form. Thus did Marxism itself become a form of nationalism, not in practice and due to constraint, but as theory, because it could not maintain the divide

between form and substance.' Sanjay Seth, *Marxist Theory and Nationalist Politics: The Case of Colonial India* (New Delhi: Sage, 1995), p. 229.

49. The aftermath of the Meerut Conspiracy Case saw caste contradictions coming to the fore *within* the Communist Party. On the one hand, Maratha Communist leaders in the city were receptive to issues of rural exploitation, for example, the anti-khot (landlord) agitation in the Konkan, which had a direct impact on the kunbi-Marathas who constituted the bulk of Bombay's industrial workforce. At the same time, the radicalization of the Indian National Congress in the aftermath of the Poona Pact also, and ironically, saw the development of a shared perception between mainstream nationalists and Communists alike, that Ambedkar was 'anti-national'. These issues came to a head after the historic elections of 1937, when Congress won major victories across the provinces. Ambedkar shifted away from the caste-class model of the ILP in favour of establishing the AISCF in 1942, even as the Cripps Mission and later, the Cabinet Mission Plan, sidelined SCs as a significant (and separate) political constituency whose interests had to be factored in in shaping the politics of independent India.

50. Andrew Sartori has recently made a similar argument with regard to 'Lockeanism', where he argues that tracking the power of a form of thought does not mean strict adherence to the methods of intellectual history or critical commentary on a thinker's works. Andrew Sartori, *Liberalism in Empire* (Berkeley: University of California Press, 2015). This becomes especially true of the relationship between Ambedkar and Marx, where Ambedkar returned, repeatedly, to distinguish his position from Marxist dogma, but where numerous organic intellectuals affiliated with the Ambedkar movement were drawn to vernacular Marxism—by which I mean forms of everyday critique that were keenly attentive to the supplementary relationship of caste and (caste) labour.

51. I believe Ambedkar's great contribution to Marxist thinking lies in asking what kind of analysis might emerge if we prioritized the social experiences of the Dalit in the place of the proletariat.

52. When Germany-returned Gangadhar Adhikari translated the *Communist Manifesto* (*Communist Jahirnama*) into Marathi in 1931, class was associated with terms such as *kashta* (hard work), *daridryata* (impoverishment, destitution), *bekaar* (unemployed, worthless) and *bhukekangal* (pauperized), to correlate with abstract labour. Class identity was also related to social forms such as the degraded Dalit classes, Dalit *varga*, Pathans (popularly associated with the 'flesh trade', moneylending, extortion and other parasitical activities that further impoverished working people) and the wild, rowdy *mavali*, identified with the communities of the Sahyadri mountain range (and their traditions of banditry and guerrilla warfare). Each of these was imprecisely identified with class, and constituted something like an excessively dispossessed multitude, rather than a proletariat class per se.

53. Anupama Rao, 'Stigma and Labour: Remembering Dalit Marxism', *Seminar*, special issue, *Caste Matters*, May 2012.

54. We could argue that Ambedkar shifted towards a national resolution of the Dalit question during the 1940s and 1950s, culminating in the dual moves of Buddhist conversion and the Constitution. However, he was equally involved in internationalizing the issue at the time. Indeed, the correspondence in 1946 between Ambedkar and W.E.B. Du Bois is well known and concerned Ambedkar's request for a copy of the National Negro Congress petition to the United Nations, which attempted to secure minority rights through the United Nations council, as he wished to make a similar representation for the Dalit cause. A recent paper also shows that Ambedkar was in active contact with Jan Smut, Churchill, and the Indian Conciliation Group and other conservative politicians. Jesus Chairez, 'B.R. Ambedkar, Partition and the internationalization of untouchability, 1939–1947', *South Asia* (forthcoming).

55. Ambedkar, 'Revolution and Counter-Revolution in India', *Dr. Babasaheb Ambedkar: Writings and Speeches,* vol. 3, pp. 269–70.

56. Ambedkar, 'Who Are the Shudras', *Dr. Babasaheb Ambedkar: Writings and Speeches,* vol.7, pp. 318–55.

57. Ambedkar was especially keen to challenge the perspective put forward by Hindu nationalists such as Tilak regarding the role of Vedic India—and later, the Bhagavad Gita—in incubating ideas of social equality and non-violence. See for example, Tilak's *Gita Rahasya*, and *Arctic Home in the Vedas.* Ambedkar dates ideas of non-violence in the Bhagavad Gita to the post-Buddhist era in 'Revolution and Counter-Revolution in Ancient India'.

58. Ambedkar describes the conflict between Kshatriyas and Brahmins by returning to Shivaji's coronation, an issue that had preoccupied anti-caste thinkers from the Deccan before him. 'Who Are the Shudras', *Dr. Babasaheb Ambedkar: Writings and Speeches,* vol. 7, pp. 175–85.

59. Ambedkar, *Revolution and Counter-Revolution* in *Dr. Babasaheb Ambedkar: Writings and Speeches,* vol. 3, 267, 269–71 and 276–77.

60. Brutalized life, flesh, is 'that zero degree of social conceptualization that does not escape concealment under the brush of discourse, or the reflexes of iconography', Hortense Spillers tells us (Hortense J. Spillers, 'Mama's Baby, Papa's Maybe: An American Grammar Book', *Diacritics* 17.2 [1987]: 64–81.) In *Black Reconstruction*, Du Bois draws on the transubstantiation of Christ, on the idea that the bread and wine become the flesh and blood of the wounded Christ, to describe black history as 'tragedy made flesh'.

## Chapter 21. Ambedkar beyond the Critique of Indology: Sexuality and Feminism in the Field of Caste

1. *Contributions to Indian Sociology*, 1957.

2. Louis Dumont (1911–98) was an eminent figure in the fields of sociology, anthropology and Indology.

3. Classical Indology is the study of old and middle Indic languages (notably Sanskrit texts on Hinduism).

4. B.S. Cohn, *An Anthropologist Among the Historians and Other Essays* (New Delhi: Oxford University Press, 1987).

5. The postcolonial critique of caste theorizes it as an orientalist construct—a discursive production of colonial rule. See B.S. Cohn, *An Anthropologist Among the Historians and Other Essays* (New Delhi: Oxford University Press, 1987); R. Inden, *Imagining India* (Oxford: Blackwell, 1990); A. Ahmad, 'Between Orientalism and Historicism: Anthropological Knowledge of India', *Studies in History* 7.1: 135–63; Nicholas B. Dirks, *Castes of Mind: Colonialism and the Making of Modern India* (Princeton: Princeton University Press, 2001). Caste, they hold, is not a traditional age-old institution inscribed in the shastra, smriti or sutra. The phenomenal rise of caste is linked to administrative discourse, like the census survey reports of the British colonizers. Aiming at a systematic homogenization of the heterogeneous mass, the strains of colonial governmentality reduced several unrelated or arbitrarily related groups into a few odd castes. See P. Kolenda, *Caste, Cult, and Hierarchy: Essays on the Culture of India* (New Delhi: Manohar Book Service, 1981); S. Jaiswal, *Caste: Origin, Function and Dimensions of Change* (New Delhi: Manohar Publishers, 1998). The defining features of caste, offered by Indologists and sociologists for a holistic understanding of the pan-Indian system—like pollution-purity, hierarchy-interdependence, restrictions on occupation, commensality, marriage—were relegated to regional differences. This view has thoroughly been criticized by many scholars who observe that ignoring the long oppressive history of the pre-colonial past, caste cannot be consigned to colonialism. 'Western influence was a necessary but not a sufficient causal factor in the rise of this particular social construction'. R. King, *Orientalism and Religion: Postcolonial Theory, India and 'the Mystic East'* (London: Routledge, 1999). However, while calling attention to the crucial role played by indigenous Brahminical ideology in the crystallization of caste and also the overall significance of caste in Indian social formations, scholars often reify it as a timeless ahistorical category. Caste is thus turned into a meta-reality which cannot be obliterated. Postcolonial thinkers are not naïve. They do not distort the pre-colonial history of India glorifying it as casteless. Rather they point at the fact that colonial rule has turned caste, repudiating its flexibilities and regional variations, into an ossified system to mark the whole population of India. The current essay tends to read Ambedkar's theorization amidst these academic impasses. His nuanced critique of the reified notion of caste historicizes the course of its institutionalization as an oppressive system.

6. G. Guru, 'How Egalitarian Are the Social Sciences in India?' *Economic and Political Weekly* 37.50 (2002): 5003–09.

7. J. Butler, 'What is Critique? An Essay on Foucault's Virtue', in *The Sensibility of Critique: Response to Asad and Mahmood. Is Critique Secular? Blasphemy,*

*Injury, and Free Speech*, eds. Judith Butler, Talal Asad, Wendy Brown and Saba Mahmood (Berkeley: Townsend Center for the Humanities, 2009), pp. 101–36.

8. Ibid, p. 109.

9. T. Fitzgerald, 'From Structure to Substance: Ambedkar, Dumont and Orientalism', *Contributions to Indian Sociology* 30.2 (1996): 282.

10. Ibid.

11. Ibid, p. 274.

12. Ignoring the academic significance of Ambedkar's theorization of caste, published almost two decades before Ghurye, is a dominant trend in Indian sociology. While Ghurye is recognized as the 'founding' father of Indian sociology, Ambedkar has been ostracized from being a legitimate contributor to sociology! Not only Ghurye, but subsequent sociologists such as Louis Dumont and M.N. Srinivas, and most others who followed later, have ignored Ambedkar's scholarship. See P.G. Jogdand and Ramesh Kamble, 'The Sociological Traditions and Their Margins: The Bombay School of Sociology and Dalits', *Sociological Bulletin* 62.2 (2013): 328.

13. T. Fitzgerald, 'From Structure to Substance: Ambedkar, Dumont and Orientalism', *Contributions to Indian Sociology* 30.2 (1996): 274.

14. L. Dumont, *Homo Hierarchicus: The Caste System and Its Implications* (Chicago: University of Chicago Press, 1980).

15. Ibid, p. 8.

16. L. Dumont, *From Mandeville to Marx: The Genesis and Triumph of Economic Ideology* (Chicago: University of Chicago Press, 1977), *Essays on Individualism: Modern Ideology in Anthropological Perspective* (Chicago: University of Chicago Press, 1986), *German Ideology: From France to Germany and Back* (Chicago: University of Chicago Press, 1994).

17. T. Fitzgerald, 'From Structure to Substance: Ambedkar, Dumont and Orientalism', *Contributions to Indian Sociology* 30.2 (1996): 274.

18. E. Said, *Orientalism* (New York: Pantheon Books, 1978).

19. E. Said, *The World, the Text, and the Critic* (Cambridge, Mass.: Harvard University Press, 1983), p. 216.

20. David Ludden, 'Orientalist Empiricism and Transformations of Colonial Knowledge', in *Orientalism and The Post-Colonial Predicament*, eds. C.A. Breckenridge and Peter Van der Veer (Philadelphia: University of Pennsylvania Press), p. 252.

21. Ibid, p. 253.

22. D. Ganguly, *Caste, Colonialism and Counter-modernity: Notes on a Postcolonial Hermeneutics of Caste* (London and New York: Routledge, 2005), p. 59.

23. Ibid.

24. Ibid, p. 60.

25. E. Said, *The World, the Text, and the Critic* (Cambridge, Mass.: Harvard University Press, 1983), p. 216.

26. D. Quigley, 'Is a Theory of Caste Still Possible?' *Sociological Review* 41.1 (1993). Quigley has been one of Dumont's scathing critics, and identifies two organizing tenets of the structural analysis of caste. First, Dumont considers caste as a systemic whole which cannot be reduced to a sum total of discrete castes. Caste as a system can only be understood in relation to other castes. This relatedness can best be comprehended in terms of a prevalent set of religious values enunciated in classical Hindu texts. Second, the ideology of the caste system is defined by the principle of hierarchy, a consensual unity over dissent and frames of inequality, which encompasses the domain of empirical facts. The Dumontian frame unifies seemingly unrelated ethnographic studies of caste, providing a dominant social and anthropological perspective.

27. Nicholas B. Dirks, *Castes of Mind: Colonialism and the Making of Modern India* (Princeton: Princeton University Press, 2001), p. 57.

28. D. Ganguly, *Caste, Colonialism and Counter-modernity: Notes on a Postcolonial Hermeneutics of Caste* (London and New York: Routledge, 2005).

29. B. Bhadra, 'Caste(s): The Archetypal Orientalist—Predicament of Sociology on India', *Indian Sociological Society Journal* 1.2 (2013): 21.

30. P. Chatterjee, Caste and Subaltern Consciousness, *Subaltern Studies VI: Writing on Southeast Asian History and Society*, ed. Ranajit Guha, (New Delhi: Oxford University Press, 1992), p. 80.

31. Dipankar Gupta, 'Continuous Hierarchies and Discrete Castes', *Economic and Political Weekly* 19.46 (1984): 1955–2053.

32. L. Dumont, *Homo Hierarchicus: The Caste System and Its Implications* ( Chicago: University of Chicago Press, 1980.

33. Ibid, p. xxx.

34. B.R. Ambedkar, 'Annihilation of Caste', in *The Essential Writings of B.R. Ambedkar*, ed. Valerian Rodrigues, (New Delhi: Oxford University Press, 2002), p. 260.

35. D. Ganguly, *Caste, Colonialism and Counter-modernity: Notes on a Postcolonial Hermeneutics of Caste* (London and New York: Routledge, 2005).

36. Nicholas B. Dirks, *Castes of Mind: Colonialism and the Making of Modern India* (Princeton: Princeton University Press, 2001), p. 294.

37. U. Bagade, 'Ambedkar's Historical Method: A Non-Brahmanic Critique of Positivist History', the Ninth Dr Ambedkar Memorial Lecture (New Delhi: Dr Ambedkar Chair, Centre for the Study of Social Systems, School of Social Sciences, Jawaharlal Nehru University, 2012), https://www.jnu.ac.in/sites/. . ./9th%20Dr.%20Ambedkar%20Memorial%20Lecture.pdf.

38. This almost coincides with the argument of the standpoint theorists advocating that the lives of women 'will generate less partial and distorted accounts not only of women's lives but also of men's lives and of the whole social order'. See S. Harding, 'Introduction: Standpoint Theory as a Site of Political, Philosophic, and Scientific Debate', in *The Feminist Standpoint Theory Reader: Intellectual and*

*Political Controversies*, ed. Sandra Harding (New York and London: Routledge, 2004), p. 128.

39. B.R. Ambedkar, 'The Untouchables: Who Were They and Why They Became Untouchables' in *Dr. Babasaheb Ambedkar: Writings and Speeches*, vol. 7, ed. Vasant Moon (Mumbai: Government of Maharashtra, 1990), p. 244.

40. Ibid.

41. Ibid.

42. S. Rege, *Against the Madness of Manu: B.R. Ambedkar's Writings on Brahmanical Patriarchy* (New Delhi: Navayana, 2013); Anupama Rao, ed. *Gender and Caste*. (New Delhi: Kali for Women, 2003); Gail Omvedt, *Ambedkar: Towards an Enlightened India* (New Delhi: Penguin Books India, 2004); Kalpana Kannabiran, 'Sociology of Caste and the Crooked Mirror: Recovering B.R. Ambedkar's Legacy', *Economic and Political Weekly* 44.4 (2009): 35–39.

43. In a forthcoming essay entitled 'Women and the Brahmanical Nation: Questions Concerning Caste and Gender', following B.R. Ambedkar's explorations on the question of woman and Gayle Rubin's conceptualization of the sex gender system, I propose a concept called the caste–gender–sexuality system. This is to underscore the structural underpinnings of caste marked by gender inequity and sexual violation. The methodological and theoretical prism of this system helps formulate a critique of the idealization of women as both emancipated and divinized figures in the nationalist discourses on recasting women. This idealization, though presented in a universalist garb, was an upper-caste project. Hence, the Dalit woman was fundamentally excluded from the Hindu nationalist project of women's reforms. The current essay, sharing some of Ambedkar's theorizations—on caste bringing out the question of woman—with the forthcoming piece, deploys the caste–gender–sexuality system to subvert the Brahminical-patriarchal hegemony of the Indological discourse.

44. S. Tharu and T. Niranjana, 'Problems for a Contemporary Theory of Gender', in Subaltern Studies IX, eds. Shahid Amin and Dipesh Chakrabarty (New Delhi: Oxford University Press, 1996).

45. S. Rege, *Against the Madness of Manu: B.R. Ambedkar's Writings on Brahmanical Patriarchy* (New Delhi: Navayana, 2013), p. 61.

46. Ambedkar believes that to ensure endogamy it is necessary to maintain a constant numerical equality between marriageable units of men and women. This can only be done if all couples die together. But if a husband dies before the wife he creates a surplus woman 'who must be disposed of, else through intermarriage she will violate the endogamy of the group'. B.R. Ambedkar, 'Caste in India: Their Mechanism, Genesis and Development', in *The Essential Writings of B.R. Ambedkar*, ed. Valerian Rodrigues, pp. 241–62 (New Delhi: Oxford University Press, 2002), p. 247.

47. Ibid, p. 245.

48. Ibid, pp. 248–49.

49. B.R. Ambedkar, 'The Rise and Fall of the Hindu Woman: Who Was Responsible for It?' In S. Rege, *Against the Madness of Manu: B.R. Ambedkar's Writings on Brahmanical Patriarchy* (New Delhi: Navayana, 2013), p. 172.

50. Ibid, p. 171.

51. Ibid, p. 176.

52. B.R. Ambedkar, 'The Rise and Fall of the Hindu Woman: Who was Responsible for It?' (1951).

53. B.R. Ambedkar, 'The Triumph of Brahminism', *Dr. Babasaheb Ambedkar: Writings and Speeches*, ed. Vasant Moon (Mumbai: Government of Maharashtra, 2014), p. 315.

54. Ibid.

55. Lata Mani, 'Contentious Traditions: The Debate on Sati in Colonial India', in *Cultural Critique* 7, *The Nature and Context of Minority Discourse II* (1987): 119–56.

56. Michel Foucault, *Power/Knowledge: Selected Interviews and Other Writings, 1972–1977*, ed. Colin Gordon (New York: Pantheon Books, 1980), p. 193.

57. B.R. Ambedkar, 'The Triumph of Brahminism', *Dr. Babasaheb Ambedkar: Writings and Speeches*, ed. Vasant Moon (Mumbai: Government of Maharashtra, 2014), p. 295.

58. Ibid.

59. Ibid, p. 323.

60. Arundhati Roy, 'The Doctor and the Saint', in *The Annihilation of Caste: The Annotated Critical Edition*, ed. S. Anand (New Delhi: Navayana, 2014).

61. B.R. Ambedkar, 'Annihilation of Caste', in *The Essential Writings of B.R. Ambedkar*, ed. Valerian Rodrigues (New Delhi: Oxford University Press, 2002), p. 289.

62. Ibid, p. 279.

63. Ibid, pp. 280–81.

64. Ibid, p. 289, emphasis in original.

65. A. Rao, 'Sexuality and the Family Form' *Economic and Political Weekly* 40.8 (2005): 716.

# A NOTE ON THE CONTRIBUTORS

**Anjani Kapoor** is a master's candidate at the Graduate Center, City University of New York. She was previously working as an associate producer in the editorial department of India Today TV. Prior to that, she was a senior reporter at Times Now, where she researched, scripted and produced television shows on political, social and international issues. She has written for the *Indian Express* and a few online portals. She completed her master's in journalism from the Symbiosis Institute of Media and Communication, Pune.

**Anupama Rao** is TOW associate professor of history and associate professor, MESAAS. She is associate director, Institute for Comparative Literature and Society, and senior editor at the journal *Comparative Studies of South Asia, Africa, and the Middle East*. She is working on a critical study of Ambedkar titled *Ambedkar in His Time and Ours*, and is in the process of publishing the English translation of the autobiography of Dalit communist R.B. Moré.

**Ashwin Desai** is professor in the department of sociology at the University of Johannesburg. His research interests include sport, political economy and social policy. His latest work on the close relationship between politics and cricket in South Africa, *Reverse Sweep: The Story of Cricket in Post-apartheid South Africa,* was published by Jacana in 2017. With Goolam Vahed, he is the co-author of *The South African Gandhi: Stretcher-bearer of Empire*.

**Bronislaw Czarnocha** is a quantum physicist and a mathematics professor at the City University of New York. He was exiled from Poland in the aftermath of the student uprising in March 1968, exactly fifty years ago. His interest in the bisociative revolution started in 1982 while analysing the process of the Revolution of Solidarity. His interest in the Dalit struggle for the annihilation of caste arose through eight years of collaboration with the Arunthathiyars of Tamil Nadu where he saw the divide between the

Marxist Left and Dalits directly on the ground. The tragic suicide of Rohith Vemula, followed by the arrest of Kanhaiya Kumar at JNU and the results of the American elections of 2016, motivated him to undertake the full process of the exploration and formulation of the principle of bisociative revolution.

**Chandraiah Gopani** is an assistant professor at the G.B. Pant Social Science Institute, Allahabad. He obtained his MA, MPhil and PhD in the discipline of political science from the University of Hyderabad. His areas of interests are political theory, caste, social movements, Dalit studies, subaltern, public policy, education and gender. He is engaged in the research and teaching of anti-caste legacies by focusing on Dalit movements, politics and literature and the role of social movements in shaping society, state and democracy. Presently he is working on mobilization and the struggles of marginalized Dalits. He regularly writes for reputed research journals, magazines and newspapers in English and Telugu.

**Gary Michael Tartakov** is professor emeritus of art and design history at Iowa State University and the editor and lead author of *Dalit Art and Visual Imagery*. Tartakov has been studying India's visual imagery and culture since 1963, when he came to study ancient temple arts of the Deccan. *The Durga Temple at Aihole* is his work from that research. More recently he has worked on orientalism and the European interpretation of traditional India. For the last two-and-a-half decades he has focused on Dalit cultural history and the visual imagery Dalits have used to establish their presence on India's public stage.

**Goolam Vahed** is a professor of history at the University of KwaZulu Natal. He has written on various aspects of the history of Indians and Muslims in South Africa, and on race and cricket. His most recent work is *Chota Motala: A Biography of Political Activism in the KwaZulu-Natal Midlands*.

**Hira Singh** teaches at the department of sociology at York University, Toronto. His areas of interest include social inequality, social theory and social movements. He has done research on feudalism in non-European and European societies, colonial rule and resistance, migrant labour and agri-business in Canada and Indian indentured labour in South Africa. His articles have been published in national and international journals and edited books. His most recent published work is *Recasting Caste: From the Sacred to the Profane*. He is working on a manuscript titled 'The Asiatic Mode of Production, Feudalism, and Social Movements: Studies in Indian Society and History'. He is currently engaged in a project on the abolition of slavery in the British empire and Indian indentured labour.

**Hugo Gorringe** is a senior lecturer in sociology at the University of Edinburgh. His research focuses on politics, social exclusion, marginalization and mobilization among Dalits in Tamil Nadu and draws on extensive ethnographic fieldwork in the state. He is the author of *Untouchable Citizens: The Dalit Panthers and Democratisation in Tamil Nadu* and *Panthers in Parliament: Dalits, Caste and Power in South India,* as well as numerous articles on identity, violence, caste and politics. He is co-editor of *From the Margins to the Mainstream: Institutionalising Minorities in South Asia*. He has written multiple commentary and analysis pieces for *The Hindu* and the *Economic and Political Weekly*, discussed his work on the BBC show *Thinking Allowed* and submitted written evidence on caste discrimination to the UK Foreign Affairs Select Committee.

**Jean Drèze**, development economist, has taught at the London School of Economics and the Delhi School of Economics and is currently visiting professor at Ranchi University. He has made wide-ranging contributions to development economics and public policy, with special reference to India. His recent books include *An Uncertain Glory: India and Its Contradictions* (with Amartya Sen) and *Sense and Solidarity: Jholawala Economics for Everyone*. Drèze is also active in various campaigns for social and economic rights as well as in the worldwide movement for peace and disarmament.

**Kevin D. Brown** is the Richard S. Melvin professor at Indiana University's Maurer School of Law, where he has been on the faculty since 1987. Brown holds a 1978 BS degree from the Kelley School of Business at Indiana University, where he majored in accounting. He graduated from Yale Law School in 1982. His research interest is primarily in the areas of race and law, particularly the African-American experience. He has published over seventy articles on issues such as school desegregation, affirmative action and African-American Immersion Schools. His books include *Race, Law and Education in the Post Desegregation Era* and *Because of Our Success: The Changing Racial and Ethnic Ancestry of Blacks on Affirmative Action*.

**Lama Choyin Rangdrol** is an African-American Buddhist educator in the Tibetan tradition. He has given lectures at Ambedkar's 125th birth anniversary at Columbia University and the Ambedkar International Conference on Social Justice, Bangalore. He has taught Buddhism to Maharashtra's Bahujan Ambedkarite community from Mumbai to Nagpur. Prior to teaching, he completed a forest retreat with Lama Tharchin Rinpoche and seven years study with Khempo Yurmed Tinly, the abbot of monasteries in Bhutan and Dharamsala. Rangdrol worked for twenty years in the mental health field at the UCLA Neuropsychiatric Hospital in California, the USC University Hospital Department of Psychiatry and state hospitals for the developmentally disabled. He dealt in forensic psychiatry and managed the cases of mentally ill and homeless populations in the Hawaiian Islands. His short volume work *Black Buddha* was featured as a classic of American Buddhism by *Buddhadharma* magazine. He has travelled and taught in London, Amsterdam, Estonia, France, Mexico, Sweden and Thailand.

**Manu Bhagavan** is professor of history and human rights at Hunter College, City University of New York. He is the author of *The Peacemakers* and *Sovereign Spheres*, and the co-editor of four other books, including *Hidden Histories*. His edited volume on India and the Cold War is forthcoming. His Quartz essay on global authoritarianism went viral internationally and was translated into German as the cover article of the May 2016 issue of Berliner Republik magazine. He is the recipient of a 2006 Fellowship from the American Council of Learned Societies and is an elected member of the Pacific Council on International Policy. He regularly appears in the media to comment on global affairs.

**Neha Mishra** is the founding director and assistant professor at the School of Legal Studies, REVA University, Bengaluru. Enrolled as an advocate at the Delhi Bar Council since 2009, she was working as an attorney in a leading law firm till she took up academics fulltime. She is one of the leading researchers on colourism in India. She teaches gender studies and human rights law. Her articles have been published in Huffington Post, US; Wire; *Asia Times* and *Washington Global Studies Review*, among others. She is the winner of the Education Award, 2016, by Indus Foundation. She has been invited as speaker and panelist at distinct international conferences.

**Nicolas Jaoul** is a CNRS research fellow in anthropology at the Institut de Recherche Interdisciplinaire Sur Les Enjeux Sociaux, Paris. He is most interested in the political ethnography of the anti-caste movement, with a special emphasis on the material mediations of bodies, objects, images and space. His fieldwork has been carried out in different regions (Bihar, Maharashtra, Punjab, Uttar Pradesh and the UK diaspora) in order to study Dalit activism in different regional contexts. Although dealing mostly with Ambedkarism, he has also studied the way other ideological traditions (Naxalism, Gandhism and Hindutva) have dealt with caste and untouchability.

**Partha Chatterjee** is professor of anthropology and of Middle Eastern, South Asian and African studies at Columbia University, New York, and honorary professor, Centre for Studies in Social Sciences, Kolkata. His books are *Nationalist Thought and the Colonial World*, *The Nation and Its Fragments: Colonial and Postcolonial Histories*, *The Politics of the Governed* and *The Black Hole of Empire: History of a Global Practice of Power*.

**Rajesh Sampath** is currently associate professor of the philosophy of justice, rights and social change at Brandeis University, Massachusetts. He completed his PhD at the University of California, Irvine, in the humanities with a focus on modern continental European philosophy and critical theory at the Critical Theory Institute. He studied under the French philosopher Jacques Derrida, the founder of deconstruction. His areas of specialization centre on the philosophy of history, historical time and epochal shifts. Subsequently, he did a postdoctoral fellowship at the University of California, Berkeley and a DAAD postdoctoral fellowship in Germany where he published articles on continental European philosophy.

**Ritu Sen Chaudhuri** teaches sociology at the West Bengal State University. She is also a visiting lecturer on women's studies at the Women's Studies Research Centre, University of Calcutta, and the School of Women's Studies, Jadavpur University. After completing a master's in sociology from the University of Calcutta, she did her doctoral research from the Centre for Studies in Social Sciences. Her areas of interest include sociological and feminist theories, gender and sexuality, caste studies, women's writing and the interfaces of sociology and literature. She has published articles on various issues including women's writing, the women's movement, feminist theory, caste and gender, Tagorean novels and film texts in academic journals and edited books. Currently, she is supervising five PhD dissertations and working on a book project.

**Rohit De** is a lawyer and historian of modern South Asia and focuses on the legal history of the Indian subcontinent and the common law world. De's book *The People's Constitution: Litigious Citizens and the Making of Indian Democracy* (forthcoming 2018) explores how the Indian Constitution, despite its elite authorship and alien antecedents, came to permeate everyday life and imagination in India during its transition from a colonial state to a democratic republic. Mapping the use and appropriation of constitutional language and procedure by diverse groups such as butchers and sex workers, street vendors and petty businessmen, journalists and women social workers, it offers a constitutional history from below. He continues to write on the social and intellectual foundations of constitutionalism in South Asia.

**Ronald E. Hall** was an expert in the first African-American skin colour discrimination case. His research includes 150 (co)-authored works. He was featured in 'Light Girls' by OWN and won the Mellen Prize for Distinguished Contribution to Scholarship. He is the author of *The Melanin Millennium.* He lectured at Bates College, Pennsylvania State University and Oxford University, Paramaribo, Suriname, Jindal Global University and the Tata Institute of Social Sciences. He was invited by a US Congressman to address skin colour and was the lead presenter at the Global Perspectives on Colorism Conference.

**Samuel L. Myers, Jr** is the director and professor, Roy Wilkins Center for Human Relations and Social Justice at the Hubert H. Humphrey School of Public Affairs, University of Minnesota. He is an oft-cited Massachusetts Institute of Technology–trained economist who has published more than a hundred studies on applied microeconomic and policy issues in leading economics and interdisciplinary journals and in books and monographs. He is a pioneer in the use of applied econometric techniques to examine racial disparities in crime, detect illegal discrimination in home mortgage lending and consumer credit markets, assess the impacts of welfare on family stability to evaluate the effectiveness of government transfers in reducing poverty and detect disparities and discrimination in government contracting. In 2008–09 he was a Senior Fulbright Fellow at the Chinese Academy of Social Sciences.

**Sukhadeo Thorat** is professor emeritus, Centre for the Study of Regional Development, School of Social Sciences, Jawaharlal Nehru University, New Delhi and distinguished professor, Savitribai Phule University, Pune,

K.R. Narayanan Chair for Human Rights and Social Justice, Mahatma Gandhi University, Kerala (Honorary), managing trustee, Indian Institute of Dalit Studies, New Delhi.

**Vanishree Radhakrishna** is a practicing lawyer at the High Court of Karnataka. She was a British Chevening Scholar and obtained her LLM in human rights from the University of Leicester in United Kingdom. She holds a bachelor's degree from the National Law School of India University. She has also undertaken graduate training in public policy analysis at American University, Washington DC and has specialized in service laws and discrimination in public employment. She has successfully fought cases against fake caste certificates in Karnataka. Her areas of interest include comparative constitutional theories, affirmative action, human rights and Buddhist psychology. She has published articles in the *Jindal Journal on Public Policy* and the *American International Journal for Research in Humanities, Arts and Social Sciences* on topics ranging from the Supreme Court and affirmative action in India, significance of the civil rights movement in America and on Jewish human rights at the dawn of the French Revolution.

# INDEX

means of production, 158, 161;
African American perspective on
common struggles, xxviii, 43–60;
awareness of the African-American
community, 50–56; African
Americans and Jews of Christian
Europe, xxvii, 32–42; capitalism,
54–55, 58; caste oppression,
217; and caste subalternity,
problem of, 340–58; Christians,
55, 103; citizenship, 291; class
analysis associated with, 185;
consciousness, 303; conversion
to Buddhism. See Buddhism,
conversion to; converts, impact
on, 230–37; dehumanization,
356, 357; equated with death,
depravity, impurity, 300; diaspora,
96, 102–03; dual discrimination
based on gender and caste, 68,
69–72. *See also* caste discrimination;
emancipation, 281–82, 285,
288; existence, 357–58; feminist
movements, 367; freedom and
equality, lack of, 153–54; human
rights, 100; iconography, social
significance of, 334; identity,
xiv, xxv, xxxiv, 102, 103, 186,
202, 204–05, 212, 215, 233, 301,
366; inequalities among, 181,
187–95, 195–99; interrogating
the category, 183–87; intra-caste
conflicts, 195, 334; and the Left,
202–05; liberation struggle. *See*
Dalit movements; Maha Dalits,
186, 193; marginality, 355;
marginalization as a source of
sociological knowledge, 360;
movement. *See* Dalit movement;
nomenclature, 184; and non-
Dalits in India, racial difference,
xix; oppression, xvii, xx, xxi, 14,

43–44, 50, 54, 58, 60, 90, 92, 120,
129, 200, 204, 216, 368;—caste
specific, 43, 51–52, 94, 104, 187,
206–10, 217, 220–21, 253, 301,
303–05, 369; participation in the
Maoist movement, 218; political
autonomy, 286; political praxis,
290; politics, 87–104, 126, 197,
200, 283, 286, 290, 330–32, 333,
338, 343, 353; private Hindu
practice and public Buddhist
practice, dichotomy, 233;
psychological damage, xviii; in
public discourse, 16, 53, 182, 184,
185, 187; radicalism, 333; religious
sects, 287; representation in the
legislatures, 132; reservation.
*See* reservation for Scheduled
Castes; rights, struggle in global
politics, 87–104; social locations
and historical trajectory, 190;
social isolation, 246; subjectivity,
355; symbolic assertion, 334–35;
symbolic exclusion, 333; thought
'untimeliness of, 357–58; ; unequal
access to reservation and state
policies, 197; universalism, xxix–
xxx, 355; vote bank, xiii, 35, 132,
236, 330, 337, 339; women, 368,
370. *See also* Depresses Castes,
Scheduled Castes, Untouchables
Dalit-Bahujan, 185
*Dalit Bandhu*, 184
*Dalit Drum*, 339
Dalit India Chamber of Commerce
and Industry, 55
Dalit Jatiya Sangh and Dalit Sarsvat
Parishat, 184
Dalit Mahasabha of Andhra Pradesh,
185
Dalit movements, liberation struggle,
xxviii, xxix, 32–42, 43–60, 87–104,

282, 285, 290; representation,
88, 113, 118, 120–21, 124, 126,
128–30, 133, 194, 344, 347;
reservations, 192; revolution, 231,
239; rights of minorities, xxx, 89,
108, 127, 192, 266, 348
politics, 20–22, 30, 104, 109, 114,
132, 161, 196, 235, 262, 329,
353, 361, 363, 370; agonistic,
357; biopolitics, 297; caste, 54,
357; communal, of majority
communalism, 125, 131–32;
of community, 343; cultural,
333; Dalits, emancipatory
politics, xxvii, 88, 92, 126,
182–83, 185, 187, 197,
200–01, 330–32, 342–43, 353;
democratic, 175–77; in defence
of, Ambedkar and political
parties, 138–41; domination
by legal professionals, 136;
electoral, xv, 177, 236; identity,
xiii, 201, 230, 333; idolatry,
332; international, 33, 87,
91; labour, 354; lawyering as,
xxx–xxxi, 134–50; Left, 352;
of minority rights, 133, 346,
349; of Muslim nationalism,
346, 348; nationalist, 123; of
Navayana Buddhism, 281–92;
outcaste, xxxv, 355; postcolonial,
xiv, 341; of regionalism, 100;
and religion, 340; right to, 344;
South African, xxx; symbolic,
330, 334–35, 337–39; vote-bank,
xv, xxvii, 35, 132, 236, 330,
337, 339; women in, 178
pollution, religious notion of, 54–55,
244, 256, 263
Poona Pact, 35, 68, 120, 125, 153,
347, 354
Portuguese, 3

postcolonial: bureaucratic order, 104;
politics, xiv, 341
post-Independence development
projects, 102
poverty and inequality, poverty and
discrimination, 19, 23, 24, 28, 57,
68, 110, 179, 225, 226, 260–61,
266, 270, 271–72, 274, 287, 298
Prabhakar, Jupudi, 197
*Prabuddha Bharat*, xi
Praja Socialists, 353
Prasad, Chandra Bhan, 54–55
Prasad, Vijay, 53
prejudice based on race, religion,
sexual orientation, or ethnicity,
61–83, 261–63
Prevention of Atrocities Act (1989),
256, 267, 269
princely states, xxxi, 118, 124, 129,
154, 155
private property, 28, 141, 142, 147,
163
*Problem of the Rupee*, 6
production relations, 342
prohibition laws, 145
property ownership, wealth and
income, inequality, 130
property rights, 147–48
prostitution, 145
Proudhon; *The Philosophy of Poverty*,
155–56
psychology of prejudice, 261–63
public facilities, obstruction of, 62
public purpose, 148
public transportation, 11
Punjab, 182, 186; disparities and
hierarchy among Dalits, 190;
Pakistan question and, 123
Punjabi Sikhs, 48
purity-impurity, notion of, 164–65,
167, 300, 301
Pushyamitra, 356